An Archaeology of Sympathy

An Archaeology

of Sympathy

The Sentimental Mode

in Literature and Cinema

JAMES CHANDLER

The University of Chicago Press *Chicago & London*

James Chandler is the Barbara E. and Richard J. Franke Distinguished Service Professor in the Department of English Language and Literature and chair of the Department of Cinema and Media Studies at the University of Chicago. He is the author of several books, including *England in 1819: The Politics of Literary Culture and the Case of Romantic Historicism*, also published by the University of Chicago Press.

The University of Chicago Press, Chicago 60637
The University of Chicago Press, Ltd., London
© 2013 by The University of Chicago
All rights reserved. Published 2013.
Printed in the United States of America

22 21 20 19 18 17 16 15 14 13   1 2 3 4 5

ISBN-13: 978-0-226-03495-9 (cloth)
ISBN-13: 978-0-226-03500-0 (e-book)
DOI: 10.7208/chicago/9780226035000.001.0001

Library of Congress Cataloging-in-Publication Data

Chandler, James, 1948– author.
    An archaeology of sympathy : the sentimental mode in literature and cinema / James Chandler.
        pages   cm
    Includes bibliographical references and index.
    ISBN 978-0-226-03495-9 (cloth : alkaline paper)
    ISBN 978-0-226-03500-0 (e-book)
    1. Sentimentalism. 2. Sentimentalism in motion pictures. 3. Capra, Frank, 1897–1991—Criticism and interpretation. 4. Sentimentalism in literature. 5. English literature—History and criticism. I. Title.
    PN56.S475C47 2013
    809'.9145—dc23
                                                                2012044801

♾ This paper meets the requirements of ANSI/NISO Z39.48-1992 (Permanence of Paper).

For

CATHERINE

and

MICHAEL

and

JONAH

and

JACK

SENTIMENTALE SEELEN

Sie weinen! ach! der Metzger schlachtet ein Kalb!
Erst brüllte die Bestie noch, jezt ist sie falb!
Sie lachen! Himmel, wie närrisch in seiner Art,
Natur, Natur! Ein Hund trägt keinen Bart!
Was sprudelt ihr hoch, als wart ihr gesonnt?
Wir hören, wie Bielams Esel gar sprechen konnt!

—KARL MARX

When I mounted my hobby horse, I never thought, or pretended to think, where I was going, or whether I should return home to dinner or supper, or the next day, or the next week. I let him take his own course; and amble, or curvet, or trot, or go a sober, sorrowful, lackadaysical pace, as it pleased him best. It was all one to me, for my temper was ever in unison with his manner of coursing it—be it what it might, I never pricked him with a spur, or struck him with a whip; but let the rein lay loosely on his neck, and he was wont to take his way without doing injury to any one.

Some would laugh at us as we passed along, and some seemed to pity us, and now and then a melancholy tender-hearted passenger would look at us and heave a sigh.—Thus have we travelled together; but my poor Rosinante did not, like Balaam's ass, stand still if he saw an Angel in the way, but directly pushed up to her, and if it were but a damsel, sitting by the fountain, who would let me take a refreshing draught from her cup, she was, surely, an angel to me.

The grand error of life is, that we look too far:—we scale the Heavens, we dig down to the centre of the earth, for systems, and we forget ourselves.—Truth lies before us; it is in the highway path; and the ploughman treads on it with his clouted shoon.

Nature defies the rule and the line;—Art raises its structures, and forms its works on their aid; but Nature has her own laws, which Art cannot always comprehend, and Criticism can never reach.

—LAURENCE STERNE

Contents

Preface

This book is about a distinctively modern rhetorical mode or mood with wide influence across forms and genres, about how it took shape in the medium of print and how it was adapted to the medium of film. I use "rhetorical" in the broad sense here to include questions of narrative, address, and moral posture. By "distinctively modern" I mean roughly "since the European Enlightenment," though important elements of my account derive from the mid-seventeenth century. The story I tell comes up to our own moment. Insofar as it claims to be an "archaeology," it might even be said to begin there. Still, the rapid social and cultural development of Britain in the mid-eighteenth century remains a special point of focus of the book because it was there and then that the term "sentimental" was first coined, there and then that what it identified really emerged. Scholars of this subject have long been aware that the first entry in the *Oxford English Dictionary* for "sentimental" involves a 1749 query about its already fashionable currency. One Lady Bradshaigh wrote to Samuel Richardson, the most influential writer of that decade, to ask, "What, in your opinion, is the meaning of the word sentimental, so much in vogue among the polite?" But even with the help of large, digitally searchable databases, antecedent instances of the term have been difficult to identify, even for the 1740s. "Sentimental" named something new under the sun in that moment, something Richardson himself had a lot to do with.

"Mode" and "mood" are interchangeable terms in some contexts—in English grammar, for example—though we more typically use the former to refer to a manner or fashion of proceeding (a modality) and the latter to indicate an affective condition, as in the title of a jazz composition by Duke Ellington, "In a Sentimental Mood," which makes an appearance in one of the 1990s neo-Capra films that I survey in chapter 1. Both terms, "mode" and "mood," are relevant to my arguments. In categorizing this thing called "the sentimental" over the course of writing *An Archaeology of Sympathy*, I have in fact found myself toggling between the two terms. So for the purposes of a preliminary exposition I propose a single term, one that connotes both mood and mode. That term is "disposition."

A disposition, nowadays, is first of all an emotional tendency or outlook. This is the sense invoked by Cornel West, in an interview at the Occupy Wall Street encampment on September 29, 2011, when he told Amy Goodman of *Democracy Now!* that President Obama should apologize to the Congressional Black Caucus for accusing its members, in effect, of whining: "I tell my brother, you got to understand the genius of Bob Marley. He called his group the Wailers, not the Whiners. The Wailers were persons who cry for help against the context of catastrophe. . . . Whining is a cry of self-pity, of a sentimental disposition." West's phrase not only captures the prevailing contemporary understanding of "disposition" as a psychological tendency; it also casts "sentimental" as unequivocally pejorative, a now-standard use of the term. The reduction of "disposition" to *attitude* and "sentimental" to *self-pitying* is precisely what this book seeks to roll back, in favor of a richer and more complex history of representational practices.

This brings me to a longer-standing set of associations with the term "disposition," one with strong roots in classical learning. In Roman rhetoric, *dispositio* is the term for how some particular matter is disposed—how its component parts are ordered, organized, and arranged. The sentimental revolution in literature that dates from the mid-eighteenth century is not just about new kinds and levels of feeling but also about new ways of ordering works and organizing the worlds represented in them. It is this aspect of that revolution that interests me most. A startling challenge to traditional forms of disposition appears in the very first line of Laurence Sterne's *Sentimental Journey through France and Italy* (1768), introduced with an extended dash: "——They order, said I, this matter better in France—."[1] The dash, the pronouns, the deictic *this*, the situation, the matter, the strange order of the sentence itself: nothing is clearly set forth in this sentence. Rather than explain himself, Parson Yorick makes his remark the occasion for plunging headlong into a journey to the Continent, where he claims to have "incontestably" arrived by the middle of page one. This would indeed be a novel novel. For all the apparent idiosyncrasy and contingency of Sterne's procedures, he was decidedly a pioneer of a new disposition, of new structuring principles in narrative art, and would eventually be recognized for this achievement in the twentieth century by Viktor Shklovsky, leading light of the Russian Formalist school of criticism.

The initial task for the *dispositio* in Roman rhetoric, following directly on *inventio* (or "finding" of the matter), is the *exordium*, the "beginning of the web." Building on writers like Shaftesbury, Richardson, and Adam Smith, Sterne developed new techniques for representing spectatorial networks, laying bare his devices as he went. My largest claim in this book is that these procedures, these structuring principles, come to matter centrally to early twentieth-century American cinema. They matter especially, but not exclusively, to the practices of cinematic *montage*, which the great film critic André Bazin once defined as "simply the ordering of images in time."[2] Mediated by a long tradition of fictional practice nowhere more evident than in Dickens, the sentimental disposition helped to order and organize the so-called classical narrative system of early Hollywood. One of its inventors, D. W. Griffith, and one of his most important disciples, Frank Capra, are both often characterized as "sentimental" in the casually pejorative sense: simpleminded and schmaltzy. Part of my aim in this book is to suggest that their approaches to film art—their practices of shooting, editing, and mise-en-scène—are deeply informed by the manner in which spectators are disposed in a sentimentally ordered world.

A final sense of "disposition" at play in this book has to do with the handling or settling of cases. There are two distinct ways in which to address what might be called the sentimental disposition of a case. The first turns on the claim that, in Adam Smith's influential *Theory of Moral Sentiments*, we find not only an explicit rejection of traditional casuistry but also an implicit representation of a new moral order premised on what I call "the sentimental case"—the situation in which one stands apprehended as an object of the sort of imaginative projection that Smith terms "sympathy." The second has to do with the origins of sentimentalism in early-modern theological efforts to deal with perceived threats to the immateriality and immortality of the soul. These efforts were based on "the vehicular hypothesis," a new theory of sensibility worked out by Henry More and the Cambridge Latitudinarians, parodied by Margaret Cavendish, and, I argue, established as a massively influential subgenre by Sterne in 1768. Thanks to Sterne's inflections, the "sentimental journey," in both literature and cinema, ultimately owes something important to this arcane theological doctrine.

In the Latitudinarian tradition, in which Sterne (like many Anglican divines) was trained, the ancient notion of the soul would be saved by a modern notion of the heart. Body and soul, matter and spirit, would be reconciled in their being sentimentalized together. The consequences of this influential negotiation have surfaced in explicit representations of matter and spirit from Shaftesbury and Sterne to Mary Shelley and Dickens to Griffith and Capra. It is admittedly a circuitous route that leads from More's vehicular hypothesis to vehicular conceits in Wim Wenders's *Kings of the Road*, but I try to signpost it as clearly as possible. In most of these cases, the relation between sensibility and sentiment, on the one hand, and materiality, on the other, proves to be surprisingly central. This recognition takes on added force when one considers the notion of a "medium" in relation to the intellectual history of materialism. A medium might be described as a means of communication that falls between what Aristotle called a material cause and an instrumental cause. Media materialism, not to say technological determinism, must be a central issue for an account that follows the successive reanimations of the sentimental disposition in theater, print, and film. I say "successive," but this history is neither quite continuous nor discontinuous. It is perhaps better described as "actively layered," to borrow Peter Galison's informal label for his and Lorraine Daston's account of modern scientific objectivity—closer, perhaps, to a focused media archaeology than a history.[3]

What I offer is an "archaeology" in this rough-and-ready sense, rather than in the more technical understanding of the scholarly genre proposed by Michel Foucault. Nonetheless, the importance I attach to cinema's literary-cultural past here distinguishes my efforts from, say, Charles Affron's *Cinema and Sentiment*, a fine book of interpretative essays on emotion and film art published over three decades ago by this press. My book intends, as Affron's does not, to produce an account of sentimental cinema's relation to earlier literary sentimentalism. Moreover, it claims to find in this story a more technical, specific, and coherent conception of cinematic sentiment in the bargain. This more focused conception of cinematic sentiment makes it possible to see the historical stratigraphy I claim to trace, and it involves several component terms that in some cases date back to those seventeenth-century issues about materialism. A quick lexicon of those keywords might be helpful.

The first is *sensibility*, a term closely connected to More's understanding of the faculty for which he coined the term "sensorium" in 1650, as indicated in Laurence Sterne's famous ejaculation in *Sentimental Journey*: "Dear sensibility! . . . great SENSORIUM of the world!"[4] Sensibility is what enables us to have fine-grained sensory experience—to feel. Sterne calls it the "fountain of our feelings." Another notion is *point of view*, a philosophical concept that develops as the sensorium is increasingly understood to be punctually located in time and space, especially in the representational practices of early fiction from Aphra Behn and Daniel Defoe to Samuel Richardson and Fanny Burney. By the mid-eighteenth century, when the term "sentimental" was coined, the notion of a point of view was well developed in both literature and philosophy. A third is *mobility*, which here specifically registers the relation between motion and emotion, the sensibility's capacity both to move and to be moved, to travel both in body and in spirit, actually or virtually. Such movement is thus associated with a fourth notion, *virtuality*, which marks the capacity of an embodied sensorium (in the new scientific understanding of that notion) to undergo circulation among a range of imagined sensory locations. For the eighteenth century, this kind of virtualized circulation generates a crucially modern epistemological structure that Hume identified as a "general point of view" and that his friend Adam Smith turned into his "impartial spectator." Point of view is the most marked index of an embedded sensorium, but since more senses than the visual are involved, it is not the whole story. *Generality* itself is central to the sentimental formation, as one of sentimentalism's opponents, William Blake, recognized when he said that truth resided in "minute particular[s]" and "to generalize is to be an idiot."[5]

Probably the key component in this conceptual cluster, however, is *sympathy*, which connects one sensorium with another by enabling us to face one another, adopt one another's points of view, and modify passion into sentiment by means of virtual circulation. The process by which the central figure of the literary spectator becomes sentimentalized over the course of the eighteenth century is, more or less, the process by which that spectator comes to be defined by a capacity for sympathy, in this specific sense of the term. The foundations of sympathy shaped a central line of cinema as we know it. Thus, important starting points for my archaeology, clues for where to dig deeper, occur in a series of films by Frank Capra. I claim these films mark steps in Capra's own gradual discovery that Hollywood's narrative system, its techniques for shooting and editing, effectively embodied the kind of regulated or networked sympathy formalized in the eighteenth century.

And finally, in explicating the Enlightenment moment in this actively layered history, I also make much of Friedrich Schiller's notion of the sentimental as dependent on *reflection*, and thus as ambivalently "reflexive," in a way that fits the conceptual repertoire I have just outlined. Relevant to such reflexivity is Niklas Luhmann's idea of secondary observation, which offers a very abstract version of some of the Enlightenment developments I trace, especially in respect to habits of generalization. Yet his account of second-order systemic processes in the eighteenth century seems itself too generalized for my purposes. I wish to preserve the specificity of something identifiable as sentiment not only in the eighteenth century of *Sentimental Journey* but also, in modified form, in the nineteenth century of *A Christmas Carol* and the twentieth century of Griffith's emotionally charged narrative system and Capra's appropriation of it.

I should alert my readers that this book's own *dispositio* is not altogether straightforward. Like Sergei Eisenstein, I view the traffic between literature and cinema as a two-way street. I do contend that the new forms of literary spectatorship of the eighteenth century provided some of the conditions for the possibility of close-ups and shot/reverse-shot techniques in classical Hollywood cinema. At the same time, the work of Eisenstein's friend Capra, increasingly self-conscious about that system as one of its early auteurs, provides a kind of aperture for seeing in fresh relief crucial features of earlier sentimental literature, especially those pertaining to the structures of sympathy in the networked spectatorship of the eighteenth century. Over two decades as an insider-outsider in Hollywood, from 1928 to 1948, Capra developed a kind of self-consciousness, so I argue, about the meaning of the classical narrative system of cinema that his hero Griffith had done much to forge. Agreeing with Eisenstein that Dickens mattered much to this system, but disagreeing with Eisenstein's account of how he mattered, I suggest that Dickens helped to sustain and evolve both the case of the eighteenth-century literary spectator and the sentimental network in which that spectator was enmeshed. I suggest that Eisenstein recognized the sentimental connection but elided it in favor of linking literature and cinema in a genealogy of Soviet montage. I argue further that Capra, by stages, came to see (1) that Hollywood cinema was a medium of sentiment in this more technical sense; (2) that the discovery had political implications for film practice; and (3) with *It's a Wonderful Life*, that the historical roots of Hollywood's narrative code could be traced into the cultural past for which his Dickens stood.

The interest and instability of that network—as developed in the early novel, formalized by Adam Smith, brought to narrative self-consciousness by Sterne, and projected in Griffith and Capra—lie in the way in which the horizontal field of mutually reflective relationships is compounded by a vertical structure of reflexive levels. The resulting scheme is thus at once a circuit of reflections and an ascending scale of reflexivity. Both metaphors—the circuit and the ascending scale—derive importantly from eighteenth-century commerical discourse: the former from the period's theories of trade, the latter from its notions of moral progress. There is tension between these two ways of imagining sentiment, and that tension appears in the rich ambivalences and ambiguities of the sentimental mode. Sympathy is a key element in each, and it is worth stressing that, while this book takes its starting clues from cinema, what it offers is an archaeology of sympathy, not of cinema itself. That latter project, of course, has its own vast and active agenda at the present time, not least in the productive work on "cinema before cinema" now being undertaken by, among others, my colleague Tom Gunning.

It will be obvious by now that the chapters of this book are not arranged in chronological order. The book begins, in medias res, with American cinema. Though I trigger the argument with some references to the Capraesque in contemporary American culture, my starting point is in his early cinema. Several dates, several moments, are crucial in Capra's productive career. One of them is 1938, when he became the first American director to appear on the cover of *Time* magazine, as self-proclaimed avatar of a new, director-centered approach to filmmaking and president of both the Academy of Motion Picture Arts and Sciences and the Screen Directors Guild. Another is 1948, which marks the beginning of the end for both Capra and the studio system. But a crucial early moment, a starting point for his career as he himself recounts it, occurs in 1922, when, with no experience as a director, Capra talked his way on to a San Francisco set and made a twelve-minute film of a narrative poem by Rudyard Kipling, *The Ballad of Fultah Fisher's Boarding House*— a film for which at least one print has miraculously survived. That same year, 1922, found him working for Erich von Stroheim on the monumental production of *Greed*, an adaptation of Frank Norris's naturalist masterpiece *McTeague*. Von Stroheim's work, as we will see, would retrospectively be taken by critics like Bazin to anticipate an alternative cinematic idiom to the one Capra (and others in the 1930s) elaborated in the new talkies. Capra, for his part, rejected von Stroheim's filmmaking in favor of Griffith's, as he explains in another significant episode from his autobiography.

Here then, in its most schematic form, is the large loop I trace in this book. From Capra's apprentice work for von Stroheim in 1922 it goes on, in part 1, to follow a path through Capra's career until 1948, and his reception up through the present. In part 2 the argument circles back to the eighteenth century to look at the internalization of theater and the virtualization of the spectator, both of which help to constitute the sentimental in the print medium. In digging deeper into the history behind this figure of "Dickens," to whom Eisenstein said we must turn to understand the cinema of Griffith, the middle part of the book examines four related eighteenth-century formations: the sentimental case, sentimental probability, the sentimental vehicle, and the sentimental monster. All are relevant to Dickens and the milieu of Victorian narrative and visual culture, yet all had their emergence in the earlier history of the sentimental as I outline it here. In part 3 the discussion works forward through the two great antisentimental movements of Romanticism and Modernism. For while there have been critiques of the sentimental almost since the time of its first appearance, these two cultural movements are often understood as defining themselves by a rejection of it. Interested as I am in the repudiations, I am also interested in the ways in which key authors in these movements nonetheless seriously engage with sentimental forms and themes, and how these engagements unavoidably leave their works marked by the sentimental mode.

A consideration of sentimentalism in James Joyce's *Ulysses*, published in 1922, enables us to return full circle to a moment of departure. If we recall that Joyce had attempted to establish the first cinema in Ireland just a few years earlier, a closing of the circuit in this way perhaps becomes a little less improbable. The two chapters of part 3 matter to the book in other ways as well. In chapter 8, which considers the response of Blake and Wordsworth to sentimentalism, I pose a question about how the features of the sentimental mode, with its novelistic scheme of interlocking points of view, can be registered within the constraints and capacities of lyric verse. My answer there is that wordplay, syntactical ambiguity, and shifting voice positions in the lyric—for example, in the rediscovery and psychologization of ballad dialogues—are made to do work that is done in the sentimental novel by syllepsis and shifting points of view. Chapter 9 approaches the problem of cinema and literary modernism not as a question about a new literature that self-consciously registers cinematic effects, nor, as David Trotter so suggestively does, as a question about how cinematic realism shapes modernist literary practice, but rather as two parallel outcomes of sentimentalism. Indeed, Conrad's studied use of quasi-cinematic close-ups and pivotal shot/ reverse-shot sequences in *Lord Jim* actually anticipates the emergence of Hollywood's classical narrative system by a decade or two. Finally, partly on account of the subtlety of these issues, the two chapters of part 3 afford the opportunity for a more extended analysis of particular literary texts than elsewhere in the book.

In its largest aims, this book seeks to bring together literary history/criticism with film history/criticism. I have tried to craft it in such a way that readers more familiar with one side of the scholarship than the other will neither be bored by what they know better nor uninterested in what they know less well. Readers interested only in cinema can probably read only part 1 with some profit. Readers interested only in the literary side can probably read the introduction and parts 2 and 3 and find themselves able to place the claims in the larger argument. My hope, of course, is that the argument will be engaged as a whole. As I write in the book's coda, I mean to recapture the mutual possibilities opened up by the encounter between Joyce and Eisenstein in 1929, where each so impressed the other. Likewise, I mean to overcome any residual resistance that might descend to us from the fact that I. A. Richards founded modern literary criticism at Cambridge in that very same year, with a book, *Practical Criticism*, grounded on the assumption that cinema was no more (nor less) than a symptom of a massive cultural problem for which the careful study of poetry was the solution.

INTRODUCTION   The Sentimental Mode

Across a range of disciplines, there has been much scholarly interest of late in what might broadly be called the world of feeling. The work that has been done in this vein identifies its subject matter with a variety of labels: the emotions, the passions, pathos, the affections, affect, sensibility. Although such differences matter, one also finds common tendencies in this scholarship. It typically tries to come to terms both with the facts of the feelings (how they work, how they relate to each other) and with the meanings of the feelings (and how their significance has been acknowledged, suppressed, or explained). Often it seeks to explore how the affective side of our lives is to be understood in relation to our cognitive or ratiocinative powers. In so doing, such work often steers clear of simple oppositions between feeling and thinking, or feeling and knowing, and turns instead toward the cognitive or rational elements in our experience of the emotions and toward their role in judgment.

In choosing *sentiment* as my focus, I necessarily join those scholars who have interested themselves in the cognitive and rational aspects of the world of feeling. In one range of its meanings, *sentiment* historically belongs in a grouping that includes terms like *observation* or *reflection*. The first definition of "sentiment" listed in Dr. Johnson's *Dictionary* is "thought; notion; opinion."

In Johnson's time, the term could refer more particularly to the propositional content of a statement—to the sentiment, one would say, as opposed to its expression or to the form in which it is couched. Thus, Johnson's somewhat awkwardly phrased second definition: "The sense considered distinctly from the language or things."[1] Johnson may well have been thinking of the sorts of "sentiment, caution, aphorism, reflection and observation" that Samuel Richardson had recently culled from his influential novel *Clarissa* (1747–1748) and placed at the conclusion of the third edition (1751). Few writers have mattered more to the early history of sentiments than Richardson, in whose hands a sentiment could take the form of a declarative sentence addressed to a specific topic. The following proposition appeared in his 1751 gleanings from *Clarissa* under the rubric "Character": "Characters very good, or extremely bad, are seldom justly given." And this one appeared under "Charity": "True Generosity is Greatness of soul: it incites us to do more by a fellow-creature than can be strictly required of us."[2] For Richardson, a sentiment could be expressed as a statement with a subject matter.

Sentiment thus was, and to a degree still is, grammatically congruent with a term like "opinion." One can speak of a person's several sentiments or opinions, and of a person's overall sentiment or opinion on a given subject, and one can also speak of *shared* sentiment, or *public* or *national* sentiment, just as in the case of opinion. Yet sentiment proves to be more involved in the affective life than opinion. This is perhaps because it came to be understood as the outcome of an *experience*, as something felt—sensed, from the Latin *sentire*—rather than just held or thought.[3] This later, affective association with sentiment may be connected with another new usage of the term (dating to the same period as Richardson's harvesting of moral sentences from *Clarissa*), in which sentiment is understood as the expression of a wish or aspiration. The clearest evidence for this connotation is to be found in another kind of collection, the extremely popular but little discussed genre of the "collection of toasts and sentiments." From the mid-eighteenth century these lists were often appended to published popular song lyrics. In the decades after 1750, one finds scores of these collections, almost all in a remarkably consistent format. Though they have had little critical attention, these collections, together with Richardson's moral sentences from *Clarissa*, mark perhaps the earliest English example of what might be called the form of the sentiment as such. And they clearly register the side of sentiments that opens not only toward opinion and judgment but also toward affect and conviviality. Both toasts and sentiments as literary performances figure signally in certain key works I discuss in this book.

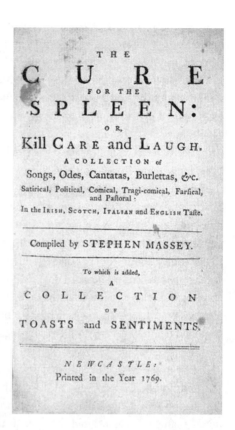

THE

C U R E

FOR THE

S P L E E N:

O R,

Kill CARE and LAUGH.

A COLLECTION of

Songs, Odes, Cantatas, Burlettas, &c.

Satirical, Political, Comical, Tragi-comical, Farſical, and Paſtoral :

In the IRISH, SCOTCH, ITALIAN and ENGLISH Taſte.

Compiled by STEPHEN MASSEY.

To which is added,

A

C O L L E C T I O N

O F

TOASTS and SENTIMENTS.

N E W C A S T L E :

Printed in the Year 1769.

Early instance of a volume of popular songs that includes "a collection of toasts and sentiments." Bodleian Library, University of Oxford, aleph no. 013591832.

Performing a grammatical function like that of opinion but carrying a semantic implication involving it in the feelings, the term "sentiment" thus, over the course of the eighteenth century, came to indicate a new kind of element in the world of ethics and aesthetics. The story of this early transformation has been told in a variety of ways, perhaps nowhere with more scholarly rigor than in Isabel Rivers's magisterial history of British religious and ethical thought.[4] Her two-volume study charts first a partial displacement of grace by reason and then a partial displacement of grace and reason by sentiment. The notion of sentiment itself underwent a crucial transformation in and beyond the decades studied by Rivers, even as it began to assume a more central place in moral and aesthetic discourse.[5]

Various stages can be distinguished in the process of this transformation. The crucial one in Britain, perhaps, comes with the first wave of "moral sense" writing, especially the early eighteenth-century publication of the work of Anthony Ashley Cooper (the third Earl of Shaftesbury) and Frances

Hutcheson, who proselytized and extended Shaftesbury's ideas in Ireland and Scotland. These founders of the moral sense school were themselves working in the wake of the writers alternately called Cambridge Platonists, Latitudinarians, or sometimes just "Latitude men." Some influential modern notions about the soul arose with these writers' responses to the radical challenges posed by materialism, mechanism, and the new science. Writers like Shaftesbury and Hutcheson took Latitudinarian thought further than the early Latitudinarians might have wished, however, and they did so precisely by making sentiment so central to their concerns. From the 1720s to the 1750s, the notion of sentiment would receive a yet more powerful elaboration by two Scottish followers of Hutcheson, David Hume and Adam Smith, for whom it became, as we shall see, closely associated with the figure of the virtualized spectator.[6] By the 1760s, there existed a robust school of thought in Britain that founded moral theory squarely on the basis of the sentiments.[7] From the eighteenth century forward, the discourse of sentiments would be closely connected to the discourse on the soul. The first instance of the adjective "sentimental" I have found in English, somewhat earlier than philologists reckoned before the advent of digitally assisted searches, is in fact the phrase "sentimental soul" in 1743.[8]

It was in the 1750s, a decade that saw both the collected sentiments of the third edition of *Clarissa* and the first rash of song books concluding with "toasts and sentiments," that the new term began to take hold, and it very quickly came to be associated with a new mode of writing and composition. This literary *façon de faire* enjoyed quick success, provoked much controversy, and survived in various guises for many decades to come. It is still with us today in a range of forms and practices. It is a mode of representation that derives in demonstrable ways from the increasingly important conceptualization of sentiment in eighteenth-century moral philosophy, even as it shaped moral philosophy in its turn: Adam Smith, a key figure in this story, once suggested that we had more to learn from modern novelists like Richardson and Riccoboni than from many classical philosophers.[9] The sentimental indeed owes much to the prior literary and cultural modes, genres, and contexts among which it took shape. These include not only that "new species of writing" called the novel, but a host of other developments as well: the transformed conventions of the theater, the burgeoning epistolary culture, modern notions of decorum, Enlightenment theories of taste and style, coffee-house culture and other elements of the new public sphere, the emergence of what would later be called the social sciences, new forms of public space, and so on.

Laurence Sterne became a major avatar for the new mode that came to be called the sentimental, and he looms large in this book for that reason and many others. The celebrity that attached to his work in the 1760s with the serial publication of *Tristram Shandy*, and that would be sustained after his untimely death in 1768, much increased the currency that the notion of the sentimental would soon acquire.[10] Though Sterne did not coin the term "sentimental," he did much to circulate it when he incorporated it in the title of his last work, *A Sentimental Journey* (1768), which, coming on the heels of *Tristram Shandy*, enjoyed perhaps even more massive popular vogue and more serious cultural influence across Europe and America and beyond. Indeed, in a scene as remote from Sterne's eighteenth-century Yorkshire as the St. Petersburg of the Russian Revolution, Viktor Shklovsky, leader of the Russian Formalist school of criticism, would announce Sterne's centrality to modern culture. Shklovsky pointedly entitled his 1923 memoir of the tumultuous 1917–1922 period *Sentimental'noe puteshestvie* (*Sentimental Journey*), after Sterne's famous book. The memoir, republished twice in the Soviet Union of the 1920s, registers Shklovsky's pivotal critical engagement with Sterne from as early as 1918 through a series of lectures and essays in which he showcases his new formalist method with a bold argument: despite its seeming eccentricity, *Tristram Shandy*'s laying bare of its fictional devices enabled it to become the very epitome of the novel as a genre. This is why Sterne's work was "revolutionary," as Shklovsky pointedly wrote in 1921.[11] For my purposes, too, Sterne's work stands as a revolution and an epitome. And since this work, especially *Sentimental Journey*, is not as familiar as it once was, it might be helpful to look briefly at Sterne's distinctive way of proceeding— to get a feel, as it were, for his sentimental mood or mode, especially in relation to his interest in how a mood modulates with alterations in what Sterne's century called "humor."

A Sentimental Mise-en-Scène

The very opening pages of Sterne's *A Sentimental Journey*—a book arranged not in chapters but in brief titled sections—alert us that the journey in question traverses more boundaries than those of place and nation.[12] In the inaugural sequence, Sterne's narrator-protagonist, Parson Yorick (a minor character in *Tristram Shandy*), traveling on impulse to France to settle a matter of etiquette, discourteously refuses alms to a Franciscan mendicant on arrival at Calais, and then immediately expresses remorse for his action. This all occurs before we come to the preface, which is supposedly written in a detached chaise in a carriage yard at Calais before the journey across France has even begun. Readers of *Tristram Shandy* will not be surprised to know that the preface comes several pages into the narrative—that is standard enough Shandean fare—but they may be struck by Yorick's signal and recurring use of the word "order," starting with that mystifying opening sentence: "——They order, said I, this matter better in France—."[13]

A posthumous sequel to the book, once thought to be written by Sterne's friend John Hall-Stevenson, has it that the matter in question concerns toasts, "the inconvenience of drinking healths whilst at meal, and toasts afterwards."[14] Toasting, it turns out, figures in at the opening of the second brief section of *Sentimental Journey*, when Yorick has found himself "incontestably in France" and therefore subject to the infamous *droits d'aubaine*, the claim of the king of France on an alien's property in the event of his death on French soil:

CALAIS

WHEN I had finish'd my dinner, and drank the King of France's health, to satisfy my mind that I bore him no spleen, but, on the contrary, high honour for the humanity of his temper—I rose up an inch taller for the accommodation.

—No—said I—the Bourbon is by no means a cruel race: they may be misled like other people; but there is a mildness in their blood. As I acknowledged this, I felt a suffusion of a finer kind upon my cheek—more warm and friendly to man, than what Burgundy (at least of two livres a bottle, which was such as I had been drinking) could have produced.

—Just God! said I, kicking my portmanteau aside, what is there in this world's goods which should sharpen our spirits, and make so many kind-hearted brethren of us, fall out so cruelly as we do by the way?

When man is at peace with man, how much lighter than a feather weighs the heaviest of metals in his hand! he pulls out his purse, and holding it airily and uncompress'd, looks round him, as if he sought for an object to share it with—In doing this, I felt every vessel in my frame dilate—the arteries beat all chearily together, and every power which sustained life, perform'd it with so little friction, that 'twould have confounded the most *physical precieuse* in France: with all her materialism, she could scarce have called me a machine—

I'm confident, said I to myself, that I should have overset her creed.

The accession of that idea, carried nature, at that time, as high as she could go—I was at peace with the world before, and this finish'd the treaty with myself—

—Now, was I a King of France, cried I—what a moment for an orphan to have begg'd his father's portmanteau of me! (3–4)

Crossing a vexed national border a scant few years after the bloody Seven Years' War (1756–1763), apparently on a mission to verify a point about formalities of toasting, Yorick himself offers a toast to the king of France, despite being angry over the *droits d'aubaine*. He enters into a mood of humane benevolence, rejoicing in his own generosity. He becomes a study, it would seem, in the figure that would come to be called "the man of feeling."

Not all, however, is as it seems in this passage, as becomes clear in retrospect when events give the lie to Yorick's self-representation: "I had scarce utter'd the words, when a poor monk of the order of St. Francis came into the room to beg something for his convent" (4). Yorick not only refuses alms to the monk but scolds and insults him. And then, just as abruptly, he suffers pangs of remorse: "My heart smote me the moment he shut the door . . . : every ungracious syllable I had utter'd, crouded back into my imagination: I reflected, I had no right over the poor Franciscan, but to deny him; and that the punishment of that was enough to the disappointed without the addition of unkind language" (7). The sequence with the monk in Calais is set off from the rest of the book by the postponed preface, thus forming a kind of preliminary set piece, a trial run, a sample of what is to come. But what does it betoken?

Thomas Jefferson, who thought Sterne the most important moralist of the age and always carried a copy of *Sentimental Journey* on his own travels, singled out this very sequence for attention when he gave his account of what makes the book compelling. For Jefferson, it demonstrates the innovative play of impulse and reflection in Sterne's writings, how this work engages readers with a vivid representation of shifts in mood. On a closer look, however, what constitutes Yorick's expansive mood in the first of the Calais sections is inextricable from the peculiarities of his way of narrating it: disposition here goes hand in hand with *dispositio*. Note that Yorick does not say he drinks a toast to the king because he bears the king high honor rather than spleen. Rather, he says he does so to "satisfy his mind" that this represents his disposition. How can a toast, such an "accommodation," as Yorick calls it, satisfy one's mind about one's disposition? That it apparently succeeds in doing so is registered in Yorick's claim that he "rose up an inch taller for [it]." It is only then, after all, that he speaks his mind on the question of the issue of the humanity of the Bourbon race more broadly, and this "acknowledgment" seems in turn to affect his body, producing a blush of benevolence "warm and friendly to man" upon his cheek, a blush not to be mistaken for the flush caused by red wine. Yorick's account of this generous impulse leads him to construe the fact of its palpable occurrence in him—what he can "feel" of it in the vessels and arteries of his frame—as evidence against a materialist or mechanistic understanding of human action.

We might speculate that the basis for this last conclusion has to do with how the "accommodation" in the toast to the health of the king and the "acknowledgment" in the sentiment about the humanity of the Bourbon race both seem to induce bodily effects (rather than the other way around). Yet in the very next section, reflecting on that refusal of alms to the monk, which seems to belie his self-described mood of humanity and fellow-feeling, Yorick declares, "There is no regular reasoning upon the ebbs and flows of our humours; they may depend upon the same causes, for ought I know, which influence the tides themselves" (4). Yorick is now sounding every bit as much the materialist as the most physical *précieuse*. The question of whether we can reason regularly about humors, or understand the nature of their causes, is thus very much in play in *Sentimental Journey*. The answers, however, seem to be caught up in contradiction and disorder.

When you examine the structure of Sterne's fiction, wrote Shklovsky, "you begin to see that the disorder is intentional," even "poetic"—"strictly regulated, like a painting by Picasso."[15] Sterne gives us several clues as to the designed disorder of how Yorick represents his heady mood in the first "Calais" section. For example, in hypothetically putting himself in the place of the king of France toward the close of the passage, Yorick seems to suggest that his expansive mood would guarantee the king's generosity in respect to the spoils of the *droits d'aubaine*. But since Yorick would be the beneficiary of this generosity, such a suggestion might itself appear self-interested, and thus ungenerous. So might the criticism Yorick levels against French materialism, by way of Molière's satirical portrait of seventeenth-century salon women in *Les précieuses ridicules* (1659). Yorick turns this figure into a *précieuse physicale*— that is, a "materialist" female *philosophe*, bred on a century of mechanism, from Descartes to La Mettrie, author of *L'homme machine* (1748).[16] And Yorick's generous feeling itself turns into a "confidence" that he should have "overset her creed." Here, as in the earlier phrase "with all of her materialism," "her" can refer either to the physical *précieuse* or to "France." In this light, the Englishman's generous praise of France's generosity carries a contradictory insinuation about her unspiritual creed.

As a final clue to the design of Sterne's disorder, there is the curious moment in this passage that slips bizarrely from general to particular, and from typification to narration. It is the moment where Yorick describes, by way of general rule, what it is to feel and act when "man is at peace with man." The verbal flourish with which Yorick describes this state must first be read, I think, as a self-consciously typifying kind of rhetoric: the coins of the emblematic man-at-peace sit lightly in his hand, and, filling out the emblem, "he pulls out his purse, and holding it airily and uncompress'd, looks round him, as if he sought for an object to share it with" (4). Clearly, Yorick seems to be offering the kind of rhetorical exemplum or generalizing figure for which the particularities of a fictional character's actual case are beside the point: this, in general, is the way of a man with an easy conscience. But suddenly the timelessness of aphorism is displaced into the time of narrative action: "In doing this, I felt every vessel of my frame dilate." That is to say, what Yorick describes in the general case of "man . . . at peace with man" are not things that we seem meant to imagine Yorick himself as actually doing. Yorick appears, therefore, to step into the role of a figure drawn from a sweeping trope of rhetorical generalization. Putting the point the other way around, we might say that the figure is made literal.

In rhetoric, the name for the trope that conflates the literal and figurative is *syllepsis*.[17] On Shklovsky's analysis, we might speculate that, while this trope matters to the novel in general—how do we draw such lines in narrative fiction, after all?—Sterne makes it especially apparent in his own practice. Adapting Shklovksy's point for my purposes, I suggest that Sterne's revolutionary act of laying bare this device contributes to the sentimental disposition. To see this more clearly, consider another example, just pages later, when a hand again figures in a moment of literalization. Having entered the carriage yard, Yorick sees the monk in conversation with a beautiful woman, worries she may be hearing about his ill treatment of the monk, and then falls into heated negotiations with the master of the carriage yard. No sooner has this contretemps subsided than Yorick reproaches himself for his anger:

> Base passion! said I, turning myself about, as a man naturally does upon a sudden reverse of sentiment—base, ungentle passion! thy hand is against every man, and every man's hand against thee—heaven forbid! said she, raising her hand up to her forehead, for I had turned full in front upon the lady I had seen in conference with the monk—she had followed us unperceived—Heaven forbid indeed! said I, offering her my own—she had a black pair of silk gloves open only at the thumb and two fore-fingers, so accepted it without reserve. (13)

The literalization of the hand here goes hand in hand with another trope, one that matches a "sudden reverse of sentiment" with a quick turnabout of the body. These are indeed just two instances among many in *Sentimental Journey* where the figure of the hand seems to be made literal flesh, as it were, in the act of narration.[18]

Between these two encounters, soon after Yorick first enters the carriage yard, occurs a passage that raises to explicitness a problem of the relation of the narrative's literal and figurative levels. Yorick, writing his preface in the desobligeant, casts doubt on the idea that in an age of enlightenment's spreading beams, one must literally travel to partake of the benefits of other countries, concluding his peroration with an apostrophe in the form of a rhetorical question: "Where then, my dear countrymen, are you going—" The question is interrupted by some Englishmen, standing outside the vehicle in which Yorick has been writing his preface:

> —We are only looking at this chaise, said they—Your most obedient servant, said I, skipping out of it, and pulling off my hat—We were wondering, said one of them. . . . what could occasion its motion.——'Twas the agitation, said I coolly, of writing a preface. (11)

Here, we might say, the figure of apostrophe—Yorick's address to his presumably absent "dear countrymen"—is made literal in the persons of the Englishmen, who seem to materialize out of nowhere, providing the rhetorical question with a comically literal response. All this raises the question: what kind of virtual or fictional world have we been drawn into with Sterne's baffling travel story? It is clearly one in which problems of virtuality have themselves been multiply complicated.

Thomas Jefferson singled out just this aspect of Sterne, in this very episode, when he wrote to his friend Robert Skipwith with such high praise for Sterne's moral project: "We neither know nor care whether Laurence Sterne really went to France, whether he was there accosted by the poor Franciscan, at first rebuked him unkindly, and gave him a peace offering; or whether the whole be not a fiction. In either case we are equally sorrowful at the rebuke, and secretly resolve we will never do so; we are pleased with the subsequent atonement, and view with emulation a soul candidly acknowledging its fault, and making a just reparation."[19] This is a partial answer to the question of what makes this journey "sentimental." Yet the logic of Shklovsky's analysis of Sterne's larger implications encourages us to press the question more closely as to just what other devices are laid bare in *Sentimental Journey*. It is one burden of *An Archaeology of Sympathy* to do just that, partly by showing what writers and artists in various genres and media saw in Sterne (or in those shaped by his work) for decades to come, even beyond Shklovsky's own moment.

Though Sterne did not coin the term "sentimental," he did invent the phrase "sentimental journey" to name his *new* new thing in the world. The phrase quickly became a kind of shibboleth for authors from many literary cultures. One measure of the novelty of the term sentimental itself in 1768 is that when a German writer attempted to translate it into German, he was obliged to coin a new word—*empfindsam*—to capture the English neologism. Marx's use of the imported adjective in his early poem "Sentimentale Seelen" matters to the work of that lyric, as we shall see, and likewise the use of the term *sentimentalisch* by the Anglophile Friedrich Schiller in 1795. Germany was in fact one of the many places in the world where Sterne and the sentimental attracted enormous interest. Indeed, Schiller and his friend Johann Wolfgang von Goethe would find themselves in an intense epistolary exchange about "sentimental journeys" in 1797, not long after the publication of Schiller's *On Naïve and Sentimental Poetry* (1795), which Goethe praised.

I take Schiller's analysis in this little treatise very seriously in my own approach to the category of the sentimental. I see his treatise as achieving for it something like what Edmund Burke had achieved for the categories of the sublime and beautiful several decades earlier. Schiller, we will see, explains the sentimental as a literary mode constituted at once by ambivalence and reflexivity—two features that stand out in those early pages of *Sentimental Journey*—and this powerful insight proves most helpful in correcting some misleading views of the matter. As both practitioner and theorist, Schiller had a keen interest in British literature and philosophy. His plays of the 1780s and 1790s borrowed heavily from Shakespeare, and, as his invocation of Sterne suggests, he attended to developments in Britain's language, thought, and culture during the decades when the sentimental was emerging there.[20] Schiller's essay serves as a reminder that the sentimental is a mode or mood defined not by a simplistic form of sincerity but rather by a complex form of modernity, one that brings difficult questions of virtuality and fictionality into play. Schiller's arguments have not had the recognition they deserve in discussions of the sentimental mood, especially among commentators who reduce it to elementary sympathy, to sincerity, or to simplicity itself.[21] It will be clear that I tend to use the term "sentiment" in this book in ways consistent with how the term took shape in the late eighteenth century, especially as inflected by Schiller's commentary.

Put most crudely, "sentiment," as I employ it, means something like distributed feeling. It is emotion that results from social circulation, passion that has been mediated by a sympathetic passage through a virtual point of view. It involves a structure of vicariousness. In such an understanding, therefore, sentiment is precisely not a "vehement passion."[22] Vehement passion draws a line around a human subject, defining and intensifying personal will, personal limits, a person's strongest emotional attachments. Vehement passion signals our invisible depths. Sentiments, by contrast, might be said to spread us thin.[23] They are the result of a projective imagination across a network or relay of regard. By "regard," I mean attention, respect, heed, care, but I also mean something closer to the French sense of regard: a look or a gaze, an act performed with the eyes. The regard in question involves a sense of how another is regarding us, what our eyes can see in the eyes of another, or more generally in the face of another.[24]

Sentiments, that is, tend to involve speculation as to the meaning of another's countenance, what it expresses and what it hides. One might say that they elaborate a system of looking at lookers looking—even, or especially, when all this looking is taking place in the virtual space of the printed page. Yorick's narration of his encounter with the monk, for example, is very much a play of eyes and faces, looks and countenances: Yorick was against the monk from "the moment [he] cast [his] eyes upon him" (5); when the monk offers "a cast upwards with his eyes," Yorick knows that he appeals to heavenly authority (6); when the monk gives "a slight glance with his eye downward upon the sleeve of his tunick," Yorick feels "the full force of the appeal" and acknowledges the monk's poverty (6). These eye-casts are echoed in "the whole cast of [the monk's] look and figure," which Yorick later berates himself "not to have been struck with" (6) when he can still bring "his figure . . . before [his] eyes" (5). All this looking and being looked at is happening on the page, and we will see that Sterne becomes even more self-conscious about the intersubjective visual field of his narrative in other more developed passages where the question of point of view is yet more insistently in play. The relation of such visual structures to ambivalence and reflexivity will be at the heart of the matter in my account of the sentimental. As Yorick says of the episode with the wife of the Parisian glove merchant: "There are certain combined looks of simple subtlety—where whim, and sense, and seriousness, and nonsense, are so blended, that all the languages of Babel set loose together could not express them—they are communicated and caught so instantaneously, that you can scarce say which party is the infecter" (46). This state of sympathetic connection, as we shall see in chapter 5, is what Latitudinarians called the "vehicular state," for which "subtlety" proves a signal term of art.

Adam Smith Goes to Hollywood

Brought into visibility by Addison and Steele, developed by innovative novelists like Richardson, theorized by Adam Smith, and turned self-consciously virtuosic in Sterne, the paradoxical figure of the spectator in printed prose in eighteenth-century Britain becomes a key player in the emergence of the sentimental as a self-conscious mode.[25] My emphasis here, then, will fall on the spectator as a paradoxically *literary* figure in this period. It is a figure strongly characterized by the notion of a "point of view." As Seymour Chatman has pointed out in his effort to recover this term for critical use, the "complexity and vagueness" of the term carries part of its interest. And he explains this interest partly by way of the Sternean trope of syllepsis, a slippage between the literal and the figurative:

> We literally stand at some point (say, the top of a skyscraper) to see something (say, the rest of the city). All three of the components of the situation—the thing seen, the place from which it is seen, and the act of seeing—are literal. But when the place "from which" becomes, figuratively, the human mind, the meanings proliferate. . . . The mind, including its perceptual equipment, can be understood either as the organ of figurative "seeing" or as the equivalent of the literal post from which the seeing takes place.[26]

The ambiguity about this term is especially rich in the context of the eighteenth century's textual embedding of the spectator, where, as in Sterne, the distinction between the literal and the figurative is blurred because of a related blurring of the distinction between the virtual and the actual.

To grasp the development of the sentimental mode as dependent on a relay of regards virtualized in a medium is to prepare for a recognition crucial to the arguments of this book. For in the course of becoming culturally central in the British Enlightenment, sentiments begin to inhabit a scheme of representation in print-cultural experience. And this scheme of features and practices, for all of their ambiguous complexity, eventually lends itself to the development of narrative cinema. In the meantime, this protocinematic eighteenth-century style took shape to impressive effect, notably in the fiction of Dickens, perhaps the most influential of all writers in the sentimental line and one whose work is saturated with the developed visual culture of his moment. "Print" itself, for Dickens's moment, was of course spectacularly pictorial in ways that he abetted.[27] Perhaps unsurprisingly, therefore, Dickens has, in his turn, often been said to anticipate the work of early filmmakers.

The features and practices in question include most prominently the registering of point of view and the precise calibration of its angle and distance, but
also the facial close-up, the reverse shot, and the eyeline match. All of these
features and practices, one might say, are part of a certain self-consciousness
about the role of the embedded spectator.

Consider Dickens's handling of the visual field in a representative early
passage from *David Copperfield*, from a chapter entitled "I Observe." David
writes that, "looking back . . . into the blank of his infancy," one of the very
first things he sees "com[ing] out of the cloud" is "our house." This sounds
straightforward enough, but as he develops his retrospection into a remembered scene at church with his nursemaid Peggotty, the vision of the house
proves to be multiply mediated:

> Here is our pew in the church. What a high-backed pew! With a window
> near it, out of which our house can be seen, and *is* seen many times during
> the morning service, by Peggotty, who likes to make herself as sure as she
> can that it's not being robbed, or is not in flames. But though Peggotty's
> eye wanders, she is much offended if mine does, and frowns to me, as I
> stand upon the seat, that I am to look at the clergyman. But I can't always
> look at him.[28]

The passage goes on to register all the things young David looks at instead
of the clergyman: "I look at a boy in the aisle, and *he* makes faces at me." And
by the end of a long paragraph we see the house as just one of the objects upon
which David looks back at himself looking at and a variety of others who are
themselves in the act of looking back at him or looking at other things. In
particular, his "house" is an object that appears framed in the church window
through his memory of Peggotty's reflected gaze. The house in turn is a
place that is partly defined by what can be seen through one of *its* windows:
his father's grave in the neighboring churchyard. In a later scene also said to
involve "looking back," David will picture himself at some length at a desk in
Salem House, where his eye, like that of all the other boys in the classroom,
carefully watches the eye of the sadistic schoolmaster Mr. Creakle. The optic
drama can become quite intense: "Now he throws his eye sideways down our
lane, and we all droop over our books and tremble."[29]

For shorthand, one can refer to this mediating system of the sentimental
mode by the term "sight lines,"[30] but I should make clear that when I associate such terms with the discourse of cinema, I really mean what is perhaps
the dominant discourse of cinema, that of the narrative system of Hollywood
cinema in its so-called classical period. This classical system is a constella-

tion of stylistic devices and procedures built on such principles as continuity editing and montage. It began to take shape among an array of other actual and imagined alternatives in the 1910s. Underpinning the peculiar rhetorical scheme of this book is a strong connection I posit between the defining practices of eighteenth-century sentimentalism and the defining practices of this central line in twentieth-century cinema, and it depends on seeing that connection as anything but adventitious. Indeed, much of what follows seeks to show the logic of it. As will become clear presently, my attempt to reveal this logic involves me in an analysis of Sergei Eisenstein's influential argument for the importance of Dickens to cinema since D. W. Griffith. The point is to establish Dickens's role as a historical zeugma, a double-sided connector in this series of reanimations, linking back to the eighteenth century and forward to the twentieth.

This book, then, is about this new thing that came into the world in mid-eighteenth century Europe and shaped cultural practices (not least cinematic practices) long afterward—a mood, or mode, or tone, or genre, or style, that came to be called the sentimental. One searches for a term because it is hard to know just what category best captures the sentimental. Friedrich Schiller refers to "*der sentimentalischen Gattung*"[31]—that is, genus or genre. We might also think of it as a "symbolic form," Erwin Panofsky's category for the Alberti-inspired system of modern perspective in painting.[32] As it happens, Panofsky was also keenly interested in the art-history category that Aby Warburg called a *Pathosformel* ("Pathos formula"), a set of guidelines and templates for the visual representation of emotions, which may be even more apposite a category to capture the sentimental.[33] Some commentators have even (in effect) produced accounts of the sentimental *Pathosformel* in the visual arts.[34] The sentimental is not, however, merely a visual phenomenon, nor is it only a literary one. It is perhaps captured by Mikhail Bakhtin's still valuable notion of a "chronotope" in the context of literature.[35] A chronotope is a form of world-making that involves not only rules for representing fictional space, time, and probability, but also, necessarily, as Bakhtin himself insists, a concomitant image of the human. All of these elements are involved in the account of the sentimental that I mean to deliver in this book. In the end, I have settled on "disposition"—or "mode," for short, with an evocation of "the sentimental mood," and a nod to Duke Ellington.[36]

In tracing a succession of chronotopes over time, Bakhtin produced a detailed account that reached as far as Rabelais, who was, with Cervantes, the great artist of prose fiction in the century before Sterne, and who was indeed, with Cervantes, one of Sterne's great favorites.[37] Another way of describing my aim in this book, therefore, is that I wish to take that next step. I seek to explain something of the structures and strategies of the sentimental, and to do so in part by producing an account of its genesis, especially its conceptual genesis in early theories of sentiment. But I also seek to show how this new thing in the world, this cultural form, was recognized and misrecognized, used and misused, embraced and resisted, in the ensuing decades. This book is more than a little concerned, in other words, with the response to the sentimental chronotope on the part of its early imitators and critics, on the part of Romantic poets, gothic novelists, sage Victorians, and even representative modernist figures such as Conrad and Joyce. It is not, however, a systematic history of the subject. It is not even clear to me what that might mean. I do not, for example, pay much attention to a figure like Harriet Beecher Stowe, central to many accounts of nineteenth-century American sentimentalism.[38]

I have suggested that some of this book's primary moves and motivations come from thinking about Hollywood cinema in the second quarter of the twentieth century. I would probably not have thought to undertake such thinking without the example of Stanley Cavell's work on just that period of cinema, which I first heard in a dazzling lecture on Preston Sturges's *The Lady Eve* in 1980. As may be already evident, though, my interests run less to philosophical questions than to historical ones, that is, to questions in literary history, cinematic history, intellectual history, and the history of media and media transformations. One of this book's grander ambitions, indeed, is to trace large and significant parallels between what we might call two media transformations—one in the eighteenth century and one in the twentieth.[39] The first involves the translation of theater into print narrative, the second, of print narrative into cinematic narrative. Both processes are messy and partial: theater no more disappears into print in the eighteenth century than theater and print do into cinema in the twentieth. Both processes matter to the sentimental archaeology that I pursue, however, and in both instances my account builds on and revises fairly well established critical arguments.

A number of scholars in recent years have suggested that eighteenth-century literary sentimentalism can be understood as a translation of earlier theatrical forms into a new print medium.[40] It is this translation that contributes crucially, for example, to what I describe as the early novel's developing interest in sight lines. Other factors play an important role as well, including the notion of the human sensorium as it emerges from the new "science of human nature" in the century from 1650 to 1750.[41] One of several paradoxical developments in the story I wish to tell is that this embodied sensorium is more and more finely articulated as the spectator turns virtual—that is, as the embodied sensorium is *embedded* in a text. Thus, the extended print culture of the eighteenth century introduced two extraordinarily influential new figures to the world, both of them quite virtual: Addison and Steele's "Mr. Spectator" and Adam Smith's "impartial spectator."[42] In both instances, the new literary form of spectatorship lends itself to circulation, and may even be said to depend on it.[43] Assimilated to print fiction, this spectator functions both inside and outside of texts, both as part of the diegesis (the story or case) and as extradiegetic witness to it.[44] The spectator faces the virtual action of the printed text, but that action is itself often constituted by the interaction of virtual faces viewed by virtual eyes. This orthogonal (or triangular) structure—the spectator who beholds what amounts to a mutual beholding on the part of two other parties—becomes a hallmark of the sentimental mode and its way of making a world, especially its recognizably new form of probability. It is a structure implicit in *Sentimental Journey*'s opening pages.

A related paradox about the emergence of the sentimental mode in the eighteenth century, one equally important to my argument, is that the topos of the face-to-face encounter becomes morally crucial at the point of its virtualization, as in the case of Yorick's encounter with the Franciscan monk. This development marks one of the ways in which the history of the face matters to my story. Another has to do with the recuperation of the face-to-face encounter in such constitutive practices of classical cinema as shot/reverse-shot and the close-up. In claiming that the pivotal figure of the literary spectator is newly virtualized in the medium of cinema, I insist that it is newly *actualized* there as well, for the face in cinema, though virtual and distributed, is nonetheless also visible.[45]

This second translation—the literary into the cinematic—is so central to this book, and the sentimental mode so crucial for it, that it demands some careful exposition. Although I am ultimately interested in showing the relationship of Frank Capra's self-consciously sentimental practices to those of Sterne, and even to the moral sentimentalism of thinkers like Adam Smith and Lord Shaftesbury, I am aware that this may seem a long gap to bridge. As a way of introducing that relationship, therefore, I wish to examine the relationship between Capra's master, D. W. Griffith, and Sterne's disciple, Charles Dickens, a connection that has long been acknowledged in critical commentary. And specifically, I want to consider in some detail the argument of Eisenstein's pioneering essay "Dickens, Griffith and Ourselves" (1944), perhaps the single most influential essay we have on the relationship of literature and cinema.[46]

The Kettle Began It

Eisenstein's argument about how to think of literature and early cinema as together supplying a genealogy of dialectical montage is anything but straightforward. An especially puzzling and telling feature of Eisenstein's analysis is its subtle play with the trope of synecdoche, the figuring of the whole by the part. This play extends to the very names in the essay's title: Eisenstein sometimes attributes significance to Griffith or Dickens in and of themselves, while at other times they stand in, respectively, for all of cinema or all of the literary past. This ambiguity makes for interesting permutations. At certain moments, Eisenstein seems to be talking simply about Griffith in relation to Dickens; at others, about Dickens in relation to all of cinema; at still others, about Griffith and all of literature. In one climactic passage, he seems to be talking about all of the above: "Let Dickens and the whole ancestral array, going back as far as the Greeks and Shakespeare, be superfluous reminders that both Griffith and our cinema prove our origins to be not solely as of Edison and his fellow inventors, but as based on an enormous cultured past; each part of this past in its own moment of world history has moved forward the great art of cinematography."[47] Eisenstein even acknowledges such confusions explicitly: "I would hate it if my comparison between Dickens and Griffith were to lose its persuasiveness ... the more so as this examination of Dickens no longer concerns Griffith's skill as a film-maker, but has begun to touch on the craft of cinema in general."[48]

Yet this kind of synecdochal ambiguity—this uncertain movement between the representative part and the represented whole—turns out to be crucial to the essay's larger burden. A great deal depends, in the end, on Eisenstein's analysis of the difference between how part-whole relationships are handled in American and Soviet cinematic practice. The essay's way with parts and wholes, in short, mimes that of the Soviet style in filmmaking that it seeks to promote. This complex argument plays out in the essay by way of the key notion of "montage," which is central to the kind of relationship Eisenstein wishes to establish between Dickens and Griffith and between Griffith and "ourselves"—that is, Soviet filmmakers like Eisenstein. Griffith stood out from all other filmmakers, Eisenstein recalls, because he was not content to settle for film as pastime or entertainment and because his ambitious work contained the "rudiments of the art." These rudiments derived from an interest in "construction and method" that Griffith imparted to Eisenstein and his fellow Soviet filmmakers. Montage, says Eisenstein, is the name that "this field, this method, this principle of construction and assembly," came to bear.[49]

The Soviets, on this account, understood that montage was even more crucial and more dynamic than what it appears to be in Griffith's practice. Griffith's chief limitation was that he approached montage "through the device of parallel action." Though he himself went no further, Griffith nonetheless made it "possible for filmmakers from the other half of the globe, from another epoch and with a different class structure, to perfect the matter definitively." How did Griffith happen to approach montage through the device of parallel action? It was, insists Eisenstein, "none other than Dickens who gave Griffith the idea of parallel action!"[50] Eisenstein's analysis of how Griffith came to montage in Dickens is not always perspicuous, though it has the advantage of being grounded in Eisenstein's citation of Griffith's own testimony, as reported on two different occasions.

The first is a comment by A. B. Walkley in the *London Times* on the occasion of Griffith's visit to London in 1922. Walkley wrote of Griffith that his "best ideas, it appears, have come to him from Dickens, who has always been his favorite author." After Dickens inspired him with one great idea in particular, his "employers" were horrified by it, but, as Walkley quotes Griffith as saying, "I went home, re-read one of Dickens's novels, and came back the next day to tell them they could either make use of my idea or dismiss me."[51] The idea in question, the central idea in Walkley's account of Griffith, "is merely that of a 'break' in the narrative, a shifting of the story from one group of characters to another group"[52]—"merely," for Walkley, because he thinks Griffith overstates his debt to Dickens in that one "might have found the same practice" by reading a host of other novelists whom he goes on to list. Walkley concedes that Griffith's citation of Dickens matters, but he explains it away by pointing to the vast general influence of Dickens. This concession is not enough for Eisenstein, though in contesting its adequacy he shifts ground to make a different point: not that Griffith learned from Dickens something he could not have learned elsewhere, but that Dickens gave "to cinematography far more guidance than that which led to the montage of parallel action alone." The special claim for such guiding influence presumed a far more ample sense of montage that resided in "Dickens's nearness to the characteristics of cinema in method, style, and especially in viewpoint and exposition."[53]

Eisenstein does in fact accept that Griffith's self-understanding of his debt to Dickens is much what Walkley takes it to be, and to make this point

Eisenstein cites a second piece of testimony, legendary in commentaries on Griffith. It has to do with a transitional one-reeler, *After Many Years* (1908), that Griffith adapted from Tennyson's "Enoch Arden." Cutting back and forth from the marooned sailor to the face of his wife awaiting him a world away, Griffith is said to have been challenged with a question: "How can you tell a story jumping about like that? The people won't know what it's about." And Griffith is supposed to have replied, "Well . . . doesn't Dickens write that way?"[54] Even as he adduces this anecdote, however, Eisenstein maintains that there is much more to Dickens's cinematic legacy, even in Griffith's own practice, than such an anecdote suggests. It isn't just about what Walkley calls the "break," nor just about telling a story by "jumping about." That is just parallel montage. Even in *After Many Years* itself, the point, for Eisenstein, has to do not with parallelism but with a qualitative transformation wrought in the shot by the editing, and vice versa. What Eisenstein emphasizes about *After Many Years* is not simply that the photographed action shifts between two locations, but that it shifts from shots that show the castaway on the desert island to *facial close-ups* of his wife. "The important thing," he says, "is *how* Griffith used close-up *for the first time as montage*."[55] Suggesting that the makings of such a practice lay in Dickens's novels, Eisenstein argues in effect that Griffith got more from Dickens's practice than he knew how to explain. This additional debt had to do, precisely, with parts and wholes. The facial close-up in the sequence of crosscuts was not merely part of a larger scene; it was a qualitative transformation of it. Such shots would, more generally, cease to be understood as just a part of montage and would demand recognition as "montage cells," a kind of molecular incorporation of the total montage process.

This notion of qualitative transformation is crucial in understanding the next step that Eisenstein claims he and his fellow Soviets were able to take with montage. For in taking that step they were in a sense incorporating into their cinematic practice all those matters of "method, style, and especially viewpoint and exposition" with which Dickens prefigured cinema in ways beyond what was capturable by the notion of the break or narrative jump between two lines of action—that is, by parallel montage. Eisenstein goes on to link the notion of parallel montage to a bourgeois frame of reference, a dual world of rich and poor presented in alternation and coming together only in artifice and fantasy. He opposes to this the more developed notion of montage, in which fusion is achieved by a qualitative alteration of everything by everything.

Virtually all of the novels Eisenstein cites in explaining the cinematic Dickens are long, multiplot works that lend themselves to the practice of "jumping around": *Oliver Twist, Martin Chuzzlewit, Dombey and Son, Tale of Two Cities*. In principle, however, what Eisenstein finds in Dickens does not depend on the multiplot format. That, after all, is exactly the mistake with which he charges Walkley: confusing the potentialities for montage in Dickens's "extraordinary optical faculty" with the contingent circumstance of his having written complex Victorian three-deckers like so many other novelists of his time.[56] Eisenstein emphatically does not allow the generic fact to mask either the specific feature of Dickens's work or the capacity that produces it.[57] On the contrary, he repeatedly gropes for new phrases to capture what makes Dickens singularly cinematic: "the astonishingly plastic quality of his novels. Their astonishing visual and optical quality."[58]

What precisely is entailed for Eisenstein in this special quality of the Dickensian imagination? Part of the answer has to do with the representation of character:

> His psychology begins with the visible; he gained his insight into character by observation of the exterior—the most delicate and fine minutiae of the outward semblance, it is true, those utmost tenuousities which only the eyes that are rendered acute by superlative imagination can perceive. Like the English philosophers, he does not begin with assumptions and suppositions, but with characteristics. He lays hold of the most inconspicuous and corporeal expressions of the soul, and by the magic of his method of caricature he brings the whole personality visibly and palpably before our eyes.[59]

Such particularities seem to be a large part of what Eisenstein means when he speaks of how Dickens contributed to cinema beyond the limits of parallel montage, especially when he claims that Dickens anticipated cinema "in his particular way of seeing, and in his exposition," or in his "particularities of exposition and style—quite apart from themes and plots."[60] Is it possible to specify these particularities more precisely, perhaps in a way that avoids the masking effect of the multiplot nineteenth-century novel?

One such way, I suggest, would be to consider the Dickens of the novella, for there the themes and plotlines are simpler. Eisenstein himself mentions a novella by Dickens, *The Cricket on the Hearth* (1845), which, as he notes, Griffith adapted in a short film that he made in 1909, the year after he made *After Many Years*. Eisenstein actually quotes the first words of the story to begin his essay—"The kettle began it!"[61]—words that for him illustrate how Dickens's focus on detail evolves into the cinematic technique of the close-up. Eisenstein does not discuss "The Cricket on the Hearth" (neither tale nor film) in much further detail—it is not clear that he even saw the film—but it offers rich evidence for his general thesis about Dickens and some productive complications as well.

The Cricket on the Hearth is a simple narrative, told in three parts, about the happy household of John Peerybingle, an honest but slow-witted "carrier" (delivery man), and his younger wife Dot. It relates how a potentially destructive shadow of doubt falls across the household and how this moral threat is overcome. Two other households are involved. One is that of Caleb Plummer, a toy maker, and his blind daughter Bertha, who are exploited by a gruff and miserly toy merchant named Tackleton, a man who despises toys and permits only ugly faces on those he sells. Tackleton is said to have "one eye wide-open, and one eye nearly shut," and "the one eye nearly shut was the expressive one"—a joke that Capra would repeat, in revised form, in *American Madness*. The other household is that of Dot Peerybingle's friend May Fielding and her mother. The triggering events of the simple plot are, first, the arrival at the Peerybingles' of an old, deaf man, called simply the Stranger, and second, the news that Tackleton has become engaged to May Fielding after persuading her mother of the advantages of the match. Dot's reaction to the Stranger strikes even John as peculiar, and later Tackleton takes umbrage at a comment by the outspoken Dot apropos his marriage to May. From this point, he keeps watch on Dot, and when all of the characters are assembled for a social occasion at the Plummers', Tackleton, who "had brought his half-shot eye to bear on her," notices a whispered exchange between Dot and the Stranger, who then leave the room together. Prompted by the cynic's wont of seeing all human motivation reduced to the level of his own, Tackleton invites the unwitting John to peer in on the clandestine meeting of his wife and the Stranger:

> The Carrier looked him in the face, and recoiled a step as if he had been struck. In one stride he was at the window, and he saw— ...
>
> He saw her with the old man; old no longer, but erect and gallant; bearing in his hand the false white hair that had won his way into their desolate and miserable home. Her saw her listening to him, as he bent his head to whisper in her ear; and suffering him to clasp her round the waist, as they moved slowly down the dim wooden gallery towards the door by which they had entered it. He saw them stop, and saw her turn—to have

the face, the face he loved so, so presented to his view!—and saw her, with her own hands, adjust the Lie upon his head, laughing, as she did it, at his unsuspicious nature! (83)

Prompted in part by the hints insidiously dropped by Tackleton ("Don't commit any violence.... You're a strong made man and you might do Murder before you know it"), John broods over his wife's imagined infidelity. That same night he takes a gun down from the mantel and approaches the door of the room where the Stranger sleeps. In the decisive moment, John's better nature prevails and he forebears. It is later revealed that the handsome young Stranger is Caleb Plummer's son Edward, betrothed to May Fielding, who has returned from three years away in South America to find her forced into an engagement with Tackleton. The denouement is straightforward. Dot helps May to wed Edward before the scheduled noon wedding with Tackleton. John sees the error of his suspicion. Dot apologizes for keeping a secret from John. Tackleton has the good grace to bring the wedding cake intended for his own party to the celebration for May and the Sailor (as the Stranger comes to be called).[62]

The Film on the Grate

So bald a summary does not do justice to the story's exemplification of what Eisenstein calls Dickens's "astonishingly optical and visual quality." But even in this sketch, it is easy to tell that the story turns on a moment of discovery—a false discovery, as it happens—with a carefully staged mise-en-scène. John's witnessing of his wife's clandestine encounter with the disguised Edward is represented as occurring from a particular point of view, and in a particular sequence of movements and perceptions. It begins as he looks at Tackleton's face at close range and "recoil[s] a step as if he had been struck." It concludes with Dot moving toward the door and turning such that her face is "presented to his view." Between these two facial moments lie the apparently incriminating actions, seen through a window on Tackleton's premises. The sense that the scene is registered precisely from John's point of view is reinforced by the suggestion of free indirect discourse with which it concludes, as John seems to be imagining his "unsuspicious nature" mocked by Dot's laughing gesture.

In Griffith's adaptation, this scene takes place at the Peerybingles' house rather than Tackleton's toy factory, and Tackleton signals John (with a nod of the head) to look at the couple through a door—actually two doors—rather

Griffith, *The Cricket on the Hearth* (1909, Biograph).
Tackleton prompts John to look in on Dot and the
Stranger.

than through a window. There are two shots of the couple on the other side of
the doors, and in each both doors are opened and someone is looking through
them: first Tackleton and then, at Tackleton's instigation, John. The camera
angle is not congruent with the internal spectator's sight line in either case,
but in both shots we are left with the impression that we are seeing what the
internal spectator is seeing. (At no time can Dot and the Stranger be seen in
the other room when the outside door is closed.) And in each case we see, in
a subsequent shot of an internal spectator, Tackleton's or John's reaction to
the spectacle of Dot and the Stranger sharing a secret pleasure—presumably
the pleasure (as we later learn) of the news that he has returned to claim May
from the clutches of Tackleton. Since Griffith sets the scene at the Peerybingles' house, he can use the same setting, the same door, for the episode
later that night when John contemplates murdering the Stranger. In the film
version, John opens the outside door, but fleetingly, and not in a way that allows the Stranger to be seen. John then drops the gun, extinguishes a candle,
and sits in relative darkness by the hearth.

What John sees inside: the
Stranger's revelation.

Dot's joy.

Door closes on the sequence.

Later, John returns to the
door, armed with a gun.

The discovery scene in Griffith's *Cricket on the Hearth* represents an early instance of the use of shot sequences to suggest the kind of "psychological causality" that film historians tend to associate with later Griffith and the Hollywood system he helped to invent.[63] The sight lines are not quite what one might imagine from reading the novella; Dickens is capable of strikingly detailed perspectival descriptions in his prose.[64] Nor does Griffith's sequence involve the use of facial close-ups, in spite of Dickens's emphasis on the moment when John recoils from Tackleton and the moment when Dot turns her face "to his view." The year before, Griffith had allegedly cited Dickens's authority for incorporating the face of Enoch Arden's wife into the sequence of intercuts between the "home" and "abroad" lines of narrative in *After Many Years*.[65] Here, however, cutting within a single scene, he does not employ the close-up, certainly not in the way of his mature feature work of 1915 and after.

Of all the visual effects in Dickens's novella, however, none perhaps is so striking as the one announced by its title: *The Cricket on the Hearth*. A strand of fantasy in the tale has it that the Peerybingles's hearth, like the hearths of all worthy households, is blessed with a spirit that takes the form of a cricket and has the capacity to induce salutary visions in those who listen to its chirping. Since the story is divided into three sections called "chirps," there is a suggestion that the tale itself is a series of cricket-inspired fantasy visions. And within the tale, the cricket's chirp plays a critical role in the pivotal scene we have just been considering, the moment of John's armed approach to the door of the Stranger's room:

> He reversed the Gun to beat the stock upon the door; he already held it lifted in the air; some indistinct design was in his thoughts of calling out to him to fly, for God's sake, by the window—
>
> When, suddenly, the struggling fire illumined the whole chimney with a glow of light; and the Cricket on the Hearth began to Chirp!
>
> No sound he could have heard; no human voice, not even hers; could so have moved and softened him. The artless words in which she had told him of her love for this same Cricket, were once more freshly spoken; her pleasant voice ... thrilled through and through his better nature, and awoke it into life and action. (89)

In Griffith's adaptation, by contrast, there is no direct representation of the cricket or its chirping. Only a viewer familiar with Dickens's story would interpret the moment of John's retreating from the door and dropping his gun as having been produced by this fantastical intervention (though such a viewer might well be part of Griffith's ideal audience). To this degree, Griffith's film remains realist in its representational assumptions.

The same pattern holds true in the crucial next steps of both Dickens's story and Griffith's adaptation of it. If the auditory intervention stays the hand of John the Carrier against the Stranger, what comes next in the story stems the tide of his jealous anger toward his wife. For when John falls back to his chair by the hearth, the "power" of the cricket adds sights to sounds and complements his auditory recollections of his wife's good offices with visual ones. The "presence" of the cricket now begins to project visual images for the sake of John's moral recovery:

> Suggesting his reflections by its power, and presenting them before him, as in a Glass or Picture.... Fairies came trooping forth. Not to stand beside him as the Cricket did, but to busy and bestir themselves. To do all honor to her image. To pull him by the skirts, and point to it when it appeared. To cluster round it, and embrace it, and strew flowers for it to tread on....
>
> His thoughts were constant to her Image. It was always there. She sat plying her needle, before the fire, and singing to herself. Such a blithe, thriving, steady little Dot! (91–92)

It is in this way, through the "reflections" depicted as on a glass or picture, that John is reconciled to his better nature, and to the spirit of his wife, even before he learns the innocent truth about her secret confidences with the Stranger. None of this second-order visuality—or at least none of these visions—can be found in Griffith's film. It would perhaps have taken a Georges Méliès to do justice to them, though Griffith certainly showed himself capable of producing visionary cinema in the conclusion to *Birth of a Nation* (1915) just six years later. Here again, in other words, Griffith remains realist.

This is not to say that Griffith's adaptation lacks a counterpart to Dickens's reflective and reflexive visionary sequence. Indeed, the shot in which we see John sitting by the fire after extinguishing the candle is worth considering in some detail, in comparison both with prior shots of the hearth and with the engravings that illustrated Dickens's story. Griffith's composition follows the 1845 print quite faithfully: in each, the hearth stands on the right side of the frame and faces left. In both Griffith's shot of John just before he picks up the gun and the Dickens illustration of John just after he puts it down, the hearth is burning, but its light is not bright. In the film version, however, as John enters into his post-gun "reflections," we see it illuminating the darkness, including the figure of John, and we see him peering into the hearth's

Griffith, *The Cricket on the Hearth*. John, head in hands before the fire.

Dickens, *The Cricket on the Hearth*. The illustration on which Griffith patterned his shot.

Griffith, *The Cricket on the Hearth*. John gazing into the hearth.

lighted surface, as if looking at a film. We do not see what he sees, and we certainly do not see John's admonitory visions of Dot, his picturing of all the goodness he remembers in her. But we do see him seeing. That is, we see his "reflections" as a kind of seeing, seeing as in a glass (mirror) or picture, or somehow both at once.[66]

Although Griffith was not yet in a position to realize cinematically all of the visual suggestiveness of Dickens's story, it is easy to understand why he chose it from the extensive oeuvre of his declared favorite author. It is not just that the story, being relatively short, could be managed in a one-reeler. The story also makes a link between its own visual techniques (such as managing point of view to suggest the virtual occupation of other viewpoints) and both the act of reflection and the shifting of mood. Further, the story connects the exercise of reflection with the possibility of overcoming rash passions and allowing for the operation of our better natures: that is, it links it with the work of sentiment. The projections abet the stream of reflections, and together they reanimate John the Carrier. They activate his conscience and restore his soul. Much the same linkage is in fact also suggested, mutatis mutandis, in Griffith's film, even though we don't see the images John sees.

Dickens, Griffith, and Capra

This constellation of features shared by Dickens and Griffith—moral reflection, point of view, conscience, animation, media reflexivity—does not figure importantly in Eisenstein's account. Indeed these are just the sort of features he sets to one side in favor of a claim for Dickens and Griffith as the forerunners of dialectical montage. I will attend much to this side of Dickens in the arguments that follow, and I won't forget about Griffith. However, for reasons that will become clear in due course, my choice to represent the sentimentalism of the Hollywood narrative system is not Griffith but Frank Capra. Capra was, I maintain, Griffith's leading disciple in the sound era, when the full potential of sentimental spectatorship in cinema was newly realized. Capra's ambitions and ideological concerns were nearly as large and influential as Griffith's, and this is no coincidence: he is all but explicit in avowing Griffith as his great exemplar. And while Capra was not the innovator in film style that Griffith was, he dominated Hollywood in the 1930s almost as thoroughly as Griffith did in the 1910s. Capra's further utility for my purposes lies in his having developed a metastyle built on Griffith's pioneering narrative system, a style that came to be called "the Capraesque," massively influential in its own right, and which came to be identified with sentimentality in a pejorative sense. By the same token, the Victorian sentimentalism of Dickens—Anthony Trollope satirized him as Mr. Popular Sentiment in *The Warden* (1855)—provides a kind of portal for the earlier history of sentimentalism, not only in Sterne but also in decades of still earlier writings by which Dickens's innovations were informed: works dealing with spectatorship, sensibility, materialism, virtuality, and the soul.

In part 1, I argue that the kind of linkage between reflection and sentiment I have outlined in Griffith and Dickens should be understood as crucial to the Capraesque, which, as I further argue, developed toward an increasing self-consciousness about its cinematic roots both in a narrative system developed by Griffith and others and in a literary past for which Dickens is a nonarbitrary synecdoche.[67] Griffith would develop his craft in the single extraordinary decade following *After Many Years* and *The Cricket on the Hearth* to bring his narrative system into something like a state of full realization with *Broken Blossoms* (1919), probably as Dickensian a feature film as he ever made, though *Orphans of the Storm* (1921) would be a close second. In *Broken Blossoms*, historians of cinema would come to find the deployment not only of parallel montage between lines of action—the story of Lucy Burrows (Lillian Gish) and her brutal father Battling Burrows (Donald Crisp) on the one side and the Yellow Man (Richard Barthelmess) on the other. They would also find point-of-view shots, shot/reverse-shot sequences, facial close-ups, primitive forms of continuity, and the like.[68] If *A Tale of Two Cities* stands behind *Orphans*, the Dickens source for *Broken Blossoms* is surely *The Old Curiosity Shop*, Dickens's full-length tour de force in the sentimental mode, and one of his most popular novels in its time, not least in America.

Capra's drive toward the fulfillment of a cinematic ambition, as I will try to show, likewise takes him to Dickens, though, like Griffith, Capra never directly adapted one of Dickens's novels, even as Thomas Bentley in Griffith's era and David Lean in Capra's would do so repeatedly.[69] Capra's circumstances differed crucially from Griffith's in that, coming to Hollywood soon after Griffith's great achievements, he had them to build on. He could avail himself of the resources of the classical narrative system, and in time he also could reflect on its meaning. Capra and Eisenstein were well acquainted, and Capra recounts a meeting with the Soviet director in Moscow in 1936 but gives few details. Did they discuss Griffith and Dickens? We cannot know for sure. But the Capra who turns to Dickens in 1946 with *It's a Wonderful Life* is unquestionably aware of the importance of Dickens, his favorite author, to Griffith, the director he most admires. Griffith's connection to Dickens is part of Hollywood lore, and it is patent enough in Griffith's body of work over the productive decade of filmmaking in the 1910s. Following the logic of Eisenstein's argument, one might say that there was cinematic potential in Dickens that Griffith found compelling but did not fully develop. Like Eisenstein, Capra develops this potential. Crucially, however, he develops it in a direction very different from the one Eisenstein claims for the Soviet response to Griffith. To be precise, and to put in a nutshell one of my central arguments in part 1: Capra emphasizes precisely the sentimentalism that Eisenstein downplays.[70]

We gain a sense of this difference when Eisenstein returns, late in his essay, to the issue of Dickens's suggestion of the close-up at the opening of *The Cricket on the Hearth*: "The kettle began it!"[71] What initially interests Eisenstein in this example is the speculation about Griffith's learning from Dickens that one could trigger a cinematic narrative with a close-up, one saturated with "atmosphere." It is a device that would become the bread and butter of Hollywood film narrative—Hitchcockian suspense, for example. Eisenstein's discussion of the device later takes a surprising turn, however, to account for the difference between the ways in which American and Soviet filmmakers refer to it. Elaborating his generalizing claim about cinema's debt to a "whole constellation" of literary ancestors, Eisenstein plays once more with synecdoche: "Each part of this great past has moved forward this great art of cinematography. Let this past be a reproach to those thoughtless people who have displayed arrogance in reference to literature, which has contributed so much to this apparently unprecedented art, and is, in the first and most important place: the art of viewing—not only the eye, but viewing—both meanings embraced in the term."[72] Eisenstein will go on to suggest that the two meanings have to do with the growth from "the *cinematic eye* to the *image of an embodied viewpoint on phenomena*" (233, his emphasis), a process he calls one of the most important developments in Soviet cinema:

> We [Soviets] say that an object or face is photographed in "large scale" . . .
> The American says: *near*, or "close-up" . . .
> Among Americans the term is attached to *viewpoint*.
> Among us—to the value of what is seen. (237–38)

In this small difference, Eisenstein insists, there is "a profound distinction in principle," one that seems to align itself with the distinction between the "cinematic eye" (the literal "viewpoint") and the Soviets' "embodied viewpoint on phenomena," the montage practice in which "[we] collect the disintegrated event into one whole, but in *our* aspect" (236).

The distinction between the cinematic eye and the embodied viewpoint on phenomena is not, I think, entirely perspicuous. It is the latter, presumably, that goes beyond technical "viewpoint" to disclose "the value of what is seen." This point seems to connect to Eisenstein's earlier one about the limits of parallel montage, which shifts between two shots that remain essentially discrete. This is in contrast to the Soviet's "montage cell," the idea that the shot is transformed in montage, its "value" altered qualitatively and not just additively. Roughly speaking, we might say that Eisenstein's objection seems to be to a practice of montage grounded in the *alternation* of viewpoint rather than the *alteration* of viewpoint. But this formulation is too crude, for even in the sentimental tradition, alternation implies alteration.

Though Eisenstein explicitly assigns Griffith as great a role in shaping Soviet cinema as the enormous role he assigns Dickens in shaping Griffith's, he goes on, soon after this discussion of point of view, to describe the limits of Griffith's contribution as a correlate of ideology: "In social attitudes Griffith was always a liberal, never departing far from the slightly sentimental humanism of the good old gentlemen and sweet old ladies of Victorian England, just as Dickens loved to picture them" (233).[73] He does not explicitly make the connection between "sentimental humanism" and the alternation of viewpoints understood as "subjective" (associated here with being "liberal"), but it seems to be implied in his logic of association. In any case, it is exactly this side of Dickens and Griffith that I will suggest is crucial to the development of the Capraesque. And it is never more fully on display than in the motion picture Capra came to regard as his most important, his return to Griffith's early source in Dickens's Christmas tales to refashion *A Christmas Carol* into *It's a Wonderful Life*. Making this film just a couple of years after Eisenstein's boast about the Soviets' having realized the unfulfilled possibilities of cinema inherent in the Dickens-Griffith connection, Capra can be taken to suggest that their truest fulfillment lies precisely in the direction from which Eisenstein and his fellow Soviet filmmakers turned away.

Plan of This Book

I will have occasion in part 1 to show these tendencies in Capra and the Capraesque, recursively formed as they were over his two decades of important work, from the end of the silent period to the advent of television. A more immediate point to be made in light of Eisenstein's analysis is simply this: Capra's Griffith and Capra's Dickens are linked precisely by their common relationship to the sentimental mood or mode that is associated at once with liberal humanism, with sympathy (understood as the capacity for passing into subjective viewpoints not our own), and with virtual mediation. Further, the understanding of cinema as a medium that can realize the full potential of certain eighteenth-century formations is, naturally enough, far more explicit and fully elaborated in Capra than in Griffith's 1909 adaptation of a Dickens Christmas tale. While the light from the "film" on the Peerybingles' hearth is vaguely suggestive of a metacinematic source of "reflections," one capable of softening desperate passion into sentiment, the metacinematic effects in *It's a Wonderful Life*—the films within the film—are striking indeed. They too, of course, have their source in a relevant Dickens text. As the many other connections between *It's a Wonderful Life* and *A Christmas Carol* tend to confirm, the two projections that reanimate George Bailey—the one in the heavens for Clarence and the one Clarence arranges for George himself—surely derive from the protocinematic projections of the three spirits who come to save Scrooge.[74] The spirits' visions, after all, show the power of Dickens's optical imagination as forcefully as anything he ever dreamed up.

To register this difference between Eisenstein and Capra yet more starkly, we can recall that, in Eisenstein's account of the Soviet fulfillment of the line of cinematographic promise inherent in Dickens and Griffith, the larger "ancestral array" is supposed to go all the way back to "Shakespeare and the Greeks." By contrast, in the Capraesque fulfillment of the line of Dickens and Griffith, the "ancestral array" goes back only to about the eighteenth century and the emergence of the sentimental as a recognizable mode, as it did for Dickens.[75] Behind Little Nell and *The Old Curiosity Shop*, as Dickens himself hinted in that novel, we find the pathos and idiosyncrasy of Laurence Sterne. In the four chapters of part 2, therefore, I examine four aspects of this Enlightenment-era literary sentimentalism, all of them relevant to both Dickens and his cinematic heirs. One aspect has to do with the articulation of a novel form of literary spectatorship within the print public sphere of the eighteenth century—"novel" as in new and "novel" as in the species of narrative writing that came to be so called in that period. This argument is conceptually centered on what I call "the sentimental case," part of eighteenth-century Britain's contribution to moral theory, especially in the work of Adam Smith. The second aspect has to do with the notion of "sensibility," so closely tied to that of "sentiment," and with how it connects to Latitudinarian thinking about the nature of the soul and its relation to modern (post-seventeenth-century) notions of experience, especially in the conflation of moving and being moved. The Latitudinarian "vehicular hypothesis" about the soul proves crucial to this analysis. The third aspect has to do with the implications of the sentimental case, and the sentimental complication of movement, for the understanding of probability—that is, for how sentimental narratives unfold. The focus here falls on what is widely recognized as the sentimental mode's breach in probabilistic decorum and a fault in its artistic execution, namely, the leap sentimental plots often take in achieving resolution. The final aspect of the Enlightenment sentimental formation concerns the way in which its associated norms and forms make it possible to reconsider the notion of moral monstrosity. This chapter on sentimental monstrosity provides a different angle on the topic of "reanimation" that runs through the book.

In reframing Eisenstein's insight, then, I also wish to take it in a direction that he could not or would not have done. The creation of the classical narrative system in early Hollywood cinema—a development perhaps most closely identified with Griffith, the self-styled "man who invented Hollywood"—depends on the theory and practice of literary spectatorship two centuries earlier. In arguing that the sentimental in film derives in large part from the sentimental in print, however, I do not suggest that this derivation is straightforward. There are sediments of sentiment in this layered history, and, as I have indicated, my claim that theatrical forms are subsumed into literary ones in the eighteenth century in no way implies the disappearance of theater. More particularly, it is impossible to think of connecting Dickens, Griffith, and Capra without some attention to melodrama, a development that took shape only after the French Revolution and one that is itself derivative of the sentimental by way of the Gothic novel and the theater of the *Sturm und Drang*.

The emergence of melodrama might be understood as passion's revenge on sentiment, or indeed as theater's revenge on the sentimental, a mode with which it remained intimately connected. Eisenstein himself stresses Dickens's relation to the melodrama: Dickens did, after all, run a theater.[76] And the cinema of Griffith and his moment is unthinkable without the context of theater and the category of melodrama.[77] Along the way, therefore, I distinguish the sentimental from the melodramatic mode. There are areas of overlap, to be sure, especially with Dickens in the mid-nineteenth century. And the relations between the two modes remain complicated even into the present. But the structures and strategies of the sentimental are in principle and in practice different from those of melodrama, and it will be of considerable help in understanding both modes to appreciate these differences. Robert Lang has written well on melodrama in Griffith and other Hollywood directors, and justifies his focus with a more general claim: "Not only is the American cinema attracted ideologically to the melodramatic . . . it is *formally* melodramatic also."[78] I mean to show the ways in which a central line in American cinema (including the later Griffith) is formally *sentimental*.

I find that the specific philological history of the term "sentimental" actually helps in finding one's bearings in the cultural form that came to be identified with it. Indeed, one of the interesting features about the term in English is that it is easier to date its emergence than it is to make clear its various denotations and connotations. I have likewise already noted that this is not a fully fledged history of sentimentalism. I make reference, for example, to the fact that the so-called "first American novel," William Hill Brown's *The Power of Sympathy* (1791), is squarely and self-consciously in the line of British sentimentalism, but there is a large secondary literature on American sentimentalism that I rely on but do not try to replicate.[79] Often, this story is closely associated with what Linda Williams calls "the American melodramatic mode," linked in ways that many recent commentators have explored since the revival of melodrama studies in the 1970s.[80]

Though I am committed to Dudley Andrew's view that Capra is "a figure worthy of continued study" as the Hollywood system's "most consistently successful practitioner," I could scarcely fail to acknowledge that the subject of Capra—and that of the sentimental itself—sometimes occasions critical embarrassment.[81] Even Griffith and Dickens seem embarrassing to some commentators. The sentimental itself has long been regarded in a pejorative light, almost from the moment of its coinage in the mid-eighteenth century.[82] Works that have come to be associated with the nominalized form of the term "sentimental"—sentimentality—have, over the ensuing two and a half centuries, been considered by many critics to be the very bane of culture. As I will suggest in part 3, Horkheimer and Adorno's 1947 critique of "the culture industry," for example, can be understood as targeting sentimentality. I would in no way deny that the sentimental mode often leaves itself vulnerable to harsh judgment, nor that it often deserves it. Nonetheless, I will have occasion in the chapters that follow to distinguish the sentimental as a cultural form from sentimentality as an object of casual pejorative judgment—not only, say, in Dickens's Victorian England or Capra's America, but even within movements such as Romanticism and Modernism.[83] Part 3 of this book means to address the embarrassments of the sentimental in ways that the first two parts merely broach, and to do so in the context of these two movements, which seem to define themselves against, and indeed often boast of resisting, the sentimental.

In sum, then, producing an archaeology of sympathy and sentiment is a way of defamiliarizing them, of denaturalizing them. It is to bring to critical attention a set of features and practices, a way of world-making, that is too often misunderstood, when it is noticed at all. I thus begin with an account of the Capraesque in contemporary American life, where the sentimental sometimes becomes so pervasive as to leave no room whatsoever for recognition or real analysis.

PART 1   The Capraesque

In the wake of the financial crisis of 2008–2009 and the government rescue of banks deemed "too big to fail," a new and focused populist movement arose in the United States to urge a specific course of coordinated action. Backed by economist Robert Johnson and media entrepreneur Arianna Huffington, the movement encouraged Americans to divest from large multinationals like Citibank and Chase and instead give their banking business to small community firms. From its inception in early 2010, the movement's website has had a header that features a merged image on a broad horizontal banner bearing the words "Move Your Money." On the left side of the image, facing right, is a photograph of the CEOs of five major banks in an appearance before Congress. On the right side, facing left—facing them, as it were—is the familiar image of a man in a fedora.

It is James Stewart playing George Bailey in Frank Capra's *It's a Wonderful Life*.

The image captures Bailey looking deeply concerned. The year is 1932, and he is about to address the worried townspeople of Bedford Falls during the run on the Bailey Building and Loan. He and his newlywed bride, Mary (Donna Reed), have just halted the taxi that was to have taken them on their honeymoon, and taken George Bailey out of town after his several previous frustrated attempts to escape its confines. What happens when George Bailey arrives at the savings and loan constitutes an iconic episode in American cinema: his opening of the doors that had been closed by the dim-witted Uncle Billy, his attempt to calm the anxious crowd about the security of their investments, his brief lecture about how banks work, his exposure of the chicanery of Mr. Potter (Lionel Barrymore), Mary's offer of the $2,000 fund intended for their honeymoon to help soothe nervous customers and tide them over, and finally the nick-of-time arrival of the bank's closing hour while two dollars yet remain in the coffer. For many Americans, the whole episode from Capra's film is instantly recalled by the image of Stewart on the Move Your Money home page, where he appears to be facing down the bankers depicted across from him, in a way that the US Congress itself did not.

Both of the images that form the composite photograph on the website header appear in the short film that was made to launch the movement's work in late 2009. Eugene Jarecki is a documentary filmmaker who had already invoked the spirit of Capra in his borrowing of the title *Why We Fight* for an antiwar film that won the Sundance Grand Jury Prize in 2005. For the "Move Your Money" film, he remixed scenes from *It's a Wonderful Life* and footage from news coverage of the financial crisis to produce a four-minute-plus quasi-documentary that was released on December 29, 2009.[1] The film is introduced by an archaic-looking set of title frames, captioned by a series of similarly archaic intertitles, and accompanied by the sound of an old projector. The simple narrative recorded in the intertitles runs like this:

Once upon a time in America, men like George Bailey ran small community banks.

They made a living, but they also made people's lives better.

But elsewhere, men like Mr. Potter had another idea.

The greed of men like Mr. Potter led to the Great Depression.

They built bigger, less regulated institutions, with little regard for their customers. When panic struck Potter & Company seized the chance to exploit people's insecurity.

But the Bailey Building and Loan stood by its customers, tiding them over through the crisis.

To make matters worse, Mr. Potter and Company even stooped to stealing taxpayers' hard-earned money.

But the people of Bedford Falls had another idea.

After this last intertitle we see a bit of the famous finale of *It's a Wonderful Life*, when George's friends and neighbors enter his home bearing handfuls of cash and securities. The final intertitles of Jarecki's film issue an appeal that acknowledges the enormous annual holiday viewership for Capra's film:

This year don't just watch "IT'S A WONDERFUL LIFE," make a resolution. If you love George Bailey, get your money away from Mr. Potter.

Move your money.

On the *Huffington Post* website alone, this short film had almost half a million viewings in the first month and a half after its release.

Though Move Your Money received less press than the Tea Party movement, or the later Occupy movement, Huffington's alternative brand of populist activism can boast some early success.[2] It attracted a certain amount of attention, as did Jarecki's film. About two weeks after its first appearance, the political satirist Stephen Colbert interviewed Jarecki on his television program, first screening clips from Jarecki's film. He also issued a comic challenge to Jarecki with a film of his own, another remix of scenes from *It's a Wonderful Life*.[3] Colbert's film was shaped and retitled in behalf of the view that Mr. Potter was technically the only "community banker" in Bedford Falls and that George Bailey was an unstable young man with a tendency to fly off the handle at colleagues, family, and even schoolteachers. That Colbert could so easily remix the film to produce a very different affect and tendency is an index of what a diverse mix of moods Capra's film comprises to begin with, a feature not lost on the film's many commentators. Indeed, the Colbert *jeu d'esprit* gets at something important both about Capra and the sentimental tradition in which I wish to set his work. The sentimental is most often characterized by markedly mixed emotions, by an abiding ambivalence in both its tendencies and its norms.

The Jarecki episode demonstrates how readily Capra's cinematic work can be mobilized for public use in our time, a point reinforced by a second example from these same weeks at the turn of the twenty-first century's second decade. Not long after Jarecki appeared on *The Colbert Report*, President Obama and his Democratic Party suffered a major defeat in Congress when Scott Brown, a Massachusetts Republican who had once posed nude for *Cosmopolitan* magazine, was elected to the US Senate seat held for nearly half a century by Ted Kennedy. This shocking defeat cost the Democrats the sixty-seat "supermajority" that had briefly afforded them protection from Republican filibuster of legislative initiatives. In particular, it seemed at the time to have cost Obama and his party the chance to produce what they billed as the country's first sweeping overhaul of health care in nearly a century.

Numerous commentators compared Brown to a character played by James Stewart in another Capra film, seven years before his turn as George Bailey: the eponymous Jefferson Smith in *Mr. Smith Goes to Washington*, a neophyte appointed to the seat of a recently deceased senator. William Kristol's editorial in the *Weekly Standard* (February 1, 2010) was just one of dozens of articles to appear under the title "Mr. Brown Goes to Washington."[4] Many of these, like Kristol's, came from the political right: Sarah Palin, for example, used the formula for a piece about Brown on her Facebook page. This spate of comparisons also called forth responses from the left, denying Brown the Capra aura. An editorial in a local alternative newspaper in Massachusetts bore the title: "Scott Brown—No Mr. Smith Goes to Washington! More Like: American Idol Comes to Massachusetts."[5] Invoking Capra's 1939 film was nothing new in Washington, and it did not stop with Scott Brown. A year later Senator Frank Lautenberg, a New Jersey Democrat, introduced a piece of legislation, widely called the "Mr. Smith Bill," to tighten Senate rules on the use of the filibuster by requiring those who want to stage a filibuster to appear on the floor and speak, as Stewart's Mr. Smith famously does in Capra's film.[6]

This is just the tip of a very large cultural iceberg. I wouldn't know how to begin to number the occasions on which the formula "Mr. [or Ms.] X Goes to Washington" has been invoked in American public discourse over the last several decades.[7] Nor would I know how to list the many allusions to *It's a Wonderful Life*. In early 2012, *New York Times* columnist David Brooks discussed the "core American debate between 'On the Road' and 'It's a Wonderful Life'" in terms of itinerancy and rootedness as alternative paths to happiness.[8] Nor indeed are these the only Capra films that seem to have become fixtures in the political and cultural landscape. In June 1992, the *Los Angeles Times* published a long article that analyzed the emergence of Independent Party candidate Ross Perot and his political movement's effect on that year's presidential campaign by way of an extended meditation on Capra's *Meet John Doe* (1941).[9] A similar comparison, with a similarly detailed account of the film, was made fifteen years earlier in a piece for the *Soho Weekly News*: "Jimmy Carter: John Doe Born Again."[10] The year 2011 alone saw prominent invocations of Capra not only in the "Mr. Smith Bill," but also in the protests against antilabor legislation in Wisconsin and in coverage of the European banking crisis.

"Maybe there never really was an America," John Cassavetes, a Capra admirer, once wrote in a Hollywood trade journal: "Maybe it was all Frank Capra."[11] How did Capra's films come to achieve such a status? Robert Sklar once argued that Capra is alone among Hollywood directors in his effort "to construct a large-scale model of American society in his films."[12] This observation is helpful, though it both goes too far (is there really such a large-scale social model in Capra's films?) and fails to go far enough (how does one distinguish the pervasive influence of Capra from that of John Ford, whose Westerns also offer a social, and indeed a political, model?).[13] The question about Cassavetes's speculation eventually points to issues that lead beyond Capra, and beyond Hollywood. A part of the answer certainly lies in the sheer scope and power of Capra's reputation in the 1930s, and indeed his extraordinary productivity from the end of the silent period of cinema through to the beginning of the television era. But another part of the story lies in the vexed history of Capra's relation to television itself, and another in the widely read literary renditions of his life, first by himself and then by Joseph McBride, in a biography that set out to dismantle piece by piece Capra's careful self-mythologization. One of the most surprising twists comes with the turn to Capra's work on the part of a host of serious directors in the 1990s. Looking beyond the present chapter to the two that follow, I'm going to be arguing that the Capra phenomenon, including that late turn to Capraesque filmmaking, has to do with three moments or phases of recursivity in which his work participates, three ways in which his project in cinematic world-making was reflexively constituted.[14] The first has to do with his status as a director with larger than usual responsibilities for his product; the second, with his relation to the medium of Hollywood cinema itself; and the third, with a longer tradition of themes and practices associated with sentiment and the sentimental.

The first moment of recursivity has to do with how Capra established himself as a director with a claim to cinematic authorship: an *auteur*, as we now say, following the later theoretical discussions of the influential *Cahiers du Cinéma* in the 1950s.[15] Capra was, as we will have occasion to explore here, one of the first American directors to declare himself the author of the films he directed, and he came to be quite preoccupied with a doctrine he early on called "one man, one film."[16] His claim to having his "name above the title" was, I will argue, inextricable from a reflective practice he developed in the two decades of his dominance in Hollywood, from 1928 to 1948, when he came repeatedly and increasingly to fashion a new film as a return to one or more of his own prior achievements in cinema: *Mr. Smith Goes to Washington* (1939), for example, invokes and rethinks *Mr. Deeds Goes to Town* (1936). These films were remakes not in the narrow sense that we associate with cinematic genres but rather in a more ambitious and far more elusive sense of cinematic self-fashioning that, for better or for worse, made him the director he was at his most signature moments. Capra's work over these two decades shows a pattern of recapitulation, remaking, and self-allegorization that lends it an increasing sense of reflexive coherence. One of the great ironies of the account I will be offering is that when Capra finally undertook a strict remake of one of his early films, in the narrower and more common sense of the term—*Riding High* (1950), a remake of *Broadway Bill* (1934)—his career was effectively over. His second such effort—*Pocketful of Miracles* (1961), a remake of his *Lady for a Day* (1933)—had a cast that included Bette Davis but proved to be the nail in the coffin.[17]

The second moment of recursivity has to do with Capra's increasing self-consciousness about what, in the chapter of his autobiography about *Mr. Smith Goes to Washington*, he calls "The Power of Film." The mid-1930s was a pivotal moment for Capra's self-consciousness about his relation to fundamental elements of Hollywood narrative filmmaking as shaped two decades earlier in the transformative period of D. W. Griffith. The early thirties was a time of more general awareness of Hollywood's moral codes, of course, as these were instantiated under the leadership of Will Hays, bureaucratized in the Hays Office, and formalized in the 1934 document *A Code to Govern the Making of Motion and Talking Pictures*.[18] Capra's allusion to the new mode of censorship—the Hays Code—is evident in Clark Gable's toying with decorum in the celebrated auto-camp scenes with Claudette Colbert in *It Happened One Night* (1934) and of course in the film's famous device: the blanket hung between the beds to form the Walls of Jericho. This much is acknowledged in the best commentaries on the film. Not acknowledged, however, is Capra's increasing self-consciousness about another sort of codification of "the making of Motion and Talking Pictures."

The debate about the Hays Code was part of a larger debate about film as a medium, and about Hollywood as an industry, among pundits and academics from a range of disciplines. It was not just the moral code of Hollywood but also its *narrative* code—what we now call the classical Hollywood system—that became an object of increased visibility in this period, especially to Capra. Central to this system is the reciprocal work of the face and the eye or gaze, what Jacques Aumont calls the "ordinary face of cinema," which, he concisely explains, assumes its dominant form in the first years of the talkies:

> The Twenties and Thirties were a period of the systematic exploration of camera angles and distances in relation to the looking and speaking face, the interest in angles and distances most often effacing all other possible interest for the eyes, even for the mouth, since these variations and these explorations were determined by this obligation to let nothing escape: everything is to be made to circulate. The gaze of the ordinary face is caught in an interminable game, comparable only to the circulation of its spoken words. One of the king genres of the Thirties will be the screwball comedy, that logorrhoeic part of American cinema that Capra and Hawks exemplified, and where the problem would be, for the dialogue, to go fast enough to catch up with the fleeting intertwining of gazes. But circulation is the unbreakable rule, and nothing, no genre, can escape it.[19]

Aumont here draws heavily on André Bazin's influential account of the prehistory of both the 1940s neorealist aesthetic and deep-focus cinematography, developments with which Bazin's critical efforts are intimately associated. "From 1930 to 1940 there seems to have grown up in the world, originating largely in the United States, a common form of cinematic language," wrote Bazin in his celebrated essay "The Evolution of the Language of Cinema."[20]

What entitled this American cinema of the thirties to be thought of as a language was its rule-boundedness, but this rule-boundedness was in turn associated by Bazin with an investment in cinematic genres: "It was the triumph in Hollywood, during that time, of five or six major kinds of film that gave it its overwhelming superiority."[21] The first of the genres that he names is "American comedy," and the only example he gives is *Mr. Smith Goes to Washington*, which he wrongly dates to 1936, the year of *Mr. Deeds Goes to Town*. For reasons that I will explain in chapter 3, Bazin's confusion of these

two Capra films is meaningful, in that *Mr. Deeds Goes to Town*, not identified by name, seems to supply Bazin with his prototype of how this cinema
works. As I show in some detail, it is this same film, *Mr. Deeds*—indeed, the
very scene from *Mr. Deeds* that supplies Bazin with his unidentified example
of the rule-bound cinema of the 1930s—that represents Capra's own crucial
moment of cinematic self-consciousness in relation to these rules and to the
form of sentiment they encode.

In evolving a certain self-consciousness about his films as films, Capra
was also, with increasing explicitness, promoting comparative attention to the
place of film among other media, in particular the print media—that is, the
print-cultural public sphere as it took shape in the eighteenth and nineteenth
centuries. Of course, Capra is hardly alone among Hollywood filmmakers
in invoking the older sphere of print publicity, which figures repeatedly as a
rival domain against which classical Hollywood cinema attempts to establish
its own cultural hegemony.[22] Think of Howard Hawks's *His Girl Friday* and
Orson Welles's *Citizen Kane*, to name just two examples from about the time
Capra made *Mr. Smith* and *Meet John Doe*. But representations of writing,
reporting, and publishing are signally important to most of Capra's more programmatic films. From as early as his 1928 Douglas Fairbanks Jr. picture, *The
Power of the Press*—through those later reporter- and writer-heroes played by
the likes of Clark Gable, Jean Arthur, and Barbara Stanwyck—Capra began
to raise the stock figure of the reporter to a larger-than-life status in a quasi-
allegorical contest over national self-representation.

Beyond recursivity about film authorship and the film medium, the third
moment of recursivity in the constitution of the Capraesque has to do with
its reputation as "Capra-corn," a charge of sentimentality that was already
very much in play in a film like *Mr. Deeds Goes to Town*. I wish to claim
that Capra increasingly saw in the narrative codes he inherited from Griffith
a capacity, precisely, for producing a certain mode or mood. In the use of
the close-up shot, the moving camera, and especially the technique of shot/
reverse-shot, Capra recognized a way of creating what for two centuries had
been known as moral sentiment. I argue further that he came, in effect, to
realize that, though coded in Hollywood's idiom of classical narration, this
capacity did not originate with it. That is, he came to see that this sentimental capacity in cinema was not limited to the technological medium of film
itself—even as he promoted his own work in this medium as potentially
world-changing. Ultimately, in other words, his reflexive relation to his own
medium and its capacities for generating affect enabled him to dramatize
the relation of his self-consciously sentimental cinema to the development

of the *literary* sentimental as it took shape from the first usages of the word in Europe in the mid-eighteenth century. As we will see, the general interest in print culture on the part of Capra and other filmmakers of the 1930s both abetted and complicated this "archaeological" recognition.[23]

Such claims may seem overly speculative in the absence of the details I adduce from the films themselves, but the Dickens link, at least, is not hard to establish. Perhaps even more than Griffith, Capra was very much in thrall to Dickens. Sydney Buchman, who collaborated with Capra on *Mr. Smith Goes to Washington*, told Capra's biographer that "Capra's great passion was Dickens. As soon as he had some money, he bought some of the rarest and most extraordinary editions of Dickens' work, and he was very proud of his collection."[24] In 1946, two years after Eisenstein wrote about Dickens and Griffith, Capra produced his own Dickensian *summa cinematica—It's a Wonderful Life*—transparently a reworking of Dickens's *A Christmas Carol*. It is a film that, precisely in its Dickensian dimension, dramatizes all three moments of recursivity that I have sketched: in respect to cinematic author-ship, to the cinematic medium, and to a trans-cinematic history of sentiment traceable back to Dickens's own sources in the eighteenth century. These three moments structure the discussion to follow in part 1.[25] For all of this to make sense, however, it will be helpful to recall at the start just what Capra achieved in his Hollywood heyday and what has become of this achievement in the decades since.

ONE Capra's America

In 1938, the year before he made *Mr. Smith Goes to Washington*, Frank Capra appeared on the cover of *Time* magazine, the first film director to be so honored. The cover story used Capra to exemplify the emergence of a new kind of American filmmaker, what would later be called a cinematic "auteur." Capra had achieved exceptional autonomy at Columbia Pictures, a so-called Poverty Row studio he had joined a decade earlier, after an early career as a gag writer with Mack Sennett and a director of Harry Langdon, part of the quartet of great film clowns of the period that included Charlie Chaplin, Buster Keaton, and Harold Lloyd.[1]

Capra was—and still is—widely credited with having carried producer Harry Cohn's studio through perilous times. When the article in *Time* appeared, Capra was about to win his third Oscar for Best Director in five years for *You Can't Take It With You* (1938). By 1934 he had already made some two dozen pictures, and that year *It Happened One Night* swept all five of the top Oscars. *Mr. Deeds Goes to Town* was the great success of 1936. And by 1938 Capra had become president both of the Motion Picture Academy *and* of the inimical Screen Directors Guild. He had toured Europe the year before and met in Moscow with Sergei Eisenstein. He had made a decisive difference in the early acting careers of stars like Barbara Stanwyck, Jean Harlow, Clark

Gable, Claudette Colbert, Jean Arthur, Gary Cooper, and James Stewart. He brought to new prominence character actors such as Thomas Mitchell and Edward Arnold. In the decade that followed, Capra would make more films with Cooper, Stanwyck, Stewart, and Arthur and would also work with Cary Grant, Donna Reed, Lionel Barrymore, Spencer Tracy, Katharine Hepburn, and the young Angela Lansbury.[2]

Over that next decade, too, Capra would make his most politically explicit films, including *Mr. Smith Goes to Washington* (1939) and *Meet John Doe* (1941). When the war broke out he enlisted in the US Army, where he took charge of making what became a series of seven films, with the collective title *Why We Fight* (1942–1945). Screened for the troops and in some cases released in theaters, these films made the case for US involvement in the war and charted its progress. Capra had left Columbia Pictures after *Mr. Smith Goes to Washington*, and in 1945 he started his own company—Liberty Films—with George Stevens, William Wyler, and Sam Briskin. In 1946 he persuaded James Stewart to join him again for the company's first film, a Christmas fantasy with a very specific historical setting in upstate New York on December 24, 1945. Two years after *It's a Wonderful Life* (1946), Liberty Films released what was, even on his own account, Capra's last interesting film, *State of the Union*, a Tracy-Hepburn film about the presidential election of 1948.

Capra has been said to have dominated the 1930s as no other director has dominated a decade. This is perhaps a defensible claim if one takes Capra's political power into account. But even as a director judged by more strictly critical standards, he was well regarded at the end of the 1930s. It was in 1939 that Lewis Jacobs published his widely read, subsequently much revised and reprinted *The Rise of the American Film: A Critical History*. As its title suggests, it is a book with a teleology, a point reinforced by the title of its sixth and final part: "Maturity (1929–39)." Within this last section of the book we find a chapter, "Contemporary Directors," that singles out six exemplary figures in the dramatic field: King Vidor, Fritz Lang, Josef von Sternberg, Rouben Mamoulian, Frank Capra, and John Ford. Only Vidor and Ford are discussed at greater length than Capra, and only Ford with demonstrably higher praise, especially for *The Informer* (1935). Moreover, all the directors are introduced and evaluated with terms taken from the lexicon that Capra was developing in the mid-1930s:

> All [six] command the highest commercial respect, receive the fullest resources of their studios, and are in a position to insist on certain material. At the same time, of course, their reputations and the costliness of their

productions deprive them of the full freedom they would like. The financial investment entailed in their pictures is so high that any experimentation is considered too speculative to be undertaken. On those occasions when they have been interested in their assignments they made distinguished motion pictures that are more than merely good commercial art.[3]

Working for the smallest studio, Capra did of course have an advantage over other directors when achievement was measured in this way, especially since the yardstick was chiefly of his own creation.

One further measure of Capra's stature has recently come to light, and it is provided, interestingly, by Eisenstein. In 1946, during the brief period between the end of World War II and the beginning of the Cold War, Eisenstein wrote to Capra in his capacity as vice-chairman of the Cinema Sector of VOKS, the All-Union Society for Cultural Relations with Foreign Countries. Recalling their meeting in a Moscow hotel room a decade earlier, Eisenstein informed Capra that he was "editing here in Moscow a series of books under the title 'Materials for the History of World Cinema.'" After explaining that two volumes had been completed, one on Griffith and one on Chaplin, Eisenstein goes on to say, "Any such set of books should be incomplete without a study about your work." Eisenstein laments that he and his team of authors "have nearly no material concerning your biography, your own comments about your art, some of the outstanding opinions about it made by Americans, stills, your own pictures, etc." He asks Capra to send "anything you should consider important directly to me," for "without all this kind of stuff the critical analysis of your work by our team would be incomplete."[4] Eisenstein is known to have sent only four such letters. The other three were written to John Ford, William Wyler, and Orson Welles. Only Capra's bears a date (January 25, 1946), and only Ford is known to have replied.

Large as Capra's reputation had grown over two decades, however, it does not explain the power of his hold on the American imagination at the turn of the twenty-first century. His star plummeted after the transformative postwar moment of 1947–1948, and it remained low for many years. It was a fate, moreover, that he had long dreaded. As he told a biographer late in life, apropos of a psychological crisis he suffered in 1935, Hollywood has no use for "has beens."[5] By 1970, the year before his autobiography appeared, Capra was certainly not in the state of degradation to which he saw Mack Sennett and D. W. Griffith reduced toward the end of their lives, but he had by then known his share of oblivion. It is by no means clear that many observers under the age of fifty would have been aware in 1970 of just how large a figure he had cut in the Hollywood of the 1930s.

Capra's troubles began not long after the Second World War. In the brief period from 1947 to 1948, great changes were afoot in the world of the screen arts: the blacklist of, initially, ten Hollywood artists charged with communist sympathies; the Supreme Court's Paramount Decree, an antitrust ruling that ended the studios' system of vertical integration and prohibited the practices of block booking and blind bidding that had been crucial to it; the establishment of the three enduring US television networks; and the challenge to the studio style from abroad in Italian neorealism, the first of Europe's cinematic "new waves." It was a decisive moment for more careers than Capra's, but for Capra's it was particularly debilitating. Between 1950 and 1961, Capra made only four films, all with casts that included major stars of the period: Bing Crosby, Colleen Gray, Jane Wyman, Frank Sinatra, Edward G. Robinson, Eleanor Parker, Carolyn Jones, Glenn Ford, and Bette Davis. But none of these films achieved critical success. Over the course of the 1950s, moreover, much of his previous work had ceased to be known. This was not a period noted for revival houses, and the technologies that now allow us to view older films in new media formats did not yet exist. As for network television, Columbia did not even begin to release its pre-1948 theatrical films until 1956. By 1957 it had sold off rights to nearly two hundred features for a cost of almost ten million dollars.[6] Though not a Columbia picture, *It's a Wonderful Life* seems to have been released only slightly earlier.[7]

Capra's most authoritative biographer, Joseph McBride, has declared that Capra's falling off after 1948 was more precipitous than that of any other American filmmaker. As we will see, McBride is no friend to Capra's reputation, but the reviews of Capra's films from the 1950s generally bear out the claim that he no longer commanded anything like the respect he once had.[8] The advent of television may well have been a small part of the problem for Capra in that decade. Later, however, it would prove to be a major part of the solution.

Capra in the Age of Television

Capra seems to have glimpsed the long-term significance of television sooner than many directors of his generation: his training as an engineer at Caltech helped him to anticipate technological change from early in his career, and this ability helped him make his reputation at Columbia in the years of the revolution in film sound. The next great change was to arrive in 1948, when television networks were a new phenomenon and Capra made *State of the Union*. The film precociously concludes with a scene involving a television news conference, in which Mary Matthews (Katharine Hepburn) is asked to stand publicly by her husband Grant (Spencer Tracy), a candidate for president, in the wake of a disclosure of his marital infidelity. Those television cameras had no part, of course, in the original 1945 stage play of *State of the Union*, which in turn hearkened back to Wendell Wilkie and the 1940 election. They were added during script development by Capra and his writers Anthony Veiler and Myles Connolly. And they were prophetic in their intimation of the coming dominance of television—anticipating the appearance of Bill and Hillary Clinton on *60 Minutes* by a half century—if not quite of the problems it would pose for cinema. Capra himself would dabble in television in the 1950s, producing two widely viewed one-off features in the area of science education but it is unclear how many viewers would have connected them with the man who made *It Happened One Night*.

Ironically, it was also television broadcasting, at least in the middle term, that introduced the postwar "baby boom" generation of Americans to what would become his signature films. With *It's a Wonderful Life*, especially, we have a fairly well documented understanding of how his work came to be so familiar to American viewers, a development chiefly of the last quarter of the twentieth century. In 1974, through a clerical oversight, the copyright on the film was not renewed, and the film fell into public domain. This legal disaster proved a *felix culpa* for the film's reception. Writing about the phenomenon in the *Wall Street Journal* ten years on, when the film had begun its ascent into canons and consciousnesses, John McDonagh reported that "Interregional Program Services has distributed the film to 152 subscribing stations from coast to coast," while "National Telefilm Associates provides it to 175 additional commercial stations." Satellite television had just taken hold. On the Sunday before Christmas of 1984, McDonagh pointed out, the film "will actually go up against itself throughout the country via satellite superstations WTBS out of Atlanta . . . and WGN in Chicago."[9] By 1986 a lavishly illustrated publication, *The "It's a Wonderful Life" Book*, was brought out by Jeanine Basinger, curator of the extensive Capra archives at Wesleyan University. The volume includes documents, memoirs by key participants, and a full script of the film as shot. More than one of this book's accounts of the film's popular reception—its popular redemption, as it were—tend to model that story on the plot of the film itself.[10]

The dramatically increased exposure of *It's a Wonderful Life* increased the esteem Capra's work enjoyed in the years before the home video explosion, but might have had less effect had it not been for another boost television provided. For early-film aficionados of the 1950s, the increase in the number of pre-1948 films available on networks and local stations (especially local stations in the big markets) was a welcome boon.[11] In the commercialized US television system, however, the opportunity to see these films came with a price: repeated interruption for advertisements. Then, in 1959, the New York affiliate of CBS attempted an experiment called Award Theater, which in time was syndicated in several other US cities. It was presented as a showcase for quality first-run and (at least initially) pre-1948 films. Only a few films were aired each year, late in the evenings, but usually on the eve of major holidays, and they were shown with minimal commercial interruption. They were offered as decidedly special occasions, introduced with pomp and fanfare and a certain atmosphere of reverence and prestige.[12] The first film so presented was *It Happened One Night*. The second was *Mr. Smith Goes to Washington*.[13] It seems that neither film had been shown before on network television in the United States.[14]

It is hard to know how to assess fully the impact of these early screenings of two of Capra's most acclaimed films of the 1930s. At the very least, we can note that the films were made available to a larger American viewership under conditions propitious to the recognition of Capra's merits. In this way, then, Capra and several of his more interesting films got a serious jump on the popular interest in pre-1948 cinema that burgeoned in the 1980s. As new video technologies made it possible for home viewers to stage repeated screenings of a studio-era film, they could come to know this period of Hollywood moviemaking with a new kind of intimacy.[15] Cable programming also whetted interest in pre-1950s films. American Movie Classics was established in the mid-1980s as a cable channel that showed studio-era films with brief introductions and without commercial interruption. By 1989 the channel was reaching thirty-nine million viewers.

Capra's special place in this revival clearly owed more than a little to the legal status of *It's a Wonderful Life*, which meant that it was available for repeated viewing as early as the mid-1970s, long before most Americans had video players. It was available in VHS format by the early 1980s, and in 1990, well into the period in which American viewers rediscovered pre-1948 studio films by way of home video libraries, it was issued in a remastered version, together with a short companion film entitled *The Making of "It's a Wonderful Life."* This short film, for which Basinger was a consultant, features insider information about work on the script, the casting of the film, the construction of the set for Bedford Falls, and so on. The companion film, which heralded now familiar video supplements on the "making of" this or that motion picture, bespeaks for its time a growing interest in Capra, in American auteurism, and in the pre-1948 era, of which *It's a Wonderful Life* became, like Michael Curtiz's *Casablanca* (1942), a late and iconic exemplar.[16]

Capra Rediscovered

With the 1990s, we enter what is perhaps the most intriguing period in the complex unfolding of Capra's long history of reception. For this decade witnessed a host of films that were recognizably made in the Capra mode, and often quite pointedly so. Consider the case of the British director Stephen Frears. In 1992, fresh from a string of critical successes that included *My Beautiful Laundrette* (1985), *Sammy and Rosie Get Laid* (1987), *Dangerous Liaisons* (1988), and *The Grifters* (1990), Frears made his markedly neo-Capraesque film, *Hero* (1992). Produced by Capra's studio, Columbia, the film reworks elements especially of *Meet John Doe*. Andy Garcia plays the role of Gary Cooper's hobo, an everyman allowing himself to be remade by a female reporter (Geena Davis, reprising Barbara Stanwyck) in the service of darkly motivated media and political interests. The cynicism of the hobo sidekick played by Walter Brennan in *Meet John Doe* is updated for Dustin Hoffman's Bernie LaPlante; the theme of identity-switching and the projective dynamics of the American everyman are carried over from one film to the other; a female reporter is again a central figure, but her worksite has been updated from newspaper office to television news station. The film's atmospherics are very much of the 1930s and 1940s, right from the opening grainy shots of a ticker tape parade on a Broadway that looks much as it might have appeared a half century earlier.

A year later, Columbia brought out another picture widely recognized at the time as invoking the spirit of Capra, Harold Ramis's brilliant comedy *Groundhog Day* (1993). A film about a man who keeps reliving the same day of his life, it has aptly been described as "like *It's a Wonderful Life* with the angel not present, only implied."[17] The Coen brothers, a year later, might be said to have restored the angel for *The Hudsucker Proxy* (1994), a film they made in the midst of a remarkable early run of films that included *Blood Simple* (1984), *Miller's Crossing* (1990), and *Fargo* (1996). It is a film that not only introduces fantastic temporality into an archaic stylization of studio-era cinema, but also relies on some of Capra's characteristic moods, looks, and devices, including a juxtaposition of snappy dialogue and angelic voice-over/oversight. The fact that its action is set in the late 1950s sets its Capraesque stylistic devices in yet higher relief. The Coen brothers often make the smallest detail telling; here the 1959 Coltrane-Ellington recording of "In a Sentimental Mood" that is playing in the beatnik hangout has roots in the heart of the early Capra era. Ellington composed and first recorded the song in 1935.

The angel figure appeared in another film that year, one with the Capraesque title *It Could Happen to You* (1994). This one had Nicolas Cage channeling James Stewart, much as Andy Garcia had channeled Gary Cooper in *Hero*. Its writer-director, Andrew Bergman, can be said to have come by his Capra heritage honestly. Before he turned to screenwriting, a career that includes credits for *Blazing Saddles*, *Fletch*, and *The Freshman* (which he also directed), he published a book about "Depression America and its films," in which Capra's thirties-era films are given extended explication and much credit for the invention of the screwball comedy genre.[18] Not only was *It Could Happen to You* received as "Capraesque," but Cage's performance was understood in some quarters as his bid to become "the Jimmy Stewart of our time."[19] Cage did not deny that he was channeling Stewart, nor that Bergman encouraged it. Jim Carrey was likewise acknowledged to be striving for a Stewart effect in *The Majestic* (2001), directed by Frank Darabont (who also directed *The Shawshank Redemption*), which again was unmistakably Capraesque in mood and mode.[20] Between these two films appeared *Phenomenon* (John Turtletaub, 1996), viewed in its moment as Capraesque for the way it connected ordinary life to the affect of wonder, as perhaps signaled by the echo of George Bailey's name in that of its protagonist, George Malley (John Travolta).

Returning to 1994, we find another pronomial Capraesque title, *I'll Do Anything*, a film written and directed by James L. Brooks. It stars Nick Nolte as a divorced father and out-of-work actor who gets involved in a remake of *Mr. Smith Goes to Washington*. Like *The Majestic*, which also echoes *Mr. Smith*, this film marks a trend in explicitly political appropriations of Capra, which also includes Ivan Reitman's *Dave* (1993), with Kevin Kline and Sigourney Weaver, and Rob Reiner's *The American President* (1995), with Michael Douglas and Annette Bening.[21] The latter was written by Aaron Sorkin, who would go on to create *The West Wing*, probably the most acclaimed American network television series of the following decade.[22] The critical reception of both films included numerous references to their relation to Capra's political cinema.[23]

In 1997, amid this increased interest in his post-1933 work, came the Capra centennial. The occasion was marked with the release of many of his best pre-1934 films in DVD format, retrospectives at theaters around the United

States, and a full-length biographical documentary, *Frank Capra's American Dream*, which included interviews with Martin Scorsese, Robert Altman, and Capra's early sound technician Edward Bernds, as well as Angela Lansbury and Peter Falk, two of the only major Capra-directed actors then still working. At this point, audience interest in the studio era was really taking off, and Capra was coming to be restored to a central place there in the eyes of the new public for old movies.[24]

The Lives of Frank Capra

Another factor that may have contributed to this preoccupation with the Capraesque in the cinema of the 1990s, and perhaps in the American public sphere more generally, is the publication, in 1971, of Capra's autobiography, *The Name above the Title*. It was a provocative book, making an insistent and often unseemly claim for Capra's status as auteur, a claim trumpeted in its very title. In the wake of its publication, Capra began to be sought out once again for interviews, and he was also invited to speak on university campuses—on his work, on the question of the director as auteur, on the studio system, on politics, and on the fate of cinema.[25] It was in the 1970s, too, that the Capra archive was established at Wesleyan University, which houses the unedited manuscript of the autobiography, somewhat more risqué than the published book. Much more came to be known about Capra, and his claims to being an auteur *avant la lettre* made him interesting to readers of, say, Andrew Sarris, who was promoting an auteur-based film criticism in his books and reviews.[26] Capra's autobiography sold reasonably well in its hardback edition, partly by virtue of its being a Book of the Month Club selection.[27]

Capra's autobiography is indeed a curious affair.[28] Having ceased to make films, he in effect set out to write a Capraesque narrative of his own life, another act of self-remaking. And having become somewhat irrelevant in his later years, he chose to focus on his heyday. The book certainly asserts, often with annoying vanity, Capra's strong claim to distinction in the golden age of the studio system, a distinction captured by his becoming the first working director to gain top billing, over both the film's title and the names of its leading actors.[29] It met with somewhat uneven critical reception, with many reviewers objecting to what one called the book's tendency toward "autohagiography."[30] This same reviewer concluded his essay by calling for a more objective and factually reliable life of Capra, a wish that would be fulfilled two decades later with a trenchantly critical biography by Joseph McBride, who aggressively undertook to set the record straight.

To compare the evidence supplied in the reviews of these two books is to confirm the sense that Capra's reputation was on the rise in the two decades between them. Reviewing (favorably) *The Name above the Title* in 1972 for *Film Comment*, Jean-Loup Bourget began by observing that "Capra's reputation has been at a low ebb for years."[31] Charles Maland, reviewing the McBride biography for *Film Quarterly* two decades later, spoke of "the renaissance in Capra's reputation following the publication of *The Name above the Title*."[32] Given to debunking Capra's own account, McBride's book was likewise widely reviewed, and one senses in reader reactions the sort of interest in Capra that might have helped to fuel the films of the 1990s.

Capra's and McBride's books belong to a reception history of Capra on the more popular or journalistic side of print culture. Another source of interest in Capra in recent decades that should not be overlooked—or overstated—is the reception he has had in the field of film criticism, which was assuming a more professionalized character precisely in the period of Capra's gradual (if partial) rehabilitation. One of the renovating principles of film criticism from the 1950s onward was, precisely, to reorient attention to film around the figure of the director as author. We rightly associate this turn to the auteur with the French film journal *Cahiers du Cinéma*, founded in 1951, and with the early criticism of François Truffaut, who, along with Jean-Luc Godard, would help to generate the French New Wave cinema with series of films each began in 1959. The leading exponent of auteurism in America was indeed Andrew Sarris, who declared in his widely read *The American Cinema* (1968) that "Capra was a genuine auteur."[33] This theme in Capra criticism culminated with the conference and volume undertaken in Italy for the Capra centennial under the heading "authorship and the studio system."[34] Surely it was partly on account of his being appropriable to auteurist understandings of cinema that Capra attracted the attention of some eminent academic commentary over the ensuing decades, including work by Stanley Cavell, Dudley Andrew, and Kaja Silverman.[35]

Since the 1970s, there has been a fair amount of academic work on Capra's filmmaking, some of it brilliant, some of it admiring, some both brilliant and admiring, like Stanley Cavell's writings about *It Happened One Night* and *Mr. Deeds Goes to Town*. But even Cavell, as he later acknowledged, was somewhat defensive about the claims he made in Capra's behalf when he included *It Happened One Night* among the comedies of remarriage he clustered so persuasively in *Pursuits of Happiness* (1981). Capra may have been a force to be reckoned with in the studio era, an early auteur, and a maker of films that could even begin to respond to the critical pressure of, say, Cavell's subtle analysis of the "Walls of Jericho" in *It Happened One Night*. At the same time, however, Capra was also something of an embarrassment.[36]

One context for the embarrassment might be the sort of critique Horkheimer and Adorno leveled against the culture industry in 1947, a few years after their arrival in Los Angeles, at the height of Capra's heyday there. As we will see in chapter 9, their essay reads in places as if it were an extended critique of Capra's project at Columbia. Perhaps even closer to home is Dwight MacDonald's blistering critique of middlebrow culture in "Masscult & Midcult" (1960).[37] Behind both of these analyses, I think it is fair to say, lies the charge of sentimentality. In Capra's case this charge had already surfaced during his heyday in the 1930s—when the phrase "Capra-corn" was in fact coined—and his response to it had, from the beginning, amounted to a combination of avowal, embrace, and denial. These two key features of Capra's reception in film criticism—his claims to being an auteur and his complex relation to sentiment—were nicely summed up in a *Washington Post* review of the fifteen-film retrospective at the American Film Institute on the occasion of the Capra centennial in 1997. The article was entitled "Auteur of Corn."[38]

Auteur of Corn

My own view of the matter is that the issue of Capra's claim to auteurism and the issue of his sentimentality are closely tied, especially by way of his self-conscious relation to the cinematic medium as he knew it. Together these issues come to be important for any explanation of Capra's recent currency in contemporary American public discourse and, more specifically, for finding an answer to the question of why so many filmmakers of note produced in the 1990s recognizable variations on Capra's way of making films. I believe that all of these questions are tied to yet another question about Capra, which it will be the task of the rest of this chapter to explore. It has to do with Capra's place not in film criticism but in film historiography.

The relevance of film historiography should be apparent when we consider that the appeal of the Capraesque in a moment of rapidly transforming screen technologies has much to do with nostalgia for older forms of cinema and spectatorship in the wake of dramatically altered viewing practices.[39] The 1970s saw many new theories of film spectatorship as an experience of dark paralysis under the exigencies of a projector's compulsory temporality. But therein lies an irony, for such theories were being generated as the spectatorial experience itself was being transformed by new cable and video technologies. It has even been suggested that a sense of this transformation is partly responsible for the way in which academic film studies began in the 1980s to historicize earlier structural accounts of cinematic spectatorship—whether Marxist (Horkheimer and Adorno's reductively materialist claim that "the triumph of invested capital" constitutes the meaningful content of every film[40]) or psycholinguistic (the spectator is necessarily "sutured" into the action by editing procedures), or both.[41]

There is a further irony, however, in recognizing that Capra's work came, in the 1990s, to stand in for a large swatch of American film history, in effect for the studio era itself and its way with movies. The irony here is that Capra is not actually accorded much of a place in the most dominant contemporary accounts of the history of American film style. No account of this system has been more influential than that of David Bordwell, Kristin Thompson, and Janet Staiger in their massive *Classical Hollywood Cinema* (1985).[42] To be sure, its methods are not intended to honor a directorial oeuvre as such. Quite the contrary. Yet Capra's many films are almost entirely neglected in the volume's several hundred double-columned pages. Bordwell's own more focused study, *On the History of Film Style*, repeats the omission, even though the book is centered squarely on Hollywood cinema.[43] Again, there is a methodological commitment that constrains the argument. Yet Ernst Lubitsch's so-called "touch" for film comedy gets some attention there, just not the equally recognizable "touch" for which Capra was once celebrated. A question therefore arises: if Bordwell can write a history of Hollywood film style as if the Capraesque style had never existed, how is it that Capra came to function so emblematically in late-twentieth-century nostalgia for the studio era? Putting the question the other way around: how is it that a director whose filmmaking is nowadays often taken by contemporary filmmakers to *epitomize* the "classical style" of Hollywood films should find no serious place in a history of that style?

The resolution of this paradox gets at an important dimension of the Capra corpus, and of the Capraesque as its modality. When Bordwell speaks of "style" he tends to refer quite explicitly to "techniques of the medium."[44] So, for example, the development of deep-focus cinematography by Gregg Toland, especially in his work for Orson Welles and William Wyler in the 1940s, is a matter that receives a full chapter in Bordwell's account.[45] The various transformations in montage practice also receive much attention, as does continuity editing, the close-up, and the realist interest in location shooting. The Capraesque style, by contrast, does not involve innovation of this sort. It is true that Capra boasted of certain technical contributions to Hollywood filmmaking, but the fact is that these are minor indeed.[46] Capra's place in the history of film, I suggest, lies not in his claim to specific technical innovations, but elsewhere.

Nor is there any other special element or ingredient that one can single out as Capra's stylistic claim to fame, though, interestingly, the question has been posed in that more general form as well. At the start of the 1990s, more than sixty years after Capra's first Columbia picture, Sheldon Leonard, who memorably played Nick the bartender in *It's a Wonderful Life* and later became a major television producer, was asked to look back on Capra's work, and he did so with a similar question in view. Leonard actually ventured to name the special element in Capra—he called it "sentiment"—and he likened it to an ingredient in a recipe: "He was a master of sentiment. It was an ingredient he added like garlic, and he knew that, like garlic, it could not be used in excess."[47] Leonard's discussion of sentiment as an element in a formula, or more precisely, an ingredient in a recipe, seems to recall—consciously or otherwise—one of Capra's own early films, *That Certain Thing* (1928), one of his last silent films before he so successfully made the transition to sound cinema and, significantly, the first picture he made at Columbia. Capra even claimed to have wrangled "control over the whole film—writing, directing, editing"—from producer Harry Cohn.[48]

Capra's claim is astonishing, given his juniority at the time, and McBride modifies it somewhat.[49] To the degree it is true, however, *That Certain Thing* must be considered the first film to qualify for his "one man, one film" aspirations, and it thus provides an insight into Capra's sense of his own filmmaking at this early, pivotal moment. *That Certain Thing* may be seen to derive in part from *It* (1926), a film that turned on a similar mystery and set the vogue for Clara Bow as the "It Girl." What was the "it" that the It Girl had? What was "that certain thing"? Capra's film starred Ralph Graves, a veteran of several films by D. W. Griffith, and its plot involves a hasty but innocent marriage between a working-class young woman and a rich young man whose father disowns him for marrying beneath himself. Without the benefit of inherited wealth, the couple starts a small business making sandwiches in boxes (an etiological myth of origin for the boxed lunch) with a special ingredient that leads to great success. (In the denouement, the mystery element is revealed to be just more meat—thus the "ingredient," in effect, is generosity.) It is no stretch, I think, to suggest that the film enacts the story of Capra's own anticipated success on Poverty Row. Indeed, over the course of the next two decades, Capra repeatedly played out this story at Columbia, and then, briefly, elsewhere. Throughout that time, observers speculated about what that certain thing was that made Capra's films, many of them produced on shoestring budgets, the successes they were taken to be. This is part of the background to Leonard's question.

With Leonard, then, I would agree that part of what explains the appeal of Capra in the cinema of the 1990s is his association with sentiment. Indeed, this association is crucial to the larger account I mean to offer in this chapter. The problem with Leonard's observation, however, goes back to the denouement of *That Certain Thing*. In the end, there is no special ingredient that makes the sandwiches taste good, and the same is true of Capra's films. Sentiment is not—as Leonard would have it—a discrete element that can be added in varying amounts according, as it were, to taste. In respect to sentiment what is called the Capraesque is not, in the final analysis, a contribution to classical Hollywood style at all. It is rather a reflection or second-order thematization of it—a *metastyle*, if you like. In the nostalgic cinema of the 1990s, Capra could so easily come to represent the golden age of Hollywood—what F. Scott Fitzgerald famously termed the "genius of the system"—because his work increasingly, though unevenly, staged an internalized *relation* to that genius.[50]

What, then, enabled Capra to gain this kind of reflexivity in and on his own work, this sense of its relation both to itself and its place in the history of the classical Hollywood style of narration? The institutional part of the explanation would point to Capra's employment at Columbia Pictures. The combination of the success of Capra's early films for Columbia and the precariously small scale of the studio meant that, while unquestionably a studio-oriented director, he could wield a degree of influence and enjoy a degree of independence rare among his colleagues at the larger studios. His liberties were hard-won, as the annals of his battles with studio head Harry Cohn amply attest.[51] Yet the results encouraged Capra to be more selective in his materials and more reflective about his work.[52] One could argue that his professional experiences also contributed to Capra's tendency to be reflective. He made his first film, *Fultah Fisher's Boarding House*, with little formal training (though more than he admitted in his autobiography). His work cutting dailies for von Stroheim's *Greed* in 1922 had allowed him to witness the kind of director he did not want to be and the kind of film he did not want to make, while in his work for Mack Sennett he had a connection at just one remove to the pioneering work of Sennett's mentor, D. W. Griffith.[53]

Looking beyond these professional experiences, one could say that Capra's life from the start was that of the insider-outsider, a bundle of paradoxes. He was born to an illiterate peasant family in Sicily who, as he notes at the outset of his autobiography, needed the local priest to read the letter sent home from Los Angeles by an older brother who had already emigrated. And yet he became a master of the most advanced of communication systems before he was thirty. Coming to America at the age of three in 1899, he grew up in a rapidly modernizing Los Angeles. Having shown early signs of intellect, he would find himself a working-class undergraduate on a scientific fast track at Caltech (then called the Throop Institute) in 1915. By his own admission he roamed the country as a low-level con man and cardsharp in the early 1920s before learning the trade in which he would present himself instead as a "man of sentiment."[54]

The pattern of self-refashioning governs both the unfolding of Capra's career and the plots of many of his films. Though these plots often derive from the formulas of the Chaplin-Keaton comedies of victimization, they also dramatize, repeatedly and from early on, processes of social dislocation and personal remaking. In *That Certain Thing*, both the working-class girl and the disinherited scion she marries have to remake themselves in the new circumstances of their sandwich business. And this line continues at least through *Meet John Doe*, where the remaking of the formerly homeless title character forms an explicit part, first, of a newspaper publicity campaign and then of a political campaign. Many American directors make films with recurring signature sets, motifs, or story lines: John Ford's use of Monument Valley, Howard Hawks's rapid-fire dialogue, and Alfred Hitchcock's misleading camera pursuit of the MacGuffin, for instance.[55] But with Capra the programmatic pattern of remaking asserts itself early. This pattern becomes both abundantly clear and thematically dominant in the "social trilogy"— *Mr. Deeds* (1936), *Mr. Smith* (1939), and *Meet John Doe* (1941). The postwar *It's a Wonderful Life* can actually be read as a kind of recapitulation of Capra's *entire* career to that point. As we shall see in chapter 2, the suicide scene in that film derives not only from *Meet John Doe* and *Mr. Deeds*, but also from *Miracle Woman* (1931) and *American Madness* (1932). The bank run also repeats a sequence in *American Madness*. In the earlier film, Walter Huston plays a banker who lends on character, like James Stewart's George Bailey, and there, in the nadir of the Depression itself, appears on screen to quiet a panicky crowd, much as the younger Bailey is shown to do, by giving a brief lecture on political economy. Most of Capra's famous films up through *It's a Wonderful Life* are also rife with slapstick gags and stunts reprised from the earliest of his vaudevillian comedies and, of course, from his work with "the King," Mack Sennett.[56]

More than any other director of the thirties and forties, indeed, Capra shows a tendency toward something like a monomaniacal program. It must be said that some of this sense of mission is driven by vanity and egotism, an attempt to claim personal credit, retrospectively, for prior collaborative efforts, especially with writer Robert Riskin.[57] These are precisely the traits so vexingly on display in the autobiography. By remaking *Mr. Deeds* as *Mr. Smith*, with writer Sydney Buchman rather than with Riskin (*Mr. Deeds Goes to Washington* was the interim title), Capra effectively declared himself the author of both films, related in tendency as they markedly were. By staging a cavalcade of his entire corpus in *It's a Wonderful Life*, without either collaborator, and indeed outside of the entire framework of Columbia Pictures, Capra could represent himself as the key agent in his many successes, the common denominator, the name above the title all along.[58] The point is that however we ascribe the motivation, the pattern of recapitulation, remaking, and self-allegorization not only lends an increasing sense of coherence to Capra's work in itself but also in its relation to the institutions of American cinema as such, and indeed beyond it to the cultural past.

TWO   Capra Remakes Capra

I have suggested that what makes Capra sentimental, and even that what makes Capra Capra, depends on what I have called "recursivity" in his work, his singular preoccupation with self-revision. This tendency develops alongside a range of reflexive structures in his films, and it generates a series of reflections (implicit and explicit) on what it means to be a maker of narrative cinema in the Hollywood of the 1930s and 1940s. Taken together, these factors lead Capra to align himself with an older kind of reflexivity born in the literary sentimentalism of the eighteenth century. I have also provided some explanation as to how Capra came to pursue this sort of recursive reflection on his work, on his medium, and on the larger contexts and longer traditions in which each was enmeshed. In this chapter and the next, I want to consider examples of such cinematic remaking in Capra's career from the end of the silent era until just into the postwar period. Carrying out this analysis proves no easy matter, though, since even at the level of what I have described as auteurist recursivity, the possible topics for discussion seem endless. From one film to another, as I have suggested, Capra reprises sight gags, props, plot motifs, character types, actors, moods, and even the whole "look" of earlier films, their mise-en-scène.

The suicide theme is a good example of how Capra redeploys elements of his own earlier work.[1] When George Bailey makes his lonely way to the bridge in *It's a Wonderful Life*, he may seem thoroughly isolated, but in effect he joins a parade of desperate forerunners running back a good decade and a half in Capra's films. Capra depicts a character's (usually a protagonist's) contemplation of suicide with Blind John Carson in *The Miracle Woman* (1931), with Walter Huston's Tom Dickson in *American Madness* (1932), with the titular Chinese warlord in *Bitter Tea of General Yen* (1933), with Gary Cooper's Longfellow Deeds in *Mr. Deeds Goes to Town* (1936), with Claude Rains's Senator Paine in *Mr. Smith Goes to Washington* (1939), and with Gary Cooper again as the title character of *Meet John Doe* (1941). Indeed, with *Meet John Doe*, the topic of suicide is introduced early and hangs over the entire film, complicating its notoriously numerous conclusions. Capraesque suicide takes self-remaking to its limit, in self-unmaking.

Or consider the motif of the "Cinderella man," usually accompanied by a sequence in which an ordinary American man, in his newly acquired wealth and equipage, plays scene with a valet or butler, who dresses him up for his improved position in life. The first such figure in Capra's work is the reporter Stew Smith who, in *Platinum Blonde* (1931), marries an heiress (Jean Harlow) and moves into the mansion where she lives with her mother and brother. Explicitly mocked as a "Cinderella man," both in print and to his face, Smith plays out a struggle to retain a sense of his own identity in comic scenes with both the butler and the valet that are perhaps the best moments in the film. Clark Gable's Peter Warne is a reporter who refuses any reward from Ellen Andrews's father in *It Happened One Night* (1934), but Gary Cooper's Longfellow Deeds is himself the heir-protagonist in *Mr. Deeds*, and his scenes with his butler and valet closely parallel those of *Platinum Blonde*. The reporter-figure in the formula becomes female with this film, in the character of Jean Arthur's Babe Bennett, who goes out on the town with Deeds by night but satirizes him as a "Cinderella man" in the articles she is writing behind his back. Arthur will of course reprise the role of reporter in *Mr. Smith Goes to Washington*. In that film, Jefferson Smith's out-of-placeness is more a matter of professional ignorance than lack of money or social sophistication, but in *Meet John Doe*, the Cinderella man theme recurs with Gary Cooper's performance in the title role. The identity he assumes is actually manufactured out of whole cloth by a reincarnation of the Jean Arthur reporter, now played by Barbara Stanwyck. Cooper's John Doe, like Stew Smith and his own Longfellow Deeds, will also play the obligatory scene in which the ordinary American man submits to being dressed by an English valet.[2]

If one multiplies these sorts of connections across a corpus of three dozen

Capra films, one quickly discovers dense layers of self-reference, even self-quotation—a daunting prospect for a brief commentary. To limit the scope of analysis, therefore, I will be looking in this chapter and its successor at pairings of films that suggest some of the ways in which the self-revisiting and self-revising practices unfold (and enfold) themselves in Capra's career as a filmmaker. Specifically, I will look at the way in which the interpolated celestial screening of George Bailey's life, when it reaches 1932, draws on Capra's bank-run sequence in *American Madness*, keying a larger set of transformations that mark the intervening fifteen-year journey of self-discovery. I then turn to *It Happened One Night* to show how it revisits the trope of the "Walls of Jericho" in Capra's best silent film, *Strong Man*, to establish principles of probability for the screwball comedy.

In chapter 3, I will look at how *Mr. Deeds* remakes *Platinum Blonde*, to decisive effect for my account of Capra's sense of his medium, and at how *Mr. Smith* in turn remakes *Mr. Deeds*, with an unprecedented focus on the issue of "film power" and his own wielding of it. After some analysis of how Capra's relation to the film medium in these films and *Meet John Doe* is astutely registered in Preston Sturges's *Sullivan's Travels* (1941), I will conclude by examining the multiply recursive aspects of *It's a Wonderful Life*. In its postwar efforts to produce a retrospective on Capra's own life and lifetime, *It's a Wonderful Life*, coming as it does after his discovery of cinema as a "medium of sentiment," opens out toward a longer retrospective on *literary* sentimentalism, exemplified in Dickens but reaching back to the eighteenth century. I seek to show not only that *It's a Wonderful Life* is in some important sense a film set in the eighteenth century, but also why this should be so.

Faith and Fidelity in 1932: *American Madness*

We return to the Capraesque episode that was our starting point—the famous bank-run sequence in *It's a Wonderful Life*. This film and the earlier *American Madness* are related through a clear set of repeated elements and patterns that make Capra's self-revisions stand out the more clearly. Because the citation reaches all the way back to a film he made in 1932, it gives us good parameters for understanding the larger shifts in his shaping of the Capraesque in respect to the three central issues of authorship, medium, and sentiment. Capra had already made nearly two dozen pictures by the time he directed *It Happened One Night* in 1934, and *American Madness*, well received in its own moment, is increasingly acknowledged to be among the best of them.[3] Columbia itself had such hopes for the film on its appearance that, in its quest to break the wealthier studios' lock on the Academy Awards (inaugurated only recently, in 1929), it promoted the film with a coin that bore the inscription "best picture of the year." It was the first original screenplay that Robert Riskin wrote for Capra (the others were *Mr. Deeds Goes to Town* and *Meet John Doe*).[4]

Made and released in 1932, and set in contemporary Manhattan, *American Madness* is a film about an independent-minded bank president, Thomas Dickson (Walter Huston), whose bank suffers a run when successive waves of rumors in a space of hours exaggerate the impact of a robbery on its financial stability. Dickson is a banker who lends "on character," like his real-life model, A. P. Giannini, and, of course, like the later George Bailey.[5] This practice is deemed dangerous by the bank's directors, with whom we see Dickson sparring at a board meeting early on. Dickson's passionate commitment to the bank and its customers is such that he neglects his wife, Phyllis (Kay Johnson). She is devoted to him, but she is also an urbane and fun-loving woman whose light flirtation with the bank's unctuous vice-president, Cyril Cluett (Gavin Gordon), plays into Cluett's need for an alibi, after he acquiesces to gangster demands that he abet a robbery in lieu of payment for heavy gambling debts. Phyllis is discovered at Cluett's apartment by Matt, the bank's chief teller (Pat O'Brien), who will himself become the main suspect in the investigation of the robbery (in which a guard is murdered) that takes place that same night.

The film thus follows two parallel lines of action: one is the investigation of the crime and the eventual exposure of Mrs. Dickson's indiscretion with Cluett (which looks far worse than it is), and the other is the run on the bank that occurs while all this is going on. The struggle between Dickson and his board of directors forms another plotline, and so does the romantic interest between Matt and Helen (Constance Cummings), Dickson's secretary. The critical plot complication is that Matt cannot provide an alibi for himself without revealing that at the time of the midnight crime he was attempting to intervene in Cluett's apparent seduction of Mrs. Dickson. Dickson can tell that Matt is protecting someone but cannot tell whom or why.

The lowest ebb in Dickson's fortunes occurs at a point when the run on the bank is reaching crisis levels, the anxiety of the crowd elevating geometrically with the spread of the news across networks of gossip, and the pace of the action accelerating accordingly. The acceleration of the action anticipates Fritz Lang's *Fury* (1936) and the reliance on telephone networks that Tom Gunning has analyzed in several of Lang's films, including in *The Testament of Dr. Mabuse* (1932), which appeared in the same year as *American*

Capra, *American Madness* (1932, Columbia). The bank run.

Madness.[6] Dickson has failed to persuade the board of directors to help him out of the crisis. He has also failed to win support from other banks in town. Cluett has confessed to abetting the gangsters who robbed the bank but insists on his innocence of the guard's murder on the grounds that he was at that very hour at home with a married woman. Pressed to the breaking point, he finally blurts out that the woman he was with was Phyllis Dickson. When Dickson phones her, expecting to hear her outraged denial of Cluett's charge, she instead stammers guiltily, whereupon Dickson confronts Matt, who cannot deny that he saw her with Cluett.[7] To this point, Dickson had been all cheerful indomitability, calming the bank's panicky clients, much as George Bailey would do in a scene set at about the same time in a film made fourteen years later. But after losing faith in his wife's fidelity, he becomes utterly despondent. He agrees to sign over control of the bank to the board of directors without further protest. He locks his office door, takes a gun from his desk drawer, and contemplates suicide while the panic rages below on the main floor of the bank.

Just here, at the film's turning point, two events occur that stand in uncertain relation to each other. Within the bank-run plot, Matt and Helen (whose relationship Dickson has done much to encourage) start to work the telephones—the medium that, in an earlier montage of close-ups, we have seen foster the panic, the woes of the bank being aggravated anew with

American Madness.

each wave of calls. Matt and Helen urgently phone some of the same small businessmen whose loans Dickson had earlier had to defend to the board of directors. Almost instantly this group begins to respond, working its way through the panicky crowd waving wads of cash and proclaiming that they are depositing money, not withdrawing it. At this point, Dickson is still locked in his office.

The second event is the arrival of Mrs. Dickson at the bank to make her explanations and apologies. In this conjunction of events, we have the two plotlines coming together over the common issues of trust and fidelity. ("Faith" was a discarded early title of the film.[8]) The precise staging of the sequence, however, produces a curious twist in the causal relationships within and between the two plotlines. Dickson is, of course, not a happy man when the board and the other banks turn down his request for help, but significantly, he does not lapse into despondent paralysis until he is confronted with the evidence of his wife's infidelity. Because he had been locked in his office until his wife's arrival, he is unaware as she speaks that the bank's prospects might be brightening. There is no sign in the countenance of Huston's Dickson, or in his demeanor, that Phyllis's plea for forgiveness has moved him. The gun still sits loaded in his right hand.

As Mrs. Dickson shifts from her apology to the subject of the bank, and to speak of Dickson's commitment to its customers, they are interrupted by an employee who bursts in exclaiming, "Mr. Dickson! Come here a minute. Look at this. Something wonderful has happened. People are bringing deposits. You won't believe it until you see it. You have to come out."[9] Even then, Dickson, however, seems only vaguely curious about the audible commotion below. He "shambles" out of the office, by no means cured of his despondency. The employee says, "Look!" and Dickson "gazes in the direction he points." From roughly Dickson's point of view, we then see the spectacle on the floor of the bank. The excitement of the new investors now matches the panic of the customers seeking withdrawal. The sight instantly revives Dickson's spirits. He enters the boardroom, brushes aside the papers that have been hastily drawn up for him to sign the bank over to the directors, and brings the directors out on to the balcony to witness what he calls "a demonstration of faith that's worth more than all the collateral in the world" (196). The directors too are impressed and pledge their considerable assets in support of Dickson. The bank is saved.

This pivotal sequence in *American Madness* is thus deeply problematic, and its strangeness is emphasized by the formal and visual structure of the film, which not only is shot in what is called the "classical" idiom of Hollywood narrative cinema but seems to trumpet its classicism in other respects. Almost all of its action unfolds within the bank—an intricate set that Capra constructed on one of Columbia's lots—creating the feeling of Aristotelian unity of place. There is also the impression of unity of time. For Aristotle, this was the span of a single day, and indeed many commentators take twenty-four hours to be the span of *American Madness*, but in fact it stretches over a forty-eight-hour period. The sense of temporal compression is encouraged by the fact that the action is bookended by formal devices, notably a sequence of scenes, and indeed shots, for day 3 that strikingly repeat those of day 1. The rough structure looks like this:

> *Morning of Day 1:* Shot of the tellers heading toward the bank's underground vault; the arrival of Matt, who opens the vault and tells his daily joke. Cut to Dickson's entrance through the bank's front door; his ritual activities, cheering the team and looking after small details; his ascent to his office and conversation with Helen.

> *Morning of Day 2:* The discovery of the robbery, which will lead to the run on the bank.

> *Morning of Day 3:* Shot of the tellers heading toward the vault; the arrival of Matt, who opens the vault and tells another joke. Cut to Dickson's en-

trance; his ritual activities; his ascent to his office and conversation with Helen, which includes his insistence that she and Matt get married, but that he and his own wife get the honeymoon.

The result is a kind of sonata form—A-B-A—that leads us to attend to other sequences and symmetries as well.

Central to the film's development, as I have suggested, is the parallel between the credit Dickson has earned for his bank and the faith he has placed in the people closest to him, especially in his wife. On the second day, the sequencing of the film's downward spiral toward a point of apparent hopelessness strongly suggests that Dickson's ability to perform as effectively as he does within the bank is a function of the trust that he has (taken for granted) in his wife. He seems able to rise to any challenge on the bank's behalf with enormous energy, until the moment when he is led by the evidence to doubt her fidelity.[10] And yet her heartfelt apology and explanation for the confusion about Cluett are not enough to restore his spirits for a renewed fight on behalf of his bank. Rather, it is the bank's customers—and specifically its borrowers rather than its investors—who turn the tide of faith and fortune on both fronts, institutional and domestic. Phyllis's discredit affects her husband's relation to the bank's credit crisis, but remarkably, the solution to the bank's credit crisis seems to be a necessary condition of his being able to restore credit in *her*. In other words, despite the expectations created by the film's formal bookending, the intertwining of the finance plot and the domestic plot is not symmetrical with their untwining. Instead of the structure we might expect, A [B-C-C-B] A, we find this one: A [B-C-B-C] A. It is as if the two forms of "faith" have become merged or confused.[11]

A Tale of Two Bankers: *It's a Wonderful Life* I

I have gone on at some length in explicating a film many readers will not know in order to highlight a connection to a far better known sequence in a more familiar film: Capra's reprise of the bank run in *It's a Wonderful Life*. Since the events in *It's a Wonderful Life* can be dated quite precisely by way of diegetic newspaper headlines and by time markers in the shooting script, it is clear that this sequence, part of the initial series of flashback episodes from George Bailey's life, also dates to about 1932.[12] There are some key differences. In *It's a Wonderful Life*, as in *American Madness*, an act of theft precipitates a bank crisis, but not the crisis seen in the flashback. Rather, in the later film the theft triggers the present-tense crisis, which dates to Christmas Eve 1945, when eight thousand dollars of bank money intended for deposit falls into the hands of the unscrupulous Potter, a man whose relation to George Bailey is strongly reminiscent of that of the bank directors to Dickson in *American Madness*. The 1932 bank run depicted in *It's a Wonderful Life* seems to have been triggered, not by a crime, but by Potter's surprise move of calling in a loan at the moment Bailey was about to leave town on his honeymoon. It is the 1945 crisis, not that of the 1932 flashback sequence, that drives Bailey to contemplate suicide.

These differences matter, as we will see, but there are nonetheless suggestive connections between the bank-run sequences themselves, connections that point in turn to more telling distinctions. Most notably, in each film there is a strong intertwining of personal and institutional issues. In each case, for example, love and money seem to allegorize each other, thus creating a link between the erotic life and the secret life of capital. But the link is formed slightly differently in the two films. In *American Madness*, the displacement of passion and the crisis of confidence associated with the bank run occurs years into the Dicksons' marriage. In *It's a Wonderful Life*, newlyweds George Bailey and Mary Hatch (Donna Reed) see the early signs of panic in the streets out the rear window of a taxi on their way out of town for their honeymoon. In each film, as well, there is a mingling of personal and institutional funds. Just as Dickson ponies up all his available personal cash to save the Union National Bank, so the Bailey Savings and Loan will eventually be saved when, with everything hanging in the balance, Mary offers George the two thousand dollars in personal savings that they had intended for their honeymoon (and for the fulfillment of George's long-deferred wish to see the world).

It's a Wonderful Life places less emphasis on questions of faith and credibility than does *American Madness* (though both are still present) and there is far less intertwining of financial credit and marital fidelity.[13] The formal intermingling of plots in *It's a Wonderful Life* plays out in a different register—that of reproduction—a theme that is strikingly absent from *American Madness*, and generally absent from the scripts on which Robert Riskin worked for Capra. When the bank doors legitimately close at 6:00 p.m., and the savings and loan has been rescued by George Bailey's intervention, just two dollars remain of the two thousand that Mary had offered to reassure and tide over the panicky citizens of Bedford Falls. The assembled members of the bank's staff hold a celebration with what little is left in Uncle Billy's flask of whiskey. At its culmination, they perform a mock ritual in which they put the two singles to bed in a small tray. With sentimental inevitability, the occasion calls for a toast: "A toast! A toast to Papa Dollar and Mama Dollar, if you want the old Building and Loan to stay in business, you better have a family real quick. . . . Let's put them in the safe and see what happens" (213). That wish will be fulfilled at the end of the film, when the harvest of wealth that issues from this union is reaped in the moving finale, and commemorated with another toast, this time by George's brother Harry.

Further, George's suggestion that they pass out wedding cigars on the occasion of the union of the two dollar bills reminds him for the first time, amid all the distractions of saving the bank, that he has already entered the evening of his own wedding day. George and Mary have not themselves managed to go to bed together at this point. When George phones Mary, she invites him to an unfamiliar address, which turns out to be the abandoned Granville Mansion, on which Mary, in his company, once made a secret wish for their future happiness. When he arrives there in the rain, he is greeted by Bert the cop and Ernie the cabdriver, who are serving as wait staff for the occasion, and who serenade the newlyweds.[14]

Nor is this the first hint of a deep connection between forms of love and forms of capital in the film. The sequence just before the wedding sequence—the preceding "day in the life," some months earlier—takes place on the occasion of Harry's return from college, as a graduate, a football star, and himself a newlywed. Now, we are to understand, it is George's turn to go off to college—Harry had gone first using the money intended for George's education, while George took over the bank from his father. But when he learns that Harry's new father-in-law has offered him an attractive job, George knows he will, despite his brother's protests to the contrary, continue to bear responsibility for running the bank. The camera tracks the evolution of feeling in George's face, from dismay (at the implications for the agreed-upon plan for Harry to take over at the bank) to sympathetic joy for his brother's good fortune. It is a scene that Cavell turns to at the end of his comparison of Eisenstein and Capra in *Pursuits of Happiness* and returns to in *Cities of Words* apropos of promises one makes to another and to oneself.[15] The protracted reaction shot is one of the most complex emotional moments of the film (and one in which Capra clearly breaks with his 1930s idiom—and his own self-imposed prohibition on drawing attention to the camera—to employ a conspicuously moving camera).[16] By the end of the day, after the celebration of Harry's marriage, he has found his way to the house of Mary Hatch, who is herself back from four years away at college. She tries to rekindle the magic of the night they spent together four years earlier, a night ended by news that George's father had died suddenly. George is unresponsive. As he is about to leave, Mary receives a telephone call from their mutual childhood friend Sam Wainwright, a successful businessman.

In the celebrated scene of George and Mary sharing a telephone while her mother eavesdrops on a receiver upstairs, Sam instructs Mary to inform George of some new investment opportunities for making plastics from soybeans. George and Mary are now aroused by their nearness. Mary hoarsely repeats for George's sake Sam's claim that "he is offering you the chance of a lifetime." At this point, George seizes Mary violently and tells her that he doesn't want any commodities, or investment opportunities, and he never wants to get married, ever, which she correctly takes as his proposal of marriage. George's proposal to Mary Hatch remains one of the strongest scenes Capra ever shot, or that either Stewart or Reed ever played. In its intermingling of business negotiation and sex, homosocial bonding and heterosexual eroticism, the scene signally prepares for the events of the wedding day, when the honeymoon money becomes, in effect, a community investment that will reap dividends large and small in the film's conclusion.[17] In this well-known finale, George returns home and the townspeople come to his home with money—the "family" that George hoped would spring from the two dollars (which Uncle Billy called "seeds") that had been bedded together in the teller's tray—much as Dickson's borrowers arrive to repay the faith he invested in them, thus rescuing the bank, at the close of *American Madness*.

Of course, where the action in *American Madness* takes place over just forty-eight hours, *It's a Wonderful Life* spans most of a lifetime. Thus, the financial harvest materializes almost instantly during the crisis in the earlier film, whereas in the later one it takes more than a dozen years beyond the crisis to mature, at which point we see the townspeople of Bedford Falls filing into George and Mary's house to shower him and his family and his bank (all funds seem to merge at this point) with their small investments (or are they gifts?). And these sums will by themselves clearly be enough to save the bank, since the lost funds totaled no more than eight thousand dollars. In *American Madness*, the small investments provide only the *sign* of credit to the serious bankers, whose deep pockets settle the bank's large-scale problem decisively.

Taking the two films whole, we can now observe that perhaps the most striking difference between them has to do with the genres they inhabit. For all of its indulgence in a comic resolution of the various plot complications,

American Madness—both in narrative mode and in representational style—retains a commitment to realism. We see both Tom Dickson and George Bailey defending their lending practices, citing specific examples, in the face of skeptical interrogation by the directors to whom they are accountable. But it seems to matter that we see Tom Dickson actually turning down some loans. The texture of the cinematography in *American Madness* suggests a realist approach that at moments seems to look forward to the coming gestures of film noir. Especially in Capra's handling of the violent robbery scene in the shadowy vault, we sense strong constraints of time and space—the film's quasi-Aristotelian unities—in ways that are only partially relevant to *It's a Wonderful Life*. In the later film, George Bailey's sense of restriction in his life to date in Bedford Falls is, after all, balanced by the film's celestial perspectives and, indeed, by the dramatization of a counterfactual universe that seems to exist alongside the one he had known to that point.

This sense of fantasy in *It's a Wonderful Life* goes along with a certain logic of wish fulfillment that, as we glimpsed earlier, seems to organize its possibilities. This is very much in keeping with the role of "toasts and sentiments" in the post-eighteenth-century tradition, associated as they are with the act of wishing. One key sequence in the screening of George's early life involves the period from the day on which he saves Mr. Gower from lethal negligence to the day on which he meets Mary Hatch and learns of the death of his father. This sequence is bracketed by two instances of George's ritual act of making a wish on the large cigar lighter in Mr. Gower's drug store. The first night he spends with Mary Hatch has the couple making wishes on the stones they hurl at the windows of the abandoned Granville Mansion in which they will one day raise a family. Indeed, the entire premise of the film, and the remedy that Clarence devises for George's despondency, turns on Clarence granting George his wish never to have been born.

One might say that the logic of wish fulfillment, celestial oversight, and counterfactuality in *It's a Wonderful Life* involves this film in the work of the imagination in a way that is not true of *American Madness*. This commitment to the imagination affects the plot differences between the two films most powerfully, perhaps, in the kind of expansive or imaginative sympathy that is so visibly in play in *It's a Wonderful Life*. The theme of sympathy is present in *American Madness* as well, where it is introduced at the very start in an episode that serves as a kind of prologue to the film's central action. Matt is carrying out his daily ritual of opening the bank vault, distributing cash allowances to the junior tellers, and telling his joke for the day—a joke that the tellers have decided in advance they will not laugh at:

MATT

(*with his back to them*)

> Say, did you boys ever hear the story of the pawn broker with the glass eye?

IST TELLER

> No Matt, what is the story about the pawnbroker with the glass eye?

MATT

(*as he continues to fiddle with the lock*)

> Well, I'll tell you. A fellow went into this shop to pawn his watch. The pawnbroker said, "I'll give you $50 for it, if you can tell me which is my glass eye." The fellow said, "All right, I'll do that. It's the right one." The pawn broker said, "That's correct. But how did you know it was the right one?" The fellow said, "Well, it's got more sympathy than the other one." (104–5)[18]

Yet, the topic, though introduced so explicitly, receives little development in *American Madness*. Dickson's banking practices might be said to depend on sympathy, but this is not a fact that is flagged. And although Matt's joke suggests a possible link between the glass eye and the camera lens, Capra does not yet, at this point in his career, call attention to emphatically sympathetic camerawork.

Sympathetic camerawork began to be marked by Capra with *Mr. Deeds Goes to Town*, and it is decidedly in play throughout *It's a Wonderful Life*. The capacity for expansive sympathy is a trait that defines the character of George Bailey as it does few other heroes of Hollywood cinema. It is perhaps expressed indirectly in George's repeatedly stated desire to travel, to see what life is like in places other than the one in which he seems fated always to remain. We see this impulse again in the early sequence that is bracketed by the two moments of wish-making on Mr. Gower's cigar lighter, in the twelve-year-old and then in the twenty-one-year-old George. Working behind the counter in Mr. Gower's drugstore, he boasts to the young Mary Hatch that he has been nominated for membership in the National Geographic Society and shows her copies of the magazine from his back pocket to prove to her that coconuts come from "Tahiti—Fiji Islands, the Coral Sea" (119). Shopping for a suitcase nine years later, he tells the shopkeeper that he wants one big enough for "labels from Italy and Baghdad, Samarkand . . ." (132). His travel, however, is destined to be in a mode he has not yet come to terms with.

A Cinema of Sympathy: *It's a Wonderful Life* II

We will explore the early-modern emergence of these tropes of sentimental travel in chapter 5, but this film supplies answers of its own if we pose the question as to how so powerful an impulse in George is accommodated in the course of his ordinary life in Bedford Falls. It all has to do with his capacity for sympathy, which is indeed nothing short of superhuman. His extraordinary moral sensibility is established early in the flashback narrative of his life, when we see the twelve-year-old boy's response to the near disaster with Mr. Gower the druggist, who has just had news of his son's death and, in a confused state, has put cyanide in a customer's prescription. Young George is sent to deliver it but knows that the capsules contain poison. Having failed to secure the help of his father, who is occupied with Potter, George returns without having delivered the medication. Mr. Gower begins to scold him and to beat him on his already damaged ear until it visibly begins to bleed. While sustaining this punishment, emotional and physical, George (sobbing) breaks through to Mr. Gower with these words: "Mr. Gower, you don't know what you're doing. You put something wrong in those capsules. I know you're unhappy. You got that telegram and you're upset. You put something bad in those capsules. It wasn't your fault, Mr. Gower. . . . I know you feel bad. . . ." (129). This is as perfect an expression of spontaneous human sympathy as the resources of English have to offer, and it is managed by young George under conditions of extreme vulnerability and adversity.[19]

It is true that the cinematography relies less on shot/reverse-shot here—George's sympathy is sufficiently established by other means—and more on an orthogonal camera angle. However, here as in other moments, such as the scene in the luggage shop, this orthogonal angle is inflected to suggest the view of an extradiegetic spectator (the cinema audience) whose sympathy with George's plight, and indeed with George's own sympathy, is elicited in a way that is modeled by our stand-in, Clarence the Angel. Clarence verbally expresses his own sympathy with George when James Stewart first appears in the film, in the scene in the luggage shop. Clarence is the sentimental intermediary who views such scenes from a position transcendent (as it were) to George, but not to us.

A less physically demanding, but perhaps equally impressive, example of George's power of sympathy is his response to Clarence just after the intervention that saves his life, in the first moments of George's experience of the world without his own role in it. George is sitting at what had been Martini's Bar with Clarence, disoriented—indeed, traumatized—by his new circum-

Capra, *It's a Wonderful Life* (1946, Liberty Films).

stances. People he recognizes are not as they were; his neighbors do not recognize him, not even when he hails them. Mr. Gower is now a homeless alcoholic, having, as George is told, "spent twenty years in jail for poisoning a kid." George is so confused that he even suspects Clarence of being a hypnotist. Beyond the confusion, he and Clarence meet a hostile reception from the once genial, now menacing bartender, Nick (Sheldon Leonard), who will shortly call them "pixies" and throw them out of the bar. In the midst of this extreme personal discomfiture, George turns to Clarence and says, "Hey, little fellow—you worry me. You got someplace to sleep?" (287). This sympathetic instinct, we must conclude, runs deep in him.[20]

We see a similar instantaneous generosity in George when he and Mary, sharing a telephone, are told by Sam Wainwright that Sam's father is about to open a factory outside of Rochester to make plastics out of soybeans and that George should get in on the ground floor. George's response is to redirect the plan to help a small town still suffering the effects of the Depression: "Why not [build it] right here? You remember that old tool and machinery works? You tell your father he can get it for a song. And all the labor he wants, too. Half the town was thrown out of work when they closed" (194). It is this instinctive sympathy for his fellow townspeople at this moment that will suddenly morph into an erotic desire for Mary that prompts his proposal of marriage, articulated in that series of fierce refusals: "Now you listen to me! I don't want any plastics! I don't want any ground floors, and I don't want to get married—ever—to anyone! You understand that? I want to do what *I* want to do. And you're . . . and you're . . ." (196). Stewart told his biographer that he did the scene in "one great, unrehearsed take."[21] Capra recounts that Stewart cut many lines in his passionate one-and-only attempt with this scene, a performance that had worried Stewart in prospect because he feared he was out of practice with on-screen lovemaking. We therefore have no clear sense of the precise terms of the relation between erotic passion and venture capitalism in the script. We do know, however, that this forsaking of the "chance of a lifetime" leads to a family of four children, who appear in quick order in the celestial screening of subsequent days in George Bailey's life.

We are reminded in the course of this screening that the depiction we and Clarence are seeing of George Bailey's life is to be understood as a kind of cinema.[22] The first time we encounter the adult George Bailey (and James Stewart), the frame freezes on his face just as he announces how large a case he wants to buy for his travels around the world, now that (so he believes) he is free to leave town. "What did you stop it for?" asks Clarence the Angel of the heavenly projectionist. We are thus also reminded that the heavenly screening has an intermediary spectator, one who is increasingly engaged in—sympathetic with—the character of George Bailey. Clarence goes on to ask a number of questions that show his capacity to sympathize with the sympathetic Bailey: "It's a good face. I like it. I like George Bailey. Tell me, did he ever tell anyone about the pills? . . . Did he ever marry the girl? Did he ever go exploring?"[23] Not only does this create self-consciousness about cinematic mediation. It helps us see how the film as a whole is structured as a series of moments in which characters are defined by the degree of their sympathetic engagement with each other. Mr. Potter, of course, is consistently defined by the absence of this capacity.[24] Further, these scenes of possible sympathetic exchange are themselves framed in settings that contain spectators and eavesdroppers, whose relationship to the characters involved in the framed action is similarly defined by degrees of sympathy.

Part of the larger dynamics of sympathy in the film is figured through a series of scenes that stage a contagious impulse to "take the plunge." The first three of these all involve literal acts of entry into water. In the first of the childhood sequences, we see George jump into the icy water in which his brother has fallen. During the celebrated graduation dance, when the floor of the gym opens to reveal a swimming pool underneath and George and Mary tumble in during the Charleston contest, one after another of their schoolmates jump in with them, until finally even the principal of the high

It's a Wonderful Life. Face of George Bailey in freeze-frame.

school folds his hands into diving position and plunges in. And then there is the doubly sympathetic moment at the start where Clarence hurls himself off the bridge on which George Bailey is contemplating suicide because he knows George will instinctively dive in after him in order to save him. These acts of sympathetically taking the plunge are all summed up in the final scene as the townspeople approach the Bailey family with their gifts, tumbling one after another into participation in a collective act of generosity. Structurally, this finale revisits the queue of lenders approaching George in the Building and Loan during the bank-run scene, but the connection to the successive dives into the high school swimming pool is also powerful. This is nowhere more pointed than in the late moment when Carter, the dour bank examiner, in an affective reprise of the principal's belated immersion, decides to take the plunge of charity along with everyone else in town, adding his contribution to the basket to relieve the Baileys instead of dunning them for the lost funds, and then turning merrily to join in the singing of "Hark! The Herald Angels Sing." This is all rendered in a series of shot/reverse-shot edits that include the grateful bewilderment of George and his family. The affective force of the bank examiner's gesture—a gesture from the Scrooge story stood rightside

It's a Wonderful Life.
School principal takes
the plunge.

It's a Wonderful Life.
Bank examiner joins
the festivities.

It's a Wonderful Life.

up again—derives from its place in this powerful metaphorical chain. And the cumulative effect of this chain of reference is one of the reasons why even seasoned film viewers report themselves unable to resist the impulse to weep at this denouement, even on repeated viewing.

We will see in chapter 4 that the notion of networked spectatorship is central to the theory of moral sentiments, as worked out by Adam Smith in a 1759 book of that title. Capra plays many variations with this big idea. Sometimes the third-party spectator is implicit, but often, as with Clarence's voice-over observations about George in the luggage shop, it is quite explicit. A different example of how the explicit third-party observer can work comes in the telephone scene, where Mary Hatch's mother, hostile to George's interest, is eavesdropping on Mary's conversations with Sam and George. In the scene around the dinner table on the night of the high school dance (and, later, Mr. Bailey's death), Annie, the Baileys' African-American housekeeper, eavesdrops sympathetically on what will prove to be George's last conversation with his father, when he expresses his filial admiration for him.[25] In the wooing scene after the dance, when George and Mary have changed into makeshift dry clothes, and George corrals her in a hydrangea bush, promising her the moon, we discover that their conversation is being overheard and perhaps overseen by a bald man on a nearby porch.[26]

Add the layer of the celestial screening for Clarence and the theatrical screening for us, and you have quite a complex relay structure of subject positions in which the achievement or frustration of sympathy is registered.[27] This relay structure is in some important sense the medium of the film's action. Or to put the point differently (and in a way I will develop in part 2 of this book), the field defined by this structure of opportunities for sympathy opens up what might be called a second dimension of the action, a second level of narrative operation. This is the structure of a sentimental network, and we shall have occasion to examine more closely both its emergence and its consequences for matters of probability.[28] Its "coordinates," as I describe them, involve a horizontal axis of mutually reflective relationships and a vertical axis of higher-order reflexive levels: roughly, a circuit and a ladder. Both structures, as I have suggested, derive from eighteenth-century discourses— the former in the theory and practice of commercial society, the latter in the notion of moral progress—and sympathy matters centrally to them both.

It is in respect to such a network, I suggest, that we must consider the superhuman sympathy of the film's protagonist: his capacity to focus on the sorrow of Mr. Gower while taking blows to a reopened ear wound, his capacity to worry about Clarence at a moment when he has entered a world-swapping thought experiment without a rulebook, and his capacity to put the interests of his fellow townspeople first in a time of personal crisis. This special moral competence marks George Bailey as a hero in this kind of cinematic narrative as surely as (to take two kinds of films popular in the postwar period) the power of focused action marks the hero of a Western or the strange masochism of the male protagonist in a film noir marks him. In *American Madness*, sentimental moral competence is not entirely absent, but it is represented differently. It is represented more as a kind of force field that emerges, then recedes with the crisis, and then returns to view at the moment when Tom Dickson directs the attention of his board to the small businessmen entering his failing bank, waving wads of cash and announcing their intention to invest. Crucially, it is conceived as "faith" in this early film, not sympathy.

The quasi-remaking of *American Madness* as *It's a Wonderful Life* thus dramatizes, quite self-consciously, where Capra had got to in this crucial decade and a half of filmmaking, and it points to several related conclusions. First, in the act of remaking, Capra becomes more emphatically the author of both films. One becomes a reflection of the other, but both become reflections of him.[29] Second, there is a high degree of cinematic reflexivity in the later film, while there had been next to none in the earlier film.[30] Part of the point of mentioning Matt's Dickensian joke about the pawnbroker's glass eye is that the opportunity to make a film that is more self-conscious about the question of sympathy goes unexploited in 1932. By contrast, *It's a Wonderful Life* calls attention to cinema as the medium of its own sympathetic operations. The fact that, with Clarence, we are attending a celestial film screening is punctuated by the freezing of the frame on George's face almost as soon as James Stewart appears on the screen for the first time. It is a moment further dilated by Clarence's question, "What did you stop it for?" This reflexivity, as I will be suggesting later, opens on to larger questions of media archaeology and the relationship of Hollywood movies to the cultural forms that precede cinema—specifically those of literary sentimentalism in the eighteenth and nineteenth centuries. Clarence is, of course, himself a citizen of the eighteenth century. Moreover, the central authority figure in the film's technologically "wired" version of the heavens is the iconic figure of the American Enlightenment, Benjamin Franklin, a practical genius associated with both print and electricity. His character figures in the film as a self-consciously pivotal figure in the history of print and of electrical technologies like the cinema.[31]

The last conclusion to which this discussion of the two films points is the later film's heightened self-consciousness about the governing principle of sentiment. As we have seen, through the thematics of sympathy, and indeed through such technical devices as the close-up of the sympathetic face, *It's a Wonderful Life* insistently and suggestively links sentiment to political economy, a link that is, at best, only dimly hinted at in *American Madness.* This observation is consistent with the clear evidence that the literary source for many of the plot elements, props, and character types in *It's a Wonderful Life* is Dickens's *A Christmas Carol.*[32] Dickens had influentially elaborated the connections between political economy and sympathy, and between sympathy and moral sentiment, in the novels whose rare editions Capra so assiduously collected. Dickens was not the first to work out such connections, as we shall see, but his was perhaps the most dominant representation of the sort of literary sentimentalism to which the Dickensian framework of *It's a Wonderful Life* effectively declares Capra a devotee.

The Walls of Jericho

Two years after *American Madness* came Capra's momentous success with *It Happened One Night*, a decisive event not only for comedy in the 1930s but also for the shape of Capra's subsequent career. There are a number of ways in which this film puts Capra on the path to the sort of recapitulative cinematic mythmaking that we find in *It's a Wonderful Life*, whose title would distantly echo it.[33] In turning to *It Happened One Night*, however, I will be stressing not only its development of the Capraesque mode and its themes, but also how it can itself already be seen as an act of self-remaking.

It Happened One Night charts the travels of Ellen Andrews (Claudette Colbert), who escapes from the Florida yacht of her powerful father (Walter Connolly) in order to make her way back to New York and the man with whom she eloped. On the night bus north, she meets Peter Warne (Clark Gable), a reporter who has just quit his New York newspaper, and who assumes the role of her protector over her own initial protestations, from motives that are initially ambiguous. Along the way, they spend three nights together, the first and third sharing rooms out of necessity, the question of propriety being settled by Gable's hanging between their beds a blanket he calls "the Walls of Jericho." The blanket allows for intimate moments of conversation between them, as, from either side, they project on to it their hopes and fears. At the end of the film, after much screwball complication—this film is said by some to have actually invented the screwball comedy—we see the walls come down, and we accept it as the consummation that the film has led us to wish for and expect.

The best single piece of criticism we have on any Capra film is probably

Stanley Cavell's chapter on *It Happened One Night* in *Pursuits of Happiness* (1981), a study of what he calls the Hollywood comedy of remarriage. Cavell offers Capra's pioneering film as a kind of prototype for this subgenre, and central to Cavell's analysis is the role of the famous blanket walls:

> The question the narrative must ask itself is how to get them to tumble. That this is a question, and the kind of question it is, is declared late in the film when the second blanket is shown unceremoniously pulled down by the suspicious owners of the second auto camp. Of course, it is easy to pull it down if you do not know what it is, or care. So an early requirement for its correct tumbling is that the pair come to share a fantasy of what is holding it up.[34]

That fantasy is elaborated in their own conversational inventions. Cavell thus notes, for example, that in spite of the obvious gendering of the Israelites and the trumpet, Peter Warne insists that he has no such instrument for bringing down the blanket. Taking a cue from Cavell's analysis of the fantasy that holds up the blanket, I would like to focus on the way in which the plot function of both the blanket and its fantasy creates a dual possibility in the film—or, better, a dual *probability*, in roughly Aristotle's sense of the term. How can it be torn down unceremoniously within one order of events in the film, but not within the order of events that comprise the sympathetic order of shared fantasy?

Characteristically, for the Capra of the 1930s, this distinction is figured in terms of publicity and privacy, a thematic that is absolutely crucial to the film's working out of its plot, and one that involves crucial elements of probability. As a newspaper reporter, Peter Warne trades in publicity, of course, and Ellen at one point explains her elopement precisely as an attempt to escape the constant vigilance of the men her overprotective father has charged with monitoring her every move. Ironically, the man she eloped with, King Westley (Jameson Thomas), is himself a publicity hound. Peter later calls him a "front page gladiator." Indeed, in the film's denouement, with the second wedding ceremony of Ellen and Westley (from which Ellen runs away, with Peter), Westley actually descends onto the site of the outdoor ceremony in a one-man helicopter. Westley *is* a vaunting public "young man on the flying trapeze," to quote the song so memorably sung by the passengers aboard the night bus with Ellen and Peter.

In Peter's wrongheaded idea of how this story should end, and how the Walls of Jericho should be pulled down, it is precisely the act of turning his story into a public commodity of questionable probability that fixates his interest. He leaves Ellen in an auto camp outside Philadelphia, drives up Route 1 to his New York newspaper office, and sits down at a typewriter to compose the story of his own marriage to Ellen. The scene of Peter at the typewriter dissolves into a close-up of the typed page, still on the platen, upon which are typed these words:

> —and that's the full and exclusive story of Ellen Andrews' adventures on the road. As soon as her marriage to King Westley is annulled, she and Peter Warne, famous newspaperman—and undoubtedly the most promising young novelist of the present era—will be married.

After this redeployment of *Platinum Blonde*'s similar story-within-the-story device, Peter goes to his boss, a benign newspaper editor whose employ he has recently quit, and tells him he has the scoop on Andrews's story, for which he is asking a thousand dollars that he desperately needs. When the editor asks what the money is for, Peter replies, "To tear down the Walls of Jericho." When Peter tells him that the man Ellen is now going to marry is none other than himself, the boss walks out. Peter follows him and convinces him of the truth of the story by making him feel that truth sympathetically. The editor then rewrites the story in terms that seem to him probable: "What a story! (picturing it) On her way to join her husband, Ellen Andrews falls in love with— . . ."[35] And they agree on Peter's plan.

However, when the owners of the auto camp where Peter has left Ellen realize that he has fled, they invade the room, tear down the blanket, and induce Ellen to call her father, who comes with a police escort to retrieve her, passing the returning Peter somewhere on Route 1 in New Jersey. Meanwhile, in the act of telling his night editor to "break down the front page" for the new story, Peter's boss is interrupted by a telephone call from a reporter who has the new story, the one leading to the remarriage of Ellen and King Westley, and so the front page is rewritten. It is by means of the newspaper that Peter finds out what happened and about the remarriage that has been planned.

Though the film's final shot shows the Walls of Jericho tumbling in a secluded auto camp somewhere in rural Michigan, we do not see Peter and Ellen themselves again after her flight from the public second wedding to Westley into Peter's car. In the end, the couple is hidden even from us. Yet what brings down the Walls of Jericho, a barrier of privacy voluntarily erected between two persons with very different ideas of publicity, is deeply mediated by publicity itself. The very mechanisms of the plot turn on key moments of publicity: Ellen's father communicates with his lost daughter by producing newspaper headlines. And the film's narrative denouement is routed through the probabilities encoded in public narrative forms: Peter reads about the intended marriage between Ellen and King Westley in a newspaper.

I noted above that there are two orders of probability in *It's a Wonderful Life*. Though I would not claim to find in *It Happened One Night* the degree of self-consciousness about such things that one finds in the later film, it does sustain a similarly self-divided conception of how its world makes sense. This aspect of *It Happened One Night* becomes clearer if we recognize it, in its turn, as a reworking of Capra's *Strong Man* (1926), a silent film and his first feature, in which the figure of the Walls of Jericho is already very much in play. *Strong Man* has many claims on our attention, not least that it represents Capra's work with the great silent-age clown Harry Langdon. Cavell is not likely to have known about this film at the time of his writing about Capra (it was remastered for laser disc release by the British Film Institute in 1985). But its relevance to his central question about *It Happened One Night* is, as I hope to suggest, most telling.

Strong Man begins in a foxhole near the end of World War I with a Belgian soldier, Paul Bergot (also called simply "the Boy"), who has long exchanged letters with a blind American girl, Mary Brown, whom he has never met. The action begins when the Boy, after a David-and-Goliath struggle with an enemy soldier, whose name turns out to be Zandow, is taken prisoner by him.[36] In the next sequence, Zandow and the Boy arrive at Ellis Island; Zandow seeks to make it in America with a strong-man act. After various escapes in New York City, with the Boy temporarily slipping away from Zandow in search of Mary, they land a job in a rum-running town on the New York–Canadian border. This just happens to be the town where Mary lives, and where her father, the town preacher, is engaged in a pitched war against the local bootleggers over the entertainments staged in the gin mill–cum–vaudeville theater that now occupies the former town hall. The sequence in which Mary and the Boy meet is handled in a repeated pattern of shot/reverse-shot.

Part of the point of bringing Langdon into the present argument is that he reminds us how much the Chaplinesque figure of the 1920s owes to the late-eighteenth-century sentimental figure of the Mackenzian man of feeling, a figure of innocent folly and pure sympathy.[37] But there is more to the connection, because, as with the literary sentimentalism of the eighteenth century, a second dimension of action opens up within or athwart that of the diegesis. This is akin to the second level of probability or causation we considered

Capra, *The Strong Man* (1926, First National).
The Boy meets Mary.

in *It Happened One Night*. Thus, in a late sequence of the film, we see the Boy battling a hostile crowd within the theater, in action that is frequently cut with theatricalized reverse shots of the Boy and the crowd.[38] Intercut with this sequence, we see Mary's father leading the pious townspeople in a march against the theater, singing "Onward Christian Soldiers" and vowing to destroy the palace of venal amusements—in his words, to bring down "the Walls of Jericho." The battle inside the walls escalates, with the Boy loading up the strong man's human cannon with barbells as the marchers reach the exterior walls. What happens if we substitute *Strong Man* for *It Happened One Night* in Cavell's line of interrogation? Under what conditions can the Walls of Jericho properly be made to tumble in this earlier film? And what is the meaning of this tumbling?

I want to suggest that in *Strong Man* the tumbling of the walls is less an event to be explained than an occasion for seeing the multiplicity of modes of probability that are at work in the film. The walls separate the interior of the theater from the exterior in more ways than one. Inside the theater, action is governed by a theatricalized sense of causality that is explicitly parodied in the Boy's performance of the strong man's act, with weight-lifting feats that seem to defy gravity. Outside the theater, the film is governed by a different kind of causality, in which the songs and prayers of the faithful are expected to have efficacy in bringing down the walls of a den of iniquity. The walls come down in the culminating moments by virtue, it seems, of the separate actions taking place both inside and outside, the Boy's use of the cannon and the protesters' reliance on faith. The tumbling of the walls is the point of perfect coincidence of these two lines of action. Brought together in this way, inside and outside together pose questions about what "strength" is, what virtue is, and how to understand the power of each.

The moment at which the Walls of Jericho come down is, finally, one in which we as audience must understand ourselves as interpolated into the modes of sympathetic or sentimental causality that we see parodied in the audience relations inside the theater. We move from the position of spectators implicated in the mutual sympathy of the reaction-shot sequences, to the position of spectators within the audience of the vaudeville comedy, to a position outside the space of this constructed spectacle in which the space of its definition is itself reconfigured. The Walls of Jericho in this film divide two different forms of probability—two distinct modes of making a world—but the causal framework in terms of which the division between them is broken down itself involves a sphere of probability far less determinate than either in its operation. It is, in a sense, for the film's spectators to determine.

The Strong Man. In the theater: the Boy and the crowd.

The Strong Man. Parallel action, outside and inside.

The Strong Man. Walls tumbling; the preacher rejoicing.

Questions of Probability

We have been considering *Strong Man*'s somewhat crudely schematic way of playing with literal and figurative orders, with distinctive modes of probability, and with realist and nonrealist narrative frameworks. The discussion is meant to serve, in the first instance, as background for recognizing subtler developments along these lines in Capra's later and more self-consciously sentimental films. We have already begun to see that these later developments lead Capra to a more involved and explicit engagement with a longer tradition of sentimentalism, a tradition that includes some distinctive variations on the handling of probability. I hinted at the start at how some of these issues play out in Sterne's complex treatment of literary spectatorship in the opening pages of *Sentimental Journey*, where the devices of hypallage and syllepsis (causal and figurative ambiguity) are, as Shklovsky would say, laid bare. We will see in part 2 that the history of so-called sentimental comedy, since its prototype in *The Conscious Lovers* (a play of 1722 written by the co-author of *The Spectator*), has long been marked by a concern with how such comedy plays fast and loose with probability. This distinctive license matters to how we understand the sentimental mode's reemergence in the medium of cinema.

This concern about sentimental comedy in particular is typically focused on a gap between plot development and denouement, a certain leap of the heart that gets to the happy resolution. One commentator on this feature of the genre calls it a form of "violence done to probability."[39] Another, in a discussion of Steele's play that generalizes about the distinctive "move" that sentimental comedy makes with its conclusions, helpfully points to a "slipping of levels, in the identification of the real and the ideal," which he calls "one definition of the sentimental."[40] Reframing the issue in relation to a splitting and slipping of levels proves helpful, because it has bearing on the issue of the sentimental's reflexivity about its medium, beginning, as we will see in chapter 6, with the very explicit staging in Steele's work of the relation of print to theater. In chapter 3, we will see this dramatized starkly in the "heart leap" denouement of the sentimental media politics in Capra's *Mr. Smith Goes to Washington*.

For now, however, I will point to a vaguely similar kind of reflexivity—a slipping of levels—in some of Capra's early sound films for Columbia, films that helped that "poverty row" studio survive the first years of the Depression in the early 1930s. Two were made with the young Barbara Stanwyck: *Ladies of Leisure* (1930), about the scion of a robber baron family, a young painter who takes under his wing a call girl/model (Stanwyck), thus allegorizing Capra's relation to Stanwyck herself in the making of the film; and *Miracle Woman* (1931), where the reflexive allegory relates the suspension of disbelief in the theater to that of the phony faith healer's tent. More typically, though, from *Platinum Blonde* (1931) through *It Happened One Night, Mr. Deeds Goes to Town* (1935), and *Meet John Doe* (1941), the operative form of reflexivity involves newspaper journalism and public print culture more broadly.

To return to the question of Capra's self-remaking, the alternative fictional orders defined by something like a faculty of imagination or locus of sensibility are very much a part of the way in which *It Happened One Night* remakes *The Strong Man*. With this early, modest act of authorial self-transformation on Capra's part comes a major step in his developing self-consciousness about medium: the theater-film issue in *The Strong Man* gives way to the print-film issue in *It Happened One Night*. The latter would define much of Capra's work from that time forward, even on an occasion when, as in *State of the Union* (1948), he was working with a screenplay adapted from the stage. Issues about the relation of print to motion-picture media tend to predominate in that film, with some precocious anticipation, as we have seen, of the coming medium of television.

In *It Happened One Night*, then, we have a film that frames its developing narrative as an implicit parallel to the story that the reporter Peter Warne is himself composing and recomposing along the way. It reveals something of Capra's kind of work with this film, I think, that Peter was not a reporter in "Night Bus," the short story from which Riskin and Capra adapted *It Happened One Night*. In making newspapers so important to the film, and in developing the reflexive relation between what the reporter is writing and how the film's own narrative unfolds, Capra and Riskin returned to *Platinum Blonde*, the first film on which they worked together. (Riskin was brought in late to doctor the script.) *Platinum Blonde* had already offered a story of a wealthy heiress and a male reporter. In that case, the reporter Stew Smith (Robert Williams), prototype of Capra's Cinderella Men, was from the start working on a novel but could not get beyond the first page. Toward the end of the film, with the help of Gallagher (Loretta Young), the female reporter for whom he breaks off his marriage to the heiress (Jean Harlow), Smith is able to write the novel in a single overnight stint. It is the story of the film we have just seen.

In *It Happened One Night*, Peter Warne's narrative of his adventures with an heiress is written and rewritten in the genre of the newspaper feature rather than in that of the novel. Indeed, newspapers even function as a form of interfamily communication in the film, as Ellen's father indicates his willingness to forgive her by way of a front-page story.[41] As I have suggested, the reflexive play in this film certainly hearkens back to *Platinum Blonde* and provides further evidence of Capra's early impulses to remake his own work and to make himself a cinematic author in the bargain.[42] These early impulses attain a new level of purposiveness, however, as we follow Capra into his far more dramatic self-transformation in the second half of the 1930s. The film that most clearly registers that transformation, *Mr. Deeds Goes to Town* (1936), also plays out a new variation of the materials developed in *Platinum Blonde*. In critical commentary on Capra's career, the transformation effected by *Mr. Deeds* is most often discussed in ideological terms. It is argued alike, both by those who approve and by those who do not, that with this film Capra's work assumes a programmatic cast, a sense of social mission. I intend neither to take sides on the evaluative question nor to quarrel with this claim. I do, however, mean to show that, however we understand Capra's ideological transformation, *Mr. Deeds* involves a transformed sense of his relation both to the medium of Hollywood narrative cinema and to the question of sentiment, which he came to see as intimately connected with that medium.

THREE Cinema as a Medium of Sentiment

By most accounts, including the one provided in his autobiography, the key transformation in Capra's career occurs in 1935–1936, and the pivotal film in his development is *Mr. Deeds Goes to Town* (1936). Even observers who disagree about whether this was a good or a bad development tend to agree on the timing. There may be some quibbling about details—even about whether to describe the breakdown as one in body or in spirit—but the crisis that Capra experienced following his capturing, after two dozen pictures, what he called "the Holy Grail" (with *It Happened One Night*) is well documented. There is also general agreement that *Mr. Deeds* represents Capra's attempt to overcome this crisis, to turn his suffering into cinematic work of a higher order.

The result was both a critical and a box office success. The film did not win quite as many Oscars as *It Happened One Night*, but in certain ways it represents a greater achievement. Clark Gable and Claudette Colbert, both under contract at MGM in 1934, were already recognized stars when Harry Cohn paid for their services in *It Happened One Night*. By contrast, Gary Cooper and Jean Arthur, the leading actors in *Mr. Deeds*, were less established before this film lifted their reputations. Otis Ferguson, one of the strongest voices in American film criticism in the 1930s, praised Capra's work highly through 1936, and suggested that *Mr. Deeds* may have surpassed *It Happened One Night* ("its logical predecessor"), on which he'd heaped praise in 1934.[1] Ferguson took the occasion of his review of *Deeds* to compare Capra's comedies favorably to those of both René Clair and Ernst Lubitsch, whom he regarded as the other comic geniuses among contemporary directors. Graham Greene, reviewing *Mr. Deeds* for the *Spectator*, called it Capra's greatest picture and praised its humanity and moral sense. (It is perhaps surprising that while Capra has three films among the first thirty-five in the American Film Institute's rankings, *Mr. Deeds* did not make the list of one hundred.)

The role of Longfellow Deeds is the first of five Capra naïfs that would be played by Cooper or James Stewart over the next decade.[2] Deeds is a sensitive and sympathetic soul, and his character surely marks Capra's most explicit and deliberate embrace of the thematics of sentiment that would increasingly orient his filmmaking from this point on. How explicit and deliberate? Deeds's occupation in Mandrake Falls, New Hampshire, is that of greeting-card poet—he expresses sentiments for a living—and he conspicuously plays the role of what in the eighteenth century began to be called "the man of feeling."[3] He represents in this respect an important step in the transition that leads from Tom Dickson in *American Madness* to George Bailey. He also marks a critical moment in the series of Capra's five films in the course of a decade that turn on the relation of a reporter and an heir or quasi-heir. In the first two, *Platinum Blonde* and *It Happened One Night*, the heiress is female (Jean Harlow, Claudette Colbert) and the reporter is male (Robert Williams, Clark Gable). In *Deeds*, as in *Mr. Smith* and *Meet John Doe* (three films about men who come into situations of wealth and power without effort or merit), the reporter is female and the heir figure is male.

Coinciding with the presentation of this man-of-feeling character type and, signally, the patent thematization of sentiment as such, we find a convergence of major developments in Capra's professional and personal lives. As already noted, he was elected president of the Academy of Motion Pictures in 1936 and, while still holding this office, of the Screen Directors Guild in 1938 (the same year the US Congress established the House Committee on Un-American Activities). These years involved immensely complicated political challenges, needless to say, but the personal crises that preceded his taking these posts involved even greater levels of psychological stress. The intense fame and heightened expectations that arrived with, especially, the success of *It Happened One Night* carried a high personal cost. Capra suffered a series of mental and physical disorders in 1935, leading him to fear his brilliant career might be over, that he might suffer the dreaded fate of the Hollywood has-been. *Mr. Deeds* is the film that emerged from this moment, and it does register something of a new, or newly self-conscious, Frank Capra. In its turn, the film that remade *Mr. Deeds, Mr. Smith Goes to Washington* (1939), did much to confirm this new Capra in his mission and to make explicit the developing rivalry between print and cinema as media for moving the nation.

The period from 1935 to 1939 is perhaps the most decisive in the formation of what has come to be called the Capraesque. It also, not coincidentally, represents Capra's most strenuous and explicit engagement with the cinema of his avowed exemplar, D. W. Griffith. In marking his fullest realization of the 1930s American film style he helped to shape, this period simultaneously witnesses his first clear acknowledgment of the rivalry of film with print. Following the implications of this last point will make it possible to see how the Capraesque incarnation of the sentimental mode increasingly opens on to Dickens and the literary tradition behind him. Of course, the late 1930s was also a time of great political movement, upheaval, and confusion: the Spanish Civil War was just a flash point for larger international conflicts between fascism and communism. Most relevant for Capra, it saw the emergence of the Popular Front.[4] Capra's complex connection to the Popular Front of the late 1930s has been well considered over the years.[5] For most commentators, it is a connection marked by a profound ambivalence on Capra's part. In showing the importance of sentimentalism to late-1930s Capra, then, I also mean to illuminate his notoriously mixed feelings about the great political issues of his time.

A Turning Point

Capra's 1971 autobiography has many twists and turns, many bad endings and new beginnings. But it also has a single pivotal moment: the personal crisis of 1935. His own account of how he came out of his depression involves a piece of storytelling that, though accepted at face value for a time, has not held up in all particulars to the inquiries of Joseph McBride. But even McBride implicitly frames this moment as the decisive one for Capra's career, as is clear from his own emphasis on Capra's response to sweeping the Oscars in 1934 with *It Happened One Night*. That much, in fact, is clear from McBride's subtitle, which he borrowed from Tennessee Williams: "The Catastrophe of Success." The story Capra tells in his autobiography concerns a visit he claims to have received during the period between the success of *It Happened One Night* and the concept for *Mr. Deeds*. On Capra's account, this was a period in which he suffered a bout of psychosomatic disease, a wave of diffidence about his ability to follow his own great last act, and worries about where to turn next for a successful film project. "I lost weight, I lost interest, I lost everything," he would later tell McBride.[6]

Then one day (so Capra's story goes), Max Winslow, who had been staying with Capra at his home during the illness, announced that there was a man at the door asking to see him but refusing to see him in his sickbed. Here is Capra's account of what followed:

> I made it across the hall and into our second-floor den. A little man rose from a chair, completely bald, wearing thick glasses—as faceless a man as you will ever see. . . .
>
> I sat down weak as a cat and just as curious. The little man sat opposite and quietly said: "Mr. Capra, you're a coward . . . but infinitely sadder—you are an offense to God. You hear that man in there?" Max had turned on the radio in my room. Hitler's raspy voice came shrieking out of it. "That evil man is desperately trying to poison the world with hate. How many can he talk to? Fifteen million—twenty million? And for how long—twenty minutes? You, sir, can talk to *hundreds* of millions, for two hours—and in the dark. The talents you have, Mr. Capra, are not your own, *not* self-acquired. God gave you those talents; they are His gifts to you, to use for His purpose. And when you don't *use* the gifts God blessed you with—you are an offense to God—and to humanity. Good day, sir."
>
> The little faceless man walked out of the room and down the stairs. In less than thirty seconds he had ripped me open with the truth: exposed the fetid pus of my vanities.[7]

Capra writes that he got up, looked at himself in the mirror, and announced that he was "going to Palm Springs," where he and Robert Riskin often met to collaborate on screenplays.

Although McBride characteristically imposes the least generous possible reading of Capra's apparent resort to fictional allegory to represent this critical moment in his career, Capra clearly intended the vignette to mark the moment of his recovery from his bout with illness and depression. He had two surgeries in this period, metaphorically coded in the reference to the man's bracing challenge as the lancing of an abscess, but he claims to have emerged from the little man's chastisement with the resolve to make films that would, as he puts it, "say something." And indeed, before the year was out, he had embarked on what he would call "my first of a series of socially minded films: *Mr. Deeds Goes to Town* . . . in which I planned to 'say' something to audiences for two hours, and in the dark."[8]

The making of *Mr. Deeds*, then, was to effect a major shift in Capra's work. It was to be a shift from the critical and commercial success of *It Happened One Night*, which had not only reaped great honors but arguably pioneered what would be an influential new genre, the screwball comedy,[9] toward a new kind of social ambition, and a new level of commitment to personal responsibility and control over the cinematic product. It also represented a new stage in Capra's self-mythologization as author-director-activist. The inspired casting of nonstars and the patient work made possible by the terms of a new contract (more generous not only in terms of remuneration but also of budget, support, and time) both contributed to the sense of a new epoch in Capra's work. Capra also claimed—in a series of articles dating to 1936 and in his later autobiography—that this work offered a major challenge in the Hollywood system more broadly.[10] That would be, after all, a central theme of the cover story about him in *Time* magazine in 1938.

An element that remained continuous across this turning point in Capra's career was the scriptwriting of Robert Riskin, who had the screenplay credit on both *American Madness* and *It Happened One Night* and would have it again with *Mr. Deeds Goes to Town*. Capra acknowledged that his altered mise-en-scène created a problem with respect to Riskin. He addressed this problem when in his autobiography he discussed the implications of this shift:

> My new "look" affected, of course, my harmonious relationship with my friend, screenplay-writer Robert Riskin. He contended, and rightly, that he had contributed greatly to my former films—which he had; and that he deserved additional credit on the screen, as my collaborator or something. I discouraged that strongly. Then he spoke of becoming a director—to fashion his own ideas in films. I encouraged him, spoke to Harry Cohn about it. In a little more than a year he got the opportunity.[11]

Capra's acknowledgement did not mean, however, that he would relent in his effort to represent all elements of *Mr. Deeds* as "his," even the core of the screenplay: "Meanwhile, Riskin did a brilliant piece of writing on *Mr. Deeds Goes to Town*, keeping what I wanted to 'say' intact."[12]

McBride, not surprisingly, takes Riskin's part in this controversy. A theory about the contrast between Riskin's politics and Capra's partly underlies McBride's views: Riskin was a New Dealer and Capra was not. But McBride does not explain why Capra remained committed to Riskin in so many films, or why he turned to a member of the Communist Party, Sydney Buchman, to write *Mr. Smith Goes to Washington*, the first major film Capra made after ending his string of successes with Riskin. Capra and Riskin would team up once more, in 1940, for *Meet John Doe*. There is, as more than one commentator has pointed out, something of a contradiction to McBride's entire project: he uses his biography of Capra the director to demolish the authorship that supplies the principle of continuity for McBride's own study of his work.[13]

In spite of McBride's predictable taking of sides here, reminiscent of the debates about Orson Welles and Herman Mankiewicz, the evidence suggests that Capra worked very closely indeed with his writers in developing ideas.[14] Capra certainly seems to have been "hands on" at every stage of the process. As Herbert Biberman wrote in an open letter to Capra about *Meet John Doe* (in which he was disappointed), praising Capra for his "purposefulness of . . . character": "You are the only director I have known who regularly calls his fellow craftsmen together to discuss scripts in advance of shooting."[15] As for Riskin, he persuaded William Wellman to direct one of his own scripts, *Magic Town* (1947), a Riskin-Capra styled film script about a town whose citizens exemplify the statistical average of the United States. Though the film even had James Stewart starring opposite Jane Wyman in the leading roles, it failed miserably. But if Riskin without Capra was a disaster, Capra (perhaps pointedly) made two of his most important pictures without Riskin: *Mr. Smith* and *It's a Wonderful Life*.[16] What matters most for our purposes here is that in *Mr. Deeds* Capra saw himself embarking on a new direction in filmmaking. And most observers, whether or not they approve of that direction, tend to agree.[17]

Alongside the question of whether to approve of Capra's mid-1930s transformation, there is, of course, the problem of interpretation. Just what should we make of it?[18] Capra himself suggested that his post–"little man" vision was torn between two principles. One was the notion that his films should now say something. The other was enshrined in a bit of wisdom he attributes to Howard Hughes: "When I want to send a message I use Western Union."[19] Another version of this antididactic position is ascribed by Capra to his friend Myles Connolly, who helped on many of Capra's scripts, and who is supposed to have counseled Capra not to change his ways and to have confidence that *It Happened One Night* was not a fluke. The comment that Capra puts in Connolly's mouth identifies some key elements of Capra's sense of his own filmmaking at this crucial juncture:

> You say *It Happened One Night* is an accident. That picture's no accident. It's *you*. Letting something out without thinking. And you know what else you've done with that picture? No, I'm sure you don't. . . . You took the old classic four of show business—hero, heroine, villain, comedian—and cut

it down to *three*, by combining hero and heroine into one person. . . . So stop worrying about saying something "big" to people for two hours and in the dark. . . . Just tell your simple tales about the Johns and the Janes, and the Henrys and the Harriets—with comedy. That's your forte. And you'll unconsciously stick in some kind of message. Because you can't help it now—you're growing up.[20]

This comment sounds the themes of "mixed feelings" and unpremeditated expression, which we have briefly noted in Sterne and will continue to trace in the long history of the sentimental. But it also registers an interesting contradiction, as Capra has Connolly stating what Capra doesn't "know"—but somehow needs to trust—about his own filmmaking. Should we conclude, then, that 1935–1936 represents a radical break, or that it marks instead a new level of maturity, with an inevitable added dimension of "content"—what Connolly calls the unconscious message? Or is there some other way to understand what happens with and in *Mr. Deeds*?

An Answer for the Little Man: *Mr. Deeds Goes to Town* I

I have suggested so far that the unfolding of Capra's career is at the same time a progressive folding *in* of prior work into each significant new film. I now want to argue that *Mr. Deeds* represents a new phase in this folding-in, one that depends on Capra's recognition of his relation to the formal features of the narrative system in which he has all along been working. It is a moment where recursive self-remaking turns into something pointedly associated with sentimental reflexivity. I wish to elaborate this point by way of a scene in *Mr. Deeds* that proves to be as pivotal for this film as the film itself is for Capra's ambitious career. It is a scene that closely parallels the story Capra tells in his autobiography about the intervention of the little man during his crisis. One may conclude that the story in the autobiography narrates an event that becomes the basis for the scene—that, as Capra suggests, *Mr. Deeds* is in effect his answer to the little man. Or one may conclude that the scene in *Mr. Deeds* became retroactively the basis for the story that Capra tells about himself. Either way the scene is crucial, I contend, because it indicates Capra's new understanding of the implications of the narrative code with which he had made his mark as a director.

Longfellow Deeds (Gary Cooper) is uprooted from his life in the town of Mandrake Falls in rural New Hampshire when he inherits twenty million dollars and finds himself placed in charge of New York's Metropolitan

Opera. He soon becomes the target of crooked lawyers and unscrupulous journalists, including Jean Arthur's character, Babe Bennett, a reporter who goes out on the town with him by night and writes satirical and anonymous features about him by day. (Arthur would play a similar role opposite James Stewart in *Mr. Smith Goes to Washington*.) Here, as in *Mr. Smith*, the Arthur character gradually falls in love with the young naïf. She forms a plan to quit her job, confess her guilt, and marry him. A turning point occurs the morning after Deeds has read a markedly sentimental poem to Babe. He is planning a lavish brunch at which he intends to propose to her but suddenly is made to see her role in making him a laughingstock. The preparations for this brunch will prove to be of critical importance to understanding the implications of the scene.

In the sequence that follows the discovery of Babe's perfidy, a deflated Deeds announces that he will return to Mandrake Falls immediately. As he is leaving his mansion, he finds himself face to face with an intruder in the foyer, a desperate farmer brandishing a gun. Having seen Deeds represented as acting frivolously in the daily newspapers, the farmer charges him with insensitivity, with not caring for the poor in the hard times of the Great Depression.[21] But before the farmer can do any harm, he collapses in front of Deeds, apparently from hunger. The sequence ends with the farmer's having been helped to the place intended for Babe at the dining table. Deeds sits opposite the farmer and watches him in silence as the farmer eats ravenously, pausing only to ask if he can take some of the food home to his family. Crucially, the entire three-part sequence is handled in shot/reverse-shot. It is followed directly by a montage sequence—a series of spinning newspaper headlines announces Deeds's intention to give his money away to the needy—after which poor people are shown queuing up in front of Deeds's mansion to receive aid from his impromptu foundation.

I will return to the montage presently, but consider first the three-part sequence handled in shot/reverse-shot. It provides a double dose of the combination of elements that Aristotle singled out as defining the best plots: discovery and reversal. Deeds's discovery that Babe Bennett has been writing satirical articles after their evenings together leads to the reversal implicit in his decision to return to Mandrake Falls. But his subsequent discovery of his own failure of responsibility, in the encounter with the farmer, leads to a second reversal: a decision to attempt to make amends.[22] These two moments of discovery and reversal are conspicuously framed by the two scenes at the lavishly appointed table. It is this framing, I contend, that gives the sequence its distinctive character and marks it as pivotal in more ways than one.

Capra, *Mr. Deeds Goes to Town* (1936, Columbia).
Shot/reverse-shot sequence with Longfellow Deeds and the out-of-work farmer.

In the opening bookend scene, Deeds enters the dining room to go over arrangements for the meal with his English butler. We know that Capra relocated this scene from Deeds's bedroom, so we can assume that he had something to say about what happened in it, especially the role of the table setting. After asking the butler in charge of the occasion to replace the flowers on the table because they are "too high"—"Won't be able to see her"—Deeds takes his intended seat and asks the butler to sit opposite him while Deeds conducts a kind of rehearsal for his brunch with Babe. What follows are some vintage sight gags in the tradition of the silent comedies on which Capra cut his teeth:

LONGFELLOW
You're too tall. Slink lower, will you?

The butler does it.

LONGFELLOW
More. Now forward.

They are practically nose to nose over the flowers.

BUTLER
(*seriously*)
How's this, sir?

Mr. Deeds Goes to Town. Longfellow Deeds's earlier rehearsal for his marriage proposal.

LONGFELLOW
(*rising*)
Perfect! Perfect!

In the closing bookend, after the encounter in the foyer, the farmer is ushered to the same seat in which the butler had rehearsed the role of Babe under Deeds's direction:

DISSOLVE TO:
EXT. INTIMATE DINING ROOM

CLOSE SHOT
At the table that was all set for Babe. The man sits, eating. He seriously bends over his food. Longfellow sits opposite him—his eyes glued on the man, absorbed in profound thought.

MAN
(*tentatively*)
Can I take some of this home with me?

Longfellow nods.

DISSOLVE TO:
INSERT: NEWSPAPER HEADLINES[23]

As shot by Capra, the two bracketing scenes around the breakfast table—the first involving Deeds and his butler, the second, Deeds and the farmer—are connected by more than narrative repetition, the return to the "intimate dining room." They also rhyme formally. The protracted final scene with the farmer at the table is shot in almost complete silence, thus emphasizing the style of visual cutting that had been one of the chief achievements of American silent film from the time of Griffith onward. The two scenes are linked, that is, by virtue of the powerful cinematic device of shot/reverse-shot, which registers an affective logic that connects them. There is no explicit call for this device in the shooting script for either scene. In the first scene, we have an establishing shot and a medium shot; in the second, an establishing shot and a close shot. Not only do the two bracketing scenes rhyme with each other in their use of this device, but each connects as well to the initial encounter with the intruding farmer.[24]

Bazinian Histories of Cinema

It was with this device, then—conspicuously and reflexively deployed—that Capra chose to encode the pivotal moment in his cinema, when he turned his former craft to more socially aware purposes. What does this tell us about the meaning of this moment for the making of the Capraesque as we have come

Mr. Deeds Goes to Town.
Out-of-work farmer
assumes place intended
for Babe Bennett

to know it? What does it mean that this is the first film by Capra—perhaps the first film by any director—in which the idea and practice of "sentiment" becomes so pointedly self-conscious?

To appreciate the full import of Capra's conspicuous use of the shot/reverse-shot device in so thematically self-conscious a way, and in so highly marked a sequence from such a pivotal film, it helps to have a clear sense of the place of this device in the early transformation of Hollywood cinema, a transformation achieved in Griffith's time and partly through Griffith's work. This transformation can be said to have ushered in what has come to be called the classical narrative system, a point about which there is both broad agreement among most film scholars and much room for debate about details. This system underlies what Jacques Aumont, in a discussion useful for my purposes, has called "ordinary cinema." Aumont sounds all the appropriate notes of caution relevant to any treatment of the subject:

> If there is a cinematic ordinary, we will look for it first in that which has so long dominated, in that which continues to emerge from the past, in classical cinema. Not more than modernity, cinematic classicism cannot be contained by dates or by definitions. One can define it by reference to fictionality, by mise-en-scène and dramaturgy, by transparency, by the adequation of a mode of production to a mode of vision, by its excellence of means. It matters little: everyone has their definition, but classical cinema exists, and it is American.[25]

Aumont's commentary is of particular interest here because he focuses on what he calls the "ordinary face of cinema" (*le visage ordinaire du cinema*), and when it comes to defining the "ordinariness" of the cinematic ordinary he centers attention on faces and eyes, and on the play of what in French he can richly imply with the word *regard* (neither "look" nor "gaze" quite captures the sense in English). The face and the eyes and how they function are special keys for Aumont in understanding what he calls the importance of "order" in the cinematic ordinary—its *dispositio*, as it were:

> It was the moment in the history of cinema that, more than others, showed the desire for order, for regularity. The Twenties and Thirties, above all the Thirties, and especially in American cinema, were the years of communication in cinematographic language—of the exchange of shot for shot and of face for face. The rapidity of these exchanges increased a bit after the middle of the 1930s. Mainly, the frequency of continuity shots founded on the crossing of sightlines grew steadily (from 20% in 1920 to about

40% at the beginning of the 1940s). These statistical data no doubt mean far less than what the myopic statisticians hope, but they can nonetheless somewhat confirm what a stylistic analysis indicates: films in the 1930s were made of relatively short shots that held abundant communication with each other by virtue of the play of crossed looks.[26]

Aumont's concern with faces and eyes is of special interest to any effort to come to terms with the sentimental in cinema, and I shall return to it presently. But it is important first to place his account of the "cinematic ordinary" in some larger contexts of film history, and specifically in the history of what he calls "cinematic language."

Most students of cinema will recognize in Aumont's phraseology an echo of what is perhaps one of the half dozen most influential essays in the canon of film criticism: André Bazin's "The Evolution of the Language of Cinema." Indeed, Aumont is following a Bazinian line on these questions—he makes no bones about this—and it is therefore useful to be reminded of the broader lines of the powerful and influential account that Bazin delivers in that essay. A composite of three essays written by Bazin from 1950 to 1955, "The Evolution of the Language of Cinema" was his attempt to situate historically developments in cinema of the 1940s that he famously championed, especially the neorealism of Roberto Rossellini and Vittorio De Sica, and the deployment of deep-focus cinematography in the work of Jean Renoir, Orson Welles, and William Wyler. To locate the new postwar cinema in a history he describes as "dialectical," Bazin produces an account of the 1930s in terms that decidedly anticipate Aumont's version of the story, and indeed many others since. "From 1930 to 1940," Bazin explains, "there seems to have grown up in the world, originating largely in the United States, a common form of cinematographic language."[27] "By 1938 or 1939," he famously added, "the talking film, particularly in France and in the United States, had reached a level of classical perfection" (30). With respect to content, Bazin connects this new language with the emergence of five or six major genres: "major varieties with clearly defined rules capable of pleasing a worldwide public, as well as a cultured elite, provided it was not inherently hostile to the cinema" (28). In respect to form, this decade offered "well-defined styles of photography and editing perfectly adapted to their subject-matter; a complete harmony of image and sound." In the best films of the 1930s, we find, in short, "all the characteristics of the ripeness of a classical art" (29).

Bazin concedes that elements of this cinematic language were present in the silent period, especially after Griffith, but for him that earlier period was marked by a tension between "those directors who put their faith in the image and those who put their faith in reality" (24). The investment in the image is an investment in what "the representation on the screen adds to the object there represented," and it is reducible, for Bazin, to two primary categories: what relates to "the plastics of the image" and what relates to "the resources of montage," the latter being, as he explains, just "the ordering of images in time" (24). This distinction can in turn be linked to Bazin's comment about the "well-defined styles of photography and editing" developed in the 1930s, though the plastics of the image for him includes more than just photography—it also includes "the style of the sets, of the make-up, and, up to a point, even of the performance" (24). The editing practice of montage, in all its three major varieties—parallel montage, accelerated montage, and montage by attraction—involves "the creation of a sense or meaning not objectively contained in the images themselves but derived exclusively from their juxtaposition" (25).

A cinema based on the image—on the "expressionism," as Bazin calls it, of montage and the plastics of the image working together—was the dominant mode of silent film. But it was challenged by those directors who put their faith in reality—among them, the documentarian Robert Flaherty, F. W. Murnau, and Erich von Stroheim. What Flaherty did with realist time (recording the actual waiting period of the hunt in *Nanook of the North*), Murnau did with cinematic space (not deforming the reality he shot but forcing it to reveal its structural depth). Von Stroheim combined their efforts in "one simple rule for direction.... Take a close look at the world, keep on doing so, and in the end it will lay bare for you all its cruelty and ugliness" (27). Von Stroheim, indeed, is a director for whom it is possible to imagine a film "composed of a single shot as long-lasting and as close-up as you like" (27).

These early directors who were committed more to reality than to the cinematic image presage the realist developments that Bazin will later celebrate in the work of Rossellini and De Sica, and to a degree the deep-focus cinematography of Renoir, Welles, and Wyler. But since Bazin's account is, by his own description, dialectical, the coalescence of the classical style of the 1930s—"ordinary cinema," as Aumont will call it—makes its own important contribution to the touted 1940s formation. The deep-focus realism of the 1940s both fulfills and surpasses the realist tendencies of von Stroheim and others by incorporating some of the 1930s developments in the cinematic image as constructed from multiple points of view.

Deep focus had been around, after all, since before 1910. It was classical cinema that turned to lenses that created softer and shallower kinds of focus, for purposes all its own. The deep focus that returns after the 1930s is altered, as Bazin explains, by what comes between:

All you need to do is compare two frames shot in depth, one from 1910, the other from a film by Wyler or Welles, to understand just by looking at the image, even apart from the context of the film, how different their functions are. The framing in the 1910 film is intended, to all intents and purposes, as a substitute for the missing fourth wall of the theatrical stage, or at least in exterior shots, for the best vantage point to view the action, whereas in the second case the setting, the lighting, and the camera angles give an entirely different reading. Between them, the director and cameraman have converted the screen into a dramatic checkerboard, planned down to the last detail. . . . [T]he sequence of shots "in depth" of the contemporary director does not exclude the use of montage—how could he, without reverting to a primitive babbling?—he makes it an integral part of his "plastic." The storytelling of Welles or Wyler is no less explicit than John Ford's but theirs has the advantage over his that it does not sacrifice the specific effects that can be derived from unity of image in space and time. . . . It would be absurd to deny that montage has added considerably to the progress of film language, but this has happened at the cost of other values, no less definitely cinematic. . . . It is not a question of thereby belittling the films of 1930 to 1940, a criticism that would not stand up in the face of the number of masterpieces, it is simply an attempt to establish the notion of a dialectic progress, the highest expression of which was found in the films of the 1940's. (34–35, 38)

The Bazin-Aumont account of film history, and of the revolutions that produced and went beyond golden-age classicism—that is, beyond the cinematic ordinary of the 1930s—is by no means the whole story. Bazin's periodization of cinema history is certainly conditioned, for example, by what films he had access to. But his way of putting things proves richly relevant to the case of Capra. In a number of particulars, Bazin's account, supplemented by Aumont's, illuminates Capra's career from his early encounter with von Stroheim through to his late collaborations with Wyler. That career in turn, and its increasing imbrication with the history of sentiment, proves something of a challenge to some of their key contentions.

An Anatomy of Cinematic Sentiment: *Mr. Deeds Goes to Town* II

As we have noted, Capra had his first serious job in cinema working with von Stroheim on *Greed* (1926), the most ambitious of his films, the one that may, in its length and detail, in its exceeding of cinematic norms of the 1920s, have suggested Bazin's fantastic hypothesis of a von Stroheim film composed of one long shot revealing reality in all its hideous particularity. Capra later claimed that he had, categorically and early on, rejected von Stroheim's approach to filmmaking and that this rejection set him on the course he pursued as a director for the next decades. Jumping to the end of Capra's career, we can speculate about his notorious collapse as a force in cinema after the Second World War: having dominated the age of the cinematic ordinary as perhaps no director save Griffith has dominated any other age in cinema, he could not adapt to the new stylistic order ushered in by Renoir and Welles and Wyler and then established on a very different aesthetic footing in Rossellini's and De Sica's films from 1945–1950, shot on location in the ruins of Europe.

After the war, Capra partnered with Wyler (and George Stevens) to form Liberty Films, for which he made *It's a Wonderful Life* and *State of the Union. It's a Wonderful Life* certainly tries to make its peace with the new cinematographic regime, including some use of deep-focus shooting and that important sequence at the railroad station in which the camera moves to reflect George Bailey's evolving emotional response to the news of his brother Harry's marriage. But it is a film in which Capra is striving to reconnect with his work of the 1930s, to refashion it. He did so in such a way as to continue to make his career look all of a piece, all a reflection of his own developing self-consciousness as an author and as a sentimental force in a newly mediated notion of national culture, very much (as I will argue) in the tradition of his hero Griffith.

It thus matters to any full understanding Capra's premature decline that *It's a Wonderful Life* lost the Best Picture Oscar for 1946 to a film about the postwar moment that is now celebrated in cinema history for its exploitation of deep-focus realism, his partner William Wyler's *The Best Years of Our Lives* (1946). It would not be George Bailey's sympathetic, face-to-face encounter with his fellow townspeople on the occasion of his brother's return from the war that became the totem of postwar American cinema. Instead, the celebrated shot of 1946 would be the deep-focus sequence in *The Best Years of Our Lives* where the story lines of the three returning war veterans are juxtaposed in a long New York–style barroom: in the foreground, Hoagy

Carmichael teaches piano to the now handless ex-sailor played by Harold Johnson; in the deep background, but still in focus, Dana Andrews, a married man and ex-pilot, makes the telephone call in which he will break off his affair with the daughter of Fredric March, an ex-army sergeant.[28] Again, the point can be overstated, since much of *It's a Wonderful Life* has the look of a 1940s film. Further, as I explain below, Capra has an ingenious solution to the problem of how to stage cinematic sympathy without excessive resort to shot/reverse-shot camerawork.

It is in Capra's relation to the middle part of the Bazin-Aumont story, the moment of the cinematic ordinary itself, in the first decade of the talkies, that the real interest of this brief history lies. Returning to that moment will return us, in turn, to the moment in *Mr. Deeds Goes to Town* that was our point of departure. Here is Bazin's sparest and most neutral summary of the narrative system that achieved dominance in the 1930s:

> Thus around 1938 films were edited, almost without exception, according to the same principle. The story was unfolded in a series of set-ups numbering as a rule about 600. The characteristic procedure was by shot-reverse-shot, that is to say, in a dialogue scene, the camera followed the order of the text, alternating the character shown with each speech.
>
> It was this fashion of editing, so admirably suitable for the best films made between 1930 and 1939, that was challenged by the shot in depth introduced by Orson Welles and William Wyler. (33)

In a later reprise of this summary, however, Bazin places the system in a more critical light:

> The relative realism of the kind of cutting that flourished around 1937 implied a congenital limitation which escaped us so long as it was perfectly suited to its subject matter. Thus American comedy reached its peak within the framework of a form of editing in which the realism of the time played no part. Dependent on logic for its effects, like vaudeville and plays on words, entirely conventional in its moral and sociological content, American comedy had everything to gain, in strict line-by-line progression, from the rhythmic resources of classical editing. (39)

Postwar cinema, by contrast, draws from the realism of pre-1930s films by directors like von Stroheim in order to regenerate "realism in storytelling," thus "bringing together real time, in which things exist, along with the duration of the action, for which classical editing had insidiously substituted mental and abstract time" (39).

It is this latter note that Aumont sounds in the variations he plays on Bazin's account, variations inflected by the account of the classical narrative system to be found in the work of David Bordwell, Janet Staiger, and Kristin Thompson. One can recognize in Aumont's commentary a variation in turn on Bazin's account. He shares with Bazin the emphasis on patterns of shot/reverse-shot as these become central to the play of faces and eyes in what Aumont calls the *"visage ordinaire du cinema."* For Aumont, the classical period is best characterized as a "systematic exploration of camera angles and distances in relation to the looking and speaking face, the interest in angles and distances most often effacing all other possible interest for the eyes."[29] In this regime, the cinematic gaze (*le regard du cinema*) is caught up in a device for which the privileged face (*figure*) would be in shot/reverse-shot, where "the sighting is on the bias and the gaze is figured in its crossing with another gaze" (56).[30]

The privileged metaphors in Aumont's account of the ordinary face of cinema are circulation and exchange. It is the face, he says, "that works unceasingly, between shots and within the shot, with an eye to the exchange of one face for another" (58). In this system of narration, "everything is to be made to circulate," and the "gaze of the ordinary face is caught in an interminable game, comparable only to the circulation of its spoken words" (55). This is Aumont's elaboration of what Bazin critically refers to as the "abstraction" of classical editing, but in Aumont it borrows a Marxist inflection from Janet Staiger's analysis in identifying this program with an economic regime and in invoking the distinction between faces bearing exchange value and faces bearing use value. In the ordinary face, the pole of "exchange value" is the dominant one. It makes of the face "a pure operator of sense [*sens*], of narrative and movement, the turning plate of narrativity and the link for the diegesis." But in both cases, use value and exchange value, "what is forgotten is the actor, his body and even his face, for the sake of an abstraction" (49). Ultimately Aumont will press, unsurprisingly but not unreasonably, to identify this system with liberalism in politics and capitalism in economics: "The ordinary cinema of Hollywood and elsewhere treated the face in the only way it could, attributing it to a subject free and equal in rights to all others, but who must incessantly put his own liberty and equality into play in confronting those of other free and equal subjects. The ordinary face of cinema is also that of Western democracy, which is to say American and capitalist. It is one of the traits of imperialism that its ordinariness is an order" (59–60). Aumont's ordinary face of cinema belongs to a *dispositio imperii*.

In thinking about Capra and the 1930s, I find I agree with a good deal of what Aumont and Bazin have to say about his relation to the editing system of classical film narrative and to the ordinary face of cinema. Indeed, my argument will be that much of what they say, though with a rather different inflection, is actually implicit in the kind of self-consciousness Capra comes to achieve in his filmmaking over this period. This is nowhere clearer than in *Mr. Deeds Goes to Town*, with its signal sequence marking the allegorical moment of both Deeds's political awakening and Capra's political recognition of the social power of a medium he had come to conceive in historically sentimental terms. What is of special interest for our purposes here, however, is the one example that Bazin elaborates for his influential account of the state of cinematic editing in the late 1930s, by which point the new system was firmly established. Illustrating his contention that "in 1938 there was an almost universal standard pattern of editing," Bazin goes on to propose a thought experiment, which he sets in 1936:

> Let us suppose . . . that we have a table covered with food and a hungry tramp. One can imagine that in 1936 it would have been edited as follows:
>
> (1) Full shot of the actor and the table.
>
> (2) Camera moves forward into a close-up of a face expressing a mixture of amazement and longing.
>
> (3) Series of close-ups of food.
>
> (4) Back to full shot of person who starts slowly towards the camera.
>
> (5) Camera pulls slowly back to a three-quarter shot of the actor seizing a chicken wing.
>
> Whatever variants one could think of for this scene, they would all have certain points in common:
>
> (1) The verisimilitude of space in which the position of the actor is always determined, even when a close-up eliminates the decor.
>
> (2) The purpose and the effects of the cutting are exclusively dramatic or psychological.[31]

Though one could conceivably make the case, I do not think that Bazin is here *necessarily* alluding to the pivotal scene in *Mr. Deeds*, the 1936 American comedy that earned Capra the Oscar for Best Picture of that year. Earlier, Capra had appeared prominently in Bazin's effort to identify the half dozen major genres that were responsible for the dominance of American film in the 1930s, the genres that the classical system was there to facilitate. The first genre Bazin mentions is "comedy"—we have seen that he often takes "American comedy" as a synecdoche for the entire genre system in this genre-dominated period of filmmaking—and the only director he mentions in that category is Capra. The year in question, moreover, is 1936. The problem is that the film he names for that year is *Mr. Smith Goes to Washington*! Did Bazin displace the scene with the tramp and the food into *Mr. Smith*? Perhaps. But another reason to doubt that Bazin is actually alluding specifically or pointedly to this scene is that his description does not match up with it in every detail.[32]

I think the better explanation would posit that the sequence in *Mr. Deeds* stuck in Bazin's critical imagination because it is reflexively marked in the way that I earlier began to suggest. It is meant to stand out, to reflect on, to emblematize, the very system that Bazin here uses a very similar scene to emblematize hypothetically. This is not, however, to suggest that Bazin reads it precisely as I have done. On the contrary, Bazin will go on to argue that the classical cinema of the 1930s avoids taking up measures that "make the audience conscious of the cutting" (32). Furthermore, his summary of this hypothetical scene produces a somewhat odd set of conclusions given the actual sequence that Capra shot, as described earlier. Here is how Bazin sums up the results of his thought experiment:

> In other words, if the scene were played on a stage and seen from a seat in the orchestra, it would have the same meaning, the episode would continue to exist objectively. The changes in point of view provided by the camera would add nothing. They would present the reality a little more forcefully, first by allowing a better view and then by putting the emphasis where it belongs. (32)

Bazin here takes a stand, let us note, that is absolutely crucial to his critique of classical cinema, a position from which he can see in the classical system of editing only an abstraction from reality and can conclude that this system adds nothing important to the episode in question.

But what if we take Bazin up on his offer to think of a variant for this scene that would look just like the scene in *Mr. Deeds*? If we imagine that *Mr. Deeds* qualifies—how could it not?—as a case in point for the kind of editing Bazin is talking about in 1936, do Bazin's summary comments still hold? It seems to me that they do not. Bazin's observations do not register the care with which Capra handles the preparation and the mise-en-scène of the sequence. In the film as Capra shot it, this is the last part of a four-part drama that unfolds in Deeds's house: the preparation of the table for brunch and the proposal to Babe Bennett, the discovery of Babe's perfidy, the arrival of the man to admonish Deeds, the man eating at the place set for Babe. Capra's way of calling attention to the manner in which the final scene is shot and edited, the alternations of shot/reverse-shot and the attention to the eyes and face of both Deeds and the man across from him, seem to make this aspect of the cinematic image more integral to the action—to the "reality" of the moment—than Bazin's summary would suggest. By having Deeds model the directorial set-up, attending to the sight lines and mise-en-scène of the breakfast at which he plans to propose, Capra works to break down precisely the separation that Bazin seeks to preserve at all costs between the reality and image, between the episode considered "objectively" and the manner in which it is shot. The sequence seems to insist that we take its shooting and editing style seriously as a part of what it is trying, as Capra might have put it, to "say."

The larger point at stake here is Bazin's claim that "if the scene were played on a stage and seen from a seat in the orchestra, it would have the same meaning." This seems to me a highly contestable position, for reasons that the scene in *Mr. Deeds* helps to make clear. It misses the reality of the medium itself, and its resources. The scene in *Mr. Deeds* makes these realities a part of what it means to be representing, a part of its "meaning." Some of the problem here lies in Bazin's direct comparison of film to theater, a subject on which he elaborated his views elsewhere.[33] Eisenstein's "literary past" does not figure in Bazin's thought experiment. By contrast, one of my major contentions in this book is that literature—in particular, the sentimental tradition of the novel—is an overlooked point of reference for the sort of thing that Capra is doing in this scene. After the literary studies of Percy Lubbock, Wayne Booth, Gérard Genette, and Mieke Bal on the history of focalization in literary narrative, is it possible to say that the "meaning" of a novel is independent of the way in which it manages point of view? I think the same answer must be rendered for film narrative.

If I am right in suggesting that the missing term in Bazin's reflection on this thought experiment for classical editing in 1936 (or 1938) is "the novel," then it becomes the more interesting to recall the famous conclusion to his essay "The Evolution of the Language of Cinema," in which Bazin invidiously compared both the silent film (which "*evoked* what the director wanted to say") and the film of the 1930s (which "*described* it") to the kind of film he championed in the 1940s: "Today we can say that at last the director writes in film" (39, my emphasis). And this notion of writing in film, *écriture cinématique*, is specifically associated with the work of the novelist in the essay's final sentence: "The film-maker is no longer the competitor of the painter and the playwright, he is, at last, the equal of the novelist" (40). In spite of Bazin's justly praised catholicity in acknowledging great filmmaking across eras, this special sense of parallelism and parity with the novelist is denied to filmmakers before his own moment. Bazin has an investment, in short, in not recognizing in a director like Capra a capacity for quasi-novelistic achievement.[34]

A related blind spot bedevils the argument of Aumont, which hews close to the Bazinian line. Aumont succeeds marvelously in placing his account of the cinematic face in the context of all the problematics of *"l'oeuil qui regard"* as these matter to facial representation in painting and photography. But he has scarcely a word to say about the history of facial representation in literature—least of all in the sentimental novel, where faces, eyes, looks, and the management of point of view become central to any account of what is happening and what it all means. It was Eisenstein, to whom we turn below, who made the argument for the relevance of the novelistic tradition to American cinema. Yet it was not his friend Capra, but their common mentor Griffith, whom Eisenstein singled out in relation to this tradition. And in connecting Griffith to Dickens he did not, for specific reasons worth exploring further, identify Dickens with the tradition of point-of-view management in the sentimental novel.

The Evolution of Cinematic Language and the Structure of Sentiment

It will be clear enough from this discussion of Bazin and Aumont—it is fairly explicit in their texts—that they are agreed in distinguishing three important transformative moments in the early history of cinema. The most recent is the one with which Bazin's critical work is most intimately associated—that of postwar realism—which for Bazin and for Aumont, and for Gilles Deleuze between them, is associated with the possibility of real time in cinema.[35] The second is that of the talkies, what Bazin refers to as the cinema of 1930–1939 and what Aumont calls ordinary cinema. The first revolution, also acknowledged by both, is that of the generation of D. W. Griffith. For some historians of cinema, this revolution is decisive. Tom Gunning has detailed how the early Griffith helped to evolve the basic elements of what became the classical style, and in what has become perhaps the most dominant account of American cinema in the long post-Griffith era, David Bordwell, Janet Staiger, and Kristin Thompson have elaborated a thesis claiming that the basic style of American cinema was effectively unchanged from about the time of Griffith's *Birth of a Nation* (1915) through to 1960.[36]

I touched briefly at the outset on the role of point of view in Griffith's early one-reeler *The Cricket on the Hearth* (1909). It is now time to say something both more general and more detailed about how point of view matters in the cinematic mode that Griffith did so much to shape and Capra to exploit. One simple way in which this innovation of the 1910s can be understood—has been understood—is in terms of a change from a mode of representation based on the *scene* to one based on the *shot* as the basic unit of represented action. The earlier and (more theatrical) mode, pre-Griffith, typically called for the actors to play their parts in front of a single stationary camera positioned close enough to make out facial expressions—at least the general facial gesture, as accentuated by makeup—but far enough away to encompass two or more actors within the frame. What replaced it was a system that involved a multiplicity of camera angles and called for shooting at a range of distances, from long to close. In this later system, of course, the process of editing became a crucial part of the work of bringing the story to life.

As a part of this shift in emphasis from scene to shot, the latter came to assume a more frequent and instant association with, precisely, the "point of view." This is a process that has been sketched out by many film historians, most of whom emphasize Griffith's role in this aspect of the transformation as well. The account offered by the French film historian Jean Mitry has been challenged in some particulars, but his terms nicely resonate with my discussion here so far. Referring to the new narrative form that "allows the audience to 'take the place' of the heroes, to see and feel 'as they do,'" Mitry writes that "it may possibly have been used previously, but only in *Broken Blossoms* and other films of the time did it become conscious of its effectiveness."[37] One celebrated example of this kind of sequence in *Broken Blossoms* occurs through the front window of the Yellow Man's shop.

Since the point-of-view shot is a way of giving us a sense of how characters in the film are looking at things, it contributes to the formation of psychological causality as the engine of classical Hollywood narrative. This is also a point many commentators have made, though it is likewise not uncontested. Further, with the emergence of the point-of-view shot comes a corresponding reliance on shot/reverse-shot techniques. We see a situation; we see a character's reaction to that situation; and next we see something that the character does as a direct consequence of the response. Early in *Tramp, Tramp, Tramp* (1926), the second film on which Capra worked with Harry Langdon, we see Langdon being pummeled by a bully. It is not until

Griffith, *Broken Blossoms* (1919, D. W. Griffith Productions).
Early Hollywood sequence in shot/reverse-shot.

Langdon has suffered this humiliation that we are made to realize that we have been taking in the episode from the point of view of the character played by the young Joan Crawford. We see Langdon humiliated; then we see Crawford's reaction to this humiliation; and next we see Crawford following Langdon away from the scene to console him and embolden him to fight back. Roughly speaking, such a sequence is the result of the evolution from scene-based cinema to shot-based cinema, and the concomitant "subjectivization" of the shot, often in shot/reverse-shot sequences that enable us to track how characters see and what they do on that basis.

An important subset of shot/reverse-shot techniques, moreover, is involved in the shooting of face-to-face encounters. This involves the positioning of cameras over the shoulders of characters who are engaged in face-to-face interaction. We see each from the point of view of the other, by turns, back and forth over the course of their exchange of words or gestures. This alternation of camera angle became so commonplace over the evolution of film and video style that we now take it for granted. But it marks a clear, if gradual, technical departure from the earlier way of shooting a face-to-face encounter—even though, to be sure, the earlier and more theatrical kind of mise-en-scène survived, to be used alongside the later innovation (e.g., for "establishing shots" and the like). The use of shot/reverse-shot carries significance with respect to the possibilities for internal spectatorship (between characters within the diegesis) but also for external spectatorship (between them and the spectator). It is this double relation that Nick Browne, in a celebrated essay on the visual rhetoric of John Ford's *Stagecoach* (1939), showed to be constitutive of the cinematic object as a "specular text"—a text constructed by the orthogonal coordinates of the mimetic and pragmatic axes of attention.[38] The year 1939 marks the culmination of the middle phase of the Bazin-Aumont account, of course, and it is also the year of *Mr. Smith Goes to Washington*, to which I turn shortly. Another way of putting the point I have made about the key sequence in *Mr. Deeds Goes to Town* is that its structure is as paradigmatic as *Stagecoach* for the 1930s version of classical style, but that it marks itself as such, and marks its relation to sentiment, by virtue of Capra's singular preoccupation with cinematic self-remaking—a preoccupation that, I have suggested, became all-consuming with the making of *Mr. Deeds*.

I should stress that this is not the first glimmer of Capra's self-consciousness about the narrative system that he inherited as a young journeyman in the early 1920s, soon after the system took formally recognizable shape. I have already argued that the remaking of the Walls of Jericho trope between *Strong Man* and *It Happened One Night* represents some special awareness of this stylistic element and its place in a larger system. With *Mr. Deeds*, however, Capra seems to begin to associate such a stylistic assemblage—what we now call the classical system—with the medium of cinema itself, as it came to be understood in the period. I noted earlier that the mid-1930s was a period in which the notion of the cinema as a medium, with powers for good or ill, had become central to many discourses about modernity, American society, moral education, the fate of children, and so on.[39] References to the cinema as a "medium" begin to be commonplace, and even, as in the case of Preston Sturges's *Sullivan's Travels*, to appear in film dialogue. Post-1935 Capra has a key role to play in this story.[40] I have already suggested how central Capra was to the institutions of Hollywood from 1936 onward, but he becomes important by the late 1930s in another way as well. He becomes a champion of cinema as a medium—of specifically *his* kind of cinema as medium, one whose potential could be recognized and developed under the "one man, one film" reform he began to argue strenuously for in 1936.

What more alert and reliable witness could we indeed want to attest to this recognition than the brilliant meta-filmmaker Preston Sturges? In *Sullivan's Travels* (1941), Sturges stages an early scene between the title character (a talented young director played by Joel McCrea) and his studio producers. Sullivan has made a string of profitable light comedies, but now seeks to persuade his bosses to back a more socially engaged production, unpromisingly titled *O Brother Where Art Thou?* (The Coen brothers would seize on this as the premise for a film they made a few years after *The Hudsucker Proxy*.) Sullivan insists that the new project would redeem his earlier cinematic dalliances. "I want this picture to be a document," he says, "something that would realize the possibilities of film as the sociological and artistic medium that it is." "Something like Capra?" reply the producers. "Yes," says Sullivan, "what's wrong with that?" What is more, Sturges goes on to link this sense of film as a "sociological and artistic medium" with commitments that align his director, Sullivan, very closely with the Capra of *Mr. Deeds* and after. (The recently released *Meet John Doe* may have been part of Sturges's implied context for the reference to Capra.)[41]

When Sullivan insists on attempting a Capra film, a film about "human suffering" in "these . . . troublous times," the producers finally challenge him on the grounds that he knows nothing about human suffering. When he concedes this point, the producers think they have won the battle. Sullivan has not, however, given up on his Capra project. Rather, he has formed a resolution to equip himself to take it on: "I'm going to get some old clothes and some old shoes from wardrobe and start out with ten cents in my pocket . . . I don't know where . . . and I'm not coming back till I know what trouble is" (547). To solidify the allusive link with Capra's films, Sturges shifts the action to a scene showing Sullivan with his valet. This scene ironically revisits and inverts the sentimental hero's relation to his valet in *Mr. Deeds*, which itself, as I noted earlier, involved Capra's remaking of a similar relationship between Stew Smith and his valet in the proto-screwball comedy *Platinum Blonde*. In both Capra films, we see the valet dressing a male protagonist who has found himself suddenly rich, and in both cases, as in the later dressing of Long John Willoughby (again Gary Cooper) in *Meet John Doe*, the scene seems to have autobiographical implications for Capra, a once-poor immigrant now living in the lap of Hollywood luxury. In *Sullivan's Travels*, the valet is dressing the rich director down, and the scene is brilliantly crafted and executed. We initially see Sullivan "in front of a three-piece tailor's mirror dressed in a fearful tramp outfit" (550). The valet quips: "I think that's overdoing it a bit, sir. There's no use breaking their hearts" (550). And part of the wit of this line is that it reveals Sullivan's attempt to experience trouble as an effort to look the part of someone doing so.

When Burroughs the butler enters, and grimaces, Sullivan asks him what's wrong. The butler responds that he's "never been sympathetic to the caricaturing of the poor and needy, sir." And when the valet explains that Burroughs "doesn't know about the expedition," Sullivan fills him in: "I'm going out on the road to find out what it's *like* to be poor and needy . . . and then I'm going

Capra, *Platinum Blonde* (1931, Columbia).

Capra, *Mr. Deeds Goes to Town.*

Sturges, *Sullivan's Travels* (1941, Paramount).

to make a picture about it" (552). The butler's critique of the performance is Sturges at his best:

THE BUTLER

If you'll permit me to say so, sir: The subject is not an interesting one. The poor know about poverty and only the morbid rich would find the topic glamorous.

SULLIVAN

(*Exasperated*)

But I'm doing it *for* the poor.

THE BUTLER

I doubt that they would appreciate, sir. They rather resent the invasion of their privacy. (553)

Questions of privacy and publicity indeed become central to Sullivan's "expedition" when the studio heads insist on having it "covered" by film and print reporters. The key point here is that the "medium" of cinema—as it appears by 1940–1941 to Sullivan, Sturges, and Capra—involves some necessary act of vicariousness and some fundamental principle of sympathy.

Such a recognition is precisely what I claim to find in that pivotal sequence in *Mr. Deeds*, where a sentimental sense of the medium is turned into something like a basis for a new form of publicness. This new form of publicness may be considered the sociological side of what Sullivan calls the "sociological and artistic medium that [film] is." The self-consciousness of cinema as a medium in this sense—a sentimental renegotiation of the means of communication in a constituted public sphere—was already hinted at, in *Mr. Deeds*, in the phrasing of the farmer's threat to Deeds in the tense moments before he relents and drops his gun: "You're about to get some more publicity, Mr. Deeds! You're about to get on the front page again! See how you're going to like it this time!"[42] As in *Platinum Blonde* and *It Happened One Night*, *Mr. Deeds* here registers a narrative running on two tracks, on the screen and on the front page. And thus the confrontation with the farmer issues in a transformation of the stories that appear on the front page, in the spinning newspaper headlines that seem to be thrown out of the sentimental vortex of the scene itself.

My larger claim, then, is that in the film that inaugurates the political sentimentalism of the Capraesque as we know it, Capra begins to make a recognizable link between the shot/reverse-shot technique and a "reflective" ethics of putting one's self in the place or case of the other (about which much more in part 2). Moreover, this connection is flagged, as we have seen, by Deeds's intradiegetic "direction" of the brunch scene to enable face-to-face positioning and correct sight lines. Such self-consciousness has implications for some central motifs in the film, especially the topos of "the front page," which matters to several of Capra's most innovative and influential films of the 1930s, from *Platinum Blonde* and *It Happened One Night* forward. This reflexivity also carries forward to *It's a Wonderful Life*, a film that begins with Clarence the Angel being assigned to the case of George Bailey, which is then screened as a film-within-the-film, for him and for us. One might also say that in reformulating the question of publicity, so crucial to the plot of the film to this point, and to others before it, the film embraces shot/reverse-shot as a cinematic norm in order to represent a new form of circulated privacy—a new practice for establishing what Jürgen Habermas, speaking of the eighteenth-century print sphere, calls "intimacy oriented toward a public."

The 1930s Rivalry of Film and Print

The manner in which Capra remade Capra in *Mr. Deeds*, then, enabled him to refigure some vital relationships: to himself as auteur, to cinema as a medium, to sentiment as a structural principle of this medium, and to the social responsibilities implied in all of the above.[43] All of these refigured relationships, moreover, became even more explicit when Capra remade *Mr. Deeds* as *Mr. Smith*, and thus continued to refashion the Capraesque. Capra's ambitions for *Mr. Smith* were large, and they were closely linked with his overriding goal, as emulated by Joel McCrea's Sullivan, to realize the full potential of film as the sociological and artistic medium that it is. The Washington setting of the plot, and indeed of its disastrous gala preview at the National Press Club in October 1939, suggests the film's ambition to supplement the political form of representation with its own representational practices—or rather to supplant the traditional supplement that print had supplied from the time of America's founding, in what Thomas Carlyle once called the age of paper. The film, we might say, offers a politics of sentiment in the new cinematic mode. And the form of the plot is itself sentimental in that it offers an apparently improbable resolution—a narrative "leap"—after the failure of a plan that is supposed to save the comic protagonists.

Crucially, however, the plan and the resolution are reflexively coded in different media. The plan concocted by Mr. Smith and Saunders (Jean Arthur) depends on the paper circuit of representation—congressional bills, daily periodicals, telegrams—to remedy corruption in the representative democracy

Washington premiere of *Mr. Smith* makes headlines.

of the Capitol, specifically to exonerate Smith from counterfeit charges of corruption. (His accusers forge his signature on a piece of paper to ensure his being found guilty.) As the sentimental plot unfolds, complete with an *Our Gang*–style rescue montage featuring little boys delivering little paper fliers that speak truth to power, we find that this circuit is inadequate to the task of saving Mr. Smith.[44] The big paper bosses crush the boys' efforts, and Smith himself is eventually crushed under an avalanche of adverse paper telegrams. In the face of such a desperate circumstance, the film achieves comic resolution in roughly two minutes. Here is a concise account of the denouement by Ray Carney:

> Smith falls to the floor in a faint, after accusing Paine of betraying his ideals. Paine, stricken with remorse and grief, is apprehended with a gun in the vestibule, apparently on the verge of committing suicide. The gun is wrested out of his hand, and he makes an emotional public confession

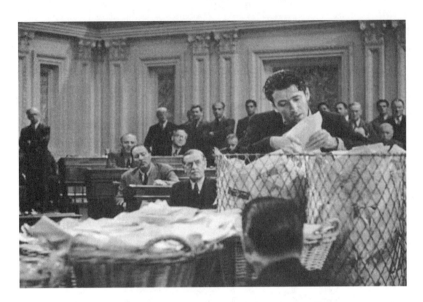

Capra, *Mr. Smith Goes to Washington* (1939, Columbia). Avalanche of adverse telegrams.

of his corruption. The whole sequence of events is speeded up almost to the point of incomprehensibility.[45]

For Carney, this finale is about the collapse of order and the triumph of "devices [that] generate extreme states of feeling."[46] By contrast, I wish to see this resolution as aligned with the "leap" that had characterized the denouement of sentimental comedy for more than two centuries, a problem of probability that stems from sympathetic relays extending beyond the diegetic field of the narrative. Smith fails to save himself in the cycle of paper. "Liberty is too precious a thing to be buried in books," he had said to Saunders earlier in the film, and neither is he able to achieve appropriate political representation in the medium of print. No, the trigger of the accelerated resolution of *Mr. Smith Goes to Washington* lies in the little sequence shots that Capra inserts just before Smith's dramatic collapse, in which the camera cuts back and forth between the face of the kneeling James Stewart and that of Harry Carey in his august seat above him. There is mutual recognition in these faces, and when Carey smiles on Smith, Smith knows what it means, and so do we.

In the end, I suggest, it is the affective medium of the film itself—this film and film as such—in which he and America find redemption. The sentimental exchange of glances between Stewart and Carey in the final moments—

handled in a subjective shot/reverse-shot sequence along calibrated sight lines, much like the one marked in *Mr. Deeds*—must be understood both to represent sympathy diegetically in the Senate and to elicit it pragmatically on the larger political stage of the nation by way of cinema and its audiences.[47] This is why Harry Carey, playing the president pro tem, is made to act so much like a movie spectator at the film's close, popping a piece of candy into his mouth, leaning back in his chair, and cupping his hands behind his head to gaze with satisfaction at the spectacle.[48] This sentimental resolution, the political apotheosis of cinema's displacement of print-mediated affect in the twentieth century, must be understood as representing, eliciting, and shaping national sentiment, all at the same time.

When powerful real-life adversaries such as Joseph Kennedy and Alben Barkley attacked the film in 1939, Capra persuaded Harry Cohn not to scrap it but instead to market it under that slogan: "Liberty is too precious a thing to be buried in books." If liberty has been buried in books, so the logic goes, it is resurrected in cinema. But cinema here is conceived as more than projected motion pictures. It is rather a particular set of practices, a particular idea of cinema, one Capra takes to be conceived in America but made for the world. And its role in the world is something Capra proclaimed in citing an article in the *Hollywood Reporter* for November 4, 1942: "*Mr. Smith Goes to Washington*, chosen by the French as the final English-language film shown before the recent Nazi-ordered countrywide ban on American and British films went into effect, was roundly cheered" with "storms of spontaneous applause."[49]

My claims about Capra's preoccupation with eye-line matches, sight lines, and the role of faces in *Mr. Smith Goes to Washington* are reinforced by Capra's extended comments in his autobiography. He recounts his new way of approaching the problem of the close-up in this film, developed partly to deal with Jean Arthur's notorious skittishness in front of the camera. It involved having Arthur play her close-ups to the voices in the master shot's playback. "Just before Jean spoke in a close-up line, I'd cut off the playback. In between her lines, I cut it back in, so she could react silently to what Jimmy Stewart, Claude Rains, and Edward Arnold were saying in the master shot." Capra encourages his readers, on their next viewing of the film, to "observe how all the close-ups meld and flow with the longer shots as smoothly as if the close-ups were photographed simultaneously." Of his little trick, Capra boasted that he "thought it was the best thing that had happened to the close-up since D. W. Griffith invented it" (275–76).

Mr. Smith Goes to Washington. Pivotal shot/reverse-shot sequence
near the film's conclusion.

Capra's comparison of his technical innovation to Griffith's alleged invention of the close-up is part of a recurring set of references to Griffith in his autobiography and in his interviews. His was probably an ambition unprecedented in American cinema since Griffith, as he himself seems to have recognized. It is indeed an important, and too little appreciated, feature of Capra's career that he so venerated Griffith. In various moments of his autobiography Capra calls Griffith "the Master," the "Unapproachable," "the giant of all filmmakers," the "Leonardo of the Screen" (61, 188, 447). He describes Griffith as "filmdom's first and perhaps greatest artist" (57). This veneration matters much to my larger argument about Capra, Eisenstein, Griffith, and the sentimental tradition that leads to Dickens. And the evidence for it is rich.

In 1971, the year in which he published *The Name above the Title*, Capra wrote the introduction for Griffith's autobiography, which was appearing more than thirty years after his death in 1939. Toward the end of this brief essay, Capra sums up the life of Griffith and asserts himself unequivocally into the central line of descent from him. He even credits Griffith with having precociously developed the auteurist notion for which Capra himself usually claimed chief credit. "David Wark Griffith," his peroration begins, "was fated to be forgotten by the great industry his art had proliferated, forgotten because he was a loner, a rebel, a proud Titan. But no one can ever again create a film art. That honor belongs solely to the Master. And all the corporation heads and all their assembly-lines could not kill Griffith's 'one man, one film' concept of artistic filmmaking. His concept took root in my small studio on Poverty Row, in the late 20's. Its seed was so fertile that the concept spread, and grew, and finally flowered in the Golden Age of Movies in the 30's and 40's."[50]

Griffith—more specifically the idea that Capra might one day become Griffith—figures centrally in the anecdote Capra tells about how he met his first wife, Helen Howell, on the set of von Stroheim's *Greed*. And, importantly for Capra's relation to the Bazinian account of the evolution of cinematic language, this anecdote condemns von Stroheim, by whom Capra was then employed. In 1922, watching von Stroheim on the set of *Greed*, for which he was processing dailies, Capra says he turned away in distaste from von Stroheim's posturings, and said to a group of bit actors, "If that Stroheim's a director, I'm D. W. Griffith."

"Maybe you will be someday," a feminine voice behind me said. . . .
"Was that supposed to be funny?" I asked her tartly.
"No, not really."[51]

Implying here that Howell's prophecy about his one day becoming Griffith was in some sense fulfilled, Capra elsewhere completes the Hollywood genealogy that suggests his line of descent from Griffith.

It completes the genealogy in the sense that Capra's own early master, the only one whose immediate influence he ever really acknowledges, was the great Mack Sennett. Capra was a gag writer for Sennett for some years before being given his chance with Sennett's great clown Harry Langdon. But as Capra explains in his autobiography, "The Golden Age of Film Comedy was fathered by Mack Sennett," a "devout student and disciple of D. W. Griffith."[52] Capra's reliable cinematographer on most of his important work for Columbia, as well as *It's a Wonderful Life*, was Joe Walker, once an apprentice to Billy Bitzer, who had long served as Griffith's cameraman. Further, Capra's recurring fear in the mid-1930s, which he refers to more than once in his autobiography, was that the bubble would burst for him and he would wind up unremembered, unknown, an alcoholic, like Mr. Gower in the alternative world unshaped by George Bailey's good influence. And the two Hollywood figures he associates with this kind of precipitous fall are indeed Sennett and Griffith. Here is how he sets up the story of his crisis after *It Happened One Night*: "Show business is brutal to has-beens. Those pushed off the top are rolled into the valley of oblivion; often into degradation. I saw it all around me: D. W. Griffith—a forgotten man; Mack Sennett—walking unnoticed in the city he once ruled as King of Comedy."[53] Capra must have feared he was next in line.

A special place is reserved both in Capra's story and in his canon for *The Birth of a Nation*. It was the first film that Capra, initially hostile to cinema, would acknowledge having gone to. To Joseph McBride he declared that he considered it the "most important film ever made."[54] And it is the only film he offers as an example of what it meant for a director to have his "name above the title" before he himself achieved that distinction as a working director.[55] There is good reason to think that Capra thought of his political films, especially *Mr. Smith Goes to Washington*, as his answer to *The Birth of a Nation*. Indeed, after Griffith's film, *Mr. Smith* may well be accounted the single most influential American film about politics.[56]

In the period between 1934 and 1939, when Capra's ascendency in Hollywood reached its apex, he also showed his preoccupation with Griffith by way of a striking gesture. For the first Academy Awards ceremony under his watch, in 1936 (the year of *Mr. Deeds*), it was Capra who came up with the idea of creating a Special Achievement award, the origin of the current Lifetime Achievement award, and presenting it to none other than D. W.

Griffith. It was an act of what might be called reverse mantle-passing, with Capra conferring on Griffith the honor of having passed the torch to himself. It was an effort to rehabilitate Griffith's reputation while at the same time avowing him as forebear.[57] I would not wish to claim for Capra the status of a figure like Griffith. If Griffith was not quite, as was implied in the title of his autobiography, "the man who invented Hollywood," he had as serious a claim to that title as anyone did. Capra and Griffith share more than what many film historians seem inclined to allow, however, not least a kind of vaunting egomaniacal ambition that stands out even in the Hollywood context.[58]

Dickens, Griffith, and Capra

A further clue to the Griffith-Capra connection can be found in the writings of Eisenstein, that giant of Soviet cinema who admired them both. Eisenstein, we have seen, placed Griffith's relationship with Dickens in the context of the kind of montage practice he and his fellow Soviet filmmakers would rework and perfect in their dialectical montage. Capra claimed the Dickensian Griffith for another teleology, the Capraesque, and in the name of another genealogy, the sentimental. Thus, as I have suggested, where Griffith adapted Dickens's 1845 Christmas story "The Cricket on the Hearth" to make a one-reeler by the same title in 1909, Capra would eventually go back to the ur-text, *A Christmas Carol*, to which "The Cricket on the Hearth" was a kind of sequel, to produce his own reworking of the sentimental Dickens for the screen in *It's a Wonderful Life*. Since Eisenstein's 1944 essay was published in Russian and unavailable in English until Jay Leyda's 1949 translation, there is no real ground for suggesting a direct connection between the two, no direct evidence that Capra was attempting to revise Eisenstein's understanding of Dickensian cinema to reclaim it for the sentimental tradition. But Eisenstein and Capra had met in Hollywood and again in Moscow in 1936, and they corresponded. Given their keen mutual interest in both Griffith and Dickens, it is easy to imagine that Eisenstein shared with Capra the thoughts that went into his 1944 essay. In any event, Capra's turn to Dickens for what he would later regard as his *summa cinematica* seems to answer, in his own cinematic terms, the argument outlined by Eisenstein.

Returning once more to our first encounter with *It's a Wonderful Life*, the film remixed by Eugene Jarecki for Move Your Money, I wish to close part 1 by noting some features of that film that are perhaps altogether obvious by now. By that, I mean Capra's distinctively sentimental conjunction of vicarious imagination, point-of-view shots, archaic elements, and references to the theory and practice of sentimental economy. These are features I will identify with the history and formal properties of what I call "the sentimental case." The framing of the entire film pointedly involves our entry into George Bailey's case, via the cinematic presentation of his life for Clarence in heaven. When Clarence is "assigned" to George's case, it is made clear that his way with it will be that of sympathy rather than analysis—we're told he "has the IQ of a rabbit" but the "faith of a child." And quite demonstrably, as in much of Capra's programmatic work after *Mr. Deeds*, the techniques of shot/reverse-shot direction emblematize sentimental practice. Indeed, Kaja Silverman has declared the entire film to be bound in a "celestial suture."[59]

To make explicit the point that will help guide us into the analyses of part 2, then, my suggestion is that Capra's invocation of Dickens indicates an increasing self-consciousness about the historical origins of the sentimental mode in the print cultural past, a point that is reinforced by the explicit references to the theory of political economy in *It's a Wonderful Life*: George Bailey's lecture on banking to the panicky townspeople during the run on the savings and loan is worthy of Adam Smith himself. Money and sentiment, as we have seen, run twin courses through this film, in which "character" and "credit" are closely coordinated. The archaic elements in the film—Mr. Potter's anachronistic horse and carriage, for example—were noted by James Agee in a review of 1946. Agee had admired *Mr. Deeds* and *Mr. Smith*, but he was troubled by *It's a Wonderful Life*. The film, he wrote, threw him back to the nineteenth century, to Dickens's period, and this observation seems fair enough as far as it goes. But I maintain that this throwback, in some telling particulars, actually points back a century further, as did Dickens's own work, to the eighteenth century.

We saw above that the double narrative of *It's a Wonderful Life* comes together in the denouement, when the money comes in and the bank is saved, along with George. It is perhaps worth emphasizing now that this conclusion is punctuated by three of the paradigmatic short expressions of sentiment that began to be popularly identified as such in the eighteenth century: the toast (Harry Bailey's "Here's to my brother George, the richest man in town"), the moral sentence (inscribed by Clarence in a copy of *Tom Sawyer*: "No man is a failure who has friends"), and the sentimental song (Burns's "Auld Lang Syne," which dates to the eighteenth century itself, sung by the community assembled in George's living room). In the case of Burns's song, Capra must be seen as going out of his way to introduce it on this occasion, since the evening in question is not New Year's Eve, after all, but Christmas Eve. Clarence the Angel wears early-modern garb and expresses a problematic taste for early-modern alcoholic beverages (flaming rum punch and mulled wine). When asked his age, he explains that he will be 293 "next May"—that is, May 1946—which means that if he died at seventy he would have died in 1722, the year of Steele's *Conscious Lovers*, the first sentimental comedy. Finally, and perhaps most tellingly, the screenplay indicates that the celestial scenes take place in the laboratory of Benjamin Franklin, who is in charge of the cinematic narration of the life of George Bailey.

It is, in other words, to the early modern period, and especially to the eighteenth century, that we are led by Capra's recursive preoccupations with his sentimental authorship in the medium of classical Hollywood narration. And it is to the eighteenth century that we turn in part 2, for an investigation into the making of the sentimental mood in literature. In his book about eighteenth-century British culture, *The Pleasures of the Imagination*, John Brewer has suggestively compared the commercially oriented cultural production of twentieth-century Los Angeles with that of eighteenth-century Britain.[60] That is the big jump to be made here, but we have a large stepping-stone in the work of Dickens. Heir to the eighteenth-century sentimental world, Dickens also, as Eisenstein insisted, did much to shape the reception of that prior world of sentiment for early American cinema.

PART 2   The Making

of Literary

Sentimentalism

I believe that the arguments of part 2 can largely stand on their own for students of eighteenth- and nineteenth-century literature. These chapters certainly aim to bring new literary angles of approach to the texts they examine and to offer some surprises for students of the field: a demonstration of Schiller's utility in gaining a better purchase on Anglo-Scottish sentiment; a revealing connection between Dickens and Sterne by way of the *Sentimental Magazine*; a demonstration of how the Latitudinarian "vehicular hypothesis" shaped the subgenre of the sentimental journey; an argument for the full importance of materialism as a backdrop of literary sentimentalism; an examination of sentimentalism's response to casuistry. I have noticed, however, that when I lecture on these literary matters, audiences respond with a new kind of interest if I begin with a film clip from Capra—the shot/reverse-shot sequence from *Mr. Deeds Goes to*

Town, for example, or the sequence in *It's a Wonderful Life* in which young George expresses sympathy for Mr. Gower even while being undeservedly beaten. The fact of that added interest led me to go further.

This procedure risks anachronism, like any treatment of past things by way of more recent ones. And I don't claim, of course, that Hollywood cinema is the only possible (or actual) development from eighteenth-century literary spectatorship—just that it is in fact one major such development. Once it becomes clear not only how literary sentimentalism shaped cinematic practice, but also that Capra's recursive self-making led him to something like that very recognition, it seems possible to want to have things both ways, both the historical account of the origins of twentieth-century cinema and the critical reframing of earlier literature at the same time. That, in any case, is my goal here.

For Eisenstein, as we have noted, the sentimental connection between Dickens's fiction and Eisenstein's filmmaking is elided or suppressed in favor of another framing: one that finds in these predecessors the basis for Soviet montage. By contrast, in the Capraesque fulfillment of the line of Dickens and Griffith, which culminates in *It's a Wonderful Life*, released just two years after Eisenstein published his essay, it is indeed the sentimental aspects of Hollywood Dickensianism that stand out. What this means in practice, as we have also seen, is that Capra seems to heighten just those elements of Griffith's Dickensian style that the dialectical materialism of Eisenstein's and his fellow Soviets' film practices is meant to transcend—interest in subjective point of view, reflexivity, symmetry, counterfactuality, moral probability, conscience, ethical formation, and indeed, interest in the "soul" itself—all features of the tradition of liberal humanism that Eisenstein wishes to bracket in his account of Griffith's debts to Dickens.

In Eisenstein's account of the Soviet fulfillment of the cinematographic promise inherent in Dickens and Griffith, the larger "ancestral array," as I have suggested, is supposed to go all the way back to "Shakespeare and the Greeks." In Capra's fulfillment of this promise, I've suggested, the ancestry traces back only to about the eighteenth century and the emergence of the sentimental as a recognizable mode or mood. Dickens's own literary debts lend support to Capra's version of the lineage. Commentators on Dickens often note the origins of his style and sensibility in the sentimentalism of the eighteenth century, though not usually in any great detail.[1] We can develop a more particularized account of Dickens's debt to this earlier sentimentalism if we consider *A Christmas Carol* in relation to a serialized magazine story of the 1770s, one from which I claim it derives. Both the theme and plot of this story, as well as the context of its publication, help to illustrate the eighteenth-century roots of Dickens's sentimentalism.

The earlier story, "The Miser Convinced of His Error," was serialized in 1773. It concerns a man named Doriman, who was "born in the very centre of commerce," to "avaricious parents," and "early initiated in their principles."[2] Like Scrooge, he "commenced [a] miser at an age when an honest heart is generally prodigal," and, like Scrooge too, he "was cruel to himself as well as others, and therefore knew not how to feel for the distresses of his fellow-creatures." And perhaps most of all like Scrooge, he "deemed humanity [in the eighteenth-century sense of "humaneness"] ridiculous, and generosity a folly": "Doriman avoided all amiable society," because "every man had been represented to him as a subtle sharper."[3] This unhappy pattern extends, as in the case of Scrooge's fatal rejection of his impoverished sweetheart, Fanny, to potentially romantic attachments. Though Doriman is "advised to marry," and does not lack candidates, "he could not find any one rich enough."[4]

Doriman is saved from his ways by the good offices of his uncle, Dolman, who is not supernatural, unlike Scrooge's spirits, but is nonetheless guided by angelic sympathies. At one point Dolman borrows money in order to help a stranger in distress, eliciting the following response: "I had no claim to your generosity. You commiserated my situation merely from knowing that I was an unfortunate father."[5] The unfortunate's distress, as the reader learns, was exacerbated by Doriman himself, who offered no relief from a usurious arrangement. The uncle confronts the nephew, who, instead of expressing re-morse, scolds the uncle for not getting a receipt (a "note of hand") for his loan to the unfortunate father. At this, the generous uncle explodes into righteous anger and disowns Doriman.

This anger is not altogether unlike that of the Spirit of Christmas Present, who mocks Scrooge with his own words, and the effect is the same. The miser becomes reflective, and the description of this moment draws on Adam Smith's account of the impartial spectator, an important figure in the history of sentiment, as an internal principle of conscientiousness born of reversed point of view—what Smith called "the man within the breast, the great judge and arbiter" of our conduct:[6]

> He returned; —he wished to banish from his memory this violent scene: he now discovered, in spight of himself, a dawn of virtue. We bear, in the centre of our hearts, an upright judge. That judge, which had been so long asleep in the heart of Doriman, was awakened at the voice of Dolman. This was the first spark of virtue which flew from that obdurate soul.

Doriman was greatly agitated; he walked about without knowing whither his footsteps guided him. An inward sentiment abased him, and he became contemptible in his own eyes.... He felt an inclination to examine his heart, and conciliate the ideas within it. He shut himself up; he reflected on what he had heard, and what he had seen: the virtuous eloquence of his uncle; that vehemence, which he could not but approve; that tenderness which shone through his noble rage. He pictured to himself the extatic pleasure which Dolman enjoyed on consoling an unfortunate father; that rapture which manifested itself by tears that were not counterfeited, but flowed spontaneously from the heart.... Is there a pleasure annexed to benevolence and munificence? It must be so, for my uncle finds himself happy, honoured, and esteemed, whilst I, (to my shame I own it) am miserable and contemptible in the very bosom of my riches.[7]

In internalizing the perspective of another, expressed as it was with tender vehemence, Doriman develops the inward sentiment constituted by a specific form of reflection, one imagined by Shaftesbury, explained by Adam Smith, deployed by Schiller, and later taken up in Dickens. It is the dual sense of reflection that combines seeing oneself in the eyes of another with the act of looking into our own hearts. As in Sterne's fiction before and Dickens's after—and in Capra's *Mr. Deeds Goes to Town*—the moment of reflection produces transformation. The next day Doriman makes the rounds to make amends, much as Scrooge does when he awakes on Christmas Day. His sentimental conversion is complete.

The publishing history of "The Miser Convinced of His Error" is as relevant as the story it tells. It appeared in the first three installments of a publication called the *Sentimental Magazine* just five years after Sterne's untimely death. The self-consciousness of this publication about its cultural provenance could scarcely be more pronounced. It explains its relation to the relatively new form of the magazine itself.[8] It also explains its relation to the emergence of what it specifically casts as a kind of sentimental modernity: "Our Ancestors placed their Amusement in Laughter, we place our's [*sic*] in Chastity of Sentiment." But the most telling marker of the magazine's programmatic orientation and strongest influences comes with the lead series that was featured just ahead of "The Miser Convinced of His Error" in the magazine's early numbers. It was entitled "A Sentimental Journey through Life," and it included various homages to the celebrated book Laurence Sterne had published five years earlier, in which he coined the phrase "sentimental journey," precisely the text that, following Viktor Shklovsky's lead, I have taken as my own template of sentimental modernity. The *Sentimental Magazine's* acts of homage to Sterne's last work include the vignette structure, the invocation of Sterne's play with the conceit of the vehicle (one of its early vignettes is in fact called "the vehicle"), and a reflexive self-interrupting preoccupation with the ongoing process of composition:

> I had now got into a train of moralizing, and had set my paper and ink-stand before me, with an intention of *honouring* the world with a narrative of my adventures, when a noise in the street broke the tread of my history, and buried every idea I had conceived, in darkness absolute.[9]

This is every bit as much an imitation of Sterne's manner as one can find in any of the numerous sequels and pastiches of *Sentimental Journey* that appeared from other hands in the years after its publication, beginning within weeks of Sterne's death.

Here, then, we have a declared organ of an emergent sentimentalism in the early 1770s that introduces itself to the world by juxtaposing two serial narratives in a manner that proves most illuminating for the genealogy I am tracing: the one story looking back a few years to Sterne and the other, just as importantly, looking forward a few decades to the Victorians. "The Miser Convinced of His Error" did indeed have a robust bibliographical afterlife. It was republished, with only slight revision, in George Wright's *The Young Moralist* (1782), a text that was itself republished in 1819 in London and in 1826 in New York.[10] There is evidence that the book had wide circulation into the Victorian period, a fact that indicates the cultural durability of Sterne-era sentimentalism, quite apart from questions about the provenance of Dickens's Christmas tale. Just as Dickens forms one link in the chain of sentimental modernity, "The Miser" forms another, which clarifies Dickens's eighteenth-century debts.

The four chapters that constitute part 2, each from a different angle, will examine early-modern contexts from which the sentimental miser emerges, especially the Latitudinarian heritage of thinking about the fate of the soul within the structures of sympathy in moral-sense philosophy. Since these chapters will also look forward, not only to Dickens but to the Capraesque, I wish to fill in the sketch I offered of that connection in part 1. As noted there, Capra's lifelong fascination with Dickens shows through much of his work, but it was not until late in the productive phase of his career that he attempted anything remotely resembling a Dickensian adaptation, with *It's a Wonderful Life's* reworking of *A Christmas Carol*. One of the ways in which Capra reinforced the film's Dickensian connection was by casting Lionel Barrymore in the role of Mr. Potter, the miserly banker. Barrymore had been identified with the role of Dickens's Scrooge since the 1930s, the period in which much of the action of *It's a Wonderful Life* is set, and in 1939 he teamed up with Orson Welles and the CBS Campbell Playhouse to produce a version of the tale for radio that defined the role of Scrooge for millions of Americans for years. A recording of this radio broadcast has survived, and audiences familiar with Barrymore's Mr. Potter will find it indeed quite uncanny to hear that persona anticipated in the grumbling complaints of his radio Scrooge.[11]

It is no trivial matter that in Capra's reworking of the story he had from Dickens, the miser is *not* convinced of his error. The miser Potter is indeed all but forgotten in the film's rousing denouement, when George experiences full redemption, both financial and emotional. It is indeed part of the interesting displacement of some key issues in the story of "The Miser Convinced of His Error" that sentimental redemption is brought not to a man who has forgot how to sympathize but, on the contrary, to the most sympathetic person in town. Scrooge doesn't know how bad off he is, and he needs supernatural intervention to find that out. The intervention in *It's a Wonderful Life* has the opposite aim: to show George how good he has it, and how miserable it would be to be the miser. Importantly, both narratives move toward a climactic emotional moment in which a supernatural agent charged with reforming the protagonist leads him to a gravesite and allows him to read the inscription on the stone. In *A Christmas Carol*, the grave, neglected of course, is Scrooge's own. In *It's a Wonderful Life*, the grave is that of George's younger brother Harry. One indicates the fate of the miser unconvinced of his error. The other indicates the fate of the world with the protagonist not there to save it. For all that, George Bailey's giddiness on being returned to his own life after Clarence's experiment decidedly reprises Scrooge's childlike glee on Christmas morning after the ministrations of the three spirits. Nowhere do the two stories come together more closely than in those moments of reawakening to the wonders, not only of Christmas Day but of ordinary life.[12]

All told, there is a sufficiently clear overlap between the two works—sufficient evidence suggesting that it is indeed *A Christmas Carol* that Capra is reworking—to establish a markedly sentimental connection between them. This evidence highlights those aspects of the sentimental mode that Capra's recursive practices led him to reanimate, and in ways that point beyond Dickens to its origins in the previous century. In part 2, then, recasting Eisenstein's analysis of Griffith and Dickens as a claim about Capra and Dickens, and as a genealogy of the sentimental chronotope rather than dialectical montage,

I wish to focus on four aspects of this connection, all leading back to the eighteenth century.

Each of the next four chapters begins thus with Capra's reworking of Dickens in *It's a Wonderful Life*, contributing to a picture of this relationship that corresponds to the one I sketched at the start in Griffith's reworking of "The Cricket on the Hearth." Each chapter focuses on a particular aspect of the Capra-Dickens connection, one that can be traced back through the sentimental line to the eighteenth century (or even earlier). These four aspects are (1) sentimental spectatorship, with its particular emphasis on a sensorium virtually embedded in a medium and the possibilities for vicarious experience; (2) the question of the sensorium itself, which leads directly to the notion of "sensibility" and the modern refiguring of the soul by way of the "vehicular hypothesis" in Latitudinarian writings; (3) the consequences of these shifts for the distinctive form of literary "probability" in the sentimental mode; and (4) the consequences of these shifts for the representation of ethical questions in the sentimental mode, especially around questions of moral deformity. Each of the chapters also involves some engagement with Sterne, our central touchstone for eighteenth-century sentimentalism.

FOUR

The Case of the

Literary Spectator

Aristotle claimed that the best tragedies combined moments of *peripeteia* (reversal) with moments of *anagnorisis* (discovery or recognition). One way Capra tends to situate himself in the Dickensian line of the sentimental is in playing a variation on this Aristotelian formula similar to Dickens's. In Capra's work, the plot structure is generally comic rather than tragic, and the narrative involves a self-recognition that depends on something like a reversal of point of view. We might say that it involves a capacity to change our case by virtue of being able to behold it. The possibility of combining reflective recognition of this sort with self-transformation is crucial to my earlier argument about that pivotal moment in *Mr. Deeds Goes to Town* in which Capra uses a highly thematized shot/reverse-shot sequence to portray the title character as coming to see himself anew. And the argument applies as well, I have suggested, to Capra's account of his own case at the time that he made the film.

In Dickens's *A Christmas Carol*, the visitations of Marley and the three spirits all have the effect of leading Scrooge to behold himself in a new way. In Jacob Marley, with whose face Scrooge has a mirrorlike encounter when he beholds it in his own door-knocker, Scrooge is pointedly given an opportunity to behold the fate of a man who is a kind of double for him. With the Spirit of Christmas Past, moreover, Scrooge is presented with scenes of his own youth. He is able from the outset to see his childhood self reading alone in a schoolroom, and he is able to weep in sympathy with that child, a topos that Dickens would further develop with the complex optics of autobiographical memory in *David Copperfield* and *Great Expectations*. In the visions of Christmas Present, Scrooge is able not only to pass into the bosom of the Cratchit family on Christmas Eve, but to witness their regard for him, their ways of seeing him.[1] And in the visions shown him by the Spirit of Christmas Future, Scrooge is able to do what Huck Finn and Tom Sawyer will do in a later work of fiction: to become a spectator to one's own funeral, where one's view of life is perforce "external" as never before.[2]

Capra's George Bailey is likewise given the chance to stand apart from his own life, and here again this externalization of perspective is constitutive of his recognizing how wonderful that life is. In turn, this recognition makes possible the reversal of fortune that gives the film its sentimental resolution. In Capra's film, there is no moment where George is allowed to see himself quite as Scrooge does in the vision of Christmas Past. Rather, his ability to behold his own life is produced, paradoxically, by seeing how things would have played out had he never been born. This counterfactual premise permits him to behold his own life, in a sense, as the shape of an absence, one with precise contours defined by the deeds he was not there to perform. He sees his own life as a hole in a world that we presume is otherwise unchanged. It is nonetheless *his* life, an absent cause, a vacancy with discernible contours. In so beholding himself, he turns himself around, as we say; here again, a kind of *peripeteia* (reversal) is attended by a kind of *anagnorisis* (discovery).[3]

In both Capra and Dickens, this conceit of standing outside one's life—seeing ourselves as others see us—is conspicuously reinforced with visual and optical emphases. In Dickens, the "extraordinary optical faculty" that Eisenstein so praised was typically harnessed to this scheme of moral self-beholding. The play of eyes and faces and particularized lines of sight is everywhere apparent in *A Christmas Carol*. Having been jolted by the frontal encounter with Marley, Scrooge soon finds himself similarly confronted with the first spirit: "The curtains of his bed were drawn aside; and Scrooge, starting up into a half-recumbent attitude, found himself face to face with the unearthly visitor who drew them: as close to it as I am now to you, and I am standing in the spirit at your elbow."[4] When this first spirit offers him a vision of his own past, the narration shows a certain care in the visual construction of the space. Dickens employs a mobile perspective that attends the pair as they (and we as readers) are transported to a country road, and from there to Scrooge's childhood schoolhouse:

> They walked along the road, Scrooge recognising every gate, and post, and tree; until a little market-town appeared in the distance, with its bridge, its church, and winding river. Some shaggy ponies now were seen trotting towards them with boys upon their backs, who called to other boys in country gigs and carts, driven by farmers. . . . The jocund travellers came on; and as they came, Scrooge knew and named them every one." (70–71)

These are Scrooge's schoolmates on the road home from the schoolhouse, where Scrooge's traveling eye is heading for an encounter with his former self.

Indeed, the approach to the schoolhouse, and to little Ebenezer within it, is managed with extraordinary attention to the question of what the two spectators within the story would be seeing along the way:

> They left the high-road, by a well-remembered lane, and soon approached a mansion of dull red brick, with a little weathercock-surmounted cupola on the roof, and a bell hanging in it. It was a large house, but one of broken fortunes; for the spacious offices were little used, their walls were damp and mossy, their windows broken, and their gates decayed. Fowls clucked and strutted in the stables; and the coach-houses and sheds were overrun with grass. Nor was it more retentive of its ancient state, within; for entering the dreary hall, and glancing through the open doors of many rooms, they found them poorly furnished, cold, and vast. There was an earthy savour in the air, a chilly bareness in the place, which associated itself somehow with too much getting up by candle-light, and not too much to eat.
>
> They went, the Ghost and Scrooge, across the hall, to a door at the back of the house. It opened before them, and disclosed a long, bare, melancholy room, made barer still by lines of plain deal forms and desks. At one of these a lonely boy was reading near a feeble fire; and Scrooge sat down upon a form, and wept to see his poor forgotten self as he used to be. (71–72)

This is a carefully managed "passage" in every sense of the term. It takes us down the road, into the lane, past the stables and coach houses, across the hall, and, through the open door, to a view of the lonely boy at one of the desks.[5] As in "The Cricket on the Hearth," the doorway represents not only a moral threshold—in crossing which Scrooge gains his first vision of himself from the outside—but also a marker of embodied sightlines in this highly particularized visual (and sensory) world. It is a world that, with Eisenstein, I want to call protocinematic.

Capra, too, stresses certain optical and visual elements in his refashioning of Dickens's tale, making use of a good deal of subjective camerawork. This is especially true of the kinds of camera angles we tend to find in the latter half of the film, where Clarence shows George the fate of the world without George in it. A clear example is the extended shot/reverse-shot sequence of George's encounter with his mother, through the door of the boardinghouse she runs in this George-less world. Important as these devices are, there is an equally important connection to be made between the fact of externalization and the idea of reversing point of view shared by Capra and Dickens, the possibilities for recognition inherent in repositioning the virtual sensorium. The recognition achieved through such a displacement is conspicuously marked by Capra for its thematic relevance in the pivotal scene from *Mr. Deeds Goes to Town*. Of course, *Mr. Deeds* is a film from the heyday of the 1930s style, of which Capra was a principal architect. With *It's a Wonderful Life*, on the other hand, we are well into the new era of Orson Welles and William Wyler. In this later film, Capra uses shot/reverse-shot techniques more sparingly, but nonetheless meaningfully, chiefly for amatory scenes between George and Mary.

Furthermore, as we noted above, the use of this device in *It's a Wonderful Life* is complicated by a persistent triangulation of spectatorship, with third-party figures repeatedly overseeing encounters and overhearing conversations. I mentioned three examples earlier: Annie, the Baileys' African-American housekeeper, during what will prove to be George's last conversation with his father; Mary's mother, during the conversation between Mary and George on the night George proposes to her; and the old bald man on the porch who listens in on George and Mary's innocent lovemaking after the graduation dance. Given Clarence's mediating presence throughout the celestial screening, this structure might even be said to subtend the entire narrative of George Bailey's life. The implicit spectatorial point of view is often Clarence's, as we saw in the signal instance when the adult George Bailey (and James Stewart) appears for the first time.[6]

In all of these instances, we might say that we have a structure in which the face-to-face encounter can itself be understood as faced, confronted, by another. Something very like this structure is anticipated in Dickens's *Christmas Carol* when, for example, Scrooge is made to face the painful face-to-face encounter in which he breaks off his engagement with a self-described "dowerless girl" (80), the only woman who ever loved him romantically:

> Again Scrooge saw himself. He was older now; a man in the prime of life. His face had not the harsh and rigid lines of later years; but it had begun to wear the signs of care and avarice. There was an eager, greedy, restless motion in the eye, which showed the passion that had taken root, and where the shadow of the growing tree would fall. (79)

The young Scrooge's restless eye looks past the love and devotion offered him by the young woman who, for her part, "look[s] mildly, but with steadiness, upon him." She asks him, apropos of their "contract," which Scrooge is prepared to honor as a contract, "'would you seek me out and try to win me now? Ah, no!'" (80). Old Scrooge, the spectator to this face-to-face encounter, is made to face the fact that he was incapable of contradicting the answer that the young woman supplied to her own question.[7] This second-order confrontation is crucial to the pathos of the scene.

In both Capra's film and Dickens's novella, we find situations representing characters in postures of visual mutuality, the objects of each other's gazes. And we find such situations complicated by a second-order spectatorship in which the encounters can themselves be reflected in the eyes of another. This is just the sort of structure, I believe, that Eisenstein found uninteresting in Griffith and Dickens. It was not part of what he and his Soviet colleagues wanted to do with Griffith or Dickens, not a direction in which they wanted to extend the rich possibilities that he invokes in this connection. By the same token, precisely this structure is crucial to what makes the Capraesque a neo-Griffithian, neo-Dickensian project: it also put us on a path back toward Sterne and Smith and the origins of eighteenth-century sentimentalism.

One final point remains to set up the following account of the case of the literary spectator, and this has to do with the term "case" itself and its relevance to the sentimental. For reasons that will become clearer as we get into the details, the notion of the case not only is helpful for thinking about the relation between an externalized point of view and its subject, but also, and not coincidentally, is a term that is most apposite to the sentimental tradition in question. It is there in Adam Smith's language about how, in the act of sympathetically imagining ourselves in the place of the other, we put ourselves in the *case* of the other: "We sometimes feel for another, a passion of which he himself seems to be altogether incapable; because, when we put ourselves in his case, that passion arises in our breast from the imagination, though it does not in his from the reality."[8] This language, as I will suggest, is to be understood in relation to Smith's critique of another model of the case as it is found in the tradition of Jesuit casuistry.

The notion of the case is operative, too, in *A Christmas Carol*. Scrooge's inquiry, as the work of the three spirits unfolds, is increasingly about what he calls his own case, about whether what is shown to him defines his real situation or whether it is just an indication of what might be. Hearing a dead man, who seems to be himself, disparaged by everyone who came into contact with him in life, Scrooge shudders and exclaims to the third spirit: "'I see, I see. The case of this unhappy man might be my own. My life tends that way, now'" (117). Likewise, George Bailey decidedly becomes a case in *It's a Wonderful Life*. He is the case that Clarence is assigned, a hard case at that. But George's case—understood as the sum of his circumstances, his situation—is also that which Clarence comes to enter into sympathetically, as his interested questions about George during the scene in the luggage shop make clear: "Tell me, did he ever . . ."[9]

It might be worth adding, though one never knows quite what to make of such an uncanny detail, that in the frozen frame about which Clarence is asking these questions, George has been caught in the act of stretching out his hands to measure the size of the case he wishes to make his own.[10] Moreover, in the window behind George Bailey, we can read "suit cases," as two words, an unusual spelling even in 1946.[11] But whatever we decide about this possible flagging of the topos, I hope these preliminary remarks prepare for the following efforts to retrace the story, back to mid-eighteenth-century Britain, when the sentimentalization of the case in the medium of print first establishes the basic parameters of a new literary mode.

Sentiment as a Structure of Feeling

It has long struck me as peculiar that Raymond Williams, our great political philologist of British culture and society in the *longue durée*, did not include "sentiment" or "sentimental" in his encyclopedia of keywords. This omission is especially odd because the period of the sentimental's emergence is the same one that often proves decisive in his historical semantics and because one of the conceptual payoffs of his work in historical lexicography was, after all, the notion of "structures of feeling."[12] Traditional philological work on the emergence of the term "sentimental" traces it to the late 1740s, though digital resources show that the adjective appears in English as early as 1743 in the phrase "sentimental soul"; such resources also show a recurring conjunction between "soul" and "sentiment" throughout the century. Phrases such as "sentimental novel" or "sentimental history," however, do not start to appear in English book titles until the mid-1750s, when the term was entering a rapid phase of development. In the British Library, the first book title to contain the word "sentimental" is *Reflections on Sentimental Differences in Points of Faith* (1752), an exercise in religious syncretism aimed at bringing persons of learning and reason closer in respect to their religious sentiments. The adjective form here, in other words, pertains to the older sense of "sentiment" (as doctrinal opinion), whose genealogy has been traced, for example, by Isabel Rivers. Yet already by 1754, in *The Friends: A Sentimental History*, the adjective form is being used in a new sense, one pertaining to a new mode of writing and feeling ("a higher Finishing of Language, and more Delicacy of Sentiment").[13]

Perhaps the appearance of those sentiments culled from Richardson's *Clarissa* for the popular third edition of the novel in 1751 helped to shift the discourse, as had Richardson's massive cultural intervention in this novel and its predecessor, *Pamela*. Perhaps the "collections of toasts and sentiments" that start to proliferate at this time played a part. There is no doubt, however, that from the 1750s the word "sentimental" was routinely associated with a new way of producing narrative, nor that Sterne's *Sentimental Journey* established the term and the mode on a lasting footing in 1768. Jean-Claude Gorjy's Sternean effort, *Le nouveau voyage sentimental* (1784), was just one of many books so titled in France.[14]

Is it possible, beyond claims about greater finish or delicacy of style, to say what the literary sentimental was in the first years of its emergence? Any such effort must allow that, early and late, the history of the term is marked by some semantic uncertainty. In 1812, decades after the term's coinage, *Barclay's Dictionary* could still begin an entry this way: "*Sentimental*: a[dj.], a word lately introduced into common use, but without any precise meaning."[15] And yet these decades also witnessed at least one serious attempt to engage philosophically with the problem, perhaps indeed the best analysis we have of it, Schiller's treatise *On Naïve and Sentimental Poetry* (1795). Even more than Kant, whose contemporary philosophical work was so deeply engaged with British writers like Burke and David Hume, Schiller had long been engaged with British literary and intellectual precedents. As a playwright he emulated Shakespeare, and as a critic he was able to write so well about the sentimental because he understood the British literary history from which it emerged.[16] Taking Schiller as a guide, one can find not only a degree of coherence in the articulation of the sentimental mode in eighteenth-century literature, but also a means of understanding certain features of its later survival and yet later reanimation in cinema.

Moreover, and critically, we also find, in Schiller's treatise, an account of the sentimental that should warn us off of some misconceptions or distortions of what it is and does. In a key section that I take as a kind of starting point for my analysis here, Schiller astutely zeros in on a complex affect that distinguishes the sentimental from the relative homogeneity he finds in the naïve mode. He argues that where the naïve poet might produce a "diversity of impression" (*verschiedene Eindruck*), this diversity nonetheless "rests solely upon the different *degree* of one and the same manner of feeling."[17] Not so with the sentimental poet, who inspires "mixed feeling," and who is always involved with "two conflicting images and feelings" (*zwei streitenden Vorstellungen und Empfindungen*).[18] Further, "the mixed feeling will always testify to this two fold source."[19] Even before we try to sort out just how the mixture of feelings relates to the conflict of representations or perceptions, it should be clear that Schiller's formulation can already be said to challenge what has become a widespread conception of the sentimental, one that would reduce it to mere simplicity or sincerity. For Schiller, quite to the contrary, the sentimental is a mode that is defined by its complexity and impurity.

We can gain perhaps a quick intimation of Schiller's sense of things in the nearly contemporary work of William Wordsworth, a poet decidedly sentimental rather than naïve, in Schiller's terms. Three years after Schiller's treatise was published, Wordsworth would travel to Germany with his Germanophile friend Samuel Taylor Coleridge. Before going, he made a return trip to Tintern Abbey, which he had visited five years earlier. He would famously take a respite from his walking tour on a bank above the River Wye, coming to rest in a spot deictically referenced as "here, under this dark sycamore," from which he could survey the surrounding landscape. The precision of his description, however, is disturbed by the recollection of what his senses registered on the earlier visit. The poet explicitly confronts his disturbed experience of two perceptions of the scene, one taking shape in his senses, the other in his memory. The double image is unmistakably associated with mixed emotions, pleasure and sadness: "The picture of the mind revives again," he wrote, "with pleasing thoughts," but also with "somewhat of a sad perplexity."[20] The resulting poem, "Lines Written a Few Miles above Tintern Abbey," came to be seen as a benchmark in English literary history. Reading the poem in relation to Schiller's treatise, one might call it a distinctively self-conscious—and self-consciously modern—verse reflection that works through both its redoubled mental image and its associated ambivalence in finding poetic resolution. One might call it sentimental.

"Tintern Abbey" has also been called protocinematic by at least one commentator.[21] But for a fuller illustration of Schiller's initial points about the sentimental, and ultimately about how they might relate to its later development and adaptation, I look not to Wordsworth but to Laurence Sterne, who was far more likely to have been in Schiller's sights. Sterne was still very much a part of Schiller's mid-1790s world. In correspondence between Schiller and Goethe in 1797, Sterne's fiction, especially the *Empfindsame Reise*, figures explicitly, by name, when they discuss Schiller's notion of the sentimental as worked out in the 1795 *Poetry* essay, a kind of follow-up, writes Goethe, "to what you yourself developed so well [in writing about the sentimental] and what is a part of our vocabulary."[22]

I wish to consider in some detail one of the most famous of all episodes in Sterne, indeed one of the most celebrated episodes in eighteenth-century sentimental culture. It is the fictional encounter with Maria of Moulines in the Normandy countryside, as narrated in the ninth and last volume of *Tristram Shandy*. The final volumes of *Tristram Shandy* overlap with *Sentimental Journey* both in the time of composition and in their way of troping on the theme of sympathetic travel: they find Tristram on the road in Continental Europe, where Yorick, in the sequel, will follow in his footsteps. The Seven Years' War was raging during the composition of the first volumes of *Tristram Shandy* (1759–1764). After the 1763 Treaty of Paris, it became easier to travel again in France. Sterne traveled to Toulouse late in that year, and he embarked on his great tour—from Calais to Italy and back—in 1765. The post-tour final volumes further complicate an already complicated notion of "progress" by adding a third dimension to Tristram's autobiography of his early years, which at this point has become preoccupied with the Widow Wadman's amorous advances and with the progress of his own narration. All three, of course, are notoriously vexed and halting, not least because of their self-conscious interconnection.

With respect to the travel narrative, we follow Tristram from his arrival in Calais, through his descent to Paris by way of Amiens, then down to Lyon and Avignon, to Narbonne and Toulouse. The encounter with Maria takes place in Normandy on the way back to England. The tour, together with his distinctively reflexive way of writing about it, gave Sterne the idea for the sequel book, *A Sentimental Journey through France and Italy*. Indeed, Parson Yorick, a central character in *Tristram Shandy* and the narrator of *Sentimental Journey*, recalls the Maria episode in *Tristram Shandy* as a prelude to telling about his own sought-for encounter with her in the later book. Together, these passages were among the most frequently anthologized of Sterne's vignettes. They appeared in many volumes promising a digest of "The Beauties of Sterne," and provoked many illustrations over the coming decades, including two remarkable paintings executed by Joseph Wright of Derby.

Maria of Moulines is a shepherdess who has half lost her senses on account of a wedding that never took place, having been blocked by a vindictive curate. She now sits by the roadside, in a somewhat disheveled state, playing the same melody over and again on her wooden flute. The episode unfolds in stages, and its denouement comes with the only words that are spoken between Tristram and Maria during their brief face-to-face encounter. The visual description of Maria is quite straightforward:

> We had got up by this time almost to the bank where Maria was sitting: she was in a thin white jacket with her hair, all but two tresses, drawn up into a silk net, with a few olive leaves twisted a little fantastically on one side——she was beautiful; and if ever I felt the full force of an honest heart-ache, it was the moment I saw her——
>
> ——God help her! poor damsel! above a hundred masses, said the postillion, have been said in the several parish churches and convents around, for her,——but without effect; we have still hopes, as she is sensible for short intervals, that the Virgin at last will restore her to herself; but her parents, who know her best, are hopeless upon that score, and think her senses are lost for ever.
>
> As the postillion spoke this, MARIA made a cadence so melancholy, so tender and querulous, that I sprung out of the chaise to help her, and found myself sitting betwixt her and her goat before I relapsed from my enthusiasm.
>
> MARIA look'd wistfully for some time at me, and then at her goat—— and then at me——and then at her goat again, and so on, alternately—
>
> ——Well, Maria, said I softly——What resemblance do you find?[23]

One contemporary reviewer suggested that Sterne's "excellence lay in the PATHETIC,"[24] and this entire episode certainly qualifies for such a description. It is full of descriptions calculated to move the feeling heart. Yet I want to insist that, here and elsewhere, his narrative turns on a kind of witticism. It is wit in the technical sense developed by studies of rhetoric popular in his own moment: it involves the yoking of two disparate images.

This proposal should not be surprising, since such forms of wit are Sterne's stock in trade. He likes nothing better than to launch a chapter, such as the one about the Widow Wadman's seductive gaze toward Uncle Toby, with a digression that assumes the following form: "An eye is for all the world exactly like a cannon, in this respect; That it is not so much the eye or the cannon, in themselves, as it is the carriage of the eye—and the carriage of the cannon, by which both the one and the other are enabled to do so much execution" (466). The passage conforms well enough to Dr. Johnson's definition of wit as "a combination of dissimilar images, or discovery of occult resemblances in things apparently unlike," and the issue of visual resemblance posed in Tristram's remark to Maria seems to belong to his recurring invocation of the tradition of wit.[25] Yet coming where it does, in a moment of tender pathos, Tristram's question ("what resemblance do you find?") suggests that wit and sentiment might be interlocking rather than antithetical modes.[26]

It is because of the persistence of wit in this episode—the mixture of representations—that the remark carries a sense of ambivalence. Though it is softly spoken, it nonetheless strikes an odd tone, establishes a peculiar mood or mode, in a way that Sterne does not want us to miss. For Tristram immediately registers his consciousness of the tonal oddity, and of the sense of ambivalence that seems to accompany it:

> I do intreat the candid reader to believe me, that it was from the humblest conviction of what a *Beast* man is,—that I ask'd the question; and that I would not have let fallen an unseasonable pleasantry in the venerable presence of Misery, to be entitled to all the wit that ever Rabelais scatter'd— and yet I own my heart smote me, and that I so smarted at the very idea of it, that I swore I would set up for Wisdom and utter grave sentences the rest of my days—and never—never attempt again to commit mirth with man, woman, or child, the longest day I had to live.
>
> As for writing nonsense to them—I believe, there was a reserve—but that I leave to the world. (523)

Tristram seeks to defend himself against the charge that his remark owes something to wit, and yet he also seems to acknowledge that his very impulse of self-defense implies a certain sense of culpability about his having lapsed into pleasantry with a person in so miserable a circumstance. His defense is that he meant only that man is a beast, but he seems to acknowledge that he has himself committed what the French postillion might have called a *bêtise*.

Like the episode with the Franciscan monk in *Sentimental Journey*, this seems to be the sort of self-conscious moment in Sterne that Thomas Jefferson singled out when he called Sterne the greatest moral writer of his time. On the one hand, Tristram's spontaneity and candor involve him in situations that bring him embarrassment and worse. As Sterne wrote to a friend about his approach to life: "When I mounted my hobby horse, I never thought, or pretended to think, where I was going."[27] On the other, what we might now call his emotional honesty enables him to acknowledge his errors as freely as he committed them, trusting in nature, as he went on to explain to his friend, which "has her own laws." These comments on his hobbyhorse are themselves reflections on his spontaneous movements. But there is something more particular to say about the matter in the Maria episode, for what is so undeniably peculiar about Tristram's acknowledgement of the *bêtise*, and of the mixed feelings that seem to have produced it, is that it reproduces pleasantry—as in *plaisanterie*—in the act of repentance for it. The apology compounds the offense. Tristram's account of his reaction to his sense of remorse is hyperbolic. He swears to "never attempt again to commit mirth with man, woman, or child"; the oath itself does seem faintly comic in its hyperbole. For evidence that he is not altogether in earnest, we need search no farther than the next sentence. The idea that a solemn oath, taken in a moment of remorse, might have a reserve clause such as one might find in an ordinary commercial contract is, clearly, a witticism.

Putting beyond doubt the centrality of performed ambivalence in this episode, Sterne closes the chapter with a final repetition of the pattern:

> Adieu, Maria!—adieu, poor hapless damsel!—some time, but not *now*, I may hear thy sorrows from thy own lips—but I was deceived; for that moment she took her pipe and told me such a tale of woe with it, that I rose up, and with broken and irregular steps walk'd softly to my chaise. —What an excellent inn at Moulins! (523)

The shift from Tristram's sadness about Maria to his relief about the inn is so abrupt that Sterne seems to be driving home a point about "mixed feelings," about the complex structure of pathos in his narrative ethics.[28]

To make matters still more complicated, the entire episode with Maria of Moulines is set within the narrative of Uncle Toby's amours in the most playful of possible arrangements. Earlier in volume 9, midway through the account of Uncle Toby and the Widow Wadman, Tristram had delivered up two blank chapters—chapters 18 and 19—presumably on the grounds that what had to be recounted in them was too difficult for the telling. After the account of the encounter with Maria, Tristram not only returns to the bawdy double entendres about "where" Uncle Toby received his war wound, but also produces the missing chapters, which, still numbered 18 and 19, take their places between chapters 25 and 26. And finally, of course, Tristram will go on from both the Maria episode and the story of Uncle Toby's amours to conclude book 9, and the novel (to the degree that it is concluded), with the coupling of Walter Shandy's bull and cow.

Schiller's Mixed Feelings

What then are we to make of Tristram's expression of remorse about a narrative indelicacy and his foreswearing of "mirth with man, woman, or child" in the context of the high hilarity in which the episode appears? If we return to Schiller, we find remarks that are quite helpful for thinking through the problems thus raised about this exemplary sentimental episode and helpful too in understanding the visual structure of literary sentimentalism. The explanation, according to Schiller, for the distinctive sense of "mixed feelings" in sentimental poetry (by contrast with the naïve) has to do with the defining practice of the sentimental poet: such a poet, he writes, "*reflects* [*reflektiert*; Schiller's emphasis] on the impression the objects make upon him, and only on the basis of that reflection is emotion founded, into which he is transported and into which he transports us" (*in die er selbst versetzt wird, und uns versetzt*).[29] The mixture of feelings is a function of the redoubled image, which in turn derives from the *reflexivity* of the generative process.

Schiller's comment resonates strikingly, I think, with the way in which Sterne has Tristram registering the significance of his comment and turning it over in his mind, pondering its implications for Maria and for himself. Schiller's claim is not, or not only, that reflection arises out of double perception and mixed feelings but rather, or also, that double perception and mixed feeling arise out of reflection. In Tristram's encounter with Maria of Moulines, for example, there is clearly a connection between the constellation of mixed feeling and double perception, on the one hand, and the act of reflection, on the other. But the connection does not seem to be unidirectional. Mixed feelings elicit reflection, but reflection also seems to elicit mixed feelings. Tristram's untimely question "reflects" on Maria's situation. Its ambivalence in turn provokes further reflection. Further reflection produces more mixed feelings, which elicit more reflection. Moreover, in light of the way the episode is contextualized among a series of self-consciously recursive and ambivalent narrations, Schiller's observations help to reveal the strong intimacy of the connection between reflexivity—the way a text redoubles itself—and mixed feelings. The most pointedly reflexive moments in Sterne's texts are moments where his ironies seem to be most unstable, the emotions in play most uncertain.

As we have already begun to see, however, in such a sprawling and notoriously self-obsessed work of fiction, a relatively simple act of reflection on Tristram's part proves to be part of a kind of hall of mirrors, a massive convolution of reflective performances and reflexive structures. That sense of recursivity is absolutely pervasive in Sterne, and is a widely acknowledged part of his cultural legacy. It was indeed captured brilliantly in the recent attempt to do what for a long time had been regarded as impossible—a film version of *Tristram Shandy*—where Michael Winterbottom's solution inevitably involved making a film about the making of a film version of *Tristram Shandy*. How then should we understand the relation between this generative "reflection" and the mixed feelings that for Schiller constitute the crucial symptom of the sentimental as a poetic mode?

To answer this question, we need to go back yet further in time, to the turn of the eighteenth century. For while Sterne nicely exemplifies the connection between reflection and emotional ambivalence, he was in large part following a set of practices and principles established for the modern era by the Earl of Shaftesbury, a writer who would himself be retrospectively saluted in the years of Sterne's celebrity as "the Head of the Sentimental school of philosophy."[30] Shaftesbury, a writer who was, like Sterne, known to Schiller,[31] classified the relevant set of practices and principles under the unusual heading of *soliloquy*, a distinctive kind of theater of self-discovery that he traces back to the earliest poets but sees reincarnated in the conventions of the Elizabethan stage—in *Hamlet*, no doubt, paradigmatically. He finds the injunction to soliloquy as far back as "that celebrated Delphic inscription, 'Recognize yourself!', which was as much as to say, 'Divide yourself!' or 'Be two!' For if the division were rightly made, all within would of course, they thought, be rightly understood and prudently managed. Such confidence they had in this home-dialect of soliloquy!"[32]

Shaftesbury's argument is long and circuitous, but central to my purposes here is the fact that he accounts for the workings of "soliloquy" with a recurring set of visual metaphors:

> We might here, therefore, as in a looking-glass, discover ourselves and see our minutest features nicely delineated and suited to our own apprehension and cognizance. . . . And—what was of singular note in these magical glasses—it would happen that, by constant and long inspection, the parties accustomed to the practice would acquire a peculiar speculative habit, so as virtually to carry about with them a sort of pocket-mirror, always ready and in use. In this, there were two faces which would naturally present themselves to our view. . . . Whatever we were employed in, whatever we set about, if once we had acquired the habit of this mirror, we should, by

virtue of the double reflection, distinguish ourselves into two different parties. And in this dramatic method, the work of self-inspection would proceed with admirable success. (87–88)

It is by way of these metaphors of redoubled personae, duplicated faces, and mirrored images that Shaftesbury elaborates his account of how we monitor our emotional lives through "self-discourse," and how we produce and negotiate mixed emotions through self-reflection. Shaftesbury's categories, in short, seem to provide in advance a key or legend for the sentimental corpus that Schiller analyzed in retrospect nearly a century later.[33]

Sterne, I maintain, navigated his sentimental travels according to some such scheme of reflection. Indeed, although we normally label *Tristram Shandy* a novel, and find ourselves well exercised to reconcile its performative and reflexive elements to the novel form, I suggest that we might do just as well to label it a Shaftesburyan soliloquy, one in which extended narrative elements have been introduced. As an episode such as the encounter with Maria of Moulines clearly shows, Tristram's is a discourse in which a dramatic process of acknowledging and correcting faults is central. Tristram's reflexive narration recurringly divides him into two parties, thus in effect repeating Sterne's own self-division, which arguably produced the character of Tristram Shandy in the first place. So when Tristram acknowledges the insensibility of his *petite bêtise* with Maria, he becomes two persons, the one who both poses the question and defends it, and the one who questions that defense, who "second guesses" that impulse. This latter is the one who swears never again to commit mirth with man, woman, or child, though the first Tristram resurfaces from that oath, with the joke about the reserve clause it contains. And so the soliloquy continues. We saw that same "dramatick method," and a similar "duplicity of soul," at the opening of *A Sentimental Journey*, in the episode where Yorick refuses alms to a poor mendicant and then, over the course of the ensuing pages, regrets his stinginess.

We saw as well that the alms episode was one of the passages singled out by an admiring Thomas Jefferson as exemplifying Sterne's reflective moral genius by showing how we are sorry for even a fictional rebuke and "view with emulation a soul candidly acknowledging its fault, and making a just reparation."[34] Might we not now speculate that the "soul," on such an account, is actually to a degree constituted by its capacity for this sort of reflection? For Sterne as for Shaftesbury, there is a moral hierarchy between the two selves involved in any moment of self-reflection, but for both writers, too, the process is ongoing. It may reach moments of temporary equilibrium, but these are indeed temporary. A "reflection" that seems to conclude one stage of an episode can be unsettled to launch the next stage, or even the next episode.

Sterne and the Sight Line

There is, however, a wider and perhaps deeper connection between Shaftesbury and Sterne, one that relates closely to the connection between mixed feeling and reflection, and that is of equal importance in the formation of the sentimental mode. To see it most clearly, it is perhaps helpful to return to Maria of Moulines and to look carefully at the way in which Sterne prepares for the tonally odd denouement that turns on Maria's ambiguous gesture and Tristram's ambivalent remark. The episode is introduced abruptly:

> ——For my uncle Toby's amours running all the way in my head, they had the same effect upon me as if they had been my own——I was in the most perfect state of bounty and good will; and felt the kindliest harmony vibrating within me, with every oscillation of the chaise alike; so that whether the roads were rough or smooth, it made no difference; every thing I saw, or had to do with, touch'd upon some secret spring either of sentiment or rapture.
>
> ——They were the sweetest notes I ever heard; and I instantly let down the fore-glass to hear them more distinctly—'Tis Maria; said the postillion, observing I was listening——Poor Maria, continued he, (leaning his body on one side to let me see her, for he was in a line betwixt us) is sitting upon a bank playing her vespers upon her pipe, with her little goat beside her.
>
> The young fellow utter'd this with an accent and a look so perfectly in tune to a feeling heart, that I instantly made a vow, I would give him a four-and-twenty sous piece, when I got to *Moulins*————And who is *poor Maria?* said I.
>
> The love and pity of all the villages around us; said the postillion——it is but three years ago, that the sun did not shine upon so fair, so quick-witted and amiable a maid; and better fate did *Maria* deserve, than to have her Banns forbid, by the intrigues of the curate of the parish who published them—He was going on, when Maria, who had made a short pause, put the pipe to her mouth and began the air again——they were the same notes;——yet were ten times sweeter: It is the evening service to the Virgin, said the young man——but who has taught her to play it—or how she came by her pipe, no one knows; we think that Heaven has

assisted her in both; for ever since she has been unsettled in her mind, it seems her only consolation——she has never once had the pipe out of her hand, but plays that *service* upon it almost night and day.

The postillion delivered this with so much discretion and natural eloquence, that I could not help decyphering something in his face above his condition, and should have sifted out his history, had not poor *Maria's* taken such full possession of me. (521–22)

We can observe, first of all, that Tristram is initially engaged with Maria of Moulines by the sound of her flute. We may therefore take it that this is, in the first instance, an aesthetic experience for him. He is prepared for this experience, to be sure, by the mood in which he finds himself after his involvement in the narration of Uncle Toby's amours. He is prepared in such a way that whatever he encounters will touch a secret spring of either sentiment or rapture. The relation between sentiment and rapture will be important in the encounter that follows, and this relation itself will be aesthetically constituted.

The initial oscillation between the sound of Maria's flute and the sound of the postillion's account of it provides a kind of model of the larger encounter. The postillion describes the source of the music to Tristram, but, though Tristram in some sense obviously registers the meaning of his words, he is taken with the *accent* and *look* that accompanies the postillion's utterance, how they are "*in tune with* a feeling heart" (my emphasis). So taken is Tristram, indeed, with the sense of attunement between the expression of pathos (look and accent) and the organ of pathos (a feeling heart) that he vows recompense for the postillion. It is true that Tristram inquires about the identity of Maria and that in response the postillion launches into the telling of her history. But the postillion has scarcely completed the first sentence of this story when Maria plays the pipe again, and this time the music strikes Tristram as "ten times sweeter." Again the postillion attempts to tell Maria's story, but the coach has been advancing during this exchange, and they have closed the distance to the place where the shepherdess sits playing. It is when she plays the flute a third time, with a cadence so moving, so transporting, that Tristram, in his "enthusiasm," is actually transported out of his chaise and onto the bank where he will commit his *petite bêtise*.

It is almost as though Sterne framed the episode to illustrate the operation of the faculty on which Shaftesbury founds his entire project, the faculty of taste understood in its ethical dimension. One might say that here in the first stage of the episode, before we reach the moment of Maria's oscillation of regard between Tristram and her goat, we are shown a more abstract kind of oscillation, one that moves between the aesthetic and the ethical. Ultimately, the instability inherent in this mixing of modes—or to put it more positively, its dynamic character—leads to the ambiguity and ambivalence with which the episode culminates. It is Tristram's sensibility that leads him on; he feels his way by taste. But in so proceeding, it turns out that he produces a response that does not feel right. It does not seem to accord with the occasion. Using Tristram's own language, we might say that his expression is not fully in tune with a sincere heart. It strikes a false note. To use terms I will come back to later, Tristram has failed to incorporate the melody played by Maria on her flute into a more complex harmony than the one he begins with. Of course, in so proceeding he also has the capacity to register this very fact: to register it in the sense of detecting the falseness of the note in the first place, and to register it in the sense of being able to acknowledge that he has struck such a note.

To see the close relation of the aesthetic and the ethical in this episode is to recognize that "sensing" is crucial to Tristram's modus operandi. It is to be reminded that we are indeed in the domain of empiricism, that the feeling in question is continuous with sensation, or with the "sensorium," to invoke the technical Latitudinarian term that Sterne will foreground when he writes the sequel of this episode for *Sentimental Journey*. It is crucial to understanding how this entire episode works, I believe, that it is triggered in the first place by a sensory impression—the sound of the flute. Moreover, the circumstances of Tristram's hearing the note are themselves precisely recorded. We know that Maria is not initially visible to Tristram. We know this because the postillion has to describe the source of the sound to him. We know also that, at the start, the chaise is close enough for the sound of the flute to reach Tristram with the window closed but not so close that he doesn't need to put the window down to hear it better.

This is another instance in which sound matters to the sensory dynamics of the episode.[35] For now I wish to stress, however, that the careful registering of the role of sense, sensation, and sensibility in the episode is most pointedly coded in Sterne's handling of visual clues. The visual unfolding of the chapter, indeed, is quite precise in showing the main stages of the episode. The details are few, but they are telling. Consider especially the emphasis on the line of sight, the apparently needless clarification on Tristram's part that, as he and the postillion approach Maria in the chaise, it is necessary for the postillion to lean to one side, "for he was in a line betwixt us."

The question on which I wish to linger here is simply this: Why this detail about the sight line? That is, why this spatial precision in the narrative? One reason for it is that it helps establish a key relation between stage one of the episode, in the chaise, and stage two, after Tristram has leapt from it to Maria's side on the bank. Geometrically considered, the movement of the postillion out of the line of sight creates a triangle, albeit a very obtuse one, out of the three characters involved. In the second stage of the episode, after Tristram suddenly places himself between Maria and her goat, a new obtuse triangle has been created, with new lines of sight. But the subject of this new triangle, at least projectively, is Maria, whose countenance betrays her oscillating, triangulating regard for both Tristram and her goat. Such details of internal spectatorship, I want to argue, emphasize the optical structure of the episode, and this structure intricately shapes our understanding of how reflection might be said to operate in it.

Stage one of the episode establishes Tristram as a spectator (one significantly located in a moving vehicle) and does so precisely enough to establish provisional lines of sight within a triangular drama. Stage two not only places him in a new triangle, with new sight lines, but also reverses the angle of vision. In her oscillating regard, Maria turns the spectator—Tristram himself—into a spectacle. Or at least he imagines himself a spectacle as seen from where she sits. One might say that the sense of embarrassment that Tristram experiences in this moment—the embarrassment that leads to his *bêtise*—is a result in part of this sense of sudden exposure, his having left the enclosure of his vehicle (after the initial, tentative opening of the window in response to the overture of Maria's musical performance) and launched himself onto the bank. In the auditory register, he becomes an element not in harmony with its setting.

Tristram's reversal of roles, from spectator to spectacle, is structurally crucial because it produces a kind of mirroring effect. Tristram, we might say, suddenly sees himself reflected in Maria's regard—reflected in his situation next to her goat. Further, this reversal of point of view, like the comparison that Tristram imagines Maria making in her oscillating gaze, creates a symmetry with the situation in stage one of the episode. For there, still in the chaise, Tristram has both Maria and the postillion in his field of vision (once the latter shifts position). In this earlier instance, it is Tristram who seems to be making the implicit comparisons between the two figures, Maria and the postillion. Tristram says that the postillion's manner of expression had interested him so much that he "should have sifted out his history, had not poor Maria's taken such full possession of me." Once on the bank, however, Tristram imagines himself the *object* of a comparative reflection.[36]

Understanding the development of the episode in this way enriches our sense of how the sentimental mode structures reflection, and, for that matter, how, as in the Schillerian account, reflection relates to mixture. Here what is seen from one spectator's point of view is mingled with a perception on the part of another spectator of the situation from which that first perception is registered. These issues of spectacle and spectatorship are not developed in Schiller's account, but they are very much a part of the Shaftesburyan transformation in moral discourse to which Schiller seems to be pointing us. Shaftesbury is quite explicit in his own deployment of the language of spectator and spectatorship when he discusses the practice of soliloquy in *Characteristics of Men*. Indeed, as for both Shaftesbury and Sterne, the kind of spectatorship in question has the structure of a double redoubling. An author (or poet) turns on himself to become a spectator to his own person, and in so doing he makes it possible to create a work in which others see themselves reflected as in a "vocal mirror."[37]

There are, however, important differences between what Shaftesbury calls for in "Advice to an Author" and what Sterne the author performs in the text of *Tristram Shandy*, especially when it comes to "the world." Two in particular should be noted here. The first is that Shaftesbury quite explicitly opposes the staging of soliloquy in a work destined for publication: "I hold it very indecent for anyone to publish his meditations, occasional reflections, solitary thoughts, or other such exercises as come under the notion of this self-discoursing practice." Authors who persist in such acts of publication defeat the point of the process and do not achieve a true self-discourse: "though they are often retired, they are never by themselves. The world is ever of the party. They have their author-character in view, and are always considering how much this or that thought would serve to complete some set of contemplations, or furnish out the commonplace Book from whence these treasured riches are to flow in plenty on the necessitous world."[38] On these terms, *Tristram Shandy* could be criticized as being what Shaftesbury calls a public "crudity." In the Maria episode, for example, Tristram clearly betrays self-consciousness about the reader's view of his remark to her. Indeed, in the novel's very first paragraph, Tristram says that the inattention of his mother and father to the circumstances of his conception was important because, "Had they duly weighed and considered all this, and proceeded accordingly,—I am verily persuaded I should have made a quite different figure in the world, from that in which the reader is likely to see me." Tristram, like Sterne behind him, is aware of his figure in the world in a way Shaftesbury disapproves of.[39]

This distinction is not trivial, but a second distinction is more telling and more germane to the later history of the sentimental mode. Sterne not only performs for the world in his fiction; he also, we might say, makes a world out of it. In a novel like *Tristram Shandy*, Shaftesbury's mental theater becomes, as we have seen, a time-space construction with its own forms of duration (the time it takes Tristram to roll up to the place where Maria is sitting), its own quasi-empirical points of view and relays of "sight lines." That this temporal-spatial construction is a scene of soliloquizing and "reflection" does not mean that it fails to make a world. This world is precisely that of the Sternean chronotope. To make this world, Sterne developed Shaftesburyan forms of theatricality and spectatorship in the direction of both increased reflexivity and increased ambivalence, much as Schiller would register in his essay of 1795. In Sterne's texts, moreover, the "drama" is played out at all times on at least three related levels. First, there is the level of the narrative diegesis, the action of the story the narrator happens to be telling (e.g., the story of Tristram's birth, or of Uncle Toby's amours). Then, there is the level of the drama of the telling itself, understood in relation to the narrator's "actual" narrative situation. And finally, there is the drama of the narration contextualized in the Sternean narrator's virtual or rhetorical situation. The passage (cited above) that leads in to the episode with Maria of Moulines, like the opening pages of *Sentimental Journey*, offers a good example both of how these three levels can be distinguished and of how they work together.

What we find in late Sterne, then, is a new sense of the spectator in eighteenth-century culture, a textualized spectator defined by the capacity to produce an affecting reflection both on/of himself and on/of the world of everyday affairs. This notion of spectatorship is absolutely crucial to the establishment of the literary mode that came to be called sentimental, one that would, much later, be reanimated in the classical system of film narration. In the passage from Shaftesburyan soliloquy to the sentimental chronotope in *Tristram Shandy*, there are three influential developments that I wish now to single out for special attention. The first, associated with Richard Steele and his partner Joseph Addison, is the emphasis on the literary spectator in the public eye. The second, associated with Samuel Richardson, is the transformation of fictional techniques for the rendering of time and space from empirically detailed points of view. The third, associated with Adam Smith, is the extension of the post-Shaftesbury Hutchesonian school of moral sentiments to produce the figure of the impartial spectator. There has been good work over the years on all three of these issues, and I draw on it liberally in bringing them together to sketch the formation of what I call the sentimental case.

Three Steps from Shaftesbury to Sterne

As to the first development, the emphasis on the literary spectator in the public eye, the two key works are, first, the series of papers inaugurated by Addison and Steele under the title of *The Spectator* and, second, *The Conscious Lovers*, the revolutionary comedy that Steele published in 1722, to which I will return in chapter 6. *The Spectator* was a daily column of reflections that was launched, as it happens, in the very year when Shaftesbury collected his published works for the omnibus publication he titled *Characteristicks* (1711). Mr. Spectator himself is an anonymous figure: we are informed in the very first paper that he must remain without name, age, or address. Yet he does give the reader sufficient account of his "History and Character," as he puts it, "to let him see I am not altogether unqualified for the Business I have undertaken." He goes on to explain his motivation for the undertaking:

> When I consider how much I have seen, read, and heard, I begin to blame my own Taciturnity; and since I have neither Time nor Inclination to communicate the Fulness of my Heart in Speech, I am resolved to do it in Writing; and to Print my self out, if possible, before I Die. I have been often told by my Friends that it is Pity so many useful Discoveries which I have made, should be in the Possession of a Silent Man. For this Reason therefore, I shall publish a Sheet full of Thoughts every Morning, for the Benefit of my Contemporaries.[40]

What Mr. Spectator takes in includes both the evidence of his senses and the erudition that comes with reading. But what he gives back is all by way of writing and, crucially, printing. His form of "ex-pression," printing out, is shaped in the active medium of the press itself. Conversely, Mr. Spectator seeks a public that is committed to the kind of reflective reading that will appreciate his transformative work: to wit, his mediation of the input of his senses by acts of writing and publishing. Already by *Spectator* no. 4, on March 5, he is reporting that he has begun to "listen after his own fame" in order to learn how he fares in the world. He is disquieted, he says, by the incapacities of some readers: "These are Mortals who have a certain Curiosity without Power of Reflection, and perused my Papers like Spectators rather than Readers." The public's proper response to the "printing out" of Mr. Spectator, in other words, is that they must engage him with their "Power of Reflection." In thus "ex-pressing himself," unburdening his full heart in his papers, Mr. Spectator renders himself a figure at once public and literary. In taking him in, his readers must become virtual spectators in their turn. They must thereby become reflective in those several senses of the word that become important to the later history of sentimentalism.

David Marshall and Jean-Christophe Agnew argued some time ago, to persuasive effect, that the figure of the literary spectator in the eighteenth century is an internalization of the theatrical spectator of the seventeenth century.[41] There has been some controversy about this claim.[42] It should certainly not be taken to imply that actual theater disappears in the eighteenth century. That is far from the case. Yet one can see in one of the century's most frequently produced plays, *The Conscious Lovers* (1722), by Richard Steele himself, that the sentimental turn in literary spectatorship is being worked out even before the term "sentimental" is coined. And it certainly left its mark in media archaeology. Though published a quarter century before the term came into currency, Steele's play has long been called the first sentimental comedy. His transformative contribution to the theater was to recenter it on *literary* principles, and he made it a point to explain in the preface to *Conscious Lovers* that the way to save British theater from its own barbarity, and above all from the barbarity of its audiences, was to insure that more plays be encountered in their printed format. Conversely, he sought to bring more readers into the theater, so that their habits of deliberation, contemplation, and sobriety could reform the carnal and licentious atmosphere of a space too accustomed to the verbal cruelty and physical vengeance of the Restoration stage. Steele, then, refigured the spectator in this distinctive conjuncture of new-mode journalism and new-mode theater.[43]

A second major step in the evolution of the literary spectator from Shaftesbury to Sterne is to be found in some key developments in new-mode fiction, especially the British novel in the run-up to its recognition in midcentury as a "new species of writing" in the world. These developments included the emergence of a commitment in practice to two apparently opposed goals for fiction. The first is to enable readers to imagine the perceptual and affective field of characters understood to be embodied in time and space, an exercise that depends on giving the sensorium of a fictional character a local habitation, embedding the sensibility in a world. Since characters move and change, this habitation must be mobile. When we track Tristram rolling down the road toward his encounter with Maria of Moulines, or Scrooge walking down the road with the first spirit toward his encounter with his former self in the schoolhouse, we are looking at later examples of that kind of mobility. The picaresque characters of the early eighteenth-century novel, from Defoe's Moll Flanders to Fielding's Tom Jones, mark an increasing sense of a sensibility moving in time and space. A second goal of the emerging novel, at least in one of its strands, is precisely to make this particularized and mobile sensorium virtual, so that a given character's world becomes imaginable by someone else—imaginable, that is, both by us, in the position of spectatorial reader, and (here is the familiar structure of sentimental triangulation) by another character in a text.

The point may seem overly familiar to readers of Ian Watt's celebrated *Rise of the Novel* and the myriad commentaries that it has spawned. And indeed there is something of what Watt calls "formal realism" about the point that I am making. My contention here has also been anticipated in the critical writings about the general problem of point of view or focalization in fiction.[44] But Cynthia Wall gets closer to the more specific issue in her account of changing descriptive practices in eighteenth-century fiction, especially in her discussion of the "implied spaces" of eighteenth-century novels. She rightly zeroes in on some developments that can demonstrably be traced in the rapidly evolving, and culturally changing, fictional practice of Samuel Richardson in the 1740s.

Identifying Richardson as the novelist who most enriches the detailed articulation of spaces that remain merely implied, Wall finds even in the small span of time between *Pamela* (1740) and *Clarissa* (1748–1749), those two massively influential novels, a shift that becomes telling for the emergence of sentimental forms over the next few decades: "Where the spaces and details of *Pamela* follow the patterns set up by Bunyan, Behn, Haywood, Defoe, and other early novelists, those in *Clarissa* are made into something else entirely."[45] In the terms that I have been suggesting from the outset, it is a shift in which the point of view of a character like Clarissa becomes more and more embodied in the fictional world, more embedded in literary space.

Wall proves her point in part by calling attention to what Clarissa can*not* see: "She is forced to spend much of her time deducing the spatial patterns of events beyond her own field of vision primarily because she spends much of the novel being locked up in one place or another."[46] The sensorium in question, of course, also necessarily includes nonvisual elements. Indeed, these become a crucial part of the embedded psyche's operations in Wall's account: Clarissa's "imperfect apprehension of the spaces beyond her immediate boundaries" means that "she needs to interpret motives, events, and possibilities by deciphering the *sounds* coming out of those spaces." And here, tellingly, Wall cites Sterne to reinforce her point: "Both Clarissa and the reader always have, in Tristram's words, 'a vivid sense of location—whether in rooms, on staircases, in passages, or as forming the containment of the house.'"[47]

It is part of my argument here that Sterne learned much of his sense of location from the influential spatializing practices developed in Richardson's novels. One perhaps already, with *Pamela*, has more of a glimpse of this new practice than Wall allows, in moments such as when Pamela hears Mr. B's carriage arrive before she looks out the window to see it, and more generally in her contingent relation to her environment.[48] But certainly *Clarissa* represents an important technical advance in fictional realism, and it coincides quite precisely, as it happens, with the early circulation of the word "sentimental" to name a new narrative mode. Together, Richardson and Sterne, with their massive international reputations, established the features of this mode as it goes forward through Dickens and indeed the classical cinema of Griffith and Capra. Wall goes on to add that *all* of the characters in *Clarissa* function in relation to the implied spaces of her account. These spaces "are positionally dependent on Clarissa's; everyone else is as acutely aware as she is of the boundaries, and their apparently central spaces are implicitly facing the banished center of Clarissa herself, wherever she is."[49] The point is a valid one, but it is also true that when these characters narrate, in the uneven turn-taking of an epistolary novel with so central a figure, they focalize the space in something like the way Clarissa does and show the capacity to identify with the spatial world she herself articulates on the page.[50]

This epistolary tradition seems especially central in how the sentimental mode develops techniques of vicariousness. One thinks here of Frances Burney, one of the most important novelists to write in English between Sterne and Jane Austen, and the way in which she embeds the sensibility of *Evelina's* titular character, as the latter writes ingenuously of her London experiences to her anxious guardian in the country. Consider the report of the Vauxhall Gardens exhibition, where Evelina is coerced into "the dark walks" of the gardens by her reckless female companions:

> Quite by compulsion, I followed them down a long alley, in which there was hardly any light.
> By the time we came near the end, a large party of gentlemen, apparently very riotous, and who were hallowing, leaning on one another, and laughing immoderately, seemed to rush suddenly from behind some trees, and meeting us face to face, put their arms at their sides, and formed a kind of circle, which first stopped our proceeding, and then our retreating, for we were presently encircled.[51]

Enriched by the technical specificities developed for the novel by Richardson and Sterne (among others), Evelina's account internalizes the spectatorial function of the many urban shows that she attends over the course of the novel. Looking back from the media culture of our own time, parts of *Eve-lina* read like an eighteenth-century first-person video game: "The Shows of London," or perhaps "The Moral Dangers of London."

We turn now to the third step in the formation of the figure of the literary spectator over the long eighteenth century. It would be left to Adam Smith, in effect, to take the notion of spectatorship implicit in the writings of Shaftesbury, Steele, and Richardson, and to develop all of this into a full-blown moral system in his *Theory of Moral Sentiments* (1759). It is here that Smith would elaborate his central concept of the "impartial spectator," a figure whom we have already encountered in "The Miser Convinced of His Error," from the first issue of the *Sentimental Magazine* in 1773. And if Smith shaped subsequent fiction, as surely he did, it is also true that his work was shaped by modern fiction like Richardson's in the first place, as he made a point of acknowledging.[52]

The Theory of Moral Sentiments offered philosophically elaborated notions of double reflection and double mirroring, both linked to a notion of sympathy, to which he gave a new and important twist. In the bargain, Smith would produce a critique of casuistry that suggested his sense of the social and historical dimensions of these issues. Though a follower, like Shaftesbury, of Cicero and Marcus Aurelius, Smith recast Shaftesbury's brand of Stoicism to produce a notion of social propriety that Shaftesbury would probably not have endorsed. True, it embraced some of the ideas implicit in Shaftesburyan soliloquy, but it relied extensively on a sense of "the world" and its view of one's conduct in a way that Shaftesbury pointedly wrote against.[53] Sterne learned something from Smith's theories, especially the way in which, as we have seen, the imagined view of an external spectator works its way recursively into the consciousness and conscience of the Sternean narrator.[54] Smith's treatise is, in fact, also a theory of moral spectatorship. It was one of the most influential books of its time, and I want to suggest that the sentimental mode in literary production—well into the age of Dickens—gains much intelligibility when it is viewed in terms both of Smith's reworking of his philosophical inheritance and Sterne's idiosyncratic performances of mental theater in the tradition of Shaftesburyan authorship. Even a brief examination of Smith's revisions to Shaftesbury's notion of soliloquy, by way of Hutcheson and Hume, can account for some of the differences we noted in the way reflective soliloquy is conceived between Shaftesbury and Sterne.

Especially important for Hume is the emphasis on "point of view" in the acts of reflection of which sentiments are composed. Humean sentiments, as Annette Baier reminds us, are not "raw feels" but rather what Hume calls "impressions of reflection."[55] In the theory of ideas that Hume and Smith alike inherited from Hutcheson, an *impression* (which is affective) leaves behind a (cognitive) trace or image of itself that Hume calls an *idea* (like the image of the candle that remains after the candle itself has been removed). These ideas can return to strike us again, in memory or imagination, to create second-order affective experience. *The impression of reflection* is Hume's term for this second-order phenomenon, so crucial to Hume's moral-sense analysis.[56] Gilles Deleuze goes so far as to argue that subjectivity itself, in Hume, is nothing other than an impression of reflection.[57]

Hume's friend Smith adds a second dimension to this account in *The Theory of Moral Sentiments*. Smith posited a deep human capacity, cultivated in the daily life of commercial civil society, both for functioning as a sympathetic spectator with regard to another person and for recognizing that, as an agent, one performs before a social world of (likewise) potentially sympathetic spectators. In developing Hume's account of sympathy from within the framework of the Hutchesonian theory of ideas, Smith also attended to Hume's comments on the importance of the "general point of view," as Hume most often called it, or alternatively what Hume called the "steady" or "common" point of view. On this basis he elaborated the innovative idea of the impartial spectator as an internal principle of general perception that is able to counteract our egotism (as the weak spirit of benevolence cannot) because it carries the force of recognition, the sense of truly seeing ourselves, for example, in our own littleness within the world.[58]

It is not such a big jump, I think, from the central ethical and aesthetic functions made possible by the redoubling mirrors of the self in Shaftesburyan soliloquy to the moral-sentiments function of the general point of view and impartial spectator in Smith. Though Smith neither employs the term "sentimental," nor concerns himself at length with the novel, his arguments about the processes of character formation by way of imaginary exchange of positions in modern commercial society are deeply congruent with early examples of sentimental fiction, especially with Richardson's highly particularized rendition of the alternation of epistolary viewpoints.

The Sentimental Case

The final pages of *The Theory of Moral Sentiments* are given over to an extended account of the argument's implications for the understanding of casuistry in the new commercial age. Smith insists that moral life is debilitated by the logic-chopping entailed in the niceties of putting hypothetical moral cases—by casuistry, as he himself calls it. Moreover, he argued, the Catholic church had perverted our basic human instinct for unburdening our minds to one another when it institutionalized the casuistical impulse under the priestly authoritarianism of auricular confession.[59]

Smith's ethics is explicitly opposed to this pernicious sort of casuistry, putting in its place the sympathy-driven moral mechanism of an expanding and circulating process of socialization. But to say that Smith's ethics is anti-casuistical in this sense is not to say that he dispenses altogether with the notion of the case.

To sympathize, Smith stipulates at the very start of his treatise, is not to feel what another person feels but rather to feel what we ourselves should feel in the same situation. It is to feel what it would be *like* to be that person. Smith repeatedly refers to this capacity as the ability to put ourselves in another person's *case*, to bring his or her case home to our own bosom. To do so is to create a point of view external to our own conduct and character, an action Smith metaphorizes, as Shaftesbury did, by way of the figure of the mirror:

> We begin, upon this account, to examine our own passions and conduct, and to consider how these must appear to them, by considering how they would appear to us if in their situation. We suppose ourselves the spectators of our own behaviour, and endeavour to imagine what effect it would, in this light, produce upon us. This is the only looking-glass by which we can, in some measure, with the eyes of other people, scrutinize the propriety of our own conduct.[60]

Smith's case is not, as in casuistry, the situation that one must ethically negotiate in respect to a set of rules, but simply the case in which one stands.[61] The casuists having been expelled from his philosophical house, the case form quietly returns, now understood as the specifiable description of a person's experiential situation—of what has befallen them. Smith enables his readers to conclude, however counterintuitively, that there is a "sentimental case."

Just as the early British novel is involved with early-modern casuistry, so the sentimental novel is connected to the sentimentalization of the case in the age of Smith and Sterne, a parallel to which I return in chapter 9. The key point for now is that the subgenre known as the sentimental journey, established by Sterne within a decade of the publication of *The Theory of Moral Sentiments*, is one in which the Smithian dynamic of sympathy with cases plays a constitutive role. The very conceit of the sentimental journey is premised on Smith's elaboration of the notion that sentiment necessarily involves a certain kind of mobility—the capacity to put oneself in the place of another—a mobility made possible by the sympathetic imagination itself. What Sterne does in the wake of Smith's account, as I've tried to suggest in my reading of Tristram Shandy's encounter with Maria of Moulines, is to dramatize a soliloquy in which one moves among different points of view in a landscape of shifting sight lines. This sort of activity characterizes the figure whom, in *Sentimental Journey*, Sterne labeled the "Sentimental Traveler," a figure for whom "moving" (shifting perspectives) and "being moved" (registering new feeling) amount to the same thing. The effect of this sort of sentimental sightseeing, as it were, is much as Schiller claimed: to blend feelings, to mix them by virtue of the juxtaposition (or superimposition) of, again in Schiller's words, "two different perceptions."

One could illustrate the impact of Sterne's Smithian contrivances in the work of Henry Mackenzie (Smith's friend and Sterne's early Scottish disciple), in Oliver Goldsmith's *The Vicar of Wakefield*, and indeed in a host of other writers over the next decades.[62] But none is more influential than Walter Scott, a Smith disciple who admired Sterne and dedicated the first of his globally influential Waverley novels to Mackenzie. *Waverley* brings the sentimental journey of Edward Waverley on both sides of the '45 Rebellion to a close with the execution of the rebel chieftain, Fergus MacIvor, under whom he had briefly served. In both the trial scene at Carlyle, and in the insistently sentimental resolution that follows, action is rendered as a relay of visual regard and space as a network of feeling. MacIvor exchanges glances with Edward at his sentencing, and is later led away. Here is Scott's rendering of the moment:

> The last of the soldiers had now disappeared from under the vaulted archway through which they had been filing for several minutes; the courtyard was now totally empty, but Waverley still stood there as if stupefied, his eyes fixed upon the dark pass where he had so lately seen the last glimpse of his friend;—at length, a female servant of the governor, struck with surprise and compassion at the stupefied misery which his countenance expressed, asked him, if he would not walk into her master's house and sit down?[63]

In this triangle of gazes—the servant of the governor who sentenced MacIvor to death responding to his countenance with sympathy—we have the makings of a process by which "horror" is softened to "melancholy" and then into yet more "soothing" emotions.[64] This is Scott's mediation of the violent conflict of his grandfather's generation, mixing feelings, as Sterne had done, by way of redoubled perception. The very action of this scene takes place in a medium of crossing viewpoints, a space of sentiment.[65]

Developed philosophically by Smith and fictionally by Sterne, Shaftesbury's practice of the mirroring soliloquy evolves into a newly articulated world of feeling and action. Schiller could not have anticipated the explorations of this model in the extraordinary explosion of world-making that was the nineteenth-century novel. Scott, massively influential as he was, represented only one of several directions in which nineteenth-century novelists would take this conception of fiction. His heir and rival, Dickens, would take things in his own direction, George Eliot and Joseph Conrad in others. But for all of them, the world of fiction is not the empty homogeneous field that Benedict Anderson associated with novels of this period. It is, rather, a medium that is itself defined by a field of virtual spectators and their "views," as we say—that is, by various lines of sight, some of them crossing, some of them matching, some of them reciprocated, some of them not. The dispersed subjectivity of such a field, structured in this way, contributes an important element to the literary sentimentalism that is to be reanimated in the classical system of narrative cinema. It is, however, only a part of the sentimentalist legacy to nineteenth-century fiction and to twentieth-century filmmaking.

FIVE

Sentimental Journeys,
Vehicular States

From eighteenth-century literature through twentieth-century cinema, the sentimental spectator proves to be a figure in motion. Able to assume multiple locations in narrative space, this figure is defined in no small part by its capacity to pass virtually into other points of view. This capacity to move and be moved—to move in and by being moved—depends on a kind of quickness that in the discourse of the sentimental comes to be called "sensibility." The concept of sensibility is nearly as crucial to this line of thought as is that of sentiment itself, and it affords an additional window of access on the developments we have been tracing. I now turn to an investigation of sentimental mobility by way of this notion of sensibility in its modern evolution, but also in the conceit that I contend it generated: the sentimental journey. Both this concept and this conceit have traceable and interconnected histories that have to do with what might be called the sentimentalization of the soul, an effort undertaken to save the soul, so to speak, from the perceived threats of early modern science. These histories involve the work of Sterne in ways that are absolutely crucial to how the sentimental mode takes recognizable shape and gets transmitted to cultural practitioners in many media. For many of them, sentiment and sensibility, or some variation on these terms, are as intimately connected as they are for Sterne.

In fiction, this intimate connection holds true for Lady Morgan's first novel, *The Wild Irish Girl*, and, in France, Germaine de Staël's first novel, *Delphine* (1803), as well as George Sand's first novel, *Indiana* (1829), whereas with the influential Irish tales of Morgan's rival and more sober contemporary, Maria Edgeworth, sentiment and sensibility tend to diverge. Edgeworth's first Continentally oriented novel, *Lenora* (1806), a rewriting of *Delphine* (1803), satirizes sensibility in behalf of something like moral sentiment. The best-known work in this vein, however, would come from Jane Austen, who learned much from Edgeworth. Austen would invidiously allegorize, and simultaneously complicate, these two tendencies in the Dashwood sisters, Elinor and Marianne, in her first published novel, *Sense and Sensibility* (1813). In the oversimplified account, Marianne's keen sensibility represents a quickness of taste uninformed by moral consideration; Elinor's good sense emphasizes the reflection of the moral-sentiment tradition, which is not to suppose, as Marianne sometimes does, that Elinor lacks sensibility. My interest here is in that line of work for which sentiment and sensibility tend to be imbricated rather than opposed. It will be the purpose of this chapter to explore this imbrication by way of the overlapping tropes of moving and being moved in the long eighteenth century and beyond. To frame the discussion in relation to the larger issues of this book, I return again to Capra and his reworking of Dickens.

The theme of travel is so pervasive in *It's a Wonderful Life* that it can almost escape notice. George Bailey is obsessed with travel, and the issue comes up repeatedly during the biographical minifilm that is screened in heaven to familiarize Clarence with George's case: young George (called Captain Cook by Uncle Billy) boasts of his membership in the National Geographic Society; he later intends to cross the ocean on a cattle boat to see places like "Italy and Baghdad, Samarkand . . ."; he is downright insulting to Mary Hatch when he tells her he has no intention of staying in Bedford Falls; even Potter recognizes George's wanderlust and appeals to it when he tries to recruit him. The logic of the film suggests that if George is to be happy in Bedford Falls, he must somehow internalize or sublimate the urge to journey to the far corners of the earth. And this is exactly what he does. He translates his desire for actual travel into a kind of virtual travel, a mobility of spirit that allows him to pass sympathetically into the point of view of those he encounters in everyday life. We have already seen a number of examples of this sort of capacity—this sensibility—on George's part. When Clarence gives George the chance to witness what Bedford Falls would look like if he had never lived, we can see an extension of this kind of sublimated travel. For George's journey represents a sublimation of the globe-trotting adventure he always wanted to undertake into a local exploration aimed at showing how the townspeople of Bedford Falls benefited from his sympathetic activities in their behalf.[1] One might say that the film reveals, by a journey in counterfactual history, what George's journey in spirit has amounted to.

Not surprisingly, the figure of the journey-in-spirit is already very much in play in Dickens's *Christmas Carol*, where it is connected with such key terms in the sentimental tradition as spirit, soul, sympathy, sentiment, and sensibility. This theme and these connections surface early, when Marley explains his circumstances to Scrooge and in so doing produces something like the converse of the principle that animates the plot of *It's a Wonderful Life*. In Dickens, the journey to the far corners of the world is the price paid for not sufficiently going forth in sympathy with one's fellow creatures:

> "It is required of every man," the Ghost returned, "that the spirit within him should walk abroad among his fellow-men, and travel far and wide; and if that spirit goes not forth in life, it is condemned to do so after death. It is doomed to wander through the world—oh, woe is me!—and witness what it cannot share, but might have shared on earth, and turned to happiness!"[2]

Recalling the famous opening of the tale, we will be cognizant of the narrator's emphasis that "Marley was dead." We are given this fact in several iterations even before the short first paragraph is concluded: "no doubt whatever about that"; the "register of his burial was signed by the clergyman, the clerk, the undertaker, and the chief mourner"; "dead as a door-nail" (45). The point of this repetition is to insist that Marley's visit to Scrooge could not be subjected to skepticism of the sort that St. Thomas expressed toward the risen Christ, that is, to emphasize that Marley's return to Scrooge involves nothing less than decisive evidence of a soul that survives a body.

At first, Scrooge has his doubts. His miserliness is part and parcel of a form of undialectical materialism. The ghost takes note of Scrooge's skepticism—"You don't believe in me"—and asks Scrooge "what evidence" he would have of the ghost's reality "beyond that of your senses." When Scrooge can't answer that question, the ghost of Marley asks why he doubts his senses in the first place. Scrooge's answer has a long history in skeptical empiricism:

> "Because," said Scrooge, "a little thing affects them. A slight disorder of the stomach makes them cheats. You may be an undigested bit of beef, a blot of mustard, a crumb of cheese, a fragment of an underdone potato. There's more of gravy than of grave about you, whatever you are!" (59)

Scrooge's effort to explain matters of the spirit by reducing spirit to matter is itself explained by the narrator as a failure of heart: "Scrooge was not much in the habit of cracking jokes, nor did he feel, in his heart, by any means waggish then. The truth is, that he tried to be smart, as a means of distracting his own attention, and keeping down his terror; for the spectre's voice disturbed the very marrow in his bones" (59–60). The episode signals a crux for the sentimental mode in the history of modern materialism, and it will be a principal aim of this chapter to investigate it.

Part of what explains this crux is the modern materialist argument, at least since Hobbes, that would reduce life to a principle of motion. Within the tradition that Dickens invokes, the soul itself is defined by a kind of motion or mobility: here it is the capacity of a "spirit within" to "travel far and wide" among our fellow human creatures. In Dickens's version of the tale, the soul that fails to go abroad in sympathy while on earth is condemned to do so after death: "My spirit never walked beyond our counting-house—mark me!—in life my spirit never roved beyond the narrow limits of our money-changing hole; and weary journeys lie before me!" (61). Travel in spirit must be undertaken one way or another, either voluntarily or involuntarily, in this world or the next.

As we shall see, the means of conveyance for such travel shares something of each world—the material world and the next one. But something of the sort is already hinted at within Dickens's tale, when Scrooge, whose materialism is matched by his literalism, attempts to deflect the force of Marley's account of himself:

"You must have been very slow about it, Jacob," Scrooge observed, in a business-like manner, though with humility and deference.

"Slow!" the Ghost repeated.

"Seven years dead," mused Scrooge. "And travelling all the time!"

"The whole time," said the Ghost. "No rest, no peace. Incessant torture of remorse."

"You travel fast?" said Scrooge.

"On the wings of the wind," replied the Ghost.

"You might have got over a great quantity of ground in seven years," said Scrooge.

The Ghost, on hearing this, set up another cry, and clanked its chain so hideously in the dead silence of the night, that the Ward would have been justified in indicting it for a nuisance. (61–62)

This rebuke again strikes fear into Scrooge's heart, in a way that leaves him chastened, more receptive to the visual admonitions to come. He becomes more sensitive, more "sensible" in the eighteenth-century sense of the term.

The conceit of the soul's journey is of course an ancient one, but the sentimental refurbishment of the conceit after the scientific revolutions of the seventeenth century couches it in the terms of sensibility, which is one of the areas of conspicuous malfunction in Scrooge's life. Both he and Bob Cratchit work in a space that, in winter, Scrooge keeps freezing cold, but only the clerk seems affected by this condition. We see Cratchit "put on his white comforter, and [try] to warm himself at the candle." But Scrooge simply does not feel: "External heat and cold had little influence on Scrooge. No warmth could warm, no wintry weather chill him. No wind that blew was bitterer than he, no falling snow was more intent upon its purpose, no pelting rain less open to entreaty. Foul weather didn't know where to have him" (46). In the curious legacy of Latitudinarian theology, sensibility is the essential quickness, the vital sensorium that supplies the soul's moving vehicle.

Sentiment and sympathy find themselves in a curious alignment, then, in both Dickens and Capra. Each of their now-familiar Christmas Eve narratives is structured by a subtle modulation from the emphasis on sympathy as passing into the point of view of another to the figure of the sentimental journey. For this modulation we can trace a partial origin, I will argue, in the notion of the "sentimental journey" as Sterne coined the phrase in 1768. Sterne's new and influential subgenre might be thought of as a sentimentalization of the picaresque. This transformed genre would have great sway in Western culture for many decades and across several media, none more palpably than cinema. The terms and tropes that constellate around Sterne's *Sentimental Journey*, I will show, derive from a semi-occulted discourse on the "sensorium" as the soul's quasi-immaterial earthly casing—its "vehicle"—and on the notion of the "vehicular state" as a condition in which the ideas of communication and transportation come almost to converge. In this tradition, the soul is gauged, one might say, by the measure of sensibility. A quick and receptive sensibility indicates largeness and robustness of soul—and vice versa. That is why George Bailey's father tells him that Mr. Potter's lack of human sympathy means that he is "sick in his soul, if he has one."[3] George's own largeness of soul, by contrast, is evidenced by his sensitivity to the emotional fragility of his father's own position, as it is in so many ways throughout the film. Scrooge's senses, we have seen, have become dead to the world. It is as if the two capacities—the capacity to sympathize and the capacity to experience sensation—were bound up in each other.

I propose, then, to explore the representation of motion and emotion within this subgenre, in which the figure of the affective "vehicle" becomes a crucially conceptualized trope. I sketch the discursive origins of the notion of the sentimental vehicle in the seventeenth century and, gesturally, its subsequent development in the nineteenth and twentieth centuries. If these disparate episodes belong to a single history, however discontinuous, it might be called the history of materialist affectivity, and its central questions might be put thus: Once the vital principle of human beings begins to be explained in terms of matter and motion, how is the soul refitted for its role as the seat of the affections, and how is communication of these affections to be accomplished? How is the body's matter to be reanimated? And how might all this relate to the sentimental mode?

A Sentimental Sequel

Having launched the discussion in the previous chapter with the celebrated vignette about the encounter with Maria of Moulines in *Tristram Shandy*, I begin this one with its sequel in *Sentimental Journey*. Yorick makes clear that it is on his friend Tristram's recommendation that he makes a detour on his Continental travels to see the forlorn shepherdess. Here again, as with its predecessor, it will serve our purposes best if we read the vignette backward—in this case from the ejaculation that serves as its coda. This is Yorick's paean to sensibility, one of the most frequently echoed passages of that age:

> —Dear sensibility! source inexhausted of all that's precious in our joys, or costly in our sorrows! thou chainest thy martyr down upon his bed of straw—and 'tis thou who lifts him up to HEAVEN—eternal fountain of our feelings!—'tis here I trace thee—and this is thy divinity which stirs within me—not, that in some sad and sickening moments, '*my soul shrinks back upon herself, and startles at destruction*'—mere pomp of words!—but that I feel some generous joys and generous cares beyond myself—all comes from thee, great—great SENSORIUM of the world! which vibrates, if a hair of our heads but falls upon the ground, in the remotest desert of thy creation.[4]

Yorick's terms usefully mark the place of this book in the discursive history of sentiment, since he not only employs the term "sensibility," but also renames it with the more technical phrase: "sensorium of the world." Yet there is a certain tension between Yorick's two implied elaborations of the sensibility at the heart of the sentimental. On the one hand, the term "sensorium" is associated with the materialist theory of "vibration," articulated famously by David Hartley some years before, though it belongs to a genealogy that even then reached back almost a century. On the other hand, Yorick associates the center and source of feeling with a transcendent and spiritual order of things, the "eternal fountain of our feelings."

In addition to this tension, the passage registers a problem between language and the feelings it references, especially in its dismissal of Addison's famous line about the soul shrinking back in on itself as "mere pomp of words." Such tensions are already latent in the narrative of the encounter that elicits Yorick's outburst. For while the vignette is itself rendered in words, it consists of a mostly wordless exchange in a face-to-face setting. As in its counterpart in *Tristram Shandy*, this is a vignette in which "looks" carry much of the communicative burden, but it takes a turn that was not anticipated in Tristram's account:

> She was dress'd in white, and much as my friend [Tristram] described her, except that her hair hung loose, which before was twisted within a silk net.—She had, superadded likewise to her jacket, a pale green ribband which fell across her shoulder to the waist; at the end of which hung her pipe.—Her goat had been as faithless as her lover; and she had got a little dog in lieu of him, which she had kept tied by a string to her girdle; as I look'd at her dog, she drew him towards her with the string.—'Thou shalt not leave me, Sylvio,' said she. I look'd in Maria's eyes, and saw she was thinking more of her father than of her lover or her little goat; for as she utter'd them the tears trickled down her cheeks.
>
> I sat down close by her; and Maria let me wipe them away as they fell with my handkerchief.—I then steep'd it in my own—and then in hers—and then in mine—and then I wiped hers again—and as I did it, I felt such indescribable emotions within me, as I am sure could not be accounted for from any combinations of matter and motion.
>
> I am positive I have a soul; nor can all the books with which the materialists have pester'd the world ever convince me of the contrary. (95)

The context of materialism and its challenge to the existence of the soul is invoked with a disarming explicitness that I want to take very seriously.

It is not new with Sterne in the history of rhetoric to suggest that words may not be adequate to the expression of emotion. But there is something more here than the familiar *occupatio* of, say, the lover's declaration. Sterne has given us a *sequence* of word-affection relations. Yorick's starting point in this episode is itself, we must recall, an encounter with the words of *Tris-*

tram Shandy, Tristram's simple description of Maria: "she was in a thin white jacket with her hair, all but two tresses, drawn up into a silk net, with a few olive leaves twisted a little fantastically on one side—she was beautiful" (522). Yorick's description is introduced as a modification of Tristram's: "much as my friend described her, except. . . ." Overall, the action of this vignette is a passage from what can be both described and redescribed—the figure of Maria—to what cannot be described at all: the emotions generated by the encounter. How, one might ask, do we pass from the redescribable picture to the indescribable feelings?

The initial move away from the redescription of Maria is the production of a story, rendered in indirect discourse, that updates the story from the final pages of *Tristram Shandy*: the goat that, in Tristram's account, with comic pathos, stood in for the absent lover has now itself been replaced by a dog. This move is followed by a shift to the passage's brief example of direct discourse (words representing themselves): Maria's command to her dog. We next move to the expression of thought by a medium other than words: it is Maria's eyes that, when "look'd in," tell Yorick what Maria is thinking of, though it is not quite clear on the face of it (as it were) how he claims to know this. Finally, there is the mutual expression of emotion without resort either to words, or to "looks," or to thoughts. This is arguably the culminating moment of pathos in all of *A Sentimental Journey*: the sharing of the handkerchief for the wiping of tears, an act that seems to occasion new tears as quickly as it absorbs the old.

Roughly speaking, then, the passage can be said to dramatize a shift from mimesis to metonymy in its mode of signifying affective states. Representational signs—description, narrative, and looks (looks that betray thoughts of some object or other)—all give way to the radical affective metonymy of the tear-soaked handkerchief. The handkerchief, we might say, becomes the material medium of emotion in this passage. At this point, however, the narrative takes a curious turn. For just at the point when the material handkerchief assumes the burden of conveying emotion, of mediating affect, Yorick becomes clear about the meaning of the scene. For him, the passage from the description/redescription of Maria to the "undescribable emotion" elicited by the handkerchief that absorbs both his and Maria's tears evidently leads to two declarations of certainty. He is certain that the "undescribable" emotions he felt at that time "could not be accounted for from any combination of matter and motion." And despite the arguments of the materialists, he is certain that he has a soul. But just *how* this passage is supposed to have led to these conclusions is not immediately clear.

The best way to interpret this sequence and its relation to these conclusions, I suggest, is to concentrate on the three parallel gradations: from verbalized emotion to nonverbal tokens, from iconic or symbolic signs to indexical signs, and from the immaterial to the material. The commingling of tears in the shared handkerchief comes at the end of a continuum that includes these other ways of signifying emotion. And yet, at each step of the way, right down to the very palpable tear-soaked handkerchief, the distinction between the emotion and its means of conveyance is maintained. Emotion does not *reduce* to a question of matter and motion, nor does soul to body. Sensibility—the sensorium—might depend on physical vibrations, as Hartley had recently argued, but the feeling that is generated is nonetheless of another order of being.[5]

As I have already hinted, there is a deeper history within which to understand Sterne's remarks about the inexplicability of feelings by reference to matter and motion, and the irreducibility of soul to body. Before I turn to it, though, I want to suggest that something else is at stake in Sterne's concern with motion and emotion. Sterne dismisses as "mere pomp of words" the idea that the response of sensibility could be captured in the exclamation of Addison's Cato: *my soul shrinks back upon herself.* He insists instead that the sensorium that vibrates at the remote fall of "a hair of our heads" affords us the capacity to feel *beyond* ourselves. It is our means of "transportation." The whole paean to sensibility expresses, indeed, what can only be described as a state of transport.[6] The passage is a reflection on what it means to be *moved*, and how this being moved is to be understood in relation to the sympathetic movement of going beyond ourselves.

The Novelty of Sterne's Vehicle

Here we come to one of Sterne's most influential innovations—his invention of the sentimental journey as something that would prove to be a more or less distinct subgenre—one that he refashions out of the tradition of the picaresque. The invocation of this tradition by way of Cervantes, perhaps already intimated in the muffled allusion to the windmills of "Moulines," is signaled more unequivocally as Yorick begins to introduce the episode:

> Just heaven![7]—it would fill up twenty volumes—and alas! I have but a few small pages left of this to croud it into—and half of these must be taken up with the poor Maria my friend, Mr. Shandy, met with near Moulines.
> The story he had told of that disorder'd maid affect'd me not a little in

the reading; but when I got within the neighbourhood where she lived, it returned so strong into my mind, that I could not resist an impulse which prompted me to go half a league out of the road to the village where her parents dwelt to enquire after her.

'Tis going, I own, like the Knight of the Woeful Countenance, in quest of melancholy adventures—but I know not how it is, but I am never so perfectly conscious of the existence of a soul within me, as when I am entangled in them. (94)

Much of the work of Sterne's refashioning of the picaresque novel is achieved in his recasting of the picaro's travels into the discourse of sensibility, the "sensorium," and the soul. Crucial to Sterne's project were the complex dynamics of sympathy—newly theorized by the moral-sense philosophers over the decades leading to the 1760s, and culminating in Smith's landmark treatise on the moral sentiments of 1759, the very year in which Sterne commenced the multiyear serial publication of *Tristram Shandy*. In the figure of the sentimental journey in particular, Sterne found a conceit in which he could figure the practice of sympathy as a kind of imaginative mobility—the capacity, as Smith had described it, of passing into points of view not one's own. Although the conceit of the sentimental journey came to be banalized in the twentieth century as traveling to places consecrated by sentiment—the trip down memory lane, as we say—it was, for Sterne, something far more complex. It was a paradoxical play between, on the one hand, the virtual representation of sentiments occasioned by actual travel and, on the other, the actual exercise of virtual travel *in* sentiment. Like Quixote, that most famous of picaros (but unlike Quixote's picaresque predecessors), Yorick's itinerary is guided by affection. His movements respond to his being moved, and they express his capacity to go beyond himself.

Part of Sterne's great genius—and his special brand of sentimental wit—was to create a textual exercise where these two dimensions could not finally be told apart. In *A Sentimental Journey*, it is not only the "characters" but also the literal and figurative modes of mimesis that are constantly changing places. Understanding this better allows us to dig deeper into the book's presiding ambiguities about "order," *ordonnance*, and causality.[8] Traditional rhetoric, as I have noted, enables us to identify this pattern as hypallage, the technical term for the trope of switching causal positions, but it is no critical imposition to speak of it in the context of Sterne's fiction, for his own Walter Shandy defines hypallage for a puzzled Uncle Toby, in vehicular terms, as putting "the cart before the horse."[9]

I will return to these questions in the next chapter's account of the emergent mode of sentimental probability in Sterne and his contemporaries. The point to be stressed here is how Sterne plays with the relation between motion and emotion, between moving and being moved. Much of the brilliance of the book lies in the way Sterne develops the twin themes of travel and affection by means of a single vocabulary, one resonant with paronomasia. Central to this vocabulary is the elusive figure of the vehicle, to which we are alerted in the curious "preface" that appears, not before the first of the book's several dozen short vignettes, but rather as the seventh of these, coming after those that tell of his reason for traveling, his arrival in Calais, and his disconcerting encounter with a Franciscan mendicant to whom he refuses alms. In this preface, Sterne's narrator, Parson Yorick, offers his taxonomy of travelers, which includes "Inquisitive Travellers," "Vain Travellers," and the "Simple Traveller" and eventually arrives at the category of the "Sentimental Traveller." Yorick expresses concern that since both his "travels and [his] observations will be altogether of a different cast from any of [his] fore-runners," he "might have insisted upon a whole nitch entirely to [himself]" (10). He renounces any claim to exclusive rights to the category, however, for fear that he "should break in upon the confines of the *Vain* Traveller, in wishing to draw attention towards me, till I have some better grounds for it, than the mere *Novelty of my Vehicle*" (10).

The phrase is a puzzle, and commentators tend to bypass it altogether. At some level, we might be warranted in suggesting that the novelty of Yorick's vehicle has to do with the "sentimental journey" itself as a new form of narrative conveyance. Like most such questions in Sterne, however, things prove both more ambiguous and more complicated on a closer look. The full title of this preface-that-is-not-a-preface is "Preface: In the Desobligeant." In the preceding chapter-vignette we learn that, having just arrived in Calais, and having already committed the offense against good manners with the Franciscan mendicant, Yorick is in the market for what he calls a "chaise"—"there being no travelling through France and Italy without [one]" (7). What is described next provides the immediate segue to the "preface" that appears as the next chapter-vignette:

> Nature generally prompting us to the thing we are fittest for, I walk'd out into the coach yard to buy or hire something of that kind to my purpose: an old Desobligeant in the furthest corner of the court, hit my fancy at first sight, so I instantly got into it, and finding it in tolerable harmony with my feelings, I ordered the waiter to call Monsieur Dessein the master

of the hôtel—but Monsieur Dessein being gone to vespers, and not caring to face the Franciscan whom I saw on the opposite side of the court, in conference with a lady just arrived, at the inn—I drew the taffeta curtain betwixt us, and being determined to write my journey, I took out my pen and ink, and wrote the preface to it in the *Desobligeant*. (7–8)

It is characteristic of Sterne's sentimental wit that the preface that locates Yorick as sentimental traveler in his own taxonomy, expressing concern that he should have some greater claim to originality in this area than "the novelty of [his] vehicle," is itself, in this account, written in a stationary vehicle in a courtyard.

We can note that this particular *chaise* seems at first to literalize the meaning of the French term *chaise*, making the carriage a mere chair, and yet even here the sentimental paronomasia is not allowed to come to rest. For, after despairing of the analysis and taxonomy of kinds of travels and travelers, Yorick goes on to raise a question as to whether one needs to travel in order to gain the benefits sought from travel, opining, "A man would act as wisely, if he could prevail upon himself, to live contented without foreign knowledge or foreign improvements, especially if he lives in a country that has no absolute want of either" (10). Such a nation, Yorick seems about to suggest, is England, a nation that sees itself as leading the way, in its own way, toward Enlightenment:

> It is an age so full of light, that there is scarce a country or corner of Europe whose beams are not crossed and interchanged with others—Knowledge in most of its branches, and in most affairs, is like music in an Italian street, whereof those may partake, who pay nothing—But there is no nation under heaven—and God is my record, (before whose tribunal I must one day come and give an account of this work)—that I do not speak it vauntingly—But there is no nation under heaven abounding with more variety of learning—where the sciences may be more fitly woo'd, or more surely won than here—where art is encouraged, and will so soon rise high—where Nature (take her all together) has so little to answer for—and, to close all, where there is more wit and variety of character to feed the mind with— (11)

It is at this moment that Yorick apostrophizes his presumably remote English readers with his admonition to stay in England—"Where then, my dear countrymen, are you going"—and to substitute virtual travel for actual travel. That is, Yorick seems to be encouraging his English compatriots to journey by way of reading a book, such as this one of Sterne's, even though its belated preface was ostensibly written in a "chair" as stationary as those in which such readers may be imagined to be sitting.

This apostrophe, sufficiently curious in itself, is then complemented by that curious interruption, in which the figure of the apostrophized reader is textually materialized: "Where then . . . are you going—" asks Yorick rhetorically. "We are only looking at this chaise, said they." The once apostrophic reader, now literalized as diegetic spectator, enters into a line of interrogation about the "occasion" of the chaise's "motion." And when Yorick replies coolly to the Englishman that it was only the "agitation . . . of writing a preface," more vehicular puns are put in play:

—I never heard, said the other, who was a *simple traveller*, of a preface wrote in a *Desobligeant*.—It would have been better, said I, in a *Vis a Vis*.
   —*As an English man does not travel to see English men,* I retired to my room. (11)

As if things were not already complicated enough, the second temporality introduced here—the metatemporality involved in writing about the moment of writing—is immediately folded back into the primary line of narrative when, in the subsequent chapter-vignette, Yorick picks up the narrative in a way that offers itself as continuous both with the preface *and* with the narrative it interrupted.

Thus, on his way back to his room, perceiving that "something darken'd the passage more than myself," Yorick meets the master of the hotel, Monsieur Dessein, who seeks to put Yorick "in mind of my wants," and Yorick reports at this point that he had "wrote myself pretty well out of conceit with the Desobligeant" (11). They nonetheless open the negotiations that set the reflexive strategy for the narrative going forward. Indeed, roughly the next dozen vignettes, several of which take place in the Remise (coach house), will concern Yorick's attempt at settling on or into a vehicle for his journey. Nor will the preface prove to be the last episode to involve events that take place in a stationary chaise. (Another will involve the woman, Mme de L***, Yorick had seen across the courtyard from the desobligeant.) In any case, this two-in-one sense of the narrative from the preface forward is accompanied by other novel effects, which it helps to inaugurate or highlight.

What are we to make of this literalization? Should we conclude that the novelty of the sentimental vehicle—however we understand the reference of that term—makes this kind of move possible? We have some sense from the Maria of Moulines episode in *Tristram Shandy* of what it means for Yorick to say that he entered the desobligeant only after finding it in "tolerable harmony with [his] feelings." But what does this peculiar sense of accord with his feelings have to do with the motion that his countrymen observe in the vehicle we had presumed to be unmoving? How is one to understand the agitation of the preface in relation to the motion of the vehicle? Is there something faintly masturbatory in the episode, especially in the suggestion that what was done in the desobligeant had been better done in a vis à vis? If these "countrymen" were, in effect, precipitated out of Sterne's apostrophe to his English readers, do they then stand for English readers? If so, what does it mean for them to be "looking at" the vehicle, and wondering about the occasion of its motion? Is the desobligeant to be understood as "disobliging"—that is, as an inhospitable or unsympathetic vehicle? How, in any event, should one interpret the contrast between the desobligeant and the vis à vis (or "face to face")? Face-to-face contact and the sympathy it generates are crucial to the emerging mid-eighteenth-century dynamics of the sentimental, as we have repeatedly seen.[10] Such celebrated episodes in *A Sentimental Journey* as the encounter with Maria of Moulines utterly depend on a face-to-face staging. What does it mean that writing the preface in the desobligeant has somehow brought Yorick "face to face" with English readers? The path to answering such puzzling questions takes us into some arcane territory in early modern intellectual history.

Travels of the Early-Modern Sensorium

I have been suggesting that there is a conjunction between Sterne's discussion of the sensorium in relation to "matter and motion," on the one hand, and, on the other, his transformation of the picaresque novel to create the new subgenre of the sentimental journey, with its paronomasia about vehicles and movement. As it happens, the term "sensorium" has a traceable history, one that is a part of a seventeenth-century debate about the soul, in which the term "vehicle" also played a central role: indeed, sensorium and vehicle appear in some texts as nearly interchangeable terms.

One of the key figures in intellectual history is Henry More, the leader of the group known as the Latitudinarians or Cambridge Platonists. More developed this vocabulary in his response to what he regarded as the mechanistic theses of Descartes, the materialist-mechanistic theses of Hobbes, and the materialist theses of Spinoza.[11] The *OED* traces the first use of the term "sensorium" to More's note for a poem he wrote during the revolutionary decade that Hobbes spanned with two major works: *De Cive* (1642) and *Leviathan* (1651). Here is More's 1647 comment: "For there is first a tactuall conjunction as it were of the representative rayes of every thing, with our sensorium before we know the things ourselves." In his prose writings of the 1650s, More redescribed his theory of the sensorium in nonmaterialist terms as part of his refutation of Hobbes and others. Hobbes's account, as his recent commentators confirm, "relied exclusively on the motions and contact actions of bodies for its explanations of all change."[12] More, however, like Ralph Cudworth and Joseph Glanvill after him, supplemented such mechanisms by adding incorporeal substances to explain things he thought mechanism alone could not explain. In particular, More "invoked individual souls, and the universal Spirit of Nature as the active principles required to drive the otherwise purely mechanical world."[13] More's concession to the new mechanistic materialism was the acknowledgment that, while the soul was distinct from the body, it was nonetheless housed or "carried" in a highly subtilized form of matter that registered perceptual vibration and effected locomotion: it was the human junction box, so to speak, between motion in and motion out. This subtilized body he called the soul's "vehicle," and he posited that this organ actually survived the death of the gross body. (The *OED* credits More's *Song of the Soul* not only with the first use of "sensorium" but also for the first use of "subtile" to refer to the state of the soul after death.) The vehicle is the soul's primary medium, her innermost casing, her second nature. "The soul," writes More, in language that would be cited by at least one later commentator, should be "consider'd as invested immediately with that tenuious [*sic*] matter which is her inward vehicle."[14]

Taken as a whole, the doctrine that More developed in his "refutations" of mechanist materialism came to be known as the "vehicular hypothesis." This issue, under this name, was debated into and through the eighteenth century. Consider Archibald Cockburn's 1722 *Essay Concerning the Intermediate State of Blessed Souls*, where the fifth "Enquiry" is couched in the following terms: "Whether souls, upon their separation from Terrestrial Bodies, transmigrate into a Subtiler Corporeality; . . . as the Vehicular Hypothesis represents." In eighteenth-century America, the views of More and the Cambridge Platonists helped to shape the new "science of the soul," worked out by Puritan divines eager, for example, to determine criteria for the successful conversion of Native Americans.[15] The controversy persisted through the period in which Sterne wrote. The great Joseph Priestley references the debate in the section "Of the Vehicle of the Soul" as late as his 1782 *Disquisitions Relating to Matter and Spirit*.[16]

Given the prominence of Sterne's position-taking on the debate about materialism, motion, and the soul—and given the centrality of his play with motion, emotion, and vehicularity—it becomes impossible not to conclude that this long discourse within the prehistory of the sentimental is part of the allusive context of some of the more puzzling moments in *A Sentimental Journey*. As we look at the unfolding of this discourse more carefully, however, we might be tempted to go further. We might speculate that the new subgenre inaugurated by Sterne's groundbreaking book was, in an important sense, actually *precipitated* out of the vehicular discourse.[17]

There are two developments in the century-and-a-half-long discussion of the vehicular state that can be especially helpful in seeing its relevance to Sterne's narrative invention: one elaborates the vehicular hypothesis in terms of transportation, the other in terms of communication. The first of these has to do with the reallegorization of the soul's vehicle in terms of a travel narrative with real-world forms of conveyance. We get an early suggestion of this in Margaret Cavendish's 1666 narrative of the travels of a duchess's soul in Nottinghamshire, where references to the vehicular state merge with references to "Horses of Manage":

> As they were thus discoursing, the Duke came out of the house into the court, to see his horses of manage; whom when the Duchess's soul perceived, she was so overjoyed, that her aerial vehicle became so splendorous, as if it had been enlightened by the sun; by which we may perceive, that the passions of souls or spirits can alter their bodily vehicles.[18]

This kind of conceit, already suggestive for Sterne's later innovation, is developed further in the great prose stylist Thomas Brown's 1690 satire of Dryden, which has the following exchange:

> *Eugenius:* There was a certain Country Gentleman, no matter for his Name, or where he lived, but he had read the *Sadducismus Triumphatus*, and was so mightily taken with Dr. *More*'s Notion of a Vehicle, that he could not rest, till he had bought him a Vehicle, call'd in *English* a Calash; so he eat and drank in his Vehicle, and slept in his Vehicle, and lay with his Wife in his Vehicle, and got an Heir Apparent upon her Virtuous body in his Vehicle; and Vehicle was his Name.
> *Bays:* And what of all this, prithee? Here's a Story with all my heart.
> *Crites:* Why, as foolish as it is, it shall serve for a Vehicle to another story, which is of a certain Tooth-drawer of my acquaintance, that lived in the *Strand.*[19]

Here we come close to the witty conceit and suggestive wordplay of the preface that Sterne has his Yorick writing in the desobligeant. But the full sentimentalization of the vehicular hypothesis would await another key publication in this tradition, also by a writer who recast this philosophical discourse into playful imaginative fiction: Abraham Tucker's *The Light of Nature Pursued* (1768). This text is one of the minor classics of eighteenth-century British moral philosophy by one of its more idiosyncratic practitioners. It was well known through the Romantic period. Hazlitt reprinted it in abridged form early in his own career (1807), and from time to time there have been critical efforts to urge attention to how Tucker's associationism influenced the great Romantic writers.[20]

The Light of Nature Pursued is a sprawling work, but the two chapters of special interest to us here are the relatively short chapter called "The Vehicular State" and the very long chapter called "A Vision." In the former, Tucker lays out the vehicular hypothesis in terms that become familiar to a reader of More and his line. It maintains the spirit/matter distinction, while conceding something to the mechanistic explanation of affect in terms of matter and motion. The spirit, after death, "does not go out naked, nor entirely disengaged from matter, but carries away with her an integument from among those wherewith she was before invested."[21]

It is in the longer, later chapter, however, that Tucker fully dramatizes the concept, producing an account of what happens when his narrator, Edward Search, has a "vision" in which he has actually entered into this state. After an initial period of confusion, Search begins to focus his perception sufficiently well to discover "a kind of sack or bag filled out like a bladder with air," with two arms and "a longish neck with a head upon it, having a meagre lank-jawed face," this curious being then introducing himself as John Locke![22] Locke welcomes Search into the vehicular state by teaching him the proper command of his new faculties, including the faculty of speech. But after some strenuous exercise along these lines, Locke tells Search about the true vernacular of the vehicular state:

> We have another language among us we call the Sentient, in distinction from the Vocal, wherein I have been speaking to you. This is carried on by applying our vehicles close to one another, and raising certain figures or motions on our outside, which communicate the like to our neighbour, and thereby excite in him the same ideas that gave rise to them in ourselves, making him, as it were, feel our thoughts.[23]

Though Search is unable to engage fully in the sentient language, his conversation with Locke is, in a sense, halfway there, in that Locke has already partly initiated him in it at the start of their exchange, when Search notices that Locke's face has no mouth:

> Nay, says he [Locke], do not stand staring me in the face, you will learn nothing there: look down upon my vehicle.—I did so, and observed little fibres bouncing up and down with great strength and agility in a kind of net-work, consisting of various shaped meshes. I can liken them to nothing so well as the little wrinkles continually changing their form in the skin on top of warm milk set in the window to cool, only they moved much quicker, and with more tremulous motion.[24]

Though this text, like the philosophical hypothesis it dramatized, remained semi-occulted through the eighteenth century, there is good evidence that it enjoyed some degree of circulation. Edward Search's preview of the afterlife might well be seen behind the not dissimilar experience of that better known E. S., Ebenezer Scrooge, but there are more explicit invocations to consider.

For example, the vehicular hypothesis makes an appearance in a sentimental novel of the 1790s, Mary Hays's *Memoirs of Emma Courtney*, a novelized account of Hays's brief affair with William Frend and her unrequited flirtation with William Godwin. Tucker's book is actually footnoted in the following interpolated letter from Emma Courtney, the Hays character, to Augustus Harley, the Frend character:

> "I wish we were in the vehicular state, and that you understood the sentient language; you might then comprehend the whole of what I mean to express, but find too delicate for *words*. But I do you injustice.
>
> "If the affections are, indeed, generated by sympathy, where the principles, pursuits, and habits, are congenial—where the *end*, sought to be attained, is—
>
> 'Something, than beauty dearer,'
>
> "You may, perhaps, agree with me, that it is *almost* indifferent on which side the sentiment originates."[25]

Bringing this home to Sterne's text, I want to suggest that Yorick and Maria of Moulines are represented as having entered the vehicular state, with something like a "sentient" wordless language established as their mode of communication, the handkerchief its vehicle.

But what of all those other vehicles in *Sentimental Journey*? What have they to do with handkerchiefs? My suggestion here is that the doctrine of sympathy, rapidly developing in the moral-sense school, made possible the narrative *merger* of the respective figurative languages for communication and transportation. As Yorick says, Addison's idea that the soul shrinks back when it is moved is a mere pomp of words. The soul, when moved, is moved "beyond" itself—it is moved elsewhere. Whatever transports the soul in such a manner—whether the movement be actual or virtual—becomes a vehicle, which likewise can be actual or virtual.

It is clear that, however puzzling it became to later readers, the language of vehicularity was immediately registered, though often without full comprehension, in the early sentimental tradition after Sterne. We saw earlier that for the first issue of the new *Sentimental Magazine* in 1773, very much in the wake of Sterne's death, a second series appeared alongside the one about the miser: "A Sentimental Journey through Life." Given the idiosyncrasy of Sterne's title, there can be little doubt that this is a derivative performance, and so perhaps it should be no more surprising that we find its highlighting of the vehicle conceit than that it features a man named Toby or a setting in Calais. In a subsection headed simply "The Vehicle," the narrator of this story suggests that we think of life by way of a new conceit: "The body is the vehicle, or *carriage* of the soul." Once we see that "our body resembles a coach, we may, without any violence, look on our lives as a journey."[26] This writer for the *Sentimental Magazine* clearly recognizes that the vehicular topos matters to the mode he wants to be working in but does not seem to know how it matters or even quite how it works! William Butler Yeats, who had a more than passing interest in Henry More, showed a keener appreciation of the figure of the soul's vehicle when he revived it a century and a half later. Citing More's authority, Yeats declared in *Mythologies* (1893) that the "vehicle of the human soul is what used to be called the animal spirits," and went on to explain that the "soul has a plastic power, and can, after death, or during life, should the vehicle leave the body for a while, mould it to any shape it will by an act of imagination."[27]

From the Literary to the Cinematic Vehicle

Most of Sterne's heirs, however, seem to take a more oblique route with the vehicular figure. The reflexivity of Wordsworth's walking topos at the start of *The Prelude* (making one's way into the landscape-in-prospect as metaphor for making one's way into the unwritten poem) recalls Sterne's recurring conceit of traveling as writerly progress. In Wordsworth, however, it is as though the sentimental traveler had dismounted from his novel vehicle, having abandoned the novel for the "real language of men."[28] Scott relied on the trope to define his distinctive mode of probability in *Waverley*—a novel he dedicated to the author of *The Man of Feeling*.[29] Dickens, as we have seen, made the metaphor of sympathetic travel central to the moral structure of *A Christmas Carol*, as when Marley tells Scrooge that he travels the earth in chains after his death because his spirit did not do so when he was alive.

Yet it is perhaps in *A Tale of Two Cities* that the vehicular conceit is given freest reign. The aptly named Mr. Lorry offers us perhaps Dickens's clearest personification of the sentimental vehicle. He is, of course, the good version of the British man of commerce, perhaps a little like what Scrooge will be when he fully emerges as no longer the man he was. And the kind of mediating emotional relay that Mr. Lorry enables throughout the book, beginning with his good offices toward Lucy Manette's unfortunate father in the opening section, is to be set (in a view of the French Revolution first explained by Edmund Burke) against the ominous vehicles that figure the extremes of the French. First, the coach of the French marquis, which kills a child under its wheels on a Paris street, before rolling on its way, and which requires a collective push from the local peasants (the "jacquerie") to make its way up a steep hill. And then its proletarian counterpart—the revolutionary tumbril, vehicle of the jacquerie itself. This vehicle is ominously glimpsed in the famous opening paragraphs about the "best of times" and the "worst of times": "It is likely enough that in the rough outhouses of some tillers of the heavy lands adjacent to Paris, there were sheltered from the weather that very day, rude carts, bespattered with rustic mire, snuffed about by pigs, and roosted in by poultry, which the Farmer, Death, had already set apart to be his tumbrils of the Revolution." The dark purposes of these vehicles, as adumbrated here, are fully revealed in the climactic final scene, when Sydney Carton, whom we may take as the embodiment of the sentimental principle of putting yourself in the place of the other, is wheeled to the guillotine in one of them.[30]

Using Dickens once again as a jumping-off point to early cinema, we can now note that the movement of the motion picture camera made it a particularly apt vehicle for representing sentimental vehicularity. As Tom Gunning has noted, one version of the "cinema of attraction" appeared in Hale's Tours, the largest theater chain before 1906 that exclusively exhibited films: not only did their films "consist in non-narrative sequences taken from moving vehicles (usually trains), but the theater itself was arranged as a train car, with a conductor who took tickets, and sound effects simulating the click-clack of wheels and the hiss of air brakes."[31] After the classical Hollywood system was established, D. W. Griffith took on board the Dickensian figure of the vehicle when he refashioned key elements from *Tale of Two Cities* as *Orphans of the Storm* (1921), which features the episode of the carriage of the French marquis running over a child in a Paris street. The tumbrils, of course, figure prominently in *Orphans* as well.

Capra, as usual, was attuned to the particular powers of the classical narrative system he inherited from Griffith and others. He was also a collector of the works of Sterne (though not as avid in this as with those of Dickens). It is a particularly uncanny fact that the last scene of Sterne's *Sentimental Journey* (immediately following the Maria of Moulines vignette) involves a rainy night, an awkwardly shared room at an inn, and an ingeniously contrived decorum-preserving barrier between two beds; all this strikingly anticipates the famous sequence of auto-camp scenes in Capra's *It Happened One Night* (1934), in which Clark Gable's character hangs a blanket between his own bed and that of the young, unmarried heiress played by Claudette Colbert.[32] Might we not regard this blanket as the vehicle of the (very age-of-sensibility) sentiments that the young lovers project upon it from their beds on either side? Can it be a coincidence, I wonder, that this film, taken from a short story entitled "Night Bus," focuses much of its recognizable action on events transpiring aboard the twentieth-century equivalent of the horse-drawn coach? Or that so many other kinds of vehicles—automobiles, airplanes, motorcycles, and, at the close, the one-person helicopter of Clark Gable's showy rival (a twentieth-century desobligeant?)—figure so prominently in the film?

A decade and a half after *It Happened One Night*, working in the subgenre of melodrama rather than screwball comedy, Max Ophüls would play variations on similar themes in *Letter from an Unknown Woman*, an adaptation of a 1922 Freudian short story by Stefan Zweig. One scene in particular is worth considering for its vehicular reflexivity. The entirety of Zweig's story takes the form of a letter written on her deathbed by Lisa Berndle, a woman seduced and abandoned by a Viennese novelist named Stefan Brand. Ophüls moves the action back to that Freudian year 1900, makes the novelist a concert pianist, and places the letter within a dramatic frame that begins and ends with carriages. At the start, a carriage deposits the debauched Brand at his apartment late one night, where he finds the letter whose content constitutes the film's central narrative. At the close, a carriage collects him to take him to a duel he had earlier planned to evade. The letter itself narrates the central line of events: Lisa's girlish infatuation with Brand, her deliberate placing of herself in his way to be seduced by him after a night at the Prater amusement park, their lovemaking, her pregnancy, her rescue by a Viennese military officer, her chance encounter with Brand not long before the writing of this letter, his failure to recognize her in the act of a second seduction, the death of her young son as a result of her recklessness, her final days.

Vehicles are important throughout the representation of the letter's story, not least that of Ophüls's famously vehicular camerawork, which involves a complex choreography with the movements of the actors. But what holds special interest for us here is arguably the central scene of the film—it occurs almost at the literal midpoint—which takes place during the fateful evening's entertainments at the Prater. Having taken a carriage to reach the park, and then been followed in their stroll through the Prater by an extended tracking shot, Brand takes Lisa into an amusement called a myorama, which consists in this case of a stationary rail carriage with different strips of scenery that can be rolled horizontally past the windows to suggest the effect of travel. The amusement is staffed by a ticket taker and a man in a conductor's outfit, who powers the movement of the scenery with a bicycle. Moments of departure and arrival (e.g., "Switzerland!") are punctuated with a conductor's whistle and announcements by the man on the bicycle.[33] It is hard not to think of this as a kind of metacinema that recalls the sorts of vehicular attractions also staged around the turn of the century at Hale's Tours.

In a kind of reflexive redundancy—perhaps reminiscent of our being introduced to Dickens's Mr. Lorry when he is riding in a vehicle—we learn, during the scene of virtual scene-changing in the stationary vehicle, that Lisa's knowledge of other places is merely virtual. What she "knows" of Rio de Janeiro does not come from having visited there. Hers is a form of travel that does not depend on moving, but rather on being moved. Her uncharacteristic emotional animation in these faux journeys, furthermore, seems to derive from the erotic attention she is receiving from Stefan and, by association, from the fond recollection of the attention she received from her father when he would don his travel coat on returning from work with travel brochures. It is an animation based, either way, in a kind of romanticism, in desire displaced as longing, its object remaining always elsewhere. Like her father, she is unable to reach the exotic locations of her fantasy, even virtually. There is always an alibi. The weather is not right. And he knows the weather everywhere but at home.

In a narrative whose titular theme is the failure of a woman to be known, this is the moment in her narrative when she most evidently seeks to make knowledge of herself available to Stefan. Moreover, this stationary vehicle is the only medium, as it were—apart from the letter that later narrates it—in which her normally regressive posture gives way to self-expression, in the

Ophüls, *Letter from an Unknown Woman* (1948, Universal).
Lisa and Stefan in the myorama at the Prater.

form of autobiographical explanation. (Here again, her voluble self-narration is matched only at the level of the letter's frame narration, and it is the only place, including the frame narration, in which she narrates her relation to her father, who does not, unlike her mother and stepfather, appear in the film in an embodied role.) The myorama sequence is also the moment when Stefan most *seems* interested in getting to know her, the moment when what Stanley Cavell calls "conversation" takes place.[34] All of this is summed up in a grammar of self-knowledge with Stefan's remark to the ticket taker after she tells him that there are no more places for them to go. He replies that they will see them all again, his throwaway line both explanation and alibi: "We're revisiting the scenes of our youth."

None of these vehicular moments are part of the Zweig story. Coming at this film through an interest in Sternean modernity, I incline to see in Ophüls's use of vehicles an index of sentimental reflection, a form of medium-self-consciousness, and this stationary vehicle—protocinematic as it is—as a way of suggesting the kind of reflective self-knowing that cinema itself can (and cannot) offer. In Zweig's novella, self-reflection is analyzed in terms derived from Freud. In Ophüls's adaptation, by contrast, cinema itself is made the medium of analysis in a way that challenges Freud in his own 1900 moment and his own Viennese backyard.[35]

The Affection-Image and the Movement-Image

The logic of the affective vehicle surfaces in surprising places. One of the most surprising, perhaps, is Gilles Deleuze's noted work on cinema from the mid-1980s.[36] Deleuze spent much of his career self-consciously championing a maverick materialist position in philosophy: by the time he wrote the cinema books, he had published individual studies of Spinoza, Hume, Nietzsche, and Bergson, and he had argued, furthermore, for their continuity. In Bergson's theories of memory, matter, and motion, Deleuze had found, in effect, the rearticulation of the seventeenth-century "sensorium," but without the Neo-Platonist overlay. And in the unfolding of twentieth-century cinema he found the incarnation of Bergson's own developing views: a sense of the human world as defined by the incoming motion of perception and the outgoing motion of action, with "affection" as the name for the interval of their transduction.

To put the matter schematically, Deleuze's mapping of cinema achieves a threefold transposition of Bergsonian philosophy into cinematic practice: first, it locates what Bergson calls the "perception image" in the work of framing shots (*cadrage*); second, it locates the Bergsonian "action image" in the work of assembling shots (*montage*); finally, it locates Bergson's "affection image" in the work of the close-up shot (*gros plan*)—the kind of shot that Jean Epstein, in a passage Deleuze himself cites, calls "the soul of cinema."[37] Taken together, these three compose the "movement-image" that is the changing whole (*le tout*) of film itself, a whole registered in the double movement internal to the shot: movement as a changing relation of the parts and movement as a mobile section of the whole. The connection of the "face" with the affection-image-as-close-up, and of both with the interval in which the movement of perception is translated into the movement of action, opens a fascinating path of speculation about the crucial place of the face in the languages of the sentimental—as evidenced, for example, in the sentimental *locus classicus* of Yorick's celebrated encounter with Maria of Moulines.

Consider briefly Deleuze's illustration of all this in Wim Wenders's *Kings of the Road* (1976), a film Deleuze had earlier cited in his discussion of "faciality" in *A Thousand Plateaus* (1980).[38] *Kings of the Road* is a picaresque narrative featuring two male protagonists on journeys that coincide for a time, one of whom, the driver of a large van, moves from town to town in West Germany repairing projection equipment in local theaters. In the cinema books, *Kings of the Road* becomes for Deleuze an illustration of how a director can dramatize the movement inherent in the shot by making fungible the movements that the camera registers and the movements that the camera itself undertakes. "What counts," says Deleuze, of the celebrated opening shot of F. W. Murnau's *The Last Laugh* or Orson Welles's *Touch of Evil*, "is that the mobile camera is like a *general equivalent* of all the means of locomotion that it shows or that it makes use of—aeroplane, car, boat, bicycle, foot, metro" (22). In *Kings of the Road*, this equivalence becomes for Deleuze the Epsteinian "soul" of the film and a principle of reflexivity. It becomes a way of "introducing into the cinema a particularly concrete reflection on the cinema" (23). This comment on Wenders leads Deleuze directly into a discussion of vehicularity:

> In other words, the essence of the cinematographic movement-image lies in extracting from vehicles or moving bodies the movement which is their common substance, or extracting from movements the mobility which is their essence. This was what Bergson wanted: beginning from the body or moving thing to which our natural perception attaches movement as if it were a vehicle, to extract a simple colored "spot," the movement-image, which "is reduced in itself to a series of extremely rapid oscillations" and "is in reality only a movement of movements." Now, because Bergson only considered what happened in the apparatus (the homogeneous abstract movement of the procession of images) he believed the cinema to be incapable of that which the apparatus is in fact most capable, eminently capable of: the movement-image—that is, pure movement extracted from bodies or moving things. This is not an abstraction, but an emancipation. (23)

"The shot is the movement-image" (22). This much Deleuze states explicitly at the start of his discussion of vehicularity. But the movement-image is "pure movement," understood as an extraction from the body or moving thing that our natural perception regards as a kind of vehicle. This emancipated, emancipating "essence" of movement is what, according to Deleuze, establishes the relationship of the parts of the framed set and expresses the changes of the film as an "open whole."

Understanding the shot in this way, the congruity of its relation to the affection-image that constitutes one of its aspects becomes a little easier to see. Both are forms of "planitude"—planar fields with two "poles" or sides.

We must recall here that the French word for shot and plane are the same: *plan*. (The "face," for Deleuze, is a plaque or "plate.") And both planes are metamovements—"movements of movements" in the phrase that Deleuze cites from Bergson. The fact that the affection-image is associated with an absence of locomotion becomes less significant when we understand that the movements in each case are actually metamovements to begin with. The resonance of this language with the discourse of the soul and the vehicle—the discourse from which the *sentimental journey* initially emerged as a form—seems to me too strong to ignore, especially in light of Deleuze's self-proclaimed, Bergson-derived materialist account of affectivity. Deleuze draws complex but highly suggestive parallels and connections among his key figures: as the close-up becomes, for Epstein, the "soul of cinema," so the relation of the moving camera and the moving object in Murnau becomes, for Wenders, the "soul" of a film.[39] As for the specific question of the "face" of sentiment in these contexts, I will have more to say in subsequent chapters.

In these last few pages, I've tried to invoke the long history of the sentimental not only as a way of explaining the congruence of the affection-image and the movement-image in the first of Deleuze's cinema books, but also as a way of showing the persistence of early-modern sentimentalism's conceptual repertoire in a key strand of film theory. The screen itself operates much as the face does, in that while it registers a translative movement it is not itself in motion. But I have also been concerned to give a similar account of those sites in the affection-image that Deleuze identifies as "any spaces whatever." The production of these sites on the plane of the movement-image threatens the work of the action-image, producing those forms of displacement Deleuze calls the *balade* and the *voyage*, labels that themselves bespeak a certain cultural archaism. My hope has been that the history of the translative vehicle and the sentimental journey might provide a sort of historical cartography for the difficult Deleuzean notion of deterritorialization.[40] Let me now close these speculations with a final reflection on another iconic moment in Capra.

Late in *It Happened One Night* we see the face of Peter Warne (Clark Gable) as he motors cheerfully down the road singing the faux-ballad "Young People in Love Are Never Hungry." Suddenly, he passes the convoy of cars bearing Ellen Andrews (Claudette Colbert) in the opposite direction, back to her father's custody, thus dashing his high spirits. His tire goes flat. The landscape is suddenly transformed—a cinematic passage that calls to mind the contrastive journeys in Browning's "Childe Roland to the Dark Tower Came." We are caught up in this face, its shifting intensities and reflections, even if the deflated tire of the old jalopy gives us a too obvious hint of allegory. We can perhaps deduce from the geography that Gable/Warne is on Route 1 between Philadelphia and New York—in other words, that he is in, well, New Jersey. Yet, within the Deleuzean logic of the sentimental journey, one would have to say that he could be in any space whatever.

six

The Emergence of
Sentimental Probability

Whether we are considering the virtuality of the spectator (as discussed in chapter 4) or the mobility of the sensible soul (as discussed in chapter 5), the centrality of sympathy in the sentimental mode poses special problems for plot and the representation of action. I have already hinted at some of these problems as they appear at different moments of my archaeology: in Sterne's narrative of the encounter with the Franciscan monk that begins *Sentimental Journey*, in Dickens's account of Scrooge's conversion, and in Capra's staging of the sudden resolution of the plot of *Mr. Smith Goes to Washington*. I have suggested that they belong to a new order of probability associated with sentimentalism, but I have not yet explained in detail what this suggestion might mean.

By "probability," in this context, I mean codes of expectation and understandings of chance, design, and causality, especially those implicit in literary and dramatic works. This is a concept that reaches back to Aristotle's *Poetics*, and it is implicit in Bakhtin's understanding of how fictional worlds are fashioned as so many varieties of chronotope. Arguments about probability in intellectual history or the history of science will be familiar enough to students of the early modern period. Probability in the sense I intend here is by no means identical with the subject of Ian Hacking's *The Emergence of Probability*, a book well known for its claim that probability achieved its distinctively modern mathematical form during the debates about casuistry among the Port-Royal Jansenists in 1662. Nor will I explore that prior development in any detail here.

In light of what I have called the new "sentimental case" in eighteenth-century Britain, however, the connection Hacking elaborates between probability and casuistry is suggestive indeed, for he argues that the statistical "case" was forged by the likes of Blaise Pascal in the fires of anti-Jesuit polemic and that that helped shape the modern notion of "opinion."[1] Since Adam Smith's theorization of the sentimental case was likewise worked out in an explicitly anti-Jesuitical frame of reference, I wish to suggest a certain parallel between Hacking's pivotal moment in seventeenth-century France and the new sentimental mode in eighteenth-century Britain. Building on an insight in Douglas Lane Patey's somewhat neglected critical study of such questions, I further speculate that the new sense of probability worked out in Sterne is at least partly a response, let's call it again Latitudinarian, to the new brand of probability achieved in the scientific revolutions of the century before.[2]

We see a transatlantic manifestation of immediately post-Sternean understandings of probability in William Hill Brown's aptly titled *The Power of Sympathy* (1790). This book is generally recognized as the "first American novel," and is in fact squarely and self-consciously in the sentimental tradition as mediated by Goethe, who so admired Sterne. *A Sentimental Journey* is extensively discussed in an early chapter (most pejoratively by the least estimable commentator), and the protagonist dies with a copy of *The Sorrows of Young Werther* at his side.[3] The very title of Brown's novel signals the new conception of moral dynamics. It seems to acknowledge "sympathy" as what one commentator calls "an essential force" to be reckoned with in the world of eighteenth-century fiction.[4] Such formulations lead us to a further challenging question: how does the new power of sympathy affect the representation of how and why things happen as they do? I address this question by way of the interrelated arguments I have so far made about the virtuality of sentimental spectatorship and the mobility of the sensible soul. Together they have implications for the kind of probabilistic issues I have already broached in my discussions of Sterne's fiction and Capra's cinema.

The sentimental notion that the soul takes shape in the social intercourse between persons means that we attain an identity for ourselves through exercises in vicariousness. We make ourselves the spectators to the actions we undertake by virtue of imagining those actions from a point of view not our own, and conversely, we enter sympathetically into the situations of other agents. In such an understanding of the world, questions of activity and passivity are never easy to decide. We move when we are moved, and we are moved when we move. Wordsworth, for example, would make much of the activity of passion and the passivity of action in explaining responses to his poetry.[5] The dynamic of the sympathetic exchange leaves it unclear who is doing what to whom, and sometimes even whether we can safely say there is a "who" to begin with.[6] We have also seen that sentimental spectatorship is structured in triangulated formations. That is, according to a scheme like Adam Smith's, the mental reflection that takes place in a face-to-face encounter can itself involve other encounters. We saw this in *A Christmas Carol* when, for example, the older Scrooge is brought face to face with a face-to-face encounter between his past self and his then-fiancée. In *It's a Wonderful Life* the levels proliferate: for example, Clarence's witnessing of the old bald man who looks on as George and Mary make innocent love around the hydrangea bush.

Such triangulated chains, as I have already begun to suggest, can be supposed to occur on a single plane of circulation, where we all reflect each other, or on an ascending scale of higher-order recognitions. Problems of causality and probability mark both the plane and the ascending moral scale. On this plane, again, the reciprocities of everyday life distribute feeling in such a way as to make it difficult to tell, as Sterne wrote of the vehicular state, "which party is the infecter." Distributed feeling poses a real problem for causal claims. On the ascending scale, by contrast, we find another problem, that the notion of reflection can be structured into higher and lower orders. This, we recall, is the principle that interested Thomas Jefferson in Sterne's moral project, the idea that we don't merely reflect but also reflect *on*. If the circulatory movement of sentimental reflection distributes feeling, this one seems to recollect it in a vertical order. What Hume called an *impression of reflection* belongs, on this view, to a second order of causality.

These two structures of reflection within the sentimental tend not to be clearly sorted, and some of what I have called, after Stuart Tave, a slipping of levels in the sentimental has to do with this fundamental unclarity. To complicate matters further, we find in the sentimental frequent playing with the diegetic frame: interference between the world of the represented action (the diegetic) and what lies outside its primary frame of representation (the extra-diegetic). We have an example of interference across the diegetic frame when Clarence the Angel reflects on George Bailey's face in the freeze-frame of the interpolated screening of George Bailey's life, or when Tristram Shandy reflects on the the reception of his own story in a way that modifies it. In such moments, the chains of reflection seem to extend even to ourselves as readers of Sterne's tale or viewers of Capra's film. Indeed, it is to our own capacities for reflection that such works make their ultimate appeal, quite explicitly at times, and this sense of practical engagement has consequences for how we might answer even a basic question like "what happens" in these works. It is also a part of the explanation for why such works do not confine themselves to the codes of realism but nonetheless make use of those codes. *A Christmas Carol* offers the stark panorama of contemporary urban poverty supplied by the Spirit of Christmas Present. *It's a Wonderful Life* gives us the grim dystopian vision of Potterville contrived by Clarence. The point we now need to address is how the shift between representational modes—the realist and the aspirational, first-order and second-order, circulatory and ascending—becomes an issue for the very movement of a plot, for how we get from beginning to end.

One symptom of this displacement of action by mediation, and vice versa, is the reliance on constitutive puns and double conceits, what I earlier described as sentimental wit. For often these are associated with causal issues. The vehicle is one such trope we have considered, and we return to it again in this chapter. Another, which specifically links *A Christmas Carol* and *It's a Wonderful Life*, is the play with the notions of saving and redemption.[7] But the more familiar feature is the ambiguity about levels produced by the crossing of narrative and rhetorical axes. We saw this with the denouement in *Mr. Smith Goes to Washington*, where Jefferson Smith seems, in the eleventh hour, to be saved by the shot/reverse-shot sequence that occurs in the medium of film itself. My contention will be that the form of probability subtending these kinds of plot developments emerges with eighteenth-century sentimentalism. I mean to analyze Sterne's seminal sentimental text of 1768 for a deeper sense of how the new probability structures a narrative mode. But I also mean to look at how probability in the sentimental novel bears on probability in eighteenth-century sentimental comic drama, especially in the line of Richard Steele.

Recognizing how literary narrative in the eighteenth century internalizes the conventions of the theater within the domain of a print public sphere, we will be able to see that the problem of probability in sentimental narrative has the structure it does at least partly because of its distinctive way of fusing national representation and national mediation. I will be describing this problem as a crossing of the mimetic and pragmatic axes of representation in the context of a national readership. In less schematic terms, I mean that probability arises as a problem when collective sentiment becomes the object of representation, in both senses of "object"—when writers aspire, that is, to move national sympathies in the act of depicting them. The formation of national sentiment depends crucially, I argue, on the cross-cutting causes and effects that come into play when writers in eighteenth-century "media culture" engage in the commerce of feeling.[8]

The Cart before the Horse

In the sixteenth chapter-vignette of *Sentimental Journey*, Sterne's Parson Yorick offers a thinly veiled satire on the travel literature of Tobias Smollett, whom he dubs the "learned SMELFUNGUS."[9] Yorick has already produced his taxonomy of travelers, and he now effectively identifies Smelfungus as a "Splenetic" traveler (9), one for whom even the most sublime objects encountered in a journey—the Pantheon or the Medici Venus—are "discoloured or distorted" (24). Smelfungus's narrative is no more than "the account of his miserable feelings":

> I popp'd upon Smelfungus again at Turin, in his return home; and a sad tale of sorrowful adventures had he to tell, "wherein he spoke of moving accidents by flood and field, and of the cannibals which each other eat: the Anthropophagi"—he had been flea'd alive, and bedevil'd, and used worse than St. Bartholomew, at every stage he had come at— . . . (24)

Yorick introduces the satire on Smelfungus as part of a comic justification for his Shandean nonprogress. Indeed, at this relatively advanced point in what is supposed to be an account of his progress across the Continent, Yorick has not only failed to get himself out of Calais—he has barely arrived there:

> Lord! said I, hearing the town clock strike four, and recollecting that I had been little more than a single hour in Calais—
> —What a large volume of adventures may be grasped within this little span of life by him who interests his heart in every thing, and who, having eyes to see, what time and chance are perpetually holding out to him as he journeyeth on his way, misses nothing he can *fairly* lay his hands on.— (23–24)

Sterne here precociously develops a notion that we tend to associate with a later moment, that of Wordsworthian Romanticism, and Wordsworth will later echo Sterne's echo of Othello in making the same point.[10] It is the idea that the heart that interests itself in every thing is the one that is able to dilate the everyday affairs of life by means of a sympathetic imagination. It has no need of sublimities or catastrophes to make it "leap" to seize passing opportunity.

We will have occasion to return, in chapter 8, to Wordworth's relation to Sterne, and to the Romantic tropes and topoi implicit in such a conception of narrative progress in relation to affect. In particular, we will be looking at Wordsworth's interest, in *Lyrical Ballads* and *The Prelude*, in challenging received expectations about certain relations of norm and fact. My point here, however, is that with both writers the issue of *narrative* movement (how the story goes from point A to point B) is closely related to that of *affective* movement (what a reader-spectator might be expected to feel about the story). Indeed, so closely are these two kinds of movement related that at times they seem to merge or change roles. Thus, one of Wordsworth's most famous formulations of his innovative understanding of narrative is a claim he makes for his poetic experiments in the 1800 preface to *Lyrical Ballads*: "the feeling therein developed gives importance to the action and situation, and not the action and situation to the feeling."[11] The reason why this relation of a story's motion and emotion is so complicated in Wordsworth, and why it is hard to identify the *site* wherein "the feeling" is "developed," is that his poetics is so thoroughly associationist in its principles. It means to show, he says, "the manner in which our feelings and ideas are associated in a state of excitement" as a way of helping to exemplify a sympathetic response "without the application of gross and violent stimulants"[12]—without, that is, "moving accidents." Wordsworth seems to suggest that the "accidents" of these poetic stories were *without* location, at large in a medium of associative affect and affective communication (even when they insist on a compensatory specificity: "There is a thorn . . ."). He is grappling with the displacement of action into medium.

Rhetorically considered, we have seen, this shift of emphasis in Wordsworth's poetry involves the extended sense of the trope known as hypallage, the trope of "exchange." In Greek poetics it referred to the practice of switching modifiers, but it was later broadened to suggest causal inversion. It is defined in the *OED*, for example, as "an interchange of two elements of a proposition, the natural relations of these being reversed." It becomes the trope of preposterousness, of explanatory ambiguity, and one apposite to a period that produced Hume's associationist critique of causal assumptions. We see a good example of such a reversal when, in a poem such as "The Thorn," we understand that the narrative gives us a map to the Old Sea Captain's affective psychology. Does the thorn tree appear so threatening to him because it is the place where something terrible has happened, or does he imagine that something terrible has happened there because it looks so terrible to him?

Sterne himself used the term, as Jonathan Lamb has shown, and already in an avowedly associationist context.[13] Though the question of hypallage has resonance throughout *Sentimental Journey*, the most explicit formulation of its relevance to Sterne's practice is to be found late in *Tristram Shandy*:

> As my father once told my uncle Toby upon the close of a long dissertation upon the subject——"You can scarce," said he, "combine two ideas together upon it, brother Toby, without an hypallage"——What's that? cried my uncle Toby.
>
> The cart before the horse, replied my father——
>
> ——And what has he to do there? cried my uncle Toby——
>
> Nothing, quoth my father, but to get in——or let it alone.
>
> Now widow Wadman, as I told you before, would do neither the one or the other.
>
> She stood however ready harnessed and caparisoned at all points to watch accidents.[14]

Lamb suggests that Walter actually produces an example of hypallage for Uncle Toby with his observation (apropos Toby's regard for the Widow Wadman) that love is "not so much a SENTIMENT as a SITUATION" (475).[15] This formula, interestingly, closely echoes the terms of Wordsworth's claim to novelty in the preface to *Lyrical Ballads*.

The point is not that Walter's proverb could stand as the moral to Wordsworth's poems. The point is rather that the grammatical opposition that structures it also structures them. Clearly, such distinctions as feeling/action, or sentiment/situation, were already undergoing a major transformation some decades before Wordsworth came forward with his claim to a bold new cultural initiative. These distinctions would be forever affected. William James—later heir to the associationist tradition, author of a book titled *The Sentiment of Rationality*, and a fan of Wordsworth—offered a celebrated hypallage, most apposite to the subject of the sentimental disposition. Against what he called the "common sense" view that we cry because we feel sorry, James asserted that "this order of sequence is incorrect" and that "the more rational statement is that we feel sorry because we cry."[16]

Moving Accidents

Since Sterne's *Sentimental Journey* had such a major impact not only on novel writing but also on magazine culture for more than a half century after its publication, it is worth looking more closely to see how questions of sentiment and situation—"movement" and "accident"—achieve such richness of implication in its pages. In fact, we need look no further than those opening chapter-vignettes, which tell of that first "hour" in Calais, and which focus primarily on Yorick's choice of a "vehicle" for his "sentimental journey," on his negotiation of various financial rituals, such as alms-giving and bargaining, and on his flirtation with Mme de L***. One immediate signal that these events are structured by metalepsis is that they involve an inscrutable character named Monsieur Dessein (French for "design") who is "master of the hotel." Although his name is no accident, almost every event in the sequence seems to occur by happenstance, and at the end of it we are left to ponder the question of what it means for Yorick to "put [himself] into motion" (23).

We recall that, in an early sequence of vignettes—three sections entitled "The Monk: Calais" and one "The Desobligeant: Calais"—Yorick relates how he begins his career in France by rudely refusing alms to a monk. His treatment of the monk becomes the occasion of a reflection on his own motives and on the cultural translatability of charity. But then, in the coach yard, the vehicle seems to become literal again when he finds and mounts a one-passenger carriage (a "desobligeant"). While waiting for Monsieur Dessein to return from vespers, Yorick writes his "Preface: In the Desobligeant," the title of the next section. In the ensuing vignette, entitled simply "Calais," as though beginning the journey anew, Yorick describes his initial encounter with "Monsieur *Dessein*" and his subsequent negotiations with him over the sale of the desobligeant. Yorick is badly outmaneuvered in the encounter and concedes, after Dessein's successful thwarting of his best ploy, that "the dose was made up exactly after my own prescription; so I could not help taking it—and returning Mons. Dessein his bow, without more casuistry we walk'd together towards his Remise to take a view of his magazine of chaises" (12). But as the defensive ratiocination of the casuistry ceases, Yorick's heart becomes active, and more than ever we become aware that we are being carried along by a new kind of narrative vehicle, one in which all this stopping and starting and starting over counts as movement.[17] Subsequent vignettes in the comically extended Calais episode—from this moment through to Yorick's consummation of a deal for a carriage and his realization that he has been in Calais for just over an hour—amount to a tour de force of sentimental narrative, in which Sterne treats the key issues of movement and accident with dizzyingly self-conscious playfulness.

A good sample of this kind of writing appears in the opening paragraphs of the next chapter-vignette, "In the Street: Calais," which opens with Yorick's reflection on his feelings. It is a passage that culminates in some sentences I showcased above, in the introduction:

It must needs be a hostile kind of a world, when the buyer (if it be but of a sorry post-chaise) cannot go further with the seller thereof into the street to terminate the difference betwixt them, but he instantly falls into the same frame of mind and views his conventionist with the same sort of eye, as if he was going along with him to Hyde-park corner to fight a duel. For my own part, being but a poor sword's-man, and no way a match for Monsieur *Dessein*, I felt the rotation of all the movements within me, to which the situation is incident—I looked at Monsieur *Dessein* through and through—ey'd him as he walked along in profile—then, *en face*—thought he look'd like a Jew—then a Turk—disliked his wig—cursed him by my gods—wished him at the devil—

—And is all this to be lighted up in the heart for a beggarly account of three or four louisd'ors, which is the most I can be over-reach'd in?—Base passion! said I, turning myself about, as a man naturally does upon a sudden reverse of sentiment—base, ungentle passion! thy hand is against every man, and every man's hand against thee—heaven forbid! said she, raising her hand up to her forehead, for I had turned full in front upon the lady whom I had seen in conference with the monk—she had followed us unperceived—Heaven forbid indeed! said I, offering her my own—she had a black pair of silk gloves open only at the thumb and two fore-fingers, so accepted it without reserve—and I led her up to the door of the Remise. (13)

The peripeteia, or reversal, here occurs in a passage from "base passion" to something gentler, something more polished, in which the commercial proliferation of possibilities and positions becomes a key to the process. The movement of this passage leads Yorick from commercial conflict, back through the sentiments of a precommercial mode of conflict resolution (the duel), and around again to the commercial reckoning of the worth of the anger thus kindled as against its costs and its risks. From the deal to the duel and back, Yorick "moves" in a full rotation, enabled to feel *all* of the "movements" to which the situation is incident. We are left unclear as to whether the emotion registered here is to be understood as located in the *rotation* of these movements or in the various *feelings* through which he moves.[18] Thus, having illustrated the sentiments to which the situation is incident, the narrative proceeds, one might say, by creating the situation to which the sentiments are incident. Not only does Yorick's rotation in space mimic his last "sudden reverse of sentiment," but also his exclamation about passion's hand and every man's hand being against each other is answered in the clasp of hands between him and Mme de L***, upon whom he has unwittingly turned "full in front."

What's crucial to see here is how the narrative's complication of the question of what counts as "moving" goes hand in hand with a complication of the question of what counts as an accident, or indeed as an "event"—a complication not only in the sense of a confusion about actions "inside" and "outside" the represented characters, but more radically, in the sense of a hypallage about what is motivating what. What kind of "coincidence" are we faced with in the moment when, performing his sudden softening reverse of sentiment as a physical turn, accompanied by a remark about a hand, Yorick turns flat into the hand of the woman for whom he has a soft spot in his heart?[19] Is this a case of a situation bringing about a sentiment, or a sentiment bringing about a situation? How does causality run in this sequence, and what might "probability" mean for it?

Thus begun, Yorick's narrative game is extended with remarkable inventiveness by means of yet another of what might be called the book's "literal figures." Monsieur Dessein discovers that he has come with the wrong key to the door of the remise, leaving Yorick and the lady comically still facing the door and still holding hands while he goes off to find the right one. "Movement" is thus suspended in the face of a blank space blocking the way to a passage yet to be unlocked by a character named "design." It is not until the beginning of the sixth section to follow this one that we are informed, "Mons. Dessein came up with the key of the Remise in his hand, and forthwith let us into his magazine of chaises" (21). The obvious point, again, is that we are allowed to witness how much can happen in a moment of suspended action, but what is less obvious is how we are to understand the episode's intentionality, its design.

During the five-chapter suspension of outward narrative progress, the topic of *dessein* intrudes itself in at least two ways. The first is by way of "drawing," as we learn in a flashback that immediately ensues from Yorick's initial view of the lady, as he explains that though he initially "had not yet seen her face" this was "not material," "for the drawing was instantly set about, and long before we had got to the door of the Remise, *Fancy* had finished the whole head" (14).[20] So the fanciful drawing of the woman's head, completed in the company of Monsieur Dessein, is also completed before it is seen. Does *dessein* inhere in incidents or does it only create an illusion of projected intelligibility after the fact? Does it come from within or without? A similar kind of question brings a second sense of *dessein* into play: design as sketch or blueprint, something that is "drawn" or "drawn up." As soon as Monsieur Dessein departs, Yorick reflects on his and the lady's extraordinary situation, and the play with drawing intensifies:

> Now a colloquy of five minutes, in such a situation, is worth one of as many ages, with your faces turned towards the street: in the latter case, 'tis drawn from the objects and occurrences without—when your eyes are fixed upon a dead blank—you draw purely from yourselves. A silence of a single moment upon Monsieur *Dessein*'s leaving us, had been fatal to the situation—she had infallibly turned about—so I begun [*sic*] the conversation instantly.—[21] (13–14)

Thus, the second chapter at the locked door (the one after the flashback to the drawing of Madame de L***'s face) opens with Yorick's attempt to break the ice without losing his grip on the situation:

> This certainly, fair lady! said I, raising her hand up a little lightly as I began, must be one of Fortune's whimsical doings: to take two utter strangers by their hands—of different sexes, and perhaps from different corners of the globe, and in one moment place them together in such a cordial situation, as Friendship herself could scarce have atchieved [*sic*] for them, had she projected it for a month— (15)

Mme de L***'s rejoinder—that Yorick's reflection on Fortune's doings reveals his embarrassment—establishes a contrapuntal movement in which fortune and propriety vie for the role of ruling principle in the narrative. A few minutes later, when, finally inside the remise, Monsieur Dessein shuts them together in a chaise and leaves again, Yorick as narrator reports the "reflection that this was the second time we had been left together by a parcel of nonsensical contingencies" (22). And again his fatalism is parried. The puzzle, then, is how we take this playful treatment of accident and "design" in the context of a narrative where "movement" seems repeatedly displaced from outside to inside and back again.

Throughout the novel, such issues about the relation between what happens by design and what happens by "a parcel of nonsensical contingencies" are correlated with the trope of syllepsis: the condition of textual uncertainty operating between the literal and figurative levels.[22] The sylleptic troping is nowhere more insistent than in Sterne's treatment of the main "object" of the opening chapters, the search for a "vehicle." Insofar as we take Sterne's narrative to be an account of *literal* travel across the Continent—however *fictionalized* it might be—to that same extent we may take literally the references to vehicles of various sorts—*desobligeant, vis à vis*, and *chaise*. Historically, however, the sense of "vehicle" as a carrier or medium actually predates its more specific reference to land transportation. It thus becomes very difficult not to read certain references to the vehicle as metaphorizing a means of travel that is, precisely, "sentimental"—that is, as the "movement" of or through sentiment itself. It is not that the travel of a "sentimental journey" is merely "figurative"; it is that the distinction between the literal and the figurative is impossible to maintain with confidence. All this becomes nearly explicit when, in the taxonomy of various kinds of travelers in the "Preface: In the Desobligeant," Yorick worries that as a sentimental traveler he may have "no better grounds for "draw[ing] attention" to himself "than the mere *Novelty of my Vehicle*" (10). In one sense, Yorick's vehicle at this point is the stationary carriage-for-one, or desobligeant. In another, as we have seen, it is the Latitudinarian vehicle of the soul, about which Sterne had published a poem, "The Unknown World," in the *Gentleman's Magazine* (1743). In yet another sense, however, it is the literary medium—we might call it the sentimental mode—in which design and accident, internal and external movement, the literal and the figurative, are joined under a given conceit.

Fictional Vehicles

I have been arguing for what might be called the "syllepsis of the vehicle" in early sentimental writing—the way in which the figural dimension of the medium is made literal in the work and play of language on the printed page. And just as the conceit of the "vehicular hypothesis" of the soul's conveyance in sensibility found its way into nineteenth-century fiction via Emma Courtney and Charles Dickens, so also the trope of the vehicle as representative mode or medium gains some traction in the subsequent history of the novel, not least by way of so influential an admirer of Sterne as Sir Walter Scott. In the novel that gave its name to the Waverley series, Scott introduces his tale of 1745, "sixty years since," and the end of antique manners in Scotland with an apology for having provided so much explanatory background for the story:

> The truth is, I cannot promise ... that this story shall be intelligible, not to say probable, without it. My plan requires that I should explain the motives on which its action proceeded; and these motives necessarily arose from the feelings, prejudices, and parties of the times. I do not invite my fair readers, whose sex and impatience give them the greatest right to

complain of these circumstances, into a flying chariot drawn by hyppo-griffs, or moved by enchantment. Mine is a humble English post-chaise, drawn upon four wheels, and keeping his majesty's highway. Those who dislike the vehicle may leave it at the next halt, and wait for the conveyance of Prince Hussein's tapestry, or Malek the Weaver's flying sentry-box.[23]

The key point here is that, for Scott, each vehicular medium is associated with a mode of probability, a style of world-making. Broadly speaking, this passage suggests, there are two kinds of narrative vehicles and two modes of probability; for shorthand we can call them romantic and novelistic. It is clear from Scott's critical writings on fiction that these two modes are associated with different stages of society, the precommercial and the commercial.[24] And just as England's commercial order, epitomized in the movement of people and information by means of the postal system, evolved its own set of motives and their interpretation (as Smith explained them in *The Theory of Moral Sentiments*), so the novel of this period offers a new realism defined in these same motivational terms.[25] Scott spells out the point in *Ivanhoe*, his next extended attempt to explain his practice as a novelist, when he writes that just as Galland had to represent the "wildness of Eastern fiction" in a probabalistic mode that would render it "interesting and intelligible" to the "feelings and habits of the Western reader," so he must perform an act of vehicular translation with his medieval materials: "I have so far explained the ancient manners in modern language, and so far detailed the characters and sentiments of my persons," that the modern reader will remain engaged.[26]

Scott's vehicle, the widely circulating printed novel, depended on the very means of transportation by which it is metaphorized, the humble English post-chaise, a vehicle not unlike the one in which we first see Mr. Lorry heading off for Paris in *Tale of Two Cities*. The metaphor suggests that, like the post-chaise itself, the novel stays close to the ground and makes no explanatory leaps. You have the sense that you understand how you are getting to where you are going, or at least how you got there after the fact. The motion, the progress, of the narrative is explicable; it can be made "intelligible." The intelligibility of the motion of the English novelistic vehicle might perhaps itself be explained by way of the new mathematical form of probability in its effect on English literary theory and practice. Barbara Shapiro, for example, argues that one effect of this new system is the forging of a new literary norm defined by enhanced precision.[27]

In any case, Scott's way of encoding modes of probability in two distinct kinds of vehicle represents only one way of sorting the world of storytelling.

Another, more to the point here, has been identified by Douglas Patey in his study of various forms of probability in eighteenth-century literature. In his discussion of "sentimental communion and probable inference" in the fiction of Mackenzie and Sterne, Patey distinguishes two kinds of probability in the eighteenth-century novel, two kinds of "conditions of knowing." The first kind is what he ascribes to the didactic manner of *Joseph Andrews* and *Tom Jones*, where the point is to teach probable judgment and to rectify expectation. This is the sort of probability that governs the relation of external signs to their causes and possible effects, and it informs the work of prudential judgment. "Judgment of [this] sort . . . is what Fielding's victimized innocents—Adams, Joseph, and Fanny—must learn in order to survive in a world full of Roasting Squires and partial Justices; it is also what in *Tom Jones* Fielding warns us he expects of his reader." [28] This first kind of probability is to be broadly associated with the practice of calculation.

The other kind of probability is explicitly located by Patey in "the sentimental novel as it is practiced in England in the last third of the eighteenth century." On this account, the sentimental novel tends to associate the first kind of prudential calculation, the kind taught in the fiction of Fielding, with villainy rather than virtue: the facility in "calculating probabilities" of this sort is just the sort of thing "that the sentimental hero typically eschews." [29] Thus, in Mackenzie's *Man of Feeling* (1771), a novel written very much in the wake of the Sterne craze, the titular hero Mr. Harley can declare, "To calculate the chances of deception is too tedious a business for the life of man." [30] In lieu of prudential calculation, the sentimental novel, as Patey sees it, "celebrates the spiritual and social advantages of a quasi-intuitive communion with the thoughts and feelings of others." [31] This is what we have been calling "sympathy," which Patey distinguishes from "judgment" in a way that suggests something of the early Victorian problematic of sympathy and judgment in the dramatic monologue. The sentimental novel of "anti-prudence and anti-probability" thus provides a testing ground for a new probabalistic mode, one based in a special intuitive facility for reading "probable signs," especially those that betray the affective state of another person. [32]

Having supplemented Shapiro's thesis with Patey's notion of a specifically sentimental form of probability, one associated with the sympathy of the face-to-face encounter, we nonetheless run afoul of a second key point made by Shapiro. Her further claim is that the new mathematical probability in England not only enhanced precision but also drastically reduced ambiguity of reference. [33] Sterne's sentimental probability, as we have begun to analyze it, would seem to depend on an extraordinarily high degree of ambiguity. If the sentimental novel did indeed offer a new mode of probabilistic intelligibility—a kind of transparency that trades in the mutual legibility of persons—then whence all the "opacity," all the destabilizing verbal play, that seems so characteristic of the sentimental novel as practiced by Sterne?

I believe that the key to this problem can unlock other matters as well, and I suggest that the best way to grasp it is to identify a central paradox of sentimental fiction, whereby the dynamics of the face-to-face encounter come to govern a cultural form (the novel) that is strongly defined by action-at-a-distance and that became part of the basic currency of Britain's dispersed and highly mediated *literary* public sphere. The problem gains resonance in relation to the ongoing debate about the question of, in Thomas Haskell's phrase, "capitalism and the origins of the humanitarian sensibility." For this debate centers not only on a "revolution in moral sensibility" in just these decades of English culture, but also, at least for Haskell, on "the power of market discipline to inculcate altered perceptions of causation in human affairs" and "new habits of causal attribution that set the stage for humanitarianism."[34] What Haskell means by "altered perceptions of causation" and "new habits of causal attribution" has to do precisely with the capacity of the new market society to establish a sense of action-at-a-distance. With the new promise-keeping "form of life" of the eighteenth-century market came "the teaching of the virtues of reflection and close attention to the distant consequences of [one's] actions."[35]

Understanding the sentimental literary implementation of this new form of life depends on recalling two linked recognitions to which we have come in previous chapters.[36] The first is that, in the course of the eighteenth century, the novel gradually took the place of theater as the dominant popular genre in Britain, and the second is that the novel gradually begins to assimilate certain theatrical features and functions to itself. These points are crucial to any understanding of how "face-to-faceness" is managed sylleptically in the sentimental novel, transforming codes of expectation and probability in the process.[37] There is, of course, one particularly apposite development within the institution of British theater during the years before its "figure" was absorbed into the sentimental novel, and that is the development we call "sentimental comedy," a genre that has long posed major problems of probability for audiences and commentators alike. The peculiarities of "sentimental comedy" form a part of the problem of probability in the sentimental mode and, as symptoms of Steele's negotiation of theatrical and print media, they can help to unpack the paradoxical commitment to face-to-faceness in a literary institution defined by action at a distance.

Steele and the Medium of the Sentimental Plot

As we have seen, what has long been called sentimental comedy is generally thought to have had its programmatic inauguration in Richard Steele's *The Conscious Lovers* (1722), a play staged on hundreds of occasions through the eighteenth century and published in at least forty-seven printed editions over that same period.[38] We have also seen that probability is an issue in the sentimental comedy crafted after Steele's model in part because of the role of coincidence in the handling of resolution.[39] Thus Stuart Tave, taking *The Conscious Lovers* as representative of the sentimental, points to Steele's questionable use of the term "Providence" to explain "what is in fact another species of thing, that convenient solution of Act V—which is such a statistically astonishing connection that it seems to defy the laws of natural probability and therefore must be credited to a heavenly intervention and reward."[40]

While it is clear enough that the two primary eighteenth-century forms of the sentimental, in fiction and drama, have issues with probability, there has been little or no critical effort to understand how these respective issues might be linked. One connection, I suggest, has to do with how the sentimental plot transcends "plotting," or what Patey, in the context of the novel, describes as the probability of prudential calculation. In Steele's sentimental comedy it is the scheme of the protagonists that must be foiled before the sentimental solution can unfold. Tave points out that Steele's plot resolution in *The Conscious Lovers* forms a variation within a larger class of productions with improbable resolutions. In such plays, "the participants in the action work madly at their job of reaching their desires by whatever, often wildly ingenious means, they can invent; and, when they've done their exhausted best to deserve success, fortunate chance steps in with the last and best trick of all."[41] When Tave describes the alternative to scheming calculation in the sentimental comedy, he calls it "fortunate chance." When Patey describes the alternative to scheming calculation in the sentimental novel, he calls it "sentimental communion." But how is it that sentimental communion can function as fortunate chance and vice versa?

A second connection takes the shape of a kind of chiasmus. Just as face-to-face encounters dramatized in the theater are mediated by a sense of a new commerce in print, so the action-at-a-distance enabled by print culture returns to theatrical face-to-faceness for its basic paradigms. On the one hand, sentimental comedy involves a very self-conscious "reform" of the more licentious mode of comedy that had been in play for several decades. This reform is launched very much from within the mode of the print culture whose burgeoning power and influence would support the great ambitions of the sentimentalized public sphere of the post-Sternean novel. On the other hand, the novel has been said to achieve a distinctive form in the eighteenth century by virtue of its internalization of theatrical forms.[42] These two developments prove to be two sides of the same coin, or at least two moments in the same process. It is true that what becomes crucial to the novel is the figure of theatrical spectatorship. But it is no less true that Steele achieved his sentimental reform of drama only after establishing himself as the author of the innovative print-cultural organ he called *The Spectator*, or indeed that he discussed reforming drama in its pages, and linked that reform to the emergence of precisely the kind of *reading* public that *The Spectator* innovatively catered to.

The "violence done to probability"[43] in Steele's comedy derives, I contend, from changes associated with the newly expanded domain of literary commerce, and the "sympathetic communion" of the sentimental novel is a function of the wider "theater" of British literate society in the later eighteenth century. But how, exactly, does knowing this connection help us to understand the way in which "the power of sympathy" becomes an "essential force" in the new form of life characterized by sentimentalized probability? We can better answer this further question if we clarify what it is that the severest critics of sentimentalism find most objectionable in it. For John Traugott, the violent improbability of sentimental comedy lies in what he calls the "unlikely oxymoron" of "worldliness and sentiment, the two darlings of the age."[44] These "opposites," he suggests, "seem to feed on each other" in this genre: "If the world is composed of nothing but masks the pretended desire of sentiment to penetrate the mask and spy out the naked heart is just another mask."[45] Tave's critique, as it happens, is grounded in a related observation. What distinguishes *The Conscious Lovers* as sentimental is, again, what Tave calls a certain "slipping of levels."[46] In *The Conscious Lovers*, the trick ending is not an artifice to be admired, a wonder to be marveled at, but rather a confusion of actual and normative orders: "the trick is a pretense that heaven is earth." The point is driven home, for Tave, when the play's hero, young Bevil Junior, defends his impressive benevolence toward his would-be lover, Indiana, whom he rescued from dire circumstances, as if it were ordinary conduct in his society: "no more than what every gentleman ought to be, and I believe very many are," as Bevil himself puts it. And just as the concluding trick of *The Conscious Lovers* is that heaven is earth, so, writes Tave, "Bevil Junior as modest hero is both the gentleman that ought to be and the gentleman that is."[47]

To prepare for a different account of this slipping of levels in the sentimental, a word about the plotline of Steele's play is in order. Although the play's resolution depends on the coincidence that Bevil's lover turns out to be the long lost daughter of his father's friend, the decisive point in the plot actually occurs in act 4, as has long been recognized. Indeed, in the preface to the printed edition of his drama, Steele himself openly acknowledges "that the whole was writ for the sake of the scene in the fourth act, wherein Mr. Bevil evades the quarrel with his friend." This scene involves Bevil and another man, Mr. Myrtle, who seeks the hand of the woman, Lucinda, whom Bevil's father has in mind for his own son. Bevil has been helping Myrtle undo the comic tangle of lovers, so that the two men can marry Indiana and Lucinda respectively. But now Myrtle has become suspicious of Bevil and begins to provoke him with insults. The more coolness Bevil shows in the face of these insults, the more angry grow Myrtle's provocations. Finally, himself in a rage he is eager to have Bevil join, Myrtle adds an insult to Bevil's beloved Indiana: "Your marriage [i.e., to Lucinda, as Myrtle thinks] goes on like common business, and in the interim you have your rambling captive, your Indian princess, for your soft moments of dalliance—your convenient, your ready Indiana" (IV.i.146–49). At this insult, Bevil's anger is finally sparked, and he agrees to a duel with Myrtle.

The pivotal moment is reached when, in the act of summoning his servant to call a coach to carry him away from Myrtle, Bevil pauses to notice the act of social discipline required to speak to his servant civilly in spite of his rage toward Myrtle. At this moment we have an aside in which Bevil "recollect[s] [him]self," and in lieu of going through with the duel decides to show Myrtle the proof (a letter) that all that Myrtle has alleged is false. On reading the letter, Myrtle is mortified by his rashness and begins to ask forgiveness, but Bevil cuts him off: "You have o'erpaid the inquietude you gave me in the change I see in you towards me. Alas, what machines are we! Thy face is altered to that of another man, to that of my companion, my friend" (IV.i.195–98). This is a necessary condition for the comic resolution that follows. A duel in this case would spell a tragic outcome, just as the violent conflict between Mercutio and Theobald turns the comic potential of *Romeo and Juliet* (whose plot is much like that of *The Conscious Lovers* for the first three acts) toward its tragic conclusion.

To understand fully the question of "levels" in Steele-inspired sentimental probability requires a grasp of the decisive moment when Bevil "recollects himself." By what principle of causality or motivation can we account for this moment? Although it is perhaps the most important "event" in the play, it takes place in a space of nonaction: a long pause of the sort that enables re-flection. The occasion of this reflection is the most ordinary behavior imagin-able—the request to a servant to call a coach. And yet the manners—and the sense of "polish"—that enable Bevil to temper his anger for that act proves to him his resources for self-control. He is allowed to recognize that, though he has been provoked, control is available to him—that his "anger" is an artifice of his circumstances and his "resentment" a decision in which he must weigh a lifetime of obligations. Steele presents a transformation of the "face-to-face" encounter: the face of the man Bevil might have killed changes in an instant to the face "of another man," his friend.

In Steele's programmatic comments about this new mode of comedy, even as he insists that this scene in act 4 was the raison d'etre for the play, he allows that such incidents "are esteemed by some people no subjects of comedy." To these people his reply is that "any thing that has its foundation in happiness and success, must be allowed to be the object of comedy," and it must have seemed obvious enough to Steele that such a "recovery" as was effected by Mr. Bevil implied a foundation in happiness and success. But such an answer does not address Tave's objection that Steele's play involves a deliberate and char-acteristically sentimental confusion of norms and facts. And indeed, Steele's comment about the point of the key scene in act 4 is instructive in this regard: "I . . . hope it may have some effect on the Goths and Vandals that frequent the theaters, or a more polite audience may supply their absence."[48] The dis-parity between the behavior of the fine gentleman Bevil, offered as at once exemplary *and* typical, and the characterization of the audience as barbarians, suggests the Traugott-Tave problem for Steele's representation—how can the gentleman Bevil typify barbarism? Presumably Bevil stands for a virtual audience. But who constitutes this more polite virtual audience that might supplant the Goths and Vandals who have held sway to this point? How does that more polite audience come to figure in the scene of the theater?

The preface from which I am quoting is in fact no part of the theatrical production itself but rather a printed text. Steele himself calls attention to the difference in media: "The greatest effect of a play in reading is to excite the reader to go see it; and when he does so, it is then a play has the effect of example and precept." The "more polite" audience that might come to sup-plant the barbarians in the theater will be drawn from readers whose interest is excited by their confrontation with the text of the play. It is in this light, I believe, that the strangely actionless quality of the key moment in *The Con-scious Lovers* establishes it as a play precisely about becoming "conscious." The consciousness that is aroused in Bevil in that long pause—his reflection on his ability to temper himself for so trivial a cause as the calling of a coach but not to avoid death or murder—is a mediated awareness, a thought aroused as if in the mind of a reader pausing over a printed text. (Myrtle's counterpart conversion actually depends on his reading of a letter.)

Bevil's soliloquy on the stage, in other words, is the reverse mirror of Shaftesbury's soliloquy on the page. For Shaftesbury's "Soliloquy" (1710) argues for the place of the soliloquy as a "dramatic method" by virtue of which an author can divide in two for "the work of introspection." On such an account, as Agnew shrewdly sums it up, conscience emerges as "less the cause than the product of reflection."[49] And "reflection" is itself produced by a dramatic method in print, which turns out to be the flip side of the "print method" of sentimental drama. There is, in this sense, less distance than one might have imagined between the Steele of *The Spectator* and the Steele of *The Conscious Lovers*. Indeed, *The Conscious Lovers* was written according to a blueprint first sketched out in *The Spectator*, for a kind of anti-Etheregean comedy, in a mode counter to that of *The Man of Mode*. The mode of *The Spectator* itself is defined in relation to Shaftesbury's soliloquy, which repurposes this Elizabethan dramatic convention for eighteenth-century print culture.

For Steele, it would seem, the wider audience that surrounds the one physically present at any given performance is the new polite reading public composed of those new gentleman and ladies who composed the readership of Shaftesbury's *Letters* and *The Spectator*. Steele's verse prologue to *The Conscious Lovers* seems to be a gesture toward just this wider audience of "Britons":

> Your aid, most humbly sought, then, Britons lend,
> And lib'ral mirth like lib'ral men defend:
> No more let ribaldry, with licence writ,
> Usurp the name of eloquence or wit;
> No more let lawless farce uncensured go,
> The lewd dull gleanings of a Smithfield show.
> 'Tis yours with breeding to refine the age,
> To chasten wit, and moralize the stage. (ll.21–28)

Here the programmatic aspects of Steele's dramaturgy become clear. And the stakes in the campaign are spelled out in the ensuing lines, which conclude with an exhortation to "judge politely for your country's fame." This capacity to judge "politely" had to do with the extension of trade—the commerce that sweetens as it polishes—and the expansion of the mercantile class.[50]

While the new reach of commerce and consciousness registered in Steele's drama had its primary development in print, print narrative increasingly depended on the conventions of drama for its virtual effects. The crossing of these crucial developments is anticipated in Shaftesbury's analysis of the incorporation of the soliloquy form into modern authorship and the production of "conscience" as an impartial spectator internalized within the writer's mind. As the century proceeded, the sentimental campaign would be waged increasingly on the grounds of narrative and expository works in print. If Sterne's Yorick, whose name marks his descent from *Hamlet*, soliloquizes in print the triumph of commercial sympathies over the impulse to violent resolution of conflict (with Monsieur Dessein), this moment is roughly the converse of that in which Bevil, on the stage, depends on the reflective capacities of a national readership to manage something like the same feat.

The Coordinates of Sentimental Probability

In the sentimental mode, what can be said to happen within the plot is often crucially connected to an imagination of the work's reception by the audience. This point depends for its force on our seeing how the subject of representation in the sentimental mode can coincide with its object: the national humanitarian sensibility taking shape in the new commercial order.[51] The mimetic task of the sentimental narrative is to represent the "sensibility" of Britain's commercial society to itself, but, as it seeks to epitomize or allegorize this sensibility, it also means to *activate* it by affective movement, and thus to shape it amelioratively—to help it to realize its full capacity. This rhetorical aim is explicitly avowed, in fact, in the long subtitle of the *Sentimental Magazine* as it appears on the title page: "Or, General Assemblage of Science, Taste, and Entertainment. Calculated to Amuse the mind, to improve the understanding, and To amend the Heart." What I have termed the *pragmatic* consideration—defined here as the rhetorical project aiming not only to display the motivations of a sensibility but to better them[52]—involves its own probabilistic dimension, its own issues of likelihood and chance. In the *Sentimental Magazine*'s announcement, for example, the apparently innocuous term "calculated" is of special relevance, since it suggests that the desired moral effects of amusement, edification, and emotional repair all require a reckoning of cases in their own right. If, for example, the heart is amended by being affected, moved, then part of the "calculation" in a sentimental narrative has to do with the question of what is likely to interest and to move the heart of the audience.[53]

By the same token, however, if the heart of the audience is to be understood as a collective—even national—sensibility, and if the characters of the story are to be understood as part of a collective national allegory—then the probabilities calculated to amend the sensibility and the probabilities on which one bases a representation of its performance can be mapped as orthogonal coordinates: the mimetic axis of probability (how the epitomized members of commercial society are likely to respond within the diegetic frame of the action) is crossed by the pragmatic axis of probability (how the members of commercial society who compose its audience are likely to respond to the action as diegetically framed). For a literary culture self-conceived in the advanced commercial state of society, and caught up in a certain fiction of general participation in a print cultural public sphere, the relation between the society represented and the society addressed can be imagined as approaching full identity.

The point can be illustrated if we return to that moment early in "The Miser Convinced of His Error," the serial narrative from the opening numbers of the *Sentimental Magazine*, when the narrator underscores the "miraculous" aspect of the transformation that will have to take place in the miser Doriman, that Scrooge prototype: "Who will take compassion on his youth? Who will undertake the task of convincing him of his error? By whom is this miracle to be performed?"[54] There is a strong sense, I want to suggest, that the miracle is performed in a character defined at the juncture between the mimetic and pragmatic axes of this plot: the Briton who is at once the audience and the referent (object and subject) of the representation. The split in the author of Shaftesbury's printed soliloquy and the split in the protagonist of Steele's dramatic comedy may each be seen as a refraction of this miraculous "person."

Of course, any plot might be said to have both a mimetic and a pragmatic (or rhetorical) axis. Any plot can be seen as rule-governed both in its diegesis (the line of action) and in its practical operation on the emotions of readers (the line of affect). And surely there is a long tradition—from *The Winter's Tale* to *Peter Pan*—of invoking audience credulity or generosity in the realization of some bit of action on the stage or page. But in the case of the sentimental as I am describing it, these two axes become curiously hinged to each other. This, I believe, is what accounts for the "slippage" identified by Tave. The improbability of the plot is a projection of the anticipated effect of the sentimental text on the collective sensibility of its readers. In a scheme of (strictly speaking) sentimental progress, such as that outlined by Steele—in an age in which the expanse of trade promotes a higher and higher degree of polish in manners and softened sentiments in daily life—the represented national subject is one that, to have its case truly captured, must improve on what it represents.[55]

Sentimental probability, then, involves a public system of self-representation in which the case of the nation can be reinvented in the process of its being represented, because it can be improved in the process of its being moved. Sterne's Abdera "Fragment" in *Sentimental Journey* nicely illustrates the logic of the point in the context of early Greek theater, a projection backward from his own moment. When Euripides's *Andromeda* is performed in the vile and profligate town of Abdera, Sterne relates, Perseus's address to Cupid so enchants the city that it reforms itself: "The fire caught—and the whole city, like the heart of one man, open'd itself to Love" (29). Sternean hypallage (causal exchange) and syllepsis (literal-figurative confusion) reinforce each other in key moments around such themes. In those early pages of the book, the literalization of the "country men" to whom Yorick as writer of the preface addresses his rhetorical question ("Where then are you going?") pointedly raises the question of where they are, and certainly of where he is. On the one hand, the "here" of Yorick's comment is the England where Sterne writes and his readers read. On the other, "here" is the coach yard in Calais where Yorick begins his journey. But "here" is also the vehicle he inhabits—now momentarily the one-passenger job—which is moved but not budged by a masturbatory "agitation" that would (presumably) have been better undertaken in a vehicle defined by the structure of the *vis à vis* or "face-to-face." Face-to-face, of course, is the structure that Sterne can achieve only figuratively in the sylleptic materialization of his readers/countrymen as the interlocutors who inquire about his solitary agitation in the first place. Completing a "rotation of movements," this little episode rounds out with a return to the generalized discourse of the proverb, in which the "literal figures" of the countrymen alongside the carriage are returned to their status as generalities: *An English man does not travel to see English men.*

Sterne and the Laws of Chance

There is a moment in *Sentimental Journey*, however, where the issue of probability is quite directly articulated in a self-consciously sentimental context, and what makes it an especially apposite passage with which to close is that it articulates sentimental probability in a pointedly national frame of reference. It is the famous vignette, involving (like so many) an impediment to movement, in which Yorick's servant, La Fleur, riding a bidet, or small horse, beside Yorick's post-chaise, encounters an obstacle in the middle of the road.

And it raises a question about the limits of my interpretation of Sterne. Here, in slightly abridged form, is the vignette:

> A dead ass, before we had got a league, put a sudden stop to La Fleur's career—his bidet would not pass by it—a contention arose betwixt them, and the poor fellow was kick'd out of his jack-boots the very first kick.
>
> La Fleur bore his fall like a French christian, saying neither more or less upon it, than Diable! so presently got up and came to the charge again astride his bidet. . . .
>
> The bidet flew from one side of the road to the other, then back again—then this way—then that way, and in short every way but by the dead ass.—La Fleur insisted upon the thing—and the bidet threw him. . . . and away he [the bidet] scamper'd back to Montriul—*Peste!* said La Fleur.
>
> It is not *mal a propos* to take notice here, that tho' La Fleur availed himself but of two different terms of exclamation in this encounter—namely, *Diable!* and *Peste!* that there are nevertheless three, in the French language; like the positive, comparative, and superlative, one or the other of which serve for every unexpected throw of the dice in life.
>
> *Le Diable!* which is the first, and positive degree, is generally used upon ordinary emotions of the mind, where small things only fall out contrary to your expectations—such as—the throwing once doublets—La Fleur's being kick'd off his horse, and so forth—cuckoldom, for the same reason, is always—*Le Diable!*
>
> But in cases where the cast has something provoking in it, as in that of the bidet's running away after, and leaving La Fleur aground in jack-boots—'tis the second degree.
>
> 'Tis then *Peste!*
>
> And for the third—
>
> —But here my heart is wrung with pity and fellow-feeling, when I reflect what miseries must have been their lot, and how bitterly so refined a people must have smarted, to have forced them upon the use of it.—
>
> Grant me, O ye powers which touch the tongue with eloquence in distress!—whatever is my *cast*, Grant me but decent words to exclaim in, and I will give my nature way.
>
> —But as these were not to be had in France, I resolved to take every evil just as it befell me without any exclamation at all.
>
> La Fleur, who had made no such covenant with himself, followed the bidet with his eyes till it was got out of sight—and then, you may imagine, if you please, with what word he closed the whole affair.

As there was no hunting down a frighten'd horse in jack-boots, there remained no alternative but taking La Fleur either behind the chaise, or into it.—

I preferred the latter, and in half an hour we got to the post-house at Nampont. (32–33)

It is an episode with far-reaching resonance in the history of sentimentalism. Wordsworth's *Peter Bell* (1819) reprises the spectacle of the peasant man beating and cursing a stubborn animal in the middle of a road (this time it is the ass itself), and the 1821 "Sentimental Journey, from Islington to Waterloo Bridge" makes pointed reference to the obsession of "sentimentalists" with encounters of this sort ("the first dead dog . . . they might meet with").[56]

Of signal interest to a discussion of probability in Sterne is the governing conceit of the dice game. Merely at the level of pun or paronomasia, for example, we can notice that, beyond the wordplay on *movement, motion, emotion, accident, turn,* and *design* in the earlier passages (many of which terms remain in play here), this later passage extends the paronomasia to *cast, case, lot, throw* (coup), *fall,* and *befall.* Ian Hacking has shown how, at an earlier moment, the language of the "equal probability of cases" merged with the language of the equal probability of chances: "chances" understood paradigmatically as possible outcomes in a game of chance such as dice.[57] Sterne frames his story as a series of "cases" in which the chance outcome (the cast) can be graded in the triadic grammar of positive, comparative, and superlative. The basis of the grading system is the degree of "provocation" registered in the sensibility of the subject who suffers the "cast." Fortune or misfortune acquires a kind of measure in the marked levels of expressive exchange between agents. The assumption that "accidents" move us is elaborated by way of the conceit that in some "casts" of the dice Fortune "provokes" or calls us forth. The person who becomes the object of Fortune's call or "cast" responds with the grammatically appropriate "invocation": *Diable, Peste,* or (one suspects) *Nom de Dieu.* Emotion can be thus closely keyed to degrees of improbability. The odds of "throwing once doublets," as the standard handbooks of games of chance would have suggested for games played with two dice, are six in thirty-six or one-sixth. One in six is an ordinary enough "case" or "befalling" of improbability to call for no more than an "ordinary emotion of the mind."

It is a key premise in the theory of sentiments that, while a vexing case of misfortune calls forth a response from the sufferer, this response in turn will affect the response of witnesses to the entire spectacle. As a third party in or to the scene, one may or may not have fellow feeling with such suffering. Adam

Smith explains that restraint in response to unlucky chance, as recommended in the disciplines of Stoicism, will, along another axis of probability, increase the likelihood of a spectator's active sympathy with the victim. Sterne tacitly relies on Smith's theory here when he prays for decent words, and he resolves, in the absence of decent words in France, to accept what befalls him "without any exclamation at all." But on a level of national sentiment, Sterne wittily suggests, one can also—as a Stoical Englishman—have fellow feeling with the case of a nation whose long-term fortunes (provocations) have been such as to "force" them to resort to such an expression as the offensive superlative.

Implicit in this articulation of sentiment and probability are many of the emergent forms and structures I have been describing. The slippage between the literal and figural levels, for example, can be seen in the connection between the governing metaphor of the "casting of the dice" and La Fleur's being kicked by and thrown from his horse. This connection is cleverly intimated in the punning use of "fall" (German for "case") as a link between "cast" and "case." Earlier, we saw the literalization of the rhetorical "countrymen" and the materialization of the "hand" of fate at the end of the arm of Mdm. de L***. Now, the slide of the syllepsis goes the other way. After we are told that "La Fleur bore his fall like a French christian," we find that this "literal" fall becomes the more metaphorical or abstract sense of how "things fall out" in relation to expectations. The "fall" becomes a "case."[58]

My final speculation about this extraordinary passage concerns its relation to the figure of "hypallage": the trope of the preposterous, strictly speaking. Is there not, I wonder, an allusion to Sterne's own account of this trope in the concluding sentences of the "Dead Ass" vignette, in which the choices confronting Yorick are reduced to "taking La Fleur either behind the chaise, or into it"? We must recall that when Sterne has Walter Shandy explain the trope of hypallage to Uncle Toby, a strikingly similar phrasing is involved: "What's that? cried my uncle Toby. The cart before the horse, replied my father——And what has he to do there? cried my uncle Toby—Nothing, quoth my father, but to get in——or let it alone." In the sentimental mode, much depends on this reversibility of the driving force and the driven object.

SEVEN

Sentimental Monstrosity

In "The Miser Convinced of His Error," the serial tale featured in the first issue of the *Sentimental Magazine* in 1773, we saw that the sensibility of Doriman is so egregiously depraved that his generous uncle is led to disown him in a moment of righteous anger. This response, on the part of so unimpeachable a character, amounts to evidence that Doriman has at this point become a moral monster. Doriman's literary descendent, Ebenezer Scrooge, is heir to this kind of moral deformity. Scrooge is so monstrous that he lacks the esteem of everyone who knows him. It takes the radical innocence of a Tiny Tim to include him in the famous Christmas toast—"God bless us every one"—but only because the formulation refuses all exclusions. It carries an implicit stipulation: "even Mr. Scrooge." Capra's Mr. Potter, likewise, is squarely in line with this character type, as Capra's casting of Lionel Barrymore, the voice of Scrooge on American radio, helps to emphasize. When Capra reworks the sentimental plot of this story, as I suggested at the start of part 2, he in effect displaces the monster from the position of protagonist to that of antagonist.

This is a true enough description, but it is not the whole story. Doriman and Scrooge must reform themselves, and to do so they must come to terms with their own moral deformity. In the feel-good American twist to the plot,

George Bailey, it seems, needs to come to terms not with his depravity but with his essential wonderfulness. The world without him proves to be a far worse and less handsome place.[1] This twist, however, gets a twist in its turn. This second twist, which turns on the relation of George Bailey to Mr. Potter, is effected at two or three key moments in the film. Perhaps the most obvious such moment occurs when Potter summons George to his office to offer him a job—on the condition, it turns out, that George turn over the Bailey Building and Loan to Potter.

This is a signal face-to-face encounter, a moment that conspicuously stages a kind of mirroring between the rival bankers. It is in fact one of the few nonromantic encounters in the film to be photographed entirely with the technique of shot/reverse-shot. Within the dominant mirror-structure of the scene, to be sure, there is a comical asymmetry: Potter has provided Bailey with a far lower chair for the interview. This provides the basis for some winning physical comedy on the part of James Stewart, who keeps trying to haul himself up to Potter's eye level. Yet a deeper sense of similarity between the men lurks beneath the surfaces, and is registered by Potter himself: "Take during the Depression, for example. You and I were the only ones who kept our heads" (226). Their connection is most powerfully established, however, by Potter's ability to understand and articulate George's innermost sentiments. Potter states George's view of his own case to George every bit as well as George might have done for himself:

> Now if this young man of twenty-eight was a common ordinary yokel, I'd say he was doing fine. But George Bailey is *not* a common, ordinary yokel. He's an intelligent, smart, ambitious young man—who hates his job— who hates the Building and Loan, almost as much as I do. A young man who's been dying to get out on his own ever since he was born. A young man . . . the smartest one of the crowd, mind you, a young man who has to sit and watch his friends go places, because he's trapped. Yes, sir, trapped into frittering his life away playing nursemaid to a lot of garlic eaters. Do I paint a correct picture, or do I exaggerate? (226)

George does not contradict Potter's account. His reaction instead confirms that it has touched home. The accuracy of the picture is all the more impressive in light of Potter's limited access to any intimacy with George, and thus all the more evidence of Potter's own powers of empathic projection, perverted as they have become.

These powers argue in turn for his similarity to George, who seems as much persuaded by Potter's perspicuity, his grasp of George's case, as he is by his blandishments. Indeed, he seems on the verge of accepting the offer at the moment he requests twenty-four hours to think it over. Potter genially grants this request, promising to draw up the papers in the meantime, and George holds out an eager hand to shake on a deal almost done. As he touches Potter's hand, however, George's alacrity turns to aversion, and then to a repugnance so strong that within seconds he is calling Potter vile names and shouting at a couple of innocent bystanders on his way out, "And that goes for you too!" What are we to make of this reaction to the touch of Potter's hand? And, thinking again back to Aristotle, what of George's sudden reversal? Is it attended by some recognition?

A later scene gives us the other side of George's repugnance at Potter's deformity,[2] for it is a moment when George himself begins to turn monstrous. The scene is part of the sequence that brings the heavenly screening of George's life back to the day on which the film opens: Christmas Eve, 1945, the day of George's suicidal crisis. George learns that morning that Uncle Billy has misplaced eight thousand dollars just in advance of the bank examiner's arrival at the Building and Loan. After failing to find the money, which has been appropriated by Potter, George turns in desperation to Potter himself, who responds only with threats of prosecution and imprisonment. When George returns to the bosom of his family with his mind thus burdened, he finds little comfort in the bustle of their Christmas preparations. He barks at three of his four young children: Janie for practicing a Christmas carol, Pete for asking spelling questions for a Christmas story ("What do I look like, a dictionary!"), and little Tommy for playing with a toy sweeper. The fourth child, Zuzu, is sick with a fever. When her teacher phones to ask after her health, George seizes the phone from his wife and tells her off, and after the teacher's husband takes the phone George adds more insults and even threats.

By the time George begins to take out his rage on the objects in the living room, toppling and smashing things, it is clear that he has become the monster in the house. An intimation to that effect comes in the unfinished answer that Mary gives to one of Pete's spelling questions.

PETE: Dad, how do you spell frankincense?
GEORGE (shouts): I don't know. Ask your mother. . . .
MARY: F–R–A–N–K–I–N . . . (259)

When his rage subsides, George is isolated on one side of the room, and in a series of shot/reverse-shots between himself and individual family members, he apologizes to them one by one. But he then barks at them all again, and orders Janie to resume playing, reducing her to tears. Mary gathers the

Capra, *It's a Wonderful Life*. George Bailey turns monstrous.

children to her side, protectively, and asks George why he must continue to torture the children. George, the child-torturing, wife-abusing, teacher-threatening monster—looking disheveled and out of control—now appeals to his wife for sympathy. She says only, "Why don't you just . . .," and he leaves the house.

Both George's mirroring of Potter and his susceptibility to acting monstrously himself thus complicate the apparent break between Capra's reworking of the miser's conversion story and its earlier sentimental sources. George's monstrous side is not born of miserliness, nor are we given reason to believe, as we are in the cases of Doriman and Scrooge, that his deformity stems from malign influences in his childhood. Nor is it quite possible, conversely, to imagine that Potter is a miser who can be convinced of his error or who is in any way redeemable. Potter is curiously neglected at the end of the film. It was actually a point of controversy in the film's early reception that, having in effect stolen eight thousand dollars from the Building and Loan, and then attempted to frame George Bailey, Potter is not in the end brought to justice.

In addressing the fourth of four key features of the sentimental as it descends to cinema from the eighteenth century, then, I would like to consider this question of the relation between sentimentalism and moral deformity. How do we best explain the implications of the moral-sentiments school for the understanding of monstrosity? How did this understanding of monstrosity come to be represented? What was the fate of this representation? If in general, monsters tell us about the normative frames of reference against which their monstrous status is defined, what can we learn about the sentimental in *its* representation of categorical deformity?[3]

I look briefly at what I take to be the emergence of the relation between beauty and deformity in the work of Shaftesbury and Adam Smith. The theme of moral monstrosity is one that surfaces explicitly in both writers, as it does in a different register with Rousseau. I then turn to what is made of this connection in the work of the Godwin circle, notably that of Mary and Percy Shelley, who developed some of the fundamental contradictions of the sentimental monster in exquisitely balanced moral tales. I next consider the fate of the figure of the sentimental monster in Victorian writers such as Dickens. And finally, I examine some renderings of the Frankenstein story in cinema in the tradition of James Whale's 1931 film. Here I aim to show how strikingly Whale upended the key assumptions of Shelleyan sentimental monstrosity. I argue that Whale's account puts itself at odds with the long sentimental tradition to which I've argued Capra is heir, and turns instead to the sort of materialist account for which the Latitudinarian notion of the soul was meant in the first place to be an answer—to a materialist *consciousness*, one might say.[4]

Moral Deformity and Moral Sentiment

I began part 2 with Schiller's definition of the sentimental as a mixed mode of writing produced by "reflection," tracing backward the sources of this notion of the sentimental: in Sterne's reflexive fiction, in Smith's notion of mirrored moral sentiments, and ultimately in Shaftesbury's practice of "soliloquy." Francis Hutcheson forms a part of this genealogy too, as a thinker who was both a disciple of Shaftesbury and a key influence on Smith and Hume. All of these writers, I have stressed, have in common a commitment to seeing moral life as centered on sentiment. In the concluding pages of *The Theory of Moral Sentiments*, Smith himself reviews the various systems of morality as he understands them, placing his own among them; these observations introduce his critique of casuistry as a method for approaching moral problems. It is here that he produces what I have described as his sentimentalization of the moral case.

In that section, entitled "Of the Manner in which different Authors have treated of the practical Rules of Morality," Smith reminds his reader of a distinction he has made between the rules of justice and the rules of all other virtues. The former, he says, are "precise and accurate," the latter "loose, vague, and indeterminate." He then offers a means of understanding this distinction by way of two familiar departments of knowledge:

> The first [the rules of justice] may be compared to the rules of grammar; the others to those which critics lay down for the attainment of what is sublime and elegant in composition, and which present us rather with a general idea of the perfection we ought to aim at, than afford us any certain and infallible directions for acquiring it.[5]

The distinction between the grammarian and the critic is invidious. It prepares for Smith's critique of those moralists who follow the path of the grammarians—writers he calls "the casuists"—who "do not content themselves with characterizing in this general manner that tenor of conduct which they would recommend to us, but endeavour to lay down exact and precise rules for the direction of every circumstance of our behaviour" (329). Conversely, it prepares for his promotion of those writers who proceed as he does—those who follow the other path, the path of "criticism." This invidious comparison indeed preoccupies Smith's attention throughout the concluding pages of his very long book. The critic's way of doing things is valued by Smith in relation to *all* of the virtues except justice—and sometimes even there (as in the case of a promise extorted by a highwayman)—because, crucially, it is the critic, rather than the grammarian/casuist, who allows for "feeling and sentiment" to be recognized as they should be in the work of judgment (339). Smith's self-identification as "critic" in this sense is fundamental to his identity as the author of *The Theory of Moral Sentiments*, which is, after all, precisely about the role of feeling and sentiment in moral judgment—in approbation, admiration, and the recognition of merit.

To advocate the path of "criticism" (so understood) over the path of grammar is to suggest a connection between moral and aesthetic issues. It is a connection that we have seen to be characteristic of the sentimental line that leads from Shaftesbury to the work of Schiller in the 1790s, especially his *Letters on Aesthetic Education*, the influential sequel to *On Naïve and Sentimental Poetry*. A crucial element in this connection is the notion of moral beauty. This notion had been around since the seventeenth century in both England and France, and it had fully entered public discourse in both national contexts by the mid-eighteenth century. By then, moral beauty was understood to be achievable, and to be recognizable, by means of well-cultivated sentiments. Reasoning about moral beauty was a secondary matter. The antonym of moral beauty in this discourse is moral deformity, which also becomes a quasi-aesthetic category. Like moral beauty, it is recognizable by the sentiment it provokes in us, and, from Shaftesbury onward, that sentiment is a kind of horror.

Smith himself writes of both moral beauty and moral deformity in key passages of *The Theory of Moral Sentiments*. These passages matter not only to Smith's argument but also to the notion of sentimental monstrosity as it emerges in the decades that follow. To see just how they matter, especially to a work like Mary Shelley's *Frankenstein*, we must register the full force of a distinction that Smith makes *within* the moral tradition that he associates with the figure of the critic. The telling difference, as Smith himself explains it, is between two ways of grounding approbation in the principle of sentiment. In one approach, that of Shaftesbury and Hutcheson, the principle of sentiment is conceived as itself founded on a distinct power in the mind. For this newly discovered power, these thinkers produce a new name: the moral sense. The idea is laid out in several places by Shaftesbury, but nowhere more explicitly than in this passage from *Characteristics of Men*:

> In a creature capable of forming general notions of things, not only the outward beings which offer themselves to the sense are the objects of the affection, but the very actions themselves and the affections of pity, kindness, gratitude and their contraries, being brought into the mind by reflection, become objects. So that by means of this reflected sense, there arises another kind of affection toward those very affections themselves, which have been already felt and have now become the subject of a new liking or dislike.[6]

This kind of "reflected sense" operates in like fashion across the divide between, on the one hand, moral subjects and, on the other, the "ordinary or common subjects of sense." In Shaftesbury's aesthetic epistemology, the mind has its own "senses," its own eye and ear:

> The shapes, motions, colors, and proportions of these latter being presented to our eye, there necessarily results a beauty or deformity, according to the different measure, arrangement, and disposition of their several parts [and] according to the regularity or irregularity of their subjects.
>
> The mind, which is spectator or auditor of other minds, cannot be without its eye and ear so as to discern proportion, distinguish sound and

scan each sentiment or thought which comes before it. . . . It feels the soft and harsh, the agreeable and the disagreeable in the affections, and finds a foul and a fair, a harmonious and dissonant, as really and truly here as in any musical numbers or in the outward forms or representations of sensible things. (172)

Beauty is expressed in sensually apprehended regularity, deformity in its absence. The ladder of moral ascent in Shaftesbury's system is the ladder of generality. This is why he describes a human being in the first instance as "a creature capable of forming a general notion of things." This principle remains strong enough in the sentimental tradition to merit William Blake's famous rebuke at the turn of the nineteenth century that to generalize is to be an idiot.

Thus, in another part of *Characteristics*, a philosophical dialogue called *The Moralists, a Philosophical Rhapsody*, the Shaftesburyan stand-in, Philocles, describes the development of the virtuous mind to his worthy interlocutor, Palemon, as an ascent through levels of generality. Because Palemon is "experienced in all the degrees and orders of beauty," he will "rise to what is more general, . . . [seeking] that which is highest in the kind" (243). The enjoyment of a single beauty is not "sufficient to satisfy such an aspiring soul." This is why such a soul "seeks how to combine more beauties . . . to form a beautiful society" (243–44). But again, not "satisfied even with public good in one community of men, it frames itself a nobler object and with enlarged affection seeks the good of mankind" (244). And so on, to the contemplation of the universal mind by which "the beauty of things and the universal order [is] happily sustained" (244). Such is the self-acknowledged enthusiasm of the teleology of "moral sense" in the Shaftesburyan conception.

For his part, Smith lays out this position clearly, with a detailed explanation of the difference between "direct" and "reflex" senses, the latter deriving from the former. Though he names Hutcheson as a representative of this school of thought, the logic of the account, even the examples cited, are those given first by Shaftesbury: "In order to perceive the harmony of a sound, or the beauty of a colour, we must first perceive the sound or the colour. The moral sense was considered a faculty of this kind" (322). And by analogy, that "faculty again by which we perceive the beauty or deformity, the virtue or vice of those different passions and emotions, was a reflex, internal sense" (322).

Once Smith has outlined the moral-sense position toward the end of *The Theory of Moral Sentiments*, he raises some objections against it in favor of the alternative position, to which he declares himself a subscriber. This is the position that explains the sentiments of approbation by the operations of sympathy, rather than by a distinct "moral sense." At this late stage of the discussion, he has already long since delivered the crucial argument in favor of the one theory over the other, which has to do with the problem of "self-deceit, this fatal weakness of mankind" (158). The argument against the moral-sense view goes like this: "So partial are the views of mankind with regard to the propriety of their own conduct, both at the time of action and after it; and so difficult is it for them to view it in the light in which any indifferent spectator would consider it," that moral sense must prove not to be what it is that grounds our approbation (158). For "if it was by a peculiar faculty, such as the moral sense is supposed to be, that they judged of their own conduct," and "if they were endued with a particular power of perception, which distinguishes the beauty or deformity of passions and affections," then we might expect that we would be better judges in our own case than in that of another: "As their own passions would be more immediately exposed to the view of this faculty, it would judge with more accuracy concerning them, than concerning those of other men, of which it had only a more distant prospect" (158). Smith argues that the rampant spectacle of human self-deception gives the lie to this view. And his account of sympathy, with its feedback loops—the whole concept of the "impartial spectator"—is his answer to the problem. Our moral judgments about ourselves must therefore be understood not to depend on a peculiar faculty of moral sense but rather to be routed through our imagined sympathy with other points of view.

One of Smith's late reinforcing arguments against the moral-sense version of the sentiment-based theory of morals is that if a faculty as important as the moral sense existed, we would have had a name for it before the eighteenth century: "When love, hatred, joy, sorrow, gratitude, resentment . . . have made themselves considerable enough to get titles to know them by, is it not surprising that the sovereign of them all should hitherto have been so little heeded . . . that nobody has yet thought to bestow a name on it?" (326). The term "conscience," he argues, does not denote but rather presupposes the existence of some such faculty" (326). "Some such" faculty, however, need not on this account be a specially designated moral sense. While "conscience" may presuppose some faculty for grounding approbation, it nonetheless in itself signifies simply "our consciousness of having acted agreeably or contrary to its directions" (326).

This line of argument again seems to follow Shaftesbury's discussion in important ways. Here is Shaftesbury on the subject of conscience:

There are two things which to a rational creature must be horridly offensive and grievous, namely to have the reflection in his mind of any unjust action or behaviour, which he knows to be naturally odious and ill-deserving, or of any foolish action or behaviour, which he knows to be prejudicial to his own interest or happiness. (208)

Only the first of these is properly understood as a reaction of conscience (and for Shaftesbury, religious conscience presupposes what he calls "moral or natural conscience" [209]). This moral or natural conscience is necessarily more forceful in its reproach to one the more one attempts to disregard it: "Inward deformity growing greater by the encouragement of unnatural affection, there must be so much the more subject for dissatisfactory reflection, the more . . . any false religion or superstition prevails" (210). Thus, continues Shaftesbury, any such notion that we cherish, or character that we affect that is "contrary to moral equity and leads to inhumanity through a false conscience or wrong sense of honour, serves only to bring a man the more under the lash of real and just conscience, shame and self-reproach" (210).

In Shaftesbury's account, therefore, conscience too seems to benefit from the capacity for generalizing reflection—"reflex affections"—that leads us through the series of expansions from the particular instance to the "universal mind," inward beauty growing by the encouragement of the natural affections. As for the case of the person who would pervert that work of benevolent expansion, his inward deformity exacerbated in the feedback loop of unnatural affections, conscience rises to the occasion accordingly: the greater the perversion of moral growth, the sharper conscience's lash. In this account of conscience by Shaftesbury, one thus begins to see the point of Smith's critique about our capacity to delude ourselves. To posit that the lash of conscience will be in proportion to the inward deformity of the person of unnatural affections is to fail to give due weight to what Smith calls self-deceit.

Monstrosity in Shaftesbury and Smith

One can perhaps best see the distinction between these two approaches to sentimentalist moral theory in the differing ways in which Shaftesbury and Smith deal with the question of monstrosity. Shaftesbury's Philocles rounds off his speech about ascending the order of moral beauty by addressing moods of melancholy and skepticism:

This, Palemon, is the labour of your soul, and this its melancholy; when, unsuccessfully pursuing the supreme beauty, it meets with darkening clouds which intercept its sight. Monsters arise, not those from Libyan deserts, but from the heart of man more fertile, and with their horrid aspect, cast an unseemly reflection upon nature. (244)

This "unseemly reflection" about how "nature errs" amounts to an "arraigning" of the world and "voiding" of the deity responsible for it. These monsters of the mind quickly prove to be the counterparts of awkward facts about animal life, facts of the sort that the virtuosi of the period recorded in their cabinets of wonder. For Shaftesbury, the sentiment of wonder that inspires such collections seems to imply a monstrous mental reflection on an order of things in which, after all, some elements must necessarily be more beautiful than others to make possible a perception of beauty in the first place: "It is . . . from this order of inferior and superior things that we admire the world's beauty" (244).

Not to recognize this principle is a mistake of enormous proportions. It is indeed to allow the mere fact of deformity in the world—a fact that for Shaftesbury amounts to a necessary condition for beauty—to affect the soul of the beholder in disastrous ways. It is indeed to turn ourselves into monsters:

> Let us not therefore wonder if, by earthquakes, storms, pestilential blasts, nether or upper fires or floods, the animal kinds are often afflicted and whole species perhaps involved at once in common ruin; but much less let us account it strange, if, either by outward shock or some interior wound from hostile matter, particular animals are deformed even in their first conception, when the disease invades the seats of generation and the seminal parts are injured and obstructed in their accurate labours. It is then alone that monstrous shapes are seen, nature still working as before and not perversely or erroneously, not faintly or with feeble endeavours, but overpowered by a superior rival and by another nature's justly conquering force.
>
> Nor need we wonder if the interior form, the soul and temper, partakes of this occasional deformity and sympathizes with its close partner. Considering the strictness of this relation, who can wonder, if from a body originally impure, corrupt, distorted, a like soul arises? Who is there can wonder either at the sickness of sense or the depravity of minds enclosed in such frail bodies and dependent on such pervertible organs? (245)

This treatment of monsters in Shaftesbury's *Philosophical Rhapsody* is telling for what it shows about how Smith will diverge from his predecessor's attempt to build a moral system on the principle of sentiment. It is especially revealing in respect to the question of sympathy. Shaftesbury's notion of sympathy seems to be precisely a relation of sharing or contagion. In his account, the soul shares the condition of monstrosity with creatures deformed by the natural shocks that flesh is heir to, whether external or internal. Partaking of this deformity, sympathizing with its close partner, the body, a distorted soul is said by Shaftesbury to arise from a distorted body.

As it happens, Shaftesbury was much exercised by the interest in monsters in his own time, an interest much documented by recent work in the history of science in the early modern period.[7] The critique of the cabinet of wonder is anticipated earlier in *Characteristics of Men*, where he laments that the tales of travels that had so consumed the English reading public in the seventeenth century had turned the nation into so many Desdemonas, hanging on the Moor's tales of monsters and moving accidents. The "same Moorish fancy," writes Shaftesbury, "prevails strongly at the present time": "Monsters and monster lands were never more in request, and we may often see a philosopher or a wit run a tale-gathering in those 'idle deserts' as familiarly as the silliest woman or mere boy" (162). This contagion model of moral monstrosity is not unlike Wordsworth's concern with the spreading of a degraded public appetite for outrageous stimulation in the 1790s, when, in a poem from *Lyrical Ballads*, he in fact alludes to the same passage from *Othello* for similar ends.[8] Shaftesbury returns to this theme late in *Characteristics of Men*, when he reflects again on the status of the inferior virtuosi:

> In seeking so earnestly after these rarities they fall in love with rarity for rareness's sake. Now the greatest rarities in the world are monsters. So that the study and relish of these gentlemen, thus assiduously employed, becomes monstrous, and their whole delight is found to consist in selecting and contemplating whatever is most monstrous, disagreeing, out of the way and to the least purpose of anything in nature. (405)

This contagion model of sympathy proves to be exactly the model that Smith rejects in his effort to base moral approbation on a principle of sentiment in a way that requires no specially designated faculty, no moral sense.

In *The Theory of Moral Sentiments*, as we have seen, Smith's account of sympathy explicitly banishes, from the outset, the idea that we can feel what others feel in favor of the notion that we feel according to how we imagine it would be to place ourselves in their situations. Because we can view our own conduct from those same externalized situations, we develop an otherwise impossible sense of propriety about our moral judgments. The impartial spectator mediates for us. When the system works, it looks like the story of the Stoic exemplar, "the wise and just man who has been thoroughly bred in the great school of self-command":

> He has never dared to forget for one moment the judgment which the impartial spectator would pass upon his sentiments and conduct. He has never dared to suffer the man within the breast to be absent one moment from his attention. . . . He has been in the constant practice and, indeed, under the constant necessity, of modeling, or of endeavouring to model, not only his outward conduct and behaviour, but, as much as he can, even his inward sentiments and feelings according to those of this awful and respectable judge. He does not merely affect the sentiments of the impartial spectator. He really adopts them. He almost identifies himself with, he almost becomes himself that impartial spectator, and scarce ever feels but as that great arbiter of his conduct directs him to feel. (146–47)

The virtuous man's emulation of the impartial spectator involves a sense of vigilance ("He has never dared to forget . . .") and a certain striving ("endeavouring to model . . ."). And yet the means by which the impartial spectator develops over the course of a life is itself a function of our everyday experience of the social world. This capacity to reflect on ourselves, this mirroring function, derives from our capacity to see ourselves as others see us (to invoke Robert Burns's famous synopsis—in "To a Louse"—of what he read with admiration in *Theory of Moral Sentiments* as a young man).

By virtue of this vicarious practice—this sympathetic exchange of places—we gain perspective on our sentiments and motives: "we remove ourselves, as it were, from our own natural station, and endeavour to view them at a certain distance from us." And the only means we have for doing so is to view them "with the eyes of other people, or as other people are likely to view them." That is, "we endeavour to examine our own conduct as we imagine any other fair and impartial spectator would examine it" (110). This impartial spectator—the little man in our breast, the internal judge—not only derives from sympathy but also makes a second-order sympathy possible:

> If, upon placing ourselves in his situation, we thoroughly enter into all the passions and motives which influenced [our conduct], we approve of it, by sympathy with the approbation of this supposed equitable judge. If otherwise, we enter into his disapprobation, and condemn it. (110)

As we have seen, this functioning of sympathy in the process of approbation has two aspects or dimensions. There is the act of placing ourselves in the situation or case of another, and there is the entering into all the passions and motives involved in that case. This second aspect in turn depends on another level of sympathy: sympathy with the approbation of the internal spectator whose judgment is impartial. On such an account of moral perfection—such a revision of Shaftesbury's view of the expanding field of reflective affections—what does serious failure look like? What is Smith's picture of monstrosity?

This picture begins to emerge, I think, in Smith's effort to explain the necessity of social experience in the development of the impartial spectator, when he speculates about the fate of a human creature who is deprived of such experience:

> Were it possible that a human creature could grow up to manhood in some solitary place, without any communication with his own species, he could no more think of his own character, of the propriety or demerit of his own sentiments and conduct, of the beauty or deformity of his own mind, than of the beauty or deformity of his own face. . . . Bring him into society, and he is immediately provided with the mirror which he wanted before. It is placed in the countenance and behaviour of those he lives with, which always mark when they enter into, and when they disapprove of his sentiments; and it is here that he first views the propriety and impropriety of his own passions, the beauty and deformity of his own mind. (110–11)

In view of how much Smith draws from Shaftesburyan sentimentalism, the distinction that opens between them on this point is again quite a deep one. To put the matter too crudely, while Shaftesbury explains monstrosity by the presence of contagious sympathy in the human creature, Smith explains it by the absence of projective sympathy there. For in Smith's account, not to be able to recognize one's moral beauty or deformity is itself to become deformed. Not to fulfill the aspiration that our capacity for projective sympathy instills in us as creatures is to become an aberration.

There is a still larger issue at stake here about sentiment and deformity, and seeing it requires an understanding of Smith's sense of the operations of judgment as he develops the notion from Claude Buffier:

> In each species of creatures, what is most beautiful bears the strongest characters of the general fabric of the species, and has the strongest resemblance to the greater part of the individuals with which it is classed. Monsters, on the contrary, or what is perfectly deformed, are always most singular and odd, and have the least resemblance to the generality of that species to which they belong. And thus the beauty of each species, though

in one sense the rarest of all things, because few individuals hit this middle form exactly, yet in another, is the most common, because all the deviations from it resemble it more than they resemble one another. (198–199)

Here we have a theory of beauty and deformity articulated precisely in relation to an understanding of the monstrous. The beautiful object or creature conforms most fully to the general traits of the species to which it belongs. The deformed object deviates from those traits. The monstrous object is "perfectly deformed" in a way that corresponds to the perfectly beautiful object, the one that has the strongest resemblance to the generality of that species with which it is classed.

Smith is quick to assert that he does not fully subscribe to "the system of this learned and ingenious Father, concerning the nature of beauty; of which the whole charm, according to him, would thus seem to arise from its falling in with the habits which custom had impressed upon the imagination, with regard to things of each particular kind" (199). He insists that the *utility* of any form, "its fitness for the useful purposes of which it was intended" (199), also plays a role. Smith's account of beauty and deformity as a relation to the common features of the species in question, however, helps to clarify something important about the impartial spectator. For it suggests that the process of seeing our mind's beauty or deformity mirrored in the countenances or behavior of others also, in principle, underlies the process of becoming less deformed and more beautiful. Why? Because the operation of sympathetic identification in the daily life of commercial society brings our minds into greater conformity, greater harmony, with one another, and this conformity tends to make all the minds in that society more beautiful, less deformed.[9]

This account of judgment helps to explain why the place of the perfectly deformed human in Smith's world would be reserved for that creature that grows up in isolation from the sort of human intercourse that makes such amelioration possible. And that description provides an excellent segue to Mary Shelley's *Frankenstein*, modernity's highest-profile treatment of the question of monstrosity and one that is, as it happens, thoroughly steeped in eighteenth-century notions of sympathy and sentiment.[10]

Mary Shelley's Creature in the Balance

Frankenstein is a novel that has perhaps had as much attention in recent decades as any novel in English, and it is one of the handful of literary works to have achieved in modern culture something like the status of a full-fledged myth. Much of the attention that has been shown the novel, furthermore, has to do precisely with its relation to the sentimental tradition. Among the most detailed of commentaries is that of David Marshall, who, having written well about the British tradition of sentiment, deals with *Frankenstein* largely in the French tradition centered in Rousseau. The case for reading *Frankenstein* through Rousseau is a compelling one, on the basis of both external and internal evidence. The external evidence, amply documented by Marshall, among others, has to do with the well-established record of Rousseau's pervasiveness among the British exiles in Geneva, among whom Mary Shelley wrote her precocious novel.[11] The internal evidence is also compelling. In Rousseau's late autobiographical works, for example, one finds a strain of hyperbole about his sense of isolation and alienation that seems to be echoed by both Victor Frankenstein and his creature in their voluble accounts of their own extreme misery. It is known that Shelley was writing *Frankenstein* as she was rereading Rousseau's *Reveries*, one of the paranoid late works in question. Surely any reader of *Frankenstein* will recognize the hyperbolic rhetoric of Shelley's characters in Rousseau's opening:

> So now I am alone in the world, with no brother, neighbour, or friend, nor any company left me but my own. The most sociable and loving of men has with one accord been cast out by all the rest. With all the ingenuity of hate they have sought out the cruelest torture for my sensitive soul, and have violently broken all the threads that bound me to them.... Wrenched somehow out of the natural order, I have been plunged into an incomprehensible chaos.[12]

Comparing his present and former state, Rousseau even announces his dismay that, amiable as he was and still is, he should now "be taken beyond all doubt for a monster."[13]

In addition to these broadly sentimental resonances with the late Rousseau, there is another sentimental context that holds relevance for Mary Shelley's fable, and it derives from Smith. The central locus is a passage from *The Theory of Moral Sentiments* about the distinction between physical and moral deformity. Here Smith makes a connection with his account of how our sympathy for the distress of others has implications for how we view the human cause of that distress:

> When we see one man oppressed or injured by another, the sympathy which we feel with the distress of the sufferer seems to serve only to animate our fellow-feeling with his resentment against the offender. We are

rejoiced to see him attack his adversary in his turn, and are eager and ready to assist him whenever he exerts himself for defence, or even for vengeance within a certain degree. If the injured should perish in the quarrel, we not only sympathize with the real resentment of his friends and relations, but with the imaginary resentment which in fancy we lend to the dead, who is no longer capable of feeling that or any other human sentiment. But as we put ourselves in his situation, as we enter, as it were, into his body, and in our imaginations, in some measure, animate anew the deformed and mangled carcass of the slain, when we bring home in this manner his case to our own bosoms, we feel upon this, as upon many other occasions, an emotion which the person principally concerned is incapable of feeling, and which yet we feel by an illusive sympathy with him. (71)

It is a passage that seems especially to call forward to *Frankenstein*, in part because it has to do with animation of the dead.[14] Physical deformity is mentioned only secondarily here. It has to do with the "deformed and mangled carcass of the slain." But what is interesting about this scenario is that Smith does not imagine such physical deformity as an obstacle to sympathetic identification with the position of the injured party in the conflict, an identification that extends to resentment against the offending party.

Mary Shelley's novel seems not only to lend fictional embodiment to Smith's figure of a creature isolated from birth "without any communication with his own species," but also to play a variation on his notion of an animating sympathy with the dead. Here the sentimental soul takes on another of its many guises. In Smith's figure of animation, it is as if the sympathetic living could bring the dead back to life. In *Frankenstein*, this figure is strangely literalized. Denied all sympathy, even from his own maker from the very moment of his revival, the creature is at risk of being denied a soul. The relation between moral and physical deformity—indeed, the physical deformity of a reanimated carcass (or assemblage of carcasses)—is not so easily parsed. Shelley makes everything turn on Victor Frankenstein's initial response to the first waking moments of the creature he has brought to life, a face-to-face encounter with the gravest consequences. The creature opens his eyes, and Victor turns from him in disgust. Victor's aversion amounts to a decisive refusal of sympathy with his creature, one which adumbrates and triggers a series of such moments in the novel. The creature, for his part, interprets these events in terms that seem to be drawn directly from the eighteenth-century discourses on sympathy and sentiment. Indeed, the sentimental seems in this novel to be elevated to the status of a structural principle, and the idea of sympathetic mobility—the notion that in imagination we participate in human circumstances not our own—is raised to the level of a vital moral necessity. In this sort of sentimental chronotope we must, if we are to be accounted fully human, both participate vicariously in the lives of others and feel that others do in ours.

Such views are articulated with astonishing explicitness in the novel's core scene of confrontation between the creature and his maker. They come especially to the fore in the culmination of this exchange, when the creature, who is of course fully conversant with *Paradise Lost* from his eavesdropping on the De Laceys, makes his demand for a mate: "You must create a female for me, with whom I can live in the interchange of those sympathies necessary for my being."[15] When Frankenstein vacillates, the creature presses his case in more elaborate and more philosophically robust terms:

> If I have no ties and no affections, hatred and vice must be my portion; the love of another will destroy the cause of my crimes, and I shall become a thing of whose existence every one will be ignorant. My vices are the children of a forced solitude that I abhor; and my virtues will necessarily arise when I live in communion with an equal. I shall feel the affections of a sensitive being, and become linked to the chain of existence and events, from which I am now excluded. (142)

It might be tempting, of course, to dismiss this line of argument as a rhetorical contrivance, something improvised by the creature to advance the campaign to achieve his desired goal. The problem is that such language also pervades the frame narrative about Captain Walton and his initial encounter with Victor Frankenstein in the frozen north. Soon after Victor's initial recovery, as Walton explains in a letter to his sister, the captain addressed himself to him in words that the creature's comment unwittingly echoes: "I spoke of my desire of finding a friend—of my thirst for a more intimate sympathy with a fellow mind than had ever fallen to my lot; and expressed my conviction that a man could boast of little happiness, who did not enjoy this blessing" (27).[16] Victor's reply raises the stakes yet further on this point of moral theory, citing his own earlier connection with the murdered Henri Clerval:

> "I agree with you," replied the stranger; "we are unfashioned creatures, but half made up, if one wiser, better, dearer than ourselves—such a friend ought to be—do not lend his aid to perfectionate our weak and faulty natures. I once had a friend, the most noble of human creatures, and am entitled, therefore, to judge respecting friendship." (27–28)

This kind of analysis, appearing as it does on every level of the narrative, is enough to encourage us to take seriously the creature's point, and perhaps as well the demand in behalf of which he makes it.

We also know that Percy Shelley, who shared in the work on his wife's novel, held similar views about the necessity of the sympathetic imagination at about this time. The year after the publication of *Frankenstein*, he framed that point negatively in his Byronic critique of Wordsworth's egotism:

> He had as much imagination
> As a pint-pot—he never could
> Fancy another situation
> From which to dart his contemplation
> Than that wherein he stood.[17]

And two years after that, he framed the same point *positively* in "A Defence of Poetry": "A man, to be greatly good, must imagine intensely and comprehensively; he must put himself in the place of another and of many others."[18] It is true that there seems to be something ultimately vindictive in the creature's response, something that puts him less in league with Percy Shelley's Prometheus, who learns to recant his vindictive impulse against Jupiter, than with his Beatrice Cenci, who, persecuted and defiled beyond all normal levels of human forbearance, finally submits to her darker angels and avenges herself on her tormentor. There might even seem to be something unsavory about certain details of the creature's case for a female companion. One of his requirements, after all, is that she be as hideous as he is. Nonetheless, the forceful terms of sentimental moral logic in which the creature makes his case, echoed as they are by both Walton and Victor, make for a serious indictment against his creator. By his massive failure of sympathetic engagement with his own creature at the moment of his reanimation, Victor has arguably put the creature on the road to perdition. For a time, the creature makes repeated efforts to forge a human connection, often going to enormous pains to ensure success. But without Victor's support and endorsement, and without a little luck (think of the unfortunate timing of the creature's approach to the De Laceys), he cannot break from the prison of his own sentimental isolation.[19]

Giving her own creation a deformity that is external but not (as in the central line of film adaptations) neurological, Mary Shelley thus poises her novel on a delicately balanced question: will no one sympathize with the creature because he is a monster, or is he a monster because no one will sympathize with him? These opposed views correspond broadly to two ideological positions available to Mary Shelley in her moment: on the one hand, the sort of expansive social perfectibilist view held by her father, William Godwin and her husband Percy; on the other, the more Hobbesian position, shared in part by her father's antagonist Thomas Malthus, who advocated a zero-sum approach to political science.[20] In the one scheme, social transformation changes human nature. In the other, human nature limits social transformation.

The novel seems to waver between these two constructions of the world and of the creature's monstrosity within it. There is some reinforcement for the former view in the sheer extremity of the creature's vindictiveness and in the utter innocence of his victims. There is some reinforcement for the latter view in Mary Shelley's handling of the trial of the virtuous Justine, who is falsely accused of the murder of young William Frankenstein and who actually confesses to the crime: "Ever since I was condemned, my confessor has besieged me; he threatened and menaced, until I almost began to think I was the monster he said I was."[21] This is the tradition of sentimental monstrosity with which I wish presently to contrast the sentimentalism of the cinematic monster that takes shape in the hands of James Whale and Boris Karloff (and indeed the pastiche of that character later fashioned by Mel Brooks and Peter Boyle).

The Shelleyan line of sentimental monstrosity had enormous influence from early on, not least in Dickens. It shapes Dickens's handling of a character like Magwitch in *Great Expectations*, interestingly named Abel (not Cain). Magwitch seems a terrible villain until one learns more about the extenuating circumstances of his childhood, and Pip pointedly alludes to *Frankenstein* in reference to Magwitch's monstrosity. Indeed, the young Pip imagines himself monstrous after he lies about his experiences in the deformed world of Miss Havisham and Estella.[22] Dickens trades in unsentimental monsters as well, of course. Dan Quilp's cruelty to Little Nell is unredeemable in *The Old Curiosity Shop*, and that remains true when Griffith refashions him as Battling Burroughs in *Broken Blossoms*. The same is again true for Fagin in *Oliver Twist*. In that novel the functional equivalent of the sentimental monster is the figure of the "prostitute with the heart of gold," incarnated in Nancy, a member of Fagin's gang from childhood who nonetheless reforms in time to save Oliver. These two Dickensian figures might be said to merge in Patty Jenkins's film *Monster* (2003), in which Charlize Theron won an Oscar for her portrayal of Aileen Wuornos, who had been a victim of abuse as a child and became a sex worker and eventually a serial killer who preyed on the clients she solicited.[23]

In *Frankenstein* itself, the delicately balanced central question as I have posed it—is the creature rejected because he is a monster or is he a monster because he is rejected?—resonates in the novel's many postures of ambivalence, its staging of mixed feelings. That is, the issues that make up the subsets of this larger question are likewise characterized by this sort of ambivalence. Such issues include the balancing of the creature's reasonable claims to require a mate in order to achieve some degree of humanity and his insistence that the mate suffer from the same deformities that have cost him so dearly. They also extend to the balancing of the creature's remarkable capacity for benevolence (that supreme virtue of the Godwin-Wollstonecraft-Shelley circle) and his eventual instinct for vengeance (that supreme vice of the same circle). Many readers have noted the novel's failure, or refusal, to make decisive judgments about the ethical and political issues it makes central. Its implied author, one might say, lacks full coherence.

Lawrence Lipking's reading of *Frankenstein* correctly emphasizes the book's irresolution (a feature almost parodically registered in Victor Frankenstein's strange oscillations of opinion in his dying remarks to Captain Walton). Lipking suggests that the depth of the book's ambivalence has been masked by a politically correct critical consensus in recent years that he says derives from "collective identification with the outcast," the "sympathy we give to outcasts" in our time.[24] Without quite agreeing with Lipking's account of recent commentary on the novel, I do subscribe to his claim that the book both stages in itself and induces in its readers a certain "ambivalence" or "doublemindedness." This ambivalence, I have tried to suggest, dramatizes a set of central problems in the eighteenth-century line of sentiment in which the book patently takes its place.

Mary Shelley's ambivalence also reminds us that, though I have spoken of certain Dickens characters as sentimental monsters, there are important differences between how monstrosity plays out in his novels and hers. To put it schematically, Magwitch and Nancy correspond to that Godwinian side of *Frankenstein* that would represent the creature's monstrosity as a function or effect of social failure, while Quilp and Fagin correspond to the Hobbesian view that would represent the creature's monstrosity as a condition or cause of social failure. It is possible, I think, to see in this difference the effect of melodrama on the tradition of the sentimental. Emerging in the same moment as Schiller's aesthetic treatises of the mid-1790s, very much in the wake of the first waves of violence in the French Revolution, melodrama sorts anew the "mixed feelings" that Schiller associated with the sentimental. This is part of the context that Wordsworth was describing in 1800 in his account of the overheating of cultural productions to match the contemporary craving for outrageous stimulation: "frantic novels, sickly and stupid German tragedies, and idle and extravagant stories in verse."[25]

Gothic fiction, the theater of the *Sturm und Drang*, the ballads of Bürger—these were all part of the immediate context for the emergence of melodrama. The more distant contexts of course extend back into the eighteenth century. In the kind of "melo-drama" christened in France in that same year, 1800, and imported into Britain in 1802, passions run high, heroes and villains are easy to pick out, and revenge is brutal. The ideological registers of melodrama, however, are not easily settled. Indeed, one of the men accused in the 1794 treason trials—Thomas Holcroft—established both the term and the genre in Britain. It was Holcroft who imported the word into English for his 1802 translation, without acknowledgment, of Guilbert de Pixérécourt's *Coeline* (1800), which Holcroft retitled *A Tale of Mystery: A Melo-drame*. The fact that one of the radical victim-heroes of the treason trials became an exponent of the melodramatic mode only begins to suggest the political complications of this affective form in the Revolutionary period.[26] In terms of the story I tell here, with melodrama the sentimental "reform" of theater inaugurated by Richard Steele by means of the medium of print is all undone. Passions rematerialize, one might say, with a vengeance.[27]

Frankenstein itself shows traces of this cultural backlash against the sentimentalism that gained hegemony in the late eighteenth century. The effects of melodrama might already be said to be present in those aspects of *Frankenstein* that deal in horror and histrionics, vindictiveness and violence. *Frankenstein* is, of course, more usually treated as an example of the gothic mode in fiction, with predecessors among those "frantic novels" Wordsworth listed among the excesses of the 1790s.[28] In its hybridization of sentimental and gothic (or melodramatic) modes, *Frankenstein* betrays mixed feelings about the conditions of possibility for social monstrosity in the form of its central ambiguity about the etiology of the creature's pathology. Dickens, I've suggested, later unmixes some of these feelings by separating his monsters into two sorts, redeemable and otherwise. Perhaps Robert Louis Stevenson's *Dr. Jekyll and Mr. Hyde* gives us the ultimate version of the Victorian solution: splitting the single character into opposing moral personae.

Changing Places, Switching Brains

The decade of Capra's emergence as dominant director of the sentimental talkies is also the decade of the great cinematic adaptations of *Frankenstein*, commencing with James Whale's *Frankenstein* (1931). It is an irony that I do not pretend to account for that in the films of this period, the era of Capra's ascendence, the sentimental structure of Shelley's novel is displaced by something like its antithesis: a plotline that excludes sentimental ambivalence in favor of a material emphasis on neuropsychology as determinative. Nor was the 1931 adaptation a one-off phenomenon. Its success was sufficient to warrant a series of sequels by Universal Pictures, and in general these followed the same formula. The Whale formula, in turn, is beautifully captured and pastiched in the much later send-up by Mel Brooks—and Gene Wilder, with whom he wrote the screenplay—*Young Frankenstein*.

Brooks's film is of course something of a series of inside jokes, marked by a self-consciousness that is registered in the way the actors address the camera. This effect, while hilarious in itself, also has the effect of heightening patterns and effects present in the Whale films. Brooks's and Wilder's penetrating understanding of the Whale films, in other words, helps reveal the logic that informs them. With an uncanny eye for the telling detail, they zero in, for example, on the apparatus of the brain-switching plot in Whale's film. There is a powerful logic in this plot that Brooks and Wilder identify and then develop with witty explicitness. Central to this logic is the notion that the creature's monstrosity is materially and biologically constituted. It is a neurological fact intrinsic to his being. Whale had already recast Mary Shelley's Dr. Waldheim to play the role of expositor of the relevant facts in the revised version of the story. The professor patiently explains moral deformity as a function of brain structure, and he demonstrates the difference between a good and a bad brain in graphically visual terms.

Viewing Brooks's and Wilder's parody without recently having screened its targets, one might easily imagine that their first brain-switching episode is very different from its source in the Whale-Karloff *Frankenstein*. One might assume that details like a jar labeled "abnormal brain" are as contrived as the notice at the entrance to the lab that says brains should be slipped under the door after 5:00 p.m. In fact, however, Whale's *Frankenstein* also features a plot twist in which an abnormal brain is used for the monster, and this after showing us a scientific lecture on the subject. Key moments from each film actually correspond quite closely, all in strong contrast with the narrative logic of Shelley's novel. Punctuating this correspondence, Brooks and Wilder play out the logic of the moment of "human error"—the insertion of the wrong brain. Soon after the moment of reanimation, Freddy Frankenstein (Wilder) observes that the creature's behavior is not what he expected in a being having the brain he thought he had implanted, that of a late scientific genius. Even after he confirms that his assistant Igor (Marty Feldman) had

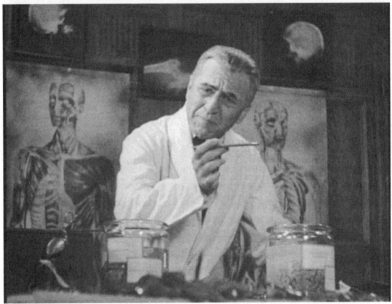

Brooks, *Young Frankenstein* (1974, 20th Century Fox). Igor with a brain in a jar.

Whale, *Frankenstein* (1931, Universal). Lecture on the criminal brain.

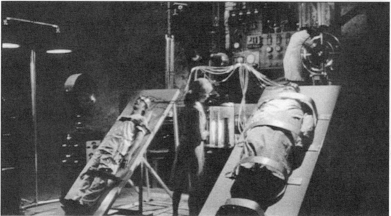

Frankenstein. Criminal brain in a jar.

Young Frankenstein. Brain-switching operation.

delivered the wrong brain, he remains sympathetic with the creature. Indeed, he eventually contrives a "solution" to the problem—surgical, not social—that involves a great sacrifice on his own part. He offers to switch his own brain with that of the creature, with hilarious erotic consequences for the parallel bedroom sequences that close the film.

Readers of Mary Shelley's novel will recall that her plot involves no brain-switching. There is no mistake of that sort, and thus no neural defect that can be assigned as the cause of Victor's alienating revelation. The novel does narrate the moment of alienation very explicitly, of course, and it comes in what Shelley later claims was the very first paragraph she wrote for the book, from Victor's account to Captain Walton of the night he made the sutured body live:

> It was on a dreary night of November that I beheld the accomplishment of my toils. With an anxiety that almost amounted to agony, I collected the instruments of life around me, that I might infuse a spark of being into the lifeless thing that lay at my feet. It was already one in the morning; the rain pattered dismally against the panes, and my candle was nearly burnt out, when, by the glimmer of the half-extinguished light, I saw the dull yellow eye of the creature open; it breathed hard, and a convulsive motion agitated its limbs.
>
> How can I describe my emotions at this catastrophe, or how delineate the wretch whom with such infinite pains and care I had endeavoured to form? (56)

In both early editions of the novel (1818 and 1831), as also in Richard Peake's influential 1823 stage adaptation, *Presumption*, the moment of Frankenstein's alienation occurs at the very moment the creature comes to life, with the opening of his dull yellow eyes. It is in this moment of eye contact that Victor notoriously turns from his creation, flees the room, and abandons the creature to fend for himself in what will prove to be a hostile world. The creature's explanation of all this comes during his confrontation with Victor on Mont Blanc, long after the creature has committed his monstrous acts of vengeance. We are left to weigh his sins in a balance with the sins against him, which arguably made him what he is.

Mary Shelley's creature is highly articulate, always a surprise to readers who come to the novel by way of the early films. He develops the equivalent of Peter Boyle's ultimate eloquence in *Young Frankenstein*, even without a second act of brain-switching, because the brain never was his problem. And this discourse (like Victor's) is characterized throughout by concern with questions of cause and effect. It is Victor's initial rejection, the creature later claims, that exposed the creature to a series of other escalating moments of rejection in the months that followed, and these collectively amount to the real cause of his having become monstrous. Hence the absolute centrality of the moment when the creature opens his eyes. In Peake's 1823 adaptation of Shelley's novel, Frankenstein simply says, "It lives!" and then, in a fashion still continuous with Shelley's novel, states his disgust directly:

> I saw the dull yellow eye of the creature open, it breached hard, and a convulsive motion agitated its limbs. What a wretch have I formed, his legs are in proportion and I had selected his features as beautiful—beautiful! Ah, horror! his cadaverous skin scarcely covers the work of muscles and arteries beneath, his hair lustrous, black, and flowing—his teeth of pearly whiteness—but these luxuriances only form more horrible contrasts with the deformities of the monster.... What have I accomplished? the beauty of my dream has vanished! and breathless horror and disgust now fill my heart.[29]

Thus in both Shelley's and Peake's presentations of the story, both on the page and on the stage, Frankenstein's initial horror and disgust at what he has brought to life is a constant and crucial component. It has to be so, really, if it is to figure as a possible cause for the creature's rejection and thus for his turning monstrous.

In the Whale films, however, the first encounter between Frankenstein and his newly animated creature is marked by anything but repugnance. The Colin Clive lines, brilliantly echoed by Gene Wilder—"Alive, it's alive . . ."— are so familiar and so often deployed in popular culture, that we may have become inured to the sense of wonder they are meant to convey. It is true that for Clive's Frankenstein in the 1931 film, the sense of wonder becomes a kind of manic glee, and true too that he may be ecstatic for not altogether admirable reasons, imagining himself to have usurped the powers of God. But he expresses no disgust at the monster's appearance, nor does he reject his person. And at the corresponding moment in Whale's 1935 sequel, *The Bride of Frankenstein*, Clive all but reprises his earlier lines: "She's alive." Brooks's version of the scene again calls attention to the logic inherent in Whale's film. That is, he has Wilder playing a kind of infantilizing love scene with the supine creature, who is just coming to consciousness on the table, a strange excess of affection that is underscored by Peter Boyle's puzzled but somehow knowing roll of the eyes in the midst of his otherwise dazed state.

The moral logic of this narrative sequence in the Whale films can be briefly summarized. The issue with the creature, at least as far as Franken-stein is concerned, has to do with his brain rather than his "person." In such a narrative framework, the claim made by the creature in Mary Shelley's novel—namely, that he is a victim of Victor's primordial abandonment—could have no force or traction. Of course, the Whale-Karloff creature lacks the capacity to make such a representation in the first place. One implication of this, we can note in passing, is that the reaction of Frankenstein to his own creature is to be distinguished from (rather than standing as exemplary for) that of the other people whom the creature encounters in his travels, the people Teri Garr's character comically refers to as "the villagers." For the Whale line of cinematic adaptation, the fact of the creature's having a brain identified a priori as "abnormal" or "criminal" is decisive. And Brooks fully plays out the implications of this premise in the final scene of *Young Franken-stein*, in which Wilder's affection for his creation extends even to a willing-ness to switch his own brain for the creature's, or at least to switch brain fluids (a biotechnological development of the twentieth century[30]). This sacrifice on Frankenstein's part leads to the eloquent elegy, premature as it turns out, by a newly humanized Peter Boyle over the body of his creator. It is a moment in which the cinematic creature, by virtue of the confusion, attains to the skill in communication that so characterizes his original in Shelley's novel. Soul, here, is all but determined by the body.

This comparison in narrative logics is helpful, I think, in identifying the sentimental constitution of both novel and creature in Mary Shelley's hands, identifying it in a way that distinguishes it from the cinematic *Frankenstein*. It is true that there is a whiff of what might be called sentimentality in Peter Boyle's speech over the body of Gene Wilder, perhaps the articulation of a strain of sentimentality that runs through the earlier Whale films. Think of the scenes in which the Whale-Karloff creature, in spite of his acts of brutal violence, is portrayed in postures of victimhood. This becomes more evident in *The Bride of Frankenstein* (1935), which picks up certain parts of the Shel-ley novel that were neglected in the 1931 film. Though the sequel does not provide a fully developed account of the creature's year of secret spectatorship and service at the cottage of the De Lacey family, it does include a version of one of its moments of climactic pathos. The creature enters the cottage of a blind man and is welcomed as a friend, creating a sense that he might be redeemable after all, only to be interrupted by humans who can see his deformity.

To be sure, Whale's films contain marked moments where the crea-ture seems to stand puzzled and victimized by his circumstances: overlong arms extended palms open, longing for human connection, calling out for a "friend"—one of the few words, most of them monosyllabic, that Karloff's monster has when, in the sequel, he does finally learn to speak a little. In the cinematic tradition, then, the sentimental element stays on the surface, since the on-screen monster is determined by a neurological fact. Though there may be moments of pathos or bathos, their significance to the plot is only local. One has no real sense of a second path for the creature: he is doomed to monstrosity from the start.

In the Whale and Brooks plots, in short, the sentimental seems at best a weakly stylistic element, what we might call "mere sentimentality." The sentimental does not define a structural principle, as it does in Shelley's novel—a key framework for issues of probability, and for the motives and identities of characters. In the novel, the principle of sympathetic mobility, as elaborated in the sentimental tradition—the notion that in imagination we participate in emotional experiences not our own—is raised to the level of a moral necessity. In this sort of sentimental chronotope, to be accounted fully human one must both share in the experience of others and have them share in one's own life. It is true that this principle comes into play less in the declarative than in the interrogative mode, that delicately balanced question about failed sympathy and achieved monstrosity at the heart of Shelley's book. It is in play nonetheless.

Her book might be said to offer a kind of apotheosis of Schiller's idea of the sentimental as mixed feelings generated by reflexivity. By contrast, the tendency of the Whale line of cinematic adaptations of *Frankenstein* seems to be to lift us clear of this sort of ambivalence and reflexivity. If, as I have argued, the tradition of the sentimental begins with the Latitudinarian attempt to save the notion of the soul from the threat of scientific materialism, then Whale's *Frankenstein*—after a century that saw both real developments in neuroscience and physiognomical theories of criminality such as those of Cesare Lombroso—seems rather to endorse that materialism, or in any case to reject the sentimental compromise. Mel Brooks, to his great credit, seems to have intuited and accentuated this intention, and driven it home with the force of a great punch line.

Of course, the Whale-Brooks sequence of *Frankenstein* adaptations is only a part of what filmmakers have tried to do with the story. There have been almost two hundred adaptations in all.[31] Some have incorporated the frame story of Captain Walton and polar exploration, which has been left out of most adaptations since Peake's *Presumption* took the stage in 1823. Some have framed the tale with a representation of Mary Shelley and her famous literary circle composing ghost stories in 1818. A good Frankenstein film to close with, perhaps, is the earliest I have found, the 1910 Edison adaptation, less than ten minutes long in its entirety. The final two scenes of the film involve the monster's assault on Victor Frankenstein's wife. This episode has been part of virtually all versions of the story, though in the twentieth-century cinema tradition, beginning with this 1910 short film, Elizabeth's life is almost always spared, as it is not in Mary Shelley's novel.

In the Edison one-reeler, the creature enters the house but cannot bring himself to commit the depredation on Elizabeth that he appears to have intended. He spares her, and then he flees. Victor follows him into the house only to find him gone. Victor then turns toward a mirror, and as he beholds himself there, his reflection becomes that of his creature. The film thus captures the doppelgänger motif, turning the creature finally into a literal reflection of his creator. While this film does not enforce the materialist reduction of the creature's monstrosity to neurology, neither does it retain the thematic importance and plot relevance that Shelley's novel attaches to Victor's sympathy, or failure of sympathy, with his creature. Insofar as anything like sympathy functions in the final scenes of the Edison *Frankenstein*, it has to do with Elizabeth, and with the creature's being overcome with affection for her—a plot twist I have found nowhere else in the Frankenstein tradition. It does, however, suggest that the theme of reflective self-recognition (or its failure) was readily available for cinematic treatment, had Whale chosen to explore it.

PART 3   Against Sentiment

When Sergei Eisenstein argued in 1944 that cinema could not be fully understood without reference to its literary traditions, his account proved as tendentious in its teleology as it was inspired in its instinct to connect literature and cinema in the first place. As we noted at the outset, the essay on Dickens and Griffith provides a genealogy of certain Soviet film practices, to the exclusion of the sorts of connections I have examined so far in this book. That is, it is concerned with dialectical montage, and perhaps dialectical materialism, rather than its sentimental alternative. Another major critical intervention of the mid-1940s, Max Horkheimer and Theodor Adorno's chapter entitled "The Culture Industry" in *Dialectic of Enlightenment*, attacked the cinema spawned by Griffith in more aggressively polemical terms. It was written during its authors' decade-long exile in Los Angeles, where they spent time with fellow exiles who had taken jobs in Hollywood, like Hanns Eisler, with whom Adorno collaborated on a book about film music. They also corresponded with other exiles, like Siegfried Kracauer, who was in New York reviewing American cinema and writing a book on German cinema.[1] The "Culture Industry" chapter represents one of the most searing indictments ever leveled at commercial cinema and at the larger system to which they saw it as central.

Horkheimer and Adorno got a close-in view of Hollywood at just about the point when Capra achieved the zenith of his influence there. Indeed, viewed in light of Capra's recursive project and his great power in Hollywood until 1948, many of their formulations seem aimed at him and his work. It is not clear how much American cinema they knew firsthand, but Capra often seems to be in their sights; there are moments in the chapter on the culture industry that read almost like a commentary on the Capraesque, especially when the subject turns to those "acts of sympathy"[2] that are often emphasized in Hollywood films:

> By emphasizing the "heart of gold," society admits the suffering it has created: everyone knows that he is now helpless in the system, and ideology has to take this into account. Far from concealing suffering under the cloak of improvised fellowship, the culture industry takes pride in looking it in the face like a man, however great the strain on self-control. The pathos of composure justifies the world which makes it necessary. That is life—very hard, but just because of that so wonderful and so healthy. (131)

Though it was probably written in 1944, the year of Eisenstein's essay, "The Culture Industry" was not published until 1947. It is thus at least conceivable that "That is life ... so wonderful" was a very contemporary allusion to Capra's 1946 tag phrase. It may also be an allusion to Griffith's dark and ironically titled *Isn't Life Wonderful?* (1924), in which the director who invented Hollywood also seemed to make a point of looking social suffering in the face, as Horkheimer and Adorno put it, like a man.

In any case, one might well take this passage to be a commentary on a high-profile Capra film such as *Mr. Deeds Goes to Town*, with that iconic sequence that puts the Capra stand-in, Gary Cooper's Longfellow Deeds, face to face with the poor farmer who speaks for the suffering of society's casualties in the mid-1930s. The scene, as we saw, involves an act of sympathy that visibly strains the sentimental protagonist's self-control. And in a sense the pathos of his composure justifies the world that makes it necessary, a world left essentially unchanged at fable's end. In 1940, even closer to the composition of "The Culture Industry," Capra brought Gary Cooper back in a far darker comedy, *Meet John Doe*, and of course Preston Sturges sent up the very idea of Hollywood looking suffering in the face with *Sullivan's Travels* (1941), which, as we saw in chapter 3, singles out Capra by name for his trumpeted aspiration to make film realize "the possibilities of the artistic and sociological medium that it is."[3]

There are certain moments in "The Culture Industry" where Horkheimer and Adorno describe the Hollywood film establishment in terms reminiscent of Capra's own frequent complaints about the system:

> The stunting of the mass-media consumer's powers of imagination and spontaneity does not have to be traced back to any psychological mechanisms; he must ascribe the loss of those attributes to the objective nature of the products themselves, especially to the most characteristic of them, the sound film. . . . Even though the effort required for his response is semi-automatic, no scope is left for the imagination. Those who are so absorbed by the world of the movie—by its images, gestures, and words— that they are unable to supply what really makes it a world, do not have to dwell on particular points of its mechanics during a screening. All the other films and products of the entertainment industry which they have seen have taught them what to expect; they react automatically. . . . From every sound film and every broadcast program the social effect can be inferred which is exclusive to none but is shared by all alike. The culture industry as a whole has moulded men as a type unfailingly reproduced in every product. (126–27)

At almost the same moment, Capra can be found making similar-sounding critical observations about the routinizing and homogenizing effects of the studio system on the quality of American cinema, as can be seen in his 1946 comments for the *New York Times* in "Breaking Hollywood's Pattern of Sameness."[4] His first programmatic film of the 1940s, *Meet John Doe*, makes such tensions between system and personhood explicit from the start, with its montage sequence playing between homogeneity and individuality, crowds and characters, during the opening credits.[5]

Yet such is the totalizing character of the cultural-industrial system described by Horkheimer and Adorno—one in which the studio system was embedded—that even would-be mavericks all must play their part in it. By a logic that Adorno often used in explaining, say, the delusive improvisatory freedom of the firmly shackled jazz musician—an analogy that he indeed makes explicit in this analysis—all deviations from the culture industry prove to support it in the end. And this holds nowhere more clearly than in cinema. Even Orson Welles, the Hollywood rebel par excellence, does not escape: "Whenever Orson Welles offends against the tricks of the trade, he is forgiven because his departures from the norm are regarded as calculated mutations which serve all the more strongly to confirm the validity of the system" (129). The principle would surely apply to Capra *a fortiori*. For his offenses against the system, after all, he was rewarded with a special contract at Columbia Studios and the dual presidencies of the Motion Picture Academy and the Screen Directors Guild.

Whether it is understood as the Capraesque itself or a more general Hollywood formation, the target of Horkheimer and Adorno's critique seems recognizably associated with sentimentality. Indeed, this is one of the ways in which their polemic is briefly characterized by other commentators.[6] The reasons for this perception are perhaps already clear enough in their emphasis on "acts of sympathy" and the "heart of gold." But the emphasis becomes even clearer in their elaboration of how commercial interests (epitomized in "advertising") flatten the inner life of the emotions:

> The way in which a girl accepts and keeps the obligatory date, the inflection on the telephone or in the most intimate situation, the choice of words in conversation, and the whole inner life as classified by the now somewhat devalued depth psychology, bear witness to man's attempt to make himself a proficient apparatus, similar (even in emotions) to the model served up by the culture industry. The most intimate reactions of human beings have been so thoroughly reified that the idea of anything specific to themselves now persists only as an utterly abstract notion: personality scarcely signifies anything more than shining white teeth and freedom from body odour and emotions. The triumph of advertising in the culture industry is that consumers feel compelled to buy and use its products even though they see through them. (167)

The mass production of affect, the commercialization of the spectator, the reification of intimacy: these have become familiar enough themes for cultural critique in recent decades. And when Adorno revisited his argument two decades later, he himself deployed the term "sentimentality" to categorize the object of his critique.[7]

Horkheimer and Adorno's critique of sentimentality has long been seen as undertaken in behalf of a modernist commitment to negative aesthetic interventions by the avant-garde. Commentaries on the connection, vexed but real, between Frankfurt School critique and modernist aesthetics have been with us for a while.[8] More recently, this kind of aesthetic project has been shown by Robert Kaufman to have strong roots in Romanticism, a movement in which Jacques Rancière locates the origins of what he calls the "aesthetic regime" as such.[9] This sense of Romanticism is to be distinguished, however, from what Adorno himself calls the generic form of "rationally supposed and adapted romanticism" when he revisits his earlier critique in 1963. For in that sense, "romanticism," lowercase, is something he associates directly with what he terms "sentimentality."[10]

For evidence that the Romantic movement in early nineteenth-century Britain manifests early stirrings of Adorno's brand of cultural critique, one need only turn to Shelley's "Defence of Poetry," as Kaufman suggests, or even to Wordsworth's preface to *Lyrical Ballads*, with its aspiration to deploy serious poetic art against modernization and massification. These latter were historical developments that Wordsworth understood as the effects of "causes unknown to former times," such as new media for the "rapid communication of intelligence," and new demographic patterns, such as "the accumulation of men in cities" where "the uniformity of their occupations" produces a craving for extraordinary stimulation, reducing their minds to "a state of almost savage torpor."[11] It was a situation in which, on his analysis, the 1790s equivalent of a culture industry fed tendencies that his own art sought specifically to counteract. At Cambridge in the 1920s, the neo-Romantic theorist I. A. Richards would reject the Schillerian idea of the "aesthetic state" as a "phantom," but would also invoke the critical language of Wordsworth, Coleridge, and Shelley to build a program of literary study very much in line with modernist values. His experiments in "practical criticism" aimed to cultivate an appreciation of serious (unsentimental) poetry against what he saw as the degraded taste of his moment.[12] And he symptomized this degradation, as I explain in the coda, by pointing to the threat of cinema.

Broadly speaking, these two movements, Romanticism and modernism, have long been understood to oppose sentimentalism. It is for this reason that I have chosen to round out this book by attending to some key encounters in each movement that seem to complicate any notion of a straightforward passage from the emergence of sentimentalism in the eighteenth century to its redeployment in early cinema. My treatment of large and vexed questions in these two antisentimental movements is obviously selective in the extreme. I mean to suggest that iconic authors in each movement—Blake and Wordsworth, Conrad and Joyce—were far more intricately engaged with the sentimental mode than we typically suppose. I will argue that their work therefore bears more of the markings of the sentimental mode than we usually recognize, and that their complex negotiations of the sentimental legacy are central to some of their signature achievements.

EIGHT   Romanticism

My discussion to this point has included several references to Romantic period writers, and we have already had glimpses of how some of them responded to sentimentalism. In chapter 6 we glanced at the "first American
novel," William Hill Brown's *The Power of Sympathy*; in chapter 7, we looked
in some detail at Mary Shelley's *Frankenstein*. We have had occasion to note
how their more celebrated contemporaries, Walter Scott and Jane Austen, responded to the sentimental. Scott's dedication of *Waverley* to Henry
Mackenzie, author of *The Man of Feeling* (1771), and Austen's handling of
the Marianne Dashwood plot in *Sense and Sensibility* are really only a small
part of the story. The career of an Anglo-Irish novelist who shaped the work
of both Scott and Austen, Maria Edgeworth, was deeply affected by her
engagements with writers representing a range of aspects of the sentimental
tradition. Edgeworth was made by her widower father to read Adam Smith
at the tender age of thirteen so that she could help him raise her siblings as
the family reassumed residence on the hereditary Irish estate. Several of her
early novels amount to extended fictional conversations with sentimentally
inflected works of her contemporaries. *Lenore* (1806) was a clear response
to Germaine de Staël's *Delphine* (1803), which Edgeworth read on her visit
to Geneva in 1803, when it was all the rage. *Ennui* (1809) and *The Absentee*

(1812) responded to Lady Morgan's *The Wild Irish Girl* (1806), in each case with a figure of good (Smithian or Burkean) sentimentalism set against the influence of bad sensibility. Much more could be said about Romantic fiction and the sentimental novel, and literary historians have indeed lately been saying it.[1]

I will return to the Romantic novel briefly in the context of chapter 9's (very selective) discussion of modernist fiction. In this chapter I intend to consider the fate of the sentimental mode in the context of poetry. There has been less attention to how the great poets of the Romantic period responded to what was after all still a very active culture of sentimentalism in their time; perhaps the most notable exception is Jerome McGann's book on Romanticism and the "poetics of sensibility."[2] The relevance of sensibility, as I have explained it here, to canonical Romanticism could certainly also be indexed by Keats's celebrated conceit of "the vale of soul-making," which hews close to the Latitudinarian line.[3] But *sensibility* names only one strand of the story I have been telling. What about questions of sympathy, spectatorship, and the sentimental case? How do we address them in the context of poetry, especially lyric poetry? Questions of point of view, for example, do not have quite the same status in the genre of the lyric as they do in prose fiction or in narrative cinema. That said, many of the issues in Romantic poetry are very much in line with those we have so far considered, such as the characteristic features of mixed feelings, slippage of levels, and interchangeability of subject positions. It is just that in short works of verse, these features tend to manifest differently. Fungible voices, for example, may do the work accomplished by fungible points of view in fiction or cinema. Compression matters, as well, in ways that demand paronomasia and other forms of poetic ambiguity. Syntactical ambiguity in particular plays a central role in some of the analyses that follow.

By way of preview, we might briefly consider Marx's early poem "Sentimental Souls," which I included as an epigraph to this book, and which, apart from a few throwaway lines by Edmund Wilson in 1940,[4] has not enjoyed much critical attention:

> Sie weinen! ach! der Metzger schlachtet ein Kalb!
> Erst brüllte die Bestie noch, jezt ist sie falb!
> Sie lachen! Himmel, wie närrisch in seiner Art,
> Natur, Natur! Ein Hund trägt keinen Bart!
> Was sprudelt ihr hoch, als wart ihr gesonnt?
> Wir hören, wie Bielams Esel gar sprechen konnt!⁵

The three couplets that constitute this poem establish voice positions that are ambiguated in ways that, by the end, make it hard to know who is speaking what. The play of pronouns is crucial. We can begin with the third-person plural *sie* that introduces the two parallel movements of the poem's first two couplets. "They cry . . . / They laugh." Presumably the referent is the "sentimental souls" of the poem's title, and the object of both their crying and laughing is the calf being slaughtered. There is also a kind of parallel between the sounds "they" make and the sounds made by the calf. That is, their crying—*weinen*—seems to be more than faintly echoed in the creature's bellowing (*brüllte*).

The syntax and the formal construction of the poem lead us to conclude that the words "Himmel, wie narrisch in seiner Art, / Natur, Natur, Ein Hund trägt keinen Bart!"—are spoken by the sentimental souls. These are the words they "laugh" (transitively, as the content of their laughter), just as "Ach! die Metzger . . ." supplies the content of what they transitively "cry." The words themselves, however, are not so easily parsed. Consider the position of the phrase "in seiner Art," between the two ejaculations, "Himmel" and "Natur, Natur!" The gender of the pronoun "seiner" means that the phrase must refer backward to "Himmel," in which case "Natur, Natur!," which follows, becomes an interruptive ejaculation, explicated as it were by the quasi-proverbial declaration: "Ein Hund trägt keinen Bart!" (That is: heaven is mad or foolish in its ways of doing things, whereas nature's ways are straightforward: a dog understood naturally cannot be said to wear a beard.) But the juxtaposition of heaven and nature in these two ejaculations prepares for a further complication of sentimentalism's play with levels in the question and answer that comprises the last two lines.

The first problem has to do with the addressee of the question, which introduces the first second-person pronoun into the poem: *ihr*. Is this addressed to the "sentimental souls" whose cry and laugh is recorded in the first four lines? If so, then presumably their crying and laughing are what is indicated by *sprudelt* (bubble up)? Or are the words to be understood as spoken by the sentimental souls to the calf about his own expressive sounds, his "bellowing"? The answer to this matters for how we read the last pronoun in the sequence, the first-person plural of the last line: "We hear. . . ." Does *wir* refer to the sentimental souls, understood here as answering or qualifying their own question, in a fashion well within the range of lyric convention? Or, in a reading equally licensed by lyric convention, is this the editorial "we" of the narrating voice, entering into the poem in the final couplet to comment on the exclamations of the sentimental souls? What light on these problems is shed by the poem's last six words, delivered with the promise of a clarification or resolution? What "we hear" is that (or how) "even Balaam's ass could speak."

The invocation of the biblical story of Balaam's ass complicates and enriches the poem that precedes it, especially in the way it highlights the question of the poem's implicit three levels: the heavenly, the human, and the animal. For Balaam's ass spoke after being beaten by Balaam for having stopped in the middle of the road. But the reason the ass stopped is that an angel of the Lord appeared to it in a way that was not evident to Balaam. The trio of the traveler, the ass, and the angel is one that Sterne explicitly invokes in describing to a friend his project in writing *Tristram Shandy*,[6] but it is also a constellation that hovers over much of the sentimental tradition. Tristram has a conversation with an ass that blocks his way at the gates of Lyons during his travels in France. He even feeds the ass a macaroon, then expresses mixed feelings about the ass's way with this morsel.[7] The same ass is soon beaten by its returning owner, who beats Tristram as well. Wordsworth's 1798 manifesto poem, *Peter Bell* (not published until 1819), plays changes on this same set of circumstances: the titular Balaam figure also beats his ass for its refusal to move, and suffers supernatural fits of remorse for his crimes. Sterne himself includes a dead ass in *Sentimental Journey*, as we have seen, an episode that involves a displacement of the Balaam story. Here the spirit of the ass, as it were, plays the angel to La Fleur's bidet (a small horse), who refuses to pass by the corpse lying in the road. Behind all of this, as Sterne himself suggests in the letter that serves as my second epigraph for this book, may lie the precedent of Sancho Panza's ass, which is itself involved in Cervantes's famous episode about a dead mule by the side of the road in the Sierra Moreno.[8]

Marx's decision to conclude a poem called "sentimental souls" with a reference to Balaam's ass, in other words, seems anything but arbitrary. It betrays the poem's knowing wink to the sentimental tradition invoked in its title, likewise his deployment of effervescent ejaculations, and his play with the question of their sources: heavenly, human, or animal. Is Marx playing on Yorick's famous paean to "Sensibility" in *Sentimental Journey*, which appears just after the encounter with Maria and her dog, and also after his claim to know now that he "has a soul" in spite of "all the books with which the materialists have pestered the world"? Sterne's passage, after all, combines the English for the ejaculation *Himmel*, with the figure of bubbling up: "Dear Sensibility! Source inexhausted of all that's costly in our joys, or costly in our sorrows! . . . HEAVEN—eternal fountain of our feelings! 'tis here I trace thee" (115). Indeed, Marx's whole poem seems marked by a distinctive kind of self-reflexive art that offers itself to the unsuspecting eye as something less complicated.

This is true not least in the use of the German word *Art*. Though *Art* is by no means reducible to *Kunst* in German, the appearance of the term here amounts to a vaguely bilingual pun. The poem marks its interest in bilingualism in its very title—we recall that the Germans had no term for "sentimental" when Sterne's *Sentimental Journey* was first published. *Art*, then, becomes a play on words not only in German—where the meaning can range from "way," to "fashion" or "manner," to something closer to art as technique—but also between German and English. Thus do the terms "nature" and "art" come to have a complex relationship that is more artful than the naturalness of its ejaculations might seem to suggest. Thus, too, does the poem motivate both of the terms in its title, showing its grasp of the sentimental mode and its sense of the stakes for the soul—heavenly, human, animal—in its deployment.

We know that the young Marx—poet, philosopher, and student of alienation—was well aware of the legacy of Schiller. It was Schiller who supplanted the German neologism *empfindsam* with the hybrid term *sentimentalisch* in his 1795 treatise, even as Marx does him one better with the French (all but English) *sentimental*.[9] There is also good evidence that Marx knew his Sterne from early days. While one biographer even describes Marx in this period as having written a "short 'humoristic novel'... under the spell of Sterne's *Tristram Shandy*," there seems to be no evidence that Marx knew Blake, whose work did not circulate widely for decades, although the temptation to relate their respective bodies of writing has been overwhelming for many commentators.[10] I am not sure that any has looked specifically at Marx's poetry in this connection, nor will I, except to say that some of the kinds of issues raised by "Sentimentale Seelen" are helpful in seeing how Blake also dealt with the discourse of the sentimental in compressed lyric form. In both cases, I stress, it is not just a matter of writing about the sentimental but rather of engaging with its forms. In both cases, and to a degree in Wordsworth, we discover a kind of *translation* of visual structures into voice structures: that is, of the sight lines that connect the points of view of sentimental spectators into echo patterns that connect the vocal positions of sentimental speakers and hearers.

Un-Huming Understanding

Although I contend that much of Blake's work is implicitly structured in and against the sentimental as a moral and aesthetic mode, his most explicit engagements with the discourse of sentiment are somewhat sparsely scattered through the letters and annotations. Consider his annotations to Boyd's *Historical Notes on Dante* (1785), and especially his comment on a passage where Boyd reflects at some length on certain characters in *The Inferno*, a text that Boyd numbers among "some Other POEMS relative to the ORIGINAL PRINCIPLES OF OUR NATURE." This is the passage in Boyd, one that echoes the idiom of Adam Smith's writing on moral sentiments:

> Such may be good poetical characters, of that mixt kind that Aristotle admits; but the most beautiful mixture of light and shade has no attraction, unless it warms the heart. It must have something that engages the sympathy, something that appeals to the moral sense, for nothing can thoroughly captivate the fancy, however artfully delineated, that does not awake the sympathy and interest the passions and appeal to our native notions of right and wrong.
>
> It is this that sets the Odyssey, in point of sentiment, so far above the Iliad. We feel the injuries of Ulysses; . . . we seem to feel the generous indignation of the young Telemachus, and we tremble at the dangers of the fair Penelope. . . . We can go along with the resentment of Ulysses, because it is just, but our feelings must tell us that Achilles carries his resentment to a savage length, a length where we cannot follow him.[11]

Blake's attitude toward the moral theory implicit in these remarks—their focus on considerations "in point of sentiment"—is revealed in the way he annotated this text. Where Boyd writes of the mixed character's failure to engage us "unless it warms the heart," Blake amends the verb to read "warms or freezes" (633). Where Boyd speaks of something that appeals to moral sense, Blake strikes "moral sense" and inserts "passions & senses." And as a comment on the entire passage, Blake writes: "If Homers [*sic*] merit was only in these Historical combinations and Moral sentiments he would be no better than Clarissa" (633). Blake's relation to Richardson is a subject upon which Leo Damrosch has touched in remarks suggesting that Blake's allegory of the worm as rapist in "The Sick Rose" ironizes Clarissa's meditation after she has been raped by Lovelace: "Thou eating canker-worm, that preyest upon the opening bud, and turnest the damask rose into livid yellowness."[12] In 1804 Blake wrote in a more laudatory vein to William Hayley about Richardson, but one suspects that this may have been one of those moments of tactical compromise with Hayley's polite culture that he later regretted.[13]

The larger point here is that Blake's specific comments on and corrections to Boyd's text reveal a firm grasp of the logic and structure of moral sentiment in their time. They certainly betray a suspicion of the sentimental mode consistent with Blake's critique of what might be termed the doctrine of the human heart, a doctrine he associated with writings he tended to call "Deist." In his "Address to the Deists," introducing chapter 3 of *Jerusalem*, Blake linked the names of Voltaire, Rousseau, Gibbon, and Hume in order to tar them all with the same brush: "You cannot escape my charge that you are Pharisees & Hypocrites, for you are constantly talking of the Virtues of the Human Heart, and particularly of your own, that you may accuse others & especially the Religious, whose errors, you by this display of pretended Virtue, chiefly design to expose" (201). I take Blake to be making a statement worthy of some attention here: not the relatively weak claim that the Deists are hypocritical *about* their human-hearted virtues, but rather the bolder one that their hypocrisy and their rhetoric of human-heartedness actually go hand in hand. Blake implies that the rhetoric of human-heartedness belongs to a project of secularization—a self-defeating attempt to overcome "religion," to contain "spirit" within "nature." This is the project that Blake saw these writers as sharing. It is also the one that he goes on to illustrate in the stanzas on "The Grey Monk" that immediately follow these comments, stanzas that include Blake's memorable line: "a Tear is an Intellectual thing" (489).

Among Blake's quartet of Deist authors, Rousseau is probably the one most routinely (if problematically) associated with the sentimental mode of writing. But Hume, too, is a dealer in sentiments, and we know that Blake once playfully mocked what he referred to as that philosopher's "Essay on Huming Understanding." I think there is good reason to believe that Blake saw Hume's escalating attack on monkish superstition as a function of what Annette Baier calls, in the title of her fine book on Hume, the "progress of sentiments."[14] To come to terms with what might be called the "Un-Huming"—or better, the "Blaking"—of understanding, we need to look more closely at the connection between secularization and sentimentalism. And to see how a tear is an intellectual thing we must come to terms, first, with why Blake revised Boyd to suggest that the attraction of great art lies in both warming *and* freezing the heart, and, additionally, with why he replaced "moral sense" with the phrase "passions & senses."

We saw earlier that Smith himself resisted the notion of the moral sense, but that is not sufficient reason to think that Blake is aligned with his position here. There is no need to repeat all that I argued earlier about Smith's notion of the sentimental case, but I would like to stress that, for Smith, to put oneself in the case of the other is to posit a kind of virtual body or virtual set of circumstances into which one projects oneself. To imagine one's self in another's case requires both an act of disembodiment and (at the same time) of virtual reembodiment. It further requires that a person's case can be somehow categorized or generalized for purposes of the imaginative translation. On one level, what is happening to me might admit of no *specific* description, in a strict sense of "specific." That is, what is happening to me might admit only of a universal description—I undergo sensations—or an ever more minutely particularized account of the sensations themselves. Understood in either of these ways, what is happening to me will not be an object of sympathetic projection—in the former instance because it is unnecessary, in the latter because it is impossible. Only if my circumstances can be *rendered* as a case—and my relation to the object world given a certain "objectivity"—can my subject position in relation to them become intelligible. Thus, one might say that to be perceived as being in a certain case is to have one's experience mediated in two related senses. It is to have it rendered in terms of a category that mediates between the universal and the particular *and* to have it rendered in a medium that permits "virtual experience."

Categories that mediate between particulars and universals are, of course, generalities. Generality admits of mediational categories and subcategories, levels of aggregation, and kinds of kinds, the whole genre-species system. And this is exactly the sort of thing that Blake famously attacked in behalf of what he called minute particulars. This is a well-known passage from late in *Jerusalem*:

> You accumulate Particulars, & murder by analyzing, that you
> May take the aggregate; & you call the aggregate Moral Law:
> And you call that Swelld & bloated Form; a Minute Particular.
> But General Forms have their vitality in Particulars: & every
> Particular is a Man; a Divine Member of the Divine Jesus. (251)

To "generalize is to be an idiot," as Blake put it in his marginalia on Joshua Reynolds's *Discourses*, in the sense that generalization depends on blind assumptions about aggregate formations and fungible relationships (641). It is to submit to a suspect kind of social science. To put my argument about Blake and sentiment in a nutshell, it is that he contrived from very early in his career, certainly well before *Jerusalem*, to dismantle both the notion of mediated virtual experience and the notion of the mediating general category. He sought to expose what he took to be the weak foundation on which such notions rest.

Blake's Mental Travel

How did Blake go about this task of exposure? Consider the example of "A Poison Tree," from *Songs of Experience*:

I was angry with my friend;
I told my wrath, my wrath did end.
I was angry with my foe:
I told it not, my wrath did grow.

And I waterd it in fears,
Night & morning with my tears:
And I sunned it with smiles,
And with soft deceitful wiles.

And it grew both day and night.
Till it bore an apple bright.
And my foe beheld it shine,
And he knew that it was mine.

And into my garden stole,
When the night had veild the pole;
In the morning glad I see;
My foe outstretchd beneath the tree. (29)

It has been argued by John Brenkman that the poem pointedly elicits two readings that prove on analysis to be mutually exclusive. The first reading takes the poem to be offering a heart-warming story about the importance of not holding in one's wrath. This is a variation on the philosophy of open-heartedness advanced by a fellow member of Blake's Joseph Johnson circle, William Godwin.[15] The second is a chilling interpretation in which the "gladness" the poet expresses in the final lines is actually about the foe who lies on the ground after being poisoned by the fruit of suppressed wrath. Both readings assume, however, that the "apple bright" is, in a straightforward sense, the fruit of the tree of suppressed wrath, watered by the speaker's tears and sunned by his smiles. Brenkman shows how the figure of the apple also works metaleptically to invert such an assumption—that is, the apple and its effects are there to remind us of a principle of envy and possessiveness that, in the first place, defines the foe as the one with whom one cannot share anything except desire for the same thing. Putting the point in slightly different terms, one might say that the poem is constructed in such a way as to both warm and freeze the heart, to make the warming and freezing of the heart inextricable from one another.[16]

I am not suggesting, even if we accept this account of the poem, that "The Poison Tree" should be recognized as the first text ever to aim at two opposed effects on the heart. *Clarissa* itself might well be said to have moments that both warm and freeze the heart—moments in Anna Howe's sisterly support for Clarissa, moments in Clarissa's response to Lovelace's calculated entrapment of her. And of course Schiller made the mixing of emotions central to his definition of the sentimental. Blake's intervention lies rather in the peculiar way in which the opposition is left suspended, unresolved. In the instance of Richardson's novel, the action is eventually resolved, in a sense, into a specific set of sentiments, ones that, from the third edition onward (1751), were in fact extracted and published at the end of the text. And before long, the list of sentiments would be detached from the work of warming and freezing, free to circulate in the virtual world of national print culture with "toasts and sentiments."

As noted above, lists of toasts and sentiments began to appear in the 1750s, typically at the ends of collections of songs, particularly songs of national sentiment. These songs, perhaps some of the same ones that Gilchrist says so impressed Blake, were commonly borrowed from the musical theaters that began to flourish in London, Dublin, and Edinburgh from the mid-eighteenth century on, and they tended to include information both about the site (for example, Ranelagh or Sadler's Wells) and the singer.[17] The politics of Union—from 1707 and 1801 and beyond—clearly freights the issue of national sentiment with a huge charge. Song collections of the sort I am describing would include, for example, *The British Melodist; or National Song Book* (1822), the subtitle of which announces that it contains "the most popular English, Scottish, and Irish Songs," and *The Harp of Orpheus; being a collection of the best English, Scotch, and Irish Songs, Catches, Glees, Duets, Trios, Quartettos, etc.* (1820). Both of these conclude with "a selection of toasts and sentiments."[18] *The Harp of Orpheus*, for instance, begins with a tribute to "England the Anchor and Hope of the World," followed by a song titled "The Death of Nelson," but also includes such songs as "Paddy O'Leary," "Paddy Carey's Fortune," and "Donald of Dundee." Or, closer to home for Blake, there is *Albion's Pride; Being a Collection of Entire New Songs for 1804, . . . To Which Is Added a Selection of New Toasts and Sentiments* (dated to 1803).[19]

The toasts and sentiments would include a mix of general desiderata (health, love, and wealth) and sometimes specifically Unionist expressions of feeling. While the sentiments aggregate the mix of ethnic songs as a Unionist formation, many of these songs had other applications, and sentiment was mobilized in response to both centripetal and centrifugal pressures. The likes of Burns and Moore—avatars of Romantic sentimentality, as we now see them—were caught up in these struggles of collective self-identification through the medium of printed sentimental collections. The forms of the festive party, and the sentimental elements of which it is composed—where these are understood as circulated and reflected emotional expression—are deeply at stake in the Union debates, and vice versa. Though I will not pursue the matter here, I suspect that these books might prove an important (and largely neglected) context for thinking about, among other things, Blake's own books of songs and proverbs in the 1790s.

My more immediate claim, however, is that, in contrast with the handling of sentiment in *Clarissa* and its various printed progeny, we find in a poem like "A Poison Tree" a good example of how, in Blake's songs, conflicting emotions are engaged in such a way as to decompose sentiment into what he called passion and sense. I mean "sense" here not only as a function of sensation but also as a function of structure and thus, ultimately, of syntax. Blake engages sentiments, in other words, to unmake the sentimental, forcing cogs to turn adversely in his system of wheels within wheels, piercing Apollyon with his own bow. It is in this way that he shows how a tear is an intellectual thing, or how a warm tear can be a spear in mental fight (to invoke one of Blake's more famous rhymes, from "The Tyger"), just as a sigh, to recall the lyric in *Jerusalem* about the Deists, is the sword of an Angel King.

This idea of using sentimental devices to overturn sentiment even extends to the reversal of cause and effect, the device that Brenkman seizes on as the key structural principle of "A Poison Tree." We have seen that in Sterne this move is called "hypallage," explained by Walter Shandy as a matter of putting the cart before the horse. I argued above that this figure of hypallage is crucial, indeed constitutive, for late Sterne, where the movement of travel becomes indistinguishable from the emotion that transports us. This kind of hypallage, likewise mobilized in the context of a sentimental topos or story line, also structures what I take to be Blake's rewriting of Sterne's *Sentimental Journey*: the poem from the Pickering Manuscript entitled "The Mental Traveller." What Blake's *mental* and Sterne's *sentimental* journeys have in common is the conjunction of virtual traveling with the thematization of pathos. But whereas in Sterne the paradoxes of this pseudo-travelogue have to do with the contradictory linkage of moving in space and being moved at

heart, in Blake the movement is between contradictory feelings that somehow beget each other:

> I traveld thro' a Land of Men
> A Land of Men & Women too
> And heard & saw such dreadful things
> As cold Earth wanderers never knew

> For there the Babe is born in joy
> That was begotten in dire woe
> Just as we Reap in joy the fruit
> Which we in bitter tears did Sow (484)

In the land of men and women where Blake's unsentimental journey occurs, we soon learn that the distinctive form of mothering involves a kind of
crucifixion, complete with crown of thorns, piercing of hands and feet, and
a special preparation of the heart: the old woman to whom the babe is given
"cuts his heart out at his side / To make it feel both cold and heat" (483).

Though one may be reminded here of Blake's revision of Boyd's commentary on Dante, it remains true that, from warming to warming-*and*-freezing
the heart, there is a key difference. This warming and freezing cannot be
plotted in Blake the way it can in both Smith's theory of the sentiments and
Sterne's practice of it—as a matter of putting oneself in the case of another,
or of imagining what it might be to be "like" them. For Blake, it is not a matter of characters changing places by way of a sympathetic imagination, not
a matter of what Dickens's Marley calls the travel of the spirit. For Blake, it
is more a matter of character categories revolving and metamorphosing into
one another. Consider the fate of the Old Woman who prepares the young
boy for crucifixion:

> Her fingers number every Nerve
> Just as a Miser counts his gold
> She lives upon his shrieks & cries
> And She grows young as he grows old

> Till he becomes a bleeding youth
> And she becomes a Virgin bright
> Then he rends up his Manacles
> And binds her down for his delight

> He plants himself in all her Nerves
> Just as a Husbandman his mould

And She becomes his dwelling place
And Garden fruitful Seventy fold (484)

This sort of vampirism is a grotesquely literalized distortion of the Smithian imaginative practice of projecting oneself into the case of the other, as if to rule out our taking Blake's poetry as a medium for a vicarious exchange of places of the sort that builds moral sentiment. The kind of crossing of terms we see in "The Mental Traveller"—its distinctively skewed Blakean chiasmus—is a part of a grammatical structure that defines his medium as inhospitable to the sentimental impulses his readers would bring to it. A similarly skewed chiasmus opens Blake's "The Human Abstract," with its crossed claims about pity and mercy, and in that case as well, the structure cues a self-consciously broken tale of organic development. Both poems resist a naturalized common sense in the name of their own distinctive forms of sense-making and unmaking.

Syntax and Sentiment

Lyric power results from compression, and elsewhere in Blake one can see such acts of hypallage performed in even briefer space, where the syntax itself seems to be doing all the work. Here is the full text of "The Shepherd," from *Songs of Innocence*:

> How sweet is the Shepherds sweet lot,
> From the morn to the evening he strays:
> He shall follow his sheep all the day
> And his tongue shall be filled with praise.
>
> For he hears the lambs innocent call,
> And he hears the ewes tender reply,
> He is watch while they are at peace,
> For they know when their shepherd is nigh. (7)

Here again, the syntax constructs the action with a crossing of categories and an exchange of functions. It is the shepherd who follows the sheep rather than the other way around; the shepherd, not the sheep, who strays; and the shepherd who heeds the call of the lamb instead of insisting that his call be heeded. Further, Blake's syntactic play in the poem turns exactly on questions of causality and exchange.

Consider in particular the apparently simple lines about these apparently simple creatures. "He hears the lambs innocent call / And he hears the ewes tender reply." The seeming primitiveness of the punctuation, in which the apostrophe is omitted in the forming of the possessive, follows the practice of the poem's opening line—"How sweet is the Shepherds sweet lot"—and indeed the practice of Blake in the *Songs* more generally. What it enables here, however, is a brilliant piece of syntactical ambiguity. For in addition to reading "call" as a noun modified by "innocent," and "reply" as a noun modified by the sentimental "tender," it becomes possible, perhaps even necessary, to take account of a second reading, in which "call" becomes an unmodified verb, "innocent" an adjective modifying "lambs," and, most striking of all, "tender" becomes an economic verb, with "reply" as its direct object, rather than a sentimental adjective. When we ourselves heed the call of Blake's poem we discover that it cannot so easily be reduced to a sentiment in the sense of a moral "sentence." It cannot, that is, be made a piece of moral sententiousness.

Or finally, to look at a poem in which the complex development of the figures of "youth" and "virgin" in "The Mental Traveller" are, in effect, condensed into a space as brief as that of "The Shepherd," consider the knotty pair of quatrains that constitute "Ah! Sun-flower":

> Ah Sun-flower! weary of time,
> Who countest the steps of the Sun:
> Seeking after that sweet golden clime
> Where the travellers journey is done.
>
> Where the Youth pined away with desire,
> And the pale Virgin shrouded in snow:
> Arise from their graves and aspire,
> Where my Sun-flower wishes to go. (25)

As is common in Blake, the syntactical joints—relative pronouns and relative adverbs especially—are where the action is. And where there is action—at least where there is *transitive* action—there must necessarily be suffering in the ancient and radical sense of the term. In Blake's poetry, the syntactical connections are the moments where action and suffering tend to converge in hypallagic ambiguity.

That particular relative adverb, "where," can itself be said to provide a set of pivots for this text, in a way brilliantly conceived for keeping the poem turning along with the wheeling Sun-flower. For it is not clear, as we read, whether these "wheres" mark the last clause in one sentence or the first in another, whether they stand in apposition with each other or constitute a sequence of place references, or whether they should be read as linear or cyclic.

"Where my Sun-Flower wishes to go," for example, can be read either as the place *to* which the Youth and the Virgin aspire, or (in apposition with the "where" of line 5) as the place *from* which they aspire.

More signally, though, Blake creates a fascinating syntactic interaction between the line about the youth and the line about the pale Virgin at the start of the second stanza. One initially reads the line "Where the Youth pined away with desire" as an incomplete dependent clause with the intransitive predicate "pined away." Coming to the next line, however, one attempts in vain to place the same syntactic construction on "the pale Virgin shrouded in snow." Here we have only a noun phrase involving a past participial modifier, "shrouded." Moreover, the verb that introduces the third line, "Arise," can only be the plural predicate of what we now must recognize as the compound subject of this sentence, the Youth and the Virgin. But what then happens to our understanding of the syntax of the first line, "Where the Youth pined away with desire"? One can—one must—now read it as itself constructed according to the model of the line about the Virgin. That is, "pined" is revealed as a past participle, parallel to "shrouded." In that function, since pine is used for burial boxes, it would mean something like "encoffined with desire." Wheels within wheels. This cycle miniaturizes that of the poem's "where" structure, and likewise does the whole poem miniaturize "The Mental Traveller," which ends with the lines reprising its opening stanzas and then suggesting the repetition of the entire cycle: "She nails him down upon the Rock / And all is done as I have told" (486).

It is entirely consistent with Blake's critique of natural religion, and of the naturalization of religion in behalf of the human heart (in his commentary on the Deists), that he should work so hard to denaturalize sentiments in his syntactic construction of songs such as "The Shepherd" and "The Sun-Flower" (and, of course, "The Fly," "The Tyger," "The Human Abstract," and others). In sum, then, and perhaps not surprisingly in view of his artisanal self-identification, Blake's emphasis on the madeness of the sentiments resists an ideological mode that, from Steele through Sterne and Smith and Mackenzie, is so evidently born of commerce—commerce "naturalized," as they argued, in a stadial history leading from hunting, to herding, to farming, to trading. The ideological mode of the sentimental is born, that is, of what J. G. A. Pocock has described as the redefinition of virtue from republican battle-worthiness to the polishing of manners in the work of deal-making.[20] More generally, Blake's emphasis on mental fight might be read in this context as reframing the national project in terms of building, rather than exchanging. Thus the tears, and smiles and frowns, associated with the virtual movements of sentimental print culture become in Blake a kind of virtual *warfare* that Blake, following a tradition at least as old as Homer, associates with labor.[21]

A further way in which this kind of argument might be used to connect Blake with a larger understanding of national sentiment in his time lies, as I hinted at the start, in its possible relevance to the Burkean concept of virtual representation. For Burke, in effect, enlisted Smith's theory of moral sentiments in behalf of a defense of the English monarchy when he laid out his view about how representatives should govern, not according to a statistical mirroring of the people by whom they are supposed to be chosen, but rather according to a notion of kinds of interest and a principle of sympathetic communion that transcends the representational mimesis of opinion. As he summed it up in 1792:

> Virtual representation is that in which there is a communion of interests and a sympathy in feelings and desires between those who act in the name of any description of people and the people in whose name they act, though the trustees are not actually chosen by them. This is virtual representation. Such a representation I think to be in many cases even better than the actual. It possesses most of its advantages, and is free from many of its inconveniences; it corrects the irregularities in the literal representation, when the shifting current of human affairs or the acting of the public interests in different ways carry it obliquely from its first line of direction. Then people may err in their choice; but common interest and common sentiment are rarely mistaken.[22]

Burke's nationalization of sentiment depends upon a naturalization of sentiment, and precisely along the lines to which Blake must have taken exception. First, Burke naturalized sentiment by seizing on the principle of generality, concerning himself with the *kinds* of interest with which a representative must have sympathy: that is, mercantile interest, agricultural interest, and so on. As long as representatives can sympathize with and speak for these aggregated generalities, the representation they provide will be fair and just. Burke's whole notion of the love of the little platoon as the basis for larger, national affections likewise depends on a logic of aggregation. Second, Burkean national sentiment presupposes a naturalization of the medium. Perhaps Burke's most famous comment on the problem of the medium is the one in which he challenges the French radicals for failing to understand something crucial about their first principles: "These metaphysic rights entering into common life, like rays of light which pierce into a dense medium, are, by the laws of Nature, refracted from their straight line."[23] Burke's own prose is such a medium, where the figure of the medium itself is one of the sources of refraction, punning as it does on the notions of *vehicle*, *means*, and *common element*.

In a way that is not true for Blake, however, the framing assumption in Burke's national sentiment is that his medium of expression is itself a thing of nature, or at least of second nature. We gain a sense of Blake's critique of second nature here if we return to his annotations to Boyd's *Historical Notes* on Dante. On page 49 of Boyd's text, Blake found the following observation: "The industrious knave cultivates the soil; the indolent good man leaves it uncultivated. Who ought to reap the harvest? . . . The natural course of things decides in favour of the villain; the natural sentiments of men in favour of the man of virtue." Next to this passage Blake scribbled, simply, "false" (634). And in explaining his charge of falsehood against a nearby passage, Blake gives a hint as to why he would denounce it: "Nature teaches nothing of Spiritual Life but only of Natural Life" (634). The notion of a second nature—of habitual and humanizing reflection on nature that is nonetheless a part of nature, a modality that, while still natural, rises to the level of spirit or "culture"—was anathema to Blake.

Blake's aim was to denaturalize the level of habitual reflection and exchange that marks the sentimental. He, by contrast, cast the syntactic joints of his affective production as mind-forg'd manacles—links that, having been made by a human being can be likewise unmade, parts of a system that, having been created by himself, kept him from enslavement by, as he put it, "another man's." This is why a tear is an intellectual thing, and why sentiment is (among other things) a national thing. It is also why, when Blake talks of tears and sighs, it is so often in the proximity of some reference to making. A brief stanza from the sentimentally entitled "On Another's Sorrow" illustrates this point quite nicely:

Think not, thou canst sigh a sigh,
And thy maker is not by.
Think not, thou canst weep a tear,
And thy maker is not near. (17)

This is making as *poesis*, and maker as poet, the framer of fearful symmetries for which the figures of sentimental balance and chiasmus prove sublimely unstable under the pressures of passion and sense.

Wordsworth, Poet of Mere Sentiment

In his seminal book on Blake, in 1947, Northrop Frye introduced his new account by way of a new historical frame of reference:

> Blake belongs neither to the Augustans nor to the Romantics, either as a representative or a rebel. He belongs to another age altogether; the age, in poetry, of Collins, Percy, Gray, Cowper, Smart, Chatterton, Burns, Ossian and the Wartons. Blake's masters in poetry were Gray, Collins, Chatterton and Ossian, and he believed to the day of his death in the authenticity of both Ossian and Rowley. But the age of Blake is not solely one of poetry; it is a broad cultural movement with ramifications in philosophy, religion, painting and politics, and takes in nearly all of that lusty half of eighteenth century culture which has nothing to do with the Age of Reason. Its chief philosopher is Berkeley and its chief prose writer is Sterne.[24]

Wonderful as it is, Frye's book does not quite fulfill the promise of this bold claim. In the body of the book, he spends more time on Locke than he does on any of these later writers to whom he thinks Blake is indebted, and Sterne, alas, gets very little attention there. The provocative claim that Blake ultimately belongs to the age of sensibility might nonetheless raise a doubt about whether he is not too easy a case to choose for my purposes, whether he even can be said to exemply any relevant understanding of Romanticism. I turn now therefore to Wordsworth, a poet who can lay as strong a claim to a central place in the English Romantic period as any poet can. His most characteristic work was, like Blake's, crucially constituted by its engagement with the sentimental, so much so that he appeared to Hazlitt, the most astute critic of his age, as a "poet of mere sentiment."[25]

Wordsworth's relation to Sterne, as I have already intimated, is a good place to start. We know that Wordsworth was reading *Tristram Shandy* as early as 1791, when he singled it out as one of the few works of modern literature to occupy his attention. At least one contemporary commentator, who admired neither Sterne nor Wordsworth, argued the case for Wordsworth as what he called "the Sterne of poetry."[26] This, I suggest, is a bold, apposite, and underappreciated perspective on the author of *Lyrical Ballads*. We tend to think of Wordsworth as anything but a sentimentalist, not least, perhaps, because he himself so routinely disparaged the writers and thinkers of the Scottish school of moral sentiments.

He disparaged many writers, of course, especially after he became hypersensitive to critical slights in midcareer. The 1815 "Essay Supplementary," appearing in the wake of the poor critical response accorded *The Excursion* (1814), attempts to explain it all away on the principle that truly great and original poets are not recognized in their time. One particularly unhandsome comment is occasioned by his converse claim about how well undeserving poets tend to fare with the public: "So strange are the obliquities of admiration, that they whose opinions are much influenced by authority will often be tempted to think that there are no fixed principles in human nature for this art to rest upon." To this declaration, Wordsworth appends the following footnote: "This opinion seems actually to have been entertained by Adam Smith, the worst critic, David Hume not excepted, that Scotland, a soil to which this sort of weed seems natural, has produced."[27]

The editor of Smith's *Lectures on Rhetoric and Belles Lettres*, J. C. Bryce, expresses understandable puzzlement at this comment: "The premise of this remark is so mistaken, and the quantity of Smith's literary criticism in the printed works, especially *Theory of Moral Sentiments* and *Essays on Philosophical Subjects* (EPS), so fragmentary and scanty, that the violence of Wordsworth's language is difficult to explain."[28] Bryce goes on to offer some help with the puzzle by pointing to a letter Wordsworth had written back in 1802, defending *Lyrical Ballads* against the charge of indelicacy. There, by way of countercharge to his critics, Wordsworth dismissively cites "the instance of Adam Smith, who, we are told, could not endure the ballad of *Clym of the Clough*, because the author had not written like a gentleman."[29] Wordsworth also offers an unflattering reflection on Smith in the penultimate book of *The Prelude*, with a pointed reference to *The Wealth of Nations*. It is elaborated into a wider critique of modern conditions of labor—"labour in excess and poverty / From day to day pre-occupy the ground / Of the affections"—and a wider lament for urbanization, for life in "cities, where the human heart is sick."[30] These remarks recall in turn Wordsworth's already published observations in the 1800 preface to *Lyrical Ballads*, where he said his new way with poetry in these experiments was meant to contrast with the cultural debasements of fin-de-siècle Britain. This was a world, he said, in which "the accumulation of men in cities" and the "uniformity of their occupations" conspired with excessive cultural stimulants to produce a new form of moral debility among his contemporaries. Their minds had been "reduced to a state of almost savage torpor."[31]

What is odd about Wordsworth's pointed allusion to Smith's *Wealth of Nations*, and about his laying so much of the blame for Britain's problems at Smith's doorstep, is that Wordsworth's analysis seems to track fairly closely in places with Smith's own meditations on similar issues in book 5 of that work.

Consider the passage where Smith enumerates the effects of that very institution—the division of labor—which had been his starting point in book 1:

> The man whose whole life is spent in performing a few simple operations, of which the effects, too are, perhaps, always the same, or very nearly the same, has no occasion to exert his understanding, or to exercise his invention in finding out expedients for removing difficulties which never occur. He naturally loses, therefore, the habit of such exertion, and generally becomes as stupid and ignorant as it is possible for a human creature to become. The torpor of his mind renders him, not only incapable of relishing or bearing a part in any rational conversation, but of conceiving any generous, noble, or tender sentiment, and consequently of forming any just judgment concerning many even of the ordinary duties of private life.[32]

"Torpor," not so common a word in late-eighteenth-century Britain, is an especially telltale echo. Wordsworth seems to be making Smith's point in Smith's own terms as part of a series of reflections that blame Smith for failing to see it at all. To be sure, there are important differences between Wordsworth's and Smith's larger representations of these adverse conditions, and certainly between their respective writerly interventions. Yet some of these differences are counterintuitive. Wordsworth, mistrustful of the "statists," puts his trust in the habits he formed in rustic life, and in those "poets in the hills," who he says will be his "second self" when he is gone (from "Michael" in *Lyrical Ballads*). Smith, by contrast, and contrary to some received views of his work, condones state intervention (at least in this instance) to ameliorate the conditions brought on by modern labor conditions. Still, the way Wordsworth echoes Smith's analysis suggests an interesting case of a writer attacking the source of his own ideas.

Wordsworth's collateral disparagement of David Hume is puzzling for similar reasons. Recall, for example, Wordsworth's stab at explaining the underlying epistemology of his account, in the preface to *Lyrical Ballads*, of how the mind "associates ideas in a state of excitement." The central principle is that "our continued influxes of feeling are modified and directed by our thoughts, which are indeed the representatives of all our past feelings."[33] Substitute "impressions" for "influxes of feelings," and "ideas" for "thoughts" representative of past feelings, and you have the articulation of the theory of ideas that opens Hume's *Treatise of Human Nature*, the groundwork of his philosophical project.

Another reason we have not paid much attention over the years to Wordsworth's relation to the sentimentalists is that he has long been read as having nothing to do with imaginative sympathy. I have already mentioned Shelley's famous indictment in "Peter Bell the Third": that "he never could / Fancy another situation / From which to dart his contemplation / Than that wherein he stood."[34] There is also Keats's famous remarks about Wordsworth as the antithesis of Shakespeare, the poet of the egotistical sublime, the writer who could *not* as easily imagine himself an Iago or an Imogene. We know, too, that Keats learned much of his theory of imaginative sympathy at the feet of Hazlitt. For Hazlitt, of course, this subject was an obsession from the start—or at least from the time of his "First Acquaintance with the Poets," in early 1798, when he argued out the issues of his *Essay on the Principles of Human Action*, a treatise very much in the British sentimentalist tradition, as its best commentators have shown.[35] It seems reasonable, then, to suppose that Hazlitt's assessments of Wordsworth on this point amount to a key source for an abiding line of critique.

Consider the last of his 1818 *Lectures on the English Poets*, "On the Living Poets," where Hazlitt set out to give Wordsworth his due—the praise with the blame. There, Hazlitt's critique of Wordsworth's alleged deficiencies in imaginative sympathy is introduced by an account of Wordsworth's Rousseauist instincts in poetry. The lecture, in other words, importantly supplies *both* an early articulation of the egotistical-sublime critique *and* of the suggestion that Wordsworth's "Muse . . . is a leveling one," as Hazlitt would put it a few years later in *The Spirit of the Age*.[36] The lecture's discussion of Wordsworth falls into roughly three parts. First comes a discussion of Wordsworth himself. Then comes the poem "Hart-Leap Well," quoted in full, followed by a third part in which Hazlitt speaks of the programmatic Wordsworth—that is, the poet "at the head of that which has been denominated the Lake school of poetry."[37] The programmatic discussion is itself divided into two parts and turns on a sharp pivot midsentence, a device characteristic of Hazlitt's criticism elsewhere and perhaps part and parcel of an analytical principle that became a leading theme in *The Spirit of the Age*: the idea that our strengths are inextricably bound up with our weaknesses.

In the lead-up to the moment of peripeteia, Hazlitt makes a long series of extravagant and dubious claims for the program of the Lake poets (Wordsworth, Coleridge, and Southey), culminating in this formulation: "They took the same method in their new-fangled ballad mongering scheme which Rousseau did in his prose paradoxes—of exciting attention by reversing established standards of opinion and estimation in the world. They were for bringing poetry back to its primitive simplicity and state of nature."[38] For all its force and finality, though, this formulation is punctuated not with a period but with a colon, and what follows the colon is a surprising completion of the thought: "so that the only thing remarkable left in the world by this change would be the persons who produced it."[39] It is at this point, and on this point, that the essay turns. What it turns into is a critique of Lakist egotism, as epitomized in Wordsworth, its *capo d'ecole*. The new direction of the essay elaborates a portrait of what Hazlitt calls "a thorough adept of this school" of poetry. We learn of this particular type that he

> is jealous of all excellence but his own. He does not like to share his reputation with his subject; for he would have it all proceed from his own power and originality of mind. . . . His egotism is in some respects a madness. . . . Few people take an interest in his writings, because he takes an interest in nothing that others do.[40]

Our strengths lie in our weaknesses, and the progressive instinct to political leveling goes hand in hand with an egotistical failure of sympathetic imagination. Hazlitt says at the start of this essay that Wordsworth is "the reverse of Walter Scott in his defects and his excellences," and in the discussion of Scott in *The Spirit of the Age*, we do in fact see the Wordsworthian character turned inside out. Scott's Shakespearean generosity of imagination is praised and praised until, again in a peripeteia that occurs midsentence, this quality in Scott is reframed as what makes him so politically retrogressive—retrogressive in the literal sense of his living entirely in the past and being unable to face or generate modernity, or even novelty.

Hazlitt's systematic adherence to his own principle—that a writer's strength and weakness must be bound up inextricably—leads him to misjudgment, often on both sides of the issue. Certainly, the claims about Wordsworth as a Rousseauist leveler will seem mistaken to those of us who are persuaded that book 5 of *The Prelude* was in fact pointedly anti-Rousseauist in its claims about education, that books 9–11 critique the state-of-nature arguments that circulated under Rousseau's name in the French Revolution, and that Wordsworth was correct to add his great paean to Burke to this poem when he wrote it years later and explicitly acknowledged its tardiness: "Genius of Burke, forgive the pen too long seduced."[41] True, Hazlitt would have seen only fragments of *The Prelude* by the time of his 1818 *Lectures*, but the point is that it was conceived and executed far closer to the time of *Lyrical Ballads* than to Wordsworth's notorious 1818 involvement in the Westmoreland elections, and that the major lyrics are not inconsistent with its tendencies.

Here, though, I am more interested in the charge about Wordsworth's failure of sympathy, which Hazlitt levels in the context of a larger claim, one that launches the first phase of the discussion in the 1818 lecture: being the reverse of Scott's writings, says Hazlitt, "Wordsworth's poetry is not external, but internal; it does not depend upon tradition, or story, or old song; he furnishes it from his own mind, and is his own subject. He is the poet of mere sentiment."[42] Nor is this an isolated remark. Hazlitt had begun to argue this view of Wordsworth in successive articles on *The Excursion* for the *Round Table*, where, on his way to a critique similar to the one he would make in 1818 ("There is nothing which excites so little sympathy in our minds as exclusive selfishness"), he defends Wordsworth's accomplishment against his many detractors: "The extreme simplicity which some persons have objected to in Mr. Wordsworth's poetry, is to be found only in the subject and the style: the sentiments are subtle and profound."[43] Meaning to explicate this point, Hazlitt goes on in the *Round Table* pieces in an enigmatic vein: he is evidently able to criticize Wordsworth's failure of sympathetic imagination while promoting his profundity of sentiment because the critic sets these terms at odds. It seems that for him, sympathy refers to the capacity to put oneself in the place of another, whereas sentiment derives from the capacity to develop practices of contemplation that are able to include their own associations—their own medium—as a part of what they contemplate.

The Strange Design of a Lyrical Ballad

In order to see whether Hazlitt is on firm ground in making the distinction he does, and as he does, I propose to turn to his own central exhibit, "Hart-Leap Well." The poem is structured in two parts, clearly delineated, and the relation of the parts is one of the reasons that it appears to be so "strangely designed."[44] But the parts are actually as odd in themselves as they are in their relation to each other. The first part presents a literary hunting ballad of a sort that might have appeared in collections like Percy's *English Reliques* or its German counterparts: Bürger's ballads are sometimes cited as a precedent for it. The story, roughly speaking, is of a knight, one Sir Walter, who pursues a deer to its death through a long and arduous day of hunting. He discovers the fatally wounded animal with "his nose [half-touching] a spring beneath a hill."[45] On looking further he sees three widely spaced hoof marks on the side of the hill, evidence that the deer made a desperate effort to reach the spring before expiring next to it. Claiming that such "sight was never seen by living eyes," Sir Walter then announces the decision that looms so momentously in the poem's little etiological account:

I'll build a Pleasure-house upon this spot,
And a small Arbour, made for rural joy;
'Twill be the traveler's shed, the pilgrim's cot,
A place of love for damsels that are coy.

A cunning Artist will I have to frame
A bason for that fountain in the dell;
And they, who do make mention of the same,
From this day forth, shall call it Hart-leap Well. (57–64)[46]

The mansion was built, along with three pillars to mark the place where the hart's hooves landed in his leap. Sir Walter lived long enough to make "merry in that pleasant bower" (72), but the first part concludes with an abrupt termination of Sir Walter's story and the promise of another:

The Knight, Sir Walter, died in course of time,
And his bones lie in his paternal vale.—
But there is matter for a second rhyme,
And I to this would add another tale. (93–96)

This promise might suggest a tandem structure for "Hart-Leap Well," one in which two stories are told either in series or in parallel. This sense is reinforced when we find that the second part also opens with the report of a man on a journey. After a brief prefatory comment, its narrative begins:

As I from Hawes to Richmond did repair,
It chanc'd that I saw standing in a dell
Three aspins at three corners of a square,
And one, not four yards distant, near a well.

What the speaker of the second part encounters, however, proves to be the ruins of the structures whose history is told in the first part. Thus, the two stories seem to be related neither in series nor in parallel, but rather in some kind of chiasmus. Indeed, it is not clear whether the poem offers different stories or one single story that is first told forward and then backward. Yet even these hypotheses do not exhaust the structural complexity of the matter, since, puzzled by the appearance of the ruin, at a loss to "divine," as he says, "what this imported," the speaker makes an inquiry to a shepherd, who, we are told, then delivers the narrative of part one: "[he] that same story told / Which in my former rhyme I have rehears'd" (121–22).

Now *this* formulation suggests a rather different relation between the two parts, one in which the second part fully contains and contextualizes the first part. And yet this structural conjecture, too, proves to have problems. For while the story of part one is left completely to inference in the shepherd's part-two discourse, the speaker goes on to quote in full the shepherd's curious commentary on the events. This commentary meditates on the questions of why the vegetation in the place has all withered away and why no animals will drink the well water. The shepherd mentions two hypotheses, both superstitious. One he dismisses: "Some say that here a murder has been done, / And blood cries out for blood" (137–38). The other, the one the shepherd favors, is that, as he puts it simply, "it was all for that unhappy Hart" (140).

At exactly this point, the search for the causes of the well's distress quickly metamorphoses into a search for why it was that the unhappy hart was so attached to the well as to have made so desperate a leap to reach it:

What thoughts must through the creature's brain have pass'd!
From the stone on the summit of the steep
Are but three bounds, and look, Sir, at this last!
O Master! it has been a cruel leap.

For thirteen hours he ran a desperate race;
And in my simple mind we cannot tell
What cause the hart might have to love this place,
And come and make his death-bed near the well.

Here on the grass perhaps asleep he sank,
Lull'd by this fountain in the summer-tide;
This water was perhaps the first he drank
When he had wander'd from his mother's side.

In April here beneath the scented thorn
He heard the birds their morning carols sing,
And he, perhaps, for aught we know, was born
Not half a furlong from that self-same spring. (141–56)

The shepherd's would seem to be an act of sympathetic imagination of a rather intense sort. He so fully enters into the case of the deer that nothing else seems to matter. Indeed, the question of the cause of the blight has been utterly displaced by the question of the causes of the hart's attraction to the well.

It is left to the speaker to suggest a larger or longer perspective, with praise for the shepherd's words and the comment that "this beast not unobserv'd by Nature fell, / His death was mourned by sympathy divine" (163–64). It is a comment, moreover, that spells out the missing step in the shepherd's reasoning on the causes of the blight on the place: that is, that they lie in a natural response to the pain of the unhappy hart. For the speaker, this is a great act of "sympathy" on the part of a higher power. The shepherd himself does not *refer* to this act of sympathy so much as he *performs* it, by virtue of his fully entering into the case of the beast that fell. There is a theology of immanence implicit in all this, as becomes clear when the speaker explicates the "sympathy divine" by laying out the basic tenet of what he calls his "creed":

> The Being, that is in the clouds and air,
> That is in the green leaves among the groves,
> Maintains a deep and reverential care
> For them the quiet creatures whom he loves. (165–68)

One might say that the shepherd's elision of the notion of nature's sympathy with the fallen hart creates the structural possibility for the narrator's projection of the shepherd's sympathy onto a divinity that is "in" the natural world. This is part of what is registered in the speaker's enigmatic comment: "Small difference lies between thy creed and mine" (162).

The position from which the speaker is able to make such a reflection marks another aspect of this small difference. For the speaker assumes a millenarian perspective on the whole affair that is only vaguely gestured toward in the shepherd's remarks. Here is the speaker's comment:

> The Pleasure-house is dust:—behind, before,
> This is no common waste, no common gloom;
> But Nature, in due course of time, once more
> Shall here put on her beauty and her bloom.
>
> She leaves these objects to a slow decay
> That what we are, and have been, may be known;
> But, at the coming of the milder day,
> These monuments shall all be overgrown. (169–76)

This passage demonstrably represents two transformations as one. The fullness of meaning in nature's scene, the entire erasure of the signs of "the hand of man," will be complete at the point when men and women need no more admonition as to what they "are and have been." That triumph of nature, however, will also be a triumph over nature, a time beyond the time when the ends of time—its purpose, design, and completion—all stand revealed. It is a matter, as Geoffrey Hartman explained years ago, of nature leading beyond itself and into the imagination of apocalypse.[47] The shepherd can see his way to the disappearance of "the trees, and stones, and fountain," but he cannot reflect on what it means to be positing such a disappearance. And yet it is the shepherd's active sympathy—his capacity to feel for passions that are not his own—that powers the poem. How, then, does the "strange design" of "Hart-Leap Well" structure these entwined issues of decipherment, apocalypse, and sympathy? And more broadly, how do we sort the issues of theology, moral philosophy, and poetics in this poem of "mere sentiment"?

Mixed Feelings, Divided Lessons

What little criticism the poem has engaged often tries to address such questions. In introducing this poem, which he quotes in full for the lecture "On the Living Poets," Hazlitt stresses that, while Wordsworth is adept at giving "fine tones of thought," he is lacking in constructive powers: "he cannot form a whole."[48] Several contemporary commentators have nonetheless taken turns attempting to imagine a whole from the parts—parts variously construed—of "Hart-Leap Well." One of the ways in which critics have made a whole of the poem is by establishing a claim about its political tendency. Two recent attempts to do so have produced radically different accounts of the unifying politics of the poem. One account sees in in the poem a reflection of a rising tide of British protest against hunting.[49] The other, finding this account misguided, offers a (more plausible) case for a poem that seeks to foreground the idea of learning from one's political mistakes.[50] Such arguments form a subset of a larger set of interpretations in which critics have tried to make a whole of the poem by ascribing a unifying role to the poet-narrator. In different ways, Hartman, Don Bialostosky, and David Bromwich have all produced variations on this argument.[51]

To make any of these arguments, however, the commentators tend to assume that the voice of the narrator is in some strong sense the voice of William Wordsworth. Bromwich, no casual reader of the *Lyrical Ballads*, goes so far as to suggest that, were Hazlitt to read this poem in voices—as he often did in delivering his lectures—he "would have impressed it on his audience that the voice which emerges at the end is Wordsworth's own."[52] This view seems to me mistaken in some important respects, among others in that it overlooks considerations that limit the integrity of both self *and* sentiment in the poem. We can approach Bromwich's argument by considering its strongest evidence, the moral that the speaker draws at the close of the poem, putatively in the poet's own voice:

> One lesson, Shepherd, let us two divide,
> Taught both by what she shews, and what conceals,
> Never to blend our pleasure or our pride,
> With sorrow of the meanest thing that feels. (177–80)

This certainly sounds like a sentiment, and one spoken with authority and finality. Furthermore, it seems to advocate a kind of purity of the sort that Hazlitt gestured toward in his epithet "the poet of mere sentiment." For Hazlitt, as for his disciple Keats, what determines that a writer has the *sympathetic* capacity, conversely, is that plasticity of imagination that brings together "the most opposite extremes": a view that ironically seems to connect Hazlitt with Schiller's earlier sense of the sentimental as involving mixed feelings that derive from a similar yoking of conflicting images or representations. The moral sentence drawn at the end of this poem, in any case, initially seems to indicate that it fails Hazlitt's test.

To bolster the case that this last stanza, and indeed the speaker's words generally in the poem, are Wordsworth's, critics sometimes adduce the blank verse lines Wordsworth wrote for the *Home at Grasmere* fragment that also narrate an experience at Hart-leap Well:

> And when the trance
> Came to us, as we stood by Hart-leap Well—
> The intimation of the milder day
> Which is to come, the fairer world than this—
> And raised us up, dejected as we were
> Among the records of that doleful place
> By sorrow for the hunted beast who there
> Had yielded up his breath, the awful trance—
> The vision of humanity and of God
> The Mourner, God the Sufferer, when the heart
> Of his poor Creatures suffers wrongfully—
> Both in the sadness and the joy we found
> A promise and an earnest that we twain,
> A pair seceding from the common world,
> Might in that hallowed spot to which our steps
> Were tending, in that individual nook,
> Might even thus early for ourselves secure,

And in the midst of these unhappy times,
A portion of the blessedness which love
And knowledge will, we trust, hereafter give
To all the Vales of earth and all mankind.[53]

Certainly the projected apocalypticism here helps to make somewhat more intelligible the puzzling references to the "milder day" in "Hart-Leap Well." The problem in explicating "Hart-Leap Well" by resort to this passage, however, is its insistence that the apocalyptic "trance," the vision of the "milder day" when nature is no more, is actually produced by a *mingling* of joy and sorrow—Schiller's "mixed feelings" again. And so the question: what bearing might this have on how we read the signs in the ostensible moral of "Hart-Leap Well"—the one drawn by the speaker—about *not* mixing sorrow with our pleasure or our pride?

While there is a distinction to be made between joy, on the one hand, and pleasure, on the other, it remains the case that where the *Home at Grasmere* fragment—which has the signature marking of Wordsworthian blank verse in an autobiographical first-person narration—insists on sorrow yoked to its opposite, the highly stylized ballad stanza with which "Hart-Leap Well" concludes insists on sorrow unalloyed. And while speaking of the "style" of this concluding ballad stanza, let it also be noted that the speaker introduces the weighty sentiment about not mixing sorrow with pleasure or pride by way of a brief injunction or invitation, which fits neatly into the space of a single line: "One lesson, Shepherd, let us two divide." Catching something peculiar in the line, Bromwich wryly notes that the Wordsworthian speaker is likely to get the lion's share in any division with the shepherd.[54] For Bromwich, the point is the Hazlittian one, that the speaker merely absorbs the shepherd, for whom he lacks true sympathy. It is a point, like Hazlitt's, that Bromwich means to be making at the poet's—that is, Wordsworth's—expense, or at least to be suggesting that Wordsworth makes at his own expense.

But there is a syntactical ambiguity that makes it very difficult to see this line as forming a coherent whole. Given the lack of case inflection in English and the conventions of subject-verb inversion in its poetry, the line can be read in two antithetical ways with equal plausibility:

1. Let us two divide one lesson

2. Let one lesson divide us two

And indeed the first interpretation involves yet another breakdown of possibilities:

1a. Let us two share a single lesson jointly.

1b. Let us two each take our separate shares of a single lesson.

I take it that these syntactical ambiguities—especially the primary one—are sufficiently obvious as not to require a great deal of arguing for. But where, in the apparently solemn context of "Hart-Leap Well," do we locate agency and motivation in such paronomasia, and how do we come to terms with its implications?[55]

In introducing lines that seem to prohibit a mixture of sorrow and pleasure/pride at the end of the sad tale of the unhappy hart, the poem has apparently framed its grave moral sentence with what we could reasonably call a certain playfulness—and even, perhaps, a prideful display of syntactical wit. Nor is this kind of element in the poem confined to syntax. It is perhaps more evident at the level of semantics and phonetics, involving especially the central figure of the hart. I have all along been echoing phrases from the poem such as "poor hart" and "unhappy hart" in order to make it possible to hear how the titular red deer is being linked with the red center of human dearness in Western iconography. I believe it is quite impossible to read the poem without hearing "hart" as "heart," all the more so in a narrative about an organism whose death is analyzed in terms of a tropism for home—a narrative that has a marked allegorical resonance, as the specific inflection of the passage in *Home at Grasmere* makes clear. Home, as they say, is where the heart is.

There does seem to be some precedent in the allegorical tradition for treating such subjects in this way. A page from a Renaissance book suggests how the "red deer" might be used to allegorize a basic human moral capacity.[56] I am not proposing that we read "Hart-Leap Well" quite as that kind of allegory, nor exactly as an allegory at all. I wish instead to press even further on the poem's wordplay, and to read it rather as a poem of "mixed feelings" than of "pure sentiment," indeed as a poem in the mode that Schiller called "sentimental," intending very different associations from Hazlitt's. We can recall here the little preface that introduces the narrative of part two of the poem:

The moving accident is not my trade;
To freeze the blood I have no ready arts:
'Tis my delight, alone in summer shade,
To pipe a simple song for thinking hearts. (97–100)

Consider the slight oddity of the phrase "thinking hearts." One might expect *feeling* hearts, or "natural hearts," as we in fact find in "Michael," also from the 1800 *Lyrical Ballads*.[57] But in reading about the fate of a "poor Hart," an "unhappy Hart," we must have been inclined to make something of "thinking hearts," even if the act of imagining the hart's thoughts did not prove—as we have seen that it does—to be absolutely crucial to the poem. When we hear the shepherd's performance of sympathy for the hart—his account of what he believes happened to cause the desolation at Hart-leap Well—he launches into an apparently unmotivated meditation on the question of, precisely, "what thoughts" passed through "that creature's brain."

It would seem, then, that from what might be called the shepherd's point of view the ideal version of the subject of the poem is a thinking hart, and that from the speaker's point of view the ideal version of the audience of the poem is a thinking heart. Perhaps another way to put the question about the unity of the poem, then, would be to ask whether there is some way of regarding these "two conflicting representations" (to reinvoke Schiller's phrase) as one?[58] What does *this* small difference—between "hart" and "heart"—signify for a compelling interpretation of "Hart-Leap Well"?

Wordsworth and Sterne

Few modern editions of "Hart-Leap Well" have failed to notice that the line about the poet's eschewing "moving accidents" alludes to *Othello*, and to the Moor's account of the adventurous tales with which he wooed and won Desdemona. Hazlitt, himself a master of allusive technique, registers the reference in his *Round Table* discussion of *The Excursion*, where he cites other phrases in Othello's speech to insist that Wordsworth's poetry offers "no hair-breadth 'scapes and perilous accidents by flood or field."[59] What tends to escape notice is that the passage echoes an earlier literary allusion to this same famous act 1 speech by Othello—the one about "moving accidents of flood and field" in Sterne's *Sentimental Journey*, which I discussed in chapter 6—and indeed that both Hazlitt and Wordsworth seem to follow Sterne's invocation of the passage. In a fashion that anticipates Wordsworth, Sterne contrasts the tale of "moving accidents" to that of the figure he terms the "sentimental traveller." And Sterne's point, like Wordsworth's, is that if your heart is quick, you can find ample gratification in ordinary things.

For Wordsworth as for Sterne, the heart that interests itself in every thing is the one that is able to dilate the everyday affairs of life by means of a sympathetic imagination. It has no need of sublimities or catastrophes to make it "leap" to seize passing opportunity. Such a heart amplifies the sense of adventure in a given moment without requiring that one venture anywhere or anything in particular. Emotional amplification is a sentimental topos that bespeaks a mode of affective proliferation parallel to the economic effects of the commercial division of labor.[60]

We have good evidence that such an understanding of the Sternean sentimental journey was still current well through the period of Wordsworth's major writings. It appears in the fashionable *London Magazine* with the narrative "A Sentimental Journey, from Islington to Waterloo Bridge, in March, 1821." Hazlitt was a regular contributor, though it is extremely unlikely that he wrote this article, which both invokes Sterne and emulates his manner:

> A traveller, said I, should have all his wits about him, and so will I. He should let nothing escape him, no more will I—he should extract reflections out of a cabbage stump, like sun-beams squeezed out of cucumbers; so will I, if I can—and he should converse with every and any one, even a fish-woman. . . . Who knows but I may make a sentimental journey, as good as Sterne's but at any rate I can write it and send it to the *London Magazine*.[61]

In producing examples of proverbial wisdom that we might call characteristically Romantic ("the meanest flower that blows . . .", "the universe in a grain of sand," or indeed, in the closing words of "Hart-Leap Well," the "meanest thing that feels"), the author of this 1821 piece, with a nod to Swift's cabbages and cucumbers, makes use of Sterne's titular phrase to frame them within a Sternean genealogy. As its author intimates, the nature of narrative will not always be a matter of self-evidence in such a conception of things.

Wordsworth, writing between these two "sentimental journeys," tags one of the *Lyrical Ballads*, "Simon Lee" (later classified by Wordsworth under "Poems of Sentiment and Reflection"), with a caveat about narrative expectations. The narrator points out that, while the poem "is no tale," it can become one in the reader's imagination: "should you think / Perhaps a tale you'll make it" (79–80). The full elaboration of this point comes in a stanza well known to readers familiar with Wordsworth's poetical experiments:

> O reader! had you in your mind
> Such stores as silent thought can bring,
> O gentle reader! you would find
> A tale in every thing. (73–76)

Similarly, but on a grander scale, Wordsworth's life's project, the multipart poem he called *The Recluse*, is a work in which the progress of an epic narrative is programmatically reduced to "a simple produce of the common day."[62]

Such productivity in the quotidian—finding "a tale in every thing"—is thoroughly anticipated in Sterne's *Journey*, where the whole question of narrative *progress*, as in *Tristram Shandy* before it, had become a seriously (and comically) vexed affair.

In the first fifteen chapter-vignettes of *Sentimental Journey*, almost nothing outward takes place. Several of these chapter-vignettes, as I noted earlier, are given over to a narrative of what ensues when Yorick and a Mme de L***, a lady he has just met, are left holding hands in front of the closed door of the carriage yard, when the landlord is unable to open its lock and abruptly abandons them there. And then, as if to emblematize the narrative's stubborn refusal to move forward, Yorick narrates two ensuing experiences in *stationary* carriages, once by himself in the carriage-for-one, or *desobligeant*, in which we are to imagine him writing his "preface," and once in a two-person coach with that same lady of his new acquaintance. In such instances, internal motion is generated by external immobilization.

Sterne's "travel" in his immobile coach thus prepares the way for Wordsworth's travel on his immobile couch—his "wander[ing] lonely as a cloud" while "on my couch I lie," in the famous lyric about the daffodils.[63] In both cases, the "sentimental journey" becomes something more (or less) than a journey to affecting places, though the latter is how Sterne's famous phrase often signifies for us nowadays. Rather, it becomes travel in and by sentiment. This is why the narrator of the 1821 "Sentimental Journey" can suggest that, while his journey may or may not prove as good as Sterne's, he "at any rate . . . can write it, and send it to the *London Magazine*."[64] This is also why this narrator can launch his narrative in the very next sentence, with the studiedly ambiguous opening: "I had hardly left the threshold of my door, ere I met, as I thought, with an adventure."[65]

Could such intricate correspondences have caught the eye of the writer for the *Gentleman's Magazine* a few years later when, in calling Wordsworth "the Sterne of Poetry," he seems to be thinking along just these lines?

> He has like his predecessor, endeavoured to extract sentiment where nobody else ever dreamt of looking for it, and has often exalted trifles into a consequence which nature never intended them to occupy; and may therefore be said to have, with Sterne, lent his aid to implanting, in certain literary departments, a tone not always auspicious to true and genuine feeling.[66]

I think this writer is on to something important about Wordsworth's generally suppressed connection to Sterne's sentimental tactics, though a more exhaustive analysis of their relationship would need to discriminate Wordsworth's forms of everyday sympathy from Sterne's. For example, where the author of the 1821 "Sentimental Journey from Islington to Waterloo Bridge" advises the sentimental traveler that "he should converse with every and any one, even a fish-woman," Wordsworth might have written "*especially* a fish-woman."

The difference is not trivial. Nor is the difference between a sentimental poem in this vein and the sort of verse that Longfellow Deeds, poet of the greeting card, produces in Capra's *Mr. Deeds Goes to Town*. We are given a sample of his writing, in the poem he reads to Babe Bennett on the night before his intended proposal:

> I tramped the earth with hopeless beat—
> Searching in vain for a glimpse of you.
> Then heaven thrust you at my very feet,
> A lovely angel—too lovely to woo.[67]

Earth and heaven, the ordinary beat of the world and the transcendent order, remain distinct in this distinctly pre-sentimental piece of doggerel. The only communication between the poet and his addressee comes with the angelic intervention, as in the tale of Balaam, but with a conventionally amorous inflection. Unsurprisingly, the sentimental redemption of the ordinary in *Mr. Deeds* does not occur at the level of the interpolated poem—which is patently an aesthetic failure. (The ridicule aimed at Deeds by the literati at the Algonquin Hotel may be cruel, but it does not produce the conviction that he is a good poet.) Capra means to achieve his goal rather on the level of cinematic poetics, in the moments where Peter Warne and Ellie Andrews eat carrots and hitchhike in *It Happened One Night*, or where George Bailey's Dickensian journey with Clarence leads him to embrace his life again.

Toward the close of the next chapter, a look at examples of high modernist fiction, I consider the reappearance of the sentimental ordinary in something close to the specific Sternean sense, specifically with the great "day in the life" novels of Joyce and Woolf in the 1920s. These, I suggest, are sentimental journeys in the Sternean line. They are perhaps unthinkable, as Shklovsky might have suggested, without Sterne's distant example. But most immediately I turn to *Lord Jim*, a travel novel that takes its readers across the high seas to distant islands such as George Bailey dreamed of visiting, even as it secures its procedures (so I argue) within the history of the sentimental mode.

NINE

Modernism

With this final chapter we shift back to an emphasis on fiction rather than poetry. We also return, by a different route, to the first decades of the twentieth century, the period of early cinema. Some fiction in this period belongs, indeed, to what David Trotter has recently called "the literature of cinema": "a literature in which people go to the movies, or in which metaphoric use is made of reference to film effects."[1] Trotter's work is part of an overdue effort in literary studies to deal with the "elephant in the room" when it comes to discussions of modernism. I mean that new motion-picture mass medium targeted explicitly by T. S. Eliot's teacher, I. A. Richards, who reinvented Anglo-American literary criticism in the 1920s. Trotter notes that from as early as Frank Norris's *McTeague* (1895), we can find fiction in which characters go to the cinema. *McTeague* itself was of course adapted to the screen by Erich von Stroheim. And it was this adaptation, as I have noted, on which the young Frank Capra worked in 1922. It was indeed while Capra was at work on *Greed*, according to his autobiography, that his twin ambitions to oppose von Stroheim's style and follow Griffith's first became evident. The literature of cinema is not itself Trotter's focus, any more than it is mine here. But whereas Trotter studies the effects of cinema on the practice of fiction writing, I am interested in the sentimental mode as it affects them both.[2]

The year 1922 is perhaps best known to historians of modern literature for witnessing the publication of *Ulysses*. Joyce and his famous book have figured prominently in recent discussions of cinema and modernism, perhaps in part because of the increasingly noted fact of Joyce's having started Dublin's first cinema, the Volta, in 1909.[3] A later episode also brings Joyce into this story, for he is known to have received Eisenstein in his Paris apartment for a long afternoon in 1929, where they discovered that their admiration was mutual. Eisenstein had acquired *Ulysses* the year before and called it "the Bible of the new cinema"—a cultural role he would later, in effect, reassign to Dickens.[4] After the meeting with Joyce, Eisenstein experimented with stream-of-consciousness writing and began to associate Joyce's formal techniques with his own ambitious project to make a film of Marx's *Capital*.[5] Joyce, for his part, later wrote to a friend that Eisenstein was one of two directors to whom he could entrust a film version of *Ulysses*.

Trotter himself joins the argument about Joyce and cinema, taking issue with some of those who see a work like *Ulysses* as shaped by the influence of Griffithian montage.[6] My own brief discussion of Joyce below, however, is not directly concerned with his immediate connection with cinema in either way. Part of my discussion will address Joyce's engagement with the products and activities of sentimental culture as these reach back to the Georgian period, when modern Dublin took architectural and cultural shape, a history nostalgically registered in "The Dead," the long final story of *Dubliners* (1913). A notable figure in that sentimental history, Thomas Moore, author of the *Irish Melodies* (or "maladies," as Joyce punningly calls them), appears by name in "The Dead," in *Ulysses*, and indeed in *Finnegans Wake*, and he provides a measure of Joyce's interest. To say that my own interest here is with sentiment rather than cinema is not to say that these issues do not overlap in Joyce's writings but only that I will be concerned with the way in which his fiction registers the legacy of sentimentalism in often marked and distinctive ways, especially in the "Nausicaa" episode of *Ulysses*.

The bulk of the discussion in this chapter, however, will address an earlier work of modernist fiction, and a seminal one: *Lord Jim*. Here again, in the work of Joseph Conrad, we find some suggestive connections to cinema, even to Capra's cinema. Capra's first collaboration with Robert Riskin, *Platinum Blonde* (1931), is a highly reflexive film that, as we have seen, established a kind of template for Capra's great reporter-centered comedies of the decade to follow, from *It Happened One Night* through *Meet John Doe*. It is a film about the writing of a play, and at its conclusion the film and the play within the screenplay merge to become the same story.[7] The recurring literary reference in the play is to the fiction of Conrad. The protagonist reporter and would-be playwright (Robert Williams) is a fan of Conrad. We see him reading Conrad, and his return of a first-edition Conrad novel to the house of the heiress (Jean Harlow) provides the alibi for their second and romantically decisive meeting. It is the injunction by the rival love interest (Loretta Young) to follow Conrad's example in writing from experience that enables the reporter's composition of his play (with much help from her). It is possible that this kind of reflexivity is meant to signal something about Conrad's own tales within tales, especially in the Marlow novels such as *Lord Jim*. Certainly Conrad was perceived as a cultural force to be reckoned with in early Hollywood. Trotter notes that Griffith himself, in describing the aims of his cinema, uncannily recalls a famous pronouncement by Conrad about the aim of his fiction: "The task I'm trying to achieve," Griffith said to Robert Grau in an interview, "is above all to make you see."[8]

As with Joyce, my discussion of Conrad emphasizes less the cross-media connections between fiction and contemporary cinema than his novel's self-conscious orientation in a history of fiction in which the sentimental holds a crucial place. Indeed, Conrad's way of structuring sight lines, reversing viewpoints, and attending to faces in a novel written at the turn of the century all *precede* the development of the classical system by about a decade and a half. My interest is partly in this anticipation and partly in an articulation of the historical development of the novel that Conrad's masterpiece encodes. This means launching my account of *Lord Jim* with a brief retrospect that will emphasize the loop my larger argument has followed so far in this book. Not coincidentally, the question of the soul's status in the modern world is overtly thematized in *Lord Jim*, as it will be again in the work of Joyce.

Conrad and the Sentimental Case

While scholars continue to debate the question of just how old the novel actually is, they now mostly agree that the narrative innovations that we associate with the fictional writings of Defoe had much to do with the "case literature" of the late seventeenth century.[9] This is a literature in which descriptions of circumstance provide hypothetical occasions for the exercise of judgment. Some of it derives from controversies in moral casuistry, raging at least since the Counter-Reformation, about how Christians were to square the obligations imposed by moral law with situations they might confront in the course of their lives. And some comes from the legal domain, in the form of published legal proceedings that tell the stories behind juridical verdicts. A number of these cases, whether in morals or at law, involve detailed representations of everyday life: "realism," in the sense in which much commentary on the early novel has employed the term since Ian Watt.[10] Others, however, involve an element of imagination, a capacity for envisioning just those circumstances that would make a judgment particularly challenging.

Clearly, realism and the imagination could work together, especially as mediated by an increasingly active sphere of public journalism. Indeed, the rise of certain journalistic practices, according to J. Paul Hunter and others, abetted casuistry's role in shaping the modern novel. Strong corroboration for the notion that at least a certain strain of the early modern novel grew out of literary techniques for "putting cases" can be found in the fiction of Samuel Richardson in the 1740s. And Richardson, we know from his biographers, elaborated his fiction precisely out of his prior exercises in composing smaller-scale hypothetical situations for moral edification. *Pamela*, for instance, arose directly out of a collection of "Familiar Letters" Richardson produced in response to two London booksellers, who asked him to write such a book to show country readers how to conduct themselves. This account of novels and cases is probably familiar enough to most recent students of the early British novel. Less familiar, perhaps, is what comes next: the sentimental moment in the history of fiction. This episode is less familiar, I think, because it is not generally recognized as another moment in the transformation of the case form.

We have seen that Adam Smith's 1759 account of the processes of character formation by way of sympathetic exchange of positions in modern commercial society draws on Richardson's early innovations in fiction and, in turn, resonates in Sterne's. The connection seems especially strong in relation to the then-fashionable epistolary method in fiction, an exercise in the alternation of views that, one might say, is very much at the center of what Smith is describing. What I want to reemphasize here is, first, Smith's concluding gesture of framing his entire treatise as both a critique of casuistry—the discursive exercise of directing conscience by the practice of putting hypothetical cases—and a challenge to the institution of auricular confession, which, in his view, likewise perverted the formation of healthy moral sentiments. The second point to reemphasize is that, in urging that we strengthen our moral constitution through the openhearted exchange of sympathies in everyday life, Smith did not altogether dispense with the notion of the case. This is because of his fundamental stipulation that "sympathy" is not feeling what another person feels but rather feeling what we ourselves should feel in a like situation. This capacity amounts to our being able to put ourselves in that person's *case*, as he repeatedly puts it. This is not, as in casuistry, a situation that they must ethically negotiate in respect to a set of rules, but simply the circumstances in which they stand.[11]

My guiding premise, then, is that what the early British novel is to the study of casuistry in the age of Defoe, the sentimental novel is to the sentimentalization of the case in the age of Sterne. As we have seen, the subgenre known as the sentimental journey, established by Sterne within a decade of the publication of *The Theory of Moral Sentiments*, is one in which the Smithian dynamic of sympathy is very much in play. The very conceit of the sentimental journey is premised, in Smith's elaboration of it, on the notion that sentiment necessarily involves a kind of mobility—the capacity to put oneself in the place of another—a mobility made possible by the sympathetic imagination itself. This premise can be seen to structure a good deal of literary work in the decades that follow—not just the so-called sentimental novel in Britain, France, Germany, and America, but, as we saw in chapter 8, a good deal of Romantic poetry and poetics as well. Blake's "The Mental Traveller" and Wordsworth's *Prelude* would be just two examples among many, though each in turn markedly revises the sentimental journey form.[12]

As I have discussed in some detail, in nineteenth-century fiction one can find the premise of sympathetically imaginative mobility in, for example, Walter Scott, Mary Shelley, and Charles Dickens. In Dickens, this holds true not just in *The Old Curiosity Shop*, a picaresque tale of the emotions that explicitly invokes Sterne's *Sentimental Journey* at its outset, but also in *A Tale of Two Cities*, with its emphasis on affective mobility and figurative vehicles. *A Christmas Carol* offered an earlier variation on the theme. When Scrooge tries to dismiss the ghost of Marley as just a bit of undigested beef, Marley replies, "It is required of every man . . . that the spirit within him should walk abroad among his fellow-men, and travel far and wide."[13] One could mount a similar argument about the novels of George Eliot. Dorothea Brooke's sympathetic mobility extends to her magnanimous exertion to assist Rosalind Lydgate even in the wake of her having apparently discovered Lydgate in an untoward intimacy with Will Ladislaw, the man she loves. In *Daniel Deronda*, the titular character is all but defined by his capacities for sympathetic mobility.[14]

One of the most enduring legacies of the Smithian problematic for the novel is indeed a critical idea developed in the wake of the Victorian novel, and made explicit in the famous prefaces of Henry James and the early criticism of Percy Lubbock. It is the idea that the crux of the matter for the developing art of fiction lies in how a novelist moves, and moves a reader, from one standpoint on the story, or in it, to another.[15] This technique is not usually connected, however, to the sentimentalization of the novelistic case. And by the same token, this interrelated history of the case form and the genre of the novel does not typically figure in discussions of modernism. Yet the example of Conrad's *Lord Jim* suggests that it ought to.

Not only can *Lord Jim* be seen as invoking the history of the sentimental case and the sentimental novel; it does so by way of a marked technical emphasis on management of point of view, a clear visual emphasis on the face, and a strong thematic emphasis on questions about the fate of the modern soul. With such thoughts in mind, then, I would like to pose a question about *Lord Jim*—in fact, about a particular sentence from a passage that occurs at almost the exact midpoint of the novel. At this midpoint, the novel's titular character, a man befriended by the narrator Marlow, has been dogged to the point of desperation across the ports of South Asia by gossip about his disgraceful conduct in a maritime emergency, when he jumped ship aboard an imperiled tramp steamer carrying eight hundred Muslim pilgrims to Arabia. The sentence in question comes just after Marlow has provided his listeners with some biographical background about a man named Stein, to whose house he has come for advice: "Such was the history of the man whom I had come to consult about Jim's case without any definite hope."[16]

The question is simply, how much pressure can be profitably put on the word "case"? In contemporary writing, the term has become so routine in its usage that it often seems to lack any function beyond some vague contribution to sentence rhythm. I have suggested that its significance for a writer like Adam Smith has accordingly been overlooked. What about here, in Conrad? What would be lost if Conrad's sentence were amended to read ". . . to consult about Jim," or "about Jim's situation" or "about Jim's problem"? To see the relevance of the sentimental case to Conrad, we must first understand his investment in the elusive figure of the case itself.

The Cases of *Lord Jim*

The question as to whether the phrase "Jim's case" does any special work here can actually be even more concretely framed. Introducing Stein to his auditors a few paragraphs earlier, Marlow tells them that he was "a naturalist of some distinction" who specialized in entomology: "This collection of *Buprestidae* and *Longicorns*—beetles all—horrible miniature monsters, looking malevolent in death and immobility, and his cabinet of butterflies, beautiful and hovering under the glass cases on lifeless wings, had spread his fame far over the earth" (192). Do these cases have anything to do with "Jim's case"?

One reason to suspect so is that the cases dominate the very scene of Marlow's consultation with Stein, as Marlow explains in describing its impression on him when he arrives:

> He welcomed me in his quiet and humorous voice. Only one corner of the vast room, the corner in which stood his writing-desk, was strongly lighted by a shaded reading-lamp, and the rest of the spacious apartment melted into shapeless gloom like a cavern. Narrow shelves filled with dark boxes of uniform shape and colour ran round the walls, not from floor to ceiling, but in a somber belt about four feet broad—catacombs of beetles. . . . The glass cases containing the collection of butterflies were ranged in three long rows upon slender-legged little tables. One of these cases had been removed from its place and stood on the desk, which was bestrewn with oblong slips of paper blackened with minute handwriting.
>
> "So you see me—so," he said. His hand hovered over the case where a butterfly in solitary grandeur spread out dark bronze wings, seven inches or more across, with exquisite white veinings and a gorgeous border of yellow spots. "Only one specimen like this they have in your London, and then—no more." . . .
>
> He bent forward in the chair and gazed intently, his chin over the case. I stood at his back. (193)

An indication of how this tableau matters to the case of Jim is that the metonymy of the glass cases reappears all through the subsequent meeting between Jim and Stein. Even as Marlow approaches Stein with his question about Jim, Stein "keeps his eyes fixed on the glass case" that houses one of his prize butterflies: "I was very anxious, but I respected the intense, almost passionate, absorption with which he looked at a butterfly, as though on the bronze sheen of these frail wings, in the white tracings, in the gorgeous markings, he could see other things, an image of something perishable and defying destruction as these delicate and lifeless tissues displaying a splendour unmarred by death" (195). Later in the conversation, Marlow reports that Stein "lowered the glass lid, the automatic lock clicked sharply, and taking up the case in both hands he bore it religiously away to its place, passing out of the bright circle of the lamp into the ring of fainter light—into the shapeless dusk at last" (199). What, if anything, is to be made of this metonymic "case," indeed of all the metonymic cases and boxes among which Marlow and Stein have their conference about the case of Jim?[17]

Conrad makes it inconvenient for an attentive reader of his novel to ignore either the metonymy or the echo. He does so partly by virtue of the way he frames the conversation after Marlow reports having filled in Stein on Jim's story:

> When I finished he uncrossed his legs, laid down his pipe, leaned forward towards me earnestly with his elbows on the arms of his chair, the tips of his fingers together.
>
> "I understand very well. He is a romantic."
>
> He had diagnosed the case for me, and first I was quite startled to find how simple it was; and indeed our conference resembled so much a medical consultation—Stein of learned aspect, sitting in an arm chair before his desk; I, anxious, in another, facing him, but a little to one side—that it seemed natural to ask—
>
> "What's good for it?"
>
> He lifted up a forefinger.
>
> "There is only one remedy! One thing alone can us from being ourselves cure!" The finger came down on the desk with a smart rap. The case which he had made to look so simple before became if possible still simpler—and altogether hopeless. (199)

The remedy that Stein proposes, and that Marlow helps to implement, is to send Jim off to the remote East Indian outpost of Patusan, where Stein had earlier established some connections, and where indeed the action of the second half of *Lord Jim* is set. As Marlow makes explicit, the language of "case" and "remedy" casts Jim's case in medical terms and thus also frames the exchange between Marlow and Stein as a kind of medical consultation.

It seems fair enough to say that this language lends pointed resonance to Marlow's earlier phrase, "Jim's case." But it doesn't yet explain the metonymic work of the cases that form both background and foreground in the scene of this conversation, work that is amplified by means of the "specimen" concept. Even before Marlow manages to tell Stein Jim's story, Stein tells Marlow a story about the butterfly in the case over which his hand gestures as he speaks, a specimen of a rare species that had long eluded him. Stein explains in detail how the butterfly appeared over the face of one of three men Stein had killed in the jungle when they had attempted to ambush him "one fine morning" long ago. As soon as the butterfly settled, Stein captured him with a "flop" (one of the many important "jumps," "leaps," and "falls" in the novel): "When I got up I shook like a leaf with excitement, and when I opened these beautiful wings and made sure what a rare and so extraordinary specimen I had, my head went round and my legs became so weak with emotion that I had to sit on the ground" (197). When Stein finally breaks out of his absorption in the butterflies to ask Marlow the reason for his visit, Marlow replies: "To tell you the truth, . . . I came here to describe a specimen" (198). When Stein asks whether the specimen is a butterfly, Marlow replies, "Nothing so perfect. . . . A man" (198).

In so introducing his account of Jim for Stein, Marlow echoes a theme already sounded in their conversation at the moment when Stein first shows him the butterfly:

> "Never heard an entomologist go on like this," I observed cheerfully. "Masterpiece! And what of man?"
>
> "Man is amazing, but he is not a masterpiece," he said, keeping his eyes fixed on the glass case. (195)

The analogical link between the two specimens, Jim and the rare butterfly, is thus introduced by way of a key difference already established between the two species. And this in turn is framed, as we shall see, by one of the most celebrated refrains in all of Conrad's fiction, one already well-rehearsed by the time we reach this scene at the rough midpoint of the novel: Marlow's repeated declaration that Jim was "one of us," that he was "of the right sort" (44, 74, 100, 112, 121, 208, 283, 289, 348–49). It is thus, in the context of such sorting, and such different *kinds* of sorting, as it were, that we arrive at Stein's diagnosis and prescribed remedy for Jim.

I hope this much is enough to show that, at the very least, Marlow's phrase "Jim's case" is no mere pleonasm. It appears within a framework of metaphors and metonymies, comparisons and contrasts, that richly structure this central episode. There is good reason to conclude, furthermore, that the episode in turn ramifies through the novel as a whole. One quick indication of the episode's importance is that it is reprised in Marlow's closing words, which are also the last words of the novel. They come after the narrative of Jim's death, when we are given a brief, final glimpse of Stein, "'preparing to leave all this; preparing to leave . . .' while he waves his hand sadly at the butterflies" (353; Conrad's ellipses).[18] How, then, do we best explore the possible implications of the case, taken both as theme and device, for Conrad's ambitions in *Lord Jim* and elsewhere? Just what kind of figure are we talking about in the case of Conrad's "cases"?

Students of Conrad's fiction are aware, of course, that his fiction often deploys symbolic motifs in ways that serve at once as topoi and tropes. In *Heart of Darkness*, there is the motif of the heart of the matter, which is also cast in the famous conceit of the shell and kernel. In *Nostromo*, there is the figure of cultural translation that is implicit in the hybridized titular epithet for the novel's silver-tinted hero; in *Chance*, the figure of the game, with its dynamics of "accident" and "design," two of the novel's key words; in *The Nigger of the "Narcissus,"* the figure of weather. In *Lord Jim*, there are other motifs besides that of the case. One of the most important of these is the motif of the "jump" or "leap," which recurs at several junctures in ways that matter to *any* account of the novel.

After his trial, Jim narrates to Marlow how, as the last of the crew aboard a pilgrim ship thought to be sinking with eight hundred Muslim souls aboard, he stood motionless for a long time, much as we know he did in a prior emergency (one involving a man overboard during a storm) already told in the novel's opening omniscient mode. Narrating this second emergency to Marlow, Jim explains that "she was going down, down, head first under me . . .," but his very next words—a famous moment in Conrad—come on the other side of a narrative ellipsis: "'I had jumped . . .' He checked himself, averted his gaze. . . . 'It seems,' he added" (124–25). This line would be pointedly echoed by Jim himself when he tells Marlow years later about the heroic moment on Patusan when he makes his great "leap" across the stream in a decisive struggle for control of the place.

More than a theme, the motif of the jump becomes a *performative* narrative trope in the novel, not just at the level of Jim's jumping over his first jump with the shift from past tense to past perfect tense ("I had jumped"), but also at the level of Conrad's overall management of the narration. Even before the introduction of Marlow, *Lord Jim* the novel, in its early omniscient mode, itself jumps over Jim's jump. Indeed, in the account of what happened aboard the *Patna* in the Arabian sea, which is painstaking in its descriptive detail up to the point of the collision, the omniscient narrator skips past the entire ship-jumping episode to Jim's trial for an alleged offense about which we have scarcely been given a clue.

Nothing could be more enigmatic. The sea is placid, we are told, and the ship's progress is smooth. Suddenly the engineer, holding forth to his shipmates, "pitched down head-first as though he had been clubbed from behind." No one understands what is going on: "Jim and the skipper staggered forward by common accord, and catching themselves up, stood very stiff and still gazing, amazed, at the undisturbed level of the sea. Then they looked upward at the stars" (62). Directly following these words comes a question that introduces the chapter's final paragraph—"What had happened?" (62)—conspicuously marked by the kind of tense shift that anticipates Jim's "I had jumped." The paragraph does not, however, tell us what had happened. The opening of the next chapter, furthermore, marks an even larger "jump": "A month or so afterwards, when Jim, in answer to pointed questions, tried to tell honestly the truth of this experience, he said, speaking of the ship: 'She went over whatever it was as easy as a snake crawling over a stick'" (63). We are now already in the scene of the inquiry, without the slightest indication of what charges Jim might be facing or, indeed, any clear sense of "what had happened."[19]

The trope/topos of *jumping* not only is crucial to *Lord Jim* but is associated with the *case* figure by way of its association with the language of "falling"; Conrad would surely have known that *Fall* is the German for case. Yet the case figure seems to stand out among this group of tropes-cum-topoi. This is partly because of its conceptual and historical richness, on which Conrad demonstrably draws, and partly because of its importance to the history of the modern novel. At least one of Conrad's own contemporaries called attention to this language in Conrad's fiction. In his review of Conrad's *Chance* (1913), one of the later Marlow tales, Henry James described the novel as "a prolonged hovering flight of the subjective over the outstretched ground of the case exposed."[20] And though some commentators on *Lord Jim* have echoed Marlow's talk of "Jim's case" in the course of making their own observations, I want to push the matter a good deal further, for I suspect that what we can read in *Lord Jim* is not only a rich meditation on, say, the relation between men and butterflies, Jim's case and Stein's cases, but also a sentimental mediation of this entire problematic sense of the case, as "specimen," with older understandings that belong to ethics and jurisprudence. Jim's dire situation at the novel's midpoint, after all, derives from both his ethical predicament during a crisis aboard the *Patna* and his legal conviction in the subsequent inquiry.

Given the importance of ethical and jurisprudential cases to the history of the novel, we can finally discern in the palimpsest-like narrative structure of *Lord Jim* a register of the British novel's long engagement with the complex history of the modern case form. If a key moment in that engagement is the moment of the sentimental transformation of the novel in the late eighteenth century, which involves a critical intervention in the history of casuistry by the British moral-sentiments school of social theory, then crucial to that transformation, as I have argued, is a sense of the relation of the case and the face. That Stein's prized specimen first appears as a shadow on a human face, in other words, turns out to be no less crucial a detail than Marlow's reference to "Jim's case" when he offers up Jim as a specimen for Stein's study.

Thinking History in Cases

The prospect of attempting a history of the case as a concept or problem, or for that matter a history of case-thinking as an intellectual style, is a daunting challenge. So much so that when some brave writer like Michel Foucault takes a stab at it, the gesture tends to attract its share of notice. Foucault's brief comments on this topic are to be found chiefly in two passages from *Discipline and Punish* (1975). The first comes in the chapter on "generalized punishment," in a discussion of how modern forms of individualization differ from what is implicit in forms of punishment meted out by the older jurisprudence. In the older system, according to Foucault, two variables—"circumstances" and "intentions"—were used to determine the punishment. This determination thus, he says, belonged "to 'casuistry' in the broad sense."[21] In the newer system, which would come to dominate in the nineteenth century, "psychological knowledge will take over the role of casuistic jurisprudence," as punishments began to refer to the defendant himself: "to his nature, to his way of life and his attitude of mind, to his past, to the 'quality' and not to the intention of his will" (99). What Foucault calls the "code-individualization link," furthermore, was provided by "the scientific models of the period":

> Natural history no doubt offered the most adequate schema: the taxonomy of species according to an uninterrupted gradation. One sought to constitute a Linnaeus of crimes and punishments, so that each particular offense and each punishable individual might come . . . within the provisions of a general law. (99)

Foucault does not at this point make explicit the terminological connection between the old casuistical or jurisprudential "case" and the new case of taxonomical individuation, but he does come round to doing so in the section of the book devoted to "discipline" in relation to the problem of "the 'clinical' sciences" and the problem of the "entry of the individual description" (191).

His declaration there—often echoed in the years since he made it—is that the answers are to be found in those "'ignoble' archives, where the modern play of coercion over bodies, gestures, and behaviour has its beginnings, and especially in the documents associated with 'the examination'":

> The examination, surrounded by all its documentary techniques, makes each individual a "case": a case which at one and the same time constitutes an object for a branch of knowledge and a hold for a branch of power. The

case is no longer, as in casuistry or jurisprudence, a set of circumstances defining an act and capable of modifying the application of a rule; it is the individual as he may be described, judged, measured, compared with others, in his very individuality; and it is also the individual who has to be trained or corrected, classified, normalized, excluded, etc. (191)

Foucault's observations on this head have been picked up by various commentators interested in the history of the case.[22] They have probably been addressed most extensively by John Forrester. While in the main accepting what he calls Foucault's "account of the genesis of the case," Forrester seeks (in behalf of a more nuanced sense of the psychoanalytic case in particular) to qualify the account in which Foucault "counterposes the case as found in 'casuistry or jurisprudence' with the case as found in the clinical sciences."[23] Forrester produces a somewhat revised "genealogy of the case in the late nineteenth century," one that resists Foucault's tendency to "[place] at a distance the writing of the individual life as a case from 'jurisprudence or casuistry.'"[24] What I find so suggestive about all of this for the analysis of *Lord Jim* is that Conrad, writing at the turn of the century, seems to be offering something like Foucault's counterposition of case forms along with something like Forrester's attempt to nuance the relationship. And Conrad's sensitivity to the sentimental case, pivotal to this history in a number of ways, is what makes this possible.

To see the relevance of both Foucault's account and Forrester's elaboration, it helps to recognize that the scene of the consultation with Stein is not the first time in the novel that Marlow uses the phrase "Jim's case." Jim's case has become a matter of explicit attention, as it happens, just after one of the narrative's remarkable "jumps," as we turn the page from the end of chapter 3 (where it is made clear that some accident has befallen the *Patna*) to the beginning of chapter 4 (where Jim is standing trial for some unexplained abrogation of duty). Readers cannot fail to be puzzled by the exceedingly sketchy picture of the trial as it takes shape in chapter 4, for while we are made aware that some sort of case is being tried, it is by no means clear what it is a case *of*. We are given a phenomenological account of the courtroom activities, with an impressionistic mise-en-scène and some fragments of a question and answer:

He [Jim] spoke slowly; he remembered swiftly and with extreme vividness; he could have reproduced like an echo the moaning of the engineer for the better information of these men who wanted facts. After his first feeling of revolt he had come round to the view that only a meticulous precision of statement would bring out the true horror behind the appalling face of things. The facts those men were so eager to know had been visible, tangible, open to the senses, occupying their place in space and time, requiring for their existence a fourteen-hundred-ton steamer and twenty-seven minutes by the watch; they made a whole that had features, shades of expression, a complicated aspect that could be remembered by the eye, and something else besides, something invisible, a directing spirit of perdition that dwelt within, like a malevolent soul in a detestable body. He was anxious to make this clear. . . . This awful activity of mind made him hesitate at times in his speech. . . . He was becoming irrelevant; a question to the point cut short his speech, like a pang of pain, and he felt extremely discouraged and weary. He was coming to that, he was coming to that, and now, checked brutally, he had to answer by yes or no. He answered truthfully by a curt "Yes, I did"; and fair of face, big of frame with young gloomy eyes, he held his shoulders upright above the box while his soul writhed within him. (64–65)

As readers, we do not know at this point that what is at issue in this exchange is the incriminating circumstance that Jim jumped ship. Nor, for that matter, are we informed of the extenuating circumstance that he was the last of his motley crew to do so. We do have a sense that the "inquiry" involves at least a quasi-legal case and that it has moral implications. We have this on the authority of the (still at this point) omniscient narrator, whose reliability we have no grounds for doubting and who tells us that Jim's "soul writhed within him." It is only in the following chapter (chapter 5)—in a second narrative jump, where narrative responsibility shifts from the omniscient narrator to Marlow—that a fuller sense emerges of what for the first time in the book is called "the Patna case." And it is only then that we glimpse the implications for what in chapter 6 will for the first time be called "Jim's case."

There is, I suggest, a subtle difference between "the Patna case," whose dim outline begins to be discernible in the course of Marlow's interpolated tale, and "Jim's case." This difference is explicable by way of one of the judges in the inquiry, a sea captain, like Marlow, who is called Big Brierly, a solid-seeming figure with an internal instability that later leads him to take his own life by leaping off his own ship. Of this man Brierly, Marlow tells his listeners:

The sting of life could do no more to his complacent soul than the scratch of a pin to the smooth face of a rock. This was enviable. As I looked at him, flanking on one side the unassuming pale-faced magistrate who presided at the inquiry, his self-satisfaction presented to me and to the world a surface as hard as granite. He committed suicide very soon after.

No wonder *Jim's case* bored him, and while I thought with something akin to fear of the immensity of his contempt for the young man under examination, he was probably holding silent inquiry into *his own case*. The verdict must have been unmitigated guilt, and he took the secret of the evidence with him in that leap into the sea. (86; italics added)

The "probably" makes clear that an analogical relationship between Jim's case and Brierly's own is established here by way of a double projection—Marlow imagining what Brierly is imagining. Since Brierly had been charged with no crime, this analogy in turn encourages a further analogy between the courts and the conscience, which is to say, between the jurisprudential case and the casuistical one.

We have already been given a clue about these kinds of distinctions toward the end of chapter 5, the first chapter under Marlow's narration, when Marlow mentions having run into one of the crew of the *Patna*, its chief engineer, at a nearby hospital just before the inquiry. Although Marlow is hoping that an interview with this man might "offer something explanatory of the famous affair from his point of view" (80), the engineer's point of view has been nullified by his delirium, apparently a combined effect of the trauma of the events and his own withdrawal from alcohol. After this encounter, Marlow meets the attending physician, who pronounces the engineer "'A curious case. D.T.s of the worst kind,'" to which he then adds, "'I never remember being so interested in a case of jim-jams before.'"[25] The doctor's interest in this case does not derive from not knowing what it is a case of. He knows that it is a case of delirium tremens. His interest derives from his sense of it as "curious." The question of whether a case "bores" (as Jim's case does Big Brierly) or "interests" (as the engineer's does the doctor) is a major part of case thinking—in the novel as in the casuistical tradition. And of course it comes to the fore in the novel's central question of Marlow's interest in Jim's case.

The engineer's case does not in itself matter to Jim's, as we learn from the parting exchange between the doctor and Marlow:

"I say," he cried after me; "he can't attend that inquiry. Is his evidence material, you think."

"Not in the least," I called back from the gateway. (83)

These are the last words of chapter 5. And since *Lord Jim* was initially serialized, these chapter breaks are also breaks between installments. The ensuing chapter will pick up this thread in a way that helps establish a distinction between the *Patna* case and Jim's case. Here are the very first words of chapter 6, in Marlow's voice:

> The authorities were evidently of the same opinion. The inquiry was not adjourned. It was held on the appointed day to satisfy the law, and it was well-attended because of its human interest, no doubt. There was no incertitude as to facts—as to the one material fact I mean. How the Patna came to be hurt it was impossible to find out; the court did not expect to find out; and in the whole audience there was not a man who cared. Yet, as I've told you, all the sailors in the port attended, and the waterside business was fully represented. Whether they knew it or not, the interest that drew them there was purely psychological—the expectation of some essential disclosure as to the strength, the power, the horror, of human emotions. Naturally nothing of the kind could be disclosed. The examination of the only man able and willing to face it was beating futilely round the well-known fact, and the play of questions upon it was as instructive as the tapping with a hammer on an iron box, were the object to find out what's inside. However, an official inquiry could not be any other thing. Its object was not the fundamental why, but the superficial how, of this affair. (84)

Underlying Marlow's words here—and much of the tale that follows—is the question of Marlow's own interest in Jim's case. It is an interest that Marlow himself characteristically avoids explaining. At the same time, this interest holds a key to the further question, raised pointedly by this whole series of transitions, as to how to understand the various senses of "the case" in the novel—from the ethical, political, legal, and medical, on the one hand, to those associated with the themes of "interest," "curiosity," and "sympathy," on the other. It is a question of just what construction we are to put on "Jim's case," and of how one engages it in a way that avoids the mistake of those whose inquiries seem merely to be tapping with a hammer on an iron box to determine what is inside. Marlow, like Conrad behind him, is here working with a conceptual understanding of the sentimental case undreamed of in either Foucault's or Forrester's casuistical genealogies.

The Face of the Case

Marlow's own answer to the question of his interest in Jim's case is that it is grounded in nothing more than "curiosity, the most obvious of sentiments"—which seems like a denial of his own involvement in a drama centering on "the strength, the power, the horror, of human emotions." Marlow's self-explanation, such as it is, is surely not to be taken at face value in a book whose central figure is so defined by mists and mystery.[26] It is almost as if Jim has to be made mysterious to justify the "obvious" arousal of curiosity that Jim occasions in Marlow. What may be more to the point, in any event, is the novel's dramatization of the mutual connection between Jim and Marlow. And perhaps the key to this connection is that the novel establishes their relationship in a series of personal encounters with a great deal of emphasis on the face.

For example, when we are finally treated to some detail about what happened aboard the *Patna*, the specifics are provided neither by the omniscient narrator, who, as we have seen, overleaps those events, nor by Marlow, at the start of his narration to the harbor-side audience, but rather in the account that Jim delivers in his face-to-face conversation with Marlow on the night after the inquiry. The narrative of the key details, that is, belongs to the doubly dramatic situation of Marlow's report of a dinner conversation between himself and Jim. Moreover, the details about the circumstances of this conversation are as striking as those about the circumstances of the events aboard the *Patna* and aboard the small lifeboat afterward. In chapters 7–12, given over to Marlow's account of his long conversation with Jim about the *Patna* affair, we see a drama played out between them that in turn depends on a conflict within Marlow between the work of judgment and the work of sympathy. And much of this conflict expresses itself through Marlow's comments on the face-to-face exchange of gestures and glances with Jim:

And all the time I had before me those blue, boyish eyes looking straight into mine, this young face, these capable shoulders, the open bronzed forehead with a white line under the roots of clustering fair hair, this appearance appealing at sight to all my sympathies: this frank aspect, the artless smile, the youthful seriousness. He was of the right sort; he was one of us. (100)

He drew quick breaths at every few words and shot quick glances at my face, as though in his anguish he were watchful of the effect. He was not speaking to me, he was only speaking before me, in a dispute with an invisible personality, an antagonistic and inseparable partner of his existence— another possessor of his soul. (111)

. . . his eyes shone . . . (113)

There was a suggestion of awful stillness in his face . . . (124)

He raised his hand deliberately to his face ... (124)

His clear blue eyes turned to me with a piteous stare ... (125)

He tried to sound me out with an attentive glance dropped on me in passing. (136)

He was looking me squarely in the face, and withdrew his gaze slowly. (139)

The very reason Jim gives for telling his story is that "[he] would like to explain—[he] would like somebody to understand—somebody—one person at least" (103). There are moments when Marlow can see Jim's efforts only as a kind of delusional, self-serving casuistry. When Jim says, "'I always believed in being prepared for the worst,'... staring anxiously in [Marlow's] face," Marlow can neither take his point nor meet his eyes: "I nodded my approval of the sound principle, averting my eyes before the subtle unsoundness of the man" (109).

At times Marlow suggests that he is being emotionally "bullied" by Jim (121). But at other times he avows being "swayed" by him (112), and he often finds he enters sympathetically into Jim's suffering:

His uneasy eyes fastened upon mine, questioned, begged, challenged, entreated. For the life of me I couldn't help murmuring, "You've been tried." (134)

In spite, or because, of the sense of compulsion in Marlow's response, moments like this have been taken by some readers to dramatize the overcoming of judgment by sympathy in Marlow's narrative. But however we judge Marlow's own reaction, we sense that sympathy and judgment may be pulling him in different directions.

In Smith's influential theory, the work of sympathy is a precondition of judgment, in two senses: first, the lifelong experience of sympathetic identification establishes the basis for judgment by strengthening the guiding viewpoint of the impartial spectator, and, second, in any given encounter, we must put ourselves in the other's case in order to form a judgment about his or her response to it.[27] As the sentimental line is extended in later literary production, however, a tension develops between judgment and sympathy.[28] This tension appears most clearly in the nineteenth century's prevalent dramatic-monologue form and, more pointedly, in the emergence of the problematic of the sentimental monster in novels by Godwin, Mary Shelley, and Dickens.[29]

Exploring *Lord Jim* in light of Foucault's genealogy of the clinical case out of the juridico-casuistical case, we have thus come up against the moment that Foucauldians (and others) tend to elide: the moment of the sentimental challenge to the juridico-casuistical case, well in advance of the nineteenth-century heyday of the clinical case form. Changes in form, however, need to be recognized in their formal or procedural dimension. Just as the sentimental challenge to casuistry in Smith is inaugurated with a proposal for a new way of proceeding in ethics, so the sentimental mode is registered in *Lord Jim* most powerfully in its procedural ramifications. It is not simply that the conversation with Jim, or even the Marlow narrative as a whole, can be read in some thematic relation to the sentimental—nor even just that a sentimental narrative or drama is conspicuously interpolated in a larger novelistic frame. Rather, the very *means* of interpolation are themselves implicated in the legacy of the sentimental novel. That is to say, the very device by which Marlow is introduced into the omniscient narration itself constitutes a crucial sentimental structure, a novelistic equivalent of the cinematic suture.

It works like this. As we near the end of chapter 4 (the last of the chapters with omniscient narration), after negotiating the swirling impressions of Jim at the inquiry and the confusing fragments of his exchanges with the judges, we arrive at a description of his gaze, roving across the faces of those assembled in the courtroom:

> Jim's eyes, wandering in the intervals of his answers, rested upon a white man who sat apart from the others, with his face worn and clouded, but with quiet eyes that glanced straight, interested and clear. . . . He met the eyes of the white man. The glance directed at him was not the fascinated stare of the others. It was an act of intelligent volition. (62)

The as yet nameless man on whom Jim's gaze comes to rest, and whose eyes meet his, turns out to be Marlow, who is immediately identified by name. And just as quickly, the omniscient narrator sets the stage for Marlow's performance some years later for a group of male auditors on a harbor-side verandah who are ready to settle into a long yarn after a good meal, the very yarn cited by the omniscient narrator of *Lord Jim*. The account of the meeting of Jim's and Marlow's eyes would be worth attending to if only because it lends omniscient authority to the sorts of details in Marlow's account of the subsequent face-to-face conversation that we considered above. Crucially, when Marlow launches into his own narrative in the next chapter, his initial position in the tale is at the vantage point, precisely, on the other side of Jim's gaze in the courtroom: "My eyes met his for the first time at that inquiry" (68). In a sudden and surprising shift in narrative perspective, Marlow's tale of Jim is thus sutured into the omniscient frame narrative by a kind of cinematic "eye-line match"—a movement of shot/reverse-shot. This is not, however, Trotter's "literature of cinema"—not a moment influenced by cinematic style. The continuity system in classical narrative cinema would not be developed for another decade or two. Rather, Conrad has effectively produced his own early-twentieth-century turn on the sentimental mode in a further anticipation of that system.

To amplify the power of this device, Conrad prepares for this striking effect with a similar kind of transition, but without the reversal in point of view. It occurs in the previous chapter transition (from chapter 3 to chapter 4)—that is, in the transition from the *Patna*'s encounter with something in the Arabian Sea to the scene of the inquiry. Here is the close of chapter 3:

> What had happened? ... The eyes of the two Malays at the wheel glittered toward the white men, but their dark hands remained closed on the spokes. The sharp hull driving on its way seemed to rise a few inches in succession through its whole length, as though it had become pliable, and settled down again rigidly to its work of cleaving the smooth surface of the sea. Its quivering stopped, and the faint noise of thunder ceased all at once, as though the ship had steamed across a narrow belt of vibrating water and of humming air. (63)

And here, with its reversal of perspective, is the description of Jim in the courtroom from the opening of chapter 4:

> He stood elevated in the witness-box, with burning cheeks in a cool lofty room: the big framework of the punkas moved gently to and fro high above his head, and from below many eyes were looking at them out of dark faces, out of red faces, out of faces attentive, spellbound, as if all these people sitting in orderly rows upon narrow benches had been enslaved by the fascination of his voice. . . . The face of the presiding magistrate, clean shaved and impassible, looked at him deadly pale between the faces of the two nautical assessors. (63)[30]

This earlier chapter transition is structured over a cut, as it were, between two scenes in which Jim stands before the eyes of others. We shift, in other words, from Jim's encounter aboard the *Patna* with the gaze of the two Malay pilots who save the ship from disaster after the desertion by the white crew—they, we later learn, stand by their stations in the crisis—to his encounter in the courtroom with the gaze of those who sit in judgment of him.

Although this "cut" involves what, in the novel's idiosyncratic figural lexicon, amounts to another performative "jump," it is more like what in cinema came to be called a match cut than a jump cut. Nor, though it involves a transition between two gazes, is it to be likened to a shot/reverse-shot transition. On the contrary, since it involves parallel rather than reciprocated glances, one might argue that the *absence* of sympathy in the first transition—either thematically *or* structurally—prepares the way for the *dramatization* of sympathy in the shot/reverse-shot transition to Marlow's narrative that comes in the next turning of chapters. The sequence of two transitions, taken together, thus highlights Conrad's structured use of point-of-view techniques in the novel. More than this, it gives a sense of the point of their deployment. It shows the affective or sentimental stakes of the way Conrad folds into the novel both Marlow's narrative and Marlow's interest in Jim's case. It is an enfolding that defines Jim's situation precisely *as* a case in the sentimental frame of reference.

Conrad, we have seen, stages the introduction to "Jim's case" by way of a series of transitions from one face-to-face situation to another: from the Malays' turn toward the white men on the ship, to the face-to-face moment in court, to the singling out of the face of Marlow in this scene, to the intimacy of the dinner at which Jim tells his story to Marlow. Only in the last of these scenes, in the context of Marlow's increasingly sympathetic audition, do we actually have the story of the events that lead to Jim's disgrace. And, of course, the account of this narration being delivered years later in Marlow's own after-dinner tale-telling session on the harbor-side verandah. Here, too, the details of feature and expression seem to draw much narrative attention: "Now and then a small red glow would move abruptly, and expanding light up the fingers of a languid hand, part of a face in profound repose, or flash a crimson gleam into a pair of pensive eyes overshadowed by a fragment of an unruffled forehead" (67). Thus, while showing that Jim's case takes shape in reference both to the early modern tradition of casuistry (the legal or ethical situation that has to be faced with rule-governed judgment) and to the late-modern sense of the case (as faceless individuation by psychological or medical practices), Conrad above all emphasizes the structure of sympathy that belongs to the sentimentalization of the case, and he actualizes it through the narrative techniques of the sentimental mode.

Can it be mere coincidence that *Lord Jim*, the Conrad novel that most energetically mobilizes the language of the case, is also the one that is most invested in the issues of sympathetic identification? A sense of this special conjunction is indirectly registered in some of the best criticism of the novel, as for example in the two chapters on *Lord Jim* that form the centerpiece of Albert Guérard's classic study of Conrad from 1958. It is in *Lord Jim* that

Guérard sees "the intense conflict of judgment and sympathy—of reason and feeling, detachment and intimacy—which is the very backbone of [Conrad's] work."[31] It is "the first novel in a new form: a form bent on involving and implicating the reader in a psycho-moral drama which has no easy solution, and bent on engaging his sensibilities more strenuously and even more uncomfortably than ever before" (126). And it is "the first major novel solidly built on a true intuitive understanding of sympathetic identification as a psychic process, and as a process which may operate both consciously and less than consciously" (147). The novel exposes the reader "to a continuous subtle and flowing interplay of intellectual appeals to his judgment and poignant appeals to his sympathy" (132); "in every chapter, on every page the double appeal to sympathy and judgment is made, though one or the other may dominate" (160).

Like a number of other critics who have written well about this novel, Guérard makes use of the language of the case. He tends to do so quite casually: "A man is what he does, which in Jim's case is very little that is not equivocal" (161). Occasionally, he does so more pointedly, suggesting that one of the novel's central questions is whether we can "recognize the full complexity of any simple case, respond both sympathetically and morally to Jim and his version of 'how to be'" (142). Other critics, too, echo the novel's case discourse. Ian Watt writes of Jim: "We are made to confront the essence of his case in all its starkness; the breakdown of one individual officer's fidelity, under conditions of total moral isolation, as the result of his mistaken but well-founded fear that a catastrophe is imminent which he will be powerless to avert."[32] But where Watt writes of the complexity of the case in its starkness, and Guérard (oxymoronically) of the complexity of the case in its simplicity, neither appreciates the way in which the novel brings a number of modalities of case logic together in a single narrative. Again, these modalities include not only the ethical/legal but also the medical/psychological—as well as the case that emerges from the Smithian critique of casuistry in favor of the operations of moral sentiment by means of sympathetic identification across a range of points of view.[33]

My contention, then, has been that the notion of point of view itself, a staple of twentieth-century narratology, emerges from a formal revision in the practice of the very kind of case-thinking on which a good deal of early-modern fiction was founded in the first place, the decisive moment of the "facing of the case" in the sentimental novel. Everything depends on seeing the connections that link the case, the face, and the point of view. The elaboration of these connections is the work of what might be called the metadrama of *Lord Jim*. This elaboration, as I have tried to show, is achieved by way of recursive gestures toward various stages of the novel's modern development, though curiously, not even readers inclined to read *Lord Jim* in light of that development have recognized such connections.[34] And when these connections are not perspicuous, the metadrama remains cloaked in metamists.

Joyce, Sterne, and the Structure of Sentiment

One specific indicator of the way in which modernism and sentimentalism were imbricated in the early twentieth century can be found in the reputation enjoyed by Laurence Sterne among certain key writers. In Sterne's work, wrote Virginia Woolf in *The Common Reader*, "we are as close to life as we can be."[35] James Joyce paid Sterne his own distinct form of homage in the chapter of *Ulysses* that has come to be known as "Oxen in the Sun." In one of the longest and most virtuosic chapters of his long and virtuosic book, Joyce narrates an allegorical episode in a Dublin maternity hospital through the reenactment of a nine-stage evolution of English prose from the medieval period to the moment of *Ulysses* itself. This evolution includes a three-page passage in imitation of Sterne's *Sentimental Journey*, unmistakably so:

> A sigh of affection gave eloquence to these words and, having replaced the locket in his bosom, he wiped his eye and sighed again. Beneficent Disseminator of blessings to all Thy creatures, how great and universal must be that sweetest of Thy tyrannies which can hold in thrall the free and the bond, the simple swain and the polished coxcomb, the lover in the heyday of reckless passion and the husband of maturer years. But indeed, sir, I wander from the point. How mingled and imperfect are our sublunary joys![36]

Joyce's dilation of the moment of giving birth at such enormous length might itself be said to reproduce *Tristram Shandy*'s protracted account of his own birth, an account that also shaped the autobiographical birth narrative in *David Copperfield*.[37] The associative method in *Ulysses* that so fascinated Eisenstein is arguably one of the central contributions of Sterne to modern fiction, and Joyce foregrounds it here, as if to point up the distinctive place of Sterne's prose within this scheme of "progress." Later, describing his first efforts with the book that became *Finnegans Wake*, Joyce wrote, "I am trying to build many planes of narrative within a single aesthetic purpose. Did you ever read Laurence Sterne?"[38]

Ulysses was published too late to figure in Viktor Shklovsky's claim about *Tristram Shandy's* typification of the novel form. But the book Eisenstein called the Bible of the new cinema is a novel that shares a number of features with Sterne's fiction in respect to its place in the history of the novel. In both, one might say, we find Irish-born writers who transformed the novel by a miscellaneous virtuosity of style and subject matter, and who transformed our very notion of literary travel in the bargain. I would also suggest that Joyce's special sensitivity to literary history led him to acknowledge Sterne's contribution to English prose style in the "Oxen of the Sun" episode. My focus here, however, will be on another episode, which, though it does not acknowledge the Sternean sentimental explicitly, comes perhaps closer to registering Sterne's long-term impact in the terms I have laid out here. The episode is "Nausicaa," where Bloom encounters several young women at Sandycove strand in the early evening, and where he becomes fixated on one of them in particular, Gerty, who is perched, like Homer's Nausicaa, on the rocks above a beach.

As with most chapters of *Ulysses*, the style of the chapter does much of its work, and that style is generally acknowledged by commentators to be "sentimental." This determination often seems to be arrived at from an encounter with the chapter's opening words: "The summer evening had begun to fold the world in its mysterious embrace. Far away in the west the sun was setting and the last glow of all too fleeting day lingered lovingly on sea and strand . . ." (449). Or again, from the introduction of Gerty: "Gerty MacDowell who was seated near her companions, lost in thought, gazing far away into the distance, was in very truth as fair a specimen of winsome Irish girlhood as one could wish to see" (452). Or again, later in the scene, after Gerty and Bloom have begun their reciprocated dumbshow: "How moving the scene there in the gathering twilight, the last glimpse of Erin, the touching chime of those evening bells" (473). But what is involved in the stylistic performance of the Nausicaa section is more than a matter of tone and diction. It also has much to do with what by now we can recognize as sentimental disposition of body and soul, matter and spirit.

A mass is being said nearby to the Blessed Virgin, "Mary, star of the sea" (449), and it is said of Gerty that "her very soul is in her eyes" (456). Yet over the course of the chapter, Gerty knowingly exposes the flesh beneath her "transparent stockings" to the prurient eyes of the lingering passerby, Leopold Bloom:

She could almost see the swift answering flush of admiration in his eyes that set her tingling in every nerve. She put on her hat so that she could see from underneath the brim and swung her buckled shoe faster for her breath caught as she caught the expression in his eyes. . . . Edy Boardman was noticing it too because she was squinting at Gerty, half smiling, with her specs, like an old maid, pretending to nurse the baby. (469)

Beyond manifesting the themes of materialism and the soul, this brief passage indicates that the formal features of the sentimental mode's matched, reversed, and triangulated sight lines are very much in play. The entire episode is articulated in the play of looks and looking, mostly between Gerty and Bloom, but also triangulated in the gaze of Edy Boardman. At the crescendo of this play of eyes and faces and various body parts, fireworks go off overhead, metaphorizing Bloom's masturbatory emission: "My fireworks. Up like a rocket, down like a stick" (483). But even after this assertion of the body's role—which leaves Bloom complaining of the stickiness in his pants—a note of sentimental soulfulness, registered in the eye-line match, is sounded again: "Their souls met in a last lingering glance and the eyes that reached her heart, full of a strange shining, hung enraptured on her sweet flowerlike face" (478). If the sentimental double-vision of Nausicaa recalls Schiller's mixed feelings, which derive from the reflection that produces "two conflicting perceptions," then perhaps it is also a variant of the theme of parallax vision, seeing with two eyes, about which Bloom speculates in Lestrygonians. Parallax vision is implicitly contrasted with the monocular nationalist vision of the Citizen, whom Bloom encounters at the pub in the "Cyclops" episode.[39]

Surely, in the play of reflected gazes Nausicaa owes something to the line of Sterne as we saw it exemplified in the episode with Maria of Moulines, details of which resurface even after Bloom resumes his meditative progress along the strand: the handkerchief, the mirrored reflection. Bloom's new train of association takes him to his daughter: "drying her handkerchief on the mirror to save ironing. Best place for an ad to catch a woman's eye on a mirror" (484). The celebrated Joycean stream of consciousness that characterizes much of the narration in *Ulysses*, including "Nausicaa" itself, might itself be understood as owing something to Sterne's narrative associationism. What Joyce would say of Sterne's importance for *Finnegans Wake*, in other words, may well already have been true of *Ulysses*. And as Woolf wrote of Sterne a decade later, just a few years after she rewrote Bloom's sentimental journey in Dublin as Mrs. Dalloway's in London: "In this preference for the windings of his own mind to the guide-book and its hammered high road, Sterne is singularly of our own age."[40] The remark is intended as a high compliment, and it can serve as yet another measure of Sterne's establishing a modern template for the novel in the act, as Shklovsky suggests, of laying bare its fundamental devices and conventions. Not even the broad field of the novel, however, offered horizon enough when Nietzsche decided on his terms of praise for Sterne: "the most liberated spirit of all time."[41]

When Woolf produced her own "day-in-the-life" book about Mrs. Dalloway's sympathetic mobility, she stretched the point-of-view techniques of the eighteenth-century novel even further, and she did so in the context of a novel in which the one serious casualty—the shell-shocked Septimus, who hurls himself from a window—arguably results from a separation enforced by physicians between him and his sympathetic wife Rezia, on the dubious medical principle that the "people we are most fond of are not good for us when we are ill."[42] Woolf came by her knowledge of the Scottish Enlightenment honestly, of course, given that her father, Leslie Stephen, was one of the greatest authorities on the subject of his time. And in *To the Lighthouse*, a novel actually set in Scotland, Woolf shows the sympathetic imagination in action in the wake of the dinner party that takes up the long first part of the novel, "The Window." The object of interest, furthermore, is itself a novel in the sentimental tradition. That is, we are given access to Mrs. Ramsey's sympathetic speculations about why her husband would have been reading *The Antiquary*, a novel of Walter Scott's published in 1817 and set in eighteenth-century Scotland.

Joyce himself made a major contribution to the literature of the dinner party in his compact masterpiece "The Dead," the concluding tale in *Dubliners* and perhaps the most autobiographical. Its relation to the sentimental tradition is perhaps even more marked than that of *Ulysses*. Joyce fusses as obsessively with the details of the party as Gabriel does with the topics of his toast, and this parallel performs an act of identification with Gabriel beyond the autobiographical origins of the story in Joyce's relation to Nora Barnacle. The signs of Joyce's sentimental investment can also be seen in other ways. We learn earlier on, when Gabriel first consults his notes, that he had thought of framing his remarks in respect to Moore's *Irish Melodies*.[43] The reference is not as casual as it seems. Joyce's own deep inhabitation of Moore's sentimental oeuvre would only become a greater obsession over the years—one assiduous pair of scholars has documented allusions in *Finnegans Wake* to all but two of Moore's 124 Irish melodies.[44]

As Greta begins her tale of Michael Furey, Gabriel becomes (sylleptically) reflective, remembering a glimpse of himself in the mirror on the way into the Gresham Hotel, when he still imagined he had the prospect of lovemaking before him: "A shameful consciousness of his own person assailed him. He saw himself as a ludicrous figure, acting as a pennyboy for his aunts, a nervous and well-meaning sentimentalist, orating to vulgarians and idealising his own clownish lusts, the pitiable fatuous fellow he caught sight of in the mirror."[45] Gabriel's self-indictment as a sentimentalist in his moment of sexual humiliation at the Gresham is more complex than it might seem. The premature departure of the Irish nationalist Miss Ivors from the party for her political meeting, soon after twitting Gabriel for being a West Briton, may well imply an ethical failing on her part when measured against the gratitude expressed in Gabriel's toast.[46]

That toast had constituted the peak of the first of the tale's two emotional crescendi. After that, we fall into the flatness of the postparty letdown and the dispersed emotions of various departures. Bartell D'Arcy's belated performance of "The Lass of Aughrim" then builds toward the second crescendo. Focalized as it is through Gabriel's perception, the story's affective level intensifies with his lusty speculations in the carriage on the way to the Gresham but reaches new levels in the story's final pages. Gabriel "wonders" about the "riot of emotion" he had felt just an hour before, and initially seeks to explain it, as Scrooge does Marley's appearance, as a digestive issue: "From what had it proceeded? From his aunt's supper?" But he moves beyond this reductive analysis and into the ventriloquized soliloquy of the story's famous closing sentences, when, Greta having fallen into sleep, he meditates on the vanished and vanishing until the tapping of the snowflakes draws his attention to the window:

His soul had approached that region where dwell the vast hosts of the dead. He was conscious of, but could not apprehend, their wayward and flickering existence. His own identity was fading out into a grey impalpable world: the solid world itself, which these dead had one time reared and lived in, was dissolving and dwindling.

A few light taps upon the pane made him turn to the window. It had begun to snow again. He watched sleepily the flakes, silver and dark, falling obliquely against the lamplight. The time had come for him to set out on his journey westward. Yes, the newspapers were right: snow was general all over Ireland. It was falling on every part of the dark central plain, on the treeless hills, falling softly upon the Bog of Allen and, farther westward, softly falling into the dark mutinous Shannon waves. It was falling, too, upon every part of the lonely churchyard on the hill where Michael Furey lay buried. It lay thickly drifted on the crooked crosses and headstones, on the spears of the little gate, on the barren thorns. His soul swooned slowly as he heard the snow falling faintly through the universe and faintly falling, like the descent of their last end, upon all the living and the dead.[47]

Gabriel's journey to the West in this quasi-soliloquy is not only a compensation for his refusal to accept Greta's invitation to join him there, but also the passage of a sentimental soul, a sentimental journey of reflection and reflexivity. It is the vehicular extension of the carriage ride that had brought himself and Greta to the Gresham a little while before. His words here, at this second crescendo, parallel those of his toast, which marked the first. They are two faces of the sentimental mood. In the end, the mirroring mirror scenes—Gabriel before the mirror and Gabriel before the window—are not to be understood as the Before and After of a therapy for sentimental narcissism but as chiastic variants of mediated, affective reciprocity. They seem to suggest that a mirror can allow you to sympathize beyond yourself, and a window can be an occasion for reflection even when the light on your side of it has been extinguished.

Coda

In 1929, the year that Joyce and Eisenstein met in Paris and discussed each other's art with such keen mutual interest, I. A. Richards published *Practical Criticism*, a book that is widely acknowledged to have set the agenda for Anglo-American literary criticism in the twentieth century. The last of Richards's pioneering books of the 1920s, *Practical Criticism* analyzed the results of his classroom experiments at Cambridge in which participants were to comment in detail on poems without the benefit of biographical, historical, or editorial information: T. S. Eliot, William Empson, and Muriel Bradbrook all took part. At this critical juncture, soon after the foundation of the English tripos at Cambridge and in a formative moment for the disciplinary formation of modern literary studies in America and elsewhere, Richards's intervention was to establish a quasi-scientific basis for the cultivation of values through the study of lyric poetry. He formalized a way of focusing attention on the effects of the printed poem, of the words themselves in their virtual sounds, their relations and associations.

Both in its theoretical grounding and in the pedagogical program that it engendered, the project of *Practical Criticism* could scarcely be more different from the tenor of Joyce's meeting with Eisenstein. Richards showed little interest in fiction. At Cambridge the advancement of novel studies would be left to Richards's rival, F. R. Leavis, who worked to establish a great tradition in the English novel, with a rehabilitated Dickens at its heart. As for cinema, Richards was overtly contemptuous toward it. Indeed, he identifies cinema as a chief symptom of the cultural problem for which his work on poetry was the proposed solution. The theoretical agenda for Richards's analysis of poetry, criticism, and culture had been set forth in an earlier book, *Principles of Literary Criticism* (1924), where he wrote, in a modernist vein, that while it might be "premature to envisage a collapse of values, a transvaluation by which popular taste replaces discrimination," nonetheless "commercialism has done stranger things: we have not yet fathomed the more sinister potentialities of the cinema and the loud-speaker."[1] Richards elsewhere uses "cinema" almost interchangeably with the phrase "bad art."[2]

It is striking (though perhaps only in retrospect) that, writing across the years of the transition from silent cinema to sound cinema, with three full decades of cinematic art behind him, Richards treats cinema indiscriminately as though it were no more than a protofascist source of mass distraction and manipulation. Setting aside the brilliant pioneering work of Méliès and the Lumière brothers, and of Griffith and Chaplin, the great art films of Fritz Lang (in Germany), Abel Gance (in France), and Carl Dreyer (in Scandinavia) had all already begun to appear when Richards was working. Dreyer's masterpiece, *The Passion of Joan of Arc*, was released while Richards was inventing practical criticism in 1928. Indeed, Jean Epstein, the French filmmaker and cineaste, was at this very time developing his notion of a *poetique du cinéma*. All of this work, not to mention the work of Eisenstein himself, is tarred by Richards with the same brush. In later decades, Richards would go on to hold very different views of the media revolutions of the twentieth century,[3] but the far-reaching consequences of his earlier program were already set in motion. Literary criticism and film criticism would tend to proceed along very different paths.[4]

This division of critical labor was part of the state of affairs, after all, that Eisenstein was protesting in his 1944 essay "Dickens, Griffith, and the Film Today" when he warned that those who sought to understand cinema ignored its literary past at their peril. It is true that by 1944 Adorno's Frankfurt School colleagues Walter Benjamin and Siegfried Kracauer had already produced the beginnings of a robust line of culturally oriented cinema criticism and that, certainly in Benjamin's case, it was coordinated with the criticism of poetry and literature (not to mention architecture and advertising). Within Cambridge English itself, a related project emerged in the work of Raymond

Williams, a fellow Welshman and an admirer of Richards, who stretched the bounds of "close reading" beyond the poem to other forms and indeed other media. Williams's first major book, *Culture and Society* (1959), which included a chapter-long critique of Richards and Leavis, effectively rewrote Arnold's *Culture and Anarchy* in more democratizing terms. Williams had problems with Richards in spite of his acknowledgement that Richards's experiments in "practical criticism" had the salutary effect of "expos[ing] the disparity between the cultural pretensions of a class and its actual capacities."[5] Williams's chief complaint was that Richards restricted his attention to poetry as the primary object of criticism and restricted criticism to mere "reading" as its core practice. Williams's own notion of criticism would be centered on his distinctive concept of a "structure of feeling"—that is, an emergent historical formation "at the very edge of semantic availability," an array of incipient "semantic figures . . . discovered in material practice" through critical engagement with a range of works in a given period.

It is not widely known that as early as the 1930s at Cambridge, Williams was a dedicated film aficionado, and a great admirer of Eisenstein in particular. In 1940 he helped to start a film society there with Michael Orrom under the auspices of the Cambridge University Socialist Club. Williams wrote about the "great future" he envisioned for a cinema "freed from its present restrictions," when "all the scientific force and frustrated art of this century will be turned to the making of real films for the people."[6] This is what, looking back on this time, he called the idea of "a film of total expression."[7] But he was, at the same time, as he later explained, not invested in social realism. He was committed to "modernism"—"Joyce was without question the most important author for us"—but "not by any means defined in exclusively literary terms."[8] He was interested in the "conceptual innovations of Eisenstein's cinema," which he associates with "Brecht's complex ways of seeing," and which he tracks forward to what he calls an excessive "concentration on the point of view at the expense of what is viewed" in the cinema of the 1960s. It was all perhaps part of an effort to sort out the complex relationships that Williams saw linking, and often confusing, "radical formalism" and "radical socialism." Moreover, even before Williams published *Culture and Society*, he had coauthored a short book entitled *Preface to Film* (to which, in the same year, 1954, he added a companion volume, *Drama in Performance*). It is in this book that Williams first announces the concept of the "structure of feeling" that later became so central to his work.[9] The sequel to *Culture and Society*, *The Long Revolution* (1961) produced a history of communication practices and technologies from the nineteenth century into its present moment as a prelude to suggesting a new way forward for what we might now call media studies, and indeed media practices.[10]

Richards's founding of his program for academic practical criticism on a deeply inimical conceptualization of poetry and cinema had far-reaching consequences for how humanities have developed in the modern university, so far-reaching at Cambridge that even a force like Raymond Williams long had difficulty in overcoming it. Williams's early, forgotten championing of cinema studies, like his later and more familiar championing of drama studies, were both carried on in behalf of a challenge to Cambridge English as Richards had helped to establish it, a critique of that program as a "theorization of reading" rather than a "theorization of composition." Film, like drama, offered objects to criticism and theory that demanded attention to issues of "composition," which in turn, presumably, had implications for the study of poetry. Working on such objects, as he put it, posed a challenge for practical criticism as it had been increasingly naturalized at Cambridge (and elsewhere), because when working on drama, as with cinema, one is "inevitably brought up against problems of form in the most direct way." That is, one is made to address "basic problems of stance and mode which were never really posed at all" within the more narrowly literary confines of the Richards program.[11]

In the foregoing chapters, I have addressed "basic problems of stance and mode" in the "composition" of the sentimental mode across fiction, poetry, cinema, and theater. I have done so, recognizing that modern literary criticism has had to overcome a programmatic institutional animosity toward cinema, dating from the modernist moment, and that, more recently, film studies has had its own suspicions about literary criticism.[12] This book has sought to dramatize some of the many ways in which criticism in each field can benefit the other. The elusive critical object on which I have focused attention—the sentimental disposition (or "composition") across media and across centuries—is one that even those who sought to go beyond it, like Joyce and Eisenstein, implicitly recognized as having something like the formal and thematic patterns I have sketched in some detail. For Sterne, Schiller, Mary Shelley, Dickens, Griffith, Capra, and others, it is something like a deep principle of intelligibility in the aesthetic and ethical structuring of experience. Not to be able to recognize it when one sees it is to fail to make sense of a vast domain of modern cultural production.

Sometimes, when I have lectured from this material in recent years, instead of beginning with a little clip from a Capra film (to be explicated with a genealogy of the sentimental), I have begun in a different and stranger place: a short passage from the close of *Braveheart* (1995), in which William Wallace (Mel Gibson) is wheeled into the castle courtyard for his torture and execution and refuses the offer of the high sheriff to relent if he repents his treasonous acts. The first glimpse of the face of Mel Gibson in the tumbril, alternated with a vehicular shot of the crowd from his point of view, often elicits titters and groans, especially in light of Gibson's subsequent follies, but the sequence often compels interest on its own terms. Once Gibson has been led to the platform where the instruments of torture have been arrayed, the film's direction attends markedly to sight lines, observing strict continuity principles that date back to Griffith's Hollywood. The sheriff and Wallace exchange glances more than once. The sheriff gestures at the instruments of torture. We see a shot of the instruments from Gibson's point of view. We see Gibson's face with his eyes focused on the instruments, and so on.

For me, the interest of the *Braveheart* sequence lies in the way in which two key moments from my story in this book are enfolded there. One is that it demonstrably inhabits the closing sequence of Capra's *Mr. Smith Goes to Washington*, when another young, wrongly prosecuted national hero collapses in public, this time on the floor of the US Senate. There are enormous differences, to be sure, especially since James Stewart's highly structured exchange of gazes with Harry Carey, who presides over *this* tribunal, conveys a promise of redemptive benignity. But there also is a signature mark of the sentimental in this iconic 1939 Capraesque sequence that I omitted from my earlier account of it. It is that the two-way exchange of gazes with Harry Carey is triangulated with Stewart's exchange of gazes with a boy who serves as page on the Senate floor. The boy's faith in Mr. Smith, once shaken, is now restored. The closing sequence in *Braveheart* involves an almost identical pair of moments in which Gibson, scanning the faces of the mostly hostile crowd, settles on the face of a small boy sitting on a man's shoulders. We see Gibson find the boy's eyes with his own. We see the boy return the gaze with sympathy and comprehension. We see Gibson subtly heartened by the exchange. Braveheart is now ready to bear the worst.

The anachronism of the scene, of course, is that it deploys a modern structure of representation for a premodern ritual spectacle that is supposed to date to 1305—indeed, the very kind of spectacle, drawing and quartering, that Michel Foucault once made paradigmatic for the premodern world.[13] This anachronism points us to another moment in the history of the sentimental mood that *Braveheart* reanimates: the passage at the close of Scott's *Waverley*, which also involves a Scottish rebel leader's public trial and execution for

Mr. Smith Goes to Washington. Congressional page and
Jefferson Smith near the film's conclusion.

Gibson, *Braveheart* (1995, Icon). Braveheart on the
scaffold and the boy who returns his gaze.

treason. *Waverley's* historical subject matter, the 1745 Jacobite Rebellion, was in a sense the final chapter of the centuries-long struggle in which William Wallace loomed so large. Scott's episode, as we saw, is structured first on an exchange of looks between Edward Waverley and Fergus McIvor (the latter-day Wallace) as the prisoner is being led out of the castle courtyard, and then through the triangulation of this exchange by way of the sympathetic female servant of the very governor who condemned Fergus to death by hanging.[14]

Set explicitly "sixty years" before Scott began work on the novel in 1805, the episode emblematizes Scott's explicitly and conspicuously anachronistic practice of representing premodern history with modern techniques. More-over, it addresses a moment when the premodern and modern vividly coex-isted in Britain, and even in Scotland. At the time of the rebellion, as Scott knew as well as anyone, Scottish writers like David Hume and Adam Smith were already developing the views on which Smith's theory of moral senti-ments would be based. For Scott, indeed, the capacity of sentiment to repre-sent distributive feeling, and modify retributive passion, is very much part of the point, part of the way forward for Scotland and England alike, though it is hard to say to what degree the point was registered by Mel Gibson and the makers of *Braveheart*. After all, the upshot of the execution scene is a transcendent meeting of eyes between Wallace and his deceased wife, and the subsequent refusal of negotiation by Robert the Bruce in favor of the passion-ate charge of the Scottish clans on which the film ends. Should we conclude that the exchange of looks with the boy in *Braveheart* tips from sentiment to sentimentality? Probably we should, but the larger point is that, without a critical lens that discloses the structuring principles of the sentimental mode across media and genres, the question cannot even be properly posed.

Acknowledgments

One of the pleasures of researching and writing this book is that I have had such great people to turn to for help with it. It has been my special good fortune to work with colleagues in Cinema and Media Studies at the University of Chicago. Before CMS existed as a program, I chaired the committee that recommended Miriam Hansen for a position here in 1991, and I was among the many whose thinking she influenced after she arrived. It was she, by both precept and example, who made me see that my work on the nineteenth century's literary public sphere needed to address film and other media if it was to move into the twentieth century. Once at Chicago, Hansen hired two brilliant colleagues who also, in their spare time, took serious charge of guiding my retooling in film studies. Tom Gunning has been a superb mentor and a steadfast friend to me in this effort; he read this entire book in manuscript and made invaluable suggestions for enriching it. I am much in his debt. Yuri Tsivian has also been extremely generous with his scarce time and vast knowledge; he was especially helpful for thinking about Eisenstein on Dickens and Shklovsky on Sterne. The program that Hansen, Gunning, and Tsivian teamed up to build is now a growing department, and one of the reasons I recently agreed to chair it was to benefit yet more intimately from the erudition and generosity of this talented group, including Dong Xinyu, who read part 1 and whose singular perspective on Capra and Hollywood comedy made her comments especially telling. I salute them all, along with other colleagues who work in cinema across the porous departmental boundaries of this university.

In film studies beyond Chicago, there are too many debts to enumerate fully. Daniel Morgan read the whole manuscript and brought his subtle intelligence productively to bear on it. Jacqueline Stewart kindly read several chapters and posed some canny questions about matters I had not sufficiently thought through. Long before I began this book, when I was doing some work on D. W. Griffith, Linda Williams delivered a series of gripping public lectures on his work at the Art Institute of Chicago. These lectures were unusually formative for my thinking about silent cinema, and so were our various discussions afterward. Ultimately, I suppose it was Stanley Cavell's 1981 lecture on Preston Sturges's *The Lady Eve*, the first of his many visits to Chicago, that initially enabled me to see how some of my particular longstanding interests in cinema might, without false pretension, become the subject of intellectual argument. I have thanked him more than once in person and do so again here.

Much of this book addresses my home fields of literary studies and cultural-intellectual history. Here I have again drawn on the unbounded intellectual energy of my friend Bill Brown, who read through the manuscript, much of it more than once, and pushed me to achieve better clarity, greater depth. He exemplifies collegiality at Chicago. A very partial list of others who have helped me with this project, in criticism and conversation, would have to include John Barrell, John Bender, Lauren Berlant, Homi Bhabha, Tim Campbell, Julie Carlson, Anne Carol, Terry Castle, Bradin Cormack, Dipesh Chakrabarty, Claire Connolly, Arnold Davidson, Peter de Bolla, Ian Duncan, Maud Ellmann, Martha Feldman, Frances Ferguson, Norma Field, Penny Fielding, Christiane Frey, Leela Gandhi, Debjani Ganguly, Luke Gibbons, Kevin Gilmartin, Harriet Guest, Paul Hamilton, Beverly Haviland, Beth Helsinger, Rob Kaufman, Bill Keach, Heather Keenleyside, Jonathan Lamb, Celeste Langan, Nigel Leask, Sandra Macpherson, Iain McCalman, Jerome McGann, Maureen McLane, Susan Manning, Jon Mee, Françoise Meltzer, Mark Miller, Tom Mitchell, Rochona Majumdar, Marc Redfield, Eric Santner, Simon Schaffer, Laurie Shannon, Vincent Sherry, Eric Slauter, Michael Steinberg, Jane Taylor, Katie Trumpener, Robin Valenza, Cynthia Wall, David Wellbery, Alison Winter, and Shamoon Zamir. I have not taught many undergraduates in the last decade, but I have been more than compensated, in this and earlier decades, by having worked with such terrific graduate students. Many of my seminars have addressed topics from this book, and I would be gratified to think that my students learned as much from our discussions as I did.

Research for this book was carried out in several archives and many libraries. I visited the Capra Archives at Wesleyan University on several occasions, and

I would particularly like to thank Jeanine Basinger, who assembled it, as well as Leith Johnson and Joan Miller for their help and hospitality. I found helpful materials as well in the rich archives of the Museum of Modern Art in New York, the Margaret Herrick Library in Los Angeles, and in the National Film and Sound Archive in Canberra, Australia. I combed the British Library for mid-eighteenth-century documents in the history of sentiment and the François-Mitterrand Library for evidence of French interest in Capra's films, especially for his claim that *Mr. Smith Goes to Washington* was the last American film screened in Free France during the war. My thanks go to all of these institutions.

An early version of arguments in chapter 6 was published in *The Age of Cultural Revolutions: Britain and France, 1750–1820*, ed. Colin Jones and Dror Warhman (Berkeley: Unversity of California Press, 2002). Part of chapter 9 appeared in *Critical Inquiry* 33 (Summer 2007). Part of chapter 5 appeared in different form in a special issue of *Textual Practice* 22 (March 2008); another was published in *Afterimages of Gilles Deleuze's Film Philosophy*, ed D. N. Rodowick (Minneapolis: University of Minnesota Press, 2010). I have also lectured widely from the arguments in this book in recent years. A partial list of venues in North America would include UCLA, the Huntington Library, Stanford University, the University of California, Berkeley, Reed College, the University of Colorado, the University of Iowa, Washington University in St. Louis, St. Olaf College, the University of Wisconsin, the Chicago Film Seminar, the Chicago Humanities Festival, the University of Notre Dame, the University of Michigan, the University of Miami, Duke University, the University of Virginia, Johns Hopkins University, Rutgers University, Columbia University, Princeton University, Yale University, Brown University, Harvard University, Bowdoin College, the University of Western Ontario, the University of Toronto, and Concordia University. Abroad, I have given talks or workshops from the book at Cambridge, Oxford, Birkbeck College (London), the University of Lancaster, the University of York, the University of Edinburgh, University College Dublin, Tel Aviv University, the University of Sydney, and the Australian National University in Canberra. Some of these events were structured to include colleagues with substantial formal responses: Jonathan Friedman, Anne Janowitz, Marjorie Levinson, Kirstie McClure, Viv Soni, and Carolyn Williams. I thank all of my interlocutors (formal and informal) at these events, and want them to know that their comments mattered to the arguments of this book.

At the University of Chicago Press, my experience has been better than ever. Alan Thomas's keen sense of how to make a book work best was especially valuable in the case of a complex set of arguments like those here. The generous and thoroughgoing readers' reports from Garrett Stewart and Deidre Lynch, as well as from an anonymous reader in film studies, offered much encouragement and a detailed map for revision. Joel Score copyedited with a keen eye and a well-gauged touch. Randy Petilos helped keep everything on track. Work on this book has been greatly enabled by research leave granted by deans Janel Mueller, Danielle Allen, and Martha Roth and by brief stints as Research Fellow at King's College, Cambridge, and as Visiting Scholar in Residence at the Australian National University. It has also had the support of some excellent work-study assistance from John Maki, Mollie Godfrey, Gina DeGiovanni, and Andrew Yale. Andrew has worked on the book the longest and the hardest, helping to push it through the late labor-intensive rounds of revision, proofing, and copyediting. I thank him heartily for the great care he took, the extra mile he went, and for his many helpful suggestions large and small.

I am grateful, finally, for the support of my wife, Elizabeth O'Connor Chandler, and our families, nuclear and extended. I dedicate this book to four people we love especially well in the next two generations.

Notes

Preface

1 Laurence Sterne, *A Sentimental Journey*, ed. Ian Jack and Tim Parnell, new ed. (Oxford: Oxford University Press, 2003), 3.

2 André Bazin, *What Is Cinema?*, 2 vols., trans. Hugh Gray (Berkeley: University of California Press, 1967), 1:24.

3 Peter Galison, "Objectivity," keynote lecture, Consortium of Humanities Centers and Institutes annual conference, Washington University, St. Louis, 2008.

4 Sterne, *Sentimental Journey*, 98.

5 *The Complete Poetry and Prose of William Blake*, ed. David V. Erdman, rev. ed. (Berkeley: University of California Press, 1982), 251, 641.

Introduction

1 Samuel Johnson, *A Dictionary of the English Language* (London, 1755). For more on the history of these terms see below, chapter 4.

2 Samuel Richardson, *Clarissa*, 3rd ed., vol. 8 (London: S. Richardson, 1751), 317, 318.

3 Marie Banfield, "From Sentiment to Sentimentality: A Nineteenth-Century Lexicographical Search," *19: Interdisciplinary Studies in the Long Nineteenth Century* 4 (2007).

4 Isabel Rivers, *Reason, Grace, and Sentiment: A Study of the Language of Religion*

and Ethics in England, 1660–1780, 2 vols. (Cambridge: Cambridge University Press, 1991, 2000).

5 For another valuable cultural history of British sentimentalism in this period, see G. J. Barker-Benfield, *The Culture of Sensibility: Sex and Society in Eighteenth-Century Britain* (Chicago: University of Chicago Press, 1992); for a more compressed history, see John Brewer, "Sentiment and Sensibility," in *The Cambridge History of English Romantic Literature*, ed. James Chandler (Cambridge: Cambridge University Press, 2009), 21–44.

6 This body of work has attracted renewed interest of late from philosophers as diverse as Christine Korsgaard, Annette Baier, Charles Griswold, Samuel Fleischacker, Michael Frazer, and Amartya Sen.

7 A parallel but by no means identical story about the development of sentiment can be told from the French point of view. One finds a good start on such an account in Jean-Jacques Courtine and Claudine Haroche, *Histoire du visage: Exprimer et taire ses émotions, XVIe–début XIXe siècle* (Paris: Rivages, 1988), especially the chapter that addresses "the anatomy of sentiment," which considers roughly the same period addressed by Rivers chiefly in England; see also the section on "the empire of sentiment." That sentiment should be so central a subject to a book about the history of the face and that physiognomy should matter so much to the account is no accident, as I hope will become clear in what follows. See also William M. Reddy, *The Navigation of Feeling: A Framework for the History of Emotions* (Cambridge: Cambridge University Press, 2001), 141–210.

8 George Alexander Stevens, *The Dramatic History of Master Edward: Miss Ann, Mrs. Llwhuddwhydd, and Others* (London: Printed for T. Waller, 1743), 20. I would like to acknowledge the ARTFL Project of the University of Chicago, which installed under its PhiloLogic software the ECCO-TCP database from the Eighteenth Century Collections Online database, available at http://artfl-project .uchicago.edu/content/ecco-tcp. This idiom survives intact in Marx's early poem "Sentimentale Seelen" and Kate Chopin's 1894 short story "A Sentimental Soul."

9 Adam Smith, *The Theory of Moral Sentiments*, ed. D. D. Raphael and A. L. Mackie (Indianapolis: Liberty Fund, 1982), 143.

10 On the rapid emergence of "celebrity" culture in this decade, see Antoine Lilti, "The Writing of Paranoia: Jean-Jacques Rousseau and the Paradoxes of Celebrity," *Representations*, no. 103 (Summer 2008), 53–83.

11 Viktor Shklovsky, "Sterne's *Tristram Shandy*: Stylistic Commentary," collected in *Russian Formalist Criticism*, trans. Lee T. Lemon and Marion J. Reis (Lincoln: University of Nebraska Press, 1965), 27.

12 These same pages also provide the "paragraphs [in which] some important terms of Yorick's class/gender strategy are set," writes Eve Kosofsky Sedgwick. Her incisive reading of the novel's opening serves as a kind of template for her larger argument about the emblematic homosociality of Sterne's fiction. See Sedgwick, "*A Sentimental Journey*: Sexualism and the Citizen of the World," in *Between*

Men: English Literature and Male Homosocial Desire (New York: Columbia University Press, 1985), 67–82. We will see below that the homosocial theme markedly recurs in the sentimental mode of works by both Dickens and Capra.

13 Laurence Sterne, *A Sentimental Journey*, ed. Ian Jack and Tim Parnell, new ed. (Oxford: Oxford University Press, 2003), 3. Further citations given parenthetically in the text.

14 From the section entitled "The Post-Chaise," in *Yorick's Sentimental Journey Continued . . . By Eugenius* (1769), quoted in Ian Jack, "'A Sentimental Journey,'" *Times Literary Supplement*, February 4, 1977, 131.

15 Shklovsky, "Sterne's *Tristram Shandy*," 28.

16 For more on materialism and female agency in this period, see Natania Meeker, *Voluptuous Philosophy: Literary Materialism in the French Enlightenment* (New York: Fordham University Press, 2006), esp. 88–125.

17 For more on syllepsis and metalepsis (slippage between narrative levels), see chapter 6.

18 Two further examples: the play of hands and gloves in the vignette with the wife of the Parisian glove merchant, and the final scene, where an unfinished sentence, "So that when I stretch'd out my hand, I caught hold of the Fille de Chambre's—" (104), leaves the narrative suspended.

19 Thomas Jefferson, "A Gentleman's Library: To Robert Skipwith, with a List of Books, Monticello, Aug. 3, 1771," in *Letters* (Raleigh, NC: Alex Catalogue; Boulder, CO: NetLibrary, n.d.), 8, http://www.netlibrary.com/urlapi.asp?action=summary&v=1&bookid=1085925. For a fuller discussion of the reception of Sterne's work in America, see Lodwick Hartley, "The Dying Soldier and the Love-Born Virgin: Notes on Sterne's Early Reception in America," in *The Winged Skull: Papers from the Laurence Sterne Bicentenary Conference*, ed. Arthur H. Cash and John M. Stedmond (Kent, OH: Kent State University Press, 1971), 159–69.

20 The extent of the influence of Shaftesbury, for example, on Schiller is a matter of debate among Schiller's commentators, but we do know that Schiller's cousin was an early German translator of Shaftesbury's disciple Adam Smith.

21 Schiller's dyad seems to have returned to vogue with *Naïve and Sentimental Music* (1997–1998), by the prominent American composer John Adams, and with the Charles Eliot Norton Lectures of the Turkish novelist Orhan Pamuk, published as *The Naïve and the Sentimental Novelist* (Cambridge, MA: Harvard University Press, 2010). Both artists take pains to show their awareness of Schiller's sophisticated distinction.

22 See Philip Fisher, *The Vehement Passions* (Princeton, NJ: Princeton University Press, 2002).

23 Cf. Alfred Gell's notion of "distributed personhood" in *Art and Agency: An Anthropological Perspective* (Oxford: Clarendon Press, 1998).

24 For its lucidity of exposition, cross-Channel approach to the issues, and strong linkages between moral philosophy and economics, Emma Rothschild's *Eco-*

nomic Sentiments: Adam Smith, Condorcet, and the Enlightenment (Cambridge, MA: Harvard University Press, 2001) has made itself indispensable. In her own attempt to explain "the indefinite idea of a sentiment," Rothschild writes, "Sentiments were feelings of which one is conscious, and on which one reflects" (9). My only quibble with this sentence has to do with its conjunctive structure. As will be clear, I see the issues of consciousness and reflection as decisively overlapping in the sentimentalists I study here.

25 The account I offer here is broadly in line with the arguments about enlightenment practices of "second-order observation," though they are made at a higher level of abstraction, in Niklas Luhmann, *Observations on Modernity*, trans. William Whobrey (Stanford, CA: Stanford University Press, 1998), esp. 9–21.

26 Seymour Chatman, "A New Point of View on 'Point of View,'" in *Coming to Terms: The Rhetoric of Narrative in Fiction and Film* (Ithaca, NY: Cornell University Press, 1990), 139.

27 See, for example, the fine essays collected in *The Victorian Illustrated Book*, ed. Richard Maxwell (Charlottesville: University of Virginia Press, 2002). For compelling work on Dickens and book history, see Robert L. Patten, "Dickens as Serial Author: A Case of Multiple Identities," in *Nineteenth-Century Media and the Construction of Identities*, ed. Laurel Blake, Bill Bell, and David Finkelstein (Basingstoke: Palgrave, 2000), 137–51, and Luisa Calé, "Dickens Extra-Illustrated: Heads and Scenes in Monthly Parts," *Yearbook of English Studies* 40 (July 2010): 8–32.

28 Charles Dickens, *David Copperfield*, ed. Nina Burgis (Oxford: Oxford University Press, 1997), 14.

29 Ibid., 86.

30 Especially important to my account of how literary sentimentalism anticipates Hollywood cinema is the notion of "spatial reversal," which, as Edward Branigan nicely summarizes it, "establishes an anchor line that allows us to move through nearby spaces by calculating new angles and distances and thereby build up a cognitive map of the spaces." Branigan, *Narrative Comprehension and Film* (London: Routledge, 1992), 235.

31 *Schillers Werke, Philosophische Schriften*, ed. Helmut Koopmann, vol. 20, pt. 1 (Weimar: Hermann Böhlaus Nachfolger, 1962), 455.

32 Erwin Panofsky, *Perspective as Symbolic Form*, trans. Christopher S. Wood (New York: Zone Books, 1991). Because of the importance of "point of view" to the sentimental mode as I describe it, post-Albertine perspective is a matter with more than casual relevance to this discussion.

33 On the *Pathosformel*, see E. H. Gombrich, *Aby Warburg: An Intellectual Biography* (Oxford: Oxford University Press, 1970), 177–85, 229–38; see also Carlo Ginzburg, "From Aby Warburg to E. H. Gombrich: A Problem of Method," in *Clues, Myths, and the Historical Method*, trans. John and Anne C. Tedeschi (Baltimore: Johns Hopkins University Press, 1989), 17–59.

34 See, for example, Peter de Bolla on "the sentimental look" in *The Education of the*

Eye: Painting, Landscape, and Architecture in Eighteenth-Century Britain (Stanford, CA: Stanford University Press, 2004) and Emma Barker, *Greuze and the Painting of Sentiment* (Cambridge: Cambridge University Press, 2005). Michael Fried's work on the beholder in eighteenth-century painting is everywhere relevant to this *Pathosformel*, though he does not tend to invoke the category of the sentimental to describe it; see Fried, *Absorption and Theatricality: Painting and Beholder in the Age of Diderot* (Berkeley: University of California Press, 1980).

35 On the "chronotope," see M. M. Bakhtin, "Forms of Time and the Chronotope in the Novel," in *The Dialogic Imagination: Four Essays*, ed. Michael Holquist, trans. Caryl Emerson and Michael Holquist (Austin: University of Texas Press, 1981), 84–258.

36 Ellington composed "In a Sentimental Mood" in 1935, in Capra's heyday, part of a fashion for such titles in the big band era. Tommy Dorsey's signature "I'm Gettin' Sentimental Over You" was 1934; Glenn Miller's signature "In the Mood," 1939; and Les Brown's "Sentimental Journey," 1944. Musical sentimentalism is beyond the scope of this study, but see Peter Kivy, *Sound Sentiment: An Essay on the Musical Emotions* (Philadelphia: Temple University Press, 1989), and Charles Rosen, *Music and Sentiment* (New Haven, CT: Yale University Press, 2010). See especially recent work by the ethnomusicologist Martin Stokes, e.g., "Adam Smith and the Dark Nightingale: On Twentieth-Century Sentimentalism," *Twentieth-Century Music* 3, no. 2 (September 2006): 201–19.

37 Shklovsky ties together Cervantes and Sterne in his pioneering formalist work on the novel, written in 1918 in a literary studio in St. Petersburg: "I was working on my articles on *Don Quixote* and Sterne. I never in my life worked the way I did that year." *A Sentimental Journey: Memoirs, 1917–1922*, trans. Richard Sheldon (Normal, IL: Dalkey Archive Press, 2004), 186.

38 Were I to try to contribute to commentary on *Uncle Tom's Cabin*, it would probably be to suggest how the cabin itself becomes a kind of virtual mobile site in the novel, such that where Tom is, there his cabin is, even aboard ship.

39 This issue points to how the book opens toward what is now called "media archaeology." See, most recently, *Media Archaeology: Approaches, Applications, and Implications*, ed. Erkki Huhtamo and Jussi Parikka (Berkeley: University of California Press, 2011). For a longer historical perspective on such questions, see the essays in "Arts of Transmission," ed. James Chandler, Arnold I. Davidson, and Adrian Johns, a special issue of *Critical Inquiry* 31 (Autumn 2004). For a collection of essays in this vein that focuses on the eighteenth century, see *This Is Enlightenment*, ed. Clifford Siskin and William Warner (Chicago: University of Chicago Press, 2010).

40 See especially David Marshall, *The Figure of Theater: Shaftesbury, Defoe, Adam Smith, and George Eliot* (New York: Columbia University Press, 1986), and Jean-Christophe Agnew, *Worlds Apart: The Market and the Theater in Anglo-American Thought, 1550–1750* (Cambridge: Cambridge University Press, 1986).

41 For a critical history of the notion of a "science of human nature" in this period, see R. G. Collingwood, *The Idea of History* (Oxford: Clarendon Press, 1946), 205–9.

42 A measure of the impact of the collected *Spectator* papers across Europe is that Rousseau named it as among the very most influential books of his youth, and then singled it out for special praise: "The *Spectator* particularly pleased me, and improved my mind." Rousseau, *The Confessions*, trans. J. M. Cohen (Harmondsworth: Penguin, 1954), 110.

43 In this emphasis on "circulation" in the culture that produced mid-eighteenth-century forms of narrative, my argument overlaps with Deidre Lynch's critical intervention in *The Economy of Character: Novels, Market Culture, and the Business of Inner Meaning* (Chicago: University of Chicago Press, 1998).

44 This feature of eighteenth-century fiction would later be partially captured with the coinage "ideal presence" by the influential Henry Home, Lord Kames, in *Elements of Criticism*, 3 vols. (Edinburgh: Printed for A. Millar, London, and A. Kincaid & J. Bell, Edinburgh, 1762), 1:112–15. For more on Kames's concept and its relation to the history/fiction distinction, see Mark Salber Phillips, *Society and Sentiment: Genres of Historical Writing in Britain, 1740–1820* (Princeton, NJ: Princeton University Press, 2000), 107–10, and Ian Duncan, *Scott's Shadow: The Novel in Romantic Edinburgh* (Princeton, NJ: Princeton University Press, 2007), 131.

45 This point became central in Béla Balázs's seminal studies of cinema. See *Theory of the Film: Character and Growth of a New Art*, trans. Edith Bone (New York: Dover, 1970), especially the chapters on "the visible man" and the "face of man" (39–46, 60–88), which rework materials from Balázs's pioneering work *Der Sichtbare Mensch; oder, Die Kultur des Films* (1924).

46 Kamilla Elliott charges Eisenstein's essay with having "mainstreamed the analogy of the cinematic novel" in *Rethinking the Novel/Film Debate* (Cambridge: Cambridge University Press, 2003), 6.

47 Sergei Eisenstein, "Dickens, Griffith and the Film Today," in *Film Form*, trans. and ed. Jay Leyda (New York: Harcourt Brace & Company, 1949), 232–33.

48 Sergei Eisenstein, "Dickens, Griffith, and Ourselves," in *Writings 1934–47*, ed. Richard Taylor, trans. William Powell, *Selected Works*, vol. 3 (London: I. B. Tauris, 2010), 205. In what follows, I move back and forth between this and the Leyda translation, depending on what they include (Leyda's text generally omits more than Taylor's, except in the case of Eisenstein's discussion of A. B. Walkley's early account of Griffith and Dickens) and on the appositeness of their formulations for my purposes.

49 Eisenstein, "Dickens, Griffith and Ourselves," 199.

50 Ibid.

51 Eisenstein, "Dickens, Griffith and the Film Today," 204.

52 Ibid., 205.

53 Ibid., 206.

54 Linda Arvidson Griffith, *When the Movies Were Young* (New York: E. P. Dutton, 1925), 66; cited in Eisenstein, "Dickens, Griffith and the Film Today," 200–201.

55 Eisenstein, "Dickens, Griffith and Ourselves," 215.

56 Ibid., 202. Eisenstein quotes a famous passage from the beginning of chapter 17 of *Oliver Twist* in which Dickens reflects on his own practice as a kind of melodramatic switching from tragic to comic, "in regular alternation, as the layers of red and white in a side of streaky bacon" (214). We shall see that another kind of alternation, less derivative of the multiplot novel, is crucial to the *sentimental* tendency in Dickens.

57 Dickens's often-noted use of panoramic technique to represent the view from Mrs. Todgers's boardinghouse in *Martin Chuzzlewit* likewise may say more about Dickens's relation to the spread of panoramas in his time than about the protocinematic plasticity of his own imagination. See Dorothy Van Ghent, "The Dickens World: A View from Todgers's," *Sewanee Review* 58, no. 3 (July–September 1950): 419–38. On Dickens's relation to Victorian visual technologies, see Joss Marsh, "Dickens and Film," in *The Cambridge Companion to Charles Dickens*, ed. John O. Jordan (Cambridge: Cambridge University Press, 2001), and Helen Groth, "Reading Victorian Illusions: Dickens's *Haunted Man* and Dr. Pepper's 'Ghost,'" *Victorian Studies* 50, no. 1 (Autumn 2007): 43–65.

58 Eisenstein, "Dickens, Griffith and Ourselves," 200.

59 Ibid, 202.

60 Ibid.

61 Charles Dickens, "The Cricket on the Hearth," in *The Christmas Books*, vol. 2 (Harmondsworth: Penguin, 1971), 43. Subsequent references cited by page number in the text.

62 Tom Gunning avers that "Dickens's story provided Griffith with a more complex plot than any of his previous films" and then produces a nuanced reading of Griffith's film to illustrate the point. *Griffith and the Origins of American Narrative Film: The Early Years at Biograph* (Urbana: University of Illinois Press, 1994), 175–77.

63 David Bordwell, Janet Staiger, and Kristin Thompson, *The Classical Hollywood Cinema: Film Style and Mode of Production to 1960* (New York: Columbia University Press, 1985), 29–33.

64 When Tackleton leaves the Peerybingles's place later in the novella, we are told, "The Carrier stood looking after him until he was smaller in the distance than his horse's flowers and favors near at hand" (101).

65 Griffith forges a thematic link between his two films by making Edward Plummer a sailor, like the absent husband in *After Many Years* who returns home to find himself displaced by another man.

66 It is hard not to recall Coleridge's seminal midwinter poem "Frost at Midnight," which involves a series of reflections prompted by what Coleridge calls the flut-

tering "film" upon the grate of his hearth, an object that is, he suggests, like himself in the act of recognizing it, everywhere seeking an "echo or mirror" of itself. His note to the poem even suggests that this object, the film on the grate, is known in English legend as "the Stranger." Was Dickens drawing on this same lore in writing *The Cricket on the Hearth*? Could Griffith have known so? Garrett Stewart speculates about a connection between Coleridge's poem and other fire-gazing moments in Dickens (*Great Expectations* and *Bleak House*) as staging acts of finding imaginative solace under duress, in *Dickens and the Trials of Imagination* (Cambridge, MA: Harvard University Press, 1974), 160–61.

67 One of those other directors who did much to shape the classical system of narration was Thomas Ince, whom Capra listed, along with Griffith, DeMille, and Chaplin, as one of the four most powerful directors of the period. In 1915, the same year Griffith made *The Birth of a Nation*, Ince made *The Italians*, a feature film Capra would scarcely have failed to notice. Part of its dénouement involves a father's recognition of his parental responsibilities in an early shot/reverse-shot sequence.

68 See, for example, Jean Mitry, *The Aesthetics and Psychology of the Cinema*, trans. Christopher King (Bloomington: Indiana University Press, 1997), 208–10.

69 *It's a Wonderful Life* is correctly omitted from the long list of adaptations of *A Christmas Carol* in the appendix to *Dickens on Screen*, ed. John Glavin (Cambridge: Cambridge University Press, 2003), 206, but elsewhere in the volume Gerhard Joseph is also correct to say that the film is "as much an adaptation of a Dickens story as any of the *Olivers* or *Copperfields*" (22). Garrett Stewart offers a shrewd account of David Lean's adaptations in his contribution to the volume: "Dickens, Eisenstein, Film," 133–43.

70 Stanley Cavell, as I was happy to discover on rereading him, has a brief meditation on the tandem of Eisenstein and Capra at the end of his introduction to *Pursuits of Happiness*, noting their common debts to Dickens and acknowledging that "this conjunction of minds might seem preposterous to . . . some partisans of each," but maintaining that "as craftsmen they seem . . . to resemble one another." Cavell, *Pursuits of Happiness: The Hollywood Comedy of Remarriage* (Cambridge, MA: Harvard University Press, 1981), 40.

71 Interestingly, Griffith does *not* begin his 1909 adaptation with a close-up of the kettle.

72 "Dickens, Griffith and the Film Today," 232–33. Further citations given parenthetically in the text. For a critical survey of how film theory deals with the "objectification of embodied vision," see Vivian Sobchak, *The Address of the Eye: The Phenomenology of Film Experience* (Princeton, NJ: Princeton University Press, 1992), 14–26.

73 The phrase translated here as "sentimental humanism" is translated by William Powell as "tender-hearted morality" (223). Eisenstein's other use of the term translated as "sentimental" gets even closer to the sense of the term that concerns

us here. In arguing that Dickens's novels "bore the same relation to them [the good old gentlemen and sweet old ladies] that the film bears to the same strata in our time," Eisenstein says that the novels "compelled the reader to live with the same passions" and "appealed to the same good and sentimental elements" ("Dickens, Griffith and the Film Today," 206). The Russian term translated as "sentimental" here is *sentimental'noe*, the same word used to translate Sterne's *Sentimental Journey*. Of course, Shklovsky had earlier made prominent both the term and its connection to Sterne in his 1923 memoir, *Sentimental'noe puteshestvie* (*Sentimental Journey*). For his generous help with these Russian texts and Soviet contexts, I thank Yuri Tsivian.

74 One finds in both *It's a Wonderful Life* and its Dickensian source a level of meta-comment on internal projection: in Dickens with the secondary projection that occurs within the first spirit's vision, when Scrooge is able to see the visions generated out of reading being done by his childhood self alone in the schoolroom, and in Capra with the angel's comment, "What did you stop it for?," in relation to the screening of the life of George Bailey on the heavenly projector.

75 See also Luisa Calé's highly suggestive use of Eisenstein in an eighteenth-century context to explain the "reconstitution of great British literature in the form of galleries of paintings." Calé, *Fuseli's Milton Gallery: "Turning Readers into Spectators"* (Oxford: Oxford University Press, 2006), 6.

76 Commentators on Griffith have in turn emphasized the importance of theatrical mediations even in Griffith's literary adaptations, not least *The Birth of a Nation*. See, for example, Rick Altman, "Dickens, Griffith, and Film Theory Today," *South Atlantic Quarterly* 88, no. 2 (1989): 321–59, and David Mayer, *Stagestruck Filmmaker: D. W. Griffith and the American Theatre* (Iowa City: University of Iowa Press, 2009), passim.

77 See Linda Williams, *Playing the Race Card: Melodramas of Black and White from Uncle Tom to O. J. Simpson* (Princeton, NJ: Princeton University Press, 2001), 96–135, and several of the fine essays collected in *Home Is Where the Heart Is*, ed. Christine Gledhill (London: British Film Institute, 1987), especially Thomas Elsaesser's and Gledhill's historical accounts of melodrama before cinema, 14–28, 43–50.

78 Robert Lang, *American Film Melodrama: Griffith, Vidor, Minnelli* (Princeton, NJ: Princeton University Press, 1989), 7, emphasis in original.

79 See my "Placing *The Power of Sympathy*: Transatlantic Sentiments and the 'First American Novel,'" in *The Atlantic Enlightenment*, ed. Susan Manning and Francis D. Cogliano (Aldershot, UK: Ashgate, 2008). A number of literary and cultural histories have picked up the story of the American sentimental after Brown's novel—i.e., in the first decades of the new Republic and beyond. See, for example, Jane Tompkins, *Sensational Designs: The Cultural Work of American Fiction, 1790–1860* (Oxford: Oxford University Press, 1985); Ann Douglas, *The Feminization of American Culture* (New York: Farrar, Straus and Giroux, 1977),

which famously offers extended discussion of what Douglas calls the "sentimentalization" of "status" and of "creed and culture"; *The Culture of Sentiment: Race, Gender, and Sentimentality in 19th-Century America*, ed. Shirley Samuels (Oxford: Oxford University Press, 1992); Julia A. Sterne, *The Plight of Feeling: Sympathy and Dissent in the Early American Novel* (Chicago: University of Chicago Press, 1997); Glenn Hendler, *Public Sentiments: Structures of Feeling in Nineteenth-Century American Literature* (Chapel Hill: University of North Carolina Press, 2001); Lori Merish, *Sentimental Materialism: Gender, Commodity Culture, and Nineteenth-Century American Literature* (Durham, NC: Duke University Press, 2000); and Ezra Tawil, *The Making of Racial Sentiment: Slavery and the Birth of the Frontier Romance* (Cambridge: Cambridge University Press, 2006).

80 Williams, *Playing the Race Card*, 10–44. For a psychoanalytic account that straddles the nineteenth and twentieth centuries, see E. Ann Kaplan, *Motherhood and Representation: The Mother in Popular Culture and Melodrama* (London: Routledge, 1992). See also Lauren Berlant, *The Female Complaint: The Unfinished Business of Sentimentality in American Culture* (Durham, NC: Duke University Press, 2008), where the issue is perhaps closer to post-Romantic melodrama than to sentimentalism understood as a set of formal and thematic developments with roots traceable to the early modern period.

81 Dudley Andrew, "Productive Discord in the System: Hollywood *Meets John Doe*," in *Meet John Doe: Frank Capra, Director*, ed. Charles Wolfe (New Brunswick, NJ: Rutgers University Press, 1989), 254.

82 Oliver Goldsmith's play *The Good-Natur'd Man* appeared in the same year as Sterne's *Sentimental Journey*, 1768, and William Cooke, looking back a quarter century from 1793, already felt positioned to offer a retrospective comment: "Sentimental writing had then got possession of the stage, and nothing but morality and sententious writing lifted upon stilts, could meet the vitiated taste of the audience." Cited in *Collected Works of Oliver Goldsmith*, ed. Arthur Friedman (Oxford: Clarendon Press, 1966), 5:5. Cooke was mistaken, however, in thinking that the sentimental had run its course.

83 See, for example, the useful discriminations of Noël Carroll, *A Philosophy of Mass Art* (Oxford: Oxford University Press, 1998), 245–90.

Introduction to Part 1

1 The news footage in Jarecki's film includes appearances by Senator Bernie Sanders of Vermont, Representatives Michael Capuano of Massachusetts and Elijah Saunders of Maryland, secretary of the treasury Timothy Geithner, and others.

2 In February 2010, Bill Bradbury, democratic candidate for the US Senate from Oregon, proposed the Move Your Money policy for his state's own investments. The idea was still alive enough in the autumn of 2011 for the Occupy movement to stage a "Move Your Money" day in October, which may have helped

to produce 650,000 new credit union accounts that month, in comparison with 600,000 for all of 2010. This was followed by a "Bank Transfer Day" on November 5, announced on the *Huffington Post* in an article with a clip of Mr. Potter from *It's a Wonderful Life*: "Move Your Money Activists Prepare for Bank Transfer Day on Nov. 5," *Huffington Post*, November 4, 2011, http://www.huffingtonpost .com/2011/11/04/move-your-money-activists_n_1076630.html.

3 *Colbert Report*, January 11, 2010.

4 Some years earlier, Britain's *New Statesman* had invoked Capra's title for the journey to Washington by another Brown, Prime Minister Gordon Brown. Andrew Stephen, "When Mr Brown Goes to Washington," *New Statesman*, May 14, 2007.

5 Rosalie Tirella, *InCity Times*, Worcester, MA, January 21, 2010.

6 See, for example, "Filibuster Change—'Mr. Smith' Bill Introduced in Senate," *Washington Post*, January 6, 2011.

7 Fess Parker—between roles for Disney Studios as Davy Crockett and Daniel Boone—played Jefferson Smith in a television series adapted from Capra's film in 1962–1963. Thirty-two years later, *The Simpsons* would generate its own parody: "Mr. Lisa Goes to Washington."

8 *New York Times*, March 9, 2012, A21.

9 Jack Matthews, "John Doe, Meet Ross Perot," *Los Angeles Times*, Sunday, June 14, 1992, 5, 34–35. The votes that Perot took from George H. W. Bush helped Bill Clinton to unseat him that November.

10 Joe Flaherty, "Jimmy Carter: John Doe Born Again," *Soho Weekly Magazine*, February 3, 1977, 9.

11 Cited by James R. Silke and Bruce Henstell in "Frank Capra: 'One Man—One Film'" (1971), in *Frank Capra: Interviews*, ed. Leland Poague (Jackson: University of Mississippi Press, 2004), 72. I have tracked the line back as far as Jeanine Basinger, "America's Love Affair with Frank Capra," *American Film* 7 (March 1982): 81.

12 Robert Sklar, *Movie-Made America: A Cultural History of American Movies* (1975; New York: Random House, 1994), 209.

13 See Robert B. Pippin, *Hollywood Westerns and American Myth: The Importance of Howard Hawks and John Ford for Political Philosophy* (New Haven, CT: Yale University Press, 2010).

14 The word "recursive" has existed in ordinary English since the late eighteenth century, when it seems to have been a variation on "recurrent." Even before its technical appropriation in logic, mathematics, linguistics, and computer science, however, it seems to have conveyed some sense of reflexive or redundant effects. Thus the *OED* cites this illustration for 1790: "Till your ear be so attuned to one particular measure, that your ideas may be spontaneously absorbed into the same revolving eddy of recursive harmony." Recursive harmony, I suggest, is not just a harmony that returns but that returns on itself, that returns on itself to build

on itself. This is also a sense that links the more recent technical meanings of the term in the fields I mention. The opening of Wordsworth's *Prelude* involves "recursivity" in this sense, a feature he comes close to identifying as such when he characterizes his distinctive form of poetic inspiration as "a vital breeze, which travelled gently on / O'er things which it had made; and is become / . . . a redundant energy" (book 1, 44–46; 1805 version).

15 Still valuable is the collection of essays on cinematic authorship edited over thirty years ago by John Caughie, *Theories of Authorship* (London: Routledge, 1981).

16 See "Frank Capra: 'One Man—One Film,'" 72–92.

17 For a "preliminary taxonomy" of "kinds of remakes" (fifteen in all), see Robert Eberwein, "Remakes and Cultural Studies," in *Play it Again, Sam: Retakes on Remakes*, ed. Andrew Horton and Stuart Y. McDougal (Berkeley: University of California Press, 1998), 28–31. None quite captures Capra's work of self-remaking through 1948.

18 There is some skepticism among film historians about the importance of the 1934 formalization of the Hays Code. For an argument that it matters, see Thomas Doherty, *Pre-Code Hollywood: Sex, Immorality, and Resurrection in American Cinema 1930–34* (New York: Columbia University Press, 1999), esp. 3–15 and, for a specific account of the Code as making a difference to Capra, 341–42.

19 Jacques Aumont, *Du visage au Cinéma* (Paris: Editions de l'Etoile/Cahiers du Cinéma [distributed by Seuil], 1992), 55; translation mine.

20 André Bazin, *What Is Cinema?*, 2 vols., trans. Hugh Gray (Berkeley: University of California Press, 1967), 1:28.

21 Ibid.

22 Print is not one of the contenders in Paul Young's *The Cinema Dreams Its Rivals: Media Fantasy Films from the Radio to the Internet* (Minneapolis: University of Minnesota Press, 2006), nor is Capra discussed there, but some of the arguments are relevant to mine here about print media.

23 David Bordwell, in an essay that seeks to challenge received critical notions of convention more broadly, counters the notion of the shot/reverse-shot convention as "arbitrary" with a view of it as a kind of "contingent universal." This overcomes what for him is a false boundary between nature and culture. On the one hand, says Bordwell, shot/reverse-shot was an "invention" of the 1910s, not used in "the first 15 years of filmmaking": "It wasn't determined by the technology of the cinema, and I can find no plausible parallels in other nineteenth-century media, such as comic strips, paintings, or lantern slides." On the other hand, it was readily enough grasped by audiences. The notion of the "contingent universal" is mobilized to explain how shot/reverse-shot could have become so intelligible to so many over the coming decades. See Bordwell, "Convention, Construction, and Cinematic Vision," in *Post-Theory: Reconstructing Film Studies*, ed. David Bordwell and Noël Carroll (Madison: University of Wisconsin Press,

1996), 87–88. In pointing to the origins of this practice in print sentimentality of the nineteenth (and indeed, eighteenth) century, I am suggesting that there are more than casually associated "parallels" with the practice in a "medium" Bordwell does not look to. "Didn't Dickens write this way?" asked Griffith. It might be pointed out that two key theorists of the sentimental, Hume and Smith, are thinkers for whom natural philosophy and moral philosophy, nature and culture, were susceptible of the same Newtonian form of inquiry. This methodological presupposition was fundamental to their deep intellectual compatibility within the Scottish Enlightenment.

24 Joseph McBride, *Frank Capra: The Catastrophe of Success* (New York: Simon & Schuster, 1992), 414.

25 I hope it is clear that my discussion of Capra in part 1 is meant to be neither an exhaustive account of his career, nor a full engagement with his films and their contexts, nor a charting of all cinematic or literary influences on his work. In addition to McBride's critical biography, there is a large body of commentary— including detailed monographs by Ray Carney, Charles Maland, Leland Poague, and Eric Smoodin—that, taken as a whole, manages to accomplish these large tasks, and I rely on it explicitly throughout. My narrower aim here is to describe the Capraesque in terms that reveal its progressive engagement over two decades of filmmaking with forms of sentimentalism that predate it by almost two centuries.

Chapter 1

1 See Walter Kerr, *The Silent Clowns* (New York: Knopf, 1975), which focuses on exactly these four comic figures.

2 On Capra's cultural influence in the 1930s, see Robert Sklar, *Movie-Made America: A Cultural History of American Movies* (1975; New York: Random House, 1994), 161–227. It is a measure of how low Capra's star had fallen, post-1948, that a similarly themed and widely read book of that same year by Michael Wood, a generous critic with eclectic tastes, should leave Capra completely out of account. Wood, *America in the Movies* (New York: Basic Books, 1975).

3 Lewis Jacobs, *The Rise of the American Film, A Critical History* (New York: Teachers College Press, 1968; first published New York: Harcourt Brace, and Company, 1939), 453–54.

4 See Sergei Kapterev, "Sergei Eisenstein's Letters to Hollywood Film-makers," *Studies in Russian and Soviet Cinema* 4, no. 2 (July 2010): 248. Eisenstein's reference to meeting Capra in his Moscow hotel room tends to confirm Capra's record of the encounter in his autobiography, which was challenged by McBride. Frank Capra, *The Name above the Title: An Autobiography* (New York: Macmillan, 1971), 209–13; McBride, *Catastrophe of Success*, 368–69.

5 McBride, *Catastrophe of Success*, 172.

6 Michele Hilmes, *Hollywood and Broadcasting: From Radio to Cable* (Urbana: University of Illinois Press, 1990), 161.

7 Liberty Films sold the rights to Paramount. Paramount did not release its pre-1948 films until 1958, but it sold *It's a Wonderful Life* in 1955, and Capra's comment in a late interview suggests that the film may have been shown on television by 1957; see Janine Basinger, *The "It's a Wonderful Life" Book* (New York: Alfred A. Knopf, 1986), 68.

8 This claim is supported by the vast majority of reviews of *Riding High* (1950), *Hole in the Head* (1959), and *Pocketful of Miracles* (1961).

9 *Wall Street Journal*, December 19, 1984. Gary Fishgall reports that in the Christmas season of 1991 the film could be seen on nine different channels in Los Angeles, five local television stations and four cable channels. Fishgall, *Pieces of Time: The Life of James Stewart* (New York: Scribner, 1997), 190.

10 The theme of the film's own rebirth is suggested in the title of Basinger's introductory essay, "The Many Lives of *It's a Wonderful Life*," in *"It's a Wonderful Life" Book*, 3–69.

11 See Hilmes, *Hollywood and Broadcasting*, for an account of the SAG agreement delimiting the pre-1948 films.

12 I myself remember these telecasts very well, as well as the sense of pomp, prestige, and festivity with which they were invested.

13 The third was also a Capra film: *Arsenic and Old Lace* (1943), with Cary Grant and Priscilla Lane.

14 Val Adams, "News of TV and Radio—Informational," *New York Times*, May 10, 1959.

15 Only the format of *Million Dollar Movie*, on WOR in New York City, with its many repeated broadcasts of a single film in the course of week, created anything like a precedent for this in the realm of home viewing.

16 See Robert B. Ray, *A Certain Tendency of the Hollywood Cinema, 1930–1980* (Princeton, NJ: Princeton University Press, 1985), 89–112 (on *Casablanca*), 179–215 (on *It's a Wonderful Life*).

17 Kristin Thompson, *Storytelling in the New Hollywood: Understanding Classical Narrative Technique* (Cambridge, MA: Harvard University Press, 1999), 132.

18 See Andrew Bergman, "Frank Capra and the Screwball Comedy, 1931–1941," in *We're in the Money: Depression America and Its Films* (New York: New York University Press, 1971; reprint, Chicago: Ivan R. Dee, 1992), 132–48.

19 One interviewer told Cage, "I noticed in *It Could Happen to You* that some of your phrasing has a Jimmy Stewart quality." Cage replied, "That was something that [director] Andrew Bergman really wanted for the character of Charlie Lang, the cop I play. He would say to me, 'More Jimmy, think more Jimmy'—that was his most recurring direction to me. So I would think about *It's a Wonderful Life*. Like, there's one line in *It Could Happen to You* when Bridget Fonda says: 'Go do whatever it is you do. Go get the cat out of the tree.' And I say, 'No, that'd be the

fire department.' And in the rhythm of that line, I very specifically tried to sell James Stewart. I think of James Stewart as a legendary actor, so it was more of a tip of the hat than a flat-out imitation." Mike Marvel, interview with Nicolas Cage, *Interview*, August 1994.

20 One perhaps overly generous review of *The Majestic* noted that "Jim Carrey practically channels the spirit of Jimmy Stewart" and that the film itself shows that "the legacy of Capra is in good hands." Rob Blackwelder, review of *The Majestic* (Castle Rock Entertainment), http://www.contactmusic.com/new/film.nsf /reviews/majestic.

21 Wes Gehring, an unabashed Capra enthusiast, places *Dave* in a "trilogy" of "mainstream extensions of the Capra tradition" that also includes *The Electric Horseman* (1979) and *Field of Dreams* (1989). Gehring, *Populism and the Capra Legacy* (Westport, CT: Greenwood Press, 1995), 54. Gehring concedes that of the three, "*Dave* owes the greatest debt to Capra" (47)—by a great margin, I would add. He also goes on to argue for a "pushing of the envelope" with the Capraesque in *The Milagro Beanfield War* (1988), *Grand Canyon* (1991), and *Hero* (57–84). Of these three, I think only *Hero* makes the connection patent.

22 Capra's grandson, Frank Capra III, was first assistant director on *The American President*. Sorkin, for his part, would go on to extend his Capraesque efforts with an HBO series, *The Newsroom*, centered on a self-consciously quixotic news anchor (Jeff Daniels) on a mission to restore integrity to American news broadcasting.

23 The increasing explicitness of Capra as a reference point for such films culminates, perhaps, in Adam Sandler's actual remake, *Mr. Deeds Goes to Town* (2002). Uncannily, as with Capra himself in the mid-twentieth century, when the actual remake happens (with *Riding High* in the earlier instance), the quasi-remaking seems to cease.

24 A counterstrand of self-conscious American filmmaking (call it antisentimental) in exactly the same period forms part of the context of this neo-Capraesque movement. It involves the emergence of a certain hip discursive and stylistic irony in the films of Quentin Tarantino, whose *Reservoir Dogs* (1992) begins with a diner scene shot as an homage to the camerawork of Martin Scorsese in *Goodfellas* (1990), in which a gang member played by Tarantino himself leads a critical discussion with other gang members on the songs of Madonna. This homage would in turn be parodied in Jon Favreau's *Swingers* (1996), in which the reflexivity is intensified: the same cinematographic style is used for a scene of critical discussion led by a character played by Favreau, who explicitly attacks *Reservoir Dogs* for being derivative of *Goodfellas*! Favreau would in turn appear, as himself, in a reflexive episode of *The Sopranos*, in search of "real-life" mobsters to consult about a new film about Joey Gallo.

25 The interviews collected in *Frank Capra: Interviews*, ed. Leland Poague (Jack-

son: University Press of Mississippi, 2004), include nothing from 1947 to 1957, and only two interviews between 1947 and the appearance of Capra's autobiography in 1971. By contrast, the book includes ten interviews with Capra from the 1970s (at the end of which he was over eighty years old), some of them lengthy and most of them published in accessible venues.

26 In Timothy Corrigan's terms, Capra would be an early "auteur star," one Corrigan would surely identify more as a "commercial auteur" (like the later Bertolucci)— directors for whom "the celebrity of their agency produces and promotes texts that . . . exceed the movie itself"—than as an "auteur of commerce" (like Alexander Kluge), who "attempts to monitor or rework the institutional manipulations of the auteurist position within the commerce of the contemporary movie industry." Corrigan, "The Commerce of Auteurism: A Voice without Authority," *New German Critique* 48 (Winter 1990): 51.

27 *Name above the Title* was issued in paperback in 1982, reprinted as a Vintage paperback in 1985, and reprinted again in paper in 1997 with a preface by Jeanine Basinger. The last edition is still in print.

28 It is an even more curious affair in the unedited version housed at the Wesleyan Film Archive. In this manuscript, the story opens with Capra sleeping off a hangover in a limousine parked in a San Francisco garage that is attended by an African-American friend. Capra's bandaged penis is exposed and the opening conversation is about the cause of the problem (an STD) and whether Capra should attempt to pass as a director in order to defraud a local film company of a small amount of money.

29 The first film to bear Capra's name above the title was *Lost Horizon* (1937), and from that point forward such billing became a condition of his contract. The other directors accorded this honor were typically producer-directors like Charles Chaplin, Orson Welles, and Alfred Hitchcock.

30 Elliott Stein, "Capra Counts His Oscars," *Sight and Sound* 41, no. 3 (Summer 1972): 164.

31 Jean-Loup Bourget, review of Frank Capra, *The Name above the Title*, *Film Comment* 7, no. 4 (Winter 1971/1972): 77.

32 Charles Maland, review of Joseph McBride, *Frank Capra: The Catastrophe of Success*, *Film Quarterly* 46, no. 2 (Winter 1992/1993): 53.

33 Andrew Sarris, *The American Cinema: Directors and Directions, 1929–1968* (New York: Dutton, 1968), 87. Writing in the 1960s, probably the nadir of Capra's reputation, Sarris broke with, say, Lewis Jacobs in removing Capra from what Sarris called "the Pantheon" of great American directors (fourteen in all) and placing him in a second group he called "The Far Side of Paradise": "directors who fall short of the Pantheon either because of a fragmentation of their personal vision or because of disruptive career problems" (83). A decade later, however, Leo Braudy and Morris Dickstein returned Capra to the (international) canon

in *Great Film Directors: A Critical Anthology* (New York: Oxford University Press, 1978).

34 Robert Sklar and Vito Zagarrio, eds., *Frank Capra: Authorship and the Studio System* (Philadelphia: Temple University Press, 1998).

35 A few years after the appearance of *The Name above the Title*, a serious collection of essays, old and new, was edited and published by Richard Glatzer and John Raeburn, *Frank Capra: The Man and His Work* (Ann Arbor: University of Michigan Press, 1975). In their observant introduction, Glatzer and Raeburn puzzle over the decline of Capra's high reputation in comparison to the critical favor then enjoyed by Howard Hawks, Orson Welles, John Ford, and Alfred Hitchcock. They offer three plausible reasons for the neglect: (1) his overwhelming commercial success back in the day; (2) his unfortunate films of the 1950s; and (3) his failure fully to appeal as an auteur to French critics of the new wave period in that "much of the world of a Mr. Deeds or a Mr. Smith or a John Doe was simply culturally unavailable to non-Americans." They also point, already in 1975, to "signs that this period of underestimating Capra's work is over" (viii).

36 In 1985, Cavell wrote a further analysis of *It Happened One Night*, extending his incisive commentary in *Pursuits of Happiness: The Hollywood Comedy of Remarriage* (Cambridge, MA: Harvard University Press, 1981). The analysis works toward a comparison of Capra with Emerson and Whitman on friendship and the open road, and at its conclusion Cavell characteristically raises the difficult issues: "Am I claiming that Capra is as good as Whitman and Emerson? Am I saying that he intended the matters I have invoked to account for my mood with a moment he has provided? These are reasoned questions, deserving of reasoned answers. Until then I may put my approach to them this way. Capra shares certain of the ambitions and the specific visions of Whitman and of Emerson, and he knows about working with film roughly what they know about working with words." But the comment quickly waxes defensive in a way that, in his reflection on the piece twenty years later, he has to apologize for: Cavell, *Cities of Words: Pedagogical Letters on a Register of the Moral Life* (Cambridge, MA: Harvard University Press, 2004), 162–63.

37 Collected in MacDonald, *Against the American Grain* (New York: Random House, 1962).

38 Stephen Hunter, "Auteur of Corn: A Film Retrospective Explores the Dark Side of Frank Capra's Sunny World," *Washington Post*, January 2, 1998.

39 One has to be careful in making such claims, since it is hard to find a time when the American cinema was not nostalgic, as we might recall from Eisenstein's writings about D. W. Griffith, probably its greatest early pioneer, where he emphasized the linkages between Griffith's interest in up-to-the-minute technology, on the one hand, and, on the other, his investment in *Birth of a Nation* in recreating an American South that was gone with the wind.

40 Max Horkheimer and Theodor W. Adorno, *Dialectic of Enlightenment: Philo-sophical Fragments*, ed. Gunzelin Schmid Noerr, trans. Edmund Jephcott (Stanford, CA: Stanford University Press, 2002), 98.

41 The "suture" depends on the kind of shot that, in Jean-Pierre Oudart's and Daniel Dayan's terms, is first seen, and then read. By "read," they mean that the shot is interpreted as involving a "lack" that is defined by the implicit point of view of some "absent one." The shot is followed with a reverse-angle shot that locates the absent one (to whose glance the first shot belongs) as a *character* within the fictional diegesis. Hence the "suturing" of the subject in the film text. Oudart, "Cinema and Suture," *Cahiers du Cinéma* (April, May 1969), 211, 212, trans. Kari Hanet, in *Screen* 18 (Winter 1978); Dayan, "The Tutor-Code of Classical Cinema," in *Movies and Methods*, ed. Bill Nichols (Berkeley: University of California Press, 1976), 448. Like Murray Smith, who draws on the resources of analytic philosophy and cognitive anthropology, I seek to offer an alternative to psychoanalytic accounts of these cinematic features. Like Smith as well, as will become clear, I am interested in positing "distinct *levels of engagement* with fictional characters, which together comprise [a] *structure of sympathy*" (his italics). My account, however, draws on the resources of intellectual and cultural history, and I do not reject the language of point of view, as he explicitly does, but rather attempt to historicize its suggestive ambiguities in the long durée of sentiment. Smith, *Engaging Characters: Fiction, Emotion and the Cinema* (Oxford: Oxford University Press, 1995), 5. More recent monographs taking a cognitive approach to these questions include Greg M. Smith, *Film Structure and the Emotion System* (Cambridge: Cambridge University Press, 2003), and Carl Plantinga, *Moving Viewers: American Film and the Spectator's Experience* (Berkeley: University of California Press, 2009).

42 Bordwell, Staiger, and Thompson, *The Classical Hollywood Cinema: Film Style and Mode of Production to 1960* (New York: Columbia University Press, 1985).

43 Bordwell, *On the History of Film Style* (Cambridge, MA: Harvard University Press, 1998).

44 Ibid., 4.

45 A book that hews even more closely to the technological account of stylistic transformation in the cinema is Barry Salt's widely read *Film Style and Technology: History and Analysis*, 2nd ed. (1983; London: Starword, 1992).

46 Capra's works make some claims to innovation. For example, his autobiography discusses an experiment with overlapping sound, as well as a deliberate effort to pick up the pace of scenes, in *American Madness* (*Name above the Title*, 139–40). This kind of speed and snap would be parodied in the Coen brothers' neo-Capraesque *The Hudsucker Proxy*, but if Capra helped set the style for Hawks's *His Girl Friday* (1940), Hawks's own source, Lewis Milestone's *The Front Page* (1931), surely must have inspired Capra first. Capra boasted of using multiple cameras early, and that is important, but many other directors were also doing that.

He had Joseph Walker use different lenses for different actors or actresses, but this too is a minor innovation and not to be accounted a stylistic breakthrough.

47 *The Making of "It's a Wonderful Life"* (1990).

48 Capra, *Name Above the Title*, 83.

49 McBride, *Catastrophe of Success*, 186–90.

50 See Thomas Schatz, *The Genius of the System: Hollywood Filmmaking in the Studio Era* (New York: Pantheon, 1988). In Schatz's account, Capra figures as the internal adversary of the system and of what Capra, in a 1939 letter to the *New York Times*, called "the six producers" who "pass on about 90 per cent of the scripts and edit about 90 per cent of the pictures" (quoted in Schatz, 8).

51 For details of these struggles see, in addition to the biographical work on Capra, Bob Thomas, *King Cohn: The Life and Times of Harry Cohn* (New York: G. P. Putnam's Sons, 1967), and Bernard F. Dick, *The Merchant Prince of Poverty Row: Harry Cohn of Columbia Pictures* (Lexington: University Press of Kentucky, 1993), 89–118.

52 René Clair would later single out Capra, along with "Preston Sturges, and sometimes Ernest Lubitsch," as one of the rare Hollywood directors who worked as deliberately and selectively as himself. In *Film Crazy: Interviews with Hollywood Legends* ed. Patrick McGilligan (New York: St. Martin's Griffin, 2000), 72.

53 Lea Jacobs has recently made the provocative argument that during the 1920s Hollywood actually turned away from sentiment and toward the sort of naturalism represented, precisely, in von Stroheim's adaptation of Frank Norris's *McTeague* with the film *Greed*. Jacobs, *The Decline of Sentiment: American Film in the 1920s* (Berkeley: University of California Press, 2008), 25–78. With the talkies, however, the trend was again somewhat reversed, and in a way that is epitomized by Capra's distaste for von Stroheim, about which more below in chapter 3. It is not that the 1930s lacks instances of what Jacobs terms naturalism; Warner Brothers made several important films arguably in that vein over the course of the decade. Nonetheless, while Capra might rightly be said to triumph over von Stroheim in the short term, the 1940s, as Bazin argues, will be another story.

54 Cynicism and sentiment have been represented as in an obverse relationship at least since Herman Melville's last major novel, *The Confidence Man* (1857). Capra routinely incorporates the cynical perspective in his programmatic work post-1935, often in the figure of a jaded reporter but also in the sidekick characters played by Lionel Stander in *Mr. Deeds Goes to Town* and Walter Brennan in *Meet John Doe*.

55 The sense of directorial signature at the end of the 1930s is illustrated in a *New Yorker* article showing, with illustrative cartoons, how Ford, Hitchcock, Lubitsch, and Capra would approach the shooting of a love scene. "It's Tricks . . . and Technique," *New Yorker*, June 25, 1940, 11–12. Capra's own "touch" was touted as early as 1935; see Paula Harrison, "The Master of the Human Touch," *Motion Picture* (July 1935), 55, 76.

56 I am mindful of the critique of an approach to film history that leads to "the focus on Sennett as 'the father of film comedy'" at the expense of the pre-Keystone films, and indeed sensitive to the more general problem of how the "'masterpiece' approach" to film comedy means neglecting "the large number of ordinary films which fill in the gaps between periods of remarkable accomplishment"; the critique is made and the problem remedied in *Classical Film Comedy*, ed. Kristine Brunovska and Henry Jenkins (New York: Routledge, 1995), 6.

57 See Ian Scott, *In Capra's Shadow: The Life and Career of Screenwriter Robert Riskin* (Lexington: University Press of Kentucky, 2006), 85–154.

58 This is exactly how Graham Greene and others received the film: "Here is Capra, without the help of Riskin, back to his finest form—the form of *Mr. Deeds*. . . . It has always been an interesting question, how much Capra owed to his faithful scenario writer. Now it is difficult to believe that Riskin's part was ever very important, for all the familiar qualities are here." Greene quoted in McBride, *Catastrophe of Success*, 409.

Chapter 2

1 This theme has been highlighted recently in several recent essays on the darker side of Capra, all collected in a volume celebrating the centenary of his birth: Robert Sklar, "A Leap into the Void: Frank Capra's Apprenticeship to Ideology"; Vito Zagarrio, "It Is (Not) a Wonderful Life: For a Counter-reading of Frank Capra"; and Charles J. Maland, "Capra and the Abyss: Self-Interest versus the Common Good in Depression America," in *Frank Capra: Authorship and the Studio System*, ed. Sklar and Zagarrio (Philadelphia: Temple University Press, 1998), 37–129.

2 Ray Carney has pointed out many more such connections among Capra's films, such as the similar endings of *Broadway Bill* and its successor, *It Happened One Night*, or what he calls the "melodramatic turn" in Capra's films from 1939 to 1948. See Carney, *American Vision: The Films of Frank Capra* (Cambridge: Cambridge University Press, 1986), 253, 339.

3 All but the first two silent films with Harry Langdon were made at Columbia Pictures.

4 *It Happened One Night* and *Lost Horizon* were both adapted from works of fiction.

5 See Edward Buscombe's analysis of the film in relation to Giannini's involvement with Columbia (where his brother served on the board), in "Notes on Columbia Pictures Corporation, 1926–1941, with a New Afterword," in *Frank Capra: Authorship and the Studio System*, ed. Sklar and Zagarrio, 255–81; reprinted from *Screen* 16, no. 3 (Autumn 1975): 65–82.

6 See Tom Gunning, *The Films of Fritz Lang: Allegories of Vision and Modernity* (London: British Film Institute, 2000), 97–98. *Fury* lost out to *Mr. Deeds* in the 1936 Academy Awards.

7 This scene will be repeated when Jean Arthur gives a stammering nonreply to Gary Cooper's question, also on the telephone, in *Mr. Deeds*. Cooper's response is similar to Huston's.

8 Fidelity here, in other words, follows some of the same sort of logic that we find with "belief" in the case of *Gaslight* (1944), as Cavell has explained it in *Contesting Tears: The Hollywood Melodrama of the Unknown Woman* (Chicago: University of Chicago Press, 1996), 47–80.

9 Robert Riskin, *Six Screenplays by Robert Riskin*, ed. Pat McGilligan (Berkeley: University of California Press, 1997), 195. Further references cited parenthetically in the text.

10 Capra's earliest exploration of the problematic of faith is his deeply ambiguous study of the overlap between the shared sentiment and the confidence game in *Miracle Woman* (1931).

11 We find a similar structural twist in the plot of *Meet John Doe*, Capra's last film with Riskin, where the suicidal despair of John Willoughby (Gary Cooper), which owes in large measure to his betrayal by Ann Mitchell (Barbara Stanwyck), seems to be overcome at the end not by her rooftop appeal to him (though she has risked her own life to make it) but by that of the common people who represent the John Doe Clubs.

12 It is perhaps worth noting that this sequence was not part of the fictional source on which Capra and his writers based their screenplay, Philip Van Doren Stern, *The Greatest Gift: A Christmas Tale* (Philadelphia: David McKay Co., 1944; New York: Penguin Studio, 1996).

13 Cf. George Bailey's being kissed by Vie (Gloria Grahame) in gratitude for a personal loan in *It's a Wonderful Life*. The kiss is innocent and matters to the plot only insofar as it colors the bank's fiduciary legitimacy in the eyes of the prudish bank examiner.

14 We see Bert and Ernie kiss before George and Mary do; the newlyweds may be presumed to reach their own makeshift bridal suite in the leaky edifice after the wedding supper that Mary has prepared for them. Another index of the saturation of American culture by Capra is the pair of puppets called Bert and Ernie who share a residence on the children's television series *Sesame Street*. There has been considerable debate as to whether Bert and Ernie are gay. Indeed, 2011 saw a movement to have the producers "out" the characters as a way of teaching children to accept the life choices of gay men.

15 Cavell, *Pursuits of Happiness: The Hollywood Comedy of Remarriage* (Cambridge, MA: Harvard University Press, 1981), 41; Cavell, *Cities of Words: Pedagogical Letters on a Register of the Moral Life* (Cambridge, MA: Harvard University Press, 2004), 254–55.

16 See Andrew Klevan's extended revisiting of Cavell's account of this sequence, with particular attention to "the scrutiny of the camera" and how James Stewart "makes visible to the camera crucial aspects of his character, while credibly keep-

ing them invisible to the other characters." Klevan, "Guessing the Unseen from the Seen: Stanley Cavell and Film Interpretation," in *Contending with Stanley Cavell*, ed. Russell B. Goodman (New York: Oxford University Press, 2005), 127.

17 The sequence observes a logic that Eve Kosofsky Sedgwick has traced, not co-incidentally, to Sterne's *Sentimental Journey*. See her *Between Men: English Literature and Male Homosocial Desire* (New York: Columbia University Press, 1985), 67–82.

18 This is roughly the joke that Dickens makes at Tackleton's expense in *The Cricket on the Hearth* (see Introduction).

19 Even Charles Affron's sensitive reading of this scene misses the key point about George's superhuman powers of sympathy in a state of duress, finding instead a "sympathy of tears" between the man and the boy at the close of the scene. Affron, *Cinema and Sentiment* (Chicago: University of Chicago Press, 1982), 7.

20 A third sequence (discussed earlier), subtler than the other two but perhaps more emblematic in its technical presentation, is that in which George reacts to the news of his brother's marriage, which has adverse implications for himself.

21 Fishgall, *Pieces of Time: The Life of James Stewart*, 186.

22 One precedent for a film about a celestial screening of ordinary life on earth is Fritz Lang's long neglected *Liliom* (1934), his first Hollywood film, in which the misdeeds of the title character (Charles Boyer) are shown on a heavenly surveillance apparatus.

23 Jeanine Basinger, The *"It's a Wonderful Life" Book* (New York: Alfred A. Knopf, 1986), 131.

24 But see below, chapter 7, where I discuss Potter's monstrous parody of this capacity.

25 Annie is a special case of the function of the third party. When she pauses from serving dinner to hear George's response to his father's expression of hope that George will return to run the Building and Loan, George playfully mocks her interest: "Annie, why don't you draw up a chair? Then you'd be more comfortable and you could hear everything that is going on." But Annie gets the best of the exchange: "I would if I thought I'd hear anything worth listening to" (143). The type of the wise, saucy, concerned servant is at least as old as Dorine in Moliere's *Tartuffe*, but Annie's race figures in her intermittent invisibility and her way of mattering/not-mattering to the action, a point confirmed by Harry Bailey's cavalier mock flirtation with her: "Annie, I'm in love with you. There's a moon out tonight" (139).

26 Man on porch: "Why don't you kiss her instead of talking her to death? . . ." George: "Hey, mister, come back out here, and I'll show you some kissing that'll put hair back on your head" (159).

27 In an explicitly Cavellian spirit, Leland Poague offers a suggestive account of *It's a Wonderful Life* by way of *Hamlet* in a chapter titled "To Be or Not to Be." Poague, *Another Frank Capra* (Cambridge: Cambridge University Press, 1994),

186–222. The account might be extended to include these structures of overseeing, overhearing, and reflexivity in the two works. The question of who over-
sees or overhears what is often crucial in *Hamlet,* even for the issue of whether
Hamlet's best-known soliloquy is performed in the knowledge that Polonius
is behind the arras. The play's devices of reflection and reflexivity, not least the
conscience-catching play within the play, famously form a part of its relation
to the tradition of revenge tragedy. Such a move is restaged in the way Richard
Steele's reflexive devices in the first sentimental comedy, *The Conscious Lovers,*
respond to the vindictive tendencies in Restoration drama. Sterne, I would suggest, registers the importance of *Hamlet* for sentimentalism not only in naming
his self-conscious protagonist Yorick but also in a series of *Hamlet* moments that
run through *Sentimental Journey.*

28 Like me, Carl Plantinga sees the relevance of Adam Smith's notions of spectatorship to Hollywood cinema, but we explain that relevance in different ways. Capra
figures not at all in his discussion, and his definition of "sentiment" is simply
"any emotion that is typically or often accompanied with crying," a problem that
makes it difficult for him to discriminate between "sentimentality" and what I
call the sentimental mode. Plantinga, *Moving Viewers: American Film and the
Spectator's Experience* (Berkeley: University of California Press, 2009), 192–93.

29 It is again important to recall that *American Madness* was the first Capra film for
which Robert Riskin had the sole screenwriting credit and that the writing team
for *It's a Wonderful Life* did not include him.

30 The telephone is the primary technology in *American Madness,* its network capacities providing the means both of spreading panic and of quelling it. The only
glimmer of self-consciousness about the film medium in *American Madness* is in
the joke Matt tells at the start.

31 Two complete scripts for *It's a Wonderful Life* survive in the Wesleyan Cinema
Archives. One is the script of the film as shot, dated March 1947, the other is
the "estimating script" of March 1946, which contains much evidence, in his own
hand, of Capra's work on the screenplay. It includes an opening sequence, set in
what is supposed to be Franklin's "workshop and office," that lends some context
to Franklin's role as a voice of authority in the heavens. Technology is fore-
grounded: "Radio parts and various electronic devices are scattered around." We
first see Franklin "examining some delicate electrical device." When Joseph walks
up to him, Franklin explains, "New radar equipment from down below— ...
They're not far behind us down there." Basinger, *"It's a Wonderful Life" Book,* 325.

32 The evidence is mainly internal, but McBride calls *A Christmas Carol* "one of
Capra's favorite books" and notes elsewhere that among the treasures in Capra's
rare book collection was a proof copy of Dickens's novella. McBride, *Frank
Capra: The Catastrophe of Success* (New York: Simon & Schuster, 1992), 522, 332.

33 There may also be an echo of the title of D. W. Griffith's late feature film *Isn't
Life Wonderful?* (1924).

34 Cavell, *Pursuits of Happiness*, 81. For Cavell, part of the explanation turns on understanding that the blanket is not only barrier but also screen, which, especially with Gable's character, "takes on the characteristics of a movie screen" (105). This claim for the film's subtle reflexivity is consistent, I think, with the analysis that I offer along different lines.

35 Riskin, *Six Screenplays*, 298.

36 He is almost certainly named for the first American bodybuilder, the Prussian-born Eugene Sandow, who died the year before this film was released.

37 Chaplin seems to belong in this line in a way that Buster Keaton, with his dead-pan face and competence with machinery, does not.

38 This kind of theatricalization characterizes some of the very first and stagiest (as it were) instances of shot/reverse-shot in early cinema, as in Griffith's *The Drunkard's Reformation* (1909).

39 John Traugott, "Heart and Mask and Genre in Sentimental Comedy," *Eighteenth-Century Life* 10 (October 1986): 143.

40 Stuart M. Tave, *Lovers, Clowns, and Fairies: An Essay on Comedies* (Chicago: University of Chicago Press, 1993), 132.

41 Cf. newspaper communication of domestic issues in *That Certain Thing*.

42 A year after *Platinum Blonde*, in *Merrily We Go to Hell* (1932), Dorothy Arzner developed a similar plot—reporter (Fredric March) marries an heiress (Sylvia Sidney) over her family's protest—with a similarly reflexive subplot: the reporter writes a play that echoes the plot of the film.

Chapter 3

1 Ferguson, "Mr. Capra Goes to Town," in *The Film Criticism of Otis Ferguson*, ed. Robert Wilson, foreword by Andrew Sarris (Philadelphia: Temple University Press, 1971), 127.

2 Cooper in *Mr. Deeds Goes to Town* and *Meet John Doe*; Stewart in *You Can't Take it With You, Mr. Smith Goes to Washington*, and *It's a Wonderful Life*.

3 So christened in Henry Mackenzie's 1771 novella *The Man of Feeling*, written in the wake of the death of Laurence Sterne. Charles Maland identifies the relevant qualities in the Capra hero in sketching one of the conventions of the work: "He has a childlike innocence (related to Langdon's comic persona) that more worldly and experienced people scoff at and take advantage of." Maland, *Frank Capra* (New York: Twayne, 1995), 93.

4 For good accounts of the larger movements, see Michael Denning, *The Cultural Front: The Laboring of American Culture in the Twentieth Century* (London: Verso, 1996), and Dudley Andrew and Steven Ungar, *Popular Front Paris and the Poetics of Culture* (Cambridge, MA: Harvard University Press, 2005). Both studies use events in 1934, on either side of the Atlantic, as their points of departure.

5 Kathleen Moran and Michael Rogin, "'What's the Matter with Capra?' *Sulli-*

van's Travels and the Popular Front," *Representations*, no. 71 (Summer 2000), 106–34; Leonard Quart, "Frank Capra and the Popular Front," in *American Media and Mass Culture: Left Perspectives*, ed. Donald Lazere (Berkeley: University of California Press, 1987), 178–83; Jeffrey Richards, "Frank Capra and the Cinema of Populism," in *Movies and Methods*, ed. Bill Nichols (Berkeley: University of California Press, 1976), 65–77. See also Leland Poague's response to Richards's influential critique in *Another Frank Capra* (Cambridge: Cambridge University Press, 1994), 23–34.

6 Joseph McBride, *Frank Capra: The Catastrophe of Success* (New York: Simon & Schuster, 1992), 319.

7 Frank Capra, *The Name above the Title: An Autobiography* (New York: Macmillan, 1971), 176.

8 Ibid., 182.

9 See Andrew Bergman, "Frank Capra and the Screwball Comedy, 1931–1941," in *We're in the Money: Depression America and its Films* (New York: New York University Press, 1971; reprint, Chicago: Ivan R. Dee, 1992), 132–48.

10 Articles by Capra appeared in the *Saturday Evening Post* and elsewhere in 1936 arguing the case for the director as auteur. In his 1971 autobiography, he wrote, "In Hollywood *Mr. Deeds* sowed the seeds of change. . . . The 'one man, one film' idea took hold, grew slowly—against stormy opposition from entrenched executives—and today [1971] many directors have a box-office value as big, or bigger, than the stars." Capra, *Name above the Title*, 186. See Thomas Schatz's partially persuasive debunking of Capra's self-portrait as proto-auteur, but note that he has to leave *It's a Wonderful Life* completely out of his account to make his case. Schatz, "Anatomy of a House Director: Capra, Cohn, and Columbia in the 1930s," in *Frank Capra: Authorship and the Studio System*, ed. Robert Sklar and Vito Zaggario (Philadelphia: Temple University Press, 1998), 10–36. Schatz's own valuable book on the studio system undermines its own anti-auteurist claims by elevating the studio's producer (e.g., Irving Thalberg, David O. Selznick) to the level of auteur. Schatz, *The Genius of the System: Hollywood Filmmaking in the Studio Era* (New York: Pantheon, 1988).

11 Capra, *Name above the Title*, 186.

12 Ibid.

13 See Charles Maland's comment in his balanced review of the book: "On the one hand, he faults the director for self-aggrandizing behavior and for minimizing the important contributions of collaborators to his films, claiming that much of what we call Capra's 'vision' is the creation of screenwriters like Robert Riskin and Myles Connolly. On the other hand, McBride often analyzes the films as very personal, albeit sometimes submerged, expressions of Capra's personality, an analytical strategy that accepts Capra's 'one man, one film' auteurism at face value, even as much of the rest of the biography seems to undermine it." Maland, review of McBride, *Catastrophe of Success*, *Film Quarterly* 46, no. 2 (Winter

1992/1993): 53. Leland Poague develops this point as part of an extended riposte to McBride in a postscript to *Another Frank Capra*, 223–43. Vito Zagarrio also notes the contradiction, in "It Is (Not) a Wonderful Life," in Sklar and Zagarrio, *Frank Capra*, 72. He observes that the debate about studio auteurs is longstanding and complicated, and faults not only McBride's ungenerous instincts but also the short shrift given the complexities of the topic (70–72).

14 McBride takes a different view of screenwriter-director relations in the equally controversial case of Mankiewicz and Welles.

15 Biberman, "Frank Capra's Characters," in *New Masses*, July 1941; reprinted in *Meet John Doe: Frank Capra, Director*, ed. Charles Wolfe (New Brunswick, NJ: Rutgers University Press, 1989), 231.

16 Of the three Capra films in the top thirty-five of the American Film Institute's 1998 ranking of the hundred greatest American films, the two that were made without Riskin rank above the Riskin-scripted *It Happened One Night* (number 35). *It's a Wonderful Life* stands at number 11, *Mr. Smith* at number 29.

17 For a negative assessment of the 1935 turning point, see, for example, Elliott Stein, "Capra Counts His Oscars," *Sight and Sound* 41, no. 3 (Summer 1972): 162; this view also surfaced during the retrospectives of the early Capra that marked his centennial in 1997.

18 So important is this question within biographically oriented studies of Capra's work that Poague devotes nearly half a chapter to reviewing the various positions on the difference made by *Mr. Deeds* before advancing his own. Poague, *Another Frank Capra*, 94–124.

19 Capra, *Name above the Title*, 178.

20 Ibid.

21 The farmer mentions a front-page story by Bennett, published with a photo of Deeds feeding doughnuts to a horse, reminiscent perhaps of Yorick's feeding macaroons to an ass in *Sentimental Journey*.

22 Deeds's plan to turn philanthropist runs him afoul of the corrupt lawyers who have other plans for his money, much as Mr. Smith's plan for the Willett Creek summer camp, in the sequel film, runs that character afoul of the bosses who have other plans for the land.

23 Robert Riskin, *Six Screenplays by Robert Riskin*, ed. Pat McGilligan (Berkeley: University of California Press, 1997), 424–25. In his effort to diminish Capra's claims to authorship of *Mr. Deeds*, McBride asserts that Capra shot the script largely as Riskin gave it to him. Of course, that script was, to begin with, a joint venture, as even McBride's own refrain would suggest: "Riskin and Capra wrote . . ." Given Capra's known involvement in all stages of the scripts, it seems odd to assume that this episode, or any episode, is Riskin's rather than Capra's. But my argument about what is crucial in the distinctive bracketing of this sequence does not depend on such speculations. What is crucial are the decisions Capra made in shooting it, which are nowhere indicated in the shooting script itself.

24 Normally such details would be indicated in the shooting script, and Riskin's screenplays do occasionally call for "reverse angle" shots, as in an earlier scene between Deeds and Walter, his valet. Ibid., 385.

25 Jacques Aumont, *Du visage au Cinéma* (Paris: Editions de l'Etoile/Cahiers du Cinéma [distributed by Seuil], 1992), 44; translation mine.

26 Ibid., 59.

27 André Bazin, "The Evolution of the Language of Cinema," in *What Is Cinema?*, 2 vols., trans. Hugh Gray (Berkeley: University of California Press, 1967), 1:28. Further references cited parenthetically in the text.

28 Bazin singled out this shot for detailed praise in an essay devoted to Wyler, "William Wyler ou le janséniste de la mise en scène," in *Qu'est-ce que le cinema?* vol. 1, *Ontologie et langage* (Paris: Cerf, 1969), 166–69. For other accounts of the iconic significance of this shot, see Charles Affron, *Cinema and Sentiment* (Chicago: University of Chicago Press, 1982), 79–82, and David Bordwell, *On the History of Film Style* (Cambridge, MA: Harvard University Press, 1998), 64, 215, 225–26. The other most famous shot of this kind in the period is Welles's depiction in *Citizen Kane* of Kane's wife, a suicide, with the pills in the foreground and Kane in the background, for which Bazin includes a frame enlargement in his "Film Language" essay.

29 Aumont also follows Bazin in emphasizing the relevance of the Kuleshov experiment with montage for this moment in cinema. Aumont, *Du visage au Cinéma*, 48–49. Further references cited parenthetically in the text.

30 Placing the cinematic face in the history of the painted face, Aumont emphasizes that such a representation of the face and how it looks means that, unlike that of many painted faces, the foreground is irrelevant to the ordinary face of cinema. Aumont, *Du visage au Cinéma*, 56.

31 Bazin, "Evolution of the Language," 1:31–32. Further references cited parenthetically in the text.

32 E.g., Capra's out-of-work man is not alone at the table, is seated rather than standing, and holds a drumstick, not a chicken wing.

33 See Bazin's two-part essay "Theater and Cinema," in *What Is Cinema?*, 1:76–124

34 Bazin elaborated his notion of cinematic *écriture* in an essay on Bresson's *Diary of a Country Priest*. For the influence of this concept on later French cinema, including on Bazin's protégé François Truffaut, see Dudley Andrew, *Film in the Aura of Art* (Princeton, NJ: Princeton University Press, 1984), 112–30.

35 See Gilles Deleuze, *Cinema 2: The Time-Image*, trans. Hugh Tomlinson and Robert Galeta (Minneapolis: University of Minnesota Press, 1989), 1–24.

36 Tom Gunning, *D. W. Griffith and the Origins of American Narrative Film*; David Bordwell, Janet Staiger, and Kristin Thompson, *The Classical Hollywood Cinema: Film Style and Mode of Production to 1960* (New York: Columbia University Press, 1985), 10. Bordwell has elaborated this thesis elsewhere, in *On the History of Film Style*, for example, and Thompson has extended its reach, with some modifica-

tions, beyond 1960 in *Storytelling in the New Hollywood*. Aumont comments on Bordwell's claims for the stability of the system from 1915 to 1960 in *Du visage au Cinéma*, 59–60. For challenges and modifications, see the essays collected in *Classical Hollywood Narrative: The Paradigm Wars*, ed. Jane Gaines (Durham, NC: Duke University Press, 1992).

37 Jean Mitry, *Aesthetics and Psychology of the Cinema*, trans. Christopher King (Bloomington: Indiana University Press, 1997), 207. I should note that this is not yet the soon-to-be-orthodox point-of-view shot at 45 degrees. The abuse, in *Broken Blossoms*, of the Girl (Lillian Gish) by the Yellow Man (Donald Crisp) in a hovel by the Thames must inevitably recall, for anyone who has read it, Quilp and Little Nell from *Old Curiosity Shop* (1841), that most sentimental of Dickens's novels. What has the plot of the opium-addicted Yellow Man to do with Dickens's novel? For starters, the First Opium War against China, resulting in the taking of Hong Kong and the creation of the treaty ports, was raging in 1841, and Dickens registered the issue in several of his writings. Further, Edwin Drood's uncle, John Jasper, visits an opium den in London in Dickens's last novel, *The Mystery of Edwin Drood* (1870).

38 Nick Browne, "The Rhetoric of the Specular Text with Reference to *Stagecoach*," *Communications* 23 (1975). I explain "mimetic and pragmatic axes" below in chapter 6. In the same year as Browne's essay, Laura Mulvey produced her seminal article "Visual Pleasure and Narrative Cinema" (*Screen* 16 [Autumn 1975], 6–18), which revolutionized critical thinking about the cinematic gaze. Mulvey breaks down what she calls "the complex interaction of looks . . . specific to film" into three kinds of cinematic gaze, two of which (that of the camera and that of the audience) are, she argues, subordinated to a third, "that of the characters at each other in the screen illusion" (17). My account of sentimental reflexivity in Capra, and of the crossing of mimetic and pragmatic axes, seems to complicate these claims somewhat in relation to his case. Clarence functions *both* as actor and as a stand-in for the cinematic audience, though Mulvey may well remind me that Clarence happens to be a "character" with a very "odd body" if he has any body at all.

39 See Garth Jowett, Ian Jarvie, and Kathryn Fuller-Seeley, *Children and the Movies: Media Influences and the Payne Fund Controversy* (New York: Cambridge University Press, 1996); see also Robert Sklar, *Movie-Made America: A Cultural History of American Movies* (1975; New York: Random House, 1994), 161–227.

40 See Eric Smoodin, *Regarding Frank Capra: Audience, Celebrity and American Film Studies, 1930–1960* (Durham, NC: Duke University Press, 2004), 76–118.

41 Preston Sturges, *Five Screenplays*, ed. Brian Henderson (Berkeley: University of California Press, 1985), 543. Further references cited parenthetically in the text. Sturges was shooting the film very much in the shadow of *Meet John Doe*, which was released on May 3, 1941. *Sullivan's Travels* went into production on May 12, and wrapped on July 22. Many of the contradictions inherent Capra's post-1934

efforts to realize the possibilities of film as a sociological and artistic medium erupt in *Meet John Doe* in ways that would not have been lost on Sturges. As Dudley Andrew points out, Capra's own "filmic system is as totalitarian and powerful as the political machinations of the film's villain, D. B. Norton." Andrew, "Productive Discord in the System: Hollywood *Meets John Doe*," in Wolfe, *Meet John Doe*, 231.

42 Riskin, *Six Screenplays*, 422.

43 For an account of the role that Capra's films began to play in American classrooms in the 1930s, see Eric Smoodin, "Film Education and Quality Entertainment for Children and Adolescents," in *Regarding Frank Capra*, 76–118.

44 The reference is not casual; Capra worked on the *Our Gang* comedies in the early 1920s.

45 Carney, *American Vision: The Films of Frank Capra* (Cambridge: Cambridge University Press, 1986), 342.

46 Ibid., 342. Carney goes on to complain about the critical fashion "to stigmatize art that uses such devices to generate extreme states of feeling . . . as sentimental." In this he seems to follow Charles Affron's more general claim that "sentimental narratives tend to generate improbabilities in proportion to the strength of the feelings they express." Affron, *Cinema and Sentiment*, 23. On my accounting, of course, the scene's resort to the sentimental has to do not with the extremity of emotion but with its distribution across the sympathetic network.

47 Nick Browne is right, I think, to connect the conclusion of *Mr. Smith* with the pivotal scene involving the farmer in *Mr. Deeds*. But he does not tie either sequence to a sort of self-consciousness about the structure of sentiment, as I outline it in this book. He focuses instead on the question of "speech" in *Mr. Smith* and the practice of ideological justification in *Mr. Deeds*. Browne, "The Politics of Narrative Form: Capra's *Mr. Smith Goes to Washington*," *Wide Angle* 3 (1979): 4–11.

48 The casting of Carey is itself a link with Griffith, for he acted in many of Griffith's films.

49 Capra, *Name above the Title*, 292–93. Further references cited parenthetically in the text.

50 *The Man Who Invented Hollywood: The Autobiography of D. W. Griffith*, ed. James Hart (Louisville: Touchstone Publishing, 1972), xii.

51 Capra, *Name above the Title*, 35–36.

52 Ibid., 57.

53 Ibid., 172.

54 McBride, *Catastrophe of Success*, 63. McBride explains that Capra was alerted to the film early because his friend Blue Washington had a bit part in it.

55 Capra, *Name above the Title*, 186.

56 On the reception history of *Birth of a Nation*, see, for example, Janet Staiger, "*The Birth of a Nation*: Reconsidering Its Reception," in *Interpreting Films: Studies in*

the Historical Reception of American Cinema (Princeton, NJ: Princeton University Press, 1992), 139–53, and Melvyn Stokes, *D. W. Griffith's "The Birth of a Nation"* (New York: Oxford, 2007), 111–70.

57 Capra, *Name above the Title*, 188. Capra told McBride that his decision to use Griffith for the 1936 Oscars led to a problem: "We didn't know where he was. We finally found him in a Kentucky saloon. It took a little doing but he finally agreed. And strangely enough, he did bring the crowd in." McBride, *Catastrophe of Success*, 337.

58 No doubt fueling Capra's rivalry with von Stroheim is the fact that von Stroheim actually worked for Griffith, and later did his part to honor him, notably in a 1948 radio address (now available as a sound recording) that also sounded the theme of Griffith's neglected late reputation.

59 Kaja Silverman, *Male Subjectivity at the Margins* (New York: Routledge, 1992), 93–103.

60 John Brewer, *The Pleasures of the Imagination: English Culture in the Eighteenth Century* (New York: Farrar, Straus and Giroux, 1997), xi.

Introduction to Part 2

1 Audrey Jaffe, for example, notes that Dickens's tale "both recalls and revises those scenes in eighteenth-century fiction that, depicting encounters between charity givers and receivers, model sympathy for readers positioned as witnesses." Jaffe, *Scenes of Sympathy: Identity and Representation in Victorian Fiction* (Ithaca, NY: Cornell University Press, 2000), 30.

2 "The Miser Convinced of His Error," *Sentimental Magazine* (March 1773), 19

3 Ibid., 20

4 Ibid., 21

5 "The Miser Convinced of His Error," *Sentimental Magazine* (April 1773), 58.

6 Adam Smith, *The Theory of Moral Sentiments*, ed. D. D. Raphael and A. L. Macfie (Indianapolis: Liberty Fund, 1982), 130.

7 "The Miser Convinced of His Error," *Sentimental Magazine* (April 1773), 59–60.

8 "To obviate these Difficulties [of long and unvarying prose writings] in the Walk of Science, has given Rise to those various Productions, which are to be met with under the Title of MAGAZINES: At the same Time that they delight by their Variety, they prevent Satiety by the Concisesness of their Essays. But Performances of this Kind, like those of the dramatic Species, must be adapted to the *Ton* [*sic*], or reigning Taste of the Times in which they were written." Advertisement, *Sentimental Magazine*, vol. 1 (March 1773).

9 "The Miser Convinced of His Error," *Sentimental Magazine* (March 1773), 5

10 Republished with slight modifications in George Wright, *The Young Moralist* (1782); in William Darnton and George Wright, *The Young Moralist* (1819); and in an American edition in 1826. See Robert D. Mayo, *The English Novel in the*

Magazines 1740–1815, with a Catalogue of 1375 Magazine Novels and Novelettes (Evanston: Northwestern University Press, 1962). See also Edward W. Pitcher, "Robert Mayo's *The English Novel in the Magazines 1740–1815*: New Facts," *Library*, ser. 5, 31, no. 1 (1976): 20–30. Mayo does not make the connection with *A Christmas Carol*, but he does suggest that these tales had a very wide circulation indeed.

11 See *A Christmas Carol*, radio broadcast, performed December 24, 1939, by Lionel Barrymore, Orson Welles, et al., Campbell Playhouse, Internet Archive audio, http://www.archive.org/details/CampbellPlayhouseAChristmasCarol12241939. For a broader survey, see James Chapman, "God Bless Us, Every One: Movie Adaptations of *A Christmas Carol*," in *Christmas at the Movies: Images of Christmas in American, British and European Cinema*, ed. Mark Connelly (London: I. B. Taurus, 2000), 9–37.

12 There is something about Dickens's and Capra's treatment that casts the Christmas experience as close to the "Sternean ordinary," despite the modern sense of holiday exceptionality that has surrounded it since the Victorian period. Harold Ramis extends the move in his Capraesque *Groundhog Day*, in which the Eternal Return, figured as redemptive acceptance of everyday life, takes place on the holiday that is as close to an ordinary day as any on the American calendar.

Chapter 4

1 Mrs. Cratchit refuses her husband's invitation to toast Scrooge, even after his urging, except for the sake of the day.

2 This staging of one's attendance at one's own funeral seems to be the primary connection between *The Adventures of Tom Sawyer*, the book that Clarence inscribes to George, and the Dickensian source story.

3 See Margaret Atwood's update of the tale in the decidedly unsentimental register of retribution: "Scrooge Nouveau," in *Payback: Debt and the Shadow Side of Wealth* (Toronto: Anansi, 2008), 162–203.

4 Charles Dickens, "A Christmas Carol," in *The Christmas Books*, vol. 1 (Harmondsworth: Penguin, 1971), 68. Further references cited parenthetically in the text.

5 Do we find in Dickens's tale a precedent for one of the most famous tracking shots in all of early cinema, in which King Vidor, in *The Crowd* (1928), has his camera scale the walls of a New York office building to find a young man amid a grid of desks, alone in the company of others?

6 The management of point of view in this scene in the luggage shop is curious. It is basically a single shot lasting almost a minute and a half, broken only by a two-second close-up of Joe the shopkeeper's face. We see him and George mostly from the side in a midrange two-shot, though the camera begins on Joe, pans to George, and freezes on George's face for more than twenty seconds. The orthogonal angle of this kind of two-shot is markedly identified with Clarence's

point of view, for when the frame freezes on the face of James Stewart, Clarence comments first (as noted earlier) on the freezing of the frame ("What'd you stop it for?") and then on what he can see in it ("It's a good face"). Much the same can be said, for example, about the orthogonal point of view on George's poignant encounter with Mr. Gower about the poison pills and on his final conversation with his father at the dining room table.

7   The proliferation of levels here, as in Capra, is suggested by the passage in which the narrator tells us that he is as near to us as Scrooge is to the spirit.

8   See Smith, *The Theory of Moral Sentiments*, ed. D. D. Raphael and A. L. Macfie (Indianapolis: Liberty Fund, 1982), 12. And so, with the dead: "[we lodge] our own living souls in their inanimated bodies, and thence conceiv[e] what would be our own emotions in this case" (13). Cf. "my emotion . . . arises from bringing your case home to myself, from putting myself in your situation, and thence conceiving what I should feel in the like circumstances" (317). See also, for example, pp. 16 and 73.

9   Screenplay in Jeanine Basinger, *The "It's a Wonderful Life" Book* (New York: Knopf, 1986), 131.

10 Garrett Stewart writes suggestively about point of view and temporality in this freeze-frame in *Between Film and Screen: Modernism's Photo Synthesis* (Chicago: University of Chicago Press, 1999), 15–16.

11 I thank Neil Verma for pointing out for me that "suit case" might have been a little less unusual in 1928, when the scene is set, which means that Capra might have had his flagging of the term without violating historical verisimilitude.

12 Raymond Williams, "Structures of Feeling," in *Marxism and Literature* (Oxford: Oxford University Press, 1977), 128–35.

13 *The Friends: A Sentimental History* (London, 1754), iii–iv. The philology of the new term "sentimental" has been worked out in some detail, including that fascinating point that the German translation of Sterne's *Sentimental Journey* in 1768 required a new German coinage, *Empfindsam*. For the most detailed philological tracing of "sentimental" and its cousins, especially in relation to Sterne's impact, see Erik Erämetsa, *A Study of the Word "Sentimental" and of other Linguistic Characteristics of Eighteenth Century Sentimentalism in England* (Helsinki: Academia Scientiarum Fennica, 1951), 18–63. Erämetsa's work is extended and supplemented in Marie Banfield, "From Sentiment to Sentimentality: A Nineteenth-Century Lexicographical Search," *19: Interdisciplinary Studies in the Long Nineteenth Century* 4 (2007). The digital archive of ECCO, aided by ARTFL, has made it possible to update this philology through the finding that the term appears in the phrase "sentimental soul" as early as 1743.

14 The title's "reference to Sterne is deliberate and self-conscious," as David J. Denby points out in *Sentimental Narrative and the Social Order in France, 1760–1820* (Cambridge: Cambridge University Press, 1994), 26.

15 *Barclay's Dictionary* (London, 1812), 780.

16 Katie Trumpener suggests that Henry Mackenzie's *Man of Feeling* (1771) may supply a particular kind of link from Schiller's essay back to Scottish Enlightenment accounts of sentiment. Trumpener, *Bardic Nationalism: The Romantic Novel and the British Empire* (Princeton, NJ: Princeton University Press, 1997), 112.

17 Friedrich Schiller, "On Naïve and Sentimental Poetry," in *Essays*, trans. Walter Hinderer and Daniel O. Dahlstrom (New York: Continuum, 1993), 204. The German citation is from *Schillers Werke, Philosophische Schriften*, ed. Benno von Wiese, vol. 20, pt. 1 (Weimar: Hermann Böhlaus Nachfolger, 1962–1963), 440.

18 Schiller, "Naïve and Sentimental Poetry," 204. Cf. *Schillers Werke, Philosophische Schriften*, 20 (pt. 1): 441.

19 Schiller, "Naïve and Sentimental Poetry," 204.

20 William Wordsworth, *William Wordsworth: The Major Works*, ed. Stephen Gill (Oxford: Oxford University Press, 2000), 133.

21 Frank D. McConnell, *The Spoken Seen: Film and the Romantic Imagination* (Baltimore: Johns Hopkins University Press, 1975), 112–14.

22 Goethe to Schiller, August 16, 1797, in *Correspondence between Goethe and Schiller, 1794–1805*, trans. Liselotte Dieckmann, Studies in Modern German Literature, vol. 60 (New York: P. Lang, 1994).

23 Laurence Sterne, *The Life and Opinions of Tristram Shandy, Gentleman*, ed. Ian Campbell Ross, rev. ed. (Oxford: Oxford University Press, 2009), 522–23. Subsequent references given parenthetically in the text.

24 Quoted in Ian Jack, introduction to *A Sentimental Journey through France and Italy* (Oxford: Oxford University Press, 1984), xi.

25 Samuel Johnson, *The Lives of the Poets*, ed. John H. Middendorf, *The Works of Samuel Johnson*, vol. 21 (New Haven, CT: Yale University Press, 2010), 26.

26 Jay Clayton helpfully connects some of these features in the survival of Dickensianism, though not of Sternean sentimentalism, in pointing to a certain "kind of irony": "Incongruity, contradiction, the juxtaposition of mismatched signifiers and ill-assorted values—these are the tokens by which Dickens travels today." Clayton, *Charles Dickens in Cyberspace: The Afterlife of the Nineteenth Century in Postmodern Culture* (Oxford: Oxford University Press, 2003), 152.

27 *The Letters of the Late Rev. Mr. Laurence Sterne, to his Most Intimate Friends, on Various Occasions*, ed. Lydia Sterne de Medalle (London: R. Sammer, 1797), 173.

28 For Adam Smith's observations on the brevity of human sympathy, see *Theory of Moral Sentiments*, 21–22.

29 Schiller, "Naïve and Sentimental Poetry," 441.

30 The phrase belongs to Andrew Kippis in the *Biographia Britannica*, 2nd edition (1789), 4:294; cited in Isabel Rivers, *Reason, Grace and Sentiment: A Study of the Language of Religion and Ethics in England, 1660–1780*, 2 vols. (Cambridge: Cambridge University Press, 1991, 2000), 2:152.

31 There is a longstanding controversy within Schiller scholarship, from Ernst Cassirer to Frederick Beiser, about just what Shaftesbury meant to Schiller. Beiser's

skeptical account can be found in *Schiller as Philosopher: A Re-Examination* (Oxford: Oxford University Press, 2005), 91–93.

32 Anthony Ashley Cooper, Third Earl of Shaftesbury, "Soliloquy, or Advice to an Author," in *Characteristics of Men, Manners, Opinions, Times*, ed. Lawrence Klein (Cambridge: Cambridge University Press, 1999), 77. Subsequent citations by page references in the text. Adam Smith, as we shall see below, adapts this figure of the mirror to represent the reflecting face of the spectator.

33 One passage in the "Soliloquy" that seems especially to anticipate Schiller's account of his famous dyad of the 1790s is Shaftesbury's account of "the great difference . . . between such persons as have been taught by nature only [he mentions "good rustics and plain artisans"] and such as by reflection and the assistance of art have learned to form those motions which on experience are found the easiest and most natural" (85).

34 See above, introduction, 7, 10.

35 Shaftesbury repeatedly asserts not only an identity of moral and aesthetic judgment, and correspondence of inward and outward sense, but also a congruence among the categories of symmetry and proportion, on the one hand, and harmony on the other. Thus, in concluding "Soliloquy," he argues that just as harmony, symmetry, and proportion have a foundation in nature, whatever may be the errors of local judgment, so "virtue has the same fixed standard": "The same numbers, harmony and proportion will have place in morals and are discoverable in the characters and affections of mankind." Shaftesbury, *Characteristics of Men*, 159. Such a system of correspondence seems to underlie Sterne's parallel mobilization of harmony and geometry to dramatize the operation of sentiment in this representative episode. Musical thematics are reprised in its sequel in *Sentimental Journey*, when Yorick touches the "string" by which Maria holds on to her dog, a replacement for the goat, and the string begins to "vibrate." See below, chapter 5.

36 The episode emblematizes the sentimentalist's interest, flagged by Marx in his poem "Sentimentale Seele" (Sentimental Souls), in the positioning of the human uncertainly between the animal world and the divine world. Heather Keenleyside offers an incisive reading of the Maria episode in "Animals and Other Persons" (PhD diss., University of Chicago, 2009).

37 Shaftesbury, *Characteristics of Men*, 74.

38 Ibid., 75. "The world . . . serves as a tutor to persons of an inferior rank" (94). It also serves as a tutor to modern authors more generally: "Our modern authors . . . are turned and modelled, as themselves confess, by the public relish and current humour of the times. They regulate themselves by the irregular fancy of the world, and frankly own they are preposterous and absurd in order to accommodate themselves to the genius of the age. In our days the audience makes the poet, and the bookseller the author, with what profit to the public or what prospect of lasting fame and honour to the writer, let anyone who has judgment imagine" (118).

39 There is an interesting complication in Shaftesbury's choice of soliloquy as the paradigm for the discipline he recommends to authors. One of the key features of the soliloquy as it was developed on the Elizabethan-Jacobean stage is the way it combines internal and external aspects of spectatorship. The soliloquy was a moment in a drama where the speaking character could be understood to be addressing most directly either himself (or herself) *or* the audience. In Michael Fried's terms, which were developed to account for theories of spectacle in the decades following Shaftesbury, we might say that the soliloquy was a moment of extreme theatricality and extreme self-absorption at one and the same time.

40 *Spectator*, no. 1 (March 2, 1711).

41 See David Marshall, *The Figure of Theater: Shaftesbury, Defoe, Adam Smith, and George Eliot* (New York: Columbia University Press, 1986), and Jean-Christophe Agnew, *Worlds Apart: The Market and the Theater in Anglo-American Thought, 1550–1750* (Cambridge: Cambridge University Press, 1986).

42 For example, Lisa A. Freeman, *Character's Theater: Genre and Identity on the Eighteenth-Century English Stage* (Philadelphia: University of Pennsylvania Press, 2002), 12–16.

43 The virtues of reflection are also central to Steele's reforming drama, in other words, and their bearing on issues of sentimental probability is discussed below in chapter 6.

44 I am thinking here of a line of critical commentary on the novel that runs from Henry James to Percy Lubbock to Wayne Booth to Gérard Genette to Mieke Bal and more recently to Dorothy Hale.

45 Cynthia Wall, *The Prose of Things: Transformations of Descriptions in the Eighteenth Century* (Chicago: University of Chicago Press, 2006), 142.

46 Ibid., 144. See also Wall's discussion of how early readers of Richardson stressed "the dramatically visual qualities of his work," in "The Spaces of *Clarissa* in Text and Film," in *Eighteenth-Century Fiction on Screen*, ed. Robert Mayer (Cambridge: Cambridge University Press, 2002), 111.

47 Wall, *Prose of Things*, 145.

48 James Grantham Turner, writing of the spirited debates about *Pamela* in the 1740s, notes that each side "assumes that producing subjectivity renders it physical, supplying a body for the fictional 'nobody,'" and that "the sentimental or internal-empathetic reception therefore relies on the scenic or external-spectatorial imagination that the novel's critics use against it." Turner, "Novel Panic: Picture and Performance in the Reception of Richardson's *Pamela*," *Representations*, no. 48 (Fall 1994), 73. Turner builds on the framework that Catherine Gallagher would make central to *Nobody's Story: The Vanishing Acts of Women Writers in the Marketplace, 1670–1820* (Berkeley: University of California Press, 1995).

49 Wall, *Prose of Things*, 146.

50 For resonances of this new sort of sentimental space in mid-eighteenth-century British and French culture more generally, see Peter de Bolla on "the culture

of visuality" in *The Education of the Eye: Painting, Landscape, and Architecture in Eighteenth-Century Britain* (Stanford, CA: Stanford University Press, 2003), 14–71, and especially his account of Smithian space in Vauxhall Gardens, 71–81. See also Emma Barker, *Greuze and the Painting of Sentiment* (Cambridge: Cambridge University Press, 2005), especially her account of Greuze's 1761 painting *L'accordee de village* (*The Village Bride*), 46–64.

51 Frances Burney, *Evelina* (Harmondsworth: Penguin, 1994), 219. Consider, too, Evelina's report of a triangulation of gazes just a few pages later, when she is being harassed by Mr. Smith: "I could not endure that Sir Clement, whose eyes followed him with looks of the most surprised curiosity, should witness his unwelcome familiarity" (225).

52 Smith, *Theory of Moral Sentiments*, 143.

53 Indeed, Smith's engagement with "the world" has led commentators since his own time to charge his moral philosophy with conventionalism and conformism. For a recent defense of Smith, and his notion of conscience, against the former charge, see Fonna Forman-Barzilai, *Adam Smith and the Circles of Sympathy* (Cambridge: Cambridge University Press, 2010), 96–102; for a recent defense against the latter charge, see Ryan Hanley, *Adam Smith and the Character of Virtue* (Cambridge: Cambridge University Press, 2009), 135–50. On Smith and masculine stoicism, see Julie Ellison, *Cato's Tears and the Making of Anglo-American Emotion* (Chicago: University of Chicago Press, 1999), 10–12.

54 For an early attempt to link the two writers, see Kenneth MacLean, "Imagination and Sympathy: Sterne and Adam Smith," *Journal of the History of Ideas* 10 (June 1949): 399–410.

55 Annette Baier, *A Progress of Sentiments: Reflections on Hume's Treatise* (Cambridge, MA: Harvard University Press, 1991), 180. And see Blakey Vermeule's elaboration of a related insight by Baier, on the "indirectness of the indirect passions," in her discussion of "The Spectator Morality of the Enlightenment." Vermeule, *The Party of Humanity: Writing Moral Psychology in Eighteenth-Century Britain* (Baltimore: Johns Hopkins University Press, 2000), 155–57.

56 In Adam Smith's version of this analysis, he cites John Locke, behind Hutcheson, as having called the faculty in question that of "reflection." Smith, *Theory of Moral Sentiments*, 322.

57 Gilles Deleuze, *Empiricism and Subjectivity: An Essay on Hume's Theory of Human Nature* (New York: Columbia University Press, 1991), 26.

58 For a good account of the tensions between Hume's and Smith's account of sentiment, as these mattered to Sterne, see Lynn Festa, *Sentimental Figures of Empire in Eighteenth-Century Britain and France* (Baltimore: Johns Hopkins University Press, 2006), 22–36, 89–90. Dror Wahrman, also "listens in" to these intellectual debates, monitoring them, and the fiction contemporary with them, for evidence to block casual assumptions about the birth in this moment of a modern self grounded in psychological interiority, 185–89. Like Festa, Jonathan Lamb con-

siders the imperial dimension of these issues in *The Evolution of Sympathy in the Long Eighteenth Century* (London: Pickering & Chatto, 2009), 111–14.

59 Smith, *Theory of Moral Sentiments*, 327–42. Smith is one of the thinkers who proposes what J. G. A. Pocock has called the commercial reinvention of "virtue." Pocock, *Virtue, Commerce, and History* (Cambridge: Cambridge University Press, 1985), 157–92. See also, of course, Albert O. Hirschman, *The Passions and the Interests: Political Arguments for Capitalism before Its Triumph* (Princeton, NJ: Princeton University Press, 1977), 9–66.

60 Smith, *Theory of Moral Sentiments*, 112. Robert Mitchell attends to these aspects of Smith, in instructive comparison with Rousseau, in *Sympathy and the State in the Romantic Era: Systems, State Finance, and the Shadows of Futurity* (New York: Routledge, 2007), 61–92. Like Mitchell, Mary Fairclough attends to sympathy as part of a nineteenth century debate about mass contagion in her forthcoming *The Romantic Crowd: Sympathy, Controversy and Print Culture* (Cambridge: Cambridge University Press, 2013).

61 Though the logic of changing point of view seems implicit in Smith's key concept of an "imaginary change of situation," with its capacity to provide external perspective on our character, Smith himself reserves the language of point of view for a different moment in the transaction, one in which we agree or disagree (and thereby approve or disapprove) of the other person's response to what has befallen them—i.e., to their case. See below, pp. 240–42.

62 See, for example, Maureen Harkin's introduction to her edition of Mackenzie's *The Man of Feeling* (Peterborough, Ontario: Broadview Press, 2005), 9–19. See also Susan J. Manning's introduction to her edition of Mackenzie's *Julia de Roubigné* (East Linton, Scotland: Tuckwell Press, 1999), xv–xxiv. Rae Greiner has lately followed the logic of Smithian sympathy into the nineteenth-century novel and beyond, where she attempts to track the emergence of the later concept of "empathy." Greiner, "Thinking of Me Thinking of You: Sympathy v. Empathy in the Realist Novel," *Victorian Studies* 53, no. 3 (2011): 417–26. And see also her helpful online essay for *BRANCH*: "1909: The Introduction of 'Empathy' into English," *Britain, Representation, and Nineteenth-Century History*, an extension of Romanticism and Victorianism on the Net (RaVoN) (2012). Though not grounded in the tradition of Smith's "impartial spectator," Amanda Anderson's argument, in *The Powers of Distance: Cosmopolitanism and the Cultivation of Detachment* (Princeton, NJ: Princeton University Press, 2001), is relevant, perhaps counterintuitively, to the reception of Smithian sympathy in the high Victorian period.

63 Sir Walter Scott, *Waverley: or 'Tis Sixty Years Since*, ed. Claire Lamont (Oxford: Oxford University Press, 1986), 328.

64 Ibid., 329.

65 The sentimental novel follows a different course in France, in part because it has a different starting point there. Margaret Jacobs, in *The Sentimental Educa-*

tion of the Novel (Princeton, NJ: Princeton University Press, 1999), suggests that sentimental poetics first emerges in France with *La nouvelle Héloïse* (1761). This seems right, but there, in Rousseau's novel, what is termed "an authentically new spectacle" is something that develops from the *failure* of modern young readers to "observe, judge, reflect" in the fashion of British sentimentalism. They do not cultivate moral sentiments but instead are deliriously "filled with the single sentiment that occupies them"—that is, precisely not the sentimental in Schiller's British-oriented sense of the term: "Inventing among themselves a world different from ours, there they create an authentically new spectacle." Rousseau, *Julie, or the New Heloise,* trans. Philip Stewart and Jean Vaché (Hanover, NH: University Press of New England, 1997), 11. One later watershed for the sentimental novel in France is surely Flaubert's *Sentimental Education* itself, the subject of an apposite analysis in terms of split-level probabilities in Pierre Bourdieu, *The Rules of Art: Genesis and Structure of the Literary Field,* trans. Susan Emanuel (Stanford, CA: Stanford University Press, 1996), esp. the section on "necessary accidents," 20–25.

Chapter 5

1 George's telephone negotiation with his childhood friend–turned-globetrotter, Sam Wainwright, in behalf of starting a plastics factory in Bedford Falls (rather than elsewhere), would be an example of this translation of travel into sympathy.
2 Charles Dickens, "A Christmas Carol," in *The Christmas Books,* vol. 1 (Harmondsworth: Penguin, 1971), 61. Further references cited parenthetically in the text.
3 Jeanine Basinger, *The "It's a Wonderful Life" Book* (New York: Knopf, 1986), 140.
4 Laurence Sterne, *A Sentimental Journey,* ed. Ian Jack and Tim Parnell, new ed. (Oxford: Oxford University Press, 2003), 98. Further references cited parenthetically in the text. This celebrated passage may well be one that Marx has in his satirical sights with his wry lyric "Sentimentale Seelen." See below, chapter 8.
5 Another part of the scene's figuration has to do with Yorick's tromping on the string by which Maria retains her dog, toward the close of the scene. In asking Maria if her heart is "still so warm," he realizes that he has "touch'd upon the string on which hung all her sorrows," for she is thrown into a "wistful disorder" that is remedied only by the playing of her flute, at which point the string "ceased to vibrate" (96–97).
6 For an exploration of this trope in the period, see Miranda Burgess, "Transport: Mobility, Anxiety, and the Romantic Poetics of Feeling," *Studies in Romanticism* 49, no. 2 (Summer 2010): 229–60. Burgess is concerned with anxiety, rather than sentiment, and looks forward to I. A. Richards on tenor and vehicle rather than back to Henry More on the vehicular hypothesis.
7 Cf. Marx's equivocal ejaculation "Himmel" in "Sentimentale Seelen." See below, chapter 8.

8 The importance of "order" in *A Sentimental Journey* is signaled in the very first sentence, produced in medias res: "—They order, said I, this matter better in France—" (3). The fact of the interruptive dash without a sense of what it is interrupting, and of the pronoun without a referent, performs a problem of "order" in itself.

9 Laurence Sterne, *The Life and Opinions of Tristram Shandy, Gentleman*, ed. Ian Campbell Ross, rev. ed. (Oxford: Oxford University Press, 2009), 445.

10 Douglas Lane Patey, *Probability and Literary Form: Philosophic Theory and Literary Practice in the Augustan Age* (Cambridge: Cambridge University Press, 1984), 221–23.

11 On More's response to Spinoza, see Jonathan I. Israel, *Radical Enlightenment: Philosophy and the Making of Modernity, 1650–1750* (Oxford: Oxford University Press, 2001), 599–609. Latitudinarian sentimentalism represents an alternative path to the Spinozist tradition that Israel usefully tracks, in this and subsequent volumes, through the eighteenth-century and beyond.

12 Daniel Garber, John Henry, Lynn Joy, and Alan Gabbey, "New Doctrines of Body and Its Powers, Place, and Space," *The Cambridge History of Seventeenth-Century Philosophy*, vol. 1, ed. Daniel Garber and Michael Ayers (New York: Cambridge University Press, 1998), 581.

13 Ibid., 590.

14 Henry More, *Immortality of the Soul* (1659), later quoted in Benjamin Camfield, *A Theological Discourse of Angels, and their Ministries* (London, 1678), 16.

15 See Sarah Rivett, *The Science of the Soul in Colonial New England* (Chapel Hill: University of North Carolina Press, 2011); for related issues in the early Republic, see Sarah Knott, "The Patient's Case: Sentimental Empiricism and Knowledge in the Early American Republic," *William and Mary Quarterly*, ser. 3, 62 (October 2010): 645–76.

16 Joseph Priestley, "Of the Vehicle of the Soul," in *Disquisitions Relating to Matter and Spirit*, vol. 1, 2nd ed. (Birmingham, 1782), 103–10.

17 There is a long line of critical commentary on the relation between the figure of the "man of feeling" and the Latitudinarian notion of sensibility, though none of it makes the connection to the vehicular conceits in Sterne and others. The seminal essay, published by R. S. Crane in the first volume of *ELH*, is "Suggestions toward a Genealogy of the 'Man of Feeling,'" reprinted in Crane, *The Idea of the Humanities*, 2 vols. (Chicago: University of Chicago Press, 1967), 1:188–213. Decades later, Donald Grene attempted a systematic demolition of Crane's arguments in "Latitudinarianism and Sensibility: The Genealogy of the 'Man of Feeling' Reconsidered," *Modern Philology* 75 (1977): 159–83. Part of Grene's critique was that Crane's account was too narrow in its line of descent. Chester Chapin reviewed the controversy in light of the role played by Shaftesbury, and the distinction between the benevolent man and the man of feeling, in "Shaftesbury and the Man of Feeling," *Modern Philology* 81 (August 1983): 47–50. On the

function of narrative fragmentation in this tradition, see Everett Zimmerman, "Fragments of History and *The Man of Feeling*: From Richard Bentley to Walter Scott," *Eighteenth-Century Studies* 23 (1990): 283–300. See also chapter 6 below.

18 Margaret Cavendish, "Description of a New World, Called The Blazing World" (1666), in *Political Writings* (Cambridge: Cambridge University Press, 2003), 80–81.

19 Thomas Brown, *The Late Converts Exposed; or, The Reasons of Mr. Bays's Changing His Religion* (London, 1690), 43.

20 Leonard Trawick featured Tucker's text in his collection *Backgrounds of Romanticism* (Bloomington: Indiana University Press, 1967).

21 Abraham Tucker, *The Light of Nature Pursued*, vol. 4 (London, 1768), 12.

22 Ibid., 125–26.

23 Ibid., 135.

24 Ibid., 130.

25 Mary Hays, *Memoirs of Emma Courtney*, vol. 1 (London, 1796), 177–78.

26 *Sentimental Magazine* (March 1773), 5.

27 W. B. Yeats, *Mythologies* (Whitefish, MT: Kessinger Publishing, 2003), 349.

28 Preface to *Lyrical Ballads* (1800), in *Prose Works of William Wordsworth*, ed. W. J. B. Owen and J. W. Smyser, 3 vols. (Oxford: Clarendon Press, 1974), 1:150. On allegories of walking in Wordsworth see Celeste Langan, *Romantic Vagrancy: Wordsworth and the Simulation of Freedom* (Cambridge: Cambridge University Press, 1995), 139–224. Langan also points to "the final collapse of any simple distinction between moving and being moved" in the symbolic world that develops around the figure of the Pedlar (255).

29 See below, chapter 6.

30 Charles Dickens, *A Tale of Two Cities*, ed. Richard Maxwell (Harmondsworth: Penguin, 2003), 5–6. In addition to the vehicular conceit deeply embedded in the Latitudinarian discourse of the soul, one suspects that Montaigne's essay "On Coaches" is at work behind these deployments by Dickens and, especially, Sterne, who was much engaged with early modern wit. See Montaigne, *The Complete Essays*, trans. M. A. Screech (Harmondsworth: Penguin, 1993), 1016–37. See also Thomas De Quincey's masterpiece essay "The English Mail-Coach," in *Selected Writings of Thomas De Quincey* (New York: Random House, 1947), 913–81, esp. the first section, "The Glory of Motion."

31 Tom Gunning, "The Cinema of Attraction: Early Film, Its Spectator and the Avant-Garde," *Wide Angle* 8, nos. 3–4 (1986): 65

32 I thank Terry Castle for pointing this out to me.

33 It is worth pointing out that other crucial scenes in the film take place at railway stations. Furthermore, two turning points in the plot involve closely parallel scenes in which Lisa says goodbye to males named Stefan, each of whom promises

to see her in "two weeks." One is her lover, the other the son she has by him. The man fails to keep his promise, and the boy dies because the railway car in which she installs him is infected with typhus.

34 Cavell, *Pursuits of Happiness: The Hollywood Comedy of Remarriage* (Cambridge, MA: Harvard University Press, 1981), 1–44.

35 Ophüls's bravura camera movement is matched by his provocative play with camera location, which explores the ambiguities of point of view implicit in the conventions of Hollywood narrative voice-over.

36 But perhaps less surprising in light of his early study of David Hume. Deleuze, *Empiricism and Subjectivity: An Essay on Hume's Theory of Human Nature*, trans. Constantin V. Boundas (New York: Columbia University Press, 1991).

37 Gilles Deleuze, *Cinema 1: The Movement-Image*, trans. Hugh Tomlinson and Barbara Habberjam (Minneapolis: University of Minnesota, 1986); Jean Epstein, *Esprit de Cinéma* (Geneva: Jeheber, 1955). Further citations to Deleuze given parenthetically in the text.

38 Gilles Deleuze and Félix Guattari, *A Thousand Plateaus: Capitalism and Schizophrenia*, trans. Brian Massumi (Minneapolis: University of Minnesota Press, 1987), 167–91.

39 Jean Epstein, "Magnification and Other Writings," trans. Stuart Liebman, *October*, no. 3 (Spring 1977), 9. "Soul," here, as Epstein goes on to explain, is connected to motion: "I have never understood motionless close-ups. They sacrifice their essence, which is movement. . . . The close-up, the keystone of the cinema, is the maximum expression of this photogeny of movement. When static, it verges on contradiction" (9–10). For two divergent recent discussions of Béla Balázs, Epstein, and the theory of the close-up, see Jacques Aumont, *Du visage au Cinéma* (Paris: Editions de l'Etoile/Cahiers du Cinéma [distributed by Seuil], 1992), 77–101, and Mary Ann Doane, "The Close-Up: Scale and Detail in the Cinema," *Differences: A Journal of Feminist Cultural Studies* 14, no. 3 (Fall 2003): 89–111. On the face of sentiment, see William Rothman, "Pathos and Transfiguration in the Face of the Camera: A Reading of Stella Dallas," in *The "I" of the Camera: Essays in Film Criticism, History and Aesthetics*, 2nd ed. (Cambridge: Cambridge University Press, 2004), 87–95. And see also Noa Steimatsky's suggestive account of primal skepticism about the cinematic face in "What the Clerk Saw: Face to Face with *The Wrong Man*," *Framework* 48 (Fall 2007), 111–36—part of a forthcoming book-length study of the close-up and the face in film.

40 On the relevance of literary history for Deleuze's concept, and vice versa, see my "Edgeworth and Scott: The Literature of Reterritorialization," in *Repossessing the Romantic Past*, ed. Heather Glen and Paul Hamilton (Cambridge: Cambridge University Press, 2006), 119–39. For a more detailed treatment of Deleuze on the affection-image and the close-up in this connection, see my "The Affection-Image and the Movement-Image," in *Afterimages of Gilles Deleuze's*

Film Philosophy, ed. D. N. Rodowick (Minneapolis: University of Minnesota Press, 2010), 235–58.

Chapter 6

1 Ian Hacking, *The Emergence of Probability* (Cambridge: Cambridge University Press, 1975), 57–62, 78–79.

2 Douglas Lane Patey, *Probability and Literary Form: Philosophic Theory and Literary Practice in the Augustan Age* (Cambridge: Cambridge University Press, 1984).

3 William Hill Brown, *The Power of Sympathy* (New York: Penguin, 1996). This book is especially interesting in the deployment of its central constellation of terms. On the one hand, it raises questions about what it would mean "to investigate the great springs by which we are actuated, or account for the operation of SYMPATHY" (77). On the other, it seeks to counter a new fashion of the 1790s that takes "sentiment" to be "out of date"—that is, it aligns itself with "sentiment" against the risks of "sensibility" (1), rather as Jane Austen will do in *Sense and Sensibility* two decades later. For more on this book in this context, see my "Placing *The Power of Sympathy*: Transatlantic Sentiments and the 'First American Novel,'" in *The Atlantic Enlightenment*, ed. Susan Manning and Francis D. Cogliano (Aldershot, UK: Ashgate, 2008).

4 Stuart M. Tave, *The Amiable Humorist: A Study in the Comic Theory and Criticism of the Eighteenth and Early Nineteenth Centuries* (Chicago: University of Chicago Press, 1960), 202–3.

5 In the 1815 "Essay Supplementary," Wordsworth wrote: "Passion . . . is derived from a word which signifies *suffering*; but the connection which suffering has with effort, with exertion, and *action*, is immediate and inseparable" (emphasis in original). Wordsworth, *Prose Works*, 3:81.

6 Audrey Jaffe suggests that "sympathy threatens the foundation of feeling on which individual identity is supposedly based" and points to scenes in Victorian fiction that "project an image of sympathetic identification as a loss of identity." Jaffe, *Scenes of Sympathy: Identity and Representation in Victorian Fiction* (Ithaca, NY: Cornell University Press, 2000), 16, 18. Jaffe had earlier published a kind of pilot essay for this book that centered, not surprisingly, on Dickens's *A Christmas Carol*. See Jaffe, "Spectacular Sympathy: Visuality and Ideology in Dickens's *A Christmas Carol*," in *Victorian Literature and the Victorian Visual Imagination*, ed. Carol T. Christ and John O. Jordan (Berkeley: University of California Press, 1995), 327–44.

7 In *It's a Wonderful Life* the happy resolution is figured in rather conspicuous terms as a form of *saving*. George Bailey is on the verge of suicide at the moment when his saving is undertaken in answer to the prayers of his family and friends. Yet saving takes multiple forms in the film. The money that flows into the Baileys' house on Christmas Eve may have its origins in the mama dollar and papa dollar that survived the run on the bank, but the means of financial

growth is not that of earned interest on savings but rather sympathetic interest on the part of the townspeople. The saving of George by Clarence, the saving of the townspeople by the Bailey Building and Loan, and the saving of the Building and Loan itself are part of a wider scheme of saving that goes back to the first vignette in the heavenly screening of George's life, when he saves his brother from drowning. The notion of saving is also thus, from the earliest moment, tied to the notion of risk, for George clearly risks his life to save his brother's. And here as throughout, this risky kind of saving is expressed by the figure of "taking a plunge." Clarence has to explain to George that he induced George to save him as a way of saving George, saving his soul. Thinking back to Dickens's own casting of his trope, we could say that Marley and the spirits come to save Scrooge's soul from his compulsion to save and hoard. Dickens is as invested in the relation of sympathy and the soul as Capra is, but, as we have seen, both the embodiment and the figuration of sympathy in Dickens take a different form.

8 William B. Warner, "Formulating Fiction: Romancing the General Reader in Early Modern Britain," in *Cultural Institutions of the Novel*, ed. Deidre Lynch and William B. Warner (Durham, NC: Duke University Press, 1996), 302–5. "Reception," as James Grantham Turner puts it, "seems too mild a word for the Pamela craze that swept through eighteenth-century Europe and inspired emulation in virtually every medium." Turner, "Novel Panic: Picture and Performance in the Reception of Richardson's *Pamela*," *Representations*, no. 48 (Fall 1994), 70.

9 Laurence Sterne, *A Sentimental Journey*, ed. Ian Jack and Tim Parnell, new ed. (Oxford: Oxford University Press, 2003), 24. Subsequent references cited by page number in the text.

10 See below, chapter 8.

11 *Prose Works of William Wordsworth*, ed. W. J. B. Owen and J. W. Smyser, 3 vols. (Oxford: Clarendon Press, 1974), 1:128.

12 Ibid., 1:126, 128.

13 Jonathan Lamb, *Sterne's Fiction and the Double Principle* (Cambridge: Cambridge University Press, 1989), 76–79.

14 Laurence Sterne, *The Life and Opinions of Tristram Shandy, Gentleman*, ed. Ian Campbell Ross, rev. ed. (Oxford: Oxford University Press, 2009), 445. Subsequent references cited by page number in the text.

15 See Lamb, *Double Principle*, 77.

16 William James, *The Principles of Psychology*, 3 vols. (Cambridge, MA: Harvard University Press, 1981), 2:1065–66.

17 In a chapter on *Sentimental Journey* in his *Laurence Sterne and the Argument about Design* (Totowa, NJ: Barnes & Noble, 1982), Mark Loveridge includes some interesting remarks about Sterne and Shaftesbury but, strangely, nothing about M. Dessein and his role in the text. Cf. Hacking's chapter on "Design" in *Emergence of Probability*, 166–75.

18 For an account of some related issues regarding what might be called "moral

mechanics" in *Tristram Shandy*, see Sigurd Burckhardt, "*Tristram Shandy's* Law of Gravity," *ELH* 28, no. 1 (March 1961): 70–88. See also my "Man Fell with Apples: The Moral Mechanics of *Don Juan*," in *Byron's Poetry and Prose*, 2nd ed., ed. Alice K. Levine (New York: W. W. Norton, 2009), 993–1008.

19 The kind of confusion inscribed here is well known to beginning students of literature when they first pass from talking about characters and their motives to talking about authors and *their* characters—an experience of metalepsis.

20 See Lamb's perceptive discussion of this kind of moment in Sterne, in *Double Principle*, 29–30.

21 A further bilingual pun can be found here in the notion of things "drawn" or taken from a source.

22 Lamb builds his account of Sterne in part on Jina Politi's account of syllepsis in *The Novel and Its Presuppositions: Changes in the Conceptual Structure of Novels in the 18th and 19th Centuries* (Amsterdam: A. M. Hakkert, 1976). "Syllepsis," Politi writes of Sterne's "world model," transcends "its mere rhetorical function as a mode of wit and becomes the great principle of union and generation" (144–45). Metalepsis, as we shall see, also plays its part.

23 Sir Walter Scott, *Waverley: or 'Tis Sixty Years Since*, ed. Claire Lamont (Oxford: Oxford University Press, 1986), 24.

24 For a fuller discussion of the novel-romance distinction in Scott, see my *England in 1819: The Politics of Literary Culture and the Case of Romantic Historicism* (Chicago: University of Chicago Press, 1998), 143–46.

25 On the Romantic novel and the postal system, see Mary Favret, *Romantic Correspondence: Women, Politics, and the Fiction of Letters* (Cambridge: Cambridge University Press, 1993), 197–213.

26 Scott, *Waverley*, 63. There are other variations on this theme. Wordsworth's sylleptic representation of walking and writing as conflated activities, so deftly analyzed by Celeste Langan, might be rethought in terms of Wordsworth's implicit claim to be working without a vehicle, without a medium—to be working out, that is, what Geoffrey Hartman long ago called "the unmediated vision." See Langan, *Romantic Vagrancy*, esp. 161–75, and Geoffrey Hartman, *The Unmediated Vision: An Interpretation of Wordsworth, Hopkins, Rilke, and Valéry* (New Haven, CT: Yale University Press, 1954).

27 Barbara J. Shapiro, *Probability and Certainty in Seventeenth-Century England: A Study of the Relationships between Natural Science, Religion, History, Law, and Literature* (Princeton, NJ: Princeton University Press, 1983), 228–32.

28 Douglas Lane Patey, *Probability and Literary Form*, 222. See also Jesse Molesworth on calculation in *Tristram Shandy*, in *Chance and the Eighteenth-Century Novel: Realism, Probability, Magic* (Cambridge: Cambridge University Press, 2010), 189–206, and Thomas M. Kavanagh on French fiction about gaming and gambling in the period, in *Enlightenment and the Shadows of Chance: The Novel*

and the Culture of Gambling in Eighteenth-Century France (Baltimore: Johns Hopkins University Press, 1993) esp. 9–29.

29 Patey, Probability and Literary Form, 220, 222.

30 Henry Mackenzie, The Man of Feeling, ed. Brian Vickers (London: Oxford University Press, 1967), 53. Among the many genealogies for the "man of feeling," one must not forget the traditions of Christian folly. But see R. S. Crane, "Suggestions toward a Genealogy of the 'Man of Feeling,'" ELH 1, no. 3 (December 1934): 205–30.

31 Patey, Probability and Literary Form, 222.

32 In a passage from Sentimental Journey noted by Patey, Sterne famously describes a kind of "short hand," which, though produced in a printed text, seeks to go beyond words of any kind to a more natural form of the exchange of human expression. It is a point that might remind us of Smith on the importance of "open-hearted commerce" as the key to a well-formed moral sensibility: "There is not a secret so aiding to the progress of sociality, as to get master of this short hand, and be quick in rendering the several turns of looks and limbs, with all their inflections and delineations, into plain words. For my own part, by long habitude, I do it so mechanically, that when I walk the streets of London, I go translating all the way; and have more than once stood behind in the circle, where not three words have been said, and have brought off twenty different dialogues with me, which I could have fairly wrote down and sworn to" (47–48).

33 Shapiro, Probability and Certainty, 256–57.

34 Thomas L. Haskell, "Capitalism and the Origins of the Humanitarian Sensibility, Part 2," American Historical Review 90, no. 3 (June 1985): 548. Part 1 was published in American Historical Review 90, no. 2 (April 1985): 339–61.

35 Haskell, "Part 2," 561. The hapless Mrs. Jellyby in Bleak House is part of Dickens's later satire of this kind of humanitarianism at a distance.

36 For an approach to Haskell's thesis in relation to the novel that emphasizes the function of descriptive particularity in the new modes of fiction, see Thomas Laqueur, "Bodies, Details, and the Humanitarian Narrative," in The New Cultural History, ed. Lynn Hunt (Berkeley: University of California Press, 1989), 176–204.

37 Hazlitt, writing at the other end of the long century, is not wrong to call his own an essentially undramatic age since his was indeed an age dominated by print; but the burden of David Marshall's and Jean-Christophe Agnew's arguments is, in effect, to call attention to the absorption or displacement of theatricality back into the print-cultural public sphere. Marshall, The Figure of Theater: Shaftesbury, Defoe, Adam Smith, and George Eliot (New York: Columbia University Press, 1986); Agnew, Worlds Apart: The Market and the Theater in Anglo-American Thought, 1550–1750 (Cambridge: Cambridge University Press, 1986). See Hazlitt's "General Reporter" column on "The Drama" in the second number of The London Magazine 1 (April 1820): 432.

38 See *The Conscious Lovers*, ed. Shirley Strum Kenny (Lincoln, NE: University of Nebraska Press, 1968), xii, xvi. Kenny notes that this play is acknowledged as the "first thoroughly sentimental English comedy" (xlv). All references to the play are to this edition. Although Steele's drama was announced and received as an innovation in its time, the word "sentimental" was not applied to this dramatic mode for some years after the first production of *The Conscious Lovers*. As we have seen, the word itself does not come into currency until the 1740s.

39 In this case the coincidence that young Indiana, the hitherto objectionable lover to Bevil Junior, turns out to be the lost daughter of his father's best friend.

40 Stuart M. Tave, *Lovers, Clowns, and Fairies: An Essay on Comedies* (Chicago: University of Chicago Press, 1993), 132.

41 Ibid., 131.

42 See above, chapter 4.

43 John Traugott, "Heart and Mask and Genre in Sentimental Comedy," *Eighteenth-Century Life* 10, no. 3 (October 1986): 143.

44 Ibid.

45 Ibid.

46 Tave, *Lovers, Clowns and Fairies*, 132.

47 Ibid.

48 Kenny, *Conscious Lovers*, 5.

49 Agnew, *Worlds Apart*, 164.

50 Agnew points out that this language of polish and politeness is already linked with the revised theatricality of commerce in Shaftesbury, in *Worlds Apart*, 164. See also, as previously mentioned, J. G. A. Pocock's analysis of the commercial redefinition of "virtue" in *Virtue, Commerce, and History* (Cambridge: Cambridge University Press, 1985), 37–50. Within the play itself, the merchant class is represented by the aptly named man of commerce, Mr. Sealand, father to Lucinda, who explains his position to Sir John Bevil: "Sir, as much a cit as you take me for, I know the town and the world; and give me leave to say that we merchants are a species of gentry that have grown into the world this last century and are as honorable and almost as useful as you landed folks that have always thought yourselves so much above us; for your trading, forsooth, is extended no farther than a load of hay or a fat ox" (IV. ii. 45–54). Both the landed gentry and the cits (citizen merchants) are involved in trade. The difference is one of "extent." But this question of extent, of quantitative spread, soon becomes a question of qualitative changes. Indeed, this shift from a quantitative spread to a qualitative change is the history told by Agnew as the story of the transformation of the market from a place to a placeless process, and by Haskell as the story of the emergence of a new humanitarian sensibility in the extended markets of eighteenth-century British capitalism.

51 As Liz Bellamy points out, "the economic system is not analyzed in the abstract, but presented through the creation of fictional characters who epitomise the

values of commercial society." Bellamy, *Commerce, Morality, and the Eighteenth-Century Novel* (Cambridge University Press, 1998), 130.

52 This problem of how to weigh the "realism" of a work against its capacities for moral elevation is, of course, a celebrated critical crux in Samuel Johnson's *Preface to Shakespeare*, published just seven years earlier.

53 This line of thought would logically lead to a revision of Patey's first-level distinction between the two kinds of probability, prudential and sentimental, discussed above.

54 "The Miser Convinced of His Error," *Sentimental Magazine* 1 (March 1773): 21.

55 This point becomes utterly explicit in Shelley's later account of the difference between the American and British systems of representation in poetry *and* politics, and his discussion of the "sentiment of the necessity of change" in *A Philosophical View of Reform*, as I attempt to show in *England in 1819*, 477–80, 515–16.

56 "Sentimental Journey, from Islington to Waterloo Bridge," 508. This is the sort of "sensibility" that Marx seems to be satirizing with his reference to Balaam's ass in "Sentimental Souls"—see chapter 8.

57 On this usage, see Hacking, *Emergence of Probability*, 122–33.

58 Might we even perhaps note the appearance of that most provocative of all dice "doublets"—snake-eyes—in the image of the two empty jackboots left on the bare road after Sterne's casting of this scene on the page?

Chapter 7

1 It should be recalled that counterfactual logic is built into George's own rhetoric: "If Potter gets hold of this Building and Loan there'll never be another decent house built in this town." Jeanine Basinger, *The "It's a Wonderful Life" Book* (New York: Knopf, 1986), 208. Further references to the screenplay cited parenthetically in the text.

2 Potter's moral deformity is awkwardly matched in the film with a physical disability. He is seen throughout the film in a wheelchair. Should this fact be connected with George's repugnance at his touch? On the issue of disability studies in relation to the late-eighteenth-century emergence of "normative bodies," see Paul Youngquist, *Monstrosities: Bodies and British Romanticism* (Minneapolis: University of Minnesota Press, 2003), xxvii–xxxi.

3 Interdisciplinary work on this subject in recent years includes two collections of essays: Jeffrey Jerome Cohen, ed., *Monster Theory: Reading Culture* (Minneapolis: University of Minnesota Press, 1996), and Régis Bertrand and Anne Carol, *Le "Monstre" Humain: Imaginaire et Société* (Aix-en-Provence: Publications de l'Université de Provence, 2005).

4 See Bill Brown, *The Materialist Unconscious: American Amusement, Stephen Crane, and the Economics of Play* (Cambridge, MA: Harvard University Press, 1996).

5 Adam Smith, *The Theory of Moral Sentiments*, ed. D. D. Raphael and A. L. Macfie

(Indianapolis: Liberty Fund, 1982), 327. Further references cited parenthetically in the text.

6 Anthony Ashley Cooper, Third Earl of Shaftesbury, *Characteristics of Men, Manners, Opinions, Times*, ed. Lawrence Klein (Cambridge: Cambridge University Press, 1999), 172. Further references cited parenthetically in the text.

7 See Lorraine Daston, "Marvelous Facts and Miraculous Evidence in Early Modern Europe," in *Questions of Evidence: Proof, Practice, and Persuasion across the Disciplines*, ed. James Chandler, Arnold I. Davidson, and Harry Harootunian (Chicago: University of Chicago Press, 1994), 243–74, and Arnold Davidson, "The Horror of Monsters," in *The Emergence of Sexuality: Historical Epistemology and the Formation of Concepts* (Cambridge, MA: Harvard University Press, 2001), 93–124. See also my response to Daston, which invokes Shaftesbury's critique of the virtuosi: "Proving a History of Evidence," in *Questions of Evidence*, 275–81.

8 See below, chapter 8.

9 On the question of conformism in Smith, see above, chapter 4, note 53.

10 For an account of "moral monstrosity" in the eighteenth century that emphasizes a different problem—that of the relation of the human-as-humane to the problem of taking pleasure in cruelty—see James A. Steintrager, *Cruel Delight: Enlightenment Culture and the Inhuman* (Bloomington: Indiana University Press, 2004), 3–17.

11 See Marshall, *The Surprising Effects of Sympathy: Marivaux, Diderot, Rousseau, and Mary Shelley* (Chicago: University of Chicago Press, 1988), 228–33. For a thoughtful recent response to Marshall's account, see David Collings, *Monstrous Society: Reciprocity, Discipline, and the Political Uncanny, c. 1780–1848* (Lewisburg, PA: Bucknell University Press, 2009), 209–11. Collings's reading builds on Maureen McLane's powerful account of *Frankenstein* as a book about species and population problems. McLane, "Literate Species: Populations, 'Humanities,' and the Specific Failure of Literature in *Frankenstein*," in *Romanticism and the Human Sciences: Poetry, Population, and the Discourse of the Species* (Cambridge: Cambridge University Press, 2006), 84–108.

12 Jean-Jacques Rousseau, *Reveries of the Solitary Walker*, trans. Peter France (Harmondsworth: Penguin, 1979), 27.

13 Ibid.

14 The notion of sentimental animation is not casual in Smith. Earlier, emphasizing that the sense of "dreary and endless melancholy" that we feel is in no way to be understood as something that the senseless dead can feel, Smith says that it "arises altogether from our joining to the change which has been produced upon them, our own consciousness of that change, from our putting ourselves in their situation, and from our lodging, if I may be allowed to say so, our own living souls in their inanimate bodies, and thence conceiving what would be our emotions in this case" (13). For more on sympathy with the dead in Smith, see Esther C. Schor, *Bearing the Dead: The British Culture of Mourning from*

the Enlightenment to Victoria (Princeton, NJ: Princeton University Press, 1994), 34–40.

15 Mary Shelley, *Frankenstein*, ed. Maurice Hindle (Harmondsworth: Penguin, 1985), 140. Subsequent citations by page reference in the text. This text is based on the 1831 edition of the novel, which includes Mary Shelley's final revisions. The text should be compared with the first edition of 1818, available in *Frankenstein; or The Modern Prometheus—The 1818 Text*, ed. James Rieger (Chicago: University of Chicago Press, 1982).

16 Victor Frankenstein in turn echoes the creature's phrase when he tells Walton that he could not reveal to his family the secret of his monstrous creation, when they tried to comfort him in his losses, in spite of "his impatient thirst for sympathy" (180).

17 Percy Bysshe Shelley, "Peter Bell the Third," 298–302, in *Shelley's Poetry and Prose*, 2nd ed., ed. Donald H. Reiman and Neil Fraistat (New York: W. W. Norton, 2002), 351.

18 Shelley, "Defence of Poetry," in *Poetry and Prose*, 517.

19 For a careful analysis of the sources of the novel's treatment of such questions, see Jeanne M. Britton, "Novelistic Sympathy in Mary Shelley's *Frankenstein*," *Studies in Romanticism* 48 (Spring 2009), 3–22.

20 See McLane, *Romanticism and the Human Sciences*, 84–108.

21 Not even Justine's physical beauty guards her against the bigotry she complains of in her confessor, though the figure of the confessor, as we know from Smith, is something of a special case in the sentimentalist line.

22 "The imaginary student pursued by the misshapen creature he had impiously made, was not more wretched than I, pursued by the creature who had made me, and recoiling from him with a stronger repulsion, the more he admired me and the fonder he was of me." Charles Dickens, *Great Expectations* (Harmondsworth: Penguin, 1996), 339.

23 The decisive rejection of this tradition of sentimental monstrosity, in a context not unlike that of *Monster*, can be found in Stieg Larsson's *The Girl with the Dragon Tattoo*, where the titular character, Lisbeth Salander, is defined by her refusals of sympathy. This is especially and explicitly marked in respect to Martin Vanger, the central victim-turned-monster in the story, in spite of the appeal of Vanger's own victim, Mikael Blomkvist, who is Salander's ally and lover. From start to finish, her refusal of sympathy is matched by her commitment to vengeance, which also locates her in a Jacobean (or any case premodern) world, for all of her tech savvy. For her, a monster is a monster, no exceptions, no excuses. The point is clear enough in both of the film adaptations of the novel, Swedish and American, but it is the latter, directed by David Fincher, that drives the point home with an explicitness that matches that of the novel.

24 Lawrence Lipking, "*Frankenstein*, the True Story; or, Rousseau Judges Jean-Jacques," in *Frankenstein*, ed. J. Paul Hunter (New York: W. W. Norton, 1996), 320.

25 Wordsworth, *Prose Works*, ed. W. J. B. Owen and J. W. Smyser, 3 vols. (Oxford: Clarendon Press, 1974), 1:128.

26 See Diane Hoeveler, "The Temple of Morality: Thomas Holcroft and the Swerve of Melodrama," *European Romantic Review* 14, no. 1 (March 2003): 49–63. For studies of melodrama in longer perspective see John Cawelti, "The Evolution of Social Melodrama," in *Imitations of Life: A Reader on Film and Television Melodrama*, ed. Marcia Landry (Detroit: Wayne State University Press, 1991), 33–49; Michael Hays and Anastasia Nikolopoulou, eds., *Melodrama: The Cultural Emergence of a Genre* (New York: St. Martin's Press, 1996); Elaine Hadley, *Melodramatic Tactics: Theatricalized Dissent in the English Marketplace, 1800–1885* (Stanford, CA: Stanford University Press, 1995); Ben Singer, *Melodrama and Modernity: Early Sensational Cinema and Its Contexts* (New York: Columbia University Press, 2001); and, for the adoption of melodrama in the work of the great nineteenth-century novelists, Peter Brooks, *The Melodramatic Imagination: Balzac, Henry James, Melodrama, and the Mode of Excess* (New Haven, CT: Yale University Press, 1976).

27 My point here therefore registers some disagreement—partly semantic, partly substantive—with influential accounts of the politics of sentiment in the 1790s that stress emotional excess and extremity. See, for example, Claudia Johnson, *Equivocal Beings: Politics, Gender and Sentimentality in the 1790s* (Chicago: University of Chicago Press, 1995), esp. 1–19, and John Barrell, *Imagining the King's Death: Figurative Treason, Fantasies of Regicide 1793–96* (Oxford: Oxford University Press, 2000), 79–100. For a more detailed response see my "The Politics of Sentiment: Notes Toward a New Account," *Studies in Romanticism* 4 (Winter 2010), 553–76.

28 A detailed treatment of the gothic as a response to sentimentalism is beyond the scope of this study. If pursued along the lines I have suggested here, it would extend the account of sight-line networks and the embedded sensorium to elaborate some of the devices of mystery and suspense in a novelist like Radcliffe; there is much technical overlap between the sentimental and gothic modes, with sentiment and passion hanging in the balance, nowhere more clearly than in *Frankenstein* itself. Such an account might also take note of Geoffrey Hartman's spare summary of *Frankenstein* in an essay titled "The Sympathy Paradox": "Gothic fiction, which testifies to our repressed feelings, is at the same time a chilling confession of their limits, of a guilty emotional coldness and the fear of being vamped." Hartman, in *The Fateful Question of Culture* (New York: Columbia University Press, 1997), 153.

29 Richard Brinsley Peake, *Presumption; or, The Fate of Frankenstein* (1823), ed. Stephen C. Behrendt, *Romantic Circles* Electronic Edition (http://www.rc.umd.edu /editions/peake/). Peake's script did, however, introduce other plot elements that would later shape the films, such as Fritz, Frankenstein's henchman.

30 I thank Alison Winter for pointing this out to me.

31 See James A. W. Heffernan, "Looking at the Monster: *Frankenstein* and Film," *Critical Inquiry* 24, no. 1 (Autumn 1997): 133–58.

Introduction to Part 3

1 The contemporaneity of this book with Eisenstein's essay is even more striking than the 1947 publication date would suggest. Adorno's recent biographer points out that the entire manuscript was ready by 1944; see Stefan Müller-Doohm, *Adorno: A Biography*, trans. Rodney Livingston (Cambridge: Polity Press, 2005), 314.

2 Max Horkheimer and Theodor Adorno, *Dialectic of Enlightenment*, trans. John Cumming (New York: Continuum, 1972), 151. Further citations given parenthetically in the text.

3 Preston Sturges, *Five Screenplays*, ed. Brian Henderson (Berkeley: University of California Press, 1985), 543. Looking back on Sturges's work in 1950 Siegfried Kracauer, a Frankfurt School colleague, would see *Sullivan's Travels* as a turning point in his career because it "betrayed what was best in his laughter." Siegfried Kracauer, "Preston Sturges or Laughter Betrayed," *Films in Review* 1, no. 1 (February 1950): 45.

4 Capra wrote on that occasion: "Mass production methods, applied so skillfully to motion pictures to achieve perfection of production, only succeeded in submerging the creative skill of the individual producer and director. . . . [I]n applying the mass-production yardstick to both the mechanics and the creative side of film-making, the latter became molded into a pattern." And he described a change that he argued was already under way and for which he claimed some credit: "You'll become aware, for example, that the pattern of sameness is no longer present. The pictures will be different. They will have individuality." Capra, "Breaking Hollywood's Pattern of Sameness," *New York Times*, May 5, 1946, 15, 57; this would have been just the time when he was at work on *It's a Wonderful Life*.

5 These issues are subtly analyzed in two of the essays collected in *Meet John Doe: Frank Capra, Director*, ed. Charles Wolfe (New Brunswick, NJ: Rutgers University Press, 1989): Dudley Andrew, "Productive Discord in the System: Hollywood *Meets John Doe*," 253–68, and Nick Browne, "System of Production/System of Representation: Industry Context and Ideological Form in Capra's Meet John Doe," 269–90.

6 See, for example, Thomas Andrae, "Adorno on Film and Mass Culture: The Culture Industry Reconsidered," *Jump Cut* 20 (1979): 34–37. See also Max Paddison, *Adorno's Aesthetics of Music* (Cambridge: Cambridge University Press, 1997): "Adorno's philosophy of art is also a philosophy of modernism [to the extent] that it seeks to understand the fragmentation and alienation which characterizes Western art in the twentieth century" (3).

7 Theodor Adorno, "Culture Industry Reconsidered" (first published 1963), *New*

German Critique 6 (Fall 1975): 12. For more on Adorno's elaboration and modification of the critique in his and Horkheimer's chapter on the culture industry, especially in respect to his 1966 essay "Transparencies on Film," see Miriam Hansen, *Cinema and Experience: Siegfried Kracauer, Walter Benjamin, and Theodore W. Adorno* (Berkeley: University of California Press, 2012), 201–50.

8   For a recent account, see J. M. Bernstein, *Against Voluptuous Bodies: Late Modernism and the Meaning of Painting* (Stanford, CA: Stanford University Press, 2006).

9   The arguments have been laid out by Robert Kaufman in a series of essays on the Frankfurt School's connection to British Romanticism: "Legislators of the Post-Everything World: Shelley's *Defence* of Adorno" *ELH* 63, no. 3 (Fall 1996): 707–33; "Aura, Still," *October*, no. 99 (Winter 2002), 45–80; "Negatively Capable Dialectics: Keats, Vendler, Adorno, and the Theory of the Avant-Garde," *Critical Inquiry* 27, no. 2 (Winter 2001): 354–384. For Rancière's discussion of the aesthetic regime, see *The Politics of Aesthetics: The Distribution of the Sensible*, trans. Gabriel Rockhill (London: Continuum, 2006). Rancière can be seen as rewriting the three-part trajectory outlined in Schiller's *On the Aesthetic Education of Man* (1794), likewise culminating in the aesthetic phase.

10 Adorno, "Culture Industry Reconsidered," 15.

11 Wordsworth, preface to *Lyrical Ballads*, in *The Prose Works of William Wordsworth*, ed. W. J. B. Owen and J. W. Smyser, 3 vols. (Oxford: Clarendon Press, 1974), 1:128.

12 In reprinting an early essay by Clive Hart, Robert Scholes notes that modernist critics, from Richards on, "had an almost pathological fear of sentimentality." He notes signs that this fear may be receding (as of 2003) and approves, since "there are a things about modernism that are not visible clearly without a proper appreciation of the sentimental." Both Scholes and Hart seem to rely, however, on a definition of the sentimental supplied by Richards himself, which tends rather to reproduce the sense of the term against which much of my argument here has been pitched: Hart and Scholes, "James Joyce's Sentimentality," *James Joyce Quarterly* 41 (Fall 2003–Winter 2004): 25–36.

Chapter 8

1   For politically inflected work on sentimental fiction in this period, see, for example, Marilyn Butler, *Jane Austen and the War of Ideas* (Oxford: Clarendon Press, 1975), 7–29; Claudia Johnson, *Equivocal Beings: Politics, Gender, and Sentimentality in the 1790s: Wollstonecraft, Radcliffe, Burney, Austen* (Chicago: University of Chicago Press, 1995); Markman Ellis, *The Politics of Sensibility: Race, Gender, and Commerce in the Sentimental Novel* (Cambridge: Cambridge University Press, 1996); Amit S. Rai, *Rule of Sympathy: Sentiment, Race, and Power, 1750–1850* (Basingstoke: Palgrave, 2002); Lynn Festa, *Sentimental Figures of Empire in Eighteenth-Century Britain and France* (Baltimore: Johns Hopkins University

Press, 2006); and Michael Goode, *Sentimental Masculinity and the Rise of History, 1790–1890* (Cambridge: Cambridge University Press, 2009). See also Catherine Gallagher, *The Body Economic: Life, Death, and Sensation in Political Economy and the Victorian Novel* (Princeton, NJ: Princeton University Press, 2006), which, though centered on a later moment, frames its argument by way of Adam Smith, 7–34.

2 Jerome McGann, *The Poetics of Sensibility: A Revolution in Literary Style* (Oxford: Oxford University Press, 1998).

3 Keats explains that each of us begins as undifferentiated bits of sensibility, to be shaped in "the medium of a world like this" according to the "horn-book" of the heart. Letter to George and Georgiana Keats, April 21, 1819, in *The Letters of John Keats, 1814–1821*, ed. Hyder E. Rollins, 2 vols. (Cambridge, MA: Harvard University Press, 1958), 2:101–2.

4 Edmund Wilson, *To the Finland Station* (New York: New York Review of Books Classics, 2003), 113.

5 Karl Marx, "Sentimentale Seelen," in *Karl Marx Werke: Artikel, Literarische Versuche bis März 1843*, Marx/Engels Gesamtausgabe, vol. 1, pt. 1 (Berlin: Dietz Verlag, 1975), 675. "They cry! Alas! The butcher is slaughtering a calf! / At first the beast screamed on, now it is pale. / They laugh! Heaven, how foolish in its way, / Nature, Nature! A dog wears no beard! / What do you bubble up, like one exposed to the sun? / We hear that even Balaam's ass could speak!" I have slightly modified a translation kindly done for me by Berthold Hoeckner.

6 Of his "hobby-horse," Sterne wrote: "Thus have we travelled together; but my poor Rosinante did not, like Balaam's ass, stand still if he saw an Angel in the way, but directly pushed up to her, and if it were but a damsel, sitting by the fountain, who would let me take a refreshing draught from her cup, she was, surely, an angel to me." *Letters of the Late Rev. Mr. Laurence Sterne, to his Most Intimate Friends, on Various Occasions*, 2 vols., ed. Lydia Sterne de Medalle (Vienna: Printed for R. Sammer, 1797), 2:173–74.

7 A Capraesque man of sentiment, played by Gary Cooper, feeds a doughnut to a horse in *Mr. Deeds Goes to Town*.

8 There is also Maria's goat in *Tristram Shandy*, and the dog that had taken its place by the time Yorick meets her in *Sentimental Journey*. And as we have seen, an 1821 magazine narrative notes that "sentimentalists" get preoccupied "with the first dead dog they meet up with" (see above, 227).

9 See Philip J. Kain, *Schiller, Hegel, and Marx: State, Society, and the Aesthetic Ideal of Ancient Greece* (Kingston, ON: McGill–Queen's University Press, 1982).

10 Francis Wheen, *Karl Marx: A Life* (New York: W. W. Norton, 2000), 25–26. On Blake and Marx, see Saree Makdisi's claim that, in "describing a mode of cooperative production already evident in the late eighteenth century, Marx is working in the same conceptual continuum" as Blake. Makdisi, *William Blake and the Impossible History of the 1790s* (Chicago: University of Chicago Press, 2003), 129.

11 *The Complete Poetry and Prose of William Blake*, ed. David V. Erdman, rev. ed., (Berkeley: University of California Press, 1982), 633. Further references cited parenthetically in the text.

12 Leopold Damrosch Jr., "Burns, Blake, and the Recovery of Lyric," *Studies in Romanticism* 21, no. 4 (Winter 1982): 637–60.

13 For more on these issues between Blake and Hayley, see Susan Matthews, *Blake, Sexuality and Bourgeois Politeness* (Cambridge: Cambridge University Press, 2011).

14 Baier, *A Progress of Sentiments*, 180–81

15 Godwin's philosophical writings are sentimental insofar as they show a deep and now well documented indebtedness to David Hume. See Peter Marshall, *William Godwin* (New Haven, CT: Yale University Press, 1984), 160–62, 199–201, and Mark Philp, *Godwin's Political Justice* (Ithaca, NY: Cornell University Press, 1986), 146–52.

16 John Brenkman, *Culture and Domination* (Ithaca, NY: Cornell University Press, 1987), 111–16.

17 Alexander Gilchrist, *The Life of William Blake*, ed. W. Graham Robinson (Mineola, NY: Dover, 1998; unabridged reprint of an earlier edition, London: John Lane, 1907), 313.

18 *The British Melodist; or National Song Book, Containing the Most Popular English, Scottish, and Irish Songs, with a Selection of More Than Four Hundred Choice Toasts and Sentiments* (London: Longman and Company, 1822); *The Harp of Orpheus; Being a Collection of the Best English, Scotch, and Irish Songs, Catches, Glees, Duets, Trios, Quartettos, &c., &c. Also, a Collection of Toasts and Sentiments* (Derby, England: H. Mozley, 1820); *Albion's Pride; Being a Collection of Entire New Songs for 1804, Including the Most Famous Airs in The Wife of Two Husbands, Family Quarrels, Love Laughs at Lock-Smiths, Cabinet, Rival Statues . . . To Which Is Added a Selection of New Toasts and Sentiments* (London: T. Hughes, [1803?]).

19 See Evan Gottlieb, *Feeling British* (Lewisburg, PA: Bucknell University Press, 2007), 26–60.

20 J. G. A. Pocock, "Virtues, Rights, and Manners: A Model for Historians of Political Thought," in *Virtue, Commerce, and History* (Cambridge: Cambridge University Press, 1985), 37–50.

21 There are moments where Blake seems to resist even this generalization, such as *Jerusalem* 27, 85–88: "In my Exchanges every Land / Shall walk, & mine in every Land / Mutual shall build Jerusalem: / Both heart in heart & hand in hand." There is something about the first-person possessive pronouns here, however, that skews, perhaps even skewers, the terms of reciprocity: "*my* exchanges," "*mine* in every Land / Mutual."

22 Edmund Burke, *A Letter to Sir Hercules Langrishe, on the Subject of the Roman Catholics in Ireland*, in *The Works of the Right Honorable Edmund Burke*, ed. George Nichols, rev. ed., 12 vols. (Boston: Little, Brown, and Company, 1865–1867), 4:293.

23 Ibid., 3:312.

24 Northrop Frye, *Fearful Symmetry: A Study of William Blake* (Princeton, NJ: Princeton University Press, 1947), 167.

25 *The Complete Works of William Hazlitt*, ed. P. P. Howe, 21 vols. (London: J. M. Dent and Sons, 1930–1934), 5:156.

26 [Alciphron], "Some Speculations on Literary Pleasures—No. VIII," *Gentleman's Magazine*, May 1828, 399–400.

27 William Wordsworth, "Essay, Supplementary to the Preface," in *The Prose Works of William Wordsworth*, ed. W. J. B. Owen and Jane Worthington Smyser, 3 vols. (Oxford: Clarendon Press, 1974), 3:71.

28 *Lectures on Rhetoric and Belles Lettres*, ed. J. C. Bryce, Glasgow Edition of the Works and Correspondence of Adam Smith (Oxford: Clarendon Press, 1983), 31–32.

29 William Wordsworth to John Wilson, June 1802, in *The Letters of William and Dorothy Wordsworth: The Early Years, 1787–1805*, 2nd ed., ed. Ernest de Selincourt, rev. Chester L. Shaver (Oxford: Clarendon Press, 1967), 354–55. Wordsworth says "we are told" because Smith's comment on the ballad is reported secondhand in an anonymous essay (frequently reprinted after Smith's death) about Smith's critical opinions on a variety of topics.

30 William Wordsworth, *The Prelude*, ed. Jonathan Wordsworth, M. H. Abrams, and Stephen Gill (New York: W. W. Norton, 1979), 444.

31 Wordsworth, preface to *Lyrical Ballads*, in *The Prose Works of William Wordsworth*, ed. W. J. B. Owen and J. W. Smyser, 3 vols. (Oxford: Clarendon Press, 1974), 1:128.

32 *An Inquiry into the Nature and Causes of the Wealth of Nations*, 2 vols., ed. R. H. Campbell, A. S. Skinner, and W. B. Todd, Glasgow Edition of the Works and Correspondence of Adam Smith (Indianapolis: Liberty Classics, 1981; reprint of Oxford: Clarendon Press, 1976), 2:782.

33 Wordsworth, preface to *Lyrical Ballads*, 1:126.

34 Percy Bysshe Shelley, "Peter Bell the Third," 290–302, in *Shelley's Poetry and Prose*, ed. Donald H. Reiman and Sharon B. Powers (New York: W. W. Norton, 1977), 334.

35 See Herschel Baker, *William Hazlitt* (Cambridge, MA: Harvard University Press, 1962), 139–52; David Bromwich, *Hazlitt: The Mind of a Critic* (New York: Oxford University Press, 1983), 46–57.

36 *Complete Works of William Hazlitt*, 11:87.

37 Ibid., 5:161.

38 Ibid., 5:163.

39 Ibid.

40 Ibid.

41 Wordsworth, *The Prelude*, 255. I elaborate these arguments at length in *Words-*

worth's Second Nature: A Study of the Poetry and Politics (Chicago: University of Chicago Press, 1984), 15–92.

42 Hazlitt, *Complete Works*, 5:156.

43 Ibid., 4:120.

44 David Chandler, "Hart-Leap Well: A History of the Site of Wordsworth's Poem," *Notes and Queries* 49 (March, 2002): 19–25.

45 Wordsworth, *Lyrical Ballads*, ed. A. R. Jones and R. L. Brett (London: Methuen, 1963; rev. ed., 1965), 128. Further references cited parenthetically, by line number, in the text.

46 The role of "cunning Art" in "Hart-Leap Well" proves a crucial issue for my account here, aligning the poem more with Schiller's sense of sentiment than with Hazlitt's.

47 Geoffrey Hartman, *Wordsworth's Poetry: 1787–1814* (New Haven, CT: Yale University Press, 1964), 17–18.

48 Hazlitt, "On the Living Poets," in *Complete Works*, 5:156.

49 David Perkins, "Wordsworth and the Polemic against Hunting: *Hart-Leap Well*," *Nineteenth-Century Literature* 58 (1998): 421–45; see also Perkins, "Barbarian Pleasures: Against Hunting," in *Romanticism and Animal Rights* (Cambridge: Cambridge University Press, 2003), 64–88.

50 Chandler, "Hart-Leap Well," 19–22.

51 Hartman has the poet subsuming the figures of the knight and the shepherd in a progression of phenomenological moments in a history of imagination. Hartman, *Wordsworth's Poetry*, 141–42. For Bialostosky, the poet subsumes the voice of the shepherd in an *identification* with Sir Walter. Dan Bialostosky, *Making Tales: The Poetics of Wordsworth's Narrative Experiments* (Chicago: University of Chicago Press, 1984), 89–91. For Bromwich, the poet's subsumption of the voice of the shepherd is so total that the poem ends up merely illustrating the point, to which Hazlitt had offered it as a partial early exception, about Wordsworth's egotistical failure to register sympathetically the presence of other persons in his poetry. David Bromwich, *Disowned by Memory: Wordsworth's Poetry of the 1790s* (Chicago: University of Chicago Press, 1998), 5.

52 Bromwich, *Disowned by Memory*, 5.

53 William Wordsworth, *Home at Grasmere: Part First, Book First, of The Recluse*, ed. Beth Darlington (Ithaca, NY: Cornell University Press, 1977), 50, 52.

54 Bromwich, *Disowned by Memory*, 5.

55 Students of Wordsworth will be familiar with his distinctive way of playing with words in other apparently solemn contexts, such as the syntactical ambiguity in the pivotal ninth stanza of the Immortality Ode, composed just a few years later—"The thought of our past years in me doth breed / Perpetual benediction"—where the phrase "our past years in me" can be read in several ways that each have deep relevance to the poem's complex movement between individual experience coded in the first-person-singular ("To me alone there

came a thought of grief") and collective experience coded in the second-person-plural ("trailing clouds of glory do we come"). See my "Wordsworth's Great Ode: Romanticism and the Progress of Poetry," in *The Cambridge Companion to British Romantic Poetry*, ed. James Chandler and Maureen N. McLane (Cambridge: Cambridge University Press, 2008), 147–52.

56 There is a rich tradition behind Wordsworth's pun. E.g., in Shakespeare's *Twelfth Night* (1.1.16–22), Curio asks, "Will you go hunt, my lord?" Orsino replies, "What, Curio?" "The hart." "Why, so I do, the noblest that I have. / O, when mine eyes did see Olivia first, / Methought she purged the air of pestilence. / That instant I was turned into a hart, / And my desires, like fell and cruel hounds, / E'er since pursue me." The deer is also a figure of inwardness in Western iconography; see Leonard Barkan, "Diana and Actaeon: The Myth as Synthesis," *ELR* 10 (1980), 317–59. My thanks to Claire McEachern for these references.

57 Wordsworth, *Lyrical Ballads*, 226.

58 Jerome McGann, thinking of Schiller's distinction, has labeled Wordsworth's preface to *Lyrical Ballads*, published with "Hart-Leap Well" in the 1800 edition, "a sentimental manifesto in the strictest sense." McGann, *The Poetics of Sensibility: A Revolution in Literary Style* (Oxford: Clarendon Press, 1996), 121.

59 Hazlitt, *Complete Works*, 4:120.

60 For a good discussion of how the theory of the division of labor ramified in British writings of the period, see John Barrell, *The Birth of Pandora and the Division of Knowledge* (Houndmills, Basingstoke: Macmillan, 1992).

61 *London Magazine* (London, 1821), 509. The reference to sunbeams squeezed from cucumbers derives from book 3 of *Gulliver's Travels*, the voyage to Laputa, but the Augustan source underscores the sentimental redeployment of the topos, as explained below.

62 Wordsworth, *Home at Grasmere*, 102.

63 William Wordsworth, *The Major Works*, ed. Stephen Gill (Oxford: Oxford University Press, 2000), 304.

64 *London Magazine*, 509.

65 Let it be noted that such narratives reproduce the structures of sentimentality even when they pretend to be contesting sentimental attitudes: "These reflections [it is later explained], and the incidents which gave rise to them, I resolved to treasure up, for they would perhaps have their use in some part of my journey. They will warn me against being too sentimental, said I" (ibid., 509–10). If such a pattern (resistance in participation) is more like a rule than an exception for sentimental writings, it is worth recalling that what Schiller described as the modernizing reflexivity of the sentimental mode tends precisely to foster proleptic gestures acknowledging or denying the sentimentality of the sentimental performance itself.

66 *Gentleman's Magazine*, 1827–28, in *Sterne, The Critical Heritage*, ed. Alan B. Howes (London: Routledge & Kegan Paul, 1974), 327.

67 Robert Riskin, *Six Screenplays by Robert Riskin*, ed. Pat McGilligan (Berkeley: University of California Press, 1997), 413.

Chapter 9

1 David Trotter, *Cinema and Modernism* (Oxford: Blackwell, 2007), 19.

2 Trotter's work has now been grouped by Julian Murphet with what he calls "new modernist studies" of literature and other media, a category that also includes work by Tim Armstrong, Sara Danius, Nancy Armstrong, Michael North, Susan McCabe, Mark Wollaeger, and Juan A. Suárez. Murphet, *Multimedia Modernism: Literature and the Anglo-American Avant-garde* (Cambridge: Cambridge University Press, 2009), 5–12. Murphet may be building on Douglas Mao and Rebecca L. Walkowitz, "The New Modernist Studies," *PMLA* 123, no. 2 (2008) 737–48.

3 A short film has even been made on the subject, *From Trieste to Dublin: James Joyce and the Volta Theater*. Trieste Film Festival Press Office, "The 20th edition of the Trieste Film Festival, 15–22 January 2009" (press release), Film New Europe, January 15, 2009, http://www.filmneweurope.com/festivals/festivals/the -20th-edition-of-the-trieste-film-festival-15-22-january-2009.

4 See Gösta Werner and Erik Gunnemark, "James Joyce and Sergei Eisenstein," *James Joyce Quarterly* 27 (Spring 1990), 504.

5 See Annette Michelson, "Reading Eisenstein Reading 'Capital' (Part 2)," *October*, no. 3 (Spring 1977), 82–89.

6 Trotter challenges this view partly on the grounds that Griffith's montage techniques are misunderstood in the first place. For him, the point of Griffith's system has at least as much to do with showing the limits of its narrative devices as with showing their constructive power. Trotter, *Cinema and Modernism*, 49–85.

7 Dorothy Arzner's early Fredric March vehicle, *Merrily We Go to Hell* (1932), employs the same trope of merging the screenplay with the play it contains, and Capra toyed with the device again in *It Happened One Night*, where Clark Gable's performance owes much to Robert Williams's in *Platinum Blonde*.

8 Quoted in Lewis Jacobs, *The Rise of the American Film: A Critical History* (New York: Teachers College Press, 1968; first published, New York: Harcourt Brace, and Company, 1939), 119. Trotter points out the striking echo of Conrad in the preface to *The Nigger of the "Narcissus"*: "the power of the written word to make you hear, to make you feel,—it is before all to make you see." Trotter, *Cinema and Modernism*, 51.

9 See G. A. Starr, *Defoe and Casuistry* (Princeton, NJ: Princeton University Press, 1971); J. Paul Hunter, *Before Novels: The Cultural Contexts of Eighteenth-Century English Fiction* (New York: W. W. Norton, 1990), 288–94; Tom Keymer, "Casuistry in *Clarissa*," in *Richardson's "Clarissa" and the Eighteenth-Century Reader* (Cambridge: Cambridge University Press, 1992), 85–141; and Sandra Macpherson's

study of liability law in eighteenth-century fiction, *Harm's Way: Tragic Responsibility and the Novel Form* (Baltimore: Johns Hopkins University Press, 2010).

10   Ian Watt, *The Rise of the Novel: Studies in Defoe, Richardson, and Fielding* (Berkeley: University of California Press, 1957), 9–34. Among the many efforts to extend and challenge Watt's account, see Michael McKeon, *The Origins of the English Novel, 1600–1740* (Baltimore: Johns Hopkins University Press, 1987), esp. 1–4.

11   This language is recurrent in Smith's *Theory of Moral Sentiments*. Two early instances: "We sometimes feel for another, a passion of which he himself seems to be altogether incapable; because, when we put ourselves in his case, that passion arises in our breast from the imagination, though it does not in his from the reality"; and so, with the dead: "[we lodge] our own living souls in their inanimated bodies, and thence conceiv[e] what would be our own emotions in this case." Smith, *The Theory of Moral Sentiments*, ed. D. D. Raphael and A. L. Macfie (Indianapolis: Liberty Fund, 1982), 12, 13.

12   And in chapter 7 I showed how an anticasuistry of the sentimental case structures Percy Shelley's views of the moral imagination.

13   Charles Dickens, "A Christmas Carol," in *The Christmas Books*, vol. 1 (Harmondsworth: Penguin, 1971), 61.

14   On sympathy in, especially, *Daniel Deronda*, see David Marshall, *The Figure of Theater: Shaftesbury, Defoe, Adam Smith, and George Eliot* (New York: Columbia University Press, 1986), 193–240; Ann Cvetkovich, *Mixed Feelings: Feminism, Mass Culture, and Victorian Sensationalism* (New Brunswick, NJ: Rutgers University Press, 1992), 128–64; Rae Greiner, "Sympathy Time: Adam Smith, George Eliot, and the Realist Novel," *Narrative* 17 (October 2009) 291–311; Adela Pinch, *Thinking about Other People in Nineteenth-Century British Writing* (Cambridge: Cambridge University Press, 2010), 139–169; and Ruth HaCohen, *Vocal Fictions of Noise and Harmony: The Music Libel against the Jews* (New Haven, CT: Yale University Press, 2011), 239–85.

15   The subsequent story of the novel and its criticism has been addressed in detail by Dorothy Hale in *Social Formalism: The Novel in Theory from Henry James to the Present* (Stanford, CA: Stanford University Press, 1998).

16   Joseph Conrad, *Lord Jim*, ed. Cedric Watts and Robert Hampson (Harmondsworth: Penguin, 1986), 195. Further references cited parenthetically in the text.

17   This form of question is one that Bill Brown has made central to his pioneering work on "things"; see, for example, his *A Sense of Things: The Object Matter of American Literature* (Chicago: University of Chicago Press, 2003).

18   It is, furthermore, a novel in which the question of "last words" becomes an explicit topic of discussion; see 208–9.

19   These patterns can perhaps be considered a subset of those examined in J. Hillis Miller, "Lord Jim: Repetition as Subversion of Organic Form," in *Joseph Conrad's "Lord Jim,"* ed. Harold Bloom (New York: Chelsea House, 1987), 99–115. See also

Miller, *Fiction and Repetition: Seven English Novels* (Cambridge, MA: Harvard University Press, 1982).

20 Henry James, "The Younger Generation," review of *Chance* by Joseph Conrad, *Times Literary Supplement*, April 2, 1914, 157.

21 Michel Foucault, *Discipline and Punish: The Birth of the Prison*, trans. Alan Sheridan (New York: Pantheon Books, 1977), 99. Further citations given parenthetically in the text.

22 See, for example, Simon During, "Literature: Nationalism's Other? The Case for Revision," in *Nation and Narration*, ed. Homi K. Bhabha (London: Routledge, 1990), 142–43, and During, *Foucault and Literature: Towards a Genealogy of Writing* (London: Routledge, 1992), 200.

23 John Forrester, "If *p*, Then What? Thinking in Cases," *History of the Human Sciences* 9, no. 3 (August 1996): 13.

24 Ibid., 14.

25 J. Hillis Miller comes close to identifying one aspect of the novel's case logic when he connects this episode with others "similar in design," in which "a man confronts a crisis testing his courage, the strength of his faith in the sovereign power enthroned in a fixed standard of conduct," and "in each case someone, the man himself or someone else, interprets the test, or rather he interprets the words which the man's reaction to the test has already generated." Miller, *Fiction and Repetition*, 33.

26 Some of Marlow's most interesting self-contradictions, in this novel and elsewhere, turn on his attempt to make his relation to his sentiments and "sentimentalism" explicit. See below.

27 This is what Henry James, in the *Art of Fiction*, called "experiment": "Art lives upon discussion, upon experiment, upon curiosity, upon variety of attempt, upon the exchange of views and the comparison of standpoints." James, *Longman's Magazine* 4 (September 1884): 502.

28 It might be more accurate to say that this tension emerges from ambiguities implicit in Smith's account as to the degree in which the "contagion" model of sympathy might be troubling to the strict "projection" model. For an effort to sort out these ambiguities, and to respond to those who see Smith's theory "infected" by the contagion model, see Samuel Fleischacker, *On Adam Smith's "Wealth of Nations": A Philosophical Companion* (Princeton, NJ: Princeton University Press, 2004), 9–10.

29 The still-standard account of the form is Robert Langbaum's chapter on sympathy versus judgment in *The Poetry of Experience: The Dramatic Monologue in Modern Literary Tradition* (New York: Random House, 1957), 75–108. For a good recent redescription of the dramatic monologue form, see Meredith Martin's chapter in *Poetic Form: An Introduction*, ed. Michael D. Hurley and Michael O'Neill, 167–88 (Cambridge: Cambridge University Press, 2012).

30 Various references to Jim as "in the witness-box" when he is being examined are inflected with the "case" discourse—by Marlow's observation that "the play of questions upon it was as instructive as the tapping with a hammer on an iron box," and of course by those "dark boxes" that hold the specimens in Stein's study.

31 Albert J. Guérard, *Conrad the Novelist* (Cambridge, MA: Harvard University Press, 1958), 58. Further references cited parenthetically in the text.

32 Ian Watt, *Conrad in the Nineteenth Century* (Berkeley: University of California Press, 1979), 266.

33 For critics who do not seem to recognize the roles played by the case in *Lord Jim*, even quite insightful accounts of the novel can involve tortuous circumlocution: "Through the perceptions of other protagonists who act as his judges or confessors, his motives and actions are expounded from a spectrum of subjective positions on matters of theory and belief, so that what Jim *is*, and the fiction is concerned to present him as an enigma to be decoded through the exercise of an innovatory system of analysis, is not the same as how he is seen, and it is how he is seen that is of significance." Benita Parry, *Conrad and Imperialism: Ideological Boundaries and Visionary Frontiers* (London: Macmillan, 1983), 77–78.

34 See, for example, Ralph Rader's account of *Lord Jim* in relation to "the formal development of the English novel," even though he in fact echoes Conrad's language of "Jim's case" and indeed notes the difficulty of Conrad's producing "sympathetic, even identificative understanding of such an act" as "Jim's jumping ship." Rader, "*Lord Jim* and the Formal Development of the English Novel," in *Reading Narrative: Form, Ethics, Ideology*, ed. James Phelan (Columbus: Ohio State University Press, 1989), 227.

35 Virginia Woolf, "The 'Sentimental Journey,'" in *The Common Reader, Second Series* (London: Hogarth Press, 1932), 79.

36 James Joyce, *Ulysses* (New York: Penguin Books, 2000), 529. Further references cited parenthetically in the text.

37 Dickens's style, too, is pastiched in "Oxen in the Sun."

38 Ian Campbell Ross, *Laurence Sterne: A Life* (Oxford: Oxford University Press, 2001), 430. Beyond Joyce, and beyond Woolf, Sterne's experimental impulses might be understood to inform later twentieth-century novelists as diverse as the John Barth of *Giles Goat-Boy*, the David Foster Wallace of *Infinite Jest*, and the John Coetzee of *Diary of a Bad Year*. For further explorations of such connections, see *Laurence Sterne in Modernism and Postmodernism*, ed. David Pierce and Jan de Voogd (Amsterdam: Rodopi, 1994).

39 I was pleased to discover, as this book was going to press, that Jay Michael Dickson has written about Joyce and the sentimental in a vein similar to what I have offered here, and with special reference to "Nausicaa." He focuses on the "sentimentalist" as a Joycean character type, but does not neglect the formal issues of "external vicarious perspective" of the sort that I address here in the sentimental

mode over three centuries, and even makes the link between this technique and Joyce's norm of parallax vision. Dickson, "Defining the Sentimentalist in *Ulysses*," *James Joyce Quarterly* 44 (Fall 2006), 19–37.

40 Woolf, *The Common Reader, Second Series*, 81.

41 Ross, *Laurence Sterne*, 430.

42 Virginia Woolf, *Mrs. Dalloway* (New York: Harcourt, 1925), 147.

43 See Harry White, *Music and the Irish Literary Imagination* (Oxford: Oxford University Press, 2009), 153–86.

44 Matthew John Caldwell Hodgart and Mabel Parker Worthington, *Song in the Works of James Joyce* (New York: published for Temple University Publications by Columbia University Press, 1959). See also Harry White, *The Keeper's Recital: Music and Cultural History in Ireland, 1770–1970* (Cork: Cork University Press, 1998), which records extensive references to Moore's music throughout Joyce's writings.

45 James Joyce, *Dubliners* (New York: Penguin Books, 1992), 221.

46 Here again, Joyce's fiction finds resonance in the tradition of Laurence Sterne, whose own *Sentimental Journey*, born with the era of published "toasts and sentiments," is launched, we must recall, in a nationalist dispute over a toast, as recorded in its very first sentence: "They order ... this matter better in France."

47 Joyce, *Dubliners*, 224–25.

Coda

1 I. A. Richards, *The Principles of Literary Criticism* (1924; London: Routledge, 2001), 31.

2 Richards wrote that "at present, bad literature, bad art, the cinema, etc., are an influence of the first importance in fixing immature and actually inapplicable attitudes to most things. ... The quite common opinion that the arts have after all very little effect upon the community shows only that too little attention is being paid to the effects of bad art" (189). Part of the interest of Stanley Cavell's earliest work in film is that his arguments in behalf of ordinary cinema emerge from and explicitly engage Michael Fried's refinements of the rigors of medium specificity in modernist art, as these were outlined by Clement Greenberg—i.e., the question Cavell poses about how cinema "can have avoided the fate of modernism." Cavell, *The World Viewed: Reflections on the Ontology of Film* (Cambridge, MA: Harvard University Press, 1971; enlarged edition, 1979), 14.

3 By 1947, after his years in China attempting to spread the word about Basic English, Richards came to see that the newly emerging electronic media were "technology's long-delayed response to writing." The man who had railed against cinema and the loudspeaker would in fact develop so keen an interest in radio and television that Jean Paul Russo develops an extended comparison of Richards's

views with Marshall McLuhan's. See *I. A. Richards: His Life and Work* (Baltimore: Johns Hopkins University Press, 1989), 498, 498–500.

4 Consider the instructive example of Claude-Edmonde Magny, *L'age du romain américain* (Paris: Edition Seuil, 1948), translated as *The Age of the American Novel: The Film Aesthetic of Fiction between the Two Wars*, trans. Eleanor Hochman (New York: Frederick Ungar, 1972). This was a pioneering work in bringing together literary and film criticism, with analyses of topics like "cutting in the movies and in the novel" (71–101). Significantly, this is a book produced in France, where its effect on French intellectuals was "electric," but was not even translated into English for nearly a quarter century. For a thoughtful review of this translation and other film-and-literature work of the moment, see Christine Geduld, "Film and Literature," *Contemporary Liteature* 15 (Winter 1974): 123–30.

5 Raymond Williams, *Politics and Letters* (London: New Left Books, 1979), 193.

6 Quoted in Dai Smith, *Raymond Williams: A Warrior's Tale* (Cardigan: Parthian, 2008), 123.

7 Williams, *Politics and Letters*, 233.

8 Ibid., 45.

9 The notion of the "structure of feeling" is first laid out in Michael Orrom and Raymond Williams, *Preface to Film* (London: Film Drama, 1954), 21. Smith, *Raymond Williams*, 364–68. For Williams's interest in Eisenstein at this time, see Williams, *Politics and Letters*, 232.

10 By the mid-1970s, Williams was able to produce one of the most influential early books on television, *Television: Technology and Cultural Form* (New York: Schocken, 1974).

11 Williams, *Politics and Letters*, 191.

12 Recent work on the history of film studies has begun to document its complex disciplinary relations with literary studies, especially in the United States. In a rich, polemical overview, Dudley Andrew notes that, as of the 1970s, many members of the Society for Cinema Studies had actually gotten into the field "by teaching art films along side literary texts," but that they had found themselves either "galvanized or intimidated" by "screen theory," with important consequences for the field. Andrew, "The Core and Flow of Film Studies," in "The Fate of Disciplines," ed. James Chandler and Arnold Davidson, a special issue of *Critical Inquiry* 35 (Summer 2009): 900. For more on this historical juncture, see Philip Rosen, "*Screen* and 1970s Film Theory," in *Inventing Film Studies*, ed. Lee Grieveson and Haidee Wason (Durham, NC: Duke University Press, 2008), 264–97. For a history of the early days, see Dana Polan, *Scenes of Instruction: The Beginnings of the U.S. Study of Film* (Berkeley: University of California Press, 2007), especially his revisionist account of film studies at Columbia in the early days of the Great Books program there, 12–13, 33–89.

13 Michel Foucault, *Discipline and Punish: The Birth of the Prison* (New York: Vin-

tage Books, 1977), 3–72. Foucault launches his account of "the disappearance of torture as a public spectacle" (7) with a graphic account of a 1757 incident of drawing and quartering, which provides a kind of benchmark for the transformation he sees taking place over the next eighty years.

14 The shared structure of these episodes points up significant gendered differences. In *Mr. Smith*, Clarissa Saunders (Jean Arthur) sits above in the gallery; her face and eyes figure in the key sequence but are not part of the male-identified triangle of exchanges on the floor of the Senate. In *Braveheart*, the eyes of Wallace meet the eyes of his deceased wife, Murron (Catherine McCormack), a ghostly apparition in the crowd, the moment before the axe falls on his neck. Only in the *Waverley* scene does the meeting of a man's and a woman's eyes take place both *mutually* and between *mortal* beings, however unequal their social status.

Index

Caughie, John, 350n15

Cavell, Stanley: *Cities of Words*, 71; on conversation, 198; on Eisenstein and Capra's common debt to Dickens, 346n70; on *Gaslight*, 359n8; influence on this study, 16; on *It Happened One Night*, 55–56, 83, 87, 362n34; on *It's a Wonderful Life*, 71; ordinary cinema supported by, 400n2; *Pursuits of Happiness: The Hollywood Comedy of Remarriage*, 55–56, 71, 83, 346n70, 355n36

Cavendish, Margaret, xvi, 191

Cervantes, Miguel de, 15, 184, 185, 268, 343n37

Chance (Conrad), 308, 309

Chandler, James, 343n39, 379n40, 386n7, 388n27, 401n12

Chapin, Chester, 377n17

Chaplin, Charlie: Capra on, 346n67; comedies of victimization of, 60; Eisenstein on, 48; Langdon and, 46, 85; Mackenzian man of feeling and, 362n37; name above the title, 354n29; Richards and, 328

Characteristics of Men, Manners, Opinions, Times (Shaftesbury), 165, 167, 235, 236, 239–40, 372n32

Chatman, Seymour, 13

"Childe Roland to the Dark Tower Came" (Browning), 201

Christmas Carol, A (Dickens): case operative in, 151; *"The Cricket on the Hearth* as sequel to, 136; externalized point of view in, 146–47; face-to-face encounter in, 147, 149–50, 205; *It's a Wonderful Life* as adaptation of, 32, 33, 45, 82, 136, 143–44, 346n69, 361n32, 369n12; Joyce's "The Dead" and, 325; meta-comment on internal projection in, 33, 347n74; "The Miser Convinced of His Error" as source of, 140–42, 224; optical and visual elements in, 147–49; saving and redemption in, 144, 206; sentimental monstrosity in, 229, 232; sentiment and sympathy in alignment in, 180; shifting between representational modes in, 206; soul's mobility in, 178, 179–80, 195, 276, 303; tension between judgment and sympathy in, 316; Tucker's Edward Search compared with Ebenezer Scrooge, 193; visual mutuality in, 150

chronotope, 15–16

"Cinderella man" motif, 63, 92

cinema: Bazin on *écriture cinematique*, 118–19, 365n34; Bazin on film and theater, 118; Dickens as influence on classical narrative system of, xviii, 13–14; Epstein's *poetique du cinéma*, 328; face-to-face encounter in classical, 17; film historiography, 56–58; film noir, 73, 81; literary criticism's programmatic institutional animosity toward, 330; literature of, 299, 318; as a medium, 33, 43, 124–25, 127; as medium of sentiment, 64, 94–138; Richards on, 328, 330, 400n2; rivalry with print, 96, 128–31; sentimental mode's scheme of representation in development of narrative, 13; shift from scene to shot, 120, 123; Soviet, 18–19; as specular text, 124; translation of print narrative into, 16; two-way traffic between literature and, xviii; Williams on, 329. *See also* cinematography; editing; film criticism; Hollywood cinema

Cinema and Sentiment (Affron), xvi

cinematography: deep-focus, 43, 57, 110, 111–12, 113–14; match cut, 319. *See also* shots

circulation: Aumont on, 43, 115; circulated privacy, 128; new literary form of spectatorship lends itself to, 17; in sentimental reflection, 205; sentiment results from social, 11–12; in Smith's ethics, 173; virtualized, xvii

Citizen Kane (Welles), 44, 365n28

Clair, René, 95, 357n52

Clarissa (Richardson): articulation of spaces in, 169, 170, 373n46; Blake on, 270; mixed emotions in, 274, 275; moral sentences from, 2, 4; shifts discourse of sentiment, 152

Clayton, Jay, 371n26

close-up shot: Bergsonian affection-image and, 199; Capra uses to create moral sentiment, 44; Dickens and evolution of, 22; face-to-face encounters in, 17; facial close-ups, 14, 20, 26, 30; Griffith seen as inventor of, 131, 134; in Griffith's *The Cricket on the Hearth*, 31; as "soul of cinema," 199, 201, 379n39

Cockburn, Archibald, 190

Griffith, D. W. (*continued*)
tradition of, xix, 29, 113, 299; Capra on his connection to Dickens, 30–31; Capra's connection to, 59; Capra's views on, 134–36; Carey in films of, 367n48; characterized as "sentimental," xv; close-up invented by, 131, 134; in context of melodrama, 34, 347n76; decline in status of, 48, 135; *The Drunkard's Reformation*, 362n38; Eisenstein on Dickens's influence on, xx, 15, 17–22, 29, 31, 119, 134, 136, 140, 144, 344n45, 346n73; Eisenstein on ideological limitations of, 32; Eisenstein volume on, 48; features shared by Dickens and, 29; in forging of classical narrative system of cinema, xviii, 34, 42, 44, 109, 119, 120; Graves in films of, 58; *Isn't Life Wonderful?*, 260, 361n33; *Mr. Deeds Goes to Town* compared with visual cutting of, 107, 109; *Orphans of the Storm*, 30, 195–96; period from 1935 to 1939 as Capra's most explicit engagement with, 96; possibility of real time in, 119; psychological causality in, 26; as realist, 27; Richards ignores, 328; Richardson and articulation of space and, 170; Sennett as disciple of, 135; sentimental reconciliation of matter and spirit in, xvi; in shift from scene to shot, 120; up-to-the-minute technologies used by, 355n39; von Stroheim works for, 368n57. See also *Birth of a Nation* (Griffith); *Broken Blossoms* (Griffith); *Cricket on the Hearth, The* (Griffith)
Grifters, The (Frears), 52
Groundhog Day (Ramis), 52, 369n12
Guérard, Albert, 319–20
Guilbert de Pixérécourt, René Charles, 250
Gunning, Tom, xix, 65, 119, 195, 345n62

Habermas, Jürgen, 128
Hacking, Ian, 203–4, 227
Hale, Dorothy, 373n44, 397n15
Hale's Tours, 195, 197
Hall-Stevenson, John, 6
Hamlet (Shakespeare), 159, 223, 360n27
Hansen, Miriam, 390n7
Harkin, Maureen, 375n62
Harlow, Jean, 46, 63, 92, 95, 301

Haroche, Claudine, 340n7
Harp of Orpheus, The (song collection), 274
Hart, Clive, 390n12
"Hart-Leap Well" (Wordsworth), 287–96; apocalypticism in, 293; Hazlitt on, 285, 291, 293, 294, 295; mixed feelings in, 292, 293, 294, 295; as poem of mere sentiment, 291, 292; reading "hart" as "heart," 294–95; Shakespeare's *Othello* alluded to, 240, 295; syntactical ambiguities in, 293–94; tandem structure of, 288–89; voice of narrator in, 291–93
Hartley, David, 182, 184
Hartman, Geoffrey, 291, 382n26, 388n28, 394n51
Haskell, Thomas, 217, 383n36, 384n50
Hawks, Howard: Capra's decline in reputation compared with stature of, 355n35; *His Girl Friday*, 44, 356n46; screwball comedies of, 43; signature elements of, 60
Hayley, William, 270
Hays, Mary, 193, 214
Hays Code, 42–43, 350n18
Hazlitt, William: *Essay on the Principles of Human Action*, 285; "First Acquaintance with the Poets," 285; on his age as undramatic, 383n37; Keats influenced by, 285; on Lake poets, 285–86; *Lectures on the English Poets*, 285, 291; and "Sentimental Journey, from Islington to Waterloo Bridge, in March, 1821" in *London Magazine*, 296; *Spirit of the Age*, 285, 286; and Tucker's *The Light of Nature Pursued*, 192; on Wordsworth, 282, 285–87, 291, 292; on Wordsworth's "Hart-Leap Well," 285, 291, 293, 294, 295
Heart of Darkness (Conrad), 307
Hero (Frears), 52, 353n21
His Girl Friday (Hawks), 44, 356n46
Historical Notes on Dante (Boyd), 270–71, 276, 281
Hitchcock, Alfred, 31, 60, 354n29, 355n35, 357n55
Hobbes, Thomas, 179, 189–90, 248
Holcroft, Thomas, 250
Hollywood cinema: Capra dominates Hollywood in 1930s, 29, 42, 47, 113; Capra seen as epitomizing classical style of,

57; Capra's reflexive relation to his own medium, 44–45, 59, 62, 100; Griffith in forging of classical narrative system of cinema, xviii, 34, 42, 44, 109, 119, 120; Hays Code, 42–43, 350n18; Horkheimer and Adorno's critique of, 261–62; literary sentimentalism's relation to, 81; as melodramatic, 35; narrative system of classical period, 14–15; rule-boundedness of, 43–44; screwball comedies, 43, 53, 64, 82, 98, 125; techniques for representing spectatorial networks in, xv. *See also* studio system

Hollywood Ten, 49

Home at Grasmere (Wordsworth), 292, 293, 294

Horkheimer, Max: on cinematic spectatorship, 57; *Dialectic of Enlightenment*, 259–63; the sentimental criticized by, 35, 56, 259–63

Hudsucker Proxy, The (Coen brothers), 52–53, 125, 356n46

Huffington, Arianna, 37, 39

Hughes, Howard, 99

Huhtamo, Erkki, 343n39

"Human Abstract, The" (Blake), 277, 279

humanism: liberal, 32–33, 140; sentimental, 32, 346n73

Hume, David: associationist critique of causality, 208; Blake on, 271; emphasis on point of view in acts of reflection, 171; "An Enquiry Concerning Human Understanding," 271; on general point of view, xvii, 172; Godwin's indebtedness to, 392n15; Hutcheson as influence on, 233; on impressions of reflection, 172, 205; natural and moral philosophy associated by, 351n24; on sentiment, 171–72; and Smith's revision of Shaftesbury's notion of soliloquy, 171; tension between Smith's notion of sentiment and, 374n58; *Treatise of Human Nature*, 284; and virtualized spectator, 4; Wordsworth on, 283, 284

Hunter, J. Paul, 302

Hutcheson, Francis: in moral sense school, 3–4, 166, 233; on sentiment as founded on distinct power of the mind, 235, 236; and

Smith's revision of Shaftesbury's notion of soliloquy, 171; theory of ideas of, 172

hypallage, 208–9; in Blake's "A Poison Tree," 273–75; in Blake's "The Shepherd," 277; in *Sentimental Journey*, 91, 185, 209, 228; and syllepsis reinforce each other in Sterne, 225; in *Tristram Shandy*, 185, 209, 228, 275; in Wordsworth, 208

I'll Do Anything (Brooks), 53

imagination: imaginative mobility, 185, 303; imaginative sympathy, 73, 285; in *It's a Wonderful Life*, 73; Keats on plasticity of, 292; in legal and moral cases, 302; sentimental plots' connection to imagination of work's reception by the audience, 223. *See also* sympathetic imagination

"I'm Gettin' Sentimental Over You" (Dorsey), 343n36

Immortality Ode (Wordsworth), 394n55

"In a Sentimental Mood" (Ellington), xiv, 15, 53, 343n36

Ince, Thomas, 346n67

Indiana (Sand), 177

Informer, The (Ford), 47

"In the Mood" (Miller), 343n36

Irish Melodies (Moore), 300, 324

Isn't Life Wonderful? (Griffith), 260, 361n33

Israel, Jonathan I., 377n11

It (Badger), 58

Italians, The (Ince), 346n67

It Could Happen to You (Bergman), 53, 352n19

It Happened One Night (Capra): on American Film Institute 1998 ranking, 364n16; Cavell on, 55–56, 355n36; "Cinderella man" motif in, 63, 358n2; cinematic poetics in, 298; Connolly on, 99–100; face in, 201–2; "front page" topos in, 128; *Mr. Deeds Goes to Town* as shift from, 98; "Night Bus" as source of, 92, 196; Oscars for, 46, 94, 96; personal cost to Capra of making, 95; publicity and privacy as theme of, 83–85; reflexivity in, 92; reporter and heiress in, 82, 95, 124, 300; as reworking of *Strong Man*, 85, 92; Riskin's role in, 92, 98, 364n16; screenplay merged with play it contains, 396n7; as screwball comedy, 82, 98; self-remaking in, 82; on television,

It Happened One Night (Capra) (*continued*)
51; two-track narrative in, 127; "Walls of
Jericho" trope in, 42–43, 64, 82–85, 87, 124,
196, 362n34

It's a Wonderful Life (Capra): acts of entry
into water, 77–78, *79*; as adaptation of *A
Christmas Carol*, 32, 33, 45, 82, 136, 143–44,
346n69, 361n32, 369n12; on American
Film Institute 1998 ranking, 364n16;
American Madness compared with, 60,
64, 65, 66, 69–70, 72–74, 81–82; archaic
elements in, 137–38; bank-run sequence
in, 38, 60, 64, 65, 66, 69, 70, 78, 137; Best
Picture Oscar lost by, 113; and Capra's
awareness of importance of Dickens
to Griffith, 30; case as operative in, 151;
Colbert's remix of, 39; complex relay
structure of, 80; deep-focus cinematography in, 113; denouement, 39, 72, 80, 137–38,
144; Dickens-Griffith line culminates in,
140; and Dickens's role in Hollywood's
narrative code, xviii; discovery and
reversal in, 147; echoes title of *It Happened
One Night*, 82; eighteenth-century setting
of, 64; externalized point of view in, 147;
face-to-face encounter in, 38, 113, 149, 205,
230; faith and fidelity as themes of, 70;
film-within-a-film in, 77, 80, 81, 128; Benjamin Franklin in, 81, 138, 361n31; George's
proposal to Mary, 72, 76–77; Horkheimer
and Adorno's critique and, 260; as iconic,
52; imagination in, 73; interference across
diegetic frame in, 205; as Liberty film,
47, 113; look of 1940s film, 114; on love
and capital, 71, 77; meta-comment on
internal projection in, 347n74; "Move
Your Money" movement uses image
from, *38*, 38–39; *Mr. Deeds Goes to Town* in
transition from *American Madness* to, 95;
optical and visual elements in, 149; point
of view in, 149, 369n6; probability in, 80,
85, 87; in public domain, 50, 51; public use
made of, 40–41; Ramis's *Groundhog Day*
compared with, 52; as recapitulation of
Capra's career to that point, 60, 61, 64, 113;
as refashioning of Capra's work of 1930s,
113; reflexivity in, 81; reproduction as
theme in, 70–71; Riskin not included in,

61, 70, 99, 361n29; saving and redemption
in, 144, 206, 380n7; scripts of, 361n31; self-
consciousness about cinematic mediation
in, 77, 81; sentimental monstrosity in,
229, 230–32, *232*, 385n2; on sentiment and
political economy, 82, 137; sentiment and
sympathy in alignment in, 180; shifting between representational modes in,
206; shot/reverse-shot in, 75, 78, 149, 230;
slapstick gags and stunts in, 60; spans a
lifetime, 72; suicide theme in, 60, 63, 78,
231; sympathetic camerawork in, 74, 75;
sympathy in, 73, 74, 75–82; telephone in,
72; on television, 49, 50, 51, 352n7, 352n9;
time markers in, 69; travel in, 74, 177–78;
triangulation of spectatorship in, 149;
Turtletaub's *Phenomenon* compared with,
53; in VHS format, 51; visual mutuality in,
150; Walker as cinematographer for, 135;
wish fulfillment in, 73

"It's a Wonderful Life" Book, The (Basinger),
50, 352n10

Ivanhoe (Scott), 215

Jacobs, Lea, 357n53
Jacobs, Lewis, 47–48, 354n33
Jacobs, Margaret, 375n65
Jaffe, Audrey, 368n1, 380n6
James, Henry, 303, 309, 398n27
James, William, 209
Jarecki, Eugene, 38–39, 136
Jefferson, Thomas, 7, 10, 156, 160, 205
Jenkins, Henry, 358n56
Jenkins, Patty, 248, 387n23
Jerusalem (Blake), 272, 275
Johns, Adrian, 343n39
Johnson, Claudia, 388n27
Johnson, Joseph, 273
Johnson, Robert, 37
Johnson, Samuel, 1–2, 156, 385n52
Joseph, Gerhard, 346n69
Joseph Andrews (Fielding), 216
Joyce, James: attempts to establish first cin-
ema in Ireland, xx, 300; "The Dead," 300,
324–25; encounter with Eisenstein, xxi,
300, 327; *Finnegans Wake*, 300, 321–22, 323,
324; on sentimental mode, 16; Williams
on, 329. See also *Ulysses* (Joyce)

judgment: in case literature, 301; versus
sympathy, 216, 234, 237, 240, 241, 242, 243,
315, 316, 320

Kames, Henry Home, Lord, 344n44
Kant, Immanuel, 152
Kaufman, Robert, 263, 390n9
Keaton, Buster, 46, 60, 362n37
Keats, John, 266, 285, 292, 391n3
Keenleyside, Heather, 372n36
Kennedy, Joseph, 131
Kenney, Shirley Strum, 384n38
Kings of the Road (Wenders), xvi, 199–200
Kipling, Rudyard, xix
Klevan, Andrew, 359n16
Kracauer, Siegfried, 260, 328, 389n3
Kristol, William, 40
Kuleshov experiment, 365n29

Ladies of Leisure (Capra), 91
Lady Eve, The (Sturges), 16
Lady for a Day (Capra), 42
Lake poets, 285–86
Lamb, Jonathan, 209, 374n58, 382n22
La Mettrie, Julien Offroy de, 8
Lang, Fritz, 65–66, 328, 360n22
Lang, Robert, 34–35
Langan, Celeste, 378n28, 382n26
Langbaum, Robert, 398n29
Langdon, Harry, 46, 85, 120, 123, 135, 358n3,
362n3
Lansbury, Angela, 47, 54
Larsson, Stieg, 387n23
Last Laugh, The (Murnau), 200
Late Converts Exposed, The (Brown), 191
Latitudinarians: man-of-feeling charac-
ter and notion of sensibility of, 377n17;
moral sense school influenced by, 4; on
sensibility in journey of the soul, 180; on
sensorium, 163; and sentimental prob-
ability, 204; on the soul, 4, 33, 145, 214, 233,
257, 266; vehicular hypothesis of, xv–xvi, 12,
33, 139, 145
Lautenberg, Frank, 40
Lean, David, 30
Leavis, F. R., 328, 329
Lectures on Rhetoric and Belles Lettres
(Smith), 283

Lectures on the English Poets (Hazlitt), 285, 291
Lenora (Edgeworth), 177, 265
Leonard, Sheldon, 58–59, 76
Letter from an Unknown Woman (Ophüls),
196–99, 378n33, 379n35
Letters on Aesthetic Education (Schiller), 234
Leyda, Jay, 136
liberalism, 32, 115, 140
Liberty Films, 47, 113
Light of Nature Pursued, The (Tucker), 192–93
Liliom (Lang), 360n22
"Lines Written a Few Miles above Tintern
Abbey" (Wordsworth), 153–54
Lipking, Lawrence, 249
literary criticism: Frankfurt School, 328;
programmatic institutional animosity
toward cinema, 330; Richards and, 263,
299, 327–30; Smith on, 234, 235; Williams
and, 328–30
literary sentimentalism: American cinema's
relation to, 81, 118; Capra relates his sentimental cinema to, 44–45, 62; cinematic
sentimentalism related to, xvi, 140; four
aspects of, 33–34; *It's a Wonderful Life* and,
64, 81, 82; making of, 139–45; materialism
as backdrop to, 139; *Strong Man* compared
with, 85; as translation of theatrical forms
into print medium, 16, 206; visual structure of, 158
literary spectatorship, 146–75; in classical
Hollywood narrative system, 34, 140;
in eighteenth-century novel, 33, 140; as
internalization of theatrical spectatorship,
168; Richardson's articulation of space in
development of, 169–70; in *Sentimental
Journey*, 91; Smith's impartial spectator
in development of, 171–72; spectatorial
reader, 169; Steele on, 166, 167–68
literature: Bazin's *écriture cinematique* and,
118–19; case literature, 301–2; of cinema,
299, 318; facial representation in, 119;
two-way traffic between cinema and,
xviii. *See also* literary criticism; novels;
poetry
Locke, John, 192–93, 282, 374n56
Lombroso, Cesare, 257
London Magazine, 296, 297
Long Revolution, The (Williams), 329–30

media materialism, xvi; Richards on media revolutions, 328, 400n3

Meet John Doe (Capra): "Cinderella man" motif in, 63; dressing scene, 125; Frears's *Hero* reworks elements of, 52; as politically explicit film, 47; politicians compared with John Doe, 41; reflexivity in, 92; reporter and heir in, 95, 300; Riskin's screenplay for, 65, 98–99; self-fashioning in, 60; structural twist in plot, 359n11; Sturges and, 125, 366n41; suicide theme in, 60, 63; tensions between studio system and personhood in, 261

Méliès, Georges, 27, 328

melodrama: emergence of, 34, 250; *It Happened One Night* as, 196; "melodramatic turn" in Capra's films, 358n2; mixed feelings, 249; sentimental mode affected by, 249–50; sentimental mode distinguished from, 34–35

Memoirs of Emma Courtney (Hays), 193, 214

"Mental Traveller, The" (Blake), 275–77, 278, 279, 303

Merrily We Go to Hell (Arzner), 362n42, 396n7

metalepsis, 210, 273, 382n19, 382n22; defined, 341n17

"Michael" (Wordsworth), 284, 294–95

Milestone, Lewis, 356n46

Miller, Glenn, 343n36

Miller, J. Hillis, 398n25

Miller's Crossing (Coen brothers), 52

mimetic and pragmatic axes of representation, 124, 206–7, 223, 224, 366n38

Miracle Woman (Capra), 60, 63, 92, 359n10

mirroring: in *A Christmas Carol*, 146; in Griffith's *The Cricket on the Hearth*, 29; in Joyce's "The Dead," 324–25, 326; and Shaftesbury's account of soliloquy, 160, 165, 172, 175; in Smith's account of sympathy, 171, 173, 241; in Sturges's *Sullivan's Travels*, 125. *See also* reflection/reflexivity

"Miser Convinced of His Error, The" (magazine story): bibliographical afterlife, 143; *A Christmas Carol* derived from, 140–42, 224; crossing of the mimetic and pragmatic axes of representation in, 224; impartial spectator in, 141, 171; *It's a Wonderful Life*

displaces key issues of, 144; publishing history of, 142; sentimental monstrosity in, 229, 232

Mitchell, Robert, 375n60

Mitry, Jean, 120

mixed feelings: in Blake's "A Poison Tree," 273–75; in Capra's work, 39–40; in Connolly's views on Capra, 100; in melodrama, 249; and reflection, 158, 161; in Richardson's *Clarissa*, 274, 275; in Romantic poetry, 266; Schiller on, 153, 158, 159, 165, 174, 233, 249, 257, 274, 292, 293, 294, 295, 323; in Scott's *Waverley*, 174–75; sentimental mode characterized by, 40; sentimental sightseeing, 174; in Shelley's *Frankenstein*, 250; in *Tristram Shandy*, 157; in *Ulysses*, 323; in Wordsworth's "Hart-Leap Well," 292, 293, 294, 295

mobility, xvii; affective, 303; of fictional character, 168; imaginative, 185, 303; relation of moving and being moved in *Sentimental Journey*, 174, 185–86; sensibility moving in space and time, 168–71; sentimental spectator as figure in motion, 176; Smith on sentiment and, 173–74, 185; of the soul, 179–80, 203, 204; sympathetic, 173–74, 246, 257, 303, 324. *See also* travel

mode, xiv

modernism, 299–326; new modernist studies, 396n2; realism and, xx; sentimental mode critiqued by, 262–64; Sterne's reputation among modernist authors, 321; Williams on, 329

modernity: "cinema as medium" in discourses about, 124; Schiller on sentimental mode and, 11; Scott and, 286; sentimental, 142, 143; Shelley's *Frankenstein* and, 243; Wordsworth's "Lines Written a Few Miles above Tintern Abbey" as self-consciously modern, 153

Molière, 8, 360n25

Moll Flanders (Defoe), 168

Monster (Jenkins), 248, 387n23

monstrosity, sentimental. *See* sentimental monstrosity

montage, xv; Bazin on, xv, 111, 112; Bergsonian action-image and, 199; in classical cinema, 15; dialectical, 18, 29, 136, 144, 259;

63; sympathy's centrality as problem for plot of, 203; on television, 51; television adaptation of, 349n7; Washington, DC, preview of, 128, *129*

Mulvey, Laura, 366n38

Murnau, F. W., 111, 200, 201

Murphet, Julian, 396n2

My Beautiful Laundrette (Frears), 52

Mystery of Edwin Drood, The (Dickens), 366n37

Mythologies (Yeats), 194

naïve mode, 153

Name above the Title, The (Capra), 54–55, 96, 134, 354n27, 354n28

Nanook of the North (Flaherty), 111

naturalism, 357n53

neorealism, 43, 49, 110

Newsroom, The (television series), 353n22

Nietzsche, Friedrich, 324

Nigger of the "Narcissus," The (Conrad), 308

Norris, Frank, xix, 357n53

North, Michael, 396n2

nostalgia, 56, 57, 355n39

Nostromo (Conrad), 307

nouveau voyage sentimental, Le (Gorjy), 152

novels: casuistry in development, 301–3, 309; epistolary, 170, 172, 302; gothic fiction, 16, 34, 250, 388n28; Hill's *The Power of Sympathy* as first American, 35, 204, 265; internalizes theatrical forms, 219, 223; literary spectatorship and the eighteenth-century, 33, 140, 168–71; in literary studies, 327–28; long engagement with case form, 309; moving from one standpoint to another, 303–4; multiple directions of nineteenth-century, 175; novelistic mode of probability, 215; takes the place of theater, 217; theatrical spectatorship in, 219. *See also* sentimental novel

Old Curiosity Shop, The (Dickens), 30, 33, 248, 249, 303, 366n37

Oliver Twist (Dickens), 21, 248, 249, 345n56

"On Another's Sorrow" (Blake), 281

On Naïve and Sentimental Poetry (Schiller), 11, 152–54, 234

Ophüls, Max, 196–99, 378n33, 379n35

Orphans of the Storm (Griffith), 30, 195–96

Orrom, Michael, 329, 401n9

Othello (Shakespeare), 207, 240, 295

Oudart, Jean-Pierre, 356n41

Our Gang comedies, 129, 367n44

Paddison, Max, 389n6

Palin, Sarah, 40

Pamela (Richardson), 152, 169, 170, 302, 373n48

Pamuk, Orhan, 11

Panofsky, Erwin, 15

Parikka, Jussi, 343n39

paronomasia, 186, 187, 189, 227, 266, 294

Pascal, Blaise, 204

passion: Blake on "passions and senses," 270, 271, 275, 281; in melodrama, 34, 250; reflection in overcoming, 29, 33; Scott on sensitivity and, 334; Smith on sympathetic imagination and, 150; sympathy modifies it into sentiment, xvii, 12; vehement, 12; Wordsworth on activity of, 205

Passion of Joan of Arc, The (Dreyer), 328

Patey, Douglas Lane, 204, 216, 218, 385n53

Pathosformel, 15, 343n34

Peake, Richard, 254, 255, 257, 388n29

perspective, 15, 342n32

Peter Bell (Wordsworth), 227, 268

"Peter Bell the Third" (Shelley), 285, 387n17

Peter Pan (Barrie), 224

Phenomenon (Turtletaub), 53

picaresque: in Dickens's *Old Curiosity Shop*, 303; in early eighteenth-century novel, 168; Sterne's refashioning of, 180, 185, 189; Wenders's *Kings of the Road* as, 199

Plantinga, Carl, 361n28

Platinum Blonde (Capra): in Capra's self-transformation in 1930s, 93; "Cinderella man" motif in, 63; Conrad referred to, 300–301; "front page" topos in, 128; Gable's performance in *It Happened One Night* influenced by, 396n7; *It Happened One Night* compared with, 84; *Mr. Deeds Goes to Town* remakes, 64; reflexivity in, 92, 300; reporter and heiress in, 63, 92, 95, 300; Riskin's role in, 92; two-track narrative in, 127; valet scene in, 63, 125, *126*

plots, sentimental. *See* sentimental plots

Poague, Leland, 351n25, 353n25, 360n27, 364n13, 364n18

Pocketful of Miracles (Capra), 42

Pocock, J. G. A., 279, 375n59, 384n50

poetique du cinéma, 328

poetry: Lake poets, 285–86; lyric verse, xx, 327; in Richards's approach to criticism, 327–30; Romantic critique of sentimental mode, 266–85

point of view, xvii; in basic style of American cinema, 120; in Bazin's account of classical cinema, 117; in deep-focus realism, 111–12; in Dickens and early cinema, 14; in Dickens's *The Cricket on the Hearth*, 23, 29, 120; externalized, 146–47, 150, 173; general, xvii, 172; in Griffith's *Broken Blossoms*, 30; in Griffith's style, 140; Hume on general, xvii, 172; Hume's emphasis on, 171; in *It's a Wonderful Life*, 149, 369n6; in *Lord Jim*, 301, 304, 319, 320–21; meaning as dependent on, 118; montage grounded in alternation of viewpoint, 32; moving the reader from one standpoint to another, 303–4; perspective in painting, 342n32; point-of-view shot, 120, 136, 366n37; reversal of, 146, 164; in Richardson's *Clarissa*, 169; in Richardson's rendering of time and space, 166; in sentimental novel, xx; sentimental spectator's capacity to pass virtually into other, 176; Smith on, 375n61; spectator characterized by, 13; sympathy as capacity for passing into points of view not our own, 32–33, 180, 185, 204–5; and transition from scene to shot, 120; in *Tristram Shandy*, 164, 174; in Wordsworth's "Hart-Leap Well," 295

"Poison Tree, A" (Blake), 273–75

Polan, Dana, 401n12

Politi, Jina, 382n22

Popular Front, 96

post-chaise, 215

Powell, William, 346n73, 347n79

Power of Sympathy, The (Hill), 35, 204, 265, 380n3

Power of the Press, The (Capra), 44

Practical Criticism (Richards), 263, 327, 329

précieuses ridicules, Les (Molière), 8

Preface to Film (Williams), 329

Preface to Shakespeare (Johnson), 385n52

Prelude (Wordsworth), 194–95, 208, 240, 283, 286, 303, 350n14

Presumption (Peake), 254, 255, 257, 388n29

Priestly, Joseph, 190

Principles of Literary Criticism (Richards), 328

print: Capra's representation of, 44; as operative form of reflexivity in Capra films, 92; reporters, 44, 63, 82, 92, 95, 124, 300; rivalry with cinema, 96, 128–31; translation into cinema, 16; translation of theater into, 16, 34, 206, 217. *See also* literature

probability, sentimental. *See* sentimental probability

puns, constitutive, 206

Rabelais, 15

Rader, Ralph, 399n34

Raeburn, John, 355n35

Ramis, Harold, 52, 369n12

Rancière, Jacques, 263, 390n9

Ray, Robert B., 352n16

reader, spectatorial, 169

realism: of *American Madness*, 73; and Bazin's account of 1930s American cinema, 114; versus capacity for moral elevation, 385n52; deep-focus, 111, 113; in eighteenth-century novel, 215; formal, 169; in legal and moral cases, 302; modernist literary practices shaped by cinematic, xx; neorealism, 43, 49, 110; possibility of real time associated with, 119; Richardson's *Clarissa* an advance in, 170; shifting between aspirational mode and, 206

reanimation: in Brooks's *Young Frankenstein*, 251; in Gibson's *Braveheart*, 331; in Griffith's *The Cricket on the Hearth*, 29; in *It's a Wonderful Life*, 33; of sentimental disposition, xvi, 15, 34, 152, 166, 175; in Shelley's *Frankenstein*, 245, 247

Recluse, The (Wordsworth), 296–97

recursivity, 349n14; in the Capraesque, 41–44, 62; in Capra's self-making, 100, 138, 140, 260; in *It's a Wonderful Life*, 45, 64, 144; in *Lord Jim*, 321; in *Mr. Deeds Goes to Town*, 100; recursive harmony, 349n14; in

Rothman, William, 379n39
Rothschild, Emma, 341n24
Rousseau, Jean-Jacques: Blake on, 271;
  Hazlitt compares Wordsworth with,
  285, 286; reading Shelley's *Frankenstein*
  through, 244; on sentimental monstros-
  ity, 233; sentimental poetics of, 376n65; on
  Spectator, 344n42
Russo, Jean Paul, 400n3

Sammy and Rosie Get Laid (Frears), 52
Sand, George, 177
Sandler, Adam, 353n23
Sandow, Eugene, 362n36
Sarris, Andrew, 54, 55, 354n33
Schatz, Thomas, 357n50, 363n10
Schiller, Friedrich: *Letters on Aesthetic
  Education*, 234; Marx influenced by, 269;
  on mixed feelings, 153, 158, 159, 165, 174, 233,
  249, 257, 274, 292, 293; on modernizing reflexivity of sentimental mode, 395n65; and
  multiple directions of nineteenth-century
  novel, 175; *On Naïve and Sentimental
  Poetry*, 11, 152–54, 234; on the sentimental as constituted by ambivalence and
  reflexivity, 11, 159, 165; on the sentimental
  as dependent on reflection, xvii–xviii;
  "sentimentalisch" used by, 11; on sentimental mode, 15, 152–54, 233; Shaftesbury's
  influence on, 159, 341n20, 371n31, 372n33; on
  Sterne, 11, 154
Scholes, Robert, 390n12
Scorsese, Martin, 54, 353n24
Scott, Walter: *The Antiquary*, 324; Hazlitt
  on Wordsworth and, 286, 287; *Ivanhoe*,
  215; Sterne admired by, 214; sympathetic
  mobility in, 303; trope of the vehicle in,
  214–16; *Waverley*, 174–75, 195, 214–16, 265,
  331, 334, 402n14
screwball comedies, 43, 53, 64, 82, 98, 125
secondary observation, xviii, 342n25
Sedgwick, Eve Kosofsky, 340n12, 360n17
Sennett, Mack, 46, 48, 59, 60, 135, 358n56
Sense and Sensibility (Austen), 177, 265
sensibility, xvi–xvii; of British commercial
  audience, 223–24; capacity to be moved as
  dependent on, 176; capitalism and origins
  of humanitarian, 217; in *A Christmas Carol*,

178, 180; as largeness of soul, 180; moving
  in time and space, 168–71; poetics of, 266;
  in *Sense and Sensibility*, 177; sensorium
  and, 145, 180; in *Sentimental Journey*, xvii,
  181–82, 268; sentiment and, 176–202; in
  Sterne's refashioning of the picaresque,
  185; vehicular hypothesis on, xv–xvi, 33
sensorium, xvii; Bergson and, 199; embedded, xvii, 17; embodied, xvii, 16–17; of
  fictional character, 168; history of, 189–94;
  materialist theory of vibration associated
  with, 182, 184; mobile, 169; possibilities
  for recognition in repositioning, 149; in
  Richardson's *Clarissa*, 169; and sensibility, 145, 180; in *Sentimental Journey*, xvii,
  181–82; in sentimental spectatorship, 145;
  in Sterne's refashioning of the picaresque,
  185; in *Tristram Shandy*, 163; vehicle associated with, 180, 189
sentiment: alignment with sympathy, 180;
  the Capraesque identified with, 29–30,
  32, 58, 59, 62; cynicism associated with,
  357n54; distinguishing sentimentality
  from, 35, 361n28; as doctrinal opinion, 152;
  elaborates system of looking at lookers
  looking, 12; face of, 201; Humean, 171–72;
  ideological mode of the sentimental,
  279–80; inhabits scheme of representation
  in print-cultural experience, 13; interference across diegetic frame, 205–6; man-
  of-feeling character, 85, 95, 265, 362n3,
  371n16, 377n17, 383n30; mere sentiment,
  257, 282, 287, 291, 292; mobility involved in,
  173–74; in moral and aesthetic discourse,
  3–4; *Mr. Deeds Goes to Town* as Capra's
  most explicit embrace of, 95; national, 2,
  131, 207, 228, 274, 280, 281; opinion associated with, 2–3, 204; range of meanings of,
  1–4; Richardson's *Clarissa* and circulation
  of "sentimental," 170; secularization and
  sentimentalism, 271; and sensibility, 176–
  202; sentimental network, xviii, 80–81;
  sentimental ordinary, 298; sentimental
  soul, 4, 151, 245, 267, 268, 323, 326, 370n13;
  sentimental vehicle, xx, 181, 188, 195;
  sentimental wit, 185, 187, 206; and situation, 208, 209–14; as structure of feeling,
  151–57, 329; and syntax in Blake, 277–81;

term as used in this study, 11–12; tipping to sentimentality from, 334; toasts and sentiments, 2, *3*, 4, 73, 152, 274–75, 400n46; vicariousness in, 12. *See also* mixed feelings; passion; sentimental case; sentimentality; sentimental mode; sentimental monstrosity; sentimental probability; sentimental spectatorship

sentimental case, 172–75; the case in *A Christmas Carol*, 151; case literature, 301–2; emergence of, xx; the face of the case in *Lord Jim*, 304, 309, 314–21; Foucault's history of the case, 310–11, 314, 316–17; history of the case, 310–14; in *It's a Wonderful Life*, 137, 151; in *Lord Jim*, 304–21, 399n33; in poetic context, 266; sentimental disposition of a case, xv–xvi; sentimentalization of the case, 151, 173, 303, 304, 319; in *Sentimental Journey*, 227; and Smith on sympathetic imagination, 150–51, 241–42, 271–72, 277, 302–3, 397n11; and statistical case, 204; two ways to address, xv. *See also* casuistry

sentimental comedy: "leap" in denouement of, 91, 130; and probability, 91, 217, 218; as self-conscious reform of licentious comedy, 218–19. See also *Conscious Lovers, The* (Steele)

Sentimental Education (Flaubert), 376n65

"Sentimentale Seelen" (Marx), 11, 266–69, 372n36, 376n4

sentimental fiction. *See* sentimental novel

sentimentality: in Brooks's *Young Frankenstein*, 256; the Capraesque identified with, 29–30, 32, 44, 56, 58, 59, 62, 127, 262; critical view of works associated with, 35; criticism reproduces structures of, 395n65; distinguishing sentiment from, 35, 361n28; Horkheimer and Adorno's critique of, 262, 263; improbability of, 219; "mere" sentimentality, 257; print, 351n23; Richards's reaction to, 390n12; Romantic, 275; tipping from sentiment to, 334; in Whale's *Frankenstein* films, 256

"Sentimental Journey" (Brown), 343n36

"Sentimental Journey, from Islington to Waterloo Bridge, in March, 1821" (*London Magazine*), 227, 296, 297, 298, 391n8

sentimental journey subgenre: banalization of, 185; as new form of narrative conveyance, 186; novelty of, 184–89; paronomasia of, 186, 189; Scott's *Waverley* in, 174–75; as sentimentalization of picaresque, 180, 189; and Smith's dynamic of sympathy with cases, 173–74, 303; in Sterne's practice of sympathy as imaginative mobility, 185; vehicular hypothesis shapes, xvi, 139, 191; Woolf's *Mrs. Dalloway* in, 323

Sentimental Journey through France and Italy (Sterne), 5–12; Abdera "Fragment," 225; ambivalence and reflexivity in, 11; Blake's rewriting of, 275; Calais episode, 6–9, 156, 160, 203, 210–11; culminating moment of pathos in, 183; "Dead Ass" vignette, 225–28, 268; designed disorder of, 8; *dessein* in, 212–13; Dickens's *Old Curiosity Shop* invokes, 303; early modern sensorium as context of, 190–92; encounter with Maria of Moulines, 181–84, 189, 193, 376n5; face-to-face encounter in, 182, 189, 211, 225; in Hill's *The Power of Sympathy*, 204; hypallage in, 91, 185, 209, 228; idea for, 154; *It's a Wonderful Life* compared with, 360n17; Jefferson on, 7; last scene of, 196; literal/figurative distinction impossible to maintain in, 214; literary spectatorship in, 91; mixed feelings in, 100; narrative progress in, 208, 297; narrator of, 5, 154; nationalist dispute over a toast in, 400n46; new structuring principles of narrative art in, xiv–xv; on order, 185, 377n8; orthogonal structure of spectator in, 17; play of hands in, 9–10, 212, 341n18; popularity of, 5; posthumous sequel, 6; postponed preface, 6, 7, 10, 186–87, 188, 210; relation of moving and being moved in, 174, 185–86; reversal of feeling in, 211–12; on sensibility, xvii, 181–82, 268; on sensorium as soul's vehicle, 180; "sentimental" firmly established by, 152; "sentimental journey" coined in, 11, 142, 180; "A Sentimental Journey through Life" as homage to, 142–43, 194; the "Sentimental Traveller," 174, 186, 295; sentiment and situation in, 209–14; sequels and pastiches of, 143; Shakespeare's *Othello* alluded to, 207, 295; on "short hand" that

structured in triangulated formations, 17, 149, 205; virtuality of, 204; Wordsworth translates visual structures into voice structures, 269

Sentiment of Rationality, The (James), 209

Sesame Street (television program), 359n14

Shaftesbury, third Earl of (Anthony Ashley Cooper): *Characteristics of Men, Manners, Opinions, Times*, 165, 167, 235, 236, 239–40, 372n32; on conscience, 237–38; Hutcheson as disciple of, 233; on moral and aesthetic judgment, 162, 372n35; in moral sense school, 3–4, 17, 374n53; revised theatricality of commerce in, 384n50; Schiller influenced by, 159, 341n20, 371n31, 372n33; on sentimental monstrosity, 233, 238–40, 242; sentimental reconciliation of matter and spirit, xvi; on sentiment as founded on distinct power of the mind, 235, 236; on soliloquy, 159–60, 165, 166, 171, 172, 174, 175, 222, 223, 233, 372n33, 373n39; Sterne on, 159; Stoicism of, 171; on sympathy as sharing, 240; three steps to Sterne from, 166–72

Shakespeare, William: *Hamlet*, 159, 223, 360n27; *Othello*, 207, 240, 295; *Romeo and Juliet*, 220; *Twelfth Night*, 395n56; *Winter's Tale*, 221

Shapiro, Barbara J., 215, 216

Shawshank Redemption, The (Darabont), 53

Shelley, Mary: Rousseau as influence on, 244; sentimental reconciliation of matter and spirit, xvi. See also *Frankenstein* (Shelley)

Shelley, Percy Bysshe: on British and American systems of representation, 385n55; "A Defence of Poetry," 247, 263; "Peter Bell the Third," 285, 387n17; on sentimental monstrosity, 233; social perfectibilism of, 248; on sympathetic imagination, 247

"Shepherd, The" (Blake), 277–78

Shklovsky, Viktor: on *Sentimental Journey*, 9, 91, 142; *Sentimental'noe puteshestvie* (*Sentimental Journey*), 5, 347n73; on Sterne and Cervantes, 343n37; on Sterne and "day in the life" novels, 298; on Sterne as pioneer of new disposition, xv; on Sterne as revolutionary, 5; on Sterne establishing modern template for novel, 324; on

structure of Sterne's fiction, 8; on *Tristram Shandy*, 322

shot/reverse-shot: in Bazin's summary of narrative system of 1930s, 114, 115; Capra stages cinematic sympathy without excessive, 114; Capra uses to create moral sentiment, 44, 137; emergence of point-of-view shot and, 120, 123; face-to-face encounter in, 17, 123–24; in Griffith's *Broken Blossoms*, 30, *121–23*; in Griffith's *The Drunkard's Reformation*, 362n38; in *It's a Wonderful Life*, 75, 78, 149, 230; in *Lord Jim*, xx, 318, 319; in *Mr. Deeds Goes to Town*, 100–107, 109, 118, 131, 139–40, 146, 149; in *Mr. Smith Goes to Washington*, 131, *132–33*, 206; new forms of literary spectatorship and possibility of, xviii; and reflective ethics, 127–28; in *Strong Man*, 85, 87; subjectivization indicated by, 123

shots: framing, 199; point-of-view shot, 120, 136, 366n37; shift in emphasis from scene to, 120, 123; subjectivization of, 123. See also close-up shot; shot/reverse-shot

"Sick Rose, The" (Blake), 270

sight lines, 14; in *A Christmas Carol*, 147, 149; in Gibson's *Braveheart*, 331; in Griffith's *The Cricket on the Hearth*, 26; in *Lord Jim*, 301; in *Mr. Deeds Goes to Town*, 128; in *Mr. Smith Goes to Washington*, 131; in "Nausicaa" episode of *Ulysses*, 323; in *Tristram Shandy*, 161–66

Silverman, Kaja, 55, 137

"Simon Lee" (Wordsworth), 296

Siskin, Clifford, 343n39

Sklar, Robert, 41, 351n2, 358n1

slippage of levels: in Romantic poetry, 266; in Steele's *The Conscious Lovers*, 91, 219–21

Smith, Adam: anti-Jesuitical context of, 204; Blake contrasted with, 271–72; on brevity of human sympathy, 371n28; on case of the other, 150–51, 241–42, 271–72, 277, 302–3, 370n8, 397n11; on casuistry, xv, 151, 171, 172–74, 233, 234, 302, 317, 320; on criticism, 234, 235; Edgeworth influenced by, 265; *Essays on Philosophical Subjects*, 283; Hutcheson as influence on, 233; and ideological mode of the sentimental, 279; on impartial spectator, xvii, 17, 141, 166,

Smith, Adam (*continued*)

171–72, 237, 240–41, 361n28; on judgment and sympathy, 234, 237, 240, 241, 242, 243, 316; *Lectures on Rhetoric and Belles Lettres*, 283; on mirrored moral sentiments, 233; on mobility as involved in sentiment, 173–74, 185; and moral sense theory, 17, 33, 80, 233, 236–37, 271, 280, 302, 320, 334, 374n53; natural and moral philosophy associated by, 351n24; on the novel and moral philosophy, 4; on point of view, 375n61; political economy of *It's a Wonderful Life* and, 137; projection model of sympathy of, xv, 242, 398n28; on restraint in response to unlucky chance, 227–28; on sentimental monstrosity, 233, 235, 240–43; sentimental network formalized by, xviii, 13; Sterne influenced by, 171, 302; Stoicism of, 171; on sympathetic spectator, 172; on sympathy as capacity for passing into points of view not our own, xv, 32–33, 180, 185; tension between Hume's notion of sentiment and, 374n58; theory of ideas of, 172; and virtualized spectator, 4; *The Wealth of Nations*, 283–84; Wordsworth on, 283–84. *See also Theory of Moral Sentiments* (Smith)

Smith, Murray, 356n41

Smollett, Tobias, 207

Smoodin, Eric, 351n25, 367n43

soliloquy: in *Sentimental Journey*, 223; Shaftesbury on, 159–60, 165, 166, 171, 172, 174, 175, 222, 223, 233, 372n33, 373n39; Smith on, 171; in Steele's *The Conscious Lovers*, 222

Song of the Soul (More), 190

Sorkin, Aaron, 53, 353n22

Sorrows of Young Werther, The (Goethe), 204

soul: associated with discourse of sentiment, 4; body as vehicle of, 190, 194; body-soul/matter-spirit distinction, 190, 192; in *A Christmas Carol*, 178, 179–80, 195, 276, 303; duplicity of, 160; Epstein on close-up as "soul of cinema," 199, 201, 379n39; in Griffith's style, 140; journey of, 180; Keats on "soul-making," 266; Latitudinarian notion of, 4, 33, 145, 214, 233, 257, 266; in *Lord Jim*, 301, 304; materialism as challenge to existence of, 182, 183–84; mobility of, 179–80, 203, 204; More on, 190; "science

of," 190; sensibility as largeness of, 180; sensorium in seventeenth-century debate about, 189; sentimentalization of, 176; sentimental soul, 4, 151, 245, 267, 268, 323, 326, 370n13; Shaftesbury on distorted, 240; in Sterne's refashioning of the picaresque, 185; *Ulysses* on, 323; vehicular hypothesis on, 33, 145, 214

spatial reversal, 342n30

spectator: Capraesque's appeal and new theories of film spectatorship, 56–57; embedded, 13, 14; Hume and virtualized, 4; as literary figure, 13; making ourselves, 204–5; moral spectatorship, 171; networked spectatorship, xviii, 80; new techniques for representing spectatorial networks, xv; in poetic context, 266; second-order spectatorship, 27, 150; sentiment elaborates system of looking at lookers looking, 12; Shaftesbury on impartial, 223; shot/reverse-shot for internal and external spectatorship, 123–24; Smith on impartial, xvii, 17, 141, 166, 171–72, 237, 240–41, 361n28; Sterne on, 166, 171; sympathetic, 172; theatrical spectatorship, 168, 219; third-party, 80, 360n25; triangular structure of, 17, 149; in *Tristram Shandy*, 164; virtual, 167, 175, 203, 204. *See also* literary spectatorship; point of view; sentimental spectatorship

Spectator (Addison and Steele), 13, 17, 167, 219, 222, 344n42

Spinoza, Baruch, 189

Spirit of the Age (Hazlitt), 285, 286

Staël, Germaine de, 177, 265

Stagecoach (Ford), 124

Staiger, Janet, 57, 115, 119–20, 365n36

Stanwyck, Barbara, 44, 46, 47, 52, 63, 91–92

State of the Union (Capra), 47, 50, 92, 113

Steele, Richard: emphasis on literary spectator in public eye, 166, 167–68; and ideological mode of the sentimental, 279; and problem of probability, 217; on reading versus seeing a play, 221; reform of theater, 218, 250; *Spectator*, 13, 17, 167, 219, 222, 344n42. *See also Conscious Lovers, The* (Steele)

Steimatsky, Noa, 379n39

Steintrager, James A., 386n10

Stephen, Leslie, 324

Stern, Philip Van Doren, 359n12

Sterne, Laurence: associationism of, 321; blurring of distinction between virtual and actual in, 13; Capra collects works of, 196; Capra's sentimental practices compared with those of, 17; and Dickens's *The Old Curiosity Shop*, 33; experimental impulses' influence, 399n38; Frye on, 282; German interest in, 11; on harmony and geometry, 372n35; on his approach to life, 156–57; on his hobby horse, 156, 391n6; and ideological mode of the sentimental, 279; Jefferson on, 7, 156, 160; in Latitudinarian tradition, xvi; as major avatar of sentimental mode, 4–5; Marx as familiar with, 269; modernist authors on, 321; new techniques for representing spectatorial networks, xv; opacity in sentimental novels of, 217; on Rabelais and Cervantes, 15, 343n37; recursivity as pervasive in, 159, 233; Richardson influences sense of location of, 169–70; Schiller on, 11, 154; on sensibility, xvii; and sentimentalization of the soul, 176; sentimental network brought to narrative self-consciousness by, xviii, 13; sentimental reconciliation of matter and spirit, xvi; sentimental wit of, 185; on Shaftesbury, 159; Smith as influence on, 171, 302; on spectator, 166, 171; and vehicular hypothesis, xvi; Woolf on, 323–24; Wordsworth's relation to, 282, 295–98. See also *Sentimental Journey through France and Italy* (Sterne); *Tristram Shandy* (Sterne)

Stevens, George, 47

Stevenson, Robert Louis, 250

Stewart, Garrett, 346n66, 346n69, 370n10

Stewart, James: as Capra naïf, 95; Capra's influence on career of, 47; in *It's a Wonderful Life*, 38, 47, 60, 72, 77, 78, 79, 230, 232, 359n16; in *Mr. Smith Goes to Washington*, 40, 130–31, 331, 332; Nicolas Cage compared with, 53, 352n19; in Wellman's *Magic Town*, 99

Stoicism, 171, 228, 241

Stowe, Harriet Beecher, 16, 343n38

stream-of-consciousness narrative, 300, 323

Strong Man (Capra): the Boy in the theater, 87, *88*; the Boy meets Mary, 85, *86*; *It Happened One Night* as reworking of, 85, 92, 124; parallel action, outside and inside, 87, *89*; the preacher rejoicing, 85, *90*; probability in, 87, 91; "Walls of Jericho" trope in, 64, 85, 87, 124; the walls tumbling, 87, *90*

structures of feeling, 151, 329, 401n9

studio system: Capra's challenge to, 98, 261, 363n10, 389n4; Capra seen as stand-in for studio era, 57; golden age of, 54; Horkheimer and Adorno's critique of, 261–62; nostalgia for, 57

Sturges, Preston: *The Lady Eve*, 16; as working deliberately as himself, 357n52. See also *Sullivan's Travels* (Sturges)

Suárez, Juan A., 396n2

suicide theme, 60, 62–63, 66, 78, 231

Sullivan's Travels (Sturges): Capra films related to, 64; Capra referred to, 125, 261; cinema-as-medium referred to, 124, 125, 127; and *Meet John Doe*, 125, 366n41; questions of privacy and publicity in, 127; seen as turning point in Sturges's career, 389n3; valet scene in, 125, *126*, 127

Swingers (Favreau), 353n24

syllepsis: and hypallage reinforce each other in Sterne, 225; in Joyce's "The Dead," 324; and point of view, 13; in *Sentimental Journey*, 9, 91, 213–14, 228; in sentimental novel, xx, 217

symbolic form, 15

sympathetic imagination: in Dickens, 303; Shelley on, 247; Smith on, xv, 150, 174; in Woolf's *To the Lighthouse*, 324; in Wordsworth, 207–8, 286, 287, 289, 295

sympathy, xvii; alignment with sentiment, 180; in *American Madness*, 73–74; as capacity for passing into points of view not our own, 32–33, 180, 185, 204–5; as central in sentimental mode, 203; in *A Christmas Carol*, 178, 180; contagion model of, 240, 242, 398n28; double reflection and double mirroring linked to, 171; face-to-face encounters generate, 189, 216; Hill's *The Power of Sympathy*, 35, 204, 265, 380n3; Horkheimer and Adorno on "acts of," 260, 262; imaginative, 73, 285; as imagina-

sympathy (*continued*)

tive mobility, 185; in *It's a Wonderful Life*,
73, 74, 75–82, 137; versus judgment, 216,
234, 237, 240, 241, 242, 243, 315, 316, 320;
as key element in circuit of reflections
and ascending scale of reflexivity, xix;
Mackenzian man of feeling as figure of,
85; moral sentiment and, 82; in poetic
context, 266; political economy and, 82;
power of, 75, 204, 219; projection model
of, xv, 242, 398n28; and representation
of how and why things happen, 204; in
sentimental networks, 80–81; Shaftesbury
on, 240; in Shelley's *Frankenstein*, 243–50;
sympathetic exchange, 77, 205, 241, 302;
sympathetic identification, 245, 316, 319,
380n6; sympathetic mobility, 173–74, 246,
257, 303, 324; sympathetic spectator, 172;
sympathetic travel, 74, 75, 154, 177–80, 195.
See also sympathetic imagination

Tale of Mystery, A (Holcroft), 250
Tale of Two Cities, A (Dickens), 21, 30, 195,
196, 197, 215, 303
Tarantino, Quentin, 353n24
Tave, Stuart, 205, 218, 219, 221, 224
television: Capra's stature and, 41, 49–52;
networks established, 49; pre-1948 films
shown on, 49, 51
Testament of Dr. Mabuse, The (Lang), 65–66
That Certain Thing (Capra), 58, 59, 60
theater: Bazin on film and, 118; melodrama
associated with, 34; novel internalizes
theatrical forms, 219, 223; Steele recenters
it on literary principles, 168; translation
into print narrative, 16, 34, 206, 217. *See also*
sentimental comedy
Theory of Moral Sentiments (Smith): on
double reflection and double mirroring,
171; on impartial spectator, 171, 172; literary
criticism in, 283; on moral sense theory,
233, 236–37; on motivations and interpretations of England's commercial order, 215;
on "open-hearted commerce," 383n32; on
sentimental animation, 244–45, 386n14; on
sentimental case, xv, 172–74; on sentimental
monstrosity, 233, 235, 240–43; Shelley's

Frankenstein influenced by, 244–45; Smith's
self-identification as critic and, 234; on
sympathetic spectator, 172; and *Tristram
Shandy*, 185

Thompson, Kristin, 57, 115, 119–20, 365n36
"Thorn, The" (Wordsworth), 208–9
"To a Louse" (Burns), 241
toasts: and sentiments, 2, 3, 4, 73, 152, 274–75,
400n46; in Sterne's *Sentimental Journey*,
6, 7–8
Toland, Gregg, 57
Tom Jones (Fielding), 216
To the Lighthouse (Woolf), 324
Touch of Evil (Welles), 200
Tramp, Tramp, Tramp (Capra), 120, 123
Traugott, John, 219, 221, 362n39
travel: Blake's "The Mental Traveller,"
275–77, 278, 279, 303; in *A Christmas Carol*,
178–80, 195, 276; in *It's a Wonderful Life*,
74, 177–78; in *Lord Jim*, 298; in *Sentimental
Journey*, 5, 154, 181, 186, 187, 213–14, 225, 275,
297; *Sentimental Journey* on Smollett's
travel literature, 207; sympathetic, 74, 75,
154, 177–80, 195; in *Tristram Shandy*, 154,
160, 268, 275; virtual, 177, 185, 187–88. *See
also* sentimental journey subgenre
Treatise of Human Nature (Hume), 284
Tristram Shandy (Sterne): account of
Tristram's birth, 321; ambivalence in,
156, 157, 158, 161, 163, 166; Balaam's ass in,
268; encounter with Maria of Moulines,
154–57, 158, 160, 161–66, 174, 181–83, 184,
188; film version of, 159; on hypallage,
185; hypallage in, 209, 228, 275; interference across diegetic frame in, 205–6; lays
bare its fictional devices, 5; Marx on, 269;
and moral sense theory, 185; narrative
progress in, 297; narrator of, 154; notion of
sentimental in, 5; as novel, 160; overlaps
with *Sentimental Journey*, 154; postponed
preface, 6; reflection in, 158–59, 160, 164,
166, 323; sensing in modus operandi of,
163; as Shaftesburyan soliloquy, 160, 174;
Shklovsky on, 5, 322; sight lines in, 161–66;
three levels of drama in, 166; as time-space
construction, 166; travel in, 154, 160, 268,
275; Wordsworth reads, 282

Trollope, Anthony, 30

Trotter, David, xx, 299, 300, 301, 318, 396n2, 396n8

Truffaut, François, 55, 365n34

Trumpener, Katie, 371n16

Tucker, Abraham, 192–93

Turner, James Grantham, 373n48, 381n8

Turtletaub, John, 53

Twelfth Night (Shakespeare), 395n56

"Tyger, The" (Blake), 275, 279

Ulysses (Joyce): associationism of, 321, 323; "Cyclops" episode, 323; Eisenstein on, 300, 321, 322; mixed feelings in, 323; Moore's *Irish Melodies* referred to, 300; "Nausicaa" episode, 300, 322–23, 399n39; "Oxen in the Sun" episode, 321, 322; passage imitating *Sentimental Journey*, 321; Sternean sentimental ordinary in, 298; stream-of-consciousness narrative in, 323

vehicle: affective, 181, 199; body as soul's vehicle, 190, 194; fictional, 214–17; in French Revolution, 195; in Hale's Tours, 195; in *It Happened One Night*, 196; from literary to cinematic, 194–99; as medium, 214; in Montaigne's "On Coaches," 378n30; motion picture camera as, 195, 200; in Ophüls's *Letter from an Unknown Woman*, 196–99, 378n33; sensorium associated with, 180, 189; sentimental, xx, 181, 188, 195; in *Sentimental Journey*, 186–89, 210, 214, 225, 297; "A Sentimental Journey through Life" on, 194; soul's, 180, 190, 194; syllepsis of the, 214; in *A Tale of Two Cities*, 195; vehicular state, 12, 180, 191–93, 205; virtual, 194. *See also* vehicular hypothesis

vehicular hypothesis, xv–xvi; debate over, 190; in Hays's *Memoirs of Emma Courtney*, 193; sentimentalization of, 192; sentimental journey genre shaped by, xvi, 139, 191; on the soul, 33, 145, 214; subtlety as important to, 12; Tucker on, 192–93

Veiler, Anthony, 50

Verma, Neil, 370n11

Vermeule, Blakey, 374n55

Vicar of Wakefield, The (Goldsmith), 174

Vidor, King, 47, 369n5

viewpoint. *See* point of view

virtuality, xvii; blurring of distinction between virtual and actual, 13; Burke on virtual representation, 280–81; face-to-face encounter becomes morally crucial at point of its virtualization, 17; Schiller on sentimental mode and, 11; sentimental mode as dependent on a relay of regards virtualized in a medium, 13; sentimental spectator's capacity to pass virtually into other points of view, 176; sentiment mediated though virtual point of view, 12; in Sterne's *Sentimental Journey*, 10; virtual audience, 221, 222; virtual circulation, xvii; virtual spectator, 167, 175, 203, 204; virtual travel, 177, 185, 187–88; virtual vehicle, 194

Voltaire, 271

von Stroheim, Erich: Bazin on, xix, 111, 113; Capra on, 113, 134, 299, 357n53, 368n57; Capra works with, xix, 112, 113, 134, 299; deep-focus realism of, 111, 114; *Greed*, xix, 59, 113, 134, 299, 357n53; works with Griffith, 368n57

Wahrman, Dror, 374n58

Walker, Joseph, 135, 356n46

Walkley, A. B., 19–20, 21

Walkowitz, Rebecca L., 396n2

Wall, Cynthia, 169, 170, 373n46

Wallace, David Foster, 399n38

Warburg, Aby, 15

Warden, The (Trollope), 30

Warner, William, 343n39

Warner Brothers, 357n53

Watt, Ian, 169, 302, 320

Waverley (Scott), 174–75, 195, 214–16, 265, 331, 334, 402n14

Wealth of Nations, The (Smith), 283–84

Welles, Orson: Capra as unable to adapt to new stylistic order of, 113; Capra's decline in reputation compared with stature of, 355n35; *Citizen Kane*, 44, 365n28; deep-focus cinematography of, 110, 111, 112, 114; Eisenstein solicits material from, 48; Horkheimer and Adorno's critique of, 262; and Mankiewicz, 99; name above the title,